CW00357928

Ist edition May 2001

© Automobile Association Developments Limited 2001

This product includes map data licensed from Ordnance Survey® with the permission of the Controller of Her Majesty's Stationery Office. © Crown copyright 2000. All rights reserved.

Licence No: 399221.

All rights reserved. No part of this publication may be reproduced, stored in a retrieval system, or transmitted in any form or by any means– electronic, mechanical, photocopying, recording or otherwise – unless the permission of the publisher has been given beforehand.

Published by AA Publishing (a trading name of Automobile Association Developments Limited, whose registered office is Norfolk House, Priestley Road, Basingstoke, Hampshire, RG24 9NY. Registered number 1878835).

Mapping produced by the Cartographic Department of The Automobile Association.

A CIP Catalogue record for this book is available from the British Library.

Printed by GRAFIASA S.A., Porto, Portugal

The contents of this atlas are believed to be correct at the time of the latest revision. However, the publishers cannot be held responsible for loss occasioned to any person acting or refraining from action as a result of any material in this atlas, nor for any errors, omissions or changes in such material. The publishers would welcome information to correct any errors or omissions and to keep this atlas up to date. Please write to Publishing, The Automobile Association, Fanum House, Basing View, Basingstoke, Hampshire, RG21 4EA.

Ref: MN042

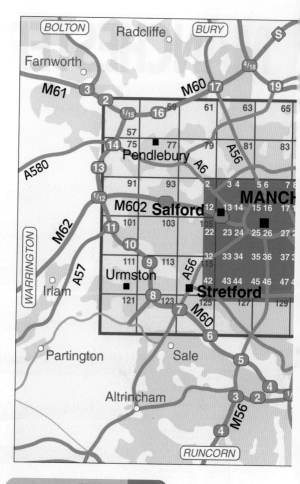

ii

Enlarged scale pages 1:10,000   6.3 inches to 1 mile

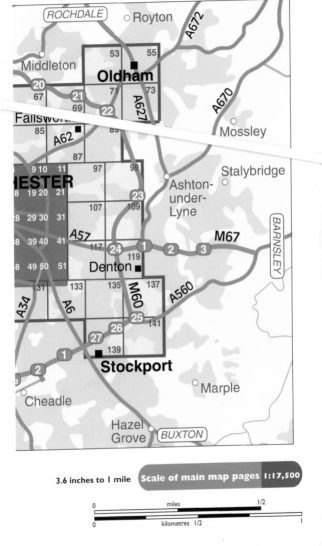

3.6 inches to 1 mile   Scale of main map pages 1:17,500

iv

Junction 9	Motorway & junction	P+ 🚌	Park & Ride
Services	Motorway service area	🚌	Bus/coach station
	Primary road single/dual carriageway	⇄	Railway & main railway station
Services	Primary road service area	⇄	Railway & minor railway station
	A road single/dual carriageway	⊖	Underground station
	B road single/dual carriageway	⊖	Light railway & station
	Other road single/dual carriageway	+++++++	Preserved private railway
	Restricted road	LC	Level crossing
	Private road	•—•—•	Tramway
← ←	One way street	- - - - - - -	Ferry route
	Pedestrian street	....	Airport runway
- - - - -	Track/ footpath	– · – · –	Boundaries- borough/ district
	Road under construction	⋁⋁⋁⋁⋁	Mounds
⌐ = = ⌐	Road tunnel	**93**	Page continuation 1:17,500
P	Parking	**7**	Page continuation to enlarged scale 1:10,000

River/canal lake, pier		Toilet with disabled facilities
Aqueduct, lock, weir		Petrol station
465 ▲ Winter Hill — Peak (with height in metres)		**PH** — Public house
Beach		**PO** — Post Office
Coniferous woodland		Public library
Broadleaved woodland		**i** — Tourist Information Centre
Mixed woodland		Castle
Park		Historic house/ building
Cemetery		Wakehurst Place NT — National Trust property
Built-up area		**M** — Museum/ art gallery
Featured building		**†** — Church/chapel
City wall		Country park
A&E — Accident & Emergency hospital		Theatre/ performing arts
Toilet		Cinema

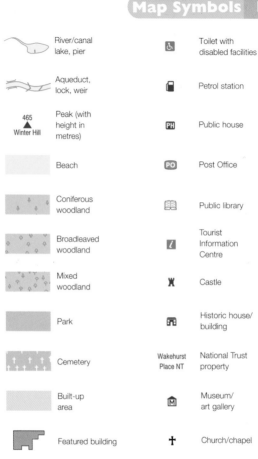

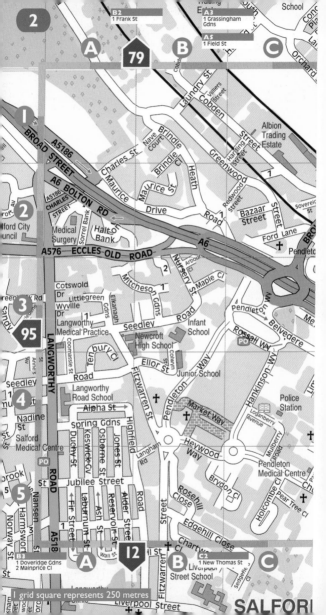

2

B2
1 Frank St

A3
1 Grassingham Gdns

A5
1 Field St

School

A   79   B   C

orchard

Laundry St
Villiers Street
Cobden Street

Nave Court
Brindle St
Charles St
Brindle Cl
Maurice St
Heath
Greenwood Street
Harling Street
Redwood Street
Albion Trading Estate

BROAD STREET
A5186

Charles St
A6 BOLTON RD
A5186 CHARLES STREET
Maurice Drive
Sorrel Bank
Halton Bank
Medical Surgery
Bazaar Street
Street
Ford Lane
Pendleto
sovereig
St
BRO

Salford City Council

A576 ECCLES OLD ROAD
A6
Pendlet

Cotswold Dr
Littlegreen
Wyville Dr
Elkanagh Gdns
Mitcheson Gdns
Nursery St
Maple Cl
Arbour
2

Langworthy Medical Practice
Seedley Road
Newcroft High School
Infant School
Pendleto
Belvedere
Me

freedk Rd
sandy

3   95

Coomassie St
Tenbury Cl
Ellor St
Conwin
Rossall WY
PO

Seedley
St
Langworthy Road School
Arne's Way
Fitzwarren St
Junior School
Pendleton Way
Hankinson WY
Loganberry Avenue
Police Station

4   St

Nadine St
Salford Medical Centre

Alpha St
Spring Gdns
Duchy St
Keswick Gv
Osborne St
Jones St
Highfield
Langham Rd
Market Way
Heywood Way
Mulberry Road
Pendleton Medical Centre
Bryson Cl

brook
St
Norway St
Harmsworth

PO
ROAD
A518

Jubilee Street
Fir Street
Laburnum St
Ash St
Reservoir St
Alder Street
Road
Street
Rosehill Close
Holcombe Cl
Pear Tree Cl
Chu

5   5

Nansen St

1   12
Wall St
Chartwell
Edgehill Close
Fitzwarren St
Sedgate
St

B3
1 Doveridge Gdns
2 Mainprice Cl

A   B
1 Liverpool
Street School

C2
1 New Thomas St
C

Langworthy
Liverpool Street

SALFORI

I grid square represents 250 metres

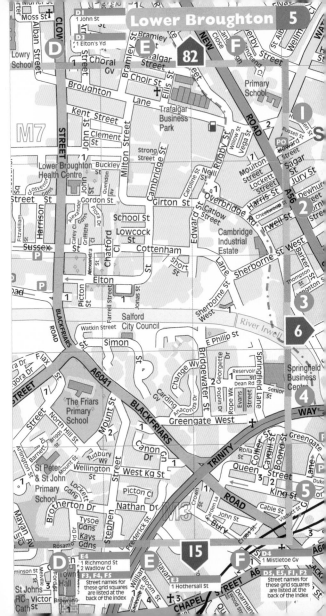

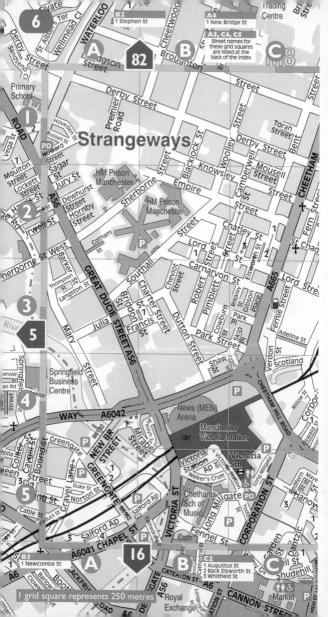

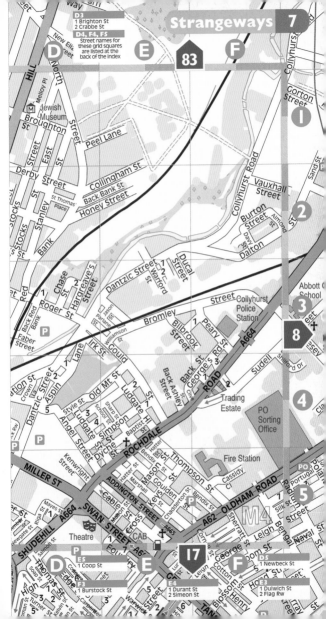

D3
1 Brighton St
2 Crabbe St

D4, F4, F5
Street names for
these grid squares
are listed at the
back of the index

83

Gorton
Street

HILL

NORTH

New Elk

Melloy Pl

M Jewish
Museum

Broughton
St

EAST STREET

DERBY STREET

Peel Lane

Collingham St

Back Bank St

Honey Street

STANLEY STREET

STOCKS

Bank

Red

Back Red
Bank

P

Faber St

Roger St

Chase
St

Hargreave's
Street

Dantzic Street

Watford
St

Ducal
Street

Sand St

Vauxhall
Street

Burton
Street

Almond St

Davy St

Dalton

Collyhurst Road

Abbott
School

Street

Bromley

Collyhurst
Police
Station

Bilbrook
Street

Peary St

Back St
George's

ROAD

A664

Sudell

Shilford Dr

8

3

4

Dantzic St

Crown St

Aspin
Lane

Style St

Old Mt St

Ludgate

Baptist St

ROCHDALE

Sharp St

School St

Simpson
St

Dyche

Hatter St

Bendix

Thompson St

Mason St

Goulden St

Cassidy
Cl

Trading
Estate

Fire Station

PO
Sorting
Office

Angel
Street

Kenwright
Street

MILLER ST

P

P

ADDINGTON STREET

Marshall

Chadderton St

Bendix St

A62 OLDHAM ROAD

Sherratt St

PO

Portugal

Silk St

Benga

Naval St

5

M4

Mayes St

St Fr

Riga St

Newgate Rd

A664

SWAN STREET

CROSS

Mason
St

P

A62

Sherratt

Leigh St

George St

Cotton

Blossom

Henry

Dulwich St

Newbeck St

Flag Rw

SHUDEHILL

Theatre

CAB

Simeon St

Thomas St

High St

Turner St

Kevin St

Warwick Street

CAB

George

Leigh

Cotton

I7

D5
1 Coop St

E5

F3
1 Burstock St

E4
1 Durant St
2 Simeon St

F
D5
1 Newbeck St

HO
1 Dulwich St
2 Flag Rw

TANS

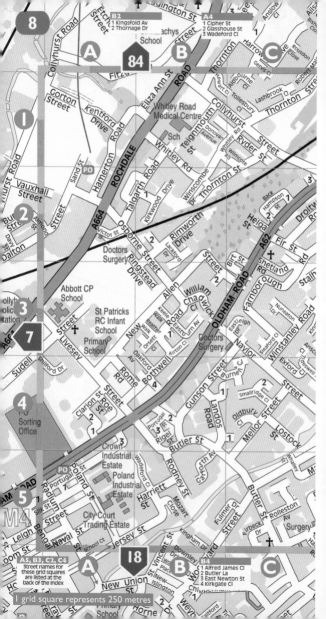

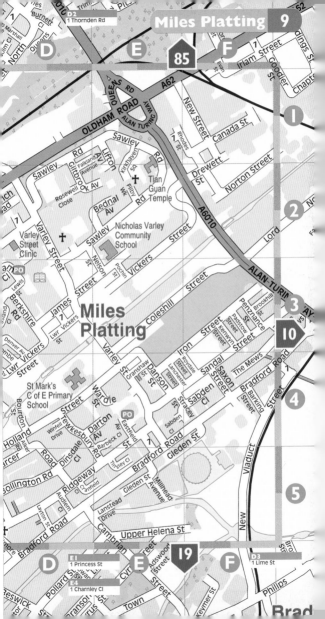

D2
1 Thornden Rd

D **E** 85 **F**

Irlam St
Goodier St
Chaptr

I

Burnett Cl
Marshall
North
QUEENS
Trimm
Pil

OLDHAM ROAD
QUEENS RD
ALAN TURING
WAY
A62

Sawley Rd
Clifton
AV
Kirkhaven
Sq
Flixt
WK
Rd
Falkland Avenue
Gilbrook
OK AV
Rosewell Close
Bednal Av

New Street
Rhodes St
Drewett St
Canada St
Norton Street

Tian Guan Temple

A6010

Lord

N

2

Nicholas Varley Community School

Varley Street Clinic

Sawley Street
Nelson Street
Pachin St
Vickers Street
Vickers Street

ALAN TURING WAY

Brookhill
Penzrance St
Padstow Street
Kenwyn Street

3

10

PO
Lewis
Berkshire Rd
Denver Av
am

James Street
Lwr Vickers Street
Coleshill Street

Iron Street
Royvale Street
Lanchester Street
Stradey
Sandal Street
Saxon Street
Sabden Cl
The Mews
Bradford Road
Barking Street
Street

4

St Mark's C of E Primary School

Varley St
Wardle Street
Granshaw St
Danson St
Sabden Cl
Gleden St
Bradford Road

Holland
Bourdon St
Alker
Mercer
Bollington Rd
Wirfell
Fewkesbury Drive
Dinsdale Cl
Darton AV
Barbeck St
Eastfield St
Ridgeway
Audlem
Armeld
PO
Stey Cl

Cleden St
Millhead Avenue
Lanstead Drive

New Viaduct Road
Bro St

5

Bradford Road
Upper Helena St
Cambrian Street
Cyr
Town

D E1
1 Princess St

E 19 **F**
Adswood Street
Keymer Sf
D3
1 Lime St

E4
1 Charnley Cl

Beswick
tor
Pollard St
Transom
Cyrus St

Phillips St
Brad

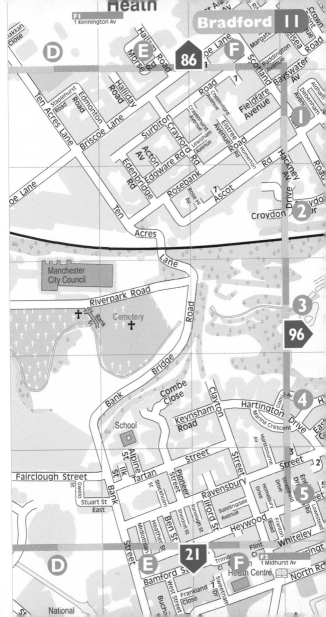

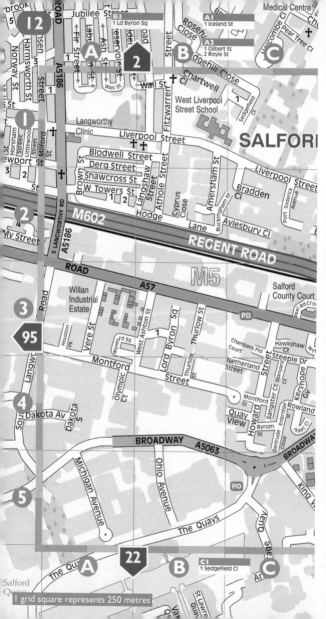

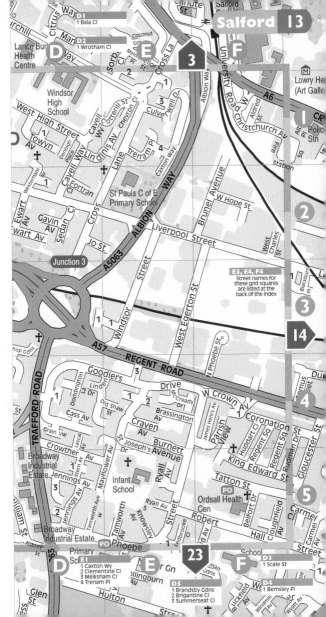

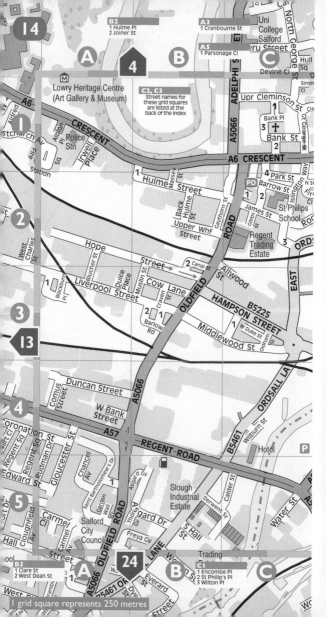

14

A

4

B

C

Uni College Salford

Peru Street

Hull Cl

North George St

Lowry Heritage Centre (Art Gallery & Museum)

M

Devine Cl

Simm Cl

Upr Cleminson St

Cle

1

A6

CRESCENT

stchurch Av

Alfred St

Albion St

Police Stn

Irwell Place

Sq

Fire station

Bank Pl

Bank St

Ct of George St

3

2

A5066

A6 CRESCENT

4 Park St

Barrow St

Islington Way

N Si

Fre

2

Massey St

1

Hulme Street

Glythorn St

Back Hulme Street

Upper Whf Street

James St

Gibbs St

St Philips School

PO

1

ROAD

Regent Trading Estate

ORDS

Rc

West Charles St

Hope Street

Bluchor St

Dulce Place

Muslin St

Cow Lane

2 Canal St

Allwood St

EAST

Liverpool Street

Blackburn Pl

1

Craven St

2

1

Barlow Rd

OLDFIELD

HAMPSON STREET

B5225

3

13

Middlewood St

W Duke St

ORDSALL LA

Duncan Street

Comus Street

W Bank Street

A5066

4

oronation St

Regent Sq

Regent Sq

Rudman Dr

Gloucester St

A57

REGENT ROAD

Chancel Av

Wilburn St

B5461

Hotel

P

dward St

5

Carmel Cl

cloughfield

Carmel Cl

Hall

Saint Bartholomew's Dr

Garden Wall

Salford City Council

Asgard Gv

Asgard Dr

Freya Gv

OLDFIELD ROAD

Slough Industrial Estate

S Hall St

Denwent St

Calder St

Water St

Trading

Street

A

24

A5066 OLDFIELD RO

B5461 OF

Everard St

Dye

Street

B

C

West

Wo

1 grid square represents 250 metres

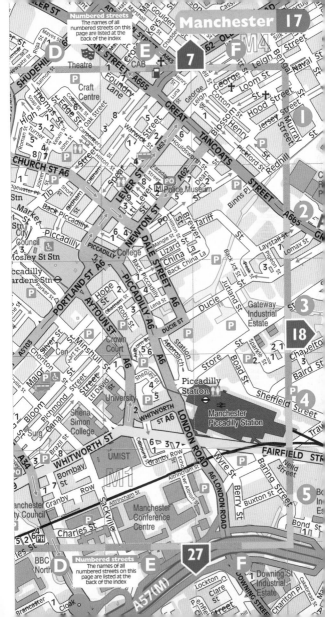

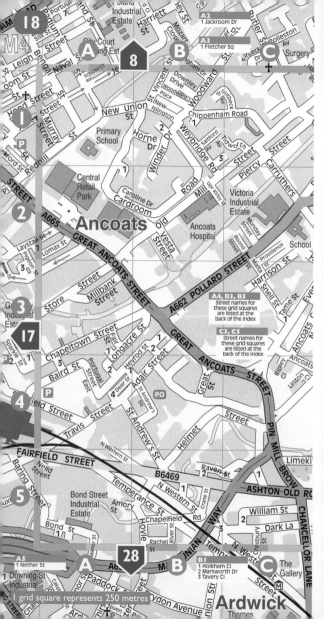

M4

A City Court ing Est

8

B

C Rolleston AV Surgery

Oland Industrial Estate

Harriett

Portu... Silk St

Leigh St

Naval St

School Ct

School St

St Vincent St

Downley Drive

Woodward

Mozart Close

Bigham Dr

Chippenham Road

I

Hood Street

Murray Street

St

Redhill

New Union St

New Islington

Horne Dr

Winder Dr

Weybridge Rd

Saltford

Tiawd Dr

Piercy St

Carruthers Street

P

xford St

Primary School

Central Retail Park

Caroline Dr

Cardroom

Uppr Kirby St

Mill Road

Victoria Industrial Estate

2 A665 **Ancoats**

Laystall St

Lomax St

Pigeon St

Old Vesta Street

Ancoats Hospital

GREAT ANCOATS STREET

Munday Street

Bond Street

Mata St

Providence St

School

Store Street

Millbank Street

A662 POLLARD STREET

Harrison St

Tame St

Anita Snell St

3

G... Industrial Este

I7

Chapeltown Street

Longacre St

Portugal Street East

Heyrod St

Adair Street

GREAT ANCOATS STREET

Ancoats

Ripley Cl

Linton

Sparkle St

P 2

Baird Street

Fall St

Deer St

St Andrew's St

PO

Great Ancoats Street

Street

PIN MILL BROW

4 ...field Street

Travis Street

St Andrew's St

Helmet Street

Limeki

N Western St

Raven St

FAIFIELD STREET

Baring Street

Nelld Street

B6469

N Western St

Crane St

ASHTON OLD RO

5

ux...

Bond Street Industrial Estate

Temperance Street

Amory St

Chapelfield

Hoyle

Rachel St

WAY

JINJAN

William St

Dark La

CHANCELLOR LANE

28

A A6...

M

B

C The Gallery

Downing St Industrial

...rydon Avenue

Ardwick

Thames

I grid square represents 250 metres

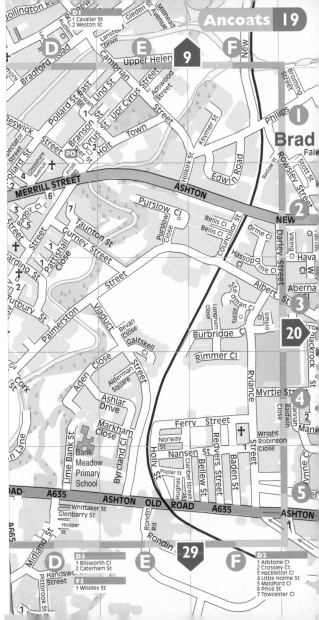

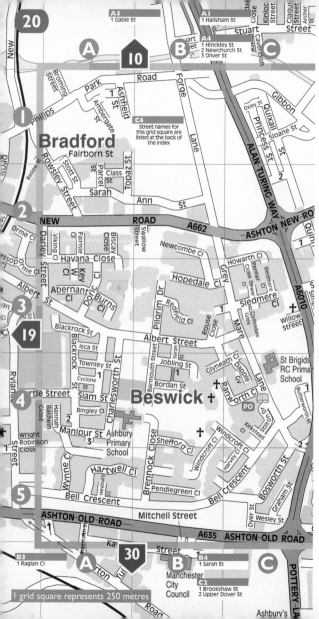

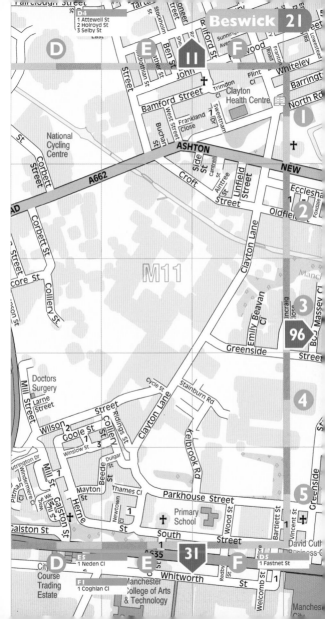

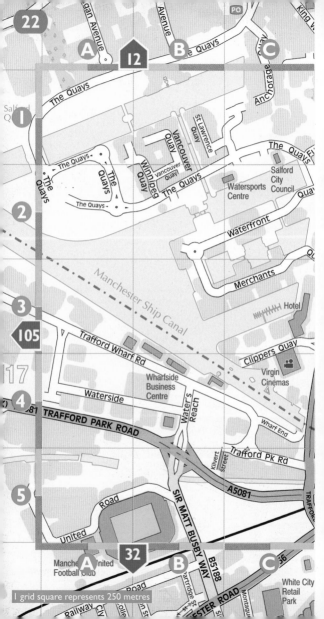

A · 12 · B · C

22

The Quays

Salford Q
1

The Quays

St Lawrence Quay

Vancouver Quay

Winnipeg Quay

Vancouver Quay

The Quays

The Quays

The Quays

Anchorage

The Quays

Watersports Centre

Salford City Council

Quay

2

Waterfront

Manchester Ship Canal

Merchants

3

105

Trafford Wharf Rd

Hotel

17

Clippers Quay

Virgin Cinemas

Wharfside Business Centre

4

Waterside

Water's Reach

Wharf End

Trafford Pk Rd

TRAFFORD PARK ROAD

5081

Kilvert Street

A5081

5

United Road

SIR MATT BUSBY WAY

B5188

TRAFFOR

Manche United Football Club

A · 32 · B · C

White City Retail Park

Railway

CHESTER ROAD

Montague

1 grid square represents 250 metres

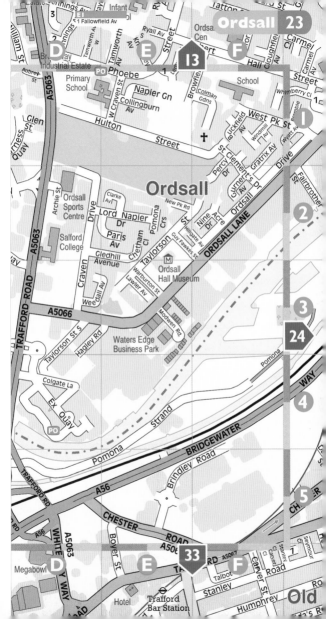

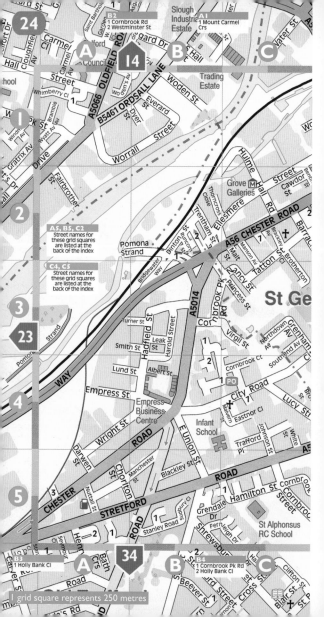

14

A B C

B2
1 Cornbrook Rd
2 Westminster St

Slough
Industrial
Estate

A1
1 Mount Carmel
Crs

Water St.

Carmel
Cl

A5066 OLDFIELD ROAD

Council

ford

gard Dr

Hall

Carmel Av

Whimberry Cl

Street

Woden's Av

B5461 ORDSALL LANE

Woden St

Everard
St

Trading
Estate

1

Gratrix Av

Drive

Bramble

Wyatt Av

Fairbrother St

Worrall Road

Dyer
St

Street

Hall

2

A5, B5, C2
Street names for
these grid squares
are listed at the
back of the index

Pomona
Strand

Bridgewater Way

Dinton St

Runcorn

Trentham St

Thorncross

Close

Ellesmere St

A56 CHESTER ROAD

Grove
Galleries

Cawdor
St

Matt

Manson Av

Tatton St

Blacker

Barra

Brotherton

3

23

C4, C5
Street names for
these grid squares
are listed at the
back of the index

Pomona
Strand

WAY

Turner St

Hadfield St

Smith St

Leak
St

Harold Street

Lund St

Albert St

Empress St

A5014

Cornbrook PK

Rd

Cor

1

2

Virgil St

Princess St

St Ge

Northndown Av

Grenham

Southend

4

Empress
Business
Centre

Wright St

Darwen St

Chorlton St

Manchester

ROAD

Blackley St

E Union St

Cornbrook Ct

PO

City Road

7

Harven

Eastnor Cl

Infant
School

Trafford
Pl

Johnson St

Lucy St

White

AF

5

CHESTER

3

Nuttall St

STRETFORD

Henry

Seymour

ROAD

Stanley Road

1

2

Sudbury D

Fernleigh Dr

ROAD

Grendale
Dr

Shrewsbur

Hamilton St

Cornbrook

street

St Alphonsus
RC School

B3
1 Holly Bank Cl

Carver St

Bath
Crs

34

A B

B4
1 Cornbrook Pk Rd
2 Holly Bank Cl

C

Road

Beever St

ford Street

Cross St

Clifton

Blair St

St P

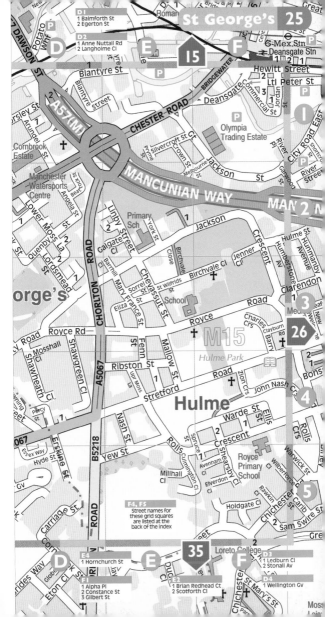

D1
1 Balmforth St
2 Egerton St

D2
1 Anne Nuttall Rd
2 Langholme Cl

E

15

F

C-Mex.Stn
Deansgate Stn

Hewitt Street

Ltl Peter St

I

DAWSON ST

Potato Whf

D

New

Roman

Great

Blantyre St

Blantyre Street

Deansgate

Commercial St

Urban

City Road East

P

CHESTER ROAD

A571(M)

Horsley St

Arundel

Cornbrook Estate

Manchester Watersports Centre

Lower Moss La

Quenby St

Lordsmead St

Angela St

Beal

Silvercroft St

Crown St

Prince

Melbourne St

Jackson St

Olympia Trading Estate

MANCUNIAN WAY

MAN 2 M

River St

Caldbeck

Shortcrs

River Street

P

Primary Sch

York St

Jackson

I

Linby Street

Galgate Cl

Barhill

Mary

Eliza

France St

Chevassut St

Sorrel St

St Wilfrids School

Birchvale Cl

Birchvale

Crescent

Jenner Cl

Hulme

Humberstone Av

Humberstone

Clarendon

Hume Avenue

Med

Leaf

New

3

Royce Rd

Mosshall Cl

Shawgreen Cl

Shawheath

CHORLTON ROAD

A5067

Fenn St

Mallow St

Royce

Road

St Wilfrids

Charles Crs

Clayburn

Barn

Charles Barn

M15

Hulme Park

Med

26

2

1

BONS

Ribston St

Upr Moss

Stretford

Road

Zion Crs

John Nash Crs

4

Percy

Hyde St

Essex Way

Nash St

Yew St

ROAD

B5218

Rolls

Cummington Cl

Millhall Cl

Hulme

Warde St

Crescent

Spruce St

Avenham

Shearsby Cl

Elverdon Cl

Ellis St

Rolls

Warwick St

Wilberforce

Rawkin Cl

Carib St

Royce Primary School

5

Carriage St

Cornbrook

St

Brides Way

Globe

Eton Cl

F-4, F-5
Street names for these grid squares are listed at the back of the index

Holdgate

Chichester

Sam Swire St

Gre

35

Loreto College

ST MARY'S ST

Chichester

Moss

orge's

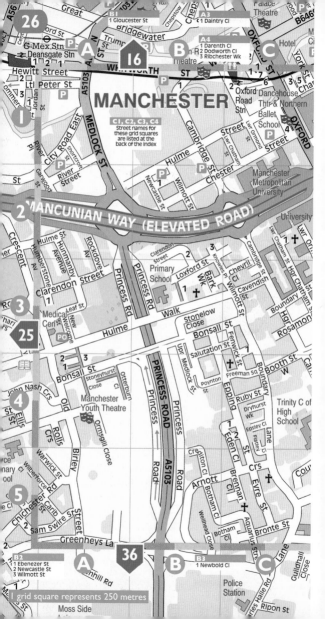

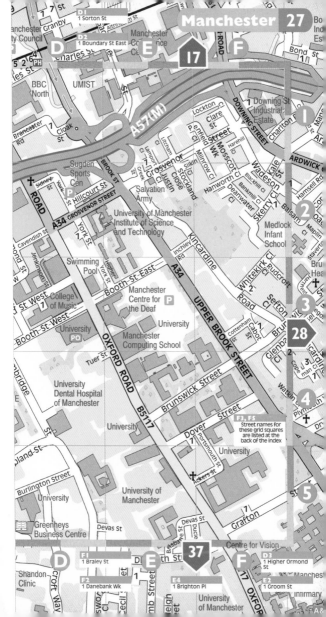

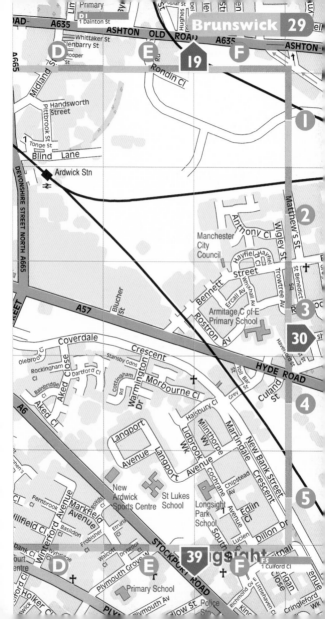

Bell Cresc
Mitchell Street
Heybury

B3
1 Skarratt Cl
2 Witterage Cl
3 Woolfall Cl

ndlegreen

A4
1 Patchett St

Ber

B1
1 Wolveton St

Dyer St

Graham St

Bosworth

ASHTON ROAD
A
20
B
A635 ASHTON OLD ROAD
C

Kay
Street
1

Gorton
Tuley St

Manchester
City
Council

Ashbury's
Station

1

POTTERY LANE

Road

Matthew's St

Wigley St
ony Cl

Vaughan Street

Regal
Industrial
Estate

Gorton Rd

Miles St

Boyd St

Aines St

A6010

2

Bennett Street

Wenlock Way

Clows

St Benedict's
Sq
Gregory St

West Gorton

Way
3
Litora

Clow
St

St

Trowtree Av
Hall St
et

Reabrook Av

Knaveton
Road

Wenlock
St
Kelsal St
2

Kempley Cl

Conquest
Benfleet

Abbotsbury

Brug
stonehur

3

Ashover
Av
Denehurst St
ord St

PO
West Gorton
Medical Centre

Street

Radbourne
Cl

A6010

29

Clowes
Ainsdale St

Beaumaris

4

HYDE ROAD
land
St

A57

Poll
Fairhaven St

Hoyland
Close
3

Gt Jon
St

Donnison St

Farnley St

Copping
St

2

1
HYDE ROAD

M12

New Bank Street
Cres

Redgate

KIRKMANSHULME LANE

5

Dillon Dr

Lane

rnall

B4
1 Deepdene St
2 Donnison St
3 Penroyson Cl

A
40
B
C

Collingt

Rigton

1 grid square represents 250 metres

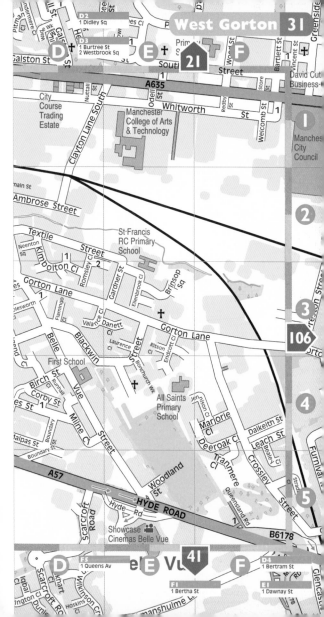

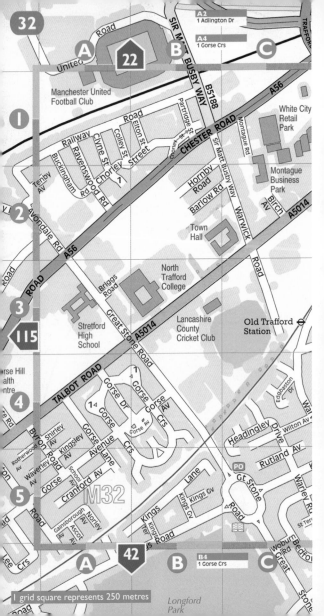

32

A2
1 Adlington Dr

A4
1 Gorse Crs

22

Manchester United
Football Club

I

White City
Retail Park

United Road

SIR MATT BUSBY WAY

A56

B5188

CHESTER ROAD

Montague Rd

Montague
Business
Park

Railway Road

Elton St

Colley St

Partridge St

Chorlton Rd

Sir Matt Busby Way

Birch AV

A5014

Clyne St

Chorley Street

Ravenswood Rd

Buckingham

Tenby AV

Hornby Road

Barlow Rd

Warwick Road

2

Avondale Rd

A56

ROAD

Town
Hall

3

ROAD

Briggs Road

North
Trafford
College

Old Trafford ⊖
Station

115

Stretford High
School

Great Stone Road

A5014

Lancashire
County
Cricket Club

orse Hill
alth
ntre

4

TALBOT ROAD

Byrom St

Gorse Dr

Gorse Crs

Gorse AV

Gorse Crs

Gorse AV

Edgbaston Dr

SIR MATT BUSBY WAY

Headingley Drive

Wilton AV

Wa

Rotherwood AV

Shirley AV

Kingsley AV

Waverley AV

Gorse Avenue

School Rd

Gorse Crs

Rutland AV

5

Gorse Road

Cranford AV

M32

Lane

Kings Lane

Kings Gv

Kings Gv

Gt Stone Road

PO

Warley Rd

Gainsborough AV

Norley AV

Ascot AV

Kings Terrace

Kings Road

Woburn Rd

Bedfo

Great

St Terr

Stone

ee
Crs

A **42** **B**

B4
1 Gorse Crs

C

I grid square represents 250 metres

Longford
Park

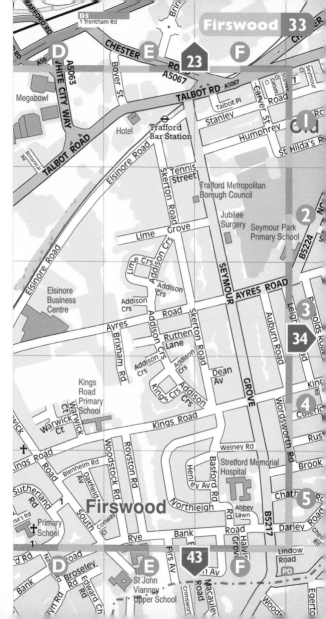

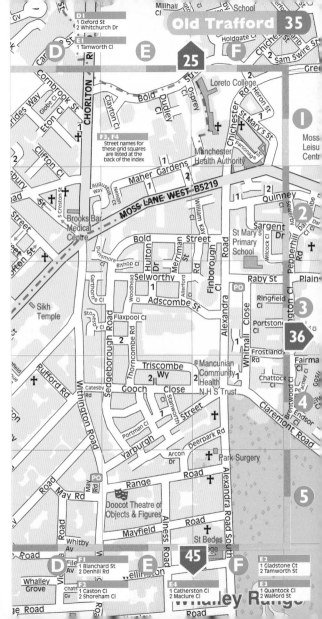

D1
1 Oxford St
2 Whitchurch Dr

E1
1 Tamworth Cl

D   E   **25**   F

Millhall   School

Holdgate   Chiche   Scarb

Sam Swire St

Gree

Car

Cornbrook Way   globe Cl   Clayton Cl   Bold   Dudley   Osprey   Loreto College

rides Way   Eton Cl   CHORLTON RD

Clifton Cl

sbury Road   S Croston St

Street   St

Brooks Bar Medical Centre

Chichester Rd   St Mary's St   Heron St

Moss Leisu Centr

I

F3, F4
Street names for these grid squares are listed at the back of the index

Manchester Health Authority

Parsonage

Augustus Way   Nelson Cl   Maher Gardens

MOSS LANE WEST-B5219

Quinney   Sewerby   be   Dar

2

Dunsmore Cl   Bishop Cl   Bold   Street

Hulton Dr   Merriman St   Finborough Rd   Rd

St Mary's Primary School

Wilcock Cl   Sargent Dr

Pepperhill Rd

Garthrop Cl   Selworthy   Woodhead Cl   Alderford   Adscombe St

Raby St   Plain

3

Sikh Temple

Sto Resbd   Flaxpool Cl

Sedgeborough Road   Thorncombe Rd

PO   Ringfield Cl

Alexandra   Portstone Cl

Whitnall Close   Frostlands Rd

36

Fairma Cl   Cosk

4

Rufford Rd   Withington Road

Catesby Rd   Triscombe Wy   Gooch   Close   Stanworth Cl   Street

Portman Cl

Mancunian Community Health N.H S Trust

Chattock Cl   Peachey Cl   Brentwood Cl   Endsor Cl

Claremont Road

Yarburgh   Arcon Dr   Deerpark Rd   Park Surgery

Road   Range   Road

PO   May Rd   Rd

Doocot Theatre of Objects & Figures

Alexandra Road South

5

Whitby Av   Mayfield   Road   Ainess   St Bedes

Road

Whalley Grove   Chats Gv

D

F1
1 Blanchard St
2 Denhill Rd

F2
1 Caston Cl
2 Shoreham Cl

File Av

Vi wellington   **45**

E   **F**

E4
1 Catherston Cl
2 Maclure Cl

E2
1 Gladstone Ct
2 Tamworth St

E3
1 Quantock St
2 Walford St

Whalley Range

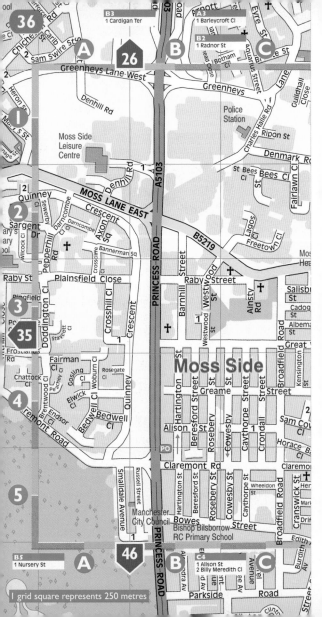

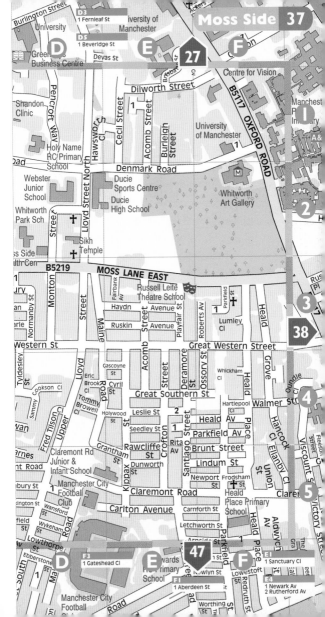

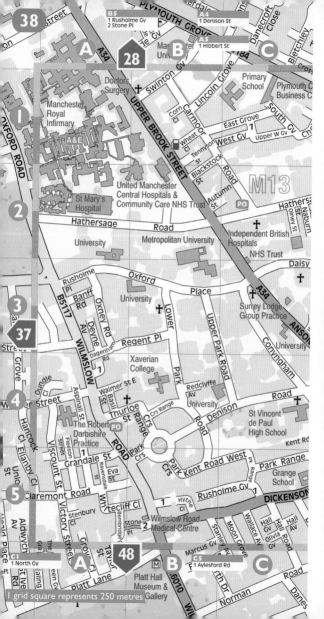

I grid square represents 250 metres

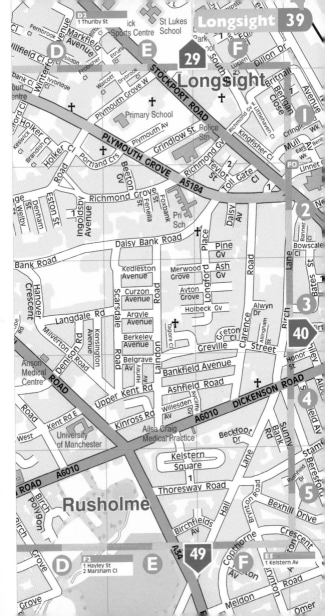

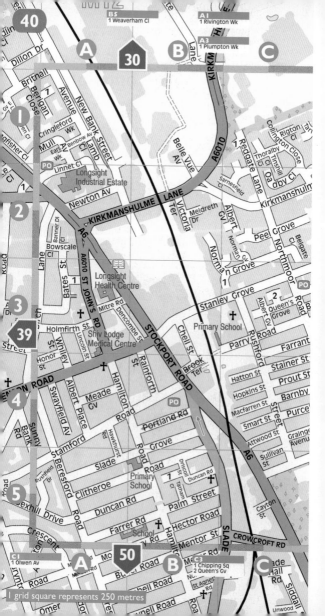

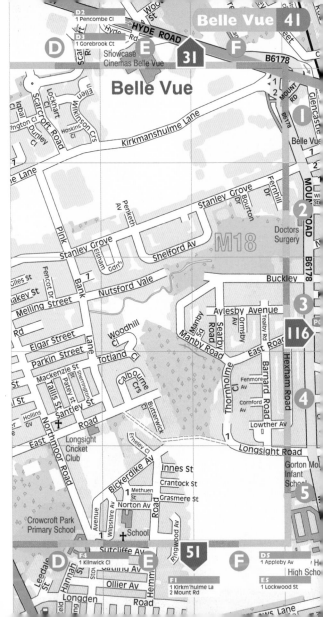

Belle Vue

Showcase Cinemas Belle Vue

31

HYDE ROAD

B6178

D2 1 Pencombe Cl
D3 1 Gorebrook Ct

Scar Rd
Rd

D

E

F

Scarcroft Road
Lockhart Cl
Ellen Wilkinson Crs
Iqbal Cl
Dunley Cl
Hoskins Cl
Wellington Cl
e Lane

I

MOUNT RD

Glencastle

Belle Vue

1

2

Kirkmanshulme Lane

Stanley Grove

Penketh Av

Elsham Gdns

Stanley Grove

Shelford Av

Bourton Dr

Fernhill Dr

M18

Doctors Surgery

MOUNT ROAD

B6178

WH St

2

Giles St
Fencot Dr
Wakey St
Meiling Street
Rd
Bank
7
Nutsford Vale

Woodhill Cl

Buckley

Aylesby Avenue

Manby St

Searby Road

Ormsby Av

Tealby Rd

East Road

3

PO

116

Elgar Street
Parkin Street
Totland Cl
Lane
Mackenzie St
Shermington St
Patey St
Santley St
Calbourne Crs

Butterwick

Thornholme Cl

Manby Road

Barnard Road

Hexham Road

Fenmore Av

Cornford Av

Lowther Av

4

St
Tallis St
Hollins GV
Santley
Road
Emeley Cl
East
Northmoor Road
Longsight Cricket Club

1

Longsight Road

Gorton Mo
Infant School

5

Bickerdike Av

Innes St
Crantock St
Grasmere St

Crowcroft Park Primary School

Avenue
Wilpshire Av
1 Methuen St
Norton Av
School
Ringwood Av
Road

Sutcliffe Av

51

D

F4 1 Kilnwick Cl
Hannah St
Gatling Av
Leedale St
Hemm
Ollier Av
Longden
Road

E

F

D5 1 Appleby Av
High Scho

E5 1 Lockwood St

F1 1 Kirkm'hulme La
2 Mount Rd

ws Lane

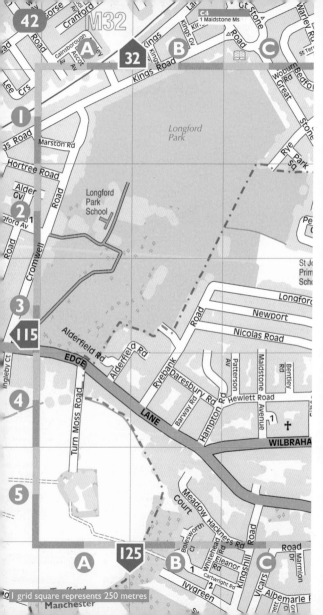

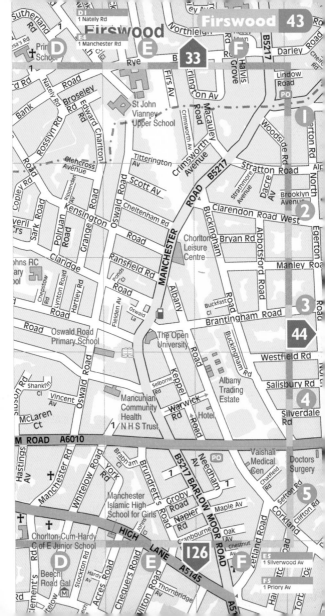

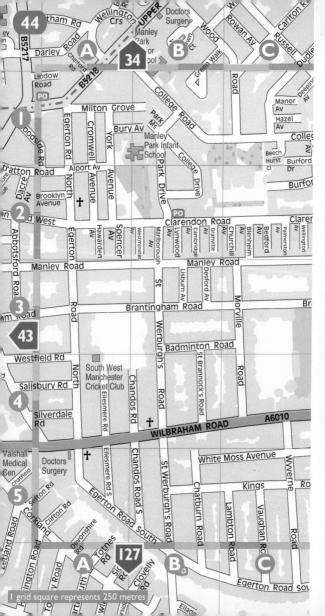

B5217

Wellington Crs

UPPER

Doctors Surgery

Rowan Av

Russell

Carlton R

Dudle

Cheltham Rd

Darley

Chelford Rd

A

Manley Park jor ool

B

Wood

Green Walk

C

Lindow Road

B5218

34

College Road

Road

Manor Av

Hazel Av

PO

Milton Grove

Park Ms

Colleg

I

Egerton Rd

Cromwell

York

Bury Av

College

Beech Hurst cl

Av

Burford

Dr

Woodside Road

Stratton Road

Dacre Av

Aiport Av

North

Avenue

Manley Park Infant School

Park Drive

College Drive

Burfor

Brooklyn Avenue

2

d West

Egerton

Hawarden Av

Spencer

Westminster Av

Clarendon Road

Marlborough

Lynwood Av

Cambridge Av

Granville Av

Churchill Av

Blenheim Av

Bedford Av

Clarer

Wellington

Palmerston

Abbotsford Road

Manley Road

St

Manley Road

3

am Road

Road

Brantingham Road

Werburgh's

Lisburn Av

Desford Av

Morville

Br

43

Badminton Road

Road

Westfield Rd

North

South West Manchester Cricket Club

Chandos Rd

Road

St Brannock's Road

4

Salisbury Rd

Ellesmere Rd

Silverdale Rd

WILBRAHAM ROAD

A6010

Vaishali Medical Cen

Chatfield

Doctors Surgery

Egerton Road South

Chandos Road S

St Werburgh's Road

White Moss Avenue

Chatburn Road

Wyverne

Kings

Ro

5

Sefton Rd

Clifton Rd

Corkland

Devonshire

Tornes Rd

127

Clovelly

A

Vaughan Rc

Road

B

C

Egerton Road Sou

Ellada

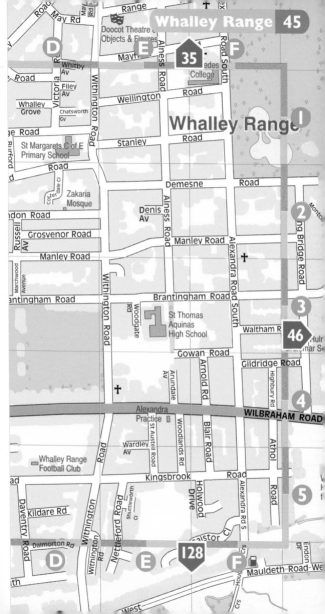

May Rd

Range

Road

Doocot Theatre
Objects & Figures

Mayfi

Alness Road

Road South

35

edes
College

Whitby
Av

Filey
Av

Chatsworth
Gv

Wellington   Road

Whalley
Grove

Victoria Rd

Withington Road

Whalley Range

Stanley   Road

I

St Margarets C of E
Primary School

Road

Cot ter dale Cl

Zakaria
Mosque

Demesne   Road   Road

2

Monton

ndon Road

Russell Av

Grosvenor Road

Denis
Av

Alness Road

ng Bridge Road

Marchwood Avenue

Manley Road

Manley Road

Alexandra Road South

antingham Road

Brantingham Road

3

Woodgate Rd

St Thomas
Aquinas
High School

Waltham R

46

Hulr
mar Se

Gowan   Road

Gildridge Road

Arundale Av

Arnold Rd

Highbury Rd

4

Alexandra
Practice

WILBRAHAM ROAD

Athol Road

Whalley Range
Football Club

Road

St Austell Road

Wardley
Av

Woodlands Rd

Blair Road

Kingsbrook   Road

Holwood Drive

Alexandra Rd S

Road

5

W
H
f

Daventry Road

Kildare Rd

Withington Road

Nettleford Road

Shuttleworth Cl

aistor

Cl

Crs

Endon Dr

D

Dalmorton Rd

E

128

F

Mauldeth Road We

th

Withington Rd

West

Hol
Crs

A
B
C

36

I

1

2

3

45

4

5

A
B
C

128

Russell Street
Bowes
Manchester Council
Bishop Bilsborrow
RC Primary School

Alexandra Av
Beresford St
Rosebery St
Cowesby St
Cranswick St
Wheeldon St

Broadfield Road

Street

Cawthorpe

Edith

Burdith

Alexandra Av
Elmswood Av
Regent Avenue
Yew Tree Av
Laurel Avenue

Parkside

Road

Clinton

Clinton Gdns

Lloyd Street

Clinton AV

Clinton Av

Clinton
Aston

Garswood
Road

Road

Manchester
Metropolitan
University

Aston Avenue

Grasscroft Cl

Montcliffe
Crescent

Spring Bridge Road

Montcliffe
Cl

Stoneyfield
Broadmeadow
Avenue

Aston Av

Aston AV

Parkway
Business
Centre

Platt
Lane

Lloyd Street South

†

Prestbury
Av

Winsford
Gatley
Avenue

Morley
Avenue

Road

Walter Road

William Hulmes
Grammar School

Highbury Rd

Bowdon
Road
Avenue

Gildridge Road

WILBRAHAM ROAD
A6010
WILBRAH

Athol
Road

Alexandra Rd S

Whalley Range
High School
for Girls

Eelsmore
Road

Sandbach
Av
Tarporley
Av

Netherton Road

Thelwall Avenue

Mellowstone
Drive

Greystoke

A5103

Doctors
Surgery
PO

Limehurst Av

Buslem
Av

Deepdale Av

1

Endon
Dr

Mauldeth Road West
Mauldeth Road West

Eddisbury Av

Coorbery Rd

Avenue

Bosley Av

Dee

PRINCESS ROAD

A5103

PRINCESS ROAD

A5103

1 grid square represents 250 metres

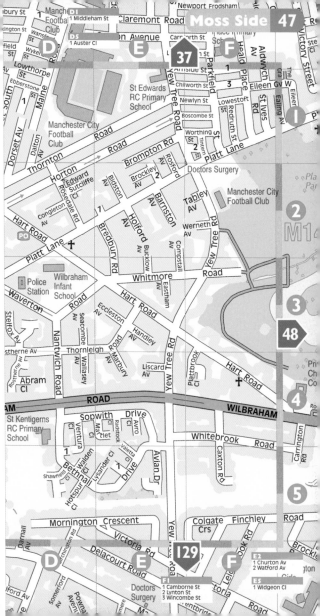

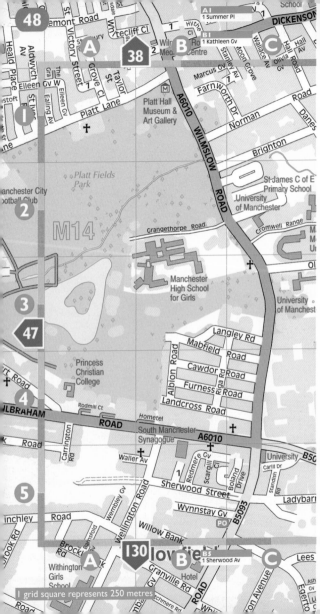

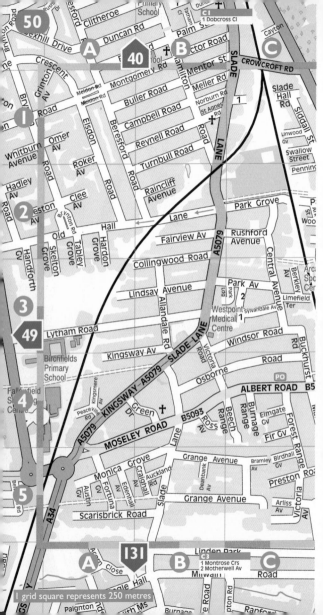

50

Rusholme Dr
Clitheroe
Primary School
Tamar C
C1
1 Dobcross Cl

Bexhill Drive
A
Duncan Rd
40
Palm St
B
Victor Road
Cayton
C
SLADE
CROWCROFT RD

Grinton Av
Crescent
Meldon Rd
Montgomery Rd
Hamilton
Mentor St
LANE
Slade Hall Rd
Siddall St

Bryon
Road
Meldon Rd
Buller Road
Meller Rd
Norburn Rd
St Agnes
1
Linwood GV

1
Whitburn Avenue
Elsdon
Beresford
Campbell Road
Road
Swallow Street
Penning

Hadley AV
Omer AV
Roker Av
Reynell Road
Turnbull Road

Preston Av
2
Byron Rd
Clee Av
Road
Raincliff Avenue

Old Skelton Grove
Tabley Grove
Hall
Hardon Grove
Lane
Park Grove

Handforth GV
Collingwood Road
Fairview Av
A5079
Rushford Avenue
Central Avenue
Berkley Av
Arca Spo Cen

3
Lytham Road
Lindsay Avenue
Alandale Rd
Park Av
Log
2
Sylvandale Av
1
Westpoint Medical Centre
Limefield Ter

49
Kingsway Av
SLADE LANE
Victoria
Windsor Road
Buckhurst Rd

Birchfields Primary School
Kingsmere
Peace Villa Rd
KINGSWAY A5079 SLADE LANE
Green
Osborne
Road
PO
ALBERT ROAD
B5

Fallowfield SI g Cen
A5079
MOSELEY ROAD
B5093
Ross Av
Beech Range
Burnage Range
Elmgate GV
Fir GV
Forest Range

4

5
A34
Bel Rd
Monica Grove
Austin GV
Fortuna Av
Craighall Av
Edenhall Av
Auckland Rd
Slade
Lane
Grange Avenue
Deanbank Av
Bramley Av
Birdhall GV
Preston Roa
Victoria
Arliss Av

Scarisbrick Road
Grange Avenue

Acon close
131
A
dale Hall
B
Milwain
Linden Park
C3
1 Montrose Crs
2 Motherwell Av
C
Road

Paignton
Burnage
e Road
xton Ms
Ranfor

1 grid square represents 250 metres

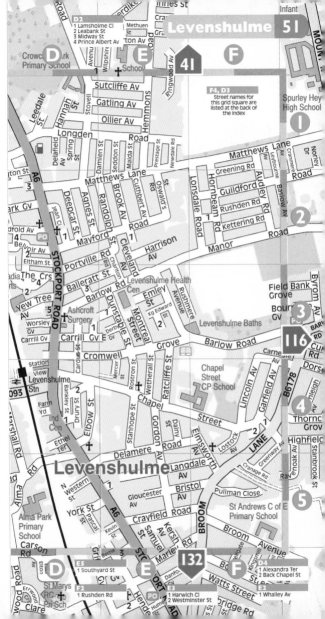

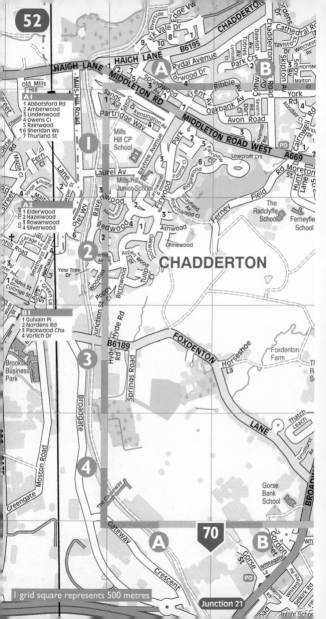

52

CHADDERTON

Junction 21

70

I grid square represents 500 metres

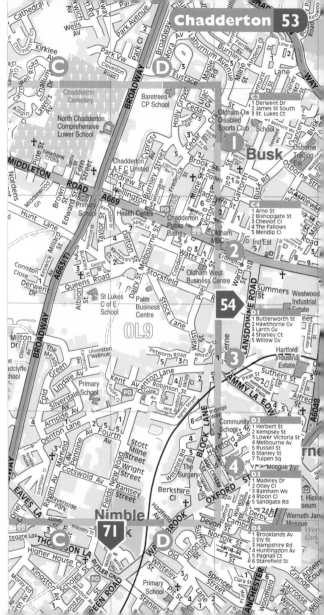

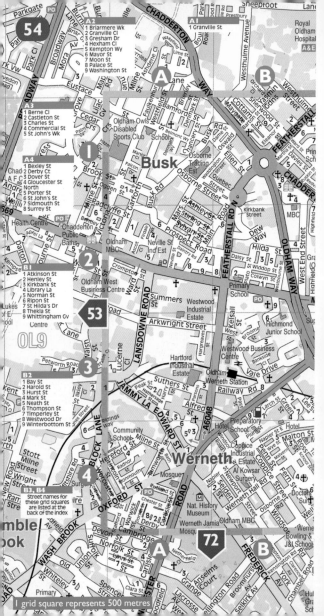

54

53 72

A2
1 Briarmere Wk
2 Granville Cl
3 Gresham Dr
4 Hexham Cl
5 Kempton Wy
6 Mayor St
7 Moon St
8 Palace St
9 Washington St

A4
1 Berne Cl
2 Castleton St
3 Charles St
4 Commercial St
5 St John's Wk

A4
1 Bexley St
2 Derby Ct
3 Dover St
4 Gloucester St North
5 Porter St
6 St John's St
7 Sidmouth St
8 Surrey St

B1
1 Atkinson St
2 Henley St
3 Kirkbank St
4 Library La
5 Norman St
6 Ripon St
7 St Hilda's Dr
8 Thekla St
9 Whittingham Gv

B2
1 Bay St
2 Harold St
3 Hurst St
4 Mark St
5 Neath St
6 Thompson St
7 Timperley St
8 Westwood Dr
9 Winterbottom St

B3, B4
Street names for these grid squares are listed at the back of the index

Busk

Werneth

OL9

1 grid square represents 500 metres

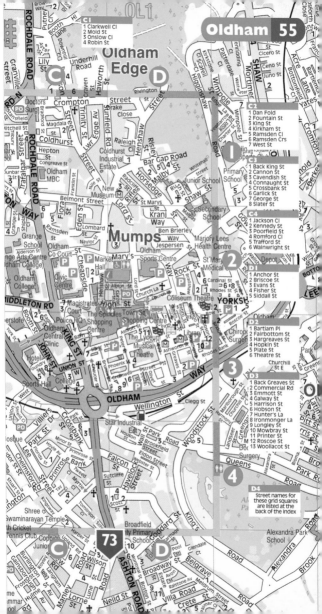

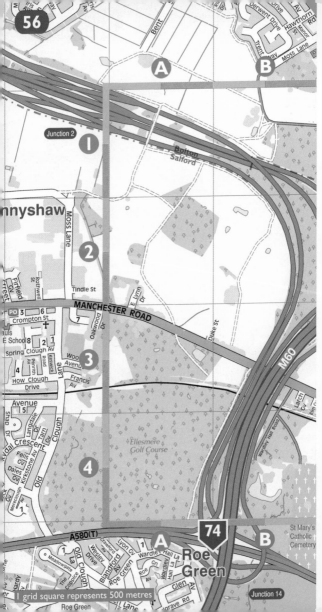

56

Junction 2

I

Bolton
Salford

nnyshaw

Moss Lane

Bent

Derwent Drive

Hawthorn

Trent Way

Moss Lane

A

B

2

Firfield

Free

Rothwell St

Tindle St

Oakmoor Dr

E Lynn Dr

Duke St

MANCHESTER ROAD

PO **3** **6**
Crompton St

7

**auls
E School** **8** **2** **1**
Spring Clough Av

Wood
Avenue

Penrith

Keswick

Road

Kirkstone

3

Francis
Av

How Clough
Drive

4

Avenue
5

Langdale

Tarn

Old

Clough

Rydal Crescent

Fells
Gv

Kirkstone Av

Dales
Gv

Mereclough

M60

Ellesmere
Golf Course

Wardley Hall Road

Larch
Gv

1

A580(T)

Lyon Gv

Wardley Hall La

A

Old Clough

The
Coppice

Meadowgate

Wesley
Mw

Blandford

Wardley
Av

Roe

74

**Roe
Green**

Clen
Av

Grave Rd

B

St Mary's
Catholic
Cemetery

Junction 14

Roe Green

I grid square represents 500 metres

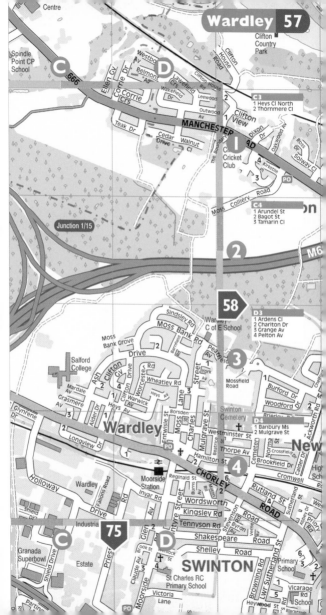

Centre

Spindle Point CP School

Clifton Country Park

Clifton House

Clifton Road

C 666 **D**

Westbo
Ellen Gv
Corrie Dr
Belmont
Av
Lawefield
Av
Corrie Crs
Wakefield
Dr
Leewood
Outwood
Av

Clifton View

C3
1 Heys Cl North
2 Thornmere Cl

MANCHESTER R D

Teak Dr
Cedar Drive
Walnut Cl

Dixon Dr
Oakwood Av
Ross Dr
Solway Cl

Cricket Club

Kirkstile
PO

Moss Colliery Road

C4
1 Arundel St
2 Bagot St
3 Tamarin Cl

on

M6

Junction 1/15

2

58

Wardley C. of E School

D3
1 Ardens Cl
2 Charlton Dr
3 Grange Av
4 Pelton Av

Moss Bank Grove

Sindsley Rd
Moss Bank Rd
Pestrfield
Av

Salford College

Moss Drive
Ash
Clifton Gv
Clifton Drive
Worcester Rd
Wheatley Rd
Heys Av
Warwick Av
Lane
Street
Moss Lane
York

3

Mossfield Road

Burford Dr
Woodford
Brierley

Mardale
Av
Grasmere
Av

Glynrene
Dr

Alden Dr
Longview Dr
Heys Av

Entwistle St
Borsden
Moss St
Charles St
Mulgrave St
Beatrice St

Swinton Cemetery

D
1 Banbury Ms
2 Mulgrave St

Ackworth Rd

Wardley

PO

Westminster St

Thorpe Av

Hamilton St

New

Orme
Crossfield
Cemetery
Brookfield Dr

High Sch

4

CHORLEY

Cromwell

Holloway

Wardley Drive

Fallons Road

Mooreside Station
Reginald St
Invar Rd
Burns St

Wordsworth

Rutland St
Sutherland St

Stevenson Rd
Byron St
Vernon St

ROAD

Wes

Shield

Industria

75

Granada Superbowl

C

Shield Drive

Estate

Priest Rd

Glen
Claude Av
Book St
Mcintyre Street
Mooreside Rd
Warlock

D

Kingsley Rd
Tennyson Rd
Shakespeare
Shelley
Road
Road

Browning Rd
Lwr Sutherland St
Heywood

Primary School

Vicarage
Rd
School

SWINTON

St Charles RC Primary School

Victoria Lane

Parting

PO

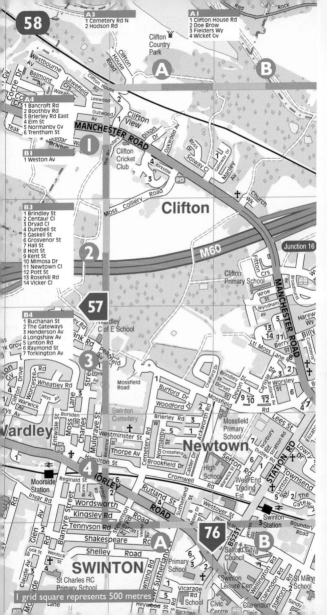

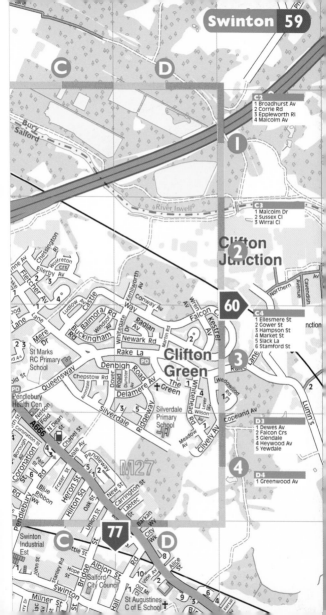

C2
1 Broadhurst Av
2 Corrie Rd
3 Eppleworth Ri
4 Malcolm Av

C3
1 Malcolm Dr
2 Sussex Cl
3 Wirral Cl

Clifton Junction

60

C4
1 Ellesmere St
2 Gower St
3 Hampson St
4 Market St
5 Slack La
6 Stamford St

Clifton Green

D3
1 Dewes Av
2 Falcon Crs
3 Glendale
4 Heywood Av
5 Yewdale

D4
1 Greenwood Av

77

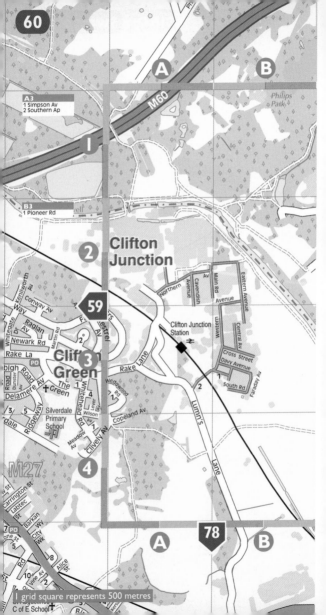

60

A B

M60

Philips Park

A3
1 Simpson Av
2 Southern Ap

I

B3
1 Pioneer Rd

2 **Clifton Junction**

Northern Avenue
Cavendish Avenue
Main Rd
Eastern Avenue
Avenue

Clifton Junction Station

Western

Central Av

Cross Street

Davy Avenue

1

South Rd

Faraday Av

59

Kenilworth Av
Conway Av
Way
Raglan
Dr Av
Whitegate
Newark Rd
Rake La
Martin Rd
Kestrel
Clif... Green
3
Rake Lane
Lumn's Lane

bigh Road
Dumster
PO
Delamere Rd
The Green
Whitehead
Lever
Wilson
Wedgwood
Copeland Av

3 5
Ridgeway
dale
Silverdale Primary School
Meadow Av
Critvely Av
4

M27

2

St
Carrington St
St
Barkan
City Wk
7 PO
St
St
Alice St
Rd
8
Wne Av
10
2
C of E School

78

A B

I grid square represents 500 metres

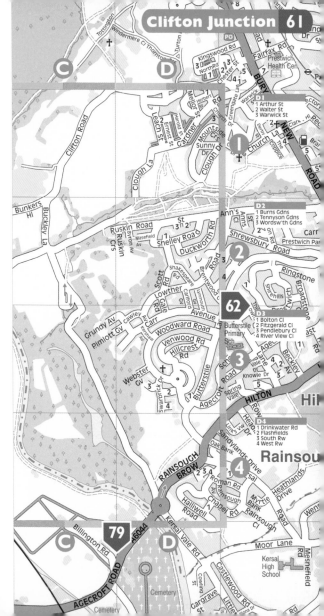

PO
Windermere Cl Thornton
Turton
Kingswood Rd
North Rd
Chester St
Warwick
Fairfax Rd
Prestwich
Health Cen

BURY

D1
1 Arthur St
2 Walter St
3 Warwick St

Herbert
Gardner
Leach St
Ernest St
Harold St
Mellor
Mountside Crs
Sunny Dr
Clough La

Church St
NEW

Clifton Road

1

ROAD

Bunkers Hi
Buckley La
Clough La

Ann's
St
Ann's
Shrewsbury Road

D2
1 Burns Gdns
2 Tennyson Gdns
3 Wordsw'th Gdns

Prestwich Par
Carr

Ruskin Road
Ruskin Crs
Byron Av
Masefield
Shelley Road
Duckworth Rd
Road

2

Ringstone
Shire hills
Broadstone

Scott
Shakespeare Rd
Brentwood
Lynmouth
Carlton
Road

Lowther
Gale
Carr
Avenue

62

Butterstile
Primary
Sch

D3
1 Bolton Cl
2 Fitzgerald Cl
3 Pendlebury Cl
4 River View Cl

Grundy Av
Pimlott Gv
Cawley Av
Keresow Av

Woodward Road
Venwood Rd
Hillcrest Rd

Webster
Gv
Butterstile
Warwick Dr
Agecroft Road

Vale
Knowle Dr
Beckley Av

3

Spring
Vale

HILTON

Hi

D4
1 Drinkwater Rd
2 Flashfields
3 South Rw
4 West Rw

Links Vw Dr
Head
Sandylands Drive
Oak Bank

Rainsou

RAINSOUGH
BROW

4

Roman Rd
Rainsough
Bank
Rainsough
Cl

Halliwell
Road
Chapel Rd
Myrtle
Heathlands
Drive

Rainsough
Road

Wen

79

C
Billington Rd
A6044
D
Kersal Vale Rd
Cowling
St
Garorave

Moor Lane
Kersal
High
School

Mesnefield
Rd
Castlewood Rd
Little

AGECROFT ROAD
Cemetery
Cemetery

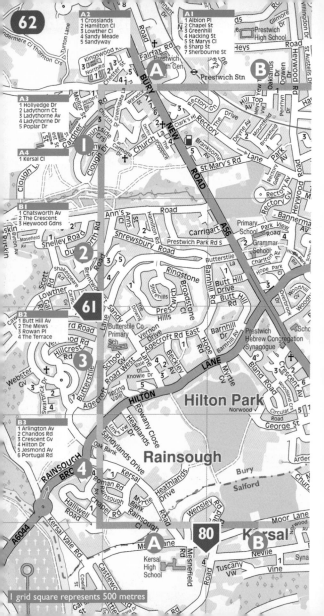

62

A2
1 Crosslands
2 Hamilton Cl
3 Lowther Cl
4 Sandy Meade
5 Sandyway

A1
1 Albion Pl
2 Chapel St
3 Greenhill
4 Hacking St
5 St Marys Cl
6 Sharp St
7 Sherbourne St

Prestwich High School

Fairfax Rd

Prestwich
th Cen

A

Prestwich Stn

B

A3
1 Hollyedge Dr
2 Ladythorn Ct
3 Ladythorne Av
4 Ladythorne Dr
5 Poplar Dr

A4
1 Kersal Cl

1

B1
1 Chatsworth Av
2 The Crescent
3 Heywood Gdns

2

61

B2
1 Butt Hill Av
2 The Mews
3 Rowan Pl
4 The Terrace

3

Prestwich Hebrew Congregation Synagogue

Hilton Park

Norwood

B3
1 Arlington Av
2 Chandos Rd
3 Crescent Gv
4 Hilton Dr
5 Jesmond Av
6 Portugal Rd

Rainsough

RAINSOUGH
BRO

4

Bury

Salford

A

80

B

Kersal High School

Kersal

I grid square represents 500 metres

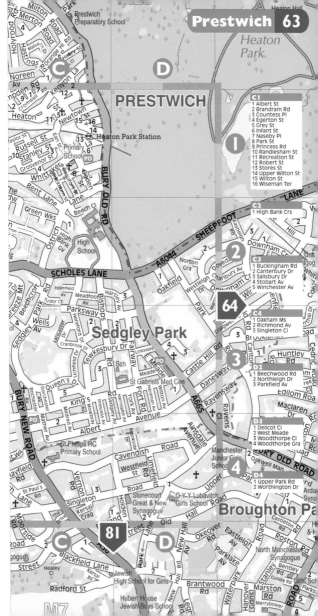

64

A3
1 Carlton Av
2 Counthill Dr
3 Links Crs

A2
1 Balmoral Gra
2 Lyndhurst Av
3 Sandringham Gra

Heaton Hall

Heaton
Park

A   **B**

MIDDLETON

P **A4** ICH
1 Inglelene Av
2 Oakwell Dr

n Park Station

Bowker Vale
Primary
School

I

A576

Northbrook
Av Welford
Rd

Edge Ware

Windle Av

B1
1 Redford Rd

LANE

Watkins Dr

Carr
Bank
Av

SHEEPFOOT

Meade

Hill

Newington

Road
Northby's

Hillwood
Av

Kendal Rd

Blackle

B2
1 Edson Rd
2 Mosslee Av
3 Southbrook Av

Downham Crs

Downham
Gdns

United
Synagogue

White
House
C
Cop

Bowker Vale Station

2

North
Gra

Dovedale Av

Charlbury Rd

Bethe

Westleigh

Downham Crs

Windsor

Edenfield Rd

Silverdale

Craigwell Rd

County

Road

Coverdale

Monica Av

63

B3
1 Bettwood Dr
2 Highclere Rd
3 Kenslow Av
4 Mountford Av

Bowker Bank Av

Carlton

Brooklands   Road

Huntley
Rd

Cedric Road

MIDDLETON

Holland

Belhaven Rd

Boardman Rd

B4
1 Alder Ct
2 Colbourne Av
3 Leicester Av
4 Nada Rd
5 Parsonage St
6 Upper Park Rd

Rothesay

Rd

Haversham
Rd Plymtree

Heaton Park
Synagogue

Dales
Av

Moorla
Av

Sch

Meade

3

PO

Carr Hill Rd

Road

Edilom Road

Ardern Road

St Gabriels Med Cen

Wilton
Rd

Haremill Rd

Danesway

Maclaren
Dr

PO

Crum

A665

Ravensway

Ravens
C

Cheetham
Hill Cricket Club

Moxley
Rd

Melford
Rd

Bennett
Rd

St Mary's Hall

Crump

FORT
Rd

York
A665

Av

AVENUE

Catherine Road

Polygon

Eaton
Rd

Redw
Rd

Cavendish

Road

Ainsdale

Avenue

Westfield
St

Limefield
Rd

BURY OLD ROAD

Manchester
Junior Girls
School

Oakwell Man Salford

King David
High School

Seymour

4

Holden
Rd

Holden

St

Lane

Old

New Hall

Upper

Park

Hall

O-Y-Y Lubavitch
Girls School

Ardath Israel
Synagogue

Jun Sch

Primary

Hanlon
Cemetery

Stonecourt
Great & New
Synagogue

Broughton Park

82

Trumpsall
roughton
nagogue

K Street

Old

New Hall
Lane

Okeover
Rd

Eastleigh
Av

Castleton
Rd

Roston
Rd

N
Manchester
Synagogue

Girls Sch

rit

George St N

Thomas st

Tyson st

PO

Wellfie
Medic
Ce

ewish
igh School for Girls

Brantwood

Parkdale

Stanley

ROAD

Bentley

Cupley Rd

Parkside
Av

George St S

Copthall
Grosvenor

Hump

Jewish Boys School

Marston
Rd

Merrybower

Crane

A

B

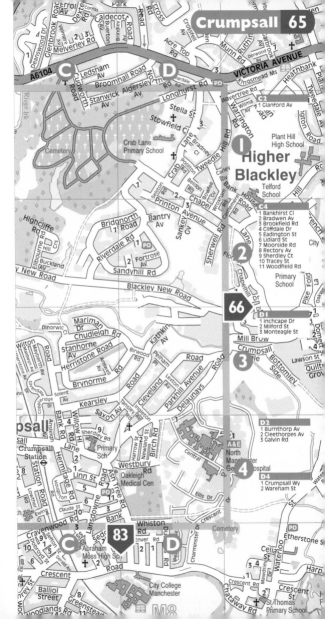

A6104

C Ledsham Av

Broomhall Road

Stanwick Aldersley Av

D

Longhurst Rd PO

VICTORIA AVENUE

Wavertree Rd

Heathbank

Tweedale

C2
1 Gianford Av

Stella St

Stowfield Cl

Crab Lane Primary School

Plant Hill High School

Higher Blackley

Telford School

C4
1 Bankhirst Cl
2 Bradwen Av
3 Brookfield Rd
4 Cliffdale Dr
5 Eadington St
6 Lidiard St
7 Moorside Rd
8 Rectory Av
9 Sherdley Ct
10 Tracey St
11 Woodfield Rd

Highcliffe Rd

Bridgnorth

Bantry Av

Printon Avenue

Chapel

Sankey Gv

Sherwell Rd

Riverdale Rd

PO

Fortrose Av

Sandyhill Rd

Blackley New Road

2

Primary School

66

D1
1 Inchcape Dr
2 Milford St
3 Monteagle St

Dinorwic

Mariman Dr

Chudleigh Rd

Stanhorne Av

Herristone Road

Wilton

Brynorme

Kathkin Av

Pelham

Cleveland Road

Parkhill Avenue

Delaunays

Mill Brow

Crumpsall

Bottomley Side

Lawson St

Quilt Gro

...psall

Crumpsall Station

Bank Av

Willow Rd

Saxon Av

Sherdley Rd

Primary Sch

Birch Rd

Harrow St

Newland St

Westbury Rd

Oakleigh Medical Cen

Central

A&E

North Manchester General Hospital

4

D2
1 Burnthorp Av
2 Cleethorpes Av
3 Calvin Rd

D4
1 Crumpsall Wy
2 Wareham St

Hermitage Road

Linn St

Claude St

Bank

Whiston Rd

Ellis Dr

Crescent

Cravenwood Rd

C

Abraham Moss High Sch

83

D

Denver Rd

Charminster Dr

Cemetery

PO

Etherstone S

Balliol Street

Greenstead

Crescent

Road

City College Manchester

M8

Chataway Rd

Crescent St

St Thomas Primary School

Celia St

Waterloo

Harp

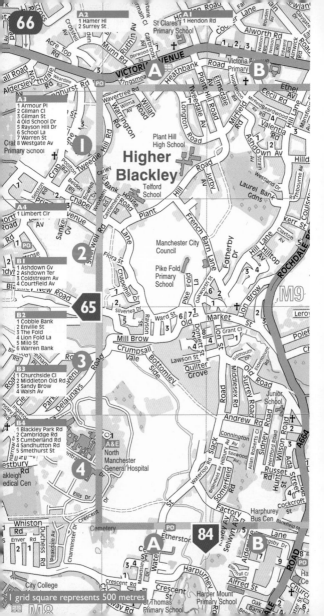

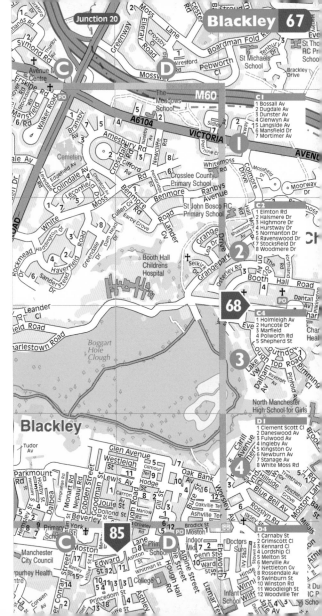

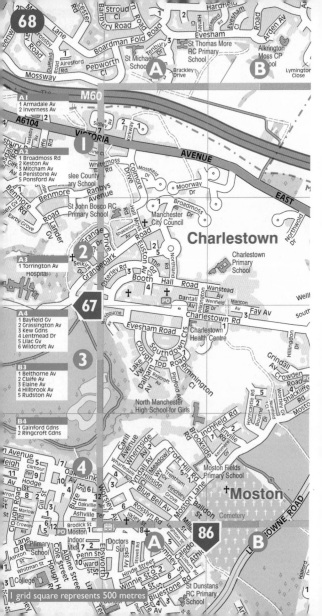

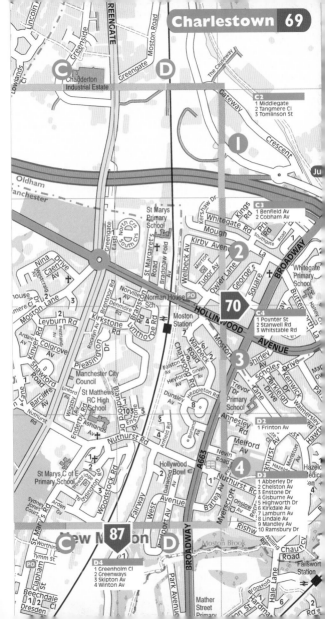

C2
1 Middlegate
2 Tangmere Ci
3 Tomlinson St

C3
1 Benfield Av
2 Cobham Av

C4
1 Poynter St
2 Stanwell Rd
3 Whitstable Rd

D2
1 Frinton Av

D3
1 Abberley Dr
2 Chelston Av
3 Enstone Dr
4 Gisburne Av
5 Highworth Dr
6 Kirkdale Av
7 Lamburn Av
8 Lindale Av
9 Mandley Av
10 Ramsbury Dr

D4
1 Greenholm Cl
2 Greenways
3 Skipton Av
4 Winton Av

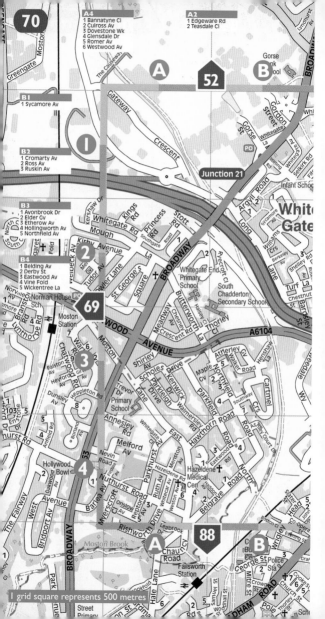

70

A4
1 Bannatyne Cl
2 Culross Av
3 Dovestone Wk
4 Glensdale Dr
5 Romer Av
6 Westwood Av

A2
1 Edgeware Rd
2 Teasdale Cl

Gorse
Bank
Pool

A 52 **B**

Gordon
Street

Gorse
St
PO
Whitegate
La

B1
1 Sycamore Av

Greengate

The Causeway

Gateway
Crescent

Junction 21

Argyll
Road

Infant School

**White
Gate**

B2
1 Cromarty Av
2 Ross Av
3 Ruskin Av

I

Kings
Rd

Princess
Rd

Stott
Road

Long
Lane

B3
1 Avonbrook Dr
2 Elder Gv
3 Etherow Av
4 Hollingworth Av
5 Northfield Av

Kershaw Dr
Whitegate Rd
Mough
Southgate La

2

Kirby Avenue

St George's
Square

Broadway

Whitegate End
Primary
School

South
Chadderton
Secondary School

B4
1 Belding Av
2 Derby St
3 Eastwood Av
4 Vine Fold
5 Wickentree La

Fowler Lane
Tudor Av

Meadway

Butterworth

Cheshire
Crescent Rd

Thorley
Cl

A6104

Turf La

Chestnut

Norville
Sch

Norman House

69

Moston
Station

WOOD

Moston
AVENUE

Shirley
Av

Scholes
Drive

Kenwick
Drive

Walmersley
Rd

Maple
Gv

Atherley
Gv

Northfield
Rd

Newel
Road

Southway

Parkfield
Crs

3

Chatworth
Av

Wall
St

Falston
Av

Heyford
Gv

Trevor
Drive

Parkfield
Drive

East
Whitegate

Hawthorn

Parkfield
Road

North
Road

Dunsley
Av

Heppleton Rd

Annesley
Rd

Melford
Av

Hazeldene Rd

Hazeldene
Medical
Cen

Eastwood
Rd

Belgrave
Road

103

Hollywood
Bowl

4

Oakwood Av

Nevin
Road

Nuthurst Road

West
Avenue

Bardsea
Av

Myerscroft
Onslow
Av

Parkham

Ruth
Av

Whitegate
Weston

Leabrook
Rd

Rishworth

A 88 **B**

The Fairway

Bridport Av

BROADWAY

Moston Brook

Hale Lane

Chauncy
Road

Failsworth
Station

George St

Police
Sta

ROAD

DHAM

Street
Primary

I grid square represents 500 metres

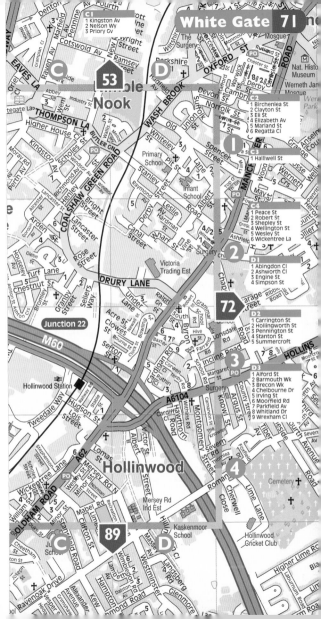

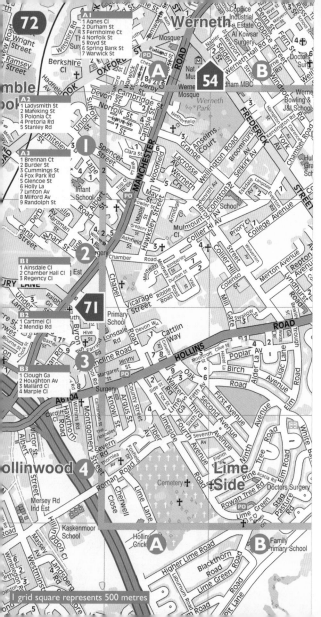

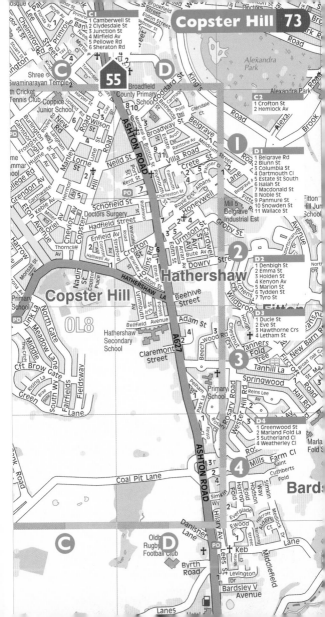

C1
1 Camberwell St
2 Clydesdale St
3 Junction St
4 Mirfield Av
5 Pellowe Rd
6 Sheraton Rd

C **D**

Shree Swaminarayan Temple

th Cricket
Tennis Club Coppice
Junior School

55

Broadfield
County Primary
School

Alexandra
Park

Alexandra Park Road

C2
1 Crofton St
2 Hemlock Av

1

D1
1 Belgrave Rd
2 Blunn St
3 Columbia St
4 Dartmouth Cl
5 Estate St South
6 Isaiah St
7 Macdonald St
8 Noble St
9 Panmure St
10 Snowden St
11 Wallace St

Doctors Surgery

Belgrave
Industrial Est

Hathershaw

2

D2
1 Denbigh St
2 Emma St
3 Holden St
4 Kenyon Av
5 Marion St
6 Tydden St
7 Tyro St

Copster Hill

OL8

Hathershaw
Secondary
School

Claremont
Street

Bellfield Avenue

Adam St

Beehive
Street

D3
1 Ducie St
2 Eve St
3 Hawthorne Crs
4 Letham St

3

Springwood

Tanhill La

Reins Lee
Av

D4
1 Greenwood St
2 Marland Fold La
3 Sutherland Cl
4 Weatherley Cl

4

Mills Farm Cl

Saint
Cuthberts
Fold

Bard

Coal Pit Lane

Danisher
Lane

Oldh
Rugby
Football Club

C **D**

Byrth
Road

Bardsley V
Avenue

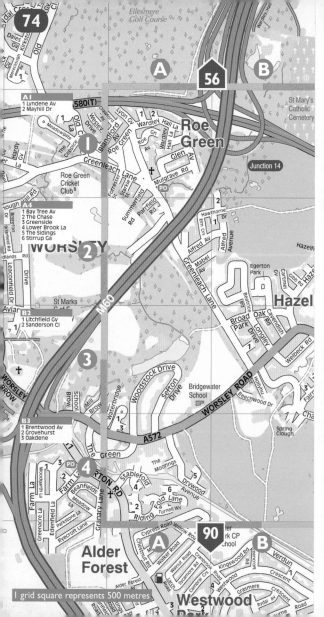

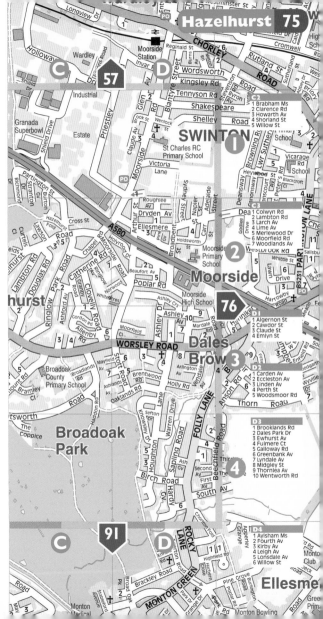

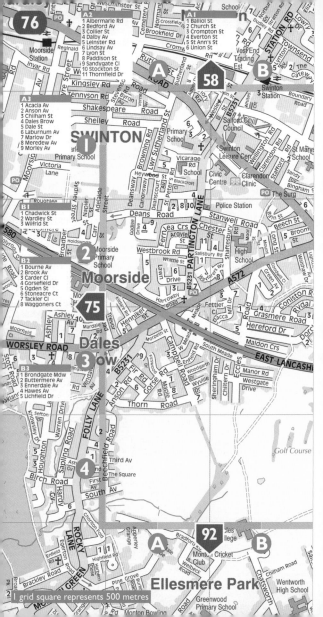

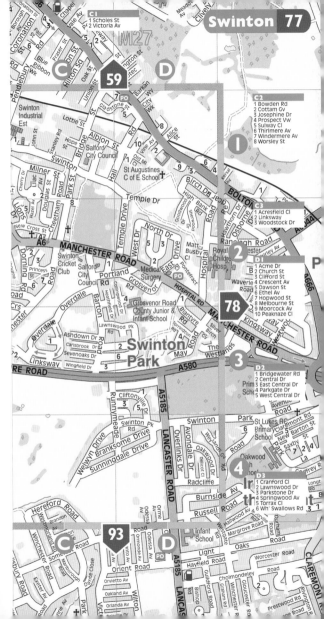

C1
1 Scholes St
2 Victoria Av

C2
1 Bowden Rd
2 Cottam Gv
3 Josephine Dr
4 Prospect Vw
5 Sulway Cl
6 Thirlmere Av
7 Windermere Av
8 Worsley St

C1
1 Acresfield Cl
2 Linksway
3 Woodstock Dr

D1
1 Acme Dr
2 Church St
3 Clifford St
4 Crescent Av
5 Dawson St
6 Ethel Av
7 Hopwood St
8 Melbourne St
9 Moorcock Av
10 Peaknaze Cl

D2
1 Bridgewater Rd
2 Central Dr
3 East Central Dr
4 Parkgate Dr
5 West Central Dr

D3
1 Cranford Cl
2 Lawnswood Dr
3 Parkstone Dr
4 Springwood Av
5 Torrax Cl
6 Wh' Swallows Rd

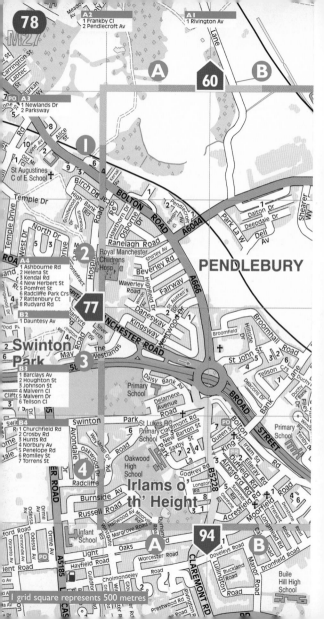

A2
1 Frankby Cl
2 Pendlecroft Av

A1
1 Rivington Av

A 60 **B**

7 PO
A3
1 Newlands Dr
2 Parksway

10

Alice Rd

Carrington Rd
Labtec
Larkin St

St Augustines
C of E School

BOLTON ROAD A6044

Birch Dr

High Bank

Hawthorn Rd

Osborne

Kersal

Pendlecroft

Park La W

Dalton Dr
Deepdale
Dell Av

Shearer Wy

Temple Dr

PENDLEBURY

West Dr
North Dr

Ranelagh Road

Royal Manchester
Childrens
Hosp.

Shirley Av

Beverley Rd

Waverley
Road

Highfield Rd

A666

Fairway

Broomhall Road

Hillside

Broomfield

A4
1 Ashbourne Rd
2 Helena St
3 Kendal Rd
4 New Herbert St
5 Pomfret St
6 Radcliffe Park Crs
7 Rattenbury Ct
8 Rudyard Rd

77

St Austells Rd

Daneway

Silver Birch

St John St

Telson

Duchy Bank

Deacons Dr

B2
1 Dauntesy Av

MANCHESTER ROAD

Kingsway

The Westlands

Swinton Park

May St

3

B3
1 Barclays Av
2 Houghton St
3 Johnson St
4 Malvern Cl
5 Malvern Dr
6 Tellson Cl

BROAD STREET

Daisy Bank Av

Primary School

Delamere
Avenue

Swinton

Park Road

St Lukes Rd
Primary
School

Claremont Rd

New Barton St

Saxby

PO

King St

Tram Sq

Ellesy Rd
Oldfield Rd

Primary
School

Wins

B4
1 Churchfield Rd
2 Crosby Av
3 Hunts Rd
4 Norbury Av
5 Penelope Rd
6 Romley St
7 Torrens St

Avondale

Weylands Gr

Oakwood Pk

Oakwood
High School

Godfrey Rd

Longton St

Alresford Rd

Moorfield Road

Longman Rd

Acresfield Rd

Denstone Rd

4

Radcliffe

Burnside

Russell Road

Hallwood Av

Moorfield

Durham Rd

Irlams o' th' Height

8

Odessa Av
Ormonde Av

Orme Rd

A5185

Infant
School

Light

Oaks

Margrove Rd

Hayfield Rd

Worcester Road

Choimondeley

Road

A 94 **B**

CLAREMONT RD

Doveleys Rd

Lillington Road

Buckland Road

Manor Road

Dronfield Road

Buile Hill High School

Prestwood Rd

Rivington Rd

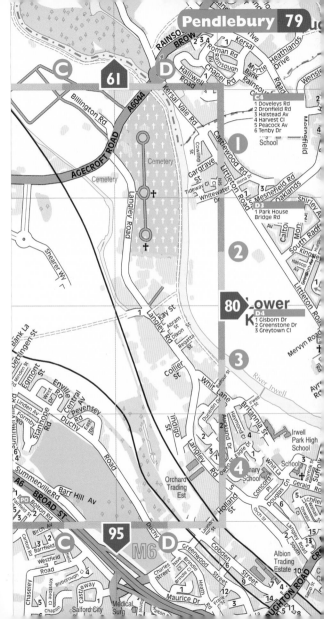

61

C **D**

RAINSO... BROW

Halliwell Road

Kersal Vale Rd

Chapel Rd

Roman Rd
Kersal
Heathlands
Drive
Rainsough
Myrtle Bank
Wensle...

C4
1 Doveleys Rd
2 Dronfield Rd
3 Halstead Av
4 Harvest Cl
5 Peacock Av
6 Tenby Dr

...igh
School

Masnefield

Billington Rd

A6044

AGECROFT ROAD

Cemetery

Cemetery

Langley Road

Shearer Wy

1

Castleford Rd

Littleton Road

Cowling St

Cargrave St

Tideway Cl

Whitewater Dr

Isis

Ilona Dr

Mesnefield Rd

Oaklands

Shirley Av

D3
1 Park House Bridge Rd

Calton

South Radf...

Kingsle...

Hasson

Gemma Gdns

2

Littleton Road

Bank La

...lderingen St

Egmont St

ENVILLE

WEST

Central Av

Pevensey

East

Duchy

Linden Av

Formby Rd

Stanhope Rd

Fairfield St

R. Minden Av

Langley Rd

Kay St

Abram St

Elixon

Regatta Rd

Collier St

Indigo St

Langley Rd

Whit Lane

Duncalm Dr

Auckland Dr

Hammond Av

Ashley Eagle St

Britannia St

Irwell St

River Irwell

Irwell Park High School

80 ... ower

K **D4**
1 Gisborn Dr
2 Greenstone Dr
3 Greytown Cl

Mervyn Road

P

Ayre... Rd

3

4

Summerville Rd

A6

BROAD ST

Barr Hill Av

Bolton Rd

Fairfield St

Linden Av

Duchy Road

Orchard Trading Est

Holland St

...mary School

Concord

Eagle Cl

Whit Lg

Douglas St

Gerald

School

Lichfiel...

Croxdel...

Langley Road

South

Albion Trading Estate

C **95** **D**

M6

Cobden St

Greenwood Street

Douglas St

...UGHTON ROAD

PO

Birch Av

Barfield

Westfield Road

Carlton Rd

Chaseley

Blyborough

Keystone

Castleway

Chapln

Salford City Medical Surg

Charles Street

Nave

Brindle

Brindle

Heath

Greenwood Street

Maurice Dr

Frank St

Salton

Cobden Street

14

10

12

Albion Trading Estate

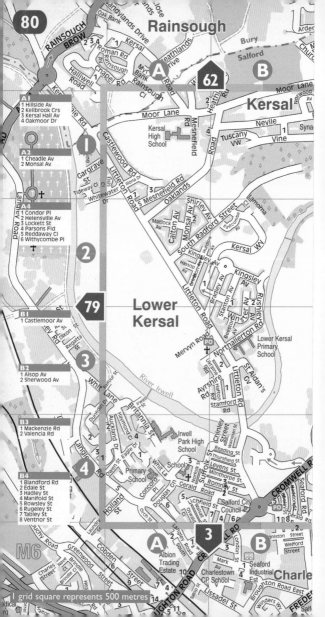

80

RAINSOUGH BROW

Rainsough

Bury
Salford

Rainsough Cl
Rainsough Rd

62

A

B

Moor Lane

Kersal

Nevile
Tuscany VW
Vine
Syna

Heathlands Drive
Oak Bank
Roman Rd
Chapel Rd
Halliwell Road
Kersal Road

A1
1 Hillside Av
2 Kellbrook Crs
3 Kersal Hall Av
4 Oakmoor Dr

A2
1 Cheadle Av
2 Monsal Av

A4
1 Condor Pl
2 Helensville Av
3 Lockett St
4 Parsons Fld
5 Reddaway Cl
6 Withycombe Pl

Moor Lane

Kersal High School

Mesnefield Rd

Castlewood Road

Gargrave St
Littleton Road
Tideway Cl
Whitewater Dr
Langley Road

Mesnefield Road
Oaklands
Illona Dr

South Radford Street
Shirley Av
Carlton Av
Matlock Av
Monsal Av
Kingsley Av
Hassop Av
Kersal Wy
Kingsley Av
Lamorna
Ramona

Bradley Av
Stanton Av
Winster Av
Rushley Av
Beecroft Av

I

2

79

B1
1 Castlemoor Av

Lower Kersal

3

B2
1 Alsop Av
2 Sherwood Av

Littleton Road

Mervyn Road
Northallerton Road
Lower Kersal Primary School

Ukraine Road
St Aidan's Cv

Regatta
Dixon
White Lane

River Irwell

Ayrshire Rd
Stamford Rd
Littleton Rd

B3
1 Mackenzie Rd
2 Valencia Rd

Whit Lane
Britannia St
Dunedin Rd
Auckland Dr
Hammond Cl
Eagle Dr
Owen St

Irwell Park High School

Chinley Street
Reading St
Thursfield St
Levens St
Milnthorpe St
Romney St
Wetmann St

4

B4
1 Blandford Rd
2 Edale St
3 Hadley St
4 Manifold St
5 Rowsley St
6 Rugeley St
7 Tabley St
8 Ventnor St

Langfield Av
Whit La
School Rd
Concord Pl
Douglas
Primary School

Gerald Road
Lichfield Rd
Suffolk St
Salford City Council

CROMWELL
Seaford Rd

M6

Holland St
Laundry

Greenwood Street
Cobden Street

Charles Street
Nave
Brindle St

A

Albion Trading Estate

3

B

Mark Charlestown CP School

Seaford Industrial Est

Charle

Langley Road South
Leighton Road

Broughton Road East
Winders Wy
FREDE

Lissadel St

I grid square represents 500 metres

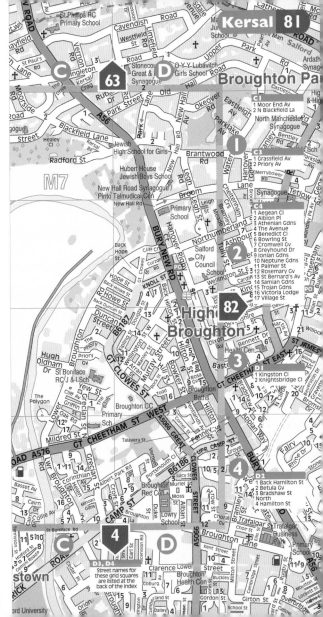

St Phillips RC Primary School
Cavendish Road
Westfield Rd
Vernon Rd
Mayfield Rd
St Paul's Lane
Singleton
C
Kersal Crag
The Drive
Rutland Dr
Park Street
A56
Blackfield Lane
Healey Cl
Radford St
Synagogue Street
Moorside Road
Road

Stonecutter Great & Synagogue
O·Y·Y Lubavitch Girls School
D
Upper Park Rd
63
New Hall Road
Okeover Rd
Old Hall
Broughton Park
Castleton
Cathedral
Kersal Man
ROAD Salford
Ardath Synagogue
High &
Cl
North Manchester Synagogue
Eastleigh
Parklake Av
Water Lane
Hanover
Bentley
Av

Merrybower Rd
Synagogue
Tetlow

1

Jewish High School for Girls
Hubert House Jewish Boys School
New Hall Road Synagogue
Pinto Talmudical Cen
New Hall Rd
Brantwood Rd
Cheltenham Crs
Ashbourne
Broom
Leigh St
Leigh St
Primary School
Northumberland
Salford City Council
Wellington
Cardiff
King
Cheshire
M7

Back Hope St
Cliff Cres
Curzon
Rigby
KNOLL ST
Hope St
Back Howe St
Howe St
Back Duncan St
Duncan Street
B6187
The Priory
Priory Gv
Knoll
Bowker

2

High Broughton

82

Dixon
Bennett St
Health Cen

3

Baste
GT. CHEETHAM ST EAST
ST JAMES
Hars St
Wilmur

Hugh Oldham Dr
St Boniface RC/J & I Sch
New St
The Polygon
Grecian
Griffin
Lower Oak
Mildred St
GT. CHEETHAM ST WEST
Broughton CC Primary
Talavera St
GT CLOWES ST
Wellington
Manley
Arran
Murray
Bowker
Todd
Rosa
Broughton Baths
Hilton
Cobnet St
Fenney St
UPR CAMP
ASCOGS GREEN
Vernon
Grove

4

Bury
Appian Way
Rhyne Rd
Fairy
Stone

ROAD A576
LWR BROUGHTON
Corinthian
Heen
Albert Park Rd
Croft St
Minoan Gdns
CAMP ST
Broughton
B6186
Lucy St
Portsmouth Cl
Broughton Rec Cen
Muriel St
Moss St
Duke St
Lowry School
Alban St
Broughton
Choral St
Bramley

Basset Av
Cairn Dr
Collie Av
St Boniface Rd
C
Gemini Road
Honford St
4
ROAD
Earl St
D
Ascension Rd
Clarence Lower Broughton Street
Coburg
Buckley
Milton Street
Trafalgar
St Trafalgar Business Park
Primary
Kent Street
Broughton Lane
Choir St
Broughton Health Cen
Gordon St
Girton St
Rugby St
Moulton St
Cambridge St
Orion
Dalley
School St
Overbridge

stown
CK
ford University

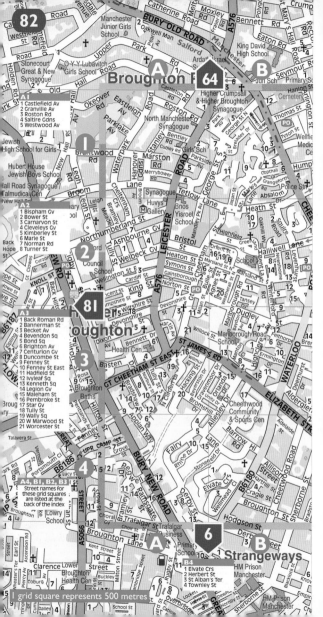

82

Catherine Road
BURY OLD ROAD
A576
Bennett
Crump

Manchester
Junior Girls
School

Oakwell Man Salford

King David
High School

Broughton P. **64**

Higher Crumpsall
& Higher Broughton
Synagogue

A1
1 Castlefield Av
2 Granville Av
3 Roston Rd
4 Saltire Gdns
5 Westwood Av

North Manchester
Synagogue

Jewish
High School for Girls

Hubert House
Jewish Boys School

Hall Road Synagogue
Talmudical Cen
New Hall

A2
1 Bispham Gv
2 Bower St
3 Carnarvon St
4 Cleveley Gv
5 Kimberley St
6 Marie St
7 Norman Rd
8 Turner St

Bnos
Yisroel
School

Bristol

81

Broughton

A3
1 Back Roman Rd
2 Bannerman St
3 Becket Av
4 Bevendon Sq
5 Bond Sq
6 Brighton Av
7 Centurion Gv
8 Duncombe St
9 Fenney St
10 Fenney St East
11 Hadfield St
12 Ivyleaf Sq
13 Kenneth Sq
14 Legion Gv
15 Maleham St
16 Pembroke St
17 Star Gv
18 Tully St
19 Wally Sq
20 W Marwood St
21 Worcester St

Broughton
Baths

Marlborough Road
School

GT CHEETHAM ST EAST

ST JAMES' RD

Cheethwood
Community
& Sports Cen

ELIZABETH STR

BURY NEW ROAD

GREAT

4

Talavera St

A4, B1, B2, B
Street names for
these grid squares
are listed at the
back of the index

Lowry
School

Broughton Lane

Kent Street

Lower
Broughton
Health Cen

Clarence

Trafalgar St
Trafalgar
Business

6

Primary
School

Strangeways

B4
1 Elvate Crs
2 Herbert St
3 St Alban's Ter
4 Towneley St

HM Prison
Manchester

HM Prison
Manchester

1 grid square represents 500 metres

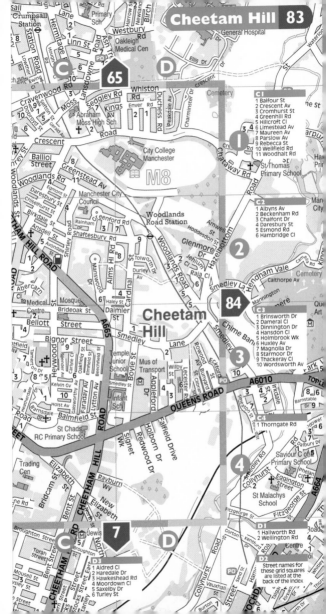

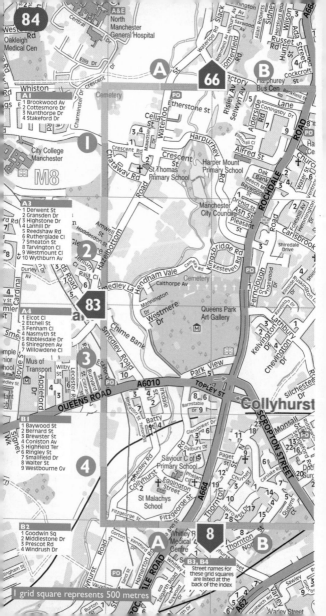

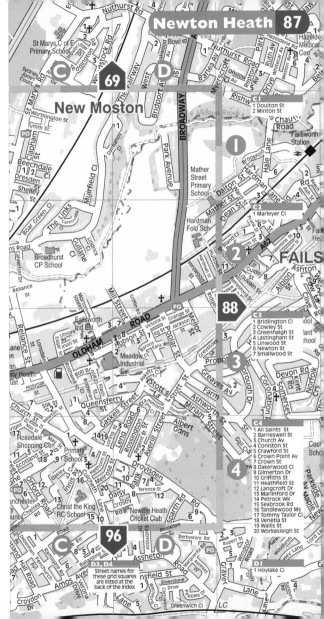

St Marys C of E
Primary School

C 69 **D**

New Moston

BROADWAY

Moston Brook

Mather
Street
Primary
School

Hardman
Fold Sch

I

C1
1 Doulton St
2 Minton St

Chauc
Road
Failsworth
Station

C2
1 Marleyer Cl

2

A62

FAILS

OLDHAM ROAD

Failsworth
Ind Est

Meadow
Industrial
Est

88

C3
1 Bridlington Cl
2 Cowley St
3 Greenhalgh St
4 Lastingham St
5 Linwood St
6 Newton St
7 Smallwood St

3

Broadhurst
CP School

Greaves
Farm

Ashworth
Street

Miriam
Street

Albert
Gdns

Devon Rd

C4
1 All Saints' St
2 Barneswell St
3 Church Av
4 Coniston St
5 Crawford St
6 Crown Point Av
7 Crown St
8 Dakerwood Cl
9 Gilmerton Dr
10 Griffiths St
11 Heathfield St
12 Langcroft Dr
13 Marlinford Dr
14 Petrock Wk
15 Seabrook Rd
16 Tandlewood Ms
17 Tommy Taylor Cl
18 Venetia St
19 Wallis St
20 Workesleigh St

4

Rosedale
Shopping Cen

Primary
School

Christ the King
RC School

Newton Heath
Cricket Club

C 96 **D**

D3, D4
Street names for
these grid squares
are listed at the
back of the index

D1
1 Hoylake Cl

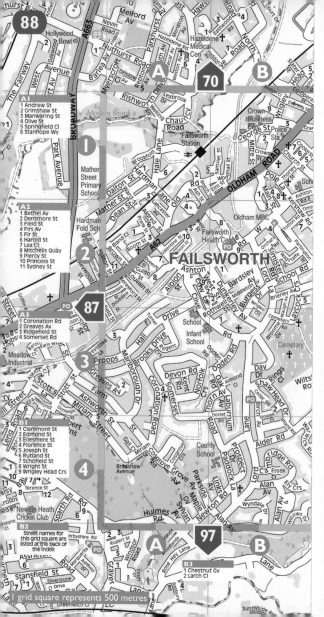

70

A

B

A1
1 Andrew St
2 Grimshaw St
3 Manwaring St
4 Olive St
5 Springfield Cl
6 Stanhope Wy

A2
1 Bethel Av
2 Densmore St
3 Field St
4 Firs Av
5 Fir St
6 Harold St
7 Lea Ct
8 Mitchells Quay
9 Piercy St
10 Princess St
11 Sydney St

A3
1 Coronation Rd
2 Greaves Av
3 Ridgefield St
4 Somerset Rd

87

B1
1 Claremont St
2 Edmund St
3 Ellesmere St
4 Florence St
5 Joseph St
6 Rutland St
7 Schofield St
8 Wright St
9 Wrigley Head Crs

B2
Street names for
this grid square are
listed at the back of
the index

B3
1 Chestnut Gv
2 Larch Cl

97

FAILSWORTH

1 grid square represents 500 metres

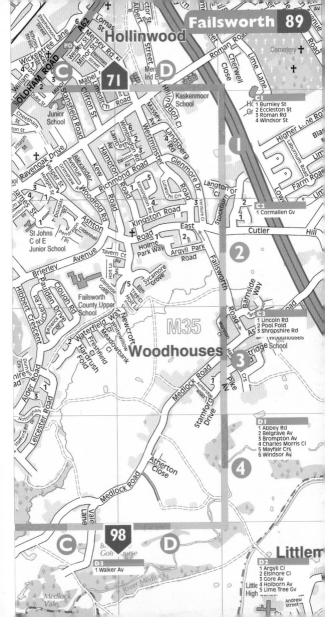

Failsworth 89

Hollinwood

Woodhouses

Littlem

A62

OLDHAM ROAD

Cemetery

71

98

Medlock Vale

Medlock Golf Course

Little High

River Medlock

Kaskenmoor School

St Johns C of E Junior School

Failsworth County Upper School

Failsworth County Junior School

Woodhouses School

M35

Roman Road

Cutler Hill

Kingston Road

Medlock Road

Vale Lane

Atherton Close

Stamford Drive

Failsworth Road

Barnside Way

Higher Lane

C1
1 Burnley St
2 Eccleston St
3 Roman Rd
4 Windsor St

C2
1 Cormallen Gv

C3
1 Lincoln Rd
2 Pool Fold
3 Shropshire Rd

D1
1 Abbey Rd
2 Belgrave Av
3 Brompton Av
4 Charles Morris Cl
5 Mayfair Crs
6 Windsor Av

D2
1 Argyll Cl
2 Elsinore Cl
3 Gore Av
4 Holborn Av
5 Lime Tree Gv

D3
1 Walker Av

C **D** **1** **2** **3** **4**

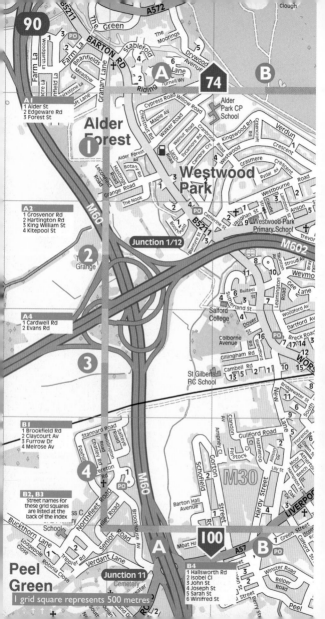

90

A
1 Alder St
2 Edgeware Rd
3 Forest St

A2
1 Grosvenor Rd
2 Hartington Rd
3 King William St
4 Kitepool St

A4
1 Cardwell Rd
2 Evans Rd

B1
1 Brookfield Rd
2 Claycourt Av
3 Furrow Dr
4 Melrose Av

B2, B3
Street names for
these grid squares
are listed at the
back of the index

B4
1 Hallsworth Rd
2 Isobel Cl
3 John St
4 Joseph St
5 Sarah St
6 Winifred St

74

100

Junction 1/12

Junction 11

Alder
Forest

Westwood
Park

Grange

Peel
Green

1 grid square represents 500 metres

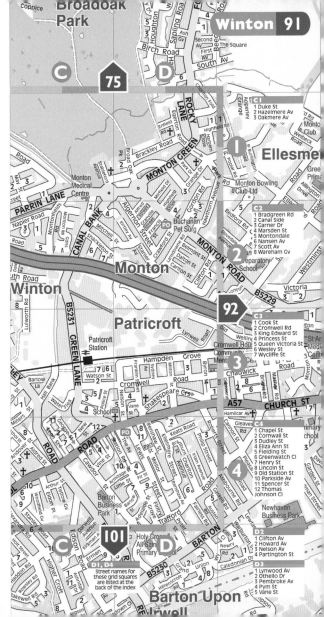

Broadoak Park

Second Av
First Av
The Square
South Av

C 75 **D**

C1
1 Duke St
2 Hazelmere Av
3 Oakmere Av

1 Ellesmer

Grange
Monto
Club
Welbeck
Gree
Prima

Monton Bowling
Club Ltd

Allington
Drive

C2
1 Bradgreen Rd
2 Canal Side
3 Garner Dr
4 Marsden St
5 Montondale
6 Nansen Av
7 Scott Av
8 Wareham Gv

Preparatory
School

2

MONTON ROAD

Westminst

Monton

Winton

Victoria
B5229

92

C3
1 Cook St
2 Cromwell Rd
3 King Edward St
4 Princess St
5 Queen Victoria St
6 Wesley St
7 Wycliffe St

Patricroft

Cromwell Hous
Community
Ment Cen

St-A
Medi
Cent

Patricroft
Station

Wellin
Road

Hampden Grove

Chadwick

Watson St

Cromwell

Shakespeare Crs

3

A57 CHURCH ST

Hamilcar Av

Gleaves

C4
1 Chapel St
2 Cornwall St
3 Dudley St
4 Eliza Ann St
5 Fielding St
6 Greenwatch Cl
7 Henry St
8 Lincoln St
9 Old Station St
10 Parkside Av
11 Spencer St
12 Thomas
   Johnson Cl

4

Newhaven
Business Park

Barton
Business Park

D2
1 Clifton Av
2 Howard Av
3 Nelson Av
4 Partington St

C 101 **D**

Holy Cross
All Sain
Primary

BARTON

Newry

D1, D4
Street names for
these grid squares
are listed at the
back of the index

B5230

Caledonian Dr

D3
1 Lynwood Av
2 Othello Av
3 Pembroke Av
4 Pym St
5 Vane St

Barton Upon
Irwell

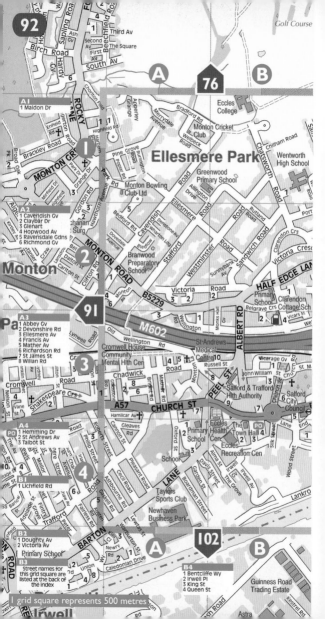

92

Golf Course

Third Av
Second Av
First Av
The Square
South Av

A **76** **B**

Eccles College

A1
1 Maldon Dr

Bradford Rd
Monton Cricket Club
Welbeck Road
Chilnam Road

Apperley Grange
Merrydale Avenue

Wentworth High School

Ellesmere Park

Highfield Rd
Pine Grove
Picture Rd

Greenwood Primary School

Enfield Rd
Park Av
Grange Dr

Allington Drive

A2
1 Cavendish Gv
2 Claybar Dr
3 Glenart
4 Hopwood Av
5 Ravensdale Gdns
6 Richmond Gv

Gordon Rd
Buchanan
Surg

Bedford Rd
Cavendish Road
Ellesmere

Denstone Av
Marlborough Lodge

Rutland Road

Monton Bowling Club Ltd

Road

Clarendon Crs
Victoria Cres

Monton

MONTON ROAD

Clifton St

Branwood Preparatory School

Westminster

Sunnybank Rd

Victoria Road

HALF EDGE LANE

Stafford

Primary School
Belgrave Crs
Clarendon Cottage Sch
Vicars Rd

A3
1 Abbey Gv
2 Devonshire Rd
3 Ellesmere Av
4 Francis Av
5 Mather Av
6 Richardson Rd
7 St James St
8 Willan Rd

Lynwell Road

91

Monton Av
Victoria Road

B5229

Monks Hall

Wellington

M602

St Andrews Medical Centre

ALBERT RD

Vicarage Gv

Old Wellington Rd

Russell St

John William St

Salford City Council

Cromwell House Community Mental Hlth Cen

Chadwick Road

Brindle St

Salford & Trafford Hlth Authority

A4
1 Hemming Dr
2 St Andrews Av
3 Talbot St

Shakespeare Crs

A57 CHURCH ST

Hamilcar Av

PEEL ST

Church Lane

B1
1 Lichfield Rd

Gleaves Rd

Oxford St

Eccles Primary School

Eccles Health Cen

The Town Hall

Eccles Recreation Cen

Silk Street

Wood Street

Roberts Street

Phillip Street

Devas St

Alma St

Lankro

B2
1 Doughty Av
2 Victoria Av

Cecil Road

Pleasant Road

Garden St

Boardman St

Irwell Pl
Irwell Gv
The Grove

Primary School

Ashcroft Rd

Gaskell St

LANE

Taylors Sports Club

Newhaven Business Park

Street names for this grid square are listed at the back of the index

BARTON

Warburton St

Newry Rd

Caledonian Drive

A **102** **B**

B4
1 Bentcliffe Wy
2 Irwell Pl
3 King St
4 Queen St

Guinness Road Trading Estate

1 grid square represents 500 metres

Irwell

Astra

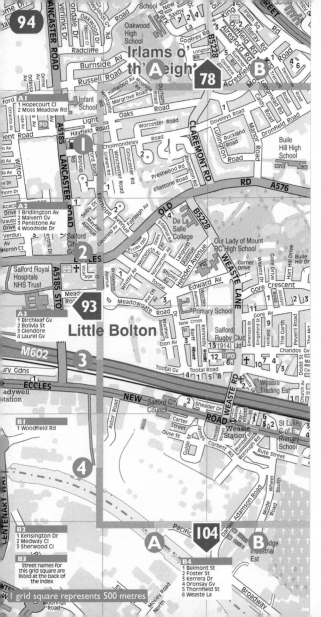

79

105

C1
1 Ashcroft Av
2 Beech Av
3 Beech Gv
4 Hemswell Cl
5 Keaton Cl
6 Monroe Cl

C2
1 Ashfield Cl
2 Castiedene Av
3 Cheviot Cl
4 Farringdon St
5 St Anne's Av

C3, D1, D3
Street names for
these grid squares
are listed at the
back of the index

C4
1 Cardigan St
2 Cumbrae Gdns
3 Dolbey St
4 Haven St
5 Heyworth St
6 Pembroke St
7 Ronaldsay Gdns
8 Rostherne St
9 Sandray Gv
10 Stowell St
11 Westray Crs

D1
1 Arbour Cl
2 Colwyn St
3 Coomassie St
4 Cotswold Dr
5 Doveridge Gdns
6 Elkanagh Gdns
7 Ellor St
8 Grass'ham Gdns
9 Littlegreen
10 Mainprice Cl
11 Seedley Rd
12 Tenbury Cl
13 Wyvllie Dr

D4
1 Buckingham St
2 Gilbert St
3 Lord Byron Sq
4 Royle St
5 Wynford Sq

Seedley

Weaste

SALFOI

M6

M602

M5

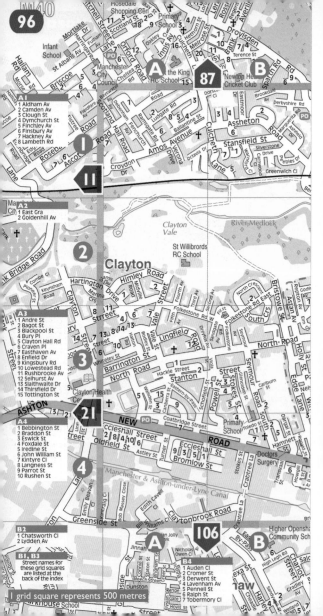

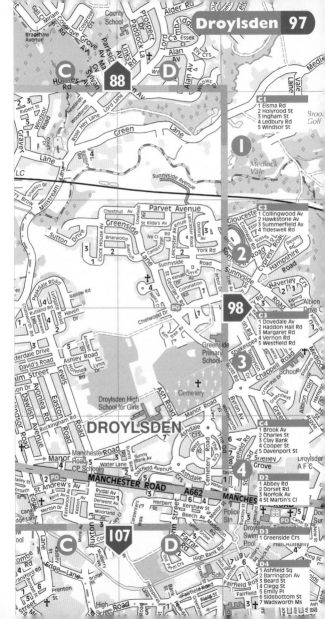

C 88 D

C1
1 Elsma Rd
2 Holyrood St
3 Ingham St
4 Ledbury Rd
5 Windsor St

1

C2
1 Collingwood Av
2 Hawkstone Av
3 Summerfield Av
4 Tideswell Rd

2

98

C3
1 Dovedale Av
2 Haddon Hall Rd
3 Margaret Rd
4 Vernon Rd
5 Westfield Rd

3

Greenside
Primary
School

Cemetery

C4
1 Brook Av
2 Charles St
3 Clay Bank
4 Cooper St
5 Davenport St

Droylsden High
School for Girls

DROYLSDEN

Shelley
Grove

Droylsden
AFC

4

D2
1 Abbey Rd
2 Dorset Rd
3 Norfolk Av
4 St Martin's Cl

MANCHESTER ROAD A662 MANCHES

Police
Stn

Droyl
Swim
Pool

D3
1 Greenside Crs

C 107 D

D4
1 Ashfield Sq
2 Barrington Av
3 Beard St
4 Clegg St
5 Emily Pl
6 Sidebottom St
7 Wadsworth Ms

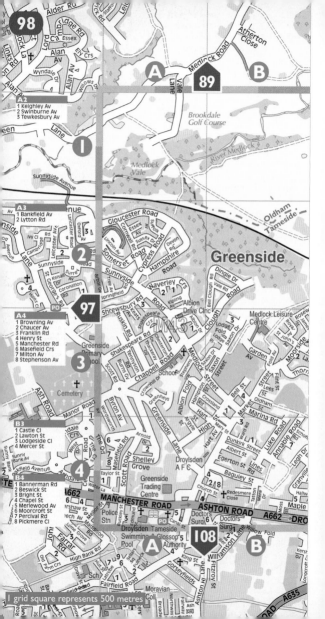

98

Alder Ru
Cambridge Rd
Essex
Alan Av
Wyndale
Alan Av
Willows

Atherton Close
Medlock Road

A **89** **B**

A2
1 Keighley Av
2 Swinburne Av
3 Tewkesbury Av

Brookdale
Golf Course

Sunnyside Avenue

Lane

Medlock
Vale

River Medlock

I

Oldham
Tameside

A3
1 Bankfield Av
2 Lytton Rd

Gloucester Road

Cornwall Rd
Essex
Av
Sussex Rd
Devon
Rd

Somerset St
Cypress Road
Hampshire Road

Greenside

Sunnyside

Naverley

Dingle Dr

Vale Rd

Leicester Av

Shrewsbury Rd

Albion
Drive Clinc

Bell Clough Rd

Medlock Leisure
Centre

2

Coronation

97

Kipling

Lodge
Fold

Clough

Garden

A4
1 Browning Av
2 Chaucer Av
3 Franklin Rd
4 Henry St
5 Manchester Rd
6 Masefield Crs
7 Milton Av
8 Stephenson Av

Greenside
Primary
School

Shakespeare Rd

Chappell Road

Medlock Street

Savon Dr

Lees
St

Oldham

Flint St

3

Scott Rd

Burns Rd

Crownmill Dr

Albion Fold

Crossland

Cemetery

Manor Road

Byron Av

Greenside Lane

Hart St

High

Marina Rd

B3
1 Castle Cl
2 Lawton St
3 Lodgeside Cl
4 Mercer St

Masefield Rd

Arnold

Shelley
Grove

Droylsden
AFC

Dunkirk Street

Albert St

Luke Rd

Baguley St

4

Greenside
Trading
Centre

Church St

Redesmere
Close

Maple

B4
1 Bannerman Rd
2 Beswick St
3 Bright St
4 Chapel St
5 Merlewood Av
6 Moorcroft St
7 Percival Rd
8 Pickmere Cl

A662

MANCHESTER ROAD

ASHTON ROAD A662

Police
Stn

Droylsden
Swimming &
Glossop
Pool

Tameside
Authority

Doctors
Surg

Doctors
Surg

Canal

A **108** **B**

Gorsefields

King St

Williamson Lane

Willow Fold

Fairfield Road

Moravian
Coll

A635

I grid square represents 500 metres

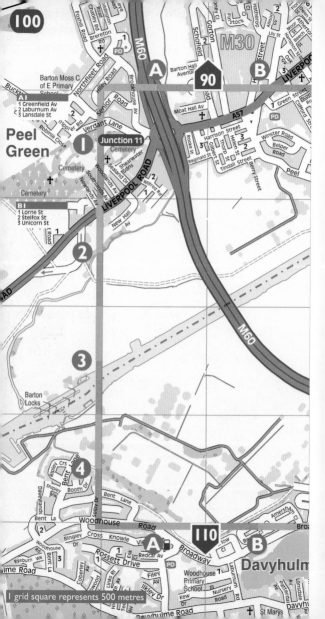

100

M30

Foxhill Road
Brereton Rd
Chifley Rd
eye

Cotton
Schofield
Hatherop
First stock
Lily st
Beech

M60

A

B

LIVERPOOL

Barton Hall
Avenue

90

Barton Moss C
of E Primary
School

Northfleet Road

Hilley Road

Brookhouse Av

Senior Road

Moat Hall Av

A57

PO

Green Street

Clifford St

A1
1 Greenfield Av
2 Laburnum Av
3 Lansdale St

mppler Rd

Verdant Lane

Harrison Street

3

Belper
Road

**Peel
Green**

Robinia Close

Southampton Av

Helen St

Winster Road

1

Cemetery

Junction 11

Cemetery

Rooke St

Gilbert St

Berry Street

Peel

Newport Av

Sealand Gdns

Shearwater

Reginald St

Tindall Street

Cemetery

Woodlands Av

Wilfred Rd

Southampton Av

LIVERPOOL ROAD

2

B1
1 Lorne St
2 Stelfox St
3 Unicorn St

d Road

New Hall
Av

2

M60

3

Barton
Locks

4

Ripley
Crs

Bent Lane

Shipley
VW

Booth Dr

Davylands

Bent La

Woodhouse

Road

Bingley
Dr

Cross

Knowle

A

Redcar Av

110

Broadway

B

Woodhouse
Primary
School

Davyhulm

Rossett Drive

Filey
Av

PO

Laburnum

ime Road

Woodhouse

Bent La

Ryeburn
Wk

Coberley

Links Rd

Eck

Ilkley Dr

Kew
Dr

Nursery
Road

Davy

St Marys

Davyhulme Road

I grid square represents 500 metres

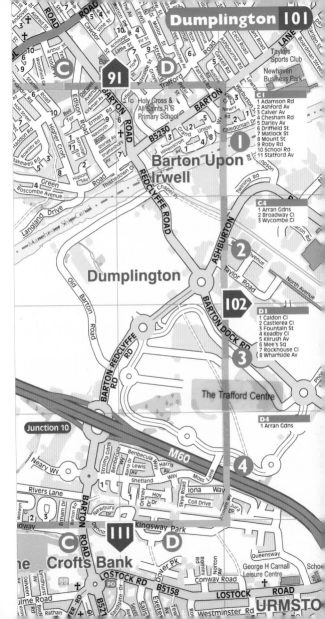

91

Taylors Sports Club

Newhaven Business Park

Holy Cross & All Saints R C Primary School

B5230

Barton Upon Irwell

REDCLYFFE ROAD

Langland Drive

Manchester Ship Canal

Boscombe Avenue

Green

Dumplington

ASHBURTON

Taylor Road

Twining Rd

North Avenue

Beacon Rd

C1
1 Adamson Rd
2 Ashford Av
3 Calver Av
4 Chesham Rd
5 Darley Av
6 Driffield St
7 Matlock St
8 Mount St
9 Roby Rd
10 School Rd
11 Stafford Av

C4
1 Arran Gdns
2 Broadway Cl
3 Wycombe Cl

102

BARTON DOCK RD

Old Barton Road

BARTON REDCLYFFE RD

D1
1 Caldon Cl
2 Castierea Cl
3 Fountain St
4 Keadby Cl
5 Kilrush Av
6 Mee's Sq
7 Rockhouse Cl
8 Wharfside Av

The Trafford Centre

D4
1 Arran Gdns

Junction 10

M60

Neary Wy

Rivers Lane

Benbecula Way

Stroma Gdns

Benbecula Dr

Lewis Av

Harris Av

Shetland

Ronay Dr

Moss Lane

Jura Dr

Way

Newbury Dr

Orkney Dr

Hoy Dr

Iona Way

Coll Drive

Kingsway Park

BARTON ROAD

Dennir

Etham Dr

Barton Rd

idway

Crofts Bank

PO

LOSTOCK RD

B5158

Dover Pk

Conway Road

Norton Rd

Romley

Queensway

George H Carnall Leisure Centre

Scho

LOSTOCK ROAD

Westminster Rd

URMSTO

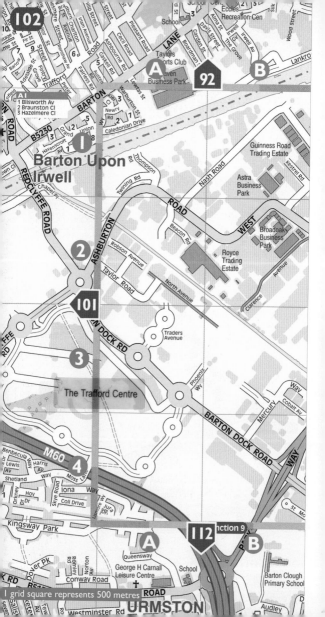

102

92

101

112

School

LANE

Taylors Sports Club

A Haven Business Park

B

Lankro

Eccles Recreation Cen

Davis Street
Alma St
The Grove
Irwell Av

Wood Street

Silk

School

A1
1 Blisworth Av
2 Braunston Cl
3 Hazelmere Cl

Pleasant Road

Cecil Road

Ashbourne Road

Lewres St

Warburton St

Newr Rd

Caledonian Drive

Union

B5230

Havenscroft Av

1

Barton Upon Irwell

REDCLYFFE ROAD

Chapel La

BARTON

Thompson Rd

Guinness Road Trading Estate

Kestrel Rd

Nash Road

Astra Business Park

ROAD

WEST

Broadoaks Business Park

Twining Rd

Beacon Rd

2

ASHBURTON

Robson Avenue

Taylor Road

North Avenue

Royce Trading Estate

Avenue

Clarence

101

RFFE RD

3

Traders Avenue

DOCK RD

The Trafford Centre

Phoenix Wy

BARTON DOCK ROAD

Mercury

Cobalt Av

WAY

St. Mo

M60

Benbecula Way
Lewis Av
Harris Way
Shetland

Moss Lane
Iona Way
Coll Drive
Jura Dr
W Jura Dr

4

Orkney
Hoy Dr
Dr

Kingsway Park

Dover PK

Conway Road

Romiley
Norton
Westmorland

Queensway

George H Carnall Leisure Centre

School

A

112 nction 9

B

Barton Clough Primary School

RD KD

Audley

| grid square represents 500 metres **ROAD**

URMSTON

Westminster Rd

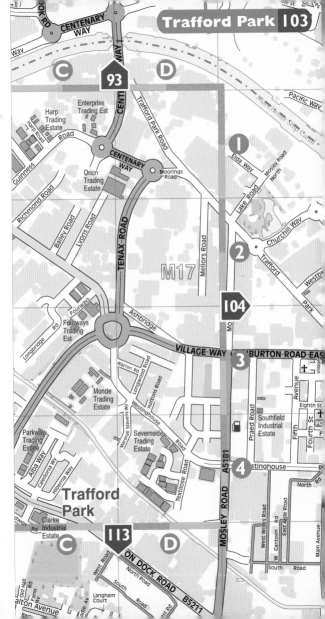

I grid square represents 500 metres

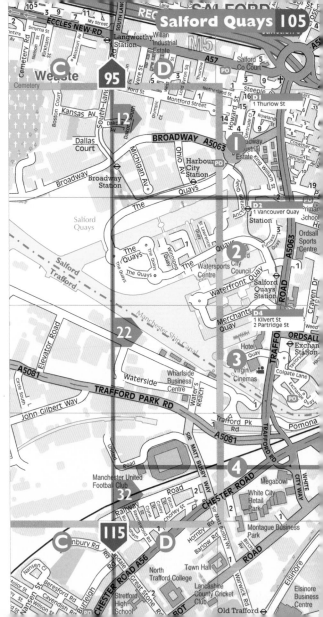

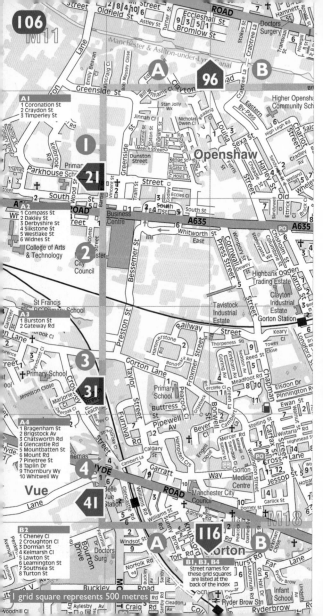

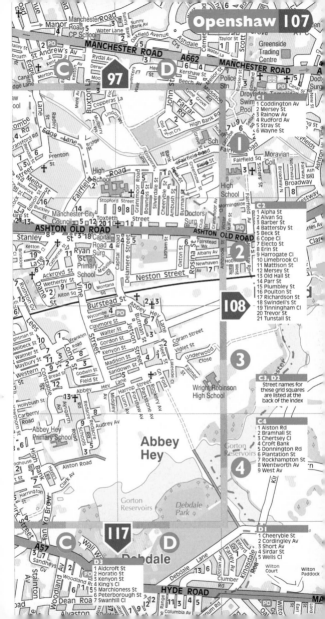

MANCHESTER ROAD

MANCHESTER ROAD A662

97

C1
1 Coddington Av
2 Mersey St
3 Rainow Av
4 Rudford Av
5 Stray St
6 Wayne St

1

Greenside
Trading
Centre

Moravian
Coll

Broadway

C2
1 Alpha St
2 Alvan Sq
3 Barber St
4 Battersby St
5 Beck St
6 Cope Cl
7 Electo St
8 Erin St
9 Harrogate Cl
10 Limebrook Cl
11 Mattison St
12 Mersey St
13 Old Hall St
14 Parr St
15 Pimley St
16 Poulton St
17 Richardson St
18 Swindell's St
19 Tinningham Cl
20 Trevor St
21 Tunstall St

ASHTON OLD ROAD

ASHTON OLD ROAD

2

108

3

Wright Robinson
High School

C3, D2
Street names for
these grid squares
are listed at the
back of the index

C4
1 Alston Rd
2 Bramhall St
3 Chertsey Cl
4 Croft Bank
5 Donnington Rd
6 Plantation St
7 Rockhampton St
8 Wentworth Av
9 West Av

Abbey
Hey

Gorton
Reservoirs

4

Abbey Hey
Primary School

Gorton
Reservoirs

Debdale
Park

D1
1 Cheeryble St
2 Cordingley Av
3 Short Av
4 Sirdar St
5 Wells Cl

117

Debdale

1 Aldcroft St
2 Horatio St
3 Kenyon St
4 King's Cl
5 Marchioness St
6 Peterborough St
7 Swanhill Cl

Wilton
Court

Wilton
Paddock

HYDE ROAD

108

STER ROAD A662 MANCHESTER

A AD

98

ON ROAD A662 DRO

B

A1
1 Annald Sq
2 B'trice Wignall St
3 Brethren's Ct
4 Durham St
5 Edward St
6 Moravian Fld
7 Outram Sq
8 Southway
9 Wood Sq

1

Droylsden Tameside Swimming & Glossop Pool Hlth Authority

Fairfield Road

Fairfield Sq

High School

Moravian Coll

Northway Fairway Broadway

Westway

MANCHESTER ROAD A635

AUDENSHA

A2
1 Hartshead Cl

ASHTON OLD ROAD

Doctors Surgery

Audenshaw Hall

Audenshaw Road

Clarendon

2

Neston Street

St Annes Primary Sch

Fairfield Station

107

Ackroyd Av

Fairfield

B1
1 Birch St
2 Florence St

Coram Street

Violet St

3

Wright Robinson High School

Manchester Tameside

King's Road

Abbey Hey

4

Gorton Reservoirs

Corn Hill Lane

Debdale Park

Denton Golf Course

Gorton Reservoirs

A

118

B

Debdale

Wilton Court

Wilton Paddock

Junction 24

A57 HYDE

MANCHESTER ROAD

1 grid square represents 500 metres

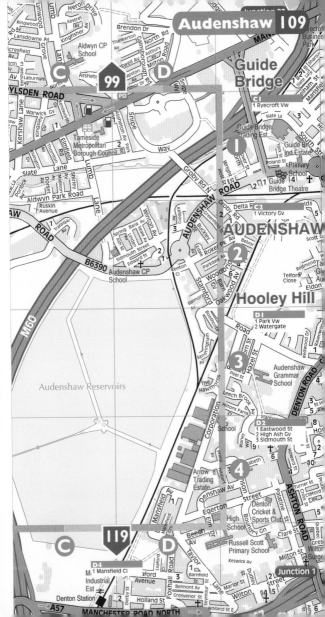

Audenshaw 109

Guide Bridge

AUDENSHAW

Hooley Hill

Audenshaw Reservoirs

C1
1 Ryecroft Vw

C2
1 Victory Gv

D1
1 Park Vw
2 Watergate

D2
1 Eastwood St
2 High Ash Gv
3 Sidmouth St

D4
1 Mansfield Cl

Tameside Metropolitan Borough Council

Audenshaw CP School

Audenshaw Grammar School

Arrow Trading Estate

Denton Cricket & Sports Club

Russell Scott Primary School

Mansfield Industrial Est

Denton Station

Aldwyn CP School

Guide Bridge Trading Est

Guide Bridge Ind Estate

Guide Bridge Primary School

Guide Bridge Theatre

The Hawthorns

99

119

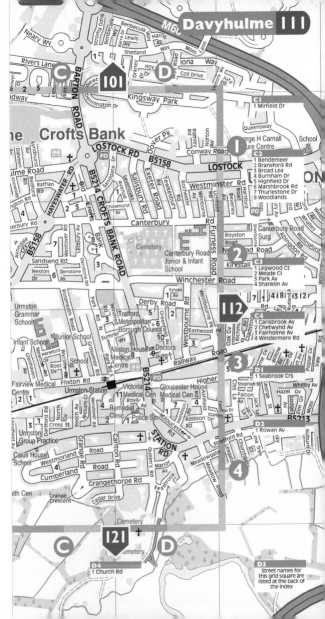

C1
1 Mirfield Dr

C2
1 Bendemeer
2 Bransford Rd
3 Broad Lea
4 Burnham Dr
5 Highfield Dr
6 Marshbrook Rd
7 Thuriestone Dr
8 Woodlands

C3
1 Legwood Ct
2 Meade Cl
3 Park Av
4 Shanklin Av

C4
1 Carisbrook Av
2 Chetwynd Av
3 Fairholme Av
4 Windermere Rd

D1
1 Seabrook Crs

D2
1 Rowan Av

D3
Street names for this grid square are listed at the back of the index

D4
1 Church Rd

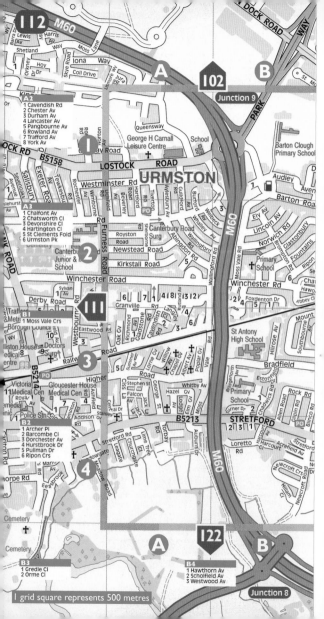

112 M60

Lewis
Harris
Shetland
Hoy Dr
Iona Way
Coll Drive

A **102**

B

Junction 9

St Mo

DOCK ROAD
WAY

PARK

Barton Clough
Primary School

A2
1 Cavendish Rd
2 Chester Av
3 Durham Av
4 Lancaster Av
5 Pangbourne Av
6 Rowland Av
7 Trafford Av
8 York Av

Queensway

George H Carnall
Leisure Centre

School

Audley
Aven

Barton Roa

I

OCK RD
B5158

Exeter Rd
Tewkesbu
Rochester
Wimborne
Lichfield
Hartford

LOSTOCK ROAD

URMSTON

Westminster Rd
Beverley
Road
Tiverton
Aylesbury Rd
Guildford
Burford
Whalley
Welbeck

PO

Ely Av
Lincoln Av
Norwich Rd
Glastonbury
Fountains
Ripon

Salisbury
Sevenoaks
Avenue
Iselhurst

Furness Road

A3
1 Chalfont Av
2 Chatsworth Cl
3 Devonshire Cl
4 Hartington Cl
5 St Clements Fold
6 Urmston Pk

Canter-
bury
Junior & In
School

Canterbury Road

Royston
Rd
Sherborne
Newstead Road

Kirkstall Road

Canterbury
Surg

Abingdon Rd
Wallingford Rd
Moss Vale Rd

Primary
School

Cha
Haw

WINCHESTER ROAD

Winchester Rd

III

Sylvan
Way

Derby Road

Granville
Richmond Av
Gladstone
Oak Gv

6 7 4 8 13 12
Langley
1
3
4
6

Rutland Rd

Foxdenton Dr

Abbey Dr

Mount

B1
1 Moss Vale Crs

Traffo
Metr
Borough Council
lliston House
Doctors
Surg

Westbourne

Eastwood

Railway

Road

Oak Gv
Summer
Lorne Gv
Willow
Chapel Av
Albert Av
Poplar Gv

St Antony
High School

Hilrose Av
Southbourne

Bradfield

3

Gloucester House
Medical Cen

B5214

PO

Higher

Royal
Av

Falcon
Central Dr
Stanley
Addison
Rd

CISS La
Stephen St
George St
Hazel Gv
Long Elm Gv
Moss

Whitby Av

Vale

Birch Av
Estonfd
Chadwick Rd
Allen Rd
Dillon Rd

Primary
School

Rock Av
Birch Rd

medical
Clinic
Police Stn

B2
1 Archer Pl
2 Barcombe Cl
3 Dorchester Av
4 Hurstbrook Dr
5 Pullman Dr
6 Ripon Crs

Stretford Rd
Churchgate
Legate

Lim
Tree

Torbay
Auburn Rd

B5213

STRETFORD

PO
2 3 1

Loretto
Rd

Newcroft Crs
William
Newcroft
Dr

Victoria
Medical Cen

rpe Rd

Manor
Easbrook

eadowgate

Meadow Road

Acrefield Av
Stretford
Harcourt

4

Cemetery

Cemetery

A **122** **B**

B3
1 Gredle Cl
2 Orme Cl

B4
1 Hawthorn Av
2 Scholfield Av
3 Westwood Av

Junction 8

M60

I grid square represents 500 metres

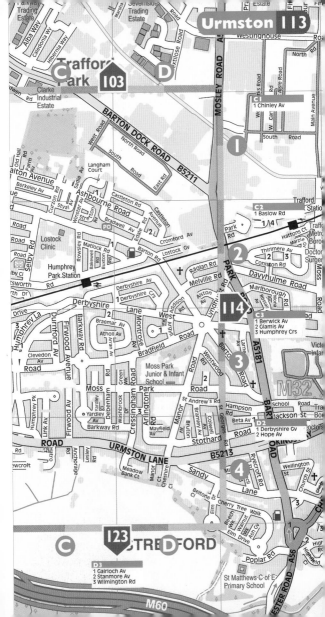

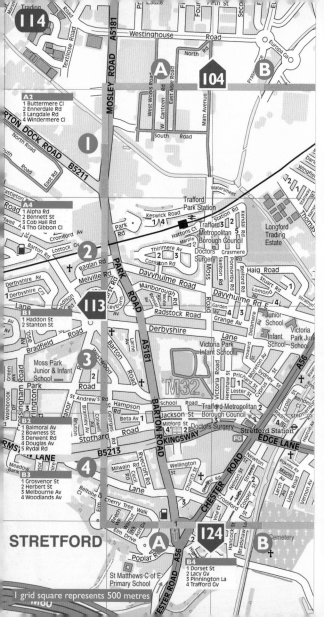

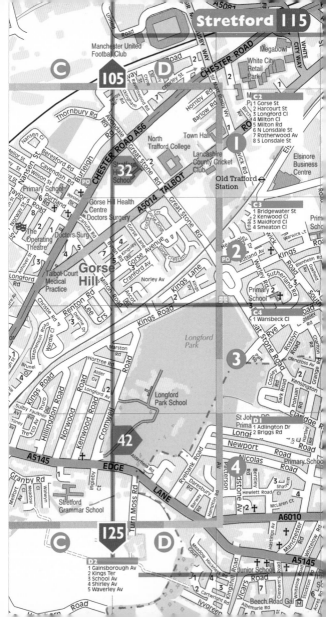

A5081

A5081

City Way

Chester Road

White City Way

Megabowl

Manchester United
Football Club

White City Retail Park

C

105

D

Chester Road

Chorley St

Hornby Rd

Barlow Rd

Sir Matt Busby Wy

M

C2
1 Gorse St
2 Harcourt St
3 Longford Cl
4 Milton Cl
5 Milton Rd
6 N Lonsdale St
7 Rotherwood Av
8 S Lonsdale St

Thornbury Rd

Arkwright

Chester Road A56

Great Stone Road

Town Hall

North Trafford College

Lancashire County Cricket Club

Wick Rd

1

RO

Elsinore Business Centre

Nansen St

Beresford Rd

Cavendish St

Burleigh

PO

Stretford High School

32

A5014 Talbot

Great Stone Rd

Old Trafford ⊖ Station

Mellor St

Wilson St

Primary School

Portland

Westby

Gorse Hill Health Centre Doctors Surgery

Gorse Avenue

Gorse Crescent

Warwick Av

Warwick Cl

C2
1 Bridgewater St
2 Kenwood Cl
3 Maldford Cl
4 Smeaton Cl

Prim Scho

Taylor's Road

8

Doctors Surg

Gorse St

Kings

Rutland Av

Warley

PO

2

Blenheim Cl

Norbreck

Rd

The Operating Theatre

4

5

Gorse Av

Cranford Av

Norley Av

Kings Lane

Sutherland Rd

Primary School

2

Longford Rd

Talbot Court Medical Practice

Renton Rd

Lee Crs

Milton Road

Kings

C4
1 Wansbeck Cl

Stone

Rosslyn

Christie Rd

Stephenson Road

Wardle Cl

Marston Rd

Kings Road

Longford Park

3

Glencross Av

Kensington

Brunel

Hortree Rd

Alder Cv

Longford Cl

Longford Park School

St John's RC
Prima

Clarendon R

D
1 Adlington Dr
2 Briggs Rd

Kings Road

Hillingdon Road

Norwood Road

Kenwood Road

Cromwell Road

42

Aldermead Rd

Newport Road

Longf

Nicolas Road

Bentley

Patterson

Primary School

Sulby

Faulkner

Tre

A5145

Edge

Lane

Turn Moss Rd

Rylebank Rd

Daresbury

Banway

Hampton

Hewlett Road

Sharston Cl

McLaren Ct

4

3

4

A6010

Granby Rd

Melfort

Meadow

Ingleby Ct

Warwi

Stretford Grammar School

1

C

125

D

Manchester

Hastings Av

Whiteleg

Junior School

A5145

D2
1 Gainsborough Av
2 Kings Ter
3 School Av
4 Shirley Av
5 Waverley Av

Meadow Hey

Kingshill

Vicars

Cartwright Rd

Road

Clements Av

Whitelow

Road

Beech Road Gar

Albemarle Rd

Ivygreen

Road

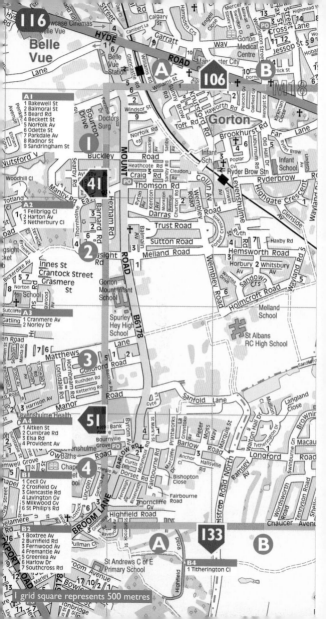

1 grid square represents 500 metres

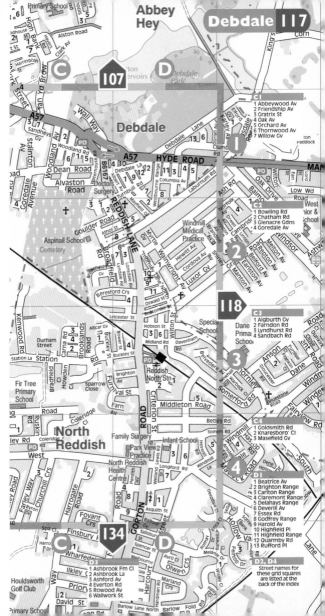

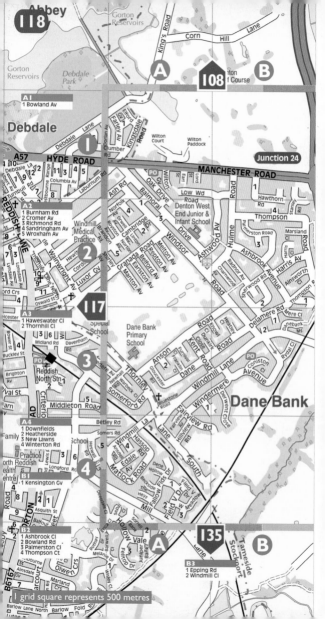

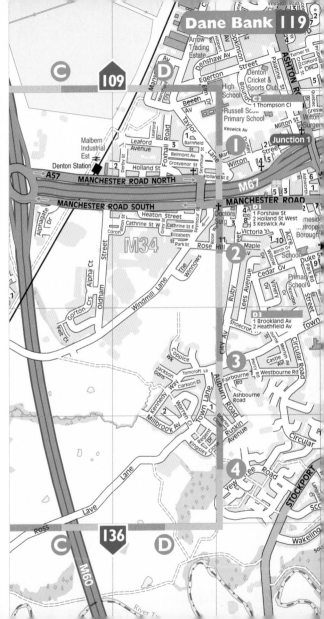

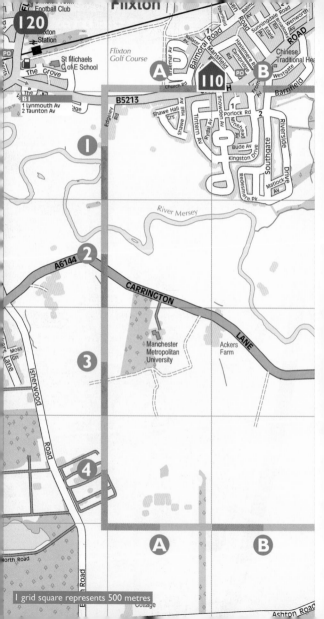

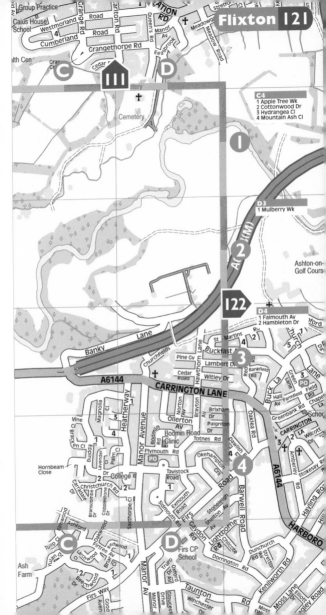

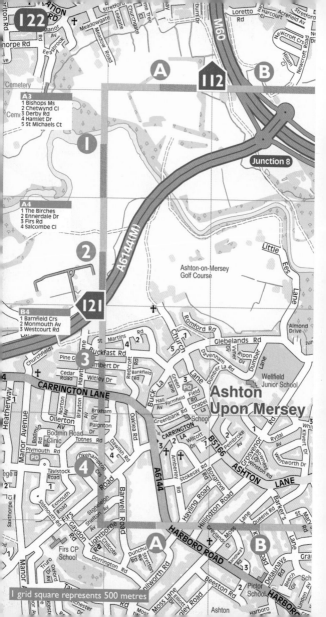

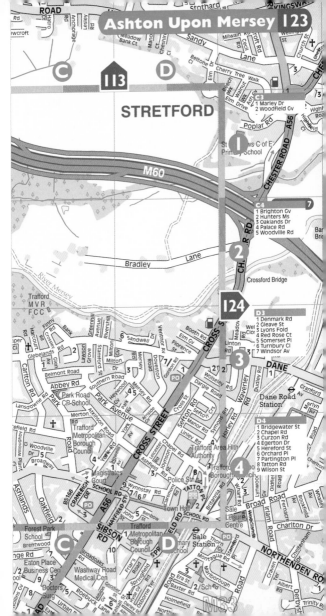

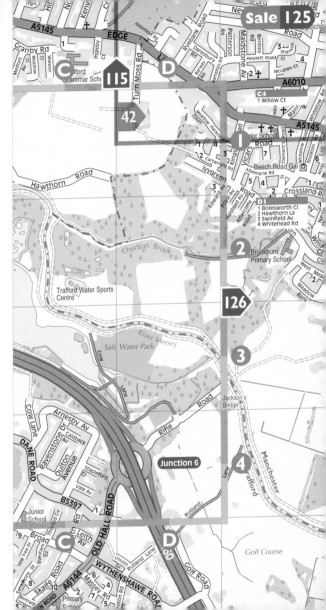

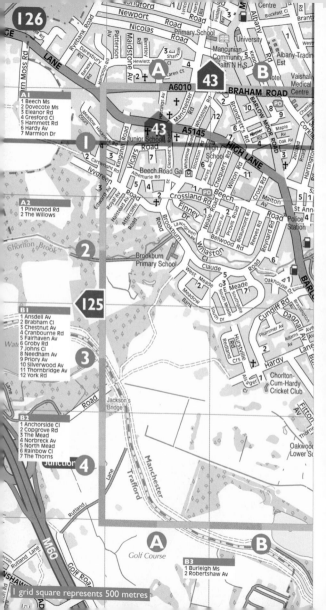

Newport
Nicolas Road
Primary School

Maidstone Av

A1
1 Beech Ms
2 Dovecote Ms
3 Eleanor Rd
4 Gresford Cl
5 Hammett Rd
6 Hardy Av
7 Marmion Dr

Mancunian
Community
Health N H S

University
Albany-Trading
Est

B

Vaishali
Medical
Centre

A

43

A6010

43 BRAHAM ROAD

PO

A5145 HIGH LANE

Junior School

Vicars Road

Beech Road Gal

Albemarle Rd

Crossland Rd

Finney
Dr

PO

Beech
Road

Maiton
Av

St Ann
Police
Station

A2
1 Pinewood Rd
2 The Willows

Chorlton Brook

Wilaston
Road

Claude

West Meade

Meade
Bank

Meadow

E Meade
Southmede

2

125

Brookburn
Primary School

B1
1 Ansdell Av
2 Brabham Cl
3 Chestnut Av
4 Cranbourne Rd
5 Fairhaven Rd
6 Groby Rd
7 Johns Cl
8 Needham Av
9 Priory Av
10 Silverwood Av
11 Thornbridge Av
12 York Rd

Cundiff Rd

Daunal

Plummer Av

Hardy

3

Hurtsville
Redland
Crs

B2
1 Anchorside Cl
2 Copgrove Rd
3 The Mead
4 Norbreck Av
5 North Mead
6 Rainbow Cl
7 The Thorns

Jackson's
Bridge

Chorlton-
Cum-Hardy
Cricket Club

4

Junction

Manchester

Trafford

M60

GOLF Road

Golf Course

A

B

B3
1 Burleigh Ms
2 Robertshaw Av

Oakwood
Lower So

1 grid square represents 500 metres

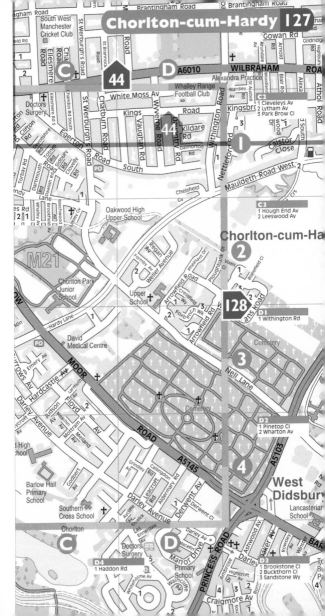

Brantingham Road

Brantingham Road

South West
Manchester
Cricket Club

Gowan Rd

Arundale Rd

Arnold Rd

Gildridge

Highbank

Cha...
Road
Ellesmere
Road

St Brannocs Road

St Werburghs Road

Road

C

44

D A6010

WILBRAHAM

Alexandra Practice

Woodlawn St

Blair Rd

Alexa...

ROA

Athol Road

Doctors
Surgery

Chandos Rds South

White Moss Av

Chatburn Road

Kings

Wyverne Road

Whalley Range
Football Club

Road

Wardley St

Austell Rd

Kingsbr...

C2
1 Cleveleys Av
2 Lytham Av
3 Park Brow Cl

Clifton
Road

Egerton Road

St Werburgh's Road

Vaughan Road

44
Kildare
Rd

Dalmorton
Rd

Withington Road

3

...wood

...st South

3 South

Caistor
Close

Torcay Rd
Torn... Rd

Sidbury Rd

Clevelly Rd

Road
South

PO

Mauldeth-Road-West

Chelsfield
Gv

Crfs

2

...les Rd

Whalley Rd
Brookfield
Beechwood

Limer Gv

Lane

Oakwood High
Upper School

C3
1 Hough End Av
2 Leeswood Av

M21

Regan...

Formby Av

Weller Avenue

Plough bank Dr

Pheasant Dr

Vixen...

Chorlton-cum-Ha

2

Bakerfield Cl

Chorlton Park
Junior
School

Upper
School

Arrowfield Road

Cresswell...

Foxb...

128

Road

ans Road

D1
1 Withington Rd

Hardy Lane

1

Arrowfield Road

David
Medical Centre

PO

Emery Av

Hardcastle Av

Darley Avenue

Floyd...

Jarmenton

Moorcroft Av

Melland Av

Judson

Meechin

2

MOOR

ROAD

Cemetery

Neil Lane

Cemetery

3

D2
1 Pinetop Cl
2 Wharton Av

A5145

...High
...school

Barlow Hall
Primary
School

Southern
Cross School

Godbert
Av

Grindley...
Al...

Callington Rd

Lestcroft...

Alderman Rd

Darley Avenue

2

Derwent Av

Derwent Cl

4

**West
Didsbur**

Lancasterian
School

Baker Av

...Rd

Rowley...

Winster Av

BA

Chorlton
...er

C

Doctors
Surgery

D

Ayclife...
Berwick Av

Ennerdale Av

Manor Drive

Primary
School

Wythenhurst Av

Highcroft

Ambrose...

Darley Av

PRINCESS ROAD

Darley...

Ashwood...

D
1 Brookstone Cl
2 Buckthorn Cl
3 Sandstone Wy

To...
Bu...
Pa...
4

D4
1 Haddon Rd

Wheatholme Av

Craigmore Av

I grid square represents 500 metres

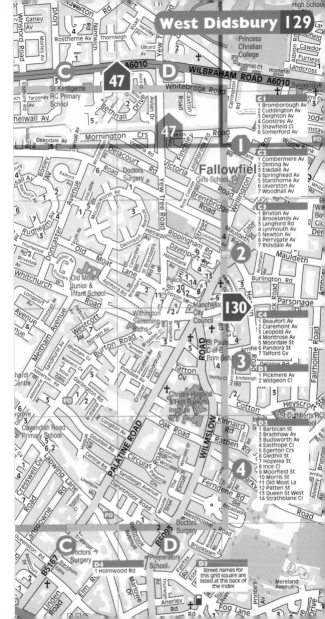

Princess Christian College

High School

WILBRAHAM ROAD A6010

47

47

Fallowfield Girls School

C1
1 Bromborough Av
2 Cuddington Av
3 Deighton Av
4 Goostrey Av
5 Shawfield Cl
6 Somerford Av

C2
1 Combermere Av
2 Dinting Av
3 Eskdale Av
4 Springhead Av
5 Stanthorne Av
6 Ulverston Av
7 Woodhall Av

C3
1 Brixton Av
2 Brooklands Av
3 Langford Rd
4 Lynmouth Av
5 Newton Av
6 Perrygate Av
7 Ridsdale Av

Manchester City Council

130

C4
1 Beaufort St
2 Claremont Av
3 Leopold Av
4 Montrose Av
5 Moordale St
6 Pandora St
7 Talford Gv

D1
1 Pickmere Av
2 Widgeon Cl

Christie Hospital & Holt Radium Institute

D2
1 Barbican St
2 Bradshaw St
3 Budsworth Av
4 Easthope Cl
5 Egerton Crs
6 Gledhill St
7 Hopelea St
8 Ince Cl
9 Moorfield St
10 Morris St
11 Old Moat La
12 Patten St
13 Queen St West
14 Strathblane Cl

D4
1 Holmwood Rd

D3
Street names for this grid square are listed at the back of the index

Mereland Avenue

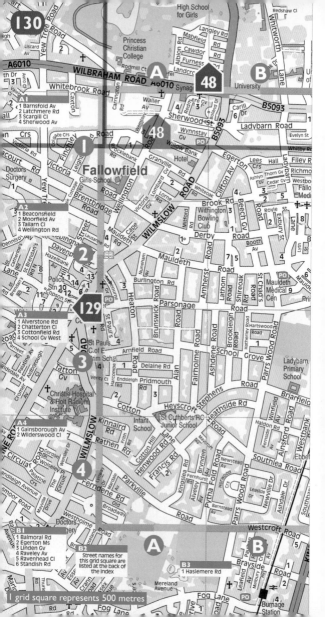

High School for Girls

Redshaw Cl

Liscard Av

Yew Tree Road

Whitworth Lane

Langley Rd

Mabfield Rd

Cawdor Rd

Princess Christian College

Furness Rd

A6010 WILBRAHAM ROAD A6010

A
48
B
University

Whitebrook Road

Waller Av

Carrington

Caxton

B5093

Sherwood St

Carill Dr

Ladybarn Road

1 Barnsfold Av
2 Latchmere Rd
3 Scargill Rd
4 Sherwood Av

A1

Crs

48

Wynnstay Gv

Evelyn St

Whitby Rd

Victoria Rd

Colgate Crs

Finchley Road

Ocklebank

Willow Bank Hotel

Leigh

PO

Fallowfield

Granville Rd

Egerton Av

Lees Crs

Hall

Filey Rd

Doctors Surgery

Girls-School

Lorne

Clifton Av

Ashlyn Gv

Cedar Gv

Westbo Fallo Medi

Victoria Road

Brentbridge Road

Wellington Road

WILMSLOW

Whitecar

Brook Rd

Beech Gv

Exbury St

1 Beaconsfield
2 Moorfield Av
3 Tallam Cl
4 Wellington Rd

A2

Mitford

Derby Rd

Withington Bowling Club

Royle St

Booth Av

Denison

Hazelbank

Davenp

Tailam Rd

Lausanne Rd

Mauldeth

Mauldeth Rd

Amherst Road

Lathom Road

Shireoak Road

St Chad's

PO

Mauldeth Medical Cen

Police Stn

2

Burlington Road

Parsonage

Road

129

PO

Heaton

Brunswick Road

St Paul's Rd

Ashdene Road

Brookleigh Road

Hartswood Road

1 Alverstone Rd
2 Chatterton Cl
3 Cottonfield Rd
4 School Gv West

A3

St Pauls C of E Prim Sch

Arnfield Road

Delaine Rd

Fairholme

Grove

Ladybarn Primary School

Briarfield

Tatton

Christie Hospital & Holt Radium Institute

Endsleigh

Pridmouth

Alan

Stephens

Road

Cotton

Heyscroft

Heathside Rd

Kinnaird

St Cuthberts RC Junior School

Haldon Rd

Winfield

Ainsford Rd

Westbank

1 Gainsborough Av
2 Wilderswood Cl

A4

WILMSLOW

Infant School

Rathen

Southlea Road

Southie

Circular

Henwood Road

Francis Rd

Pytha Fold Road

Parrs Wood Road

Ashdale Dr

Ferndene

Parkville

Broadway

Kingslea

Fernhurst

Alveley

Leaside Dr

Newville Dr

Road

Doctors

Westholme

Westcroft Road

1 Balmoral Rd
2 Egerton Ms
3 Linden Gv
4 Raveley Av
5 Ravenhead Cl
6 Standish Rd

B1

A

Street names for this grid square are listed on the back of the index

B2

Brayside Rd

B

1 Haslemere Rd

B3

Mereland Avenue

Fog Lane

PO

Burnage Station

1 grid square represents 500 metres

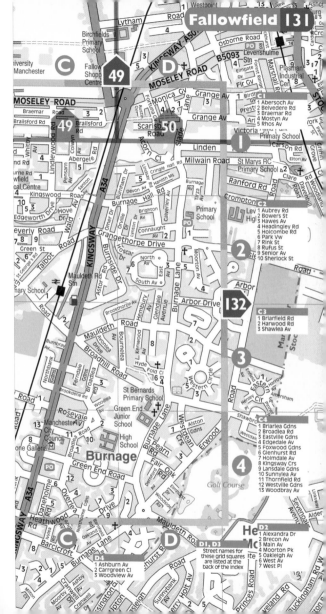

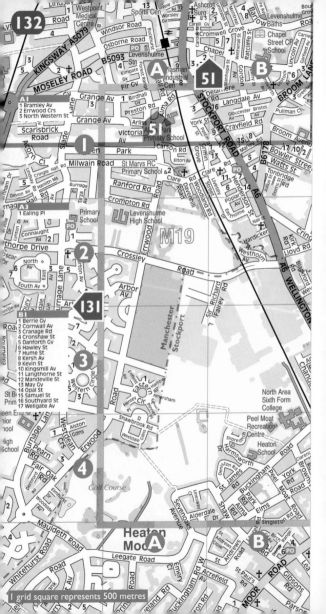

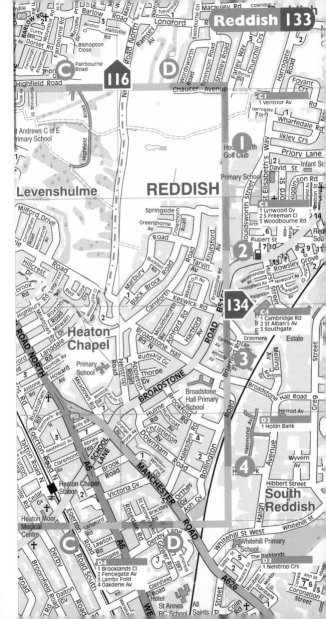

PO
BARLOW RD
Barlow
Longford
Macauley Rd
Coleridge
Swinburne
Tytheringt
Road
Dorset Rd
Curtis
Molyneux Rd
Radcliffe Rd
Fairbourne Rd
Anchor
Hallsville Rd
Road North
Ramsey St
Wordsworth Road
Shelley Road
Farley Way
Churchill Crs
Harrogate Rd
Bishopton Close
Fenleigh
Rosemarie
thon
C Fairbourne Road
Fovant Crs

116

D
Highfield Road
Chaucer Avenue
C1
1 Ventnor Av
Harrogate Dr
Wharfedale Rd
Ilkley Crs

St Andrews C of E Primary School
Highfield Road
House North Golf Club
St Elisabeth's Way
Priory Lane
David St
ord St
Ilkley Crs
Infant Sc
lson Rd

Levenshulme
REDDISH
Primary School
Arth
1 Lynwood Gv
2 S Freeman Cl
3 Woodbourne Rd
14

Milford Drive
Springside
Greenthorne Av
Crowthorn Road
Mouldsworth Street
Rupert St
6
Marg
Red Sou

Corringham Rd
Merlewood
Hillcrest Dr
Road
Knutsford Rd
Tarvin Av
2 7 10
13 8 9
11
Rowsley Grove

brook Rd
Highbury Rd
Lingcrest Rd
Cres
Marbury
Black Brook Rd
Buckden Rd
Milford Drive
Rd
Keswick Rd
Waverton Av
Broadstone rd
Westminster Av
Springfield Av
Newport Av
Paignton Gv
Newquay
Newcombe

Roxton Road
Milward
Meadows Rd
Langdale
Carnforth
Mouldsworth Rd
Ashford Rd
Hartford Av
Arnside
134
C4
1 Cambridge Rd
2 St Alban's Av
3 Southgate
Estate

Heaton Chapel
Norfolk Av
Howard Av
Primary School
Rudyard Gv
Broadstone Hall Rd N
Carmel Av
ROAD
Grasmere
Melling
Everton

ford Road North
Alstone Rd
Weston
Meadows Rd
Neistrop
Appleton
Thorpe Gv
Broadstone
BROADSTONE
3
Broadstone Hall Road
Herrod Av

Buckingham Rd
Egerton Road
Tatton Rd
A6
Claremont Av
Cedar
SCHOOL LANE
Abney
Holly Rd
Crange Rd
Hulme Rd
Huncoat
Christleton Rd
Downham Rd
Halesden Rd
Bollington Rd
ROAD
Hammond Av
D2
1 Hollin Bank
Avenue
Wyvern
4
H rook
Hibbert Street

Heaton Moor
PO
Heaton Chapel Station
Whitney Gv
Brook Road
Victoria Gv
St Leonards Gv
MANCHESTER
Ortnes Gv
Agn Gv
Brackley Rd
Halgn
South Reddish
Whitehill St West
Whitehill Primary School

Medical Centre
Derby
Road South
Broomfield Rd
Dalton Gv
Langford Rd
Lawton Rd
A6
Rosedale Rd
Denby Lane
Gower Rd
Endress
ROAD
Whitehill St West
Selby St
The Barklands
1 Neistrop Crs

C
D4
1 Brooklands Cl
2 Fencegate Av
3 Lambs Fold
4 Oakdene Av
D
Glenfield Road
Hotel
St Annes RC School
All Saints
WE
A626
Coronation Street

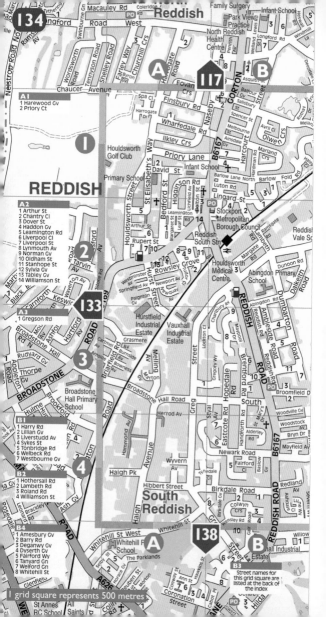

REDDISH

134

117

133

138

1 grid square represents 500 metres

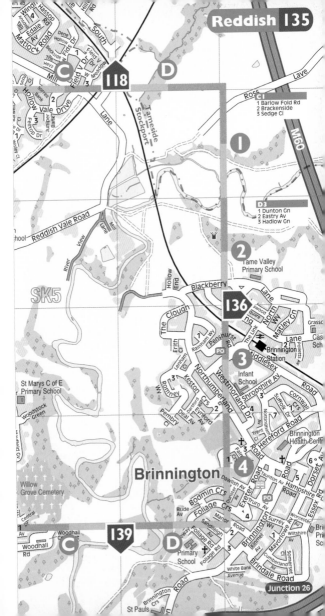

C
118
D

I

C1
1 Barlow Fold Rd
2 Brackenside
3 Sedge Cl

M60

D3
1 Dunton Gn
2 Eastry Av
3 Hadlow Gn

Ross Lane

Tameside Stockport

Reddish Vale Road

School

River View

SK5

Hollow End

Mill Lane

Blackberry

2
Tame Valley
Primary School

136

Northwood Grove

Matley Gn

North Lane

Grassc
Cas
Sch

The Clough

Erith Cl
Rainham Wy
Penshurst Rd

The Link

Brinnington
Station

Middlesex

PO

3
Infant
School

Keston Crs
Lenham Wy
Romney Wy

Northumberland

Westmoreland

Shropshire Av

Cornwall

Suffolk Cl

Nottingham

Road

St Marys C of E
Primary School

Woodstock Green

Pembry Cl
Deal Av
Eynford

Garford

Trent

Hereford Road

Brinnington
Health Centr

Willow
Grove Cemetery

Brinnington

4

Dawlish Av

Taunton Rd

Hampshire Av

Dorset

6

Bodmin Crs
Foliage
Bude

Truro Av
Exeter Road
Surrey

PO

Essex Av

Worcester

Bri
Pri
Sc

Central Av

Woodhall

139

D

Manor Road
Sandleigh
Foliage Rd

Primary
School

Foliage Rd

Brinnington

Wy

Mayfour

Wiltshire

Cumberland

Somerset

Woodhall
Rd

White Bank
Avenue

Brindale Road

Brinnington Road

St Pauls

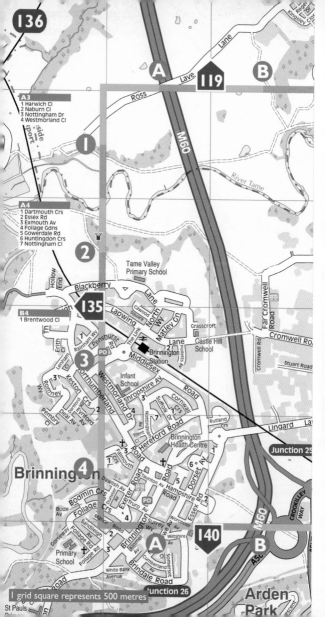

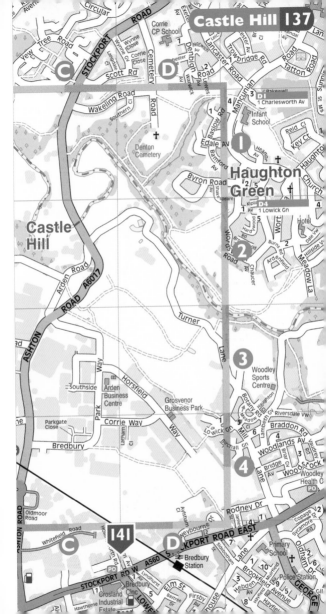

Circular

Avenue

STOCKPORT ROAD

Corrie CP School

Exeter

Lewis

Chester Av

Lancaster Road

Trowbridge Rd

Kendal

Tatton

Road

Sunnis

Yew Tree Road

Wynne Close

Langdale Cl

Corrie Close

Cemetery

Chester

Denbigh

Warwick

Lawes

Manchunian

D1 Bakewell

1 Charlesworth Av

Key Ct

Reid Cl

Haughton

C

Scott Rd

D

Wakeling Road

Southern

Road

Baslow Rd

Edale Av

Bamford

Infant School

Headworth

Denton Cemetery

Byron Road

Shakespeare

Haughton Green

Haughton Church

Kipling Av

Hardy

Wortham

D4

1 Lowick Gn

Castle Hill

Words Road

Chaucer

Arde

Burns Rd

Dale Av

Hillside La

Hotel

2

Arden Road

A6017

ASHTON ROAD

Turner Lane

3

Woodley Sports Centre

Botany

Haughton

Meadow Rd

Riversdale Vw

Horsfield

Southside

Arden Business Centre

Grosvenor Business Park

Park Way

Latham

Lowick Gn

Birchall

Mill

Lambeth Gn

Braddon Rd

Woodlands Av

Briar Gv

4

Bridge La

Woodley Health C

Parkgate Close

Corrie Way

Bredbury

PO

Oldmoor Road

Rodney Dr

Copage

Sycamore

ASHTON ROAD

Whitefield Road

C

141

D

STOCKPORT ROAD EAST

Aylsham

Neybourne

Lane

Sidebotham

Primary School

Oldham Rd

D6

Police Station

GEORGE

PO

STOCKPORT RD W

A560

Bredbury Station

Lyndhurst

Elm St

Firsby

Brookfield

Hebden Av

Havisham Avenue

Gill

Crosland Clnc

Bredbury

Bavtree Dr

Lowfield

Hawthorne Industrial Estate

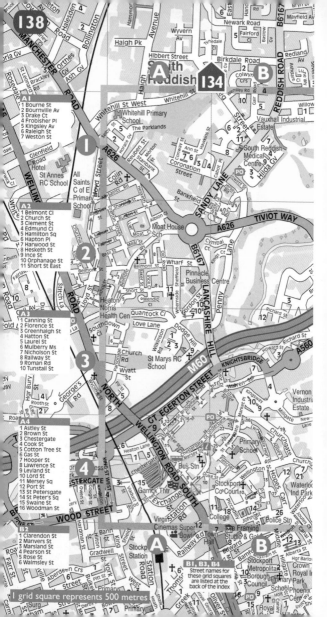

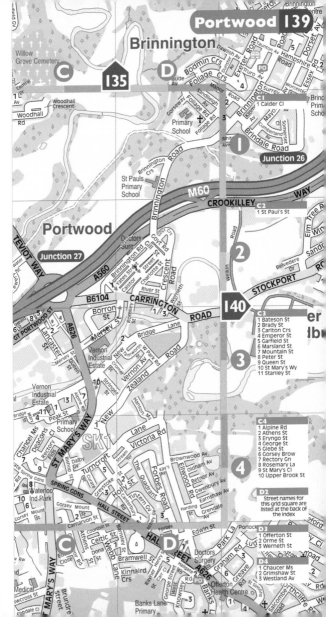

Brinnington

Willow Grove Cemetery

C **135** **D**

Woodhall Crescent

Woodhall Rd

St Pauls Primary School

Primary School

Portwood

Junction 27

A560

Doctors Surgery

Junction 26

I

Brindale Road

M60

CROOKILLEY

C2
1 St Paul's St

STOCKPORT WAY

2

B6104

CARRINGTON ROAD

140

Borron St

C3
1 Bateson St
2 Brady St
3 Carlton Crs
4 Emperor St
5 Garfield St
6 Marsland St
7 Mountain St
8 Peter St
9 Queen St
10 St Mary's Wy
11 Stanley St

Vernon Industrial Estate

3

Vernon Industrial Estate

Primary School

SKi

Victoria Rd

Brownwood Av.

C4
1 Alpine Rd
2 Athens St
3 Eryngo St
4 George St
5 Glebe St
6 Gorsey Brow
7 Rectory Gn
8 Rosemary La
9 St Mary's Ci
10 Upper Brook St

4

D2
Street names for this grid square are listed at the back of the index

SPRING GDNS

HALL STREET

Holly St

Forbes Road

D3
1 Offerton St
2 Orme St
3 Werneth Av

C **D**

Celtic St

Webb Lane

HALL STREET

Doctors Surgery

D4
1 Chaucer Ms
2 Grimshaw St
3 Westland Av

Bramwell St

Kinnaird Crs

Offerton Health Centre

Banks Lane Primary

ST MARY'S WAY

Medical

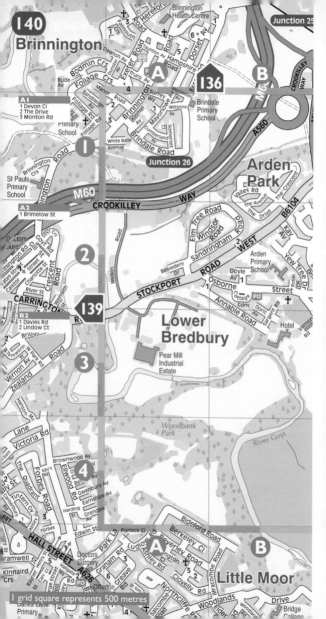

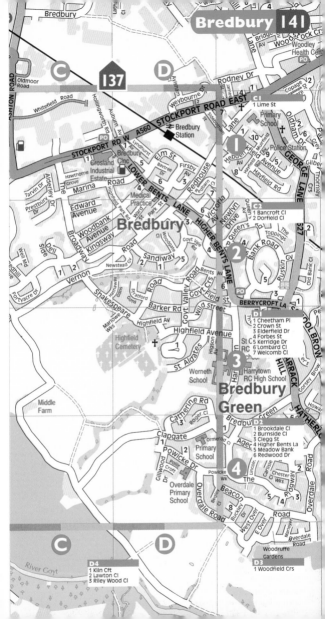

Abbey Hey	107	D4
Ancoats	18	A2
Arden Park	140	B1
Ardwick	28	B1
Ashton-under-Lyne	99	D3
Ashton Upon Mersey	122	B3
Barton Upon Irwell	101	D1
Belle Vue	41	E1
Beswick	20	A4
Blackley	67	C4
Bradford	19	F1
Bredbury	141	D2
Brinnington	135	D4
Broadoak Park	75	C4
Broughton Park	64	A4
Brunswick	28	A3
Burnage	131	C4
Castle Hill	137	C2
Chadderton	52	A2
Charlestown	3	E1
Charlestown	68	A2
Cheetam Hill	83	D3
Chorlton-cum-Hardy	127	D2
Clayton	96	A2
Clifton	58	A2
Clifton Green	59	D3
Clifton Junction	60	A2
Collyhurst	84	B3
Copster Hill	73	C2
Crofts Bank	111	C1
Crumpsall	64	B4
Dales Brow	75	D3
Dane Bank	118	B3
Davyhulme	110	B1
Debdale	117	D1
Droylsden	97	C4
Dumplington	101	C2
Eccles	93	C4
Ellesmere Park	92	A1
Failsworth	88	A2
Fairfield	108	A2
Fallowfield	129	D1
Firswood	33	D5
Flixton	110	A4
Gorse Hill	115	C2
Gorton	116	A1
Greenside	98	B2
Harpurhey	85	C2
Hathershaw	73	D2
Hazelhurst	74	B3
Heaton Chapel	133	C3
Higher Blackley	66	A1
Higher Broughton	81	D3
Hilton Park	62	A3
Hollinwood	71	C4
Hulme	25	E4
Irlams o' th' Height	78	A4
Kersal	80	B1
Levenshulme	51	D5
Levenshulme	133	C1
Lime Side	72	B4
Little Bolton	93	D3
Littlemoss	99	C1
Longsight	39	E1
Lower Bredbury	140	A3
Lower Broughton	4	B2
Lower Kersal	80	A3
Manchester	29	F4
Miles Platting	9	D3
Monton	91	D2
Moorside	75	D2
Moss Side	36	B4
Moston	68	B4
Mumps	55	C2
New Moston	87	C1
Newton Heath	86	A4
Newtown	58	A4
Nimble Nook	71	C1
North Reddish	117	C4
Old Trafford	34	A1
Openshaw	106	A1
Ordsall	23	E2
Patricroft	91	C3
Pendlebury	78	A2
Pendleton	2	C4
Portwood	139	D1
Prestwich	63	D1
Rainsough	62	A4
Reddish	133	D1
Roe Green	74	A1
Rusholme	39	D5
St George's	24	C3
Salford	12	C1
Sedgley Park	63	C3
Seedley	95	C2
South Reddish	134	A4
Strangeways	6	A1
Stretford	123	C1
Swinton	75	D1
Swinton Park	77	D3
Trafford Park	103	C4
Urmston	112	A1
Wardley	57	C4
Weaste	95	C4
Werneth	54	A4
West Didsbury	128	A4
West Gorton	30	A3
Westwood Park	90	A1
Whalley Range	45	E1
White Gate	70	B2
Winton	91	C2
Woodhouses	89	D3

USING THE STREET INDEX

Street names are listed alphabetically. Each street name is followed by its postal
town or area locality, the Postcode District, the page number, and the reference
to the square in which the name is found.

Example: **Abberley Dr** *NEWH/MOS* M40..............................**69** D3 🚹

Some entries are followed by a number in a blue box. This number indicates the
location of the street within the referenced grid square. The full street name is
listed at the side of the map page.

GENERAL ABBREVIATIONS

ACC	ACCESS	FM	FARM
ALY	ALLEY	FT	FORT
AP	APPROACH	FWY	FREEWAY
AR	ARCADE	FY	FERRY
ASS	ASSOCIATION	GA	GATE
AV	AVENUE	GAL	GALLERY
BCH	BEACH	GDN	GARDEN
BLDS	BUILDINGS	GDNS	GARDENS
BND	BEND	GLD	GLADE
BNK	BANK	GLN	GLEN
BR	BRIDGE	GN	GREEN
BRK	BROOK	GND	GROUND
BTM	BOTTOM	GRA	GRANGE
BUS	BUSINESS	GRG	GARAGE
BVD	BOULEVARD	GT	GREAT
BY	BYPASS	GTWY	GATEWAY
CATH	CATHEDRAL	GV	GROVE
CEM	CEMETERY	HGR	HIGHER
CEN	CENTRE	HL	HILL
CFT	CROFT	HLS	HILLS
CH	CHURCH	HO	HOUSE
CHA	CHASE	HOL	HOLLOW
CHYD	CHURCHYARD	HOSP	HOSPITAL
CIR	CIRCLE	HRB	HARBOUR
CIRC	CIRCUS	HTH	HEATH
CL	CLOSE	HTS	HEIGHTS
CLFS	CLIFFS	HVN	HAVEN
CMP	CAMP	HWY	HIGHWAY
CNR	CORNER	IMP	IMPERIAL
CO	COUNTY	IN	INLET
COLL	COLLEGE	IND EST	INDUSTRIAL ESTATE
COM	COMMON	INF	INFIRMARY
COMM	COMMISSION	INFO	INFORMATION
CON	CONVENT	INT	INTERCHANGE
COT	COTTAGE	IS	ISLAND
COTS	COTTAGES	JCT	JUNCTION
CP	CAPE	JTY	JETTY
CPS	COPSE	KG	KING
CR	CREEK	KNL	KNOLL
CREM	CREMATORIUM	L	LAKE
CRS	CRESCENT	LA	LANE
CSWY	CAUSEWAY	LDG	LODGE
CT	COURT	LGT	LIGHT
CTRL	CENTRAL	LK	LOCK
CTS	COURTS	LKS	LAKES
CTYD	COURTYARD	LNDG	LANDING
CUTT	CUTTINGS	LTL	LITTLE
CV	COVE	LWR	LOWER
CYN	CANYON	MAG	MAGISTRATE
DEPT	DEPARTMENT	MAN	MANSIONS
DL	DALE	MD	MEAD
DM	DAM	MDW	MEADOWS
DR	DRIVE	MEM	MEMORIAL
DRO	DROVE	MKT	MARKET
DRY	DRIVEWAY	MKTS	MARKETS
DWGS	DWELLINGS	ML	MALL
E	EAST	ML	MILL
EMB	EMBANKMENT	MNR	MANOR
EMBY	EMBASSY	MS	MEWS
ESP	ESPLANADE	MSN	MISSION
EST	ESTATE	MT	MOUNT
EX	EXCHANGE	MTN	MOUNTAIN
EXPY	EXPRESSWAY	MTS	MOUNTAINS
EXT	EXTENSION	MUS	MUSEUM
F/O	FLYOVER	MWY	MOTORWAY
FC	FOOTBALL CLUB	N	NORTH
FK	FORK	NE	NORTH EAST
FLD	FIELD	NW	NORTH WEST
FLDS	FIELDS	O/P	OVERPASS
FLS	FALLS	OFF	OFFICE
FLS	FLATS	ORCH	ORCHARD

OV	OVAL
PAL	PALACE
PAS	PASSAGE
PAV	PAVILION
PDE	PARADE
PH	PUBLIC HOUSE
PK	PARK
PKWY	PARKWAY
PL	PLACE
PLN	PLAIN
PLNS	PLAINS
PLZ	PLAZA
POL	POLICE STATION
PR	PRINCE
PREC	PRECINCT
PREP	PREPARATORY
PRIM	PRIMARY
PROM	PROMENADE
PRS	PRINCESS
PRT	PORT
PT	POINT
PTH	PATH
PZ	PIAZZA
QD	QUADRANT
QU	QUEEN
QY	QUAY
R	RIVER
RBT	ROUNDABOUT
RD	ROAD
RDG	RIDGE
REP	REPUBLIC
RES	RESERVOIR
RFC	RUGBY FOOTBALL CLUB
RI	RISE
RP	RAMP
RW	ROW
S	SOUTH
SCH	SCHOOL
SE	SOUTH EAST
SER	SERVICE AREA
SH	SHORE

SHOP	SHOPPING
SKWY	SKYWAY
SMT	SUMMIT
SOC	SOCIETY
SP	SPUR
SPR	SPRING
SQ	SQUARE
ST	STREET
STN	STATION
STR	STREAM
STRD	STRAND
SW	SOUTH WEST
TDG	TRADING
TER	TERRACE
THWY	THROUGHWAY
TNL	TUNNEL
TOLL	TOLLWAY
TPK	TURNPIKE
TR	TRACK
TRL	TRAIL
TWR	TOWER
U/P	UNDERPASS
UNI	UNIVERSITY
UPR	UPPER
V	VALE
VA	VALLEY
VIAD	VIADUCT
VIL	VILLA
VIS	VISTA
VLG	VILLAGE
VLS	VILLAS
VW	VIEW
W	WEST
WD	WOOD
WHF	WHARF
WK	WALK
WKS	WALKS
WLS	WELLS
WY	WAY
YD	YARD
YHA	YOUTH HOSTEL

POSTCODE TOWNS AND AREA ABBREVIATIONS

ALT	Altrincham
ANC	Ancoats
AUL	Ashton-under-Lyne
AULW	Ashton-under-Lyne west
BKLY	Blackley
BNG/LEV	Burnage/Levenshulme
BRO	Broughton
BRUN/LGST	Brunswick/Longsight
CCHDY	Choriton-cum-Hardy
CHAD	Chadderton
CHD/CHDH	Cheadle (Gtr. Man)/ Cheadle Hulme
CHH	Cheetham Hill
CMANE	Central Manchester east
CMANW	Central Manchester west
CSLFD	Central Salford
DID/WITH	Didsbury/Withington
DROY	Droylsden
DTN/ASHW	Denton/Audenshaw
DUK	Dukinfield
ECC	Eccles
EDGY/DAV	Edgeley/Davenport
FAIL	Failsworth
FWTH	Farnworth
GTN	Gorton
HALE/TIMP	Hale/Timperley
HTNM	Heaton Moor
HULME	Hulme

HYDE	Hyde
IRL	Irlam
MDTN	Middleton (Gtr. Man)
MPL/ROM	Marple/Romiley
NEWH/MOS	Newton Heath/Moston
NTHM/RTH	Northern Moor/Roundthorn
OFTN	Offerton
OLDS	Oldham south
OLDTF/WHR	Old Trafford/Whalley Range
OP/CLY	Openshaw/Clayton
PART	Partington
PWCH	Prestwich
RAD	Radcliffe
RDSH	Reddish
RUSH/FAL	Rusholme/Fallowfield
SALE	Sale
SALQ/ORD	Salford Quays/Ordsall
SLFD	Salford
STKP	Stockport
STLY	Stalybridge
STRET	Stretford
SWIN	Swinton
TRPK	Trafford Park
URM	Urmston
WALK	Walkden
WGTN/LGST	West Gorton/Longsight
WHTF	Whitefield
WYTH/NTH	Wythenshawe/Northenden

A

Abberley Dr NEWH/MOS M40 ...... 69 D3 🔒
Abberton Rd DID/WITH M20........ 129 C3
Abbey Cl URM M41....................... 112 B2
Abbey Dr SWIN M27 .... 76 A1
Abbey Gv CHAD OL9 .... 71 C1
　　ECC M30 .... 92 A3 🔒
Abbey Hey La GTN M18 .... 107 C3
Abbey Lawn OLDTF/WHR M16 ...... 33 F5
Abbey Rd DROY M43 .... 97 D2 🔒
　　FAIL M35 .... 89 D1 🔒
　　SALE M33 .... 123 C3
Abbeywood Av GTN M18 .... 117 C1 🔒
Abbotsbury Cl WGTN/LGST M12... 30 C3
Abbots Cl SALE M33 .... 124 B4 🔒
Abbotsford Rd CCHDY M21 .... 43 F2
　　CHAD OL9 .... 52 A1 🔒
Abbotside Cl OLDTF/WHR M16...... 34 C4
Abercarn Cl CHH M8 .... 83 C2
Abercrombie St SALE M33 .... 124 B4 🔒
Aberdeen St HULME M15 .... 37 F1
Abergele Rd RUSH/FAL M14 .... 131 C1
Abernant Cl OP/CLY M11 .... 20 A3
Abersoch Av RUSH/FAL M14 .... 131 C1
Abingdon Cl CHAD OL9 .... 71 D1 🔒
Abingdon Rd RDSH SK5............... 112 A2
　　URM M41 .... 134 B2
Abingdon St CMANE M1 .... 16 C4
Abney Rd HTNM SK4 .... 133 C4
Abram Cl RUSH/FAL M14 .... 47 D4
Abram St SLFD M6 .... 79 D3
Absalom Dr CHH M8 .... 82 B1
Acacia Av SWIN M27 .... 76 A3 🔒
Acacia Dr SLFD M6 .... 93 D2
Acacia Gv RDSH SK5................... 138 B1 🔒
Acacia Rd OLDS OL8 .... 72 B4
Acheson St GTN M18 .... 106 B4 🔒
Ackers St BRUN/LGST M13 .... 27 E5
Ackroyd Av GTN M18 .... 108 A3
Ackroyd St OP/CLY M11 .... 107 C2
Ackworth Rd SWIN M27 .... 77 D1 🔒
Acme Dr SWIN M27 .... 37 E1
Acomb St HULME M15 .... 37 E1
　　RUSH/FAL M14 .... 37 E4
Acrefield Av URM M41 .... 112 B4
Acrefield Rd DTN/ASHW M34 .... 98 B4
Acresfield Cl SWIN M27 .... 77 C5 🔒
Acresfield Rd SLFD M6 .... 78 B4
Acres Rd CCHDY M21 .... 126 A1
Acre St CHAD OL9 .... 71 C3
Acton Av NEWH/MOS M40 .... 11 E1
Adair St CMANE M1 .... 18 B4
Adams Av CCHDY M21 .... 126 B3
Adamson Rd ECC M30 .... 101 C1 🔒
Adam St OLDS OL8 .... 73 D3
Ada St BKLY M9 .... 7 E5
Addington St ANC M4 .... 18 B4
Addison Cl BRUN/LGST M13 .... 28 A4
Addison Crs OLDTF/WHR M16 ...... 33 E3
Addison Rd STRET M32 .... 113 D3
　　URM M41 .... 111 D4
Adelaide St CHH M8 .... 82 B4
　　ECC M30 .... 91 D4
　　SWIN M27 .... 75 D2
Adeline St ANC M4 .... 6 C3
Adelphi St CSLFD M3 .... 14 C1
Aden Cl WGTN/LGST M12............. 19 D4
Adlington Dr STRET M32 .... 32 A2 🔒
Adrian St NEWH/MOS M40 .... 86 A2

Adscombe St OLDTF/WHR M16 ...... 35 E3
Adstone Cl ANC M4 .... 19 D2 🔒
Adswood St NEWH/MOS M40 .... 19 E1
Aegean Cl BRO M7 .... 81 C4 🔒
Agecroft Rd SWIN M27 .... 78 A2
Agecroft Rd East PWCH M25 .... 62 A3
Agecroft Rd West PWCH M25 .... 61 D3
Agnes Cl CHAD OL9 .... 72 A1 🔒
Agnes St BNG/LEV M19 .... 51 D2
　　BRO M7 .... 82 B2
　　CHAD OL9 .... 53 D4
Agnew Pl SLFD M6 .... 3 D2 🔒
Agnew Rd GTN M18 .... 106 A4
Aigburth Gv RDSH SK5 .... 117 C3 🔒
Ailsa Cl NEWH/MOS M40 .... 84 B4 🔒
Aines St WGTN/LGST M12 .... 30 C2
Ainsdale Cl OLDS OL8 .... 72 B1 🔒
Ainsdale Gv RDSH SK5 .... 134 B3
Ainsdale St WGTN/LGST M12 .... 30 A4
Ainsford Rd DID/WITH M20 .... 130 B4
Ainsty Rd RUSH/FAL M14 .... 36 C3
Ainsworth Cl DTN/ASHW M34 ...... 118 B2
Aintree St OP/CLY M11 .... 21 F2
Airton Cl NEWH/MOS M40.............. 8 B3
Aitken St BNG/LEV M19 .... 116 A4 🔒
Aked Cl WGTN/LGST M12 .... 29 D4
Alan Av FAIL M35 .... 88 B4
Alan Rd DID/WITH M20 .... 130 A3
Alan Turing Wy NEWH/MOS M40.... 9 E1
Alasdair Cl CHAD OL9 .... 52 B1
Alba Cl ECC M30 .... 91 D4 🔒
Alban St BRO M7 .... 81 D4
Albany Av OP/CLY M11 .... 107 D2
Albany Ct URM M41 .... 110 B2
Albany Rd CCHDY M21................... 43 E3
　　ECC M30 .... 90 B2 🔒
Alba Wy STRET M32 .... 103 C4
Albemarle Av DID/WITH M20 .... 129 C3
Albemarle Rd CCHDY M21 .... 126 A1
Albemarle Rd RUSH/FAL M14 .... 36 C3
Albermarle Rd SWIN M27 .... 76 A2 🔒
Albert Av GTN M18 .... 117 C1
　　PWCH M25 .... 63 C4
　　URM M41 .... 112 A3
Albert Gdns NEWH/MOS M40 .... 87 D4
Albert Gv WGTN/LGST M12 .... 40 C3
Albert Park Rd BRO M7 .... 81 C4
Albert Pl BRUN/LGST M13 .... 40 A4
　　ECC M30 .... 92 B3
Albert Pl BNG/LEV M19 .... 50 C4
Albert Rd CHAD OL9 .... 71 D2 🔒
　　DROY M43 .... 98 B4
　　OLDS OL8 .... 71 D4
　　OLDTF/WHR M16 .... 24 B4
　　OP/CLY M11 .... 19 F3
　　PWCH M25 .... 63 C1 🔒
Albert Rd West FAIL M35 .... 87 D3 🔒
Albine St NEWH/MOS M40 .... 85 D1
Albion St HTNM SK4 .... 138 A2
Albion Dr DROY M43 .... 98 A3
Albion Fold DROY M43 .... 98 A3
Albion Pl BRO M7 .... 81 C4 🔒
　　PWCH M25 .... 62 A1 🔒
　　SALQ/ORD M5 .... 14 A1
Albion Rd RUSH/FAL M14 .... 48 B3
　　ECC M30 .... 53 C3
Albion St CHAD OL9 .... 16 A5
　　CMANE M1 .... 88 A2
　　FAIL M35 .... 55 D2
　　OLD OL1 .... 34 C2
　　OLDTF/WHR M16 .... 77 C1
　　SWIN M27 .... 77 C1

Albion Wy *SALQ/ORD* M5 .... 13 E2
Albyns Av *CHH* M8 .... 83 C2 🔟
Alcester St *CHAD* OL9 .... 71 C2
Aldborough Cl *DID/WITH* M20 .. 129 D3
Aldbourne Cl *NEWH/MOS* M40.. 8 C1
   NEWH/MOS M40 .... 84 B2 🔟
Aldcroft St *GTN* M18 .... 107 D3 🔟
Alder Ct *CHH* M8 .... 64 B4 🔟
Alderdale Dr *DROY* M43 .... 96 B3
   HTNM SK4 .... 132 A4
Alder Dr *SWIN* M27 .... 57 C4
Alderfield Rd *CCHDY* M21 .... 42 A4
Alder Forest Av *ECC* M30 .... 90 A1
Alderglen Rd *CHH* M8 .... 82 B5
Alder Gv *STRET* M32 .... 115 C3
Alder La *OLDS* OL8 .... 72 B3
Alderley Dr *MPL/ROM* SK6 .... 141 C1
Alderley Rd *RDSH* SK5 .... 134 B4
   URM M41 .... 110 A3
Alderman Sq *WGTN/LGST* M12 .... 19 E4
Aldermary Rd *CCHDY* M21 .... 127 D4
Aldermoor Cl *OP/CLY* M11 .... 106 B3 🔟
Alder Rd *FAIL* M35 .... 88 B4
Alderside Rd *BKLY* M9 .... 84 B1
Aldersley Av *BKLY* M9 .... 65 D1
Alderson St *CHAD* OL9 .... 55 C2
   SLFD M6 .... 3 D1
Alder St *ECC* M30 .... 90 A1 🔟
   SLFD M6 .... 2 A5
Aldham Av *NEWH/MOS* M40 .. 96 A1 🔟
Aldred Cl *CHH* M8 .... 83 D3 🔟
Aldred St *ECC* M30 .... 91 C4
   FAIL M35 .... 88 A2
   SALQ/ORD M5 .... 13 F1
Aldsworth Dr *NEWH/MOS* M40.. 85 C4 🔟
Aldwych Av *RUSH/FAL* M14 .... 37 F5
Aldwyn Park Rd *DTN/ASHW* M34.. 109 C2
Alexander Av *FAIL* M35 .... 89 C1
Alexander Gdns *BRO* M7 .... 5 D2
Alexander St *SLFD* M6 .... 95 C3 🔟
Alexandra Av *RUSH/FAL* M14 .... 46 B1
Alexandra Dr *BNG/LEV* M19 .. 131 D2 🔟
Alexandra Rd *ECC* M30 .... 90 B4
   OLDTF/WHR M16 .... 35 F3
Alexandra Rd South
   OLDTF/WHR M16 .... 35 F3
Alexandra St *BRO* M7 .... 5 D3
Alexandra Ter *BNG/LEV* M19 .. 51 D4 🔟
Alford Av *DID/WITH* M20 .... 129 C1
Alford Rd *HTNM* SK4 .... 132 B3
Alford St *CHAD* OL9 .... 71 D3 🔟
Alfred Av *WALK* M28 .... 74 A2
Alfred James Cl *NEWH/MOS* M40 .. 8 B4 🔟
Alfred St *BKLY* M9 .... 84 B1
   CHAD OL9 .... 54 A3
   ECC M30 .... 91 D2
Algernon St *ECC* M30 .... 91 D2
   SWIN M27 .... 75 D1 🔟
Alice St *SWIN* M27 .... 77 D1
Alison St *RUSH/FAL* M14 .... 36 C4 🔟
Alker Rd *NEWH/MOS* M40 .... 9 D4
Allandale Rd *BNG/LEV* M19 .... 50 B3
Allan Roberts Cl *BKLY* M9 .... 66 B4
Allenby Rd *SWIN* M27 .... 75 C3
Allen Rd *URM* M41 .... 112 B4
Allen St *OLDS* OL8 .... 54 B3 🔟
Allerford Cl *OLDTF/WHR* M16 .. 35 E3
Allesley Dr *CHH* M8 .... 82 B4
Alligin Cl *OLDS* OL9 .... 53 C1
Allingham St *BRUN/LGST* M13 .. 39 F3
Allington Dr *ECC* M30 .... 92 A1
Allison Gv *ECC* M30 .... 90 B4
Allison St *CHH* M8 .... 82 B4

All Saints' St *NEWH/MOS* M40 .. 87 C4 🔟
Allwood St *SALQ/ORD* M5 .... 14 B3
Alma Rd *BNG/LEV* M19 .... 51 D5
   HTNM SK4 .... 132 B4
Alma St *ECC* M30 .... 92 B4
Alminstone Cl *NEWH/MOS* M40 .. 96 B1 🔟
Almond Cl *FAIL* M35 .... 88 B3
   SLFD M6 .... 3 D5
Almond Dr *SALE* M33 .... 122 B3
Almond St *NEWH/MOS* M40 .... 7 F2
Alms Hill Rd *CHH* M8 .... 83 C2
Alness Rd *OLDTF/WHR* M16 .... 35 E5
Alpha Ct *DTN/ASHW* M34 .... 119 C2
Alphagate Dr *DTN/ASHW* M34 .. 119 C2
Alpha Pl *HULME* M15 .... 25 F1 🔟
Alpha Rd *STRET* M32 .... 114 A4 🔟
Alpha St *OP/CLY* M11 .... 107 C2 🔟
   SLFD M6 .... 2 A4
Alpha St West *SLFD* M6 .... 95 C2 🔟
Alphonsus St *OLDTF/WHR* M16 .. 34 B2
Alpine Rd *STKP* SK1 .... 139 C4 🔟
Alpine St *OP/CLY* M11 .... 11 E5
Alport Av *OLDTF/WHR* M16 .... 44 A2
Alresford Rd *SLFD* M6 .... 78 B3
Alsager Cl *CCHDY* M21 .... 126 B3
Alsop Av *BRO* M7 .... 80 B2 🔟
Alston Av *STRET* M32 .... 113 D2
Alstone Rd *HTNM* SK4 .... 133 C3
Alston Gdns *BNG/LEV* M19 .... 131 D4
Alston Rd *GTN* M18 .... 107 C4 🔟
Altair Pl *BRO* M7 .... 4 B2
Altcar Gv *RDSH* SK5 .... 117 C3
Alton Sq *OP/CLY* M11 .... 107 C2
Alton St *OLDS* OL8 .... 73 D2
Altrincham St *CMANE* M1 .... 17 E5
Alvan Sq *OP/CLY* M11 .... 107 C2 🔟
Alvaston Rd *GTN* M18 .... 117 C1
Alveley Av *DID/WITH* M20 .... 130 A4
Alverstone Rd *DID/WITH* M20 .. 130 A3 🔟
Alwyn Dr *BRUN/LGST* M13 .... 39 F3
Ambergate St *OP/CLY* M11 .... 20 A1
Amberley Rd *SALE* M33 .... 122 A4
Amber St *ANC* M4 .... 7 D5
Amberwood *CHAD* OL9 .... 52 A1 🔟
Ambleside Rd *RDSH* SK5 .... 134 B3
Ambrose St *WGTN/LGST* M12 .. 30 C2
Ambush St *OP/CLY* M11 .... 107 D2
Amersham Cl *URM* M41 .... 100 B4
Amersham Pl *BNG/LEV* M19 .. 132 A3 🔟
Amersham St *SALQ/ORD* M5 .. 12 B2
Amesbury Gv *RDSH* SK5 .... 134 B1 🔟
Amesbury Rd *BKLY* M9 .... 67 C1
Amherst Rd *DID/WITH* M20 .... 37 C1
Amory St *WGTN/LGST* M12 .... 18 A5
Amos Av *NEWH/MOS* M40 .... 96 A1
Amos St *BKLY* M9 .... 85 D2
   SLFD M6 .... 95 C3
Ampney Cl *ECC* M30 .... 90 A4
Amwell St *CHH* M8 .... 83 D2
Anaconda Dr *CSLFD* M3 .... 5 E4
Anchorage Quay *SALQ/ORD* M5 .. 22 C1
Anchorage Rd *URM* M41 .... 113 C4
Anchor Cl *BNG/LEV* M19 .... 116 A4
Anchorside Cl *CCHDY* M21 .. 126 B2 🔟
Anchor St *OLD* OL1 .... 55 D1 🔟
Ancoats Gv *ANC* M4 .... 18 C3
Ancoats Gv North *ANC* M4 .... 18 C3
Andoc Av *ECC* M30 .... 93 C4
Andover Av *ECC* M30 .... 91 C4
Andre St *OP/CLY* M11 .... 96 A3 🔟
Andrew Rd *BKLY* M9 .... 66 C4
Andrew St *CHAD* OL9 .... 53 C1
   DROY M43 .... 99 C1

FAIL M35 ..... 88 A1 🔲
Anfield Rd *NEWH/MOS* M40 ..... 69 D4
SALE M33 ..... 124 A4 🔲
Angela St *HULME* M15 ..... 25 D2
Angel St *ANC* M4 ..... 7 D4
Angora Dr *CSLFD* M3 ..... 4 C4
Annable Rd *DROY* M43 ..... 98 B4
GTN M18 ..... 107 C3 🔲
MPL/ROM SK6 ..... 140 B2
Annald Sq *DROY* M43 ..... 108 A1
Anne Nuttall St *HULME* M15 ..... 25 D2 🔲
Annesley Rd *NEWH/MOS* M40 ..... 69 D4
Annie St *SALQ/ORD* M5 ..... 95 C3
Annisdale Cl *ECC* M30 ..... 138 A1
Ann St *RDSH* SK5 .....
Anscombe Cl *NEWH/MOS* M40 ..... 8 C3
Ansdell Av *CCHDY* M21 ..... 126 B1 🔲
Ansdell Dr *DROY* M43 ..... 97 C3
Ansdell Rd *RDSH* SK5 ..... 118 A4
Ansdell St *CHH* M8 ..... 83 C2
Ansell Cl *GTN* M18 ..... 106 B5 🔲
Anselms Ct *OLDS* OL8 ..... 72 A1
Ansleigh Av *CHH* M8 ..... 65 C4
Anslow Cl *NEWH/MOS* M40 ..... 84 B3 🔲
Anson Dr *SWIN* M27 ..... 76 A3 🔲
Anson Rd *DTN/ASHW* M34 ..... 118 A3
RUSH/FAL M14 ..... 38 C3
SWIN M27 ..... 76 A3
Anson St *ECC* M30 ..... 90 B2
Answell Av *CHH* M8 ..... 65 C3
Antares Av *BRO* M7 ..... 4 C3
Anthony Cl *WGTN/LGST* M12 ..... 29 F2
Apfel La *CHAD* OL9 ..... 53 D2
Apperley Gra *ECC* M30 ..... 92 A1
Appian Wy *BRO* M7 ..... 82 A4
Appleby Av *WGTN/LGST* M12 ..... 41 D5 🔲
Appleford Dr *CHH* M8 ..... 83 D3
Appleton Rd *HTNM* SK4 ..... 133 D3
Apple Tree Wk *SALE* M33 ..... 121 C4 🔲
Apsley Gv *WGTN/LGST* M12 ..... 28 B3
Apsley St *STKP* SK1 ..... 138 B4
Aquarius La *SLFD* M6 ..... 4 A1 🔲
Aquarius St *HULME* M15 ..... 26 C5
Arbor Av *BNG/LEV* M19 ..... 132 A2
Arbor Dr *BNG/LEV* M19 ..... 131 D2
Arbor Gv *DROY* M43 ..... 97 D2
Arbory Av *NEWH/MOS* M40 ..... 86 B1
Arbour Cl *SLFD* M6 ..... 2 B3
Arbroath St *OP/CLY* M11 ..... 96 B4
Archer Pl *URM* M41 ..... 112 B2 🔲
Archer St *OP/CLY* M11 ..... 10 C5
Archie St *SALQ/ORD* M5 ..... 23 D2
Arcon Dr *OLDTF/WHR* M16 ..... 35 E5
Ardale Av *NEWH/MOS* M40 ..... 69 C3
Arden Gv *NEWH/MOS* M40 ..... 69 C4
Arden Rd *MPL/ROM* SK6 ..... 137 C2
Ardens Cl *SWIN* M27 ..... 57 D3 🔲
Arden St *CHAD* OL9 ..... 71 C2
Ardent Wy *BRO* M7 ..... 62 B4
Ardern Rd *CHH* M8 ..... 64 B4
Ardwick Gn North *WGTN/LGST* M12 ..... 28 A1
Ardwick Gn South *BRUN/LGST* M13 ..... 28 A1
Argus St *OLDS* OL8 ..... 72 A3
Argyle Av *RUSH/FAL* M14 ..... 39 E3
Argyle St *DROY* M43 ..... 98 A4
GTN M18 ..... 106 B4 🔲
SWIN M27 ..... 76 A2
Argyll Av *STRET* M32 ..... 113 D3
Argyll Cl *FAIL* M35 ..... 89 D2 🔲
Argyll Park Rd *FAIL* M35 ..... 89 D2
Argyll Rd *CHAD* OL9 ..... 70 B2
Arkle Dr *CHAD* OL9 ..... 52 B1
Ark St *BNG/LEV* M19 ..... 50 C2

Arkwright St *CHAD* OL9 ..... 54 A3
Arley Av *DID/WITH* M20 ..... 128 B4
Arlington Av *PWCH* M25 ..... 62 B3 🔲
SWIN M27 ..... 75 D3
Arlington Rd *STRET* M32 ..... 64 B4
Arlington St *CHH* M8 ..... 5 D4
CSLFD M3 ..... 5 D4
Arliss Av *BNG/LEV* M19 ..... 50 C5
Armadale Av *BKLY* M9 ..... 68 A1 🔲
Armitage Cl *OLDS* OL8 ..... 72 A2
Armitage St *ECC* M30 ..... 91 C4
Armour Pl *BKLY* M9 ..... 66 A3 🔲
Arnesby Av *SALE* M33 ..... 125 C3
Arne St *CHAD* OL9 ..... 53 C4 🔲
Arnfield Rd *DID/WITH* M20 ..... 130 A3
Arnold Dr *DROY* M43 ..... 98 A4
Arnold Rd *OLDTF/WHR* M16 ..... 45 F4
Arnott Crs *HULME* M15 ..... 26 B5
Arnside Av *CHAD* OL9 ..... 53 C4
HTNM SK4 ..... 133 D3
Arnside Dr *SLFD* M6 ..... 93 D2 🔲
Arnside Gv *SALE* M33 ..... 123 D4
Arnside St *RUSH/FAL* M14 ..... 47 E1
Arran Av *OLDS* OL8 ..... 73 D2
STRET M32 ..... 113 C3
Arran Gdns *URM* M41 ..... 101 D4 🔲
URM M41 ..... 101 C4 🔲
Arran St *BRO* M7 ..... 81 D3
NEWH/MOS M40 ..... 85 D1 🔲
Arras Gv *DTN/ASHW* M34 ..... 117 D2 🔲
Arrowfield Rd *CCHDY* M21 ..... 127 D3
Arrow St *BRO* M7 ..... 81 D4
Arthur Rd *OLDTF/WHR* M16 ..... 34 A4
Arthur St *ECC* M30 ..... 91 C4
PWCH M25 ..... 61 D1 🔲
RDSH SK5 ..... 134 A2 🔲
SWIN M27 ..... 75 D2
Artillery St *CSLFD* M3 ..... 15 F4
Arundale Av *OLDTF/WHR* M16 ..... 45 E4
Arundel St *HULME* M15 ..... 25 D1
SWIN M27 ..... 57 C4 🔲
Ascension Rd *BRO* M7 ..... 4 C1
Ascot Av *STRET* M32 ..... 32 A5
Ascot Cl *CHAD* OL9 ..... 54 A2
Ascot Pde *BNG/LEV* M19 ..... 131 D3 🔲
Ascot Rd *NEWH/MOS* M40 ..... 11 F2
Ascroft St *OLD* OL1 ..... 55 D3
Asgard Dr *SALQ/ORD* M5 ..... 14 B5
Asgard Gv *SALQ/ORD* M5 ..... 14 B5
Ashbourne Gv *BRO* M7 ..... 82 A4
Ashbourne Rd *ECC* M30 ..... 92 A4
SLFD M6 ..... 78 A4 🔲
STRET M32 ..... 113 C1
Ashbridge *TRPK* M17 ..... 103 D3
Ashbridge Rd *FAIL* M35 ..... 89 D3
Ashbrook Av *DTN/ASHW* M34 ..... 118 B2
Ashbrook Cl *DTN/ASHW* M34 ..... 118 B2 🔲
Ashbrook Farm Cl *RDSH* SK5 ..... 117 D3 🔲
Ashbrook La *RDSH* SK5 ..... 117 D2 🔲
Ashbrook St *OP/CLY* M11 ..... 108 A2
Ashburn Av *BNG/LEV* M19 ..... 131 D4 🔲
Ashburton Rd West *URM* M41 ..... 101 D2
Ashcroft Av *SLFD* M6 ..... 95 C1 🔲
Ashdale Cl *RDSH* SK5 ..... 134 B4
Ashdale Crs *DROY* M43 ..... 97 D3
Ashdale Dr *DID/WITH* M20 ..... 130 B4
Ashdene Rd *DID/WITH* M20 ..... 130 B3
Ashdown Av *BKLY* M9 ..... 66 B1
Ashdown Dr *SWIN* M27 ..... 77 C3
Ashdown Gv *BKLY* M9 ..... 66 B1 🔲
Ashdown Ter *BKLY* M9 ..... 66 B1 🔲
Ash Dr *SWIN* M27 ..... 57 C3
Ashfield Cl *SLFD* M6 ..... 95 C2 🔲

Ashfield Dr *NEWH/MOS* M40 .... **96** B1
Ashfield Gv *GTN* M18 .... **117** D2 🔟
Ashfield Rd *BRUN/LGST* M13 .... **39** E4
  SALE M33 .... **123** D4
  URM M41 .... **111** D3
Ashfield Sq *DROY* M43 .... **97** D4 🔟
Ashfield St *OLDS* OL8 .... **72** A2
  OP/CLY M11 .... **20** A1
Ashford Av *ECC* M30 .... **101** C1 🔟
  RDSH SK5 .... **117** D3 🔟
  SWIN M27 .... **75** C3
Ashford Rd *DID/WITH* M20 .... **129** C2
  HTNM SK4 .... **133** D3
Ash Gv *DROY* M43 .... **133** D3
  HTNM SK4 .... **108** A1
  RUSH/FAL M14 .... **39** F3
  STRET M32 .... **124** A1
  SWIN M27 .... **75** D4
Ashkirk St *GTN* M18 .... **106** B4 🔟
Ashlands *SALE* M33 .... **123** C4
Ashlands Av *NEWH/MOS* M40 .... **69** C4
  SWIN M27 .... **75** C3
Ashlar Dr *WGTN/LGST* M12 .... **19** E4
Ashley Av *OLDTF/WHR* M16 .... **34** C3
  SWIN M27 .... **75** D3
Ashley Court Dr *NEWH/MOS* M40 .... **70** B4
Ashley Crs *SWIN* M27 .... **75** D2
Ashley Dr *SWIN* M27 .... **75** D3
Ashley La *BKLY* M9 .... **85** D1
Ashley Rd *DROY* M43 .... **97** C3
Ashley St *CHAD* OL9 .... **54** A1
  SLFD M6 .... **95** C3
Ashlyn Gv *RUSH/FAL* M14 .... **130** B1
Ashover Av *WGTN/LGST* M12 .... **30** A3
Ashover St *STRET* M32 .... **115** C2
Ashridge Dr *ECC* M30 .... **101** C1
Ash Rd *DROY* M43 .... **97** D3
  DTN/ASHW M34 .... **118** A1
Ash St *BKLY* M9 .... **84** B2
  DTN/ASHW M34 .... **109** D2
  FAIL M35 .... **88** A1
  SLFD M6 .... **2** A5
Ashton Crs *CHAD* OL9 .... **71** C2
Ashton Hill La *DROY* M43 .... **108** A1
Ashton La *SALE* M33 .... **122** B4
Ashton New Rd *OP/CLY* M11 .... **20** C2
  WGTN/LGST M12 .... **19** E2
Ashton Old Rd *OP/CLY* M11 .... **20** C5
  WGTN/LGST M12 .... **18** C5
Ashton Rd *DROY* M43 .... **98** A4
  MPL/ROM SK6 .... **137** C5
  OLDS OL8 .... **73** D1
Ashton Rd East *FAIL* M35 .... **88** B1
Ashton Rd West *FAIL* M35 .... **88** B1
Ashton St *BKLY* M9 .... **85** D1
  CHAD OL9 .... **70** B2
Ash Tree Av *DROY* M43 .... **97** D3
Ash Tree Rd *CHH* M8 .... **65** C4
Ashville Ter *NEWH/MOS* M40 .... **67** D4
Ashwood *CHAD* OL9 .... **52** A2
Ashwood Av *DTN/ASHW* M34 .... **118** A2
Ashworth Cl *CHAD* OL9 .... **71** D2 🔟
Ashworth St *CHH* M8 .... **82** A4 🔟
  FAIL M35 .... **87** D3
  OLD OL1 .... **55** D3
Askett Cl *NEWH/MOS* M40 .... **87** D3
Aspen Wood Dr *CHAD* OL9 .... **52** A2
Aspinall St *RUSH/FAL* M14 .... **38** A4
Aspin La *ANC* M4 .... **7** D4
Asquith St *RDSH* SK5 .... **117** D3
Assheton Av *DTN/ASHW* M34 .... **99** C4
Assheton Crs *NEWH/MOS* M40 .... **96** B1 🔟
Assheton Rd *NEWH/MOS* M40 .... **96** B1

Astan Av *DROY* M43 .... **96** B2
Astbury Av *DTN/ASHW* M34 .... **99** D4
Astley St *EDGY/DAV* SK3 .... **138** A4 🔟
  OP/CLY M11 .... **96** A4
Aston Av *RUSH/FAL* M14 .... **46** C3
Astor Rd *BNG/LEV* M19 .... **131** C2
  SALO/ORD M5 .... **94** A4
Athenian Gdns *BRO* M7 .... **81** C4 🔟
Athens St *STKP* SK1 .... **139** C4 🔟
Atherley Gv *NEWH/MOS* M40 .... **70** B3
Atherstone Av *CHH* M8 .... **64** B3
Atherton Cl *FAIL* M35 .... **89** D4
Atherton St *CSLFD* M3 .... **15** E4
  ECC M30 .... **90** B4
Athlone Av *NEWH/MOS* M40 .... **86** A1
Athole St *SALO/ORD* M5 .... **12** B2
Atholl Av *STRET* M32 .... **113** C3
Athol Rd *OLDTF/WHR* M16 .... **45** F4
Athol St *ECC* M30 .... **90** B4
  GTN M18 .... **117** C2
Atkinson Rd *SALE* M33 .... **123** C3
  URM M41 .... **111** D3 🔟
Atkinson St *CHAD* OL9 .... **54** B1 🔟
  CSLFD M3 .... **15** F3
Attercliffe Rd *CCHDY* M21 .... **126** A2
Attewell St *OP/CLY* M11 .... **21** D4 🔟
Attleboro Rd *NEWH/MOS* M40 .... **86** A2
Attwood St *WGTN/LGST* M12 .... **40** C4
Atwood St *CMANE* M1 .... **16** C5
Aubrey Rd *DID/WITH* M20 .... **131** C2 🔟
Aubrey St *SALO/ORD* M5 .... **13** D5
Auburn Av *MPL/ROM* SK6 .... **141** C1
Auburn Dr *URM* M41 .... **112** A4
Auburn Rd *DTN/ASHW* M34 .... **119** D3
  OLDTF/WHR M16 .... **33** F3
Auburn St *CMANE* M1 .... **17** E4 🔟
Auckland Dr *SLFD* M6 .... **80** A4
Auckland Rd *BNG/LEV* M19 .... **50** B5
Auden Cl *OP/CLY* M11 .... **96** B1
Audenshaw Hall Gv
  DTN/ASHW M34 .... **108** B2
Audenshaw Rd *DTN/ASHW* M34 .... **108** B2
Audlem Cl *NEWH/MOS* M40 .... **9** D5
Audley Av *STRET* M32 .... **112** B1
Audley Rd *BNG/LEV* M19 .... **51** F2
Audrey Av *GTN* M18 .... **107** C4
Audrey St *BKLY* M9 .... **85** D1
Augustine Webster Cl *BKLY* M9 .... **85** C1 🔟
Augustus St *CSLFD* M3 .... **6** C2 🔟
Augustus Wy *OLDTF/WHR* M16 .... **35** D2
Austen Rd *ECC* M30 .... **90** D4
Auster Cl *RUSH/FAL* M14 .... **47** D5 🔟
Austin Gv *BNG/LEV* M19 .... **50** A5
Autumn St *BRUN/LGST* M13 .... **38** B2
Avebury Cl *CHH* M8 .... **82** B3 🔟
Avenham Cl *HULME* M15 .... **25** F5 🔟
Avenue St *STKP* SK1 .... **138** B3 🔟
The Avenue *BRO* M7 .... **81** C4 🔟
  ECC M30 .... **91** D4
  MPL/ROM SK6 .... **140** B2
Averill St *NEWH/MOS* M40 .... **87** D4
Aveson Av *CCHDY* M21 .... **126** B3
Avian Dr *RUSH/FAL* M14 .... **47** E5
Avonbrook Dr *NEWH/MOS* M40 .... **70** B3
Avondale *SWIN* M27 .... **59** C3
Avondale Crs *URM* M41 .... **111** C3
Avondale Dr *SLFD* M6 .... **77** D4
Avondale Rd *STRET* M32 .... **115** C1
Avondale St *CHH* M8 .... **83** C2
Avonlea Dr *BNG/LEV* M19 .... **131** C3
Avonlea Rd *DROY* M43 .... **97** C3
Avon Rd *BNG/LEV* M19 .... **131** D3 🔟
  CHAD OL9 .... **52** B1

Avon St *OLDS* OL8 .... 73 D1
Avril Cl *RDSH* SK5 .... 134 B1
Avro Cl *RUSH/FAL* M14 .... 47 E4
Axford Cl *BRO* M7 .... 82 B3 🔢
Axon Sq *OLDTF/WHR* M16 .... 36 A2
Aycliffe Av *CCHDY* M21 .... 127 D4
Aycliffe Gv *BRUN/LGST* M13 .... 39 E4
Aylesbury Av *URM* M41 .... 112 A1
Aylesbury Cl *SALQ/ORD* M5 .... 12 B2
Aylesby Av *GTN* M18 .... 41 F3
Aylesford Rd *RUSH/FAL* M14 .... 38 C5 🔢
Aylsham Cl *MPL/ROM* SK6 .... 137 D4
Aylsham Ms *SWIN* M27 .... 75 D4 🔢
Ayr Av *OLDS* OL8 .... 73 D2
Ayres Rd *OLDTF/WHR* M16 .... 33 E5
Ayrshire Rd *BRO* M7 .... 80 A3
Aysgarth Av *GTN* M18 .... 107 C3
Ayton Gv *RUSH/FAL* M14 .... 39 E3
Aytoun St *CMANE* M1 .... 17 E4 🔢
Azalea Av *GTN* M18 .... 106 B3 🔢

B

Back Acton St *CMANE* M1 .... 17 E4 🔢
Back Ashley St *ANC* M4 .... 7 E4
Back Balloon St *ANC* M4 .... 6 C5 🔢
Back Bank St *CHH* M8 .... 7 D2
Back Bridge St *CSLFD* M3 .... 16 A2
Back Camp St *BRO* M7 .... 81 D4 🔢
Back Chapel St *BNG/LEV* M19 .... 51 D4 🔢
Back China La *CMANE* M1 .... 17 E3
Back College Land *CSLFD* M3 .... 16 A2 🔢
Back Duncan St *BRO* M7 .... 81 C2
Back Elsworth St *CSLFD* M3 .... 6 C2 🔢
Back George St *CMANE* M1 .... 16 C4 🔢
  CMANE M1 .... 16 C3 🔢
Back Greaves St *OLD* OL1 .... 55 D3 🔢
Back Halliwell La *CHH* M8 .... 82 B2 🔢
Back Hamilton St *BRO* M7 .... 81 D2 🔢
Back Hampson St *NEWH/MOS* M40 .... 8 C2 🔢
Back Hilton St *BRO* M7 .... 81 D2
Back Hope St *SLFD* M6 .... 81 D2
Back Howe St *BRO* M7 .... 81 C2
Back Hulme St *SALQ/ORD* M5 .... 14 B2
Back Junction St *CMANE* M1 .... 17 F2
Back King St *OLD* OL1 .... 55 C3 🔢
Back Piccadilly *CMANE* M1 .... 17 E2 🔢
Back Pool Fold *CMANW* M2 .... 16 B2 🔢
Back Quay St *CSLFD* M3 .... 15 E3 🔢
Back Red Bank *ANC* M4 .... 7 D3
Back Roman St *BRO* M7 .... 82 A3 🔢
Back St George's Rd *ANC* M4 .... 7 E4
Back St Mark's La *CHH* M8 .... 82 B1 🔢
Back Scott St *OLDS* OL8 .... 55 D4 🔢
Back South Pde *CSLFD* M3 .... 16 A2
Back Spear St *CMANE* M1 .... 17 E1 🔢
Back Thomas St *ANC* M4 .... 17 D1 🔢
Back Turner St *ANC* M4 .... 17 D1 🔢
Back Water St *STKP* SK1 .... 138 B3 🔢
Bacup St *NEWH/MOS* M40 .... 86 A1
Badby Cl *ANC* M4 .... 19 D2
Baden St *OP/CLY* M11 .... 19 F5
Badminton Cl *CCHDY* M21 .... 44 B3
Bagot St *OP/CLY* M11 .... 96 A3 🔢
  SWIN M27 .... 57 C4 🔢
Baguley St *DROY* M43 .... 98 B4
Baildon St *NEWH/MOS* M40 .... 68 A4
Bailey Rd *TRPK* M17 .... 103 C2
Bailey St *OP/CLY* M11 .... 96 B4
The Bails *BRO* M7 .... 81 C3
Bainbridge Cl *WGTN/LGST* M12 .... 29 D4

Bain St *SWIN* M27 .... 76 B2
Baird St *CMANE* M1 .... 18 A4
Baker St *HTNM* SK4 .... 138 A2
Bakewell Rd *DROY* M43 .... 97 C3
  ECC M30 .... 100 B1
  STRET M32 .... 113 C2
Bakewell St *GTN* M18 .... 116 A1 🔢
Bala Cl *SALQ/ORD* M5 .... 13 D1 🔢
Baldwin Rd *BNG/LEV* M19 .... 131 D3 🔢
Bale St *CMANW* M2 .... 16 B4
Balfour Gv *RDSH* SK5 .... 117 D4
Balfour Rd *URM* M41 .... 110 B3
Balfour St *CHH* M8 .... 83 C1 🔢
  SLFD M6 .... 79 D3
Ballantine St *NEWH/MOS* M40 .... 96 A1
Ballater Av *URM* M41 .... 110 A4
Ballbrook Av *DID/WITH* M20 .... 129 D4
Balleratt St *BNG/LEV* M19 .... 51 D3
Balliol St *CHH* M8 .... 83 C1
  SWIN M27 .... 76 A1 🔢
Balmain Av *GTN* M18 .... 116 A2
Balmain Rd *URM* M41 .... 110 B2
Balmfield St *CHH* M8 .... 83 C4
Balmforth St *HULME* M15 .... 25 D1 🔢
Balmoral Av *DTN/ASHW* M34 .... 109 D2
  STRET M32 .... 114 B2 🔢
  URM M41 .... 110 B4
Balmoral Dr *DTN/ASHW* M34 .... 118 A1
Balmoral Gra *PWCH* M25 .... 64 A2 🔢
Balmoral Rd *RUSH/FAL* M14 .... 49 D5
  SWIN M27 .... 59 C3
  URM M41 .... 110 A4
Balmoral St *GTN* M18 .... 116 A1 🔢
Balsam Cl *BRUN/LGST* M13 .... 27 F2
Baltic St *SALQ/ORD* M5 .... 95 C3 🔢
Baltimore St *NEWH/MOS* M40 .... 85 D4
Bamford Av *DTN/ASHW* M34 .... 137 D1
Bamford St *CHAD* OL9 .... 54 A1
  OP/CLY M11 .... 21 E1
Banbury Ms *SWIN* M27 .... 57 D4 🔢
Banbury Rd *FAIL* M35 .... 97 C1
Banbury St *STKP* SK1 .... 138 B4 🔢
Bancroft Cl *MPL/ROM* SK6 .... 141 C2 🔢
Bancroft Rd *SWIN* M27 .... 58 A4 🔢
Banff Rd *RUSH/FAL* M14 .... 38 A3
Bangor St *RDSH* SK5 .... 138 B1 🔢
Bank Bridge Rd *OP/CLY* M11 .... 11 E4
Bankfield Av *BRUN/LGST* M13 .... 39 E4
  DROY M43 .... 98 A3
Bankfield Rd *SALE* M33 .... 122 A3
Bankfield St *BKLY* M9 .... 66 B4
  HTNM SK4 .... 138 A1
Bankhirst Cl *CHH* M8 .... 65 C4 🔢
Bank House Rd *BKLY* M9 .... 66 A1
Bank La *SLFD* M6 .... 78 B3
Bankley St *BNG/LEV* M19 .... 51 D4
Bankmill Cl *BRUN/LGST* M13 .... 27 F2
Bank Pl *CSLFD* M3 .... 14 C1
Bank Rd *CHH* M8 .... 65 C3
Bankside *CHAD* OL9 .... 54 B3
Bank St *BRO* M7 .... 82 B1 🔢
  CSLFD M3 .... 14 C1
  DROY M43 .... 107 D1
  OP/CLY M11 .... 11 E5
  OP/CLY M11 .... 11 D3
  SALE M33 .... 124 A2 🔢
Banky La *SALE* M33 .... 121 C3
Bannatyne Cl *NEWH/MOS* M40 .... 70 A4 🔢
Banner Dale *BRUN/LGST* M13 .... 40 A2
Bannerman Av *PWCH* M25 .... 62 B2
Bannerman Rd *DROY* M43 .... 98 B4
Bannerman Sq *OLDTF/WHR* M16 .... 36 A2
Bannerman St *BRO* M7 .... 82 A3 🔢

Bantry Av *BKLY* M9 .... 65 D2
Baptist St *ANC* M4 .... 7 E4
Barbeck Cl *NEWH/MOS* M40 .... 9 E5
Barber St *OP/CLY* M11 .... 107 C2 ▣
Barbican St *DID/WITH* M20 .... 129 D2 ▣
  DID/WITH M20 .... 129 D2 ▣
Barclays Av *SLFD* M6 .... 78 B3 ▣
Barcliffe Av *NEWH/MOS* M40 .... 69 C3
Barcombe Cl *URM* M41 .... 112 B2 ▣
Bardsley Av *FAIL* M35 .... 88 B2
Bardsley St *CHAD* OL9 .... 70 B2
  NEWH/MOS M40 .... 87 D4 ▣
Barff Rd *SALQ/ORD* M5 .... 94 A3
Barfoot Br *SALE* M33 .... 124 A2
Bar Gap Rd *OLD* OL1 .... 55 D1
Baring St *CMANE* M1 .... 17 F5
Barkan Wy *SWIN* M27 .... 77 D1
Barker Rd *MPL/ROM* SK6 .... 141 D2 ▣
Barker's La *SALE* M33 .... 122 B4
Barker St *CSLFD* M3 .... 6 A2
Barking St *NEWH/MOS* M40 .... 9 F4
Bark Wk *HULME* M15 .... 26 B3
Barkway Rd *STRET* M32 .... 113 C3
Barlea Av *NEWH/MOS* M40 .... 69 D4
Barleycroft Cl *OLDTF/WHR* M16 .... 36 A3 ▣
Barlow Fold Rd *RDSH* SK5 .... 135 C1 ▣
Barlow La *ECC* M30 .... 91 C3
Barlow La North *RDSH* SK5 .... 134 B3
Barlow Moor Rd *CCHDY* M21 .... 43 E5
Barlow Pl *BRUN/LGST* M13 .... 28 A2 ▣
Barlow Rd *BNG/LEV* M19 .... 51 D3
  SALQ/ORD M5 .... 14 B3
  STRET M32 .... 32 B2
Barlow's Cft *CSLFD* M3 .... 15 F1
Barlow St *ECC* M30 .... 91 D4
Barmouth St *OP/CLY* M11 .... 20 B4
Barmouth Wk *OLDS* OL8 .... 71 D3 ▣
Barnard Rd *GTN* M18 .... 41 F4
Barnby St *WGTN/LGST* M12 .... 40 C4
Barnes Av *BNG/LEV* M19 .... 51 D3
  STRET M32 .... 32 B2
Barnett Dr *CSLFD* M3 .... 5 D5
Barnfield *URM* M41 .... 120 D1
Barnfield Crs *SALE* M33 .... 122 B4 ▣
Barnfield Rd *SWIN* M27 .... 57 D3
Barnfield St *DTN/ASHW* M34 .... 119 D1
Barn Gv *DTN/ASHW* M34 .... 109 D2
Barnhill Av *PWCH* M25 .... 62 B3
Barnhill Dr *PWCH* M25 .... 62 B3
Barnhill Rd *PWCH* M25 .... 62 A2
Barnhill St *RUSH/FAL* M14 .... 36 B3
Barnsdale Dr *CHH* M8 .... 83 C3
Barnsfold Av *RUSH/FAL* M14 .... 130 A1 ▣
Barnstable Dr *NEWH/MOS* M40 .... 84 A3
Barnstead Av *DID/WITH* M20 .... 130 B4
Barnston Av *RUSH/FAL* M14 .... 47 E2
Barn St *OLD* OL1 .... 55 C3
Baroness Gv *BRO* M7 .... 4 B1 ▣
Barons Ct *FAIL* M35 .... 87 D3
Barrack St *HULME* M15 .... 24 C2
Barra Dr *URM* M41 .... 101 D4
Barrass St *OP/CLY* M11 .... 106 B3 ▣
Barrfield Rd *SLFD* M6 .... 95 C1
Barr Hill Av *SLFD* M6 .... 79 C4
Barrhill Cl *HULME* M15 .... 25 E3
Barrington Av *DROY* M43 .... 97 D3 ▣
Barrington St *OP/CLY* M11 .... 96 A3
Barrow Hill Rd *CHH* M8 .... 82 B4
Barrow St *CSLFD* M3 .... 14 C2
Barry Lawson Cl *CHH* M8 .... 82 B2 ▣
Barry Rd *RDSH* SK5 .... 134 B4 ▣
Bartlam Pl *OLD* OL1 .... 55 D2 ▣
Bartlett St *OP/CLY* M11 .... 21 F5
Barton Av *URM* M41 .... 110 B3

Barton Dock Rd *STRET* M32 .... 113 C1
  URM M41 .... 101 D2
Barton Hall Av *ECC* M30 .... 90 A4
Barton La *ECC* M30 .... 101 D1
Barton Rd *ECC* M30 .... 101 C1
  STRET M32 .... 112 B1
  STRET M32 .... 124 A1 ▣
  SWIN M27 .... 77 C2
  URM M41 .... 101 C4
Barton St *CSLFD* M3 .... 15 F5
  OLD OL1 .... 54 B1
Barway Rd *CCHDY* M21 .... 42 B4
Barwell Cl *RDSH* SK5 .... 135 C1
Barwell Rd *SALE* M33 .... 122 A4
Basford Rd *OLDTF/WHR* M16 .... 33 F5
Basildon Cl *BRUN/LGST* M13 .... 29 D5
Basil St *RUSH/FAL* M14 .... 38 A4
Baslow Av *BNG/LEV* M19 .... 51 F2
Baslow Gv *RDSH* SK5 .... 134 B4
Baslow Rd *DROY* M43 .... 97 C2
  DTN/ASHW M34 .... 137 D1
  STRET M32 .... 113 C2
Baslow St *OP/CLY* M11 .... 19 F2
Basset Av *SLFD* M6 .... 81 C4
Basten Dr *BRO* M7 .... 81 D3
Batchelor Cl *CCHDY* M21 .... 128 A2 ▣
Bateson St *STKP* SK1 .... 139 C3 ▣
Bates St *BRUN/LGST* M13 .... 40 A3
Bath Crs *OLDTF/WHR* M16 .... 34 A1
Bath St *CHAD* OL9 .... 54 A4
Batley St *BKLY* M9 .... 85 C1
Battersby St *OP/CLY* M11 .... 107 C4 ▣
Batty St *CHH* M8 .... 84 A4
Baxter St *OLDS* OL8 .... 71 D3
Baydon Av *CHH* M8 .... 82 B3
Bayfield Gv *NEWH/MOS* M40 .... 68 A4 ▣
Bay St *CHAD* OL9 .... 54 B2 ▣
Bayswater Av *NEWH/MOS* M40 .... 11 F1
Baytree Av *CHAD* OL9 .... 52 A1
Bay Tree Av *WALK* M28 .... 74 A4 ▣
Baytree Dr *MPL/ROM* SK6 .... 141 D1
Baywood St *BKLY* M9 .... 84 B1 ▣
Bazaar St *SLFD* M6 .... 2 C2
Beacon Rd *TRPK* M17 .... 102 A2
Beaconsfield *RUSH/FAL* M14 .... 130 A2 ▣
Bealey Cl *GTN* M18 .... 31 F4
Beamish Cl *BRUN/LGST* M13 .... 28 A3
Beard Rd *GTN* M18 .... 116 A1 ▣
Beard St *DROY* M43 .... 97 D4 ▣
Beardwood Rd *BKLY* M9 .... 66 B1
Beatrice Av *GTN* M18 .... 117 D1
Beatrice Rd *WALK* M28 .... 74 B2
Beatrice St *SWIN* M27 .... 57 D4
Beatrice Wignall St *DROY* M43 ...... 108 A1 ▣
  DROY M43 .... 108 A1 ▣
Beattock St *HULME* M15 .... 25 D2
Beaufort Av *DID/WITH* M20 .... 129 C4 ▣
  SWIN M27 .... 75 D2
Beaufort St *CSLFD* M3 .... 15 E5 ▣
  ECC M30 .... 90 B2 ▣
  PWCH M25 .... 63 C1
Beaumaris Cl *WGTN/LGST* M12 .... 30 B3
Beaumont Rd *CCHDY* M21 .... 126 B2
Beaver St *CMANE* M1 .... 16 C5
Bebbington St *OP/CLY* M11 .... 96 A4 ▣
Beckenham Rd *CHH* M8 .... 83 C2 ▣
Becket Av *BRO* M7 .... 82 A3 ▣
Beckett St *GTN* M18 .... 116 A1 ▣
Beckfoot Dr *BRUN/LGST* M13 .... 39 F4
Beckford St *NEWH/MOS* M40 .... 85 C4
Beckhampton Cl *BRUN/LGST* M13 .... 28 B5
Beckley Av *PWCH* M25 .... 62 A3
Beckside *RDSH* SK5 .... 118 A4

Beck St *CSLFD* M3....................... 15 E1
   OP/CLY M11............................. 107 C2 🔢
Bedford Av *OLDTF/WHR* M16........ 44 C2
   SWIN M27.................................. 76 A2 🔢
Bedford Rd *ECC* M30.................... 92 A2
   OLDTF/WHR M16....................... 32 C5
   URM M41.................................... 111 C1
Bedford St *RDSH* SK5.................. 134 A2
Bednal Av *NEWH/MOS* M40............ 9 E2
Bedwell Cl *OLDTF/WHR* M16......... 36 A4
Beech Av *DROY* M43...................... 97 D4
   DTN/ASHW M34........................ 119 D1
   SLFD M6..................................... 95 C1 🔢
   URM M41.................................... 111 C4
Beech Cl *PWCH* M25..................... 63 C2
Beechcroft *PWCH* M25.................. 63 C3
Beechcroft Cl *NEWH/MOS* M40...... 8 C4 🔢
Beechdale Cl *NEWH/MOS* M40...... 110 C2 🔢
Beechfield Av *URM* M41................. 76 A4
Beechfield Rd *SWIN* M27.............. 83 C3
Beechfield St *CHH* M8................... 95 C1 🔢
Beech Gv *RUSH/FAL* M14............. 130 B1
   SLFD M6..................................... 95 C1 🔢
Beech Hurst Cl *OLDTF/WHR* M16.. 44 C1
Beech Ms *CCHDY* M21................. 126 A1 🔢
Beech Mt *BKLY* M9....................... 84 B1
Beech Range *BNG/LEV* M19......... 50 C4
Beech Rd *CCHDY* M21.................. 126 B1
Beech St *ECC* M30....................... 90 B4
   FAIL M35.................................... 88 A1
   SWIN M27.................................. 76 B2
Beech Wk *STRET* M32.................. 124 A1
Beechwood Av *CCHDY* M21......... 127 C1
Beechwood Dr *WALK* M28............. 74 B3
Beechwood Gv *BKLY* M9............. 85 C2 🔢
Beechwood Rd *OLDS* OL8............ 73 D3
   PWCH M25................................ 63 D2 🔢
Beede St *OP/CLY* M11.................. 21 E5
Beehive St *OLDS* OL8.................. 73 D2
Beeley St *SLFD* M6...................... 80 B4
Beeston Av *BRO* M7..................... 80 B4
Beeston St *BKLY* M9.................... 85 C2
Beeth St *OP/CLY* M11................. 106 B3
Beeton Gv *BRUN/LGST* M13......... 39 E1
Beever St *OLDTF/WHR* M16......... 34 B1
Begley St *MPL/ROM* SK6........... 141 D4
Belding Av *NEWH/MOS* M40........ 70 B4 🔢
Beldon Rd *BKLY* M9..................... 65 D1
Belfield Rd *PWCH* M25................ 64 C1
Belford Av *DTN/ASHW* M34......... 118 A2
Belford Rd *STRET* M32................ 13 F5
Belfort Dr *SALQ/ORD* M5............ 40 C2
Belgate Cl *WGTN/LGST* M12....... 40 C2
Belgrave Av *FAIL* M35................. 89 D1 🔢
   RUSH/FAL M14......................... 39 E4
Belgrave Crs *ECC* M30................ 92 A2
Belgrave Rd *NEWH/MOS* M40...... 70 A4
   OLDS OL8................................. 73 D1 🔢
Belhaven Rd *CHH* M8.................. 64 B3
Bell Clough Rd *DROY* M43........... 98 B2
Bell Crs *OP/CLY* M11.................. 20 A5
Belle Vue Av *WGTN/LGST* M12.... 40 B1
Belle Vue St *WGTN/LGST* M12..... 31 D3
Bellew St *OP/CLY* M11................. 19 F5
Bellfield Av *OLDS* OL8................. 73 D3
Bellis Cl *WGTN/LGST* M12........... 19 F2
Bellott St *CHH* M8........................ 83 C3
Bells Croft Av *NEWH/MOS* M40.... 86 B2 🔢
Bell St *DROY* M43........................ 98 B3
Bell Ter *ECC* M30........................ 101 C1
Belmont Av *DTN/ASHW* M34....... 119 D1
   SLFD M6..................................... 93 C2 🔢
Belmont Cl *HTNM* SK4............... 138 A2 🔢

Belmont Rd *SALE* M33................ 123 C3
Belmont St *ECC* M30................... 91 D2
   OLD OL1.................................... 55 C1
   OLDTF/WHR M16....................... 34 C1
   SALQ/ORD M5........................... 94 B4 🔢
Belmont Wy *CHAD* OL9................ 54 A1
   HTNM SK4................................ 138 A2
Belper Rd *ECC* M30.................... 100 B1
Belthorne Av *BKLY* M9................ 68 B3 🔢
Beltone Cl *STRET* M32............... 113 D4
Belvedere Av *RDSH* SK5............ 117 D3
Belvedere Dr *MPL/ROM* SK6..... 140 A2
Belvedere Rd *RUSH/FAL* M14.... 49 F5
   SLFD M6....................................... 2 C3
Belvedere St *SLFD* M6.................. 3 E5
Belvoir Av *BNG/LEV* M19............ 51 D2
Belwood Rd *CCHDY* M21........... 126 A2
Bembridge Cl *RUSH/FAL* M14..... 38 A5
Bemsley Pl *SALQ/ORD* M5.......... 13 D4 🔢
Benbecula Wy *URM* M41............ 101 D4
Benbow Av *WGTN/LGST* M12..... 40 A1
Benbow St *SALE* M33................. 123 D4
Ben Brierley Wy *OLD* OL1.......... 55 D2
Bendall St *OP/CLY* M11.............. 107 C1
Bendemeer *URM* M41.............. 111 C2 🔢
Bendix St *ANC* M4....................... 7 E5
Benedict Cl *BRO* M7................... 81 C4 🔢
   SLFD M6....................................... 4 A1
Benfield Av *NEWH/MOS* M40...... 69 C3 🔢
Benfleet Cl *WGTN/LGST* M12..... 30 C3
Bengal St *ANC* M4........................ 7 F5
Benmore Rd *BKLY* M9................. 67 D2
Bennett Dr *BRO* M7..................... 82 A3
Bennett Rd *CHH* M8.................... 64 B4
Bennett St *STRET* M32............. 114 A4 🔢
   WGTN/LGST M12....................... 29 F3
Benny La *DROY* M43.................... 99 D2
Benson Cl *BRO* M7.................... 82 A4 🔢
Ben St *OP/CLY* M11.................... 11 E5
Bentcliffe Wy *ECC* M30............. 92 B4 🔢
Bentinck St *HULME* M15............ 24 C2
Bent La *CHH* M8.......................... 82 B2
   PWCH M25............................... 63 C1
   URM M41.................................. 100 A4
Bentley Rd *BRO* M7.................... 82 A1
   CCHDY M21.............................. 42 C4
Bentley St *CHAD* OL9................. 53 D2
Benton St *BKLY* M9................... 85 D2 🔢
Bents Av *MPL/ROM* SK6........... 141 D2
Bent St *CHH* M8........................... 6 C1
   CHH M8.................................... 83 C4
Beresford Crs *RDSH* SK5......... 117 C2
Beresford Rd *BRUN/LGST* M13... 40 A5
   STRET M32............................. 115 C1
Beresford St *FAIL* M35............... 88 A2
   RUSH/FAL M14......................... 36 B4
Berigan Cl *WGTN/LGST* M12..... 70 B2
Berkeley Av *CHAD* OL9.............. 53 D4
   RUSH/FAL M14......................... 39 E3
   STRET M32............................. 113 C1
Berkley Av *BNG/LEV* M19.......... 50 C3
Berkshire Cl *CHAD* OL9............. 53 D4
Berkshire Rd *NEWH/MOS* M40.... 9 D3
Bermondsay St *SALQ/ORD* M5... 13 E4 🔢
Bernard St *BKLY* M9.................. 84 B1 🔢
Berne Cl *CHAD* OL9.................... 54 A3 🔢
Bernice Av *CHAD* OL9................ 53 D3
Berrie Gv *BNG/LEV* M19........... 132 B1 🔢
Berry Brow *NEWH/MOS* M40...... 17 F5
Berry St *CMANE* M1.................... 17 F5
   ECC M30................................. 100 B1
   SWIN M27................................. 58 B3
Bertha St *OP/CLY* M11............... 31 F1 🔢

Bertram St *WGTN/LGST* M12 ...... **31** D4 **1**
Berwick Av *URM* M41 ...... **113** C3 **1**
Bessemer St *OP/CLY* M11 ...... **106** A2
Beswick Dr *FAIL* M35 ...... **89** C3
Beswick Rw *ANC* M4 ...... **6** C5
Beswick St *ANC* M4 ...... **18** C1
    DROY M43 ...... **98** B4 **2**
Beta Av *STRET* M32 ...... **114** A4
Bethel Av *FAIL* M35 ...... **88** A2 **1**
Bethesda St *OLDS* OL8 ...... **73** D1
Bethnal Dr *RUSH/FAL* M14 ...... **47** D5
Betley Rd *RDSH* SK5 ...... **117** D4
Betley St *CMANE* M1 ...... **18** A4 **1**
Betnor Av *STKP* SK1 ...... **139** D4
Bettwood Dr *CHH* M8 ...... **64** B3 **1**
Betula Gv *BRO* M7 ...... **81** D2 **1**
Bevan Cl *WGTN/LGST* M12 ...... **19** E3
Bevendon Sq *BRO* M7 ...... **82** A3 **4**
Beveridge St *RUSH/FAL* M14 ...... **37** D5 **1**
Beverley Av *URM* M41 ...... **112** A1
Beverley Rd *SWIN* M27 ...... **78** A2
Beverley Rd *BKLY* M9 ...... **67** C4
Beverly Rd *RUSH/FAL* M14 ...... **130** B2
Beverston Dr *BRO* M7 ...... **82** A3
Bewley St *OLDS* OL8 ...... **72** B2
Bexhill Dr *BRUN/LGST* M13 ...... **39** F5
Bexley Cl *URM* M41 ...... **110** B1
Bexley Sq *CSLFD* M3 ...... **15** D1 **1**
Bexley St *CHAD* OL9 ...... **54** A4 **1**
Beyer Cl *GTN* M18 ...... **106** A4
Bibby La *BNG/LEV* M19 ...... **131** D3 **1**
Bickerdike Av *WGTN/LGST* M12 ...... **41** E5
Bideford Rd *OFTN* SK2 ...... **140** A4
Bidston Av *RUSH/FAL* M14 ...... **47** E2
Bignor St *CHH* M8 ...... **83** C3
Bilbrook St *ANC* M4 ...... **7** E3
Billing Av *WGTN/LGST* M12 ...... **28** A1
Billington Rd *SWIN* M27 ...... **79** C1
Bill Williams Cl *OP/CLY* M11 ...... **106** A1
Billy La *SWIN* M27 ...... **58** B3
Billy Meredith Cl *RUSH/FAL* M14 ...... **36** C4 **2**
Bindloss Av *ECC* M30 ...... **93** C2
Bingham St *SWIN* M27 ...... **76** B1
Bingley Cl *OP/CLY* M11 ...... **20** A4
Binns Pl *CMANE* M1 ...... **17** F2
Birchacre Gv *RUSH/FAL* M14 ...... **130** B2 **1**
Birchall Gn *MPL/ROM* SK6 ...... **137** D4
Birch Av *FAIL* M35 ...... **88** B3
    OLDS OL8 ...... **72** B3
    OLDTF/WHR M16 ...... **32** C2
    SLFD M6 ...... **95** C1
Birch Dr *SWIN* M27 ...... **77** D1
Birchenall St *NEWH/MOS* M40 ...... **85** D1 **2**
Birchenlea St *CHAD* OL9 ...... **71** C2 **1**
The Birches *SALE* M33 ...... **122** A4 **1**
Birchfields Av *BRUN/LGST* M13 ...... **39** E5
Birchfields Rd *BRUN/LGST* M13 ...... **49** F1
Birch Gv *RUSH/FAL* M14 ...... **38** C5
Birch Hall La *BRUN/LGST* M13 ...... **49** F1
Birchington Rd *DID/WITH* M20 ...... **129** C1
Birchin Pl *ANC* M4 ...... **17** D2 **1**
Birch La *BRUN/LGST* M13 ...... **40** A3
Birchleaf Gv *SALQ/ORD* M5 ...... **94** A3 **1**
Birch Polygon *RUSH/FAL* M14 ...... **39** D5
Birch Rd *CHH* M8 ...... **65** D4
    SWIN M27 ...... **75** D4
Birch St *DROY* M43 ...... **108** B1 **1**
    WGTN/LGST M12 ...... **30** C4
Birchvale Cl *HULME* M15 ...... **25** E2
Birchwood *CHAD* OL9 ...... **52** A2
Birdhall Gv *BNG/LEV* M19 ...... **50** C5
Birkdale Gv *ECC* M30 ...... **92** B3 **1**
    RDSH SK5 ...... **134** B4
Birkdale Rd *RDSH* SK5 ...... **134** B4
Birkdale St *CHH* M8 ...... **83** C2
Birtles Av *RDSH* SK5 ...... **117** D2 **3**
Birt St *NEWH/MOS* M40 ...... **8** C3
Birwood Rd *CHH* M8 ...... **65** D3
Biscay Cl *OP/CLY* M11 ...... **20** A2
Bishop Cl *OLDTF/WHR* M16 ...... **35** E3
Bishopgate St *CHAD* OL9 ...... **53** C4 **2**
Bishop Marshall Cl
    NEWH/MOS M40 ...... **84** B4 **3**
Bishop Rd *SLFD* M6 ...... **93** D1
Bishopsgate *CMANW* M2 ...... **16** B4
Bishops Ms *SALE* M33 ...... **122** A3 **1**
Bishops Rd *PWCH* M25 ...... **63** C3
Bishop St *STKP* SK1 ...... **139** C4
Bishopton Cl *BNG/LEV* M19 ...... **116** A4
Bisley Cl *OLDS* OL8 ...... **54** B3 **2**
Bisley St *OLDS* OL8 ...... **54** B3 **2**
Bispham Av *RDSH* SK5 ...... **117** D2 **1**
Bispham St *BRO* M7 ...... **82** A2 **1**
Bittern Dr *DROY* M43 ...... **99** C2
Blackberry La *RDSH* SK5 ...... **135** D2
Black Brock La *HTNM* SK4 ...... **133** D2
Blackburn Pl *SALQ/ORD* M5 ...... **14** A3
Blackburn St *CSLFD* M3 ...... **4** C4
    OLDTF/WHR M16 ...... **34** B1 **1**
    PWCH M25 ...... **63** C1
Blackcroft Cl *SWIN* M27 ...... **76** A1
Blackfield La *BRO* M7 ...... **5** D3
Blackford Rd *BNG/LEV* M19 ...... **132** B2
Blackfriars Rd *BRO* M7 ...... **5** D3
    CSLFD M3 ...... **5** E4
Blackhill Cl *BRUN/LGST* M13 ...... **27** F2
Blackley New Rd *BKLY* M9 ...... **64** B3
Blackley Park Rd *BKLY* M9 ...... **66** B4 **1**
Blackley St *OLDTF/WHR* M16 ...... **24** B5
Blacklock St *CSLFD* M3 ...... **6** B2
Blackpool St *OP/CLY* M11 ...... **96** A3 **3**
Blackrock St *OP/CLY* M11 ...... **20** A3
Blackstock St *BRUN/LGST* M13 ...... **38** B2
Blackwin St *WGTN/LGST* M12 ...... **31** D3
Bladon St *CMANE* M1 ...... **17** E4 **1**
Blairhall Av *NEWH/MOS* M40 ...... **86** A2
Blair Rd *OLDTF/WHR* M16 ...... **45** F4
Blair St *OLDTF/WHR* M16 ...... **34** C1
Blakey St *WGTN/LGST* M12 ...... **40** C3
Blanchard St *HULME* M15 ...... **35** F1 **1**
Bland Cl *FAIL* M35 ...... **88** A2
Blandford Dr *NEWH/MOS* M40 ...... **69** C3
Blandford Rd *ECC* M30 ...... **90** B3
    SLFD M6 ...... **80** B2 **1**
Bland Rd *PWCH* M25 ...... **62** B3
Blanefield Cl *CCHDY* M21 ...... **128** A2
Blantyre Rd *SWIN* M27 ...... **77** D3
Blantyre St *ECC* M30 ...... **90** A2
    HULME M15 ...... **25** D1
    SWIN M27 ...... **75** D1
Blanwood Dr *CHH* M8 ...... **83** D2 **1**
Bledlow Cl *ECC* M30 ...... **92** A2
Blenheim Av *OLDTF/WHR* M16 ...... **44** C2
Blenheim Rd *OLDTF/WHR* M16 ...... **33** D5
Bletchley Cl *BRUN/LGST* M13 ...... **28** C5
Blinco Rd *URM* M41 ...... **112** B4
Blind La *WGTN/LGST* M12 ...... **29** D1
Blisworth Av *ECC* M30 ...... **102** A1 **1**
Blisworth Cl *ANC* M4 ...... **19** D3 **1**
Block La *CHAD* OL9 ...... **53** D4
Blodwell St *SLFD* M6 ...... **12** A1
Bloom St *CMANE* M1 ...... **16** C5
    CSLFD M3 ...... **15** E1
Blossom St *ANC* M4 ...... **17** F1 **1**
    CSLFD M3 ...... **5** F5 **1**
Blucher St *SALQ/ORD* M5 ...... **14** A3
    WGTN/LGST M12 ...... **29** E3

Blue Bell Av *NEWH/MOS* M40 .... 68 A4
Blue Ribbon Wk *SWIN* M27 .... 59 C4
Bluestone Rd *DTN/ASHW* M34 ...... 118 A3
   NEWH/MOS M40 .... 86 A1
Blunn St *OLDS* OL8 .... 73 D1 ▯
Blyborough Cl *SLFD* M6 .... 95 C1
Boad St *CMANE* M1 .... 17 F4
Boardman Rd *CHH* M8 .... 64 B3
Boardman St *ECC* M30 .... 92 A4
Boar Green Cl *NEWH/MOS* M40 ...... 87 C2
Bob Brook Cl *FAIL* M35 .... 87 C3
Bob Massey Cl *OP/CLY* M11 .... 106 A1
Bodley St *OP/CLY* M11 .... 96 A3
Bodmin Crs *RDSH* SK5 .... 135 D4
Bodmin Rd *SALE* M33 .... 48 C5
Boland Dr *RUSH/FAL* M14 .... 35 E1
Bold St *HULME* M15 .... 35 E1
   OLDTF/WHR M16 .... 35 E2
   SWIN M27 .... 58 B3
Bolesworth St *CCHDY* M21 .... 125 D1 ▯
Bolivia St *SALQ/ORD* M5 .... 94 A3 ▯
Bollington Rd *HTNM* SK4 .... 133 D4
   NEWH/MOS M40 .... 8 C5
Bolton Cl *PWCH* M25 .... 61 D3 ▯
Bolton St *SLFD* M6 .... 2 A2
   SWIN M27 .... 59 C4
Bolton St *CSLFD* M3 .... 15 E1
   RDSH SK5 .... 134 A2
Bombay St *CMANE* M1 .... 17 D5 ▯
Bonchurch Wk *WGTN/LGST* M12 .... 106 A3
Bonchurch Wk *WGTN/LGST* M12 .... 106 A3
Bandmark Rd *GTN* M18 .... 82 A3 ▯
Bond Sq *BRO* M7 .... 18 A5
Bond St *WGTN/LGST* M12 .... 18 A5
Bonsall St *HULME* M15 .... 26 A4
Boond St *ANC* M4 .... 18 C2
   CSLFD M3 .... 5 F5
Booth Av *RUSH/FAL* M14 .... 130 B2
Boothby Rd *SWIN* M27 .... 58 A2 ▯
Boothcote *DTN/ASHW* M34 .... 109 D3
Boothfield *ECC* M30 .... 90 A2
Booth Hall Rd *BKLY* M9 .... 68 A2
Booth St *DTN/ASHW* M34 .... 108 A2
   OLDTF/WHR M16 .... 34 A5
   SALE M33 .... 123 D3
Booth St *CHAD* OL9 .... 55 C2
   CMANW M2 .... 16 A1
   CSLFD M3 .... 16 B3
   FAIL M35 .... 88 A2
Booth St East *BRUN/LGST* M13 ...... 27 E3
Booth St West *HULME* M15 .... 26 C4
Bootle St *CSLFD* M3 .... 16 A3
Bordale Av *BKLY* M9 .... 85 D2
Bordan St *OP/CLY* M11 .... 20 B4
Boringdon Cl *NEWH/MOS* M40 ...... 86 B3 ▯
Borland Av *NEWH/MOS* M40 .... 69 D4
Borough Av *SWIN* M27 .... 59 C4
Borough Rd *SALQ/ORD* M5 .... 94 B4
Borron St *STKP* SK1 .... 139 C3
Borsden St *SWIN* M27 .... 57 C3
Borwell St *GTN* M18 .... 106 B3
Boscombe Av *ECC* M30 .... 101 C1
Boscombe St *RDSH* SK5 .... 117 D3
   RUSH/FAL M14 .... 47 E1
Bosley Av *DID/WITH* M20 .... 129 C1
Bossall Av *BKLY* M9 .... 67 C1 ▯
Boston Cl *FAIL* M35 .... 70 B4
Boston Ct *SALQ/ORD* M5 .... 105 C1
Boston St *OLDS* OL8 .... 73 D1
Boswell Av *DTN/ASHW* M34 .... 99 D4
Bosworth St *OP/CLY* M11 .... 20 C5
Botanical Av *OLDTF/WHR* M16 ...... 33 D1
Botany Rd *ECC* M30 .... 90 A1
Botham Cl *HULME* M15 .... 26 B5

Bothwell Rd *NEWH/MOS* M40 .... 8 B3 ▯
Bottesford Av *DID/WITH* M20 ...... 128 B4 ▯
Bottomley Side *BKLY* M9 .... 66 A3
Boundary La *HULME* M15 .... 26 C4
Boundary Rd *SWIN* M27 .... 76 B1
Boundary St *WGTN/LGST* M12 .... 31 D4
Boundary St East *CMANE* M1 .... 27 D2 ▯
Boundary St West *HULME* M15 ...... 26 C3
The Boundary *SWIN* M27 .... 57 D1
Bourdon St *NEWH/MOS* M40 .... 9 D4
Bourget St *CHH* M8 .... 82 B1 ▯
Bourne Av *SWIN* M27 .... 76 B2 ▯
Bourne Dr *NEWH/MOS* M40 .... 68 B4
Bournelea Av *BNG/LEV* M19 .... 131 D3
Bourne St *CHAD* OL9 .... 71 D3
   HTNM SK4 .... 138 A1 ▯
Bournville Av *HTNM* SK4 .... 138 A1 ▯
Bournville Gv *BNG/LEV* M19 .... 51 F5
Bourton Dr *GTN* M18 .... 41 F2
Bowden Rd *SWIN* M27 .... 77 C2 ▯
Bowdon Av *RUSH/FAL* M14 .... 46 B3
Bowers Av *URM* M41 .... 110 B1
Bowers St *RUSH/FAL* M14 .... 131 C2 ▯
Bower St *BRO* M7 .... 82 A2 ▯
   NEWH/MOS M40 .... 85 D4
   RDSH SK5 .... 117 D3
Bower Ter *DROY* M43 .... 99 C2
Bowes St *RUSH/FAL* M14 .... 36 B5
Bowfell Gv *BKLY* M9 .... 65 D2
Bowfell Rd *URM* M41 .... 110 B3
Bowker Bank Av *CHH* M8 .... 64 B3
Bowker St *BRO* M7 .... 81 D3
Bowland Av *GTN* M18 .... 118 A1 ▯
Bowland Rd *DTN/ASHW* M34 ...... 118 B2 ▯
Bow La *CMANW* M2 .... 16 B3
Bowler St *BNG/LEV* M19 .... 117 C2 ▯
Bowling Rd *GTN* M18 .... 71 D3
Bowling St *CHAD* OL9 .... 71 D3
Bowness Av *HTNM* SK4 .... 134 A3
Bowness Dr *SALE* M33 .... 122 B4
Bowness Rd *OP/CLY* M11 .... 107 D2
   STRET M32 .... 114 B2 ▯
Bowring St *BRO* M7 .... 81 C4 ▯
Bowscale Cl *BRUN/LGST* M13 .... 40 C3
Bow St *CMANW* M2 .... 16 A3 ▯
   OLD OL1 .... 55 D1
Boxgrove Rd *SALE* M33 .... 122 A4
Boxtree Av *GTN* M18 .... 116 B2 ▯
Boyd St *WGTN/LGST* M12 .... 30 C2
Boyer St *OLDTF/WHR* M16 .... 25 E5
Boyle St *CHH* M8 .... 83 D3
Brabham Cl *CCHDY* M21 .... 43 E5
Brabham Ms *SWIN* M27 .... 75 C2 ▯
Bracken Cl *DROY* M43 .... 99 C3
   SALE M33 .... 121 C4
Brackenside *RDSH* SK5 .... 135 C1 ▯
Brackley Av *HULME* M15 .... 24 C2
Brackley Rd *ECC* M30 .... 91 D1
   HTNM SK4 .... 133 D1
Bradburn Cl *ECC* M30 .... 91 D2 ▯
Bradburn St *ECC* M30 .... 91 D4
Bradden Cl *SALQ/ORD* M5 .... 12 C3
Braddon Av *URM* M41 .... 111 D3 ▯
Braddon St *OP/CLY* M11 .... 96 A3 ▯
Brade Cl *OP/CLY* M11 .... 106 A1
Bradfield Av *SLFD* M6 .... 94 A3
Bradfield Cl *RDSH* SK5 .... 117 C3
Bradfield Rd *STRET* M32 .... 113 D3
   URM M41 .... 112 B3
Bradford Rd *ECC* M30 .... 92 A1
   NEWH/MOS M40 .... 19 D1
Bradford St *OLD* OL1 .... 55 C1
Bradgreen Rd *ECC* M30 .... 91 C2 ▯

Bradley Av *BRO* M7 .... 80 B2
Bradley La *STRET* M32 .... 123 D2
Bradleys Count *CMANE* M1 ...... 17 E2 🔢
Bradley St *CMANE* M1 .... 17 E1 🔢
Bradney Cl *BKLY* M9 .... 49 F5
Bradshaw Av *DID/WITH* M20 .... 129 D2 🔢
  NEWH/MOS M40 .... 88 A4
Bradshaw Fold Av *NEWH/MOS* M40 .. 69 D2
Bradshaw La *STRET* M32 .... 124 B3
Bradshaw St *ANC* M4 .... 6 C5 🔢
  BRO M7 .... 82 A3
  OLD OL1 .... 55 D2
Bradshaw St North *BRO* M7 ...... 81 D2 🔢
Bradstone Rd *CHH* M8 .... 82 B4
Bradwell Av *DID/WITH* M20 ...... 128 B3
  STRET M32 .... 113 C2
Bradwen Av *CHH* M8 .... 65 C4 🔢
Brady St *STKP* SK1 .... 139 C3 🔢
Braemar Av *STRET* M32 .... 113 C3
  URM M41 .... 110 A4
Braemar Rd *RUSH/FAL* M14 ...... 49 E5
Brae Side OL8 .... 73 C3
Bragenham St *GTN* M18 .... 106 A4 🔢
Brailsford Rd *RUSH/FAL* M14 .... 49 F5
Brakenhurst Dr *BRO* M7 .... 82 B3 🔢
Braley St *CMANE* M1 .... 27 F1 🔢
Bramble Av *SALQ/ORD* M5 .... 24 A1
Brambling Cl *DTN/ASHW* M34 ... 99 C3
Bramhall St *GTN* M18 .... 107 C4 🔢
Bramley Av *BNG/LEV* M19 .... 50 C5 🔢
  STRET M32 .... 113 D3
Bramley Cl *SWIN* M27 .... 75 C3
Bramley Meade *BRO* M7 .... 82 A2
Bramley St *BRO* M7 .... 5 E1 🔢
Bramwell Dr *BRUN/LGST* M13 .... 28 A3
Brancaster Rd *CMANE* M1 .... 27 D1
Brandish Cl *BRUN/LGST* M13 ..... 39 D1
Brandon Av *DTN/ASHW* M34 .... 117 D2 🔢
  ECC M30 .... 93 C1
Brandon Rd *SLFD* M6 .... 77 D4
Brandram Rd *PWCH* M25 .... 63 C1 🔢
Brandsby Gdns *SALQ/ORD* M5 ... 13 D5 🔢
Branksome Av *PWCH* M25 .... 62 A1
Branksome Dr *SLFD* M6 .... 77 C4
Bransby Av *BKLY* M9 .... 67 C1
Branscombe Dr *SALE* M33 .... 121 C4
Bransford Rd *OP/CLY* M11 ...... 106 B1
  URM M41 .... 111 C2 🔢
Branson St *NEWH/MOS* M40 ..... 19 D1
Branston Rd *NEWH/MOS* M40 .... 69 D3
Brantingham Rd *CCHDY* M21 .... 43 F3
Brantwood Rd *BRO* M7 .... 81 D1
Brantwood Ter *BKLY* M9 .... 85 D2 🔢
Brassington Av *CCHDY* M21 ..... 126 B2 🔢
  SALQ/ORD M5 .... 13 E4
Braunston Cl *ECC* M30 .... 102 A1 🔢
Bray Av *ECC* M30 .... 90 B2
Brayton Av *SALE* M33 .... 121 D4
Brazennose St *CSLFD* M3 .... 16 A3
Brazil St *CMANE* M1 .... 17 D5
Bread St *GTN* M18 .... 107 C3
Breck Rd *ECC* M30 .... 90 B3
Brecon Av *BNG/LEV* M19 .... 131 D2 🔢
Brecon Wk *OLDS* OL8 .... 71 D3 🔢
Bredbury Park Wy *MPL/ROM* SK6 .. 137 C4
Bredbury Rd *RUSH/FAL* M14 ..... 47 E2
Bredbury St *CHAD* OL9 .... 53 D4
Breeze Mt *PWCH* M25 .... 62 B3
Brendon Av *NEWH/MOS* M40 .... 86 A2
  RDSH SK5 .... 134 B3 🔢
Brendon Dr *DTN/ASHW* M34 .... 99 C3
Brennan Cl *HULME* M15 .... 26 C5
Brennan Ct *OLDS* OL8 .... 72 A3 🔢

Brennock Cl *OP/CLY* M11 .... 20 B5
Brentbridge Rd *RUSH/FAL* M14 .. 129 D1
Brentfield Av *CHH* M8 .... 82 B3
Brentford Rd *RDSH* SK5 .... 134 B3
Brentford St *BKLY* M9 .... 85 C2
Brentnor Rd *NEWH/MOS* M40 ... 69 C3
Brentwood *SLFD* M6 .... 95 C2
Brentwood Av *URM* M41 .... 111 D3 🔢
  WALK M28 .... 74 B3 🔢
Brentwood Cl *OLDTF/WHR* M16 .. 36 A4
  RDSH SK5 .... 136 B4 🔢
Brentwood Ct *PWCH* M25 .... 61 D2
Brentwood Dr *ECC* M30 .... 91 D1 🔢
Brentwood Rd *SWIN* M27 .... 75 D3
Breslyn St *CSLFD* M3 .... 6 B4
Brethren's Ct *DROY* M43 .... 108 A1 🔢
Brettargh St *SLFD* M6 .... 3 D2
Brewer St *CMANE* M1 .... 17 E2
Brewery Rd *BKLY* M9 .... 84 B1 🔢
Brewster St *BKLY* M9 .... 84 B1 🔢
Brian Av *DROY* M43 .... 99 C2 🔢
Brian Redhead Ct *HULME* M15 ... 25 E2 🔢
Briar Cl *URM* M41 .... 110 A2
Briarfield Rd *BNG/LEV* M19 ..... 131 C3 🔢
  DID/WITH M20 .... 130 B3
  HTNM SK4 .... 134 A3
Briarlea Gdns *BNG/LEV* M19 .... 131 C4 🔢
Briarmere Wk *CHAD* OL9 .... 54 A2 🔢
Briarwood Av *DROY* M43 .... 97 C2
Brickley St *ANC* M4 .... 6 C3
Brick St *ANC* M4 .... 17 D1 🔢
Bridcam St *CHH* M8 .... 83 C4
Briddon St *CSLFD* M3 .... 6 A3
Brideoak St *CHH* M8 .... 83 C3
Bridgefield St *STKP* SK1 .... 138 A3 🔢
Bridgelea Ms *DID/WITH* M20 ... 129 D3 🔢
Bridgelea Rd *DID/WITH* M20 .... 129 D3
Bridgend Cl *WGTN/LGST* M12 .... 30 C1 🔢
Bridgenorth Av *URM* M41 .... 112 B3
Bridge St *CSLFD* M3 .... 15 F2 🔢
  CSLFD M3 .... 15 F5
  DROY M43 .... 107 C1
  STKP SK1 .... 138 B3 🔢
  SWIN M27 .... 77 C1
Bridgewater Pl *ANC* M4 .... 16 C2
Bridgewater Rd *SWIN* M27 ...... 77 D2 🔢
Bridgewater St *CSLFD* M3 .... 5 F3
  CSLFD M3 .... 15 E5 🔢
  ECC M30 .... 90 B3
  SALE M33 .... 123 D4 🔢
  STRET M32 .... 115 C3 🔢
Bridgewater Viad *HULME* M15 ... 25 F1
Bridgewater Wy *HULME* M15 .... 24 B3
  OLDTF/WHR M16 .... 23 E5
Bridgnorth Rd *BKLY* M9 .... 65 C2
Bridle Cl *DROY* M43 .... 99 C3
Bridlington Av *SLFD* M6 .... 94 A2 🔢
Bridlington Cl *NEWH/MOS* M40 .. 87 C3 🔢
Bridport Av *NEWH/MOS* M40 .... 87 D1
Bridson St *SALQ/ORD* M5 .... 95 C4
Briercliffe Cl *GTN* M18 .... 106 A3
Brierley Av *FAIL* M35 .... 88 B2
Brierley Rd West *SWIN* M27 ..... 58 A4 🔢
Brierley St *CHAD* OL9 .... 54 A1
  OLDS OL8 .... 73 D2
Brigadier Cl *DID/WITH* M20 ..... 129 D3
Brigantine Cl *SALQ/ORD* M5 ..... 13 D5 🔢
Briggs Rd *STRET* M32 .... 32 A3
Briggs St *CSLFD* M3 .... 5 D4
Brigham St *OP/CLY* M11 .... 106 A1
Brightman St *GTN* M18 .... 106 B3
Brighton Av *BNG/LEV* M19 ...... 131 D2
  BRO M7 .... 82 A3 🔢

RDSH SK5 .... 117 D3
Brighton Gv *RUSH/FAL* M14 .... 48 C1
   SALE M33 .... 123 C4 🔢
Brighton Pl *BRUN/LGST* M13 .... 27 E4 🔢
Brighton Range *GTN* M18 .... 117 D1 🔢
Brighton St *ANC* M4 .... 7 D5 🔢
Bright Rd *ECC* M30 .... 92 A3
Bright St *CHAD* OL9 .... 71 C2
   DROY M43 .... 98 B4 🔢
   OLDS OL8 .... 54 B4 🔢
Brigstock Av *GTN* M18 .... 106 B4 🔢
Brimelow St *MPL/ROM* SK6 .... 140 A2 🔢
Brindale Rd *RDSH* SK5 .... 140 A1
Brindle Cl *SLFD* M6 .... 2 B2
Brindle Heath Rd *SLFD* M6 .... 2 B1
Brindle Pl *HULME* M15 .... 26 C4 🔢
Brindley Av *SALE* M33 .... 124 A1 🔢
Brindley Rd *OLDTF/WHR* M16 ...... 23 E5 🔢
Brindley St *ECC* M30 .... 90 B2 🔢
   SWIN M27 .... 58 B3 🔢
Brinklow Cl *OP/CLY* M11 .... 107 C2
Brinnington Crs *RDSH* SK5 .... 139 D1
Brinnington Rd *RDSH* SK5 .... 140 A1
   STKP SK1 .... 139 C2
Brinsop Sq *GTN* M18 .... 31 E3
Brinsworth Dr *CHH* M8 .... 85 C3 🔢
Brisbane St *HULME* M15 .... 37 E1
Briscoe La *NEWH/MOS* M40 .... 10 B3
Briscoe St *OLD* OL1 .... 55 D1 🔢
Bristol Av *BNG/LEV* M19 .... 51 E5
Bristol St *BRO* M7 .... 82 A2
Bristowe St *OP/CLY* M11 .... 96 B2
Britannia Rd *SALE* M33 .... 123 D4
Britannia St *SLFD* M6 .... 80 A3
Britnall Av *WGTN/LGST* M12 .... 39 F1
Brixham Dr *SALE* M33 .... 121 D3
Brixham Rd *OLDTF/WHR* M16 .... 33 E3
Brixton Av *DID/WITH* M20 .... 129 C3 🔢
Brierley Rd East *SWIN* M27 .... 58 A4 🔢
Broadbent St *SWIN* M27 .... 75 D2
Broadfield Gv *RDSH* SK5 .... 117 C3
Broadfield Rd *GTN* M18 .... 117 C2
   RUSH/FAL M14 .... 46 C1
Broadhill Rd *BNG/LEV* M19 .... 131 C3
Broadhurst Av *SWIN* M27 .... 58 B2
Broadlands Rd *SWIN* M27 .... 75 C3
Broad Lea *URM* M41 .... 111 C2 🔢
Broadlea Rd *BNG/LEV* M19 .... 131 C4 🔢
Broadmeadow Av *OLDTF/WHR* M16.. 46 A3
Broadmoss Dr *BKLY* M9 .... 68 A2 🔢
Broadmoss Rd *BKLY* M9 .... 68 A2 🔢
Broad Oak Pk *ECC* M30 .... 91 D1
   WALK M28 .... 74 B3
Broadoaks Rd *URM* M41 .... 110 B4
Broad Rd *SALE* M33 .... 124 A4
Broadstone Cl *PWCH* M25 .... 62 A2
Broadstone Hall Rd North
   HTNM SK4 .... 133 D3
Broadstone Hall Rd South
   HTNM SK4 .... 134 A3
Broadstone Rd *HTNM* SK4 .... 133 D2
Broad St *SLFD* M6 .... 79 C4
   SWIN M27 .... 78 B3
Broadway *CHAD* OL9 .... 52 B4
   DROY M43 .... 108 A1
   FAIL M35 .... 87 D1
   SALE M33 .... 123 C4
   SALQ/ORD M5 .... 12 C5
   URM M41 .... 110 A1
Broadway Cl *URM* M41 .... 101 C4 🔢
Broadway North *DROY* M43.......... 108 A1
Broadway St *OLDS* OL8 .... 75 D1
The Broadway *MPL/ROM* SK6 ...... 141 C1

Broadwell Dr *BKLY* M9 .... 85 C2
Brocade Cl *CSLFD* M3 .... 4 C4
Brock Cl *OP/CLY* M11 .... 106 B2
Brocklehurst St *BKLY* M9 .... 86 A2 🔢
Brockley Av *RUSH/FAL* M14 .... 47 E2
Brock St *CMANE* M1 .... 17 F2 🔢
Brodick St *NEWH/MOS* M40 .... 85 D1
Brodie Cl *ECC* M30 .... 90 B3 🔢
Brogan St *GTN* M18 .... 106 B4 🔢
Bromborough Av
   DID/WITH M20 .... 129 C1 🔢
Bromfield Av *BKLY* M9 .... 66 B4
Broming St *OP/CLY* M11 .... 20 A1
Bromley St *ANC* M4 .... 7 E3
   CHAD OL9 .... 71 C3
Bromlow St *OP/CLY* M11................... 96 A4
Brompton Av *FAIL* M35 .... 89 D1 🔢
Brompton Rd *RUSH/FAL* M14 .... 47 E2
   STRET M32 .... 112 B2
Bromsgrove Av *ECC* M30 .... 90 B3 🔢
Bromshill Dr *BRO* M7 .... 82 A3
Brondgate Meadow *SWIN* M27 .... 76 B3 🔢
Bronte St *HULME* M15 .... 26 C5
Brook Av *BNG/LEV* M19 .... 51 E2
   DROY M43 .... 97 C4 🔢
   HTNM SK4 .... 133 D4
   SWIN M27 .... 76 B2 🔢
Brookburn Rd *CCHDY* M21 .... 126 A2
Brookdale Av *NEWH/MOS* M40 ...... 96 B1
Brookdale Cl *MPL/ROM* SK6 .... 141 D2 🔢
Brookdale St *FAIL* M35 .... 87 D2
Brookdene Rd *BNG/LEV* M19 .... 131 C3
Brookfield *PWCH* M25 .... 62 B1
Brookfield Av *CCHDY* M21 .... 127 C2
   SLFD M6 .... 94 A2
   URM M41 .... 110 A3 🔢
Brookfield Dr *SWIN* M27 .... 58 A4
Brookfield Rd *CHH* M8 .... 65 C4 🔢
   ECC M30 .... 90 B1 🔢
Brookfield St *OLDS* OL8 .... 55 D4
Brookfold *FAIL* M35 .... 88 A1
Brookfold Rd *HTNM* SK4 .... 133 D3
Brook Green La *GTN* M18 .... 117 D2 🔢
Brookhead Av *DID/WITH* M20 ...... 128 B2 🔢
Brookhill St *NEWH/MOS* M40 .... 9 F3
Brookhouse Av *ECC* M30 .... 90 A4
Brookhurst Rd *GTN* M18 .... 116 B1
Brookland Av *DTN/ASHW* M34 .... 119 D3 🔢
Brooklands Av *CHAD* OL9 .... 53 D4 🔢
   DID/WITH M20 .... 129 C3 🔢
Brooklands Cl *HTNM* SK4 .... 133 D4 🔢
Brooklands Dr *DROY* M43 .... 99 C2
Brooklands Rd *PWCH* M25 .... 64 A3 🔢
   RDSH SK5 .... 117 C3
   SWIN M27 .... 75 D3 🔢
Brookleigh Rd *DID/WITH* M20 ...... 130 B3
Brooklyn Av *OLDTF/WHR* M16 ...... 43 F2
Brook Rd *HTNM* SK4........................ 133 C4
   RUSH/FAL M14................................ 130 A2
   URM M41 .... 110 A2
Brooks Dr *FAIL* M35 .... 88 A3
Brookshaw St *OP/CLY* M11 .... 20 C2 🔢
Brookside Av *DROY* M43 .... 99 C2 🔢
Brookside Dr *PWCH* M25 .... 63 D4
Brookside Rd *NEWH/MOS* M40 ...... 68 A4
Brook's Rd *OLDTF/WHR* M16 .... 34 A5
Brookstone Cl *CCHDY* M21 .... 127 D3 🔢
Brook St *CHAD* OL9............................ 53 D1
   CMANE M1 .... 27 D1
   FAIL M35 .... 87 D3 🔢
   SALE M33 .... 124 A4 🔢
   SLFD M6 .... 3 E1
   SWIN M27 .... 75 D1

Brook Ter *BRUN/LGST* M13 ...... **40** B4
Brookthorpe Av *BNG/LEV* M19 ...... **131** C3
Brookwood Av *CHH* M8 ...... **84** A1 ▯
Broom Av *BNG/LEV* M19 ...... **51** F5
  BRO M7 ...... **82** A1
  RDSH SK5 ...... **134** B3 ▯
Broome Gv *FAIL* M35 ...... **88** B3
Broome St *CHAD* OL9 ...... **54** B3
Broomfield *SWIN* M27 ...... **78** B3
Broomfield Cl *RDSH* SK5 ...... **134** B3 ▯
Broomfield Dr *CHH* M8 ...... **82** B2 ▯
  RDSH SK5 ...... **134** B3
Broomhall Rd *SWIN* M27 ...... **78** B3
Broomhurst Av *OLDS* OL8 ...... **72** B1
Broom La *BNG/LEV* M19 ...... **51** F5
  BRO M7 ...... **81** D1
Broom St *SWIN* M27 ...... **76** B2
Broseley Rd *OLDTF/WHR* M16 ...... **43** D1
Brotherton Cl *HULME* M15 ...... **24** C2
Brotherton Dr *CSLFD* M3 ...... **5** D5
Broughton La *BRO* M7 ...... **2** C2
Broughton Rd *RDSH* SK5 ...... **138** B3 ▯
  SLFD M6 ...... **2** C2
Broughton Rd East *SLFD* M6 ...... **3** E2
Broughton St *CHH* M8 ...... **7** D1
Browfield Av *SALQ/ORD* M5 ...... **23** F1
Brownacre St *DID/WITH* M20 ...... **129** D3 ▯
Browncross St *CSLFD* M3 ...... **15** E2
Brownhill St *OP/CLY* M11 ...... **20** C4 ▯
Browning Av *DROY* M43 ...... **98** A4 ▯
Browning Rd *RDSH* SK5 ...... **116** B4
  SWIN M27 ...... **76** A1
Browning St *CSLFD* M3 ...... **15** D1
  HULME M15 ...... **24** C4
Brown St *CHAD* OL9 ...... **53** C2
  CMANW M2 ...... **16** C2
  CSLFD M3 ...... **15** F1
  FAIL M35 ...... **88** A2
  SLFD M6 ...... **12** A2
  STKP SK1 ...... **138** A4 ▯
Brownsville Rd *HTNM* SK4 ...... **132** B4
Brownwood Av *STKP* SK1 ...... **139** D4
Broxton St *NEWH/MOS* M40 ...... **10** A4 ▯
Broxwood Cl *GTN* M18 ...... **106** B3 ▯
Bryan Rd *CCHDY* M21 ...... **42** F2
Bryant Cl *BRUN/LGST* M13 ...... **28** B5
Brydon Av *WGTN/LGST* M12 ...... **28** B1
Brydon Cl *SLFD* M6 ...... **2** B5
Brynden Av *DID/WITH* M20 ...... **130** A4
Bryn Dr *RDSH* SK5 ...... **134** B4
Brynorange Rd *CHH* M8 ...... **65** C3
Brynton Rd *BRUN/LGST* M13 ...... **39** F3
Buchanan St *SWIN* M27 ...... **58** B4 ▯
Buchan St *OP/CLY* M11 ...... **21** E1
Buckden Rd *HTNM* SK4 ...... **133** D2
Buckfast Cl *CCHDY* M21 ...... **43** F3
Buckfast Rd *SALE* M33 ...... **121** D3
Buckfield Av *SALQ/ORD* M5 ...... **23** F1
Buckhurst Rd *BNG/LEV* M19 ...... **50** C3
Buckingham Av *SLFD* M6 ...... **94** B3 ▯
Buckingham Rd *CCHDY* M21 ...... **42** F2
  DROY M43 ...... **97** C4
  HTNM SK4 ...... **132** B4

Buckingham St *SALQ/ORD* M5 ...... **12** B2
Buckland Av *BKLY* M9 ...... **65** C2
Buckland Rd *SLFD* M6 ...... **94** B1
Buck La *SALE* M33 ...... **122** A3
Buckley Av *GTN* M18 ...... **116** A1
Buckley La *PWCH* M25 ...... **61** C2
Buckley Rd *GTN* M18 ...... **41** F3
Buckley St *BRO* M7 ...... **5** D1
  CHAD OL9 ...... **53** C2
  DROY M43 ...... **108** A1
  DTN/ASHW M34 ...... **109** D2
  OP/CLY M11 ...... **107** C2
  RDSH SK5 ...... **117** C3
Bucklow Av *RUSH/FAL* M14 ...... **47** E2
Buckthorn Cl *CCHDY* M21 ...... **127** D3 ▯
Buddleia Gv *BRO* M7 ...... **81** D3 ▯
Bude Av *RDSH* SK5 ...... **135** D4
  URM M41 ...... **120** B1
Budsworth Av *DID/WITH* M20 ...... **129** D2 ▯
Bugle St *HULME* M15 ...... **15** F5 ▯
Buile Hill Dr *SALQ/ORD* M5 ...... **94** B2
Buile St *BRO* M7 ...... **82** A2
Buller Rd *BRUN/LGST* M13 ...... **50** A1
Buller St *DROY* M43 ...... **108** A1
Bulteel St *ECC* M30 ...... **90** B2
Bunkers HI *PWCH* M25 ...... **61** C2
Bunsen St *CMANE* M1 ...... **17** E2 ▯
Bunyard St *CHH* M8 ...... **83** D3
Burbridge Cl *OP/CLY* M11 ...... **19** F3
Burdale Dr *SLFD* M6 ...... **93** D1 ▯
Burder St *OLDS* OL8 ...... **72** A3 ▯
Burdith Av *RUSH/FAL* M14 ...... **46** C1
Burford Av *OLDTF/WHR* M16 ...... **44** C1
  URM M41 ...... **112** A1
Burford Dr *OLDTF/WHR* M16 ...... **44** C1
  SWIN M27 ...... **58** A3
Burford Rd *OLDTF/WHR* M16 ...... **44** C2
Burgess Dr *FAIL* M35 ...... **88** B2
Burland St *BRO* M7 ...... **81** D4 ▯
Burleigh Ms *CCHDY* M21 ...... **126** B3 ▯
Burleigh Rd *STRET* M32 ...... **115** C1
Burleigh St *HULME* M15 ...... **37** E1
Burlington Av *OLDS* OL8 ...... **73** C1
Burlington Rd *DID/WITH* M20 ...... **130** A2
  ECC M30 ...... **92** A1
Burlington St *HULME* M15 ...... **27** D5
Burman St *OP/CLY* M11 ...... **107** C3
Burnaby St *OLDS* OL8 ...... **54** B4 ▯
Burnage Av *BNG/LEV* M19 ...... **131** D1
Burnage Hall Rd *BNG/LEV* M19 ...... **131** C2
Burnage La *BNG/LEV* M19 ...... **131** D4
Burnage Range *BNG/LEV* M19 ...... **50** C3
Burnbray Av *BNG/LEV* M19 ...... **131** C3
Burnell Cl *NEWH/MOS* M40 ...... **8** B4
Burnett Av *SALQ/ORD* M5 ...... **13** E4
Burnett Cl *NEWH/MOS* M40 ...... **84** B4 ▯
Burnfield Rd *GTN* M18 ...... **116** B2 ▯
  RDSH SK5 ...... **117** D2 ▯
Burnham Av *RDSH* SK5 ...... **117** D4 ▯
Burnham Dr *BNG/LEV* M19 ...... **131** D2
  URM M41 ...... **111** C2 ▯
Burnham Rd *DTN/ASHW* M34 ...... **118** A2 ▯
Burnley Rd *CHAD* OL9 ...... **53** D2
  FAIL M35 ...... **89** C1 ▯
Burns Av *SWIN* M27 ...... **57** D4
Burns Cl *OP/CLY* M11 ...... **20** A3
Burns Gdns *PWCH* M25 ...... **61** D2 ▯
Burns Gv *DROY* M43 ...... **98** A3
Burnside Av *HTNM* SK4 ...... **134** A3
  SLFD M6 ...... **77** D4

Burnside Cl *MPL/ROM* SK6 .... 141 D2 🔟
Burnside Dr *BNG/LEV* M19 .... 131 C2
Burnthorpe Av *BKLY* M9 .... 65 D2 🔟
Burrows Av *CCHDY* M21 .... 126 B3
Burslem Cl *DID/WITH* M20 .... 129 C1
Burstead St *GTN* M18 .... 7 E3 🔟
Burstock St *ANC* M4 .... 107 C3
Burston St *GTN* M18 .... 106 A3 🔟
Burton Gv *WALK* M28 .... 75 C1
Burton St *HTNM* SK4 .... 138 A2 🔟
   NEWH/MOS M40 .... 7 F2
Burton Wk *CSLFD* M3 .... 5 D5 🔟
Burtree St *WGTN/LGST* M12 .... 31 D3 🔟
Bury Av *OLDTF/WHR* M16 .... 44 A1
Bury New Rd *BRO* M7 .... 81 D2
Bury Pl *OP/CLY* M11 .... 96 A3 🔟
Bury St *CSLFD* M3 .... 5 F5
   RDSH SK5 .... 138 B2
Bush St *NEWH/MOS* M40 .... 85 C4
Busk Rd *CHAD* OL9 .... 54 A1
Bute Av *OLDS* OL8 .... 73 D2
Bute St *NEWH/MOS* M40 .... 67 D4
   SALQ/ORD M5 .... 94 B4
Butler Gn *CHAD* OL9 .... 71 C1
Butler La *NEWH/MOS* M40 .... 8 B4 🔟
Butler St *ANC* M4 .... 8 B5
Butman St *GTN* M18 .... 107 D3
Butter La *CSLFD* M3 .... 16 A2 🔟
Buttermere Av *SWIN* M27 .... 76 B3 🔟
Buttermere Cl *STRET* M32 .... 114 A2 🔟
Butterstile La *PWCH* M25 .... 61 D3
Butterwick Cl *WGTN/LGST* M12 .... 41 E4
Butterworth La *CHAD* OL9 .... 70 A2
Butterworth St *CHAD* OL9 .... 53 D1 🔟
   OP/CLY M11 .... 20 C4
Butt Hill Av *PWCH* M25 .... 62 B2 🔟
Butt Hill Dr *PWCH* M25 .... 62 B2
Butt Hill Rd *PWCH* M25 .... 62 B2
Buttress St *GTN* M18 .... 106 A3
Buxton Av *DID/WITH* M20 .... 128 B3 🔟
Buxton La *DROY* M43 .... 107 C1
Buxton Rd *STRET* M32 .... 113 C2
Buxton St *CMANE* M1 .... 17 F5
Byrcland St *WGTN/LGST* M12 .... 19 E5
Byrom Av *BNG/LEV* M19 .... 116 A4
Byrom St *CSLFD* M3 .... 15 F3
   OLDTF/WHR M16 .... 34 C2
   SALQ/ORD M5 .... 12 C4
Byron Av *DROY* M43 .... 98 A3
   PWCH M25 .... 61 D2
   SWIN M27 .... 76 A1
Byron Gv *RDSH* SK5 .... 117 C4
Byron Rd *DTN/ASHW* M34 .... 137 D1 🔟
   STRET M32 .... 115 C2
Byron St *ECC* M30 .... 91 D3
   OLDS OL8 .... 71 D3

C

Cable St *ANC* M4 .... 7 D5
   CSLFD M3 .... 5 F5
Cabot Pl *RDSH* SK5 .... 138 B1
Cabot St *BRUN/LGST* M13 .... 27 F3
Cadogan St *RUSH/FAL* M14 .... 36 C3
Caen Av *NEWH/MOS* M40 .... 81 C4
Cairn Dr *SLFD* M6 .... 66 C2
Cairnwell Rd *CHAD* OL9 .... 52 B1
Caistor Cl *OLDTF/WHR* M16 .... 128 A1
Caistor St *STKP* SK1 .... 139 D2
Cakebread St *WGTN/LGST* M12 .... 28 A1
Calbourne Crs *WGTN/LGST* M12 .... 41 E4

Caldbeck Av *SALE* M33 .... 125 C4
Calder Cl *RDSH* SK5 .... 139 C1 🔟
Calder Dr *SWIN* M27 .... 58 A4
Calder St *SALQ/ORD* M5 .... 14 C5
Caldon Cl *ECC* M30 .... 101 D1 🔟
Caldy Rd *SLFD* M6 .... 94 B1
Caledon Av *NEWH/MOS* M40 .... 86 A1
Caledonian Dr *ECC* M30 .... 102 A1
Caledonia Wy *STRET* M32 .... 103 C3
Caley St *CMANE* M1 .... 26 C1 🔟
Calgary St *GTN* M18 .... 106 A4
Calico Cl *CSLFD* M3 .... 4 C4
Callingdon Rd *CCHDY* M21 .... 127 D4
Calthorpe Av *BKLY* M9 .... 84 A2
Calton Av *BRO* M7 .... 80 A2
Calver Av *ECC* M30 .... 101 C1 🔟
Calverley Av *BNG/LEV* M19 .... 131 D2
Calverton Dr *NEWH/MOS* M40 .... 87 C2
Calvert Rd *ECC* M30 .... 90 B3
Cambell Rd *SALQ/ORD* M5 .... 94 A4
Cambert La *GTN* M18 .... 106 B4
Camberwell St *CSLFD* M3 .... 6 C2
   OLDS OL8 .... 73 C1 🔟
Camborne St *RUSH/FAL* M14 .... 47 F1 🔟
Cambrai Crs *ECC* M30 .... 90 A1
Cambrian St *NEWH/MOS* M40 .... 9 E5
Cambridge Av *OLDTF/WHR* M16 .... 44 B2 🔟
Cambridge Dr *DTN/ASHW* M34 .... 118 A2
Cambridge Gv *ECC* M30 .... 92 B3 🔟
Cambridge Rd *BKLY* M9 .... 66 B4 🔟
   DROY M43 .... 97 D2
   FAIL M35 .... 88 A4
   HTNM SK4 .... 133 C4 🔟
   URM M41 .... 110 B4
Cambridge St *BRO* M7 .... 5 E2
   CHAD OL9 .... 72 A1
   HULME M15 .... 26 B1
Camden Av *NEWH/MOS* M40 .... 96 A1 🔟
Camelia Rd *BKLY* M9 .... 84 A2
Cameron St *CMANE* M1 .... 16 A5 🔟
Campbell Rd *BRUN/LGST* M13 .... 50 A1
   SWIN M27 .... 76 A3
Campbell St *RDSH* SK5 .... 117 D4 🔟
Camp St *CSLFD* M3 .... 15 F4
Canada St *NEWH/MOS* M40 .... 9 F1
Canal Bank *ECC* M30 .... 91 C2
Canal Bridge La *OP/CLY* M11 .... 97 C4
Canal Side *ECC* M30 .... 91 C2 🔟
Canal St *CHAD* OL9 .... 71 D2
   CMANE M1 .... 17 D4
   DROY M43 .... 98 A4
   SALQ/ORD M5 .... 14 B2
Canberra St *OP/CLY* M11 .... 96 A3 🔟
Candleford Rd *DID/WITH* M20 .... 129 D3 🔟
Canning St *HTNM* SK4 .... 138 A3 🔟
Cannon Ct *CSLFD* M3 .... 16 B1
Cannon St *ANC* M4 .... 16 B1
   CHAD OL9 .... 55 C3 🔟
   CSLFD M3 .... 4 C5
   ECC M30 .... 92 A4
Canon Green Dr *CSLFD* M3 .... 5 E4
Canons Gv *NEWH/MOS* M40 .... 85 C4
Canonsleigh Cl *CHH* M8 .... 82 A4 🔟
Canonsway *SWIN* M27 .... 76 A2
Canterbury Dr *PWCH* M25 .... 63 C3 🔟
Canterbury Gdns *SALQ/ORD* M5 .... 93 D3 🔟
Canterbury Rd *STKP* SK1 .... 139 D4
   URM M41 .... 110 B2
Canterfield Cl *DROY* M43 .... 99 D3 🔟
Cantrell St *OP/CLY* M11 .... 21 F2
Canute Rd *STRET* M32 .... 115 C2
Canute St *SLFD* M6 .... 3 E5
Cape St *DID/WITH* M20 .... 130 A2

Capital Rd *OP/CLY* M11 .... 107 D2
Capricorn Wy *SLFD* M6 .... 4 A1 🔢
Capstan St *BKLY* M9 .... 85 C1
Carberry Rd *GTN* M18 .... 107 C4
Carden Av *SWIN* M27 .... 75 D2 🔢
Carder Cl *SWIN* M27 .... 76 B2 🔢
Cardiff Cl *OLDS* OL8 .... 71 D4
Cardiff St *BRO* M7 .... 82 A2
Cardigan Rd *OLDS* OL8 .... 71 D3
Cardigan St *SLFD* M6 .... 95 C4 🔢
Cardigan Ter *RUSH/FAL* M14 ..... 36 B3 🔢
Cardinal St *CHH* M8 .... 83 D3
  OLD OL1 .... 55 D2
Carding Gv *CSLFD* M3 .... 5 E4
Cardroom Rd *ANC* M4 .... 18 A2
Cardus St *BNG/LEV* M19 .... 51 D4
Cardwell Rd *ECC* M30 .... 90 A4 🔢
Cardwell St *OLDS* OL8 .... 73 D2
Carey Cl *BRO* M7 .... 5 D2
Carfax St *GTN* M18 .... 106 B4
Carib St *HULME* M15 .... 26 A5
Carill Av *NEWH/MOS* M40 .... 68 A4
Carill Dr *RUSH/FAL* M14 .... 48 C5
Carina Pl *BRO* M7 .... 4 B2
Carisbrook Av *URM* M41 .... 111 C4 🔢
Carisbrook Dr *SWIN* M27 .... 77 C3
Carisbrook St *BKLY* M9 .... 84 B2
Carlburn St *OP/CLY* M11 .... 96 B3
Carley Gv *BKLY* M9 .... 65 D1
Carlford Gv *PWCH* M25 .... 61 D2
Carlisle St *CHAD* OL9 .... 54 A4
  SWIN M27 .... 58 B3
Carlton Av *PWCH* M25 .... 64 A3 🔢
  RUSH/FAL M14 .... 37 E5
Carlton Crs *STKP* SK1 .... 139 C3 🔢
Carlton Dr *PWCH* M25 .... 64 A3
Carlton Range *GTN* M18 .... 117 D1 🔢
Carlton Rd *OLDTF/WHR* M16 ...... 34 C5
  SALE M33 .... 123 C3
  SLFD M6 .... 95 C1
  URM M41 .... 111 C4
Carlton St *ECC* M30 .... 91 D2
  OLDTF/WHR M16 .... 34 B3
Carlyle Cl *CHH* M8 .... 83 C3
Carlyn Av *SALE* M33 .... 124 B4
Carmel Av *SALQ/ORD* M5 .... 24 A1
Carmel Cl *SALQ/ORD* M5 .... 14 A5
Carmona Dr *PWCH* M25 .... 62 A1
Carmoor Rd *BRUN/LGST* M13 ..... 38 B1
Carnaby St *BKLY* M9 .... 67 C4 🔢
Carna Rd *RDSH* SK5 .... 117 C3
Carnarvon St *BRO* M7 .... 82 A2 🔢
  CSLFD M3 .... 6 B3
  OLDS OL8 .... 71 D3
Carnegie Av *BNG/LEV* M19 .... 51 F3
Carnforth Av *CHAD* OL9 .... 53 C3
Carnforth Rd *HTNM* SK4 .... 133 D3
Carnforth St *RUSH/FAL* M14 ..... 37 E5
Carnoustie St *NEWH/MOS* M40 ... 87 C2
Carnwood Cl *NEWH/MOS* M40 ..... 96 A5
Caroline Dr *ANC* M4 .... 18 A2
Caroline St *BRO* M7 .... 5 D1
Carpenters La *ANC* M4 .... 17 D1
Carpenters Wk *DROY* M43 .... 107 D2
Carradale Dr *SALE* M33 .... 121 C4
Carr Av *PWCH* M25 .... 61 D3
Carr Bank Av *CHH* M8 .... 64 B2 🔢
Carrgreen Cl *BNG/LEV* M19 ...... 131 D4 🔢
Carriage St *OLDTF/WHR* M16 .... 25 D5
Carrigart *PWCH* M25 .... 62 A1
Carrill Gv *BNG/LEV* M19 .... 51 D3
Carrill Gv East *BNG/LEV* M19 .... 51 D3
Carrington La *SALE* M33 .... 121 D3

  SALE M33 .... 122 A4
Carrington Rd *RUSH/FAL* M14 .... 48 A5
  STKP SK1 .... 139 D2
Carrington St *CHAD* OL9 .... 71 D2 🔢
  SWIN M27 .... 59 D4
Carron Av *BKLY* M9 .... 67 C4
Carr St *SWIN* M27 .... 75 D2
Carrsvale Av *URM* M41 .... 110 B2
Carruthers St *ANC* M4 .... 18 C1
Carslake Rd *NEWH/MOS* M40 ..... 84 B4
Carson Rd *BNG/LEV* M19 .... 51 D5
Carstairs Cl *CHH* M8 .... 82 B2 🔢
Carter St *BRO* M7 .... 81 D4 🔢
  SALQ/ORD M5 .... 94 A4
Carthage St *OLDS* OL8 .... 73 D1
Cartmel Av *HTNM* SK4 .... 133 D3
Cartmel Cl *OLDS* OL8 .... 72 B2 🔢
Cartmel Crs *CHAD* OL9 .... 70 B3
Cartmel Gv *WALK* M28 .... 74 B2
Cartwright Rd *CCHDY* M21 .... 125 D1
Carver Cl *OLDTF/WHR* M16 ...... 33 F1
Carver St *OLDTF/WHR* M16 ...... 33 F1
Cascade Dr *CHH* M8 .... 82 A4 🔢
Cass Av *SALQ/ORD* M5 .... 13 D4
Cassidy Cl *ANC* M4 .... 7 F5
Casson St *FAIL* M35 .... 88 B2 🔢
Castle Cl *DROY* M43 .... 98 B3 🔢
Castledene Av *SLFD* M6 .... 95 C2 🔢
Castlefield Av *BRO* M7 .... 82 A1 🔢
Castle Hill Rd *PWCH* M25 .... 63 D3
Castlemere Rd *BKLY* M9 .... 66 A2
Castlemoor Av *BRO* M7 .... 80 B1 🔢
Castlerea Cl *ECC* M30 .... 101 D1 🔢
Castle St *CSLFD* M3 .... 15 E5
  ECC M30 .... 92 B3 🔢
Castleton Av *STRET* M32 .... 113 D2
Castleton Rd *BRO* M7 .... 64 A4
  STRET M32 .... 113 C1
Castleton St *CHAD* OL9 .... 54 A3 🔢
Castleway *SLFD* M6 .... 95 C1
Castlewood Rd *BRO* M7 .... 79 D1
Caston Cl *OLDTF/WHR* M16 ..... 35 F2 🔢
Cateaton St *CSLFD* M3 .... 16 B1
Caterham St *ANC* M4 .... 19 D3 🔢
Catesby Rd *OLDTF/WHR* M16 .... 35 D4
Cathedral Ap *CSLFD* M3 .... 6 B5
Cathedral Gates *CSLFD* M3 ..... 16 B1 🔢
Cathedral St *ANC* M4 .... 16 B1
Catherine Rd *CHH* M8 .... 64 A4
  MPL/ROM SK6 .... 141 D4
  SWIN M27 .... 75 C2
Catherine St *ECC* M30 .... 90 A2
  OP/CLY M11 .... 107 C2
Catherston Cl *OLDTF/WHR* M16 ... 35 E4 🔢
Cathrine St East *DTN/ASHW* M34 . 119 D3
Cathrine St West *DTN/ASHW* M34 . 119 D3
Catlow La *ANC* M4 .... 17 D1 🔢
Catlow St *BRO* M7 .... 5 F2
Cattlin Wy *OLDS* OL8 .... 72 A3
Cavalier St *NEWH/MOS* M40 ... 19 D1 🔢
Cavanagh Cl *BRUN/LGST* M13 .. 28 C4
Cavell St *CMANE* M1 .... 17 E2 🔢
Cavell Wy *SALQ/ORD* M5 ...... 13 D4
  SLFD M6 .... 13 D1
Cavendish Av *DID/WITH* M20 .. 128 B3 🔢
  SWIN M27 .... 60 A2
Cavendish Gv *ECC* M30 .... 92 A2 🔢
Cavendish Pl *OP/CLY* M11 .... 10 C5
Cavendish Rd *BRO* M7 .... 63 D4
  DID/WITH M20 .... 128 B3
  ECC M30 .... 92 A2
  STRET M32 .... 115 C1

URM M41 .... 112 A2 🔟
WALK M28 .... 74 B3
Cavendish St CHAD OL9 .... 55 C3 🔟
HULME M15 .... 26 C3
Caversham Dr BKLY M9 .... 85 C1 🔟
Cawdor Rd RUSH/FAL M14 .... 48 B4
Cawdor St ECC M30 .... 91 C4
HULME M15 .... 24 C2
SWIN M27 .... 75 D1 🔟
Cawley Av PWCH M25 .... 61 D3
Cawood Sq RDSH SK5 .... 136 A3
Caxton Rd RUSH/FAL M14............. 47 F4
Caxton St CSLFD M3 .... 15 F1 🔟
Caxton Wy SALQ/ORD M5 .... 13 E1 🔟
Caygill St CSLFD M3 .... 5 F5
Caythorpe St RUSH/FAL M14 .... 36 C5
Cayton St WGTN/LGST M12............ 40 C5
Cecil Gv GTN M18 .... 116 B1 🔟
Cecil Rd BKLY M9 .... 66 B1
ECC M30 .... 92 A4
STRET M32 .... 114 A4
Cecil St HULME M15 .... 37 E1
Cedar Crs CHAD OL9 .... 53 D1
Cedar Dr DROY M43 .... 99 C3
SWIN M27 .... 57 D1
URM M41 .... 111 C4
Cedar Gv HTNM SK4 .... 133 C4
RUSH/FAL M14.......................... 130 B1
Cedar Pl BRO M7 .... 4 B1
Cedar Rd FAIL M35 .... 88 B3
SALE M33 .... 121 D3
Cedric Rd CHH M8 .... 64 A3
Cedric St SALQ/ORD M5 .... 94 B3
Celia St CHH M8 .... 84 A1
Cemetery Rd DROY M43 .... 97 C4
FAIL M35 .... 88 B3
SALQ/ORD M5 .... 95 C4
SWIN M27 .... 58 A4
Cemetery Rd North SWIN M27 ... 58 A3 🔟
Centaur Cl SWIN M27 .... 58 B3 🔟
Centenary Wy SALQ/ORD M5 ...... 93 C4
Central Av BNG/LEV M19 .... 50 C2
SLFD M6 .... 79 C3
SWIN M27 .... 60 B3
Central Dr RDSH SK5 .... 135 C4
SWIN M27 .... 77 D2 🔟
URM M41 .... 111 D3
Central St DID/WITH M20............. 129 C4
Central St CMANW M2 .... 16 B3
Centurion Gv BRO M7 .... 82 A3 🔟
Century St CSLFD M3 .... 15 F5
Ceylon St NEWH/MOS M40 .... 86 A3
Chadderton St ANC M4 .... 7 E5
Chadderton Wy CHAD OL9 .... 54 B1
Chadwick Rd ECC M30 .... 92 A3
URM M41 .... 112 B3
Chadwick St SWIN M27 .... 76 B1 🔟
Chaffinch Cl DROY M43 .... 99 C2 🔟
Chain St CMANE M1 .... 16 C3
Chalfont Av URM M41 .... 112 A3 🔟
Chalfont Dr CHH M8 .... 83 C2 🔟
Challum Dr CHAD OL9 .... 53 C1
Chamber Hall Cl OLDS OL8 .... 72 B1 🔟
Chamber Rd OLDS OL8 .... 72 A2
Chambers Field Ct SALQ/ORD M5 ... 12 C3
Chancel Av SALQ/ORD M5............. 14 A5
Chancellor La WGTN/LGST M12 .... 18 C5
Chancel Ms STKP SK1................. 139 C4
Chancery La CMANW M2 .... 16 B3
Chancery St CHAD OL9 .... 54 A1
Chandos Gv SALQ/ORD M5 .... 94 B3
Chandos Rd CCHDY M21 .... 44 A4
HTNM SK4 .... 132 B3

PWCH M25 .... 62 B3 🔟
Chandos Rd South CCHDY M21 ..... 44 B5
Change Wy CSLFD M3 .... 5 E4
Chantry Cl RDSH SK5 .... 134 A2 🔟
Chapelfield Dr WGTN/LGST M12 ... 18 B5
Chapel Gv URM M41 .... 112 A3
Chapelhill Dr BKLY M9 .... 66 A2
Chapel La BKLY M9 .... 65 D2
SALE M33 .... 122 A3
Chapel Pl URM M41 .... 101 D1
Chapel Rd OLDS OL8 .... 72 A2
PWCH M25 .... 61 D4
SALE M33 .... 123 D4 🔟
SWIN M27 .... 75 C2
Chapel St BNG/LEV M19 .... 51 E4
CSLFD M3 .... 15 E1
DROY M43 .... 98 B4 🔟
ECC M30 .... 91 C4 🔟
PWCH M25 .... 62 A1 🔟
SWIN M27 .... 59 C4
Chapeltown St CMANE M1 .... 18 A4
Chapel Wks CMANW M2 .... 16 B2 🔟
Chaplin Cl SLFD M6....................... 95 C1
Chapman Ms GTN M18 .... 106 B4 🔟
Chapman St GTN M18 .... 106 B3
Chappell Rd DROY M43 .... 98 A3
Chapter St NEWH/MOS M40 .... 10 A1
Charfield St NEWH/MOS M40 .... 87 D4 🔟
Chariot St OP/CLY M11 .... 106 B3
Charlbury Av PWCH M25 .... 63 D3
RDSH SK5 .... 134 B3
Charles Av DTN/ASHW M34......... 108 A2
Charles Barry Crs HULME M15 ...... 25 F3
Charles Halle Rd HULME M15 .... 36 C1
Charles Morris Cl FAIL M35 .... 89 D1 🔟
Charles St CHAD OL9 .... 54 A3 🔟
CMANE M1 .... 17 D5
DROY M43 .... 97 C4 🔟
SLFD M6 .... 2 A2
SWIN M27 .... 57 D4
Charleston Sq URM M41 .... 110 B2 🔟
Charleston St OLDS OL8 .... 73 D1
Charlestown Rd BKLY M9 .... 66 B3
Charlesworth Av
DTN/ASHW M34 .... 137 D1 🔟
Charlesworth St OP/CLY M11........ 20 A4
Charley Av BRO M7 .... 4 C2
Charlotte St CMANW M2 .... 16 C3 🔟
STKP SK1 .... 139 D2
Charlton Av ECC M30 .... 91 D4
PWCH M25 .... 62 B2
Charlton Dr SWIN M27 .... 57 D3 🔟
Charlton Pl CMANE M1 .... 27 F1
Charlton Rd BNG/LEV M19 .... 51 E2
Charminster Dr CHH M8 .... 83 D1
Charnley Cl NEWH/MOS M40 .... 9 E4 🔟
Charnwood Av DTN/ASHW M34..... 118 B2
Charter St CSLFD M3 .... 6 B3
Chartwell Cl SALQ/ORD M5 .... 12 B1
Chaseley Rd SLFD M6 .... 95 C1
Chase St ANC M4 .... 7 D3
The Chase WALK M28 .... 74 A4 🔟
Chassen Av URM M41 .... 110 B3 🔟
Chassen Rd URM M41 .... 110 B4
Chataway Rd CHH M8 .... 83 D1
Chatburn Rd CCHDY M21 .... 44 B5
Chatfield Rd CCHDY M21............... 43 F5
Chatford Cl BRO M7 .... 5 E3
Chatham Gv DID/WITH M20 .... 129 C3
Chatham Rd GTN M18 .... 117 C2 🔟
OLDTF/WHR M16....................... 33 F5
Chatham St CMANE M1 .... 17 E3
Chatley St CSLFD M3 .... 6 B2

Chatsworth Av PWCH M25 .... 62 B1 🡑
Chatsworth Cl DROY M43 .... 96 B2 🡑
   URM M41 .... 112 A3 🡑
Chatsworth Gv OLDTF/WHR M16 ...... 45 D1
Chatsworth Rd DROY M43 .... 97 C2
   ECC M30 .... 92 B1
   GTN M18 .... 106 A4 🡑
   STRET M32 .... 112 B2
   SWIN M27 .... 74 B4
Chatterton Cl DID/WITH M20 .... 130 A3 🡑
Chattock Cl OLDTF/WHR M16 .... 35 F4
Chatwood Rd NEWH/MOS M40 .... 88 A1
Chaucer Av DROY M43 .... 98 A4 🡑
   RDSH SK5 .... 133 D1
Chaucer Ms STKP SK1 .... 139 D4 🡑
Chaucer St OLD OL1 .... 55 C3
Chauncy Rd NEWH/MOS M40 .... 88 A1
Chaytor Av NEWH/MOS M40 .... 86 B2 🡑
Cheadle Av BRO M7 .... 80 A2 🡑
Cheadle St OP/CLY M11 .... 106 B1
Cheapside CMANW M2 .... 16 B2
   OLD OL1 .... 55 C2
Cheddar St GTN M18 .... 106 B4 🡑
Cheeryble St DROY M43 .... 107 D1 🡑
   OP/CLY M11 .... 107 D2
Cheetham Hill Rd ANC M4 .... 6 C4
   CHH M8 .... 6 C2
Cheetham Pl MPL/ROM SK6 .... 141 D1 🡑
Cheetham Rd SWIN M27 .... 77 C2
Cheetham St FAIL M35 .... 89 C1
   NEWH/MOS M40 .... 85 C4 🡑
Cheetwood Rd CHH M8 .... 82 B4
Cheetwood St CHH M8 .... 5 F2
Chelbourne Dr OLDS OL8 .... 71 D3 🡑
Chelford Cl BRUN/LGST M13 .... 38 C1
Chelford Dr SWIN M27 .... 58 A3
Chelford Rd OLDTF/WHR M16 .... 34 A5
Chell St WGTN/LGST M12 .... 40 B3
Chelmsford Av NEWH/MOS M40 .... 11 F1
Chelmsford St OLDS OL8 .... 55 C4
Chelsea Rd NEWH/MOS M40 .... 87 C4
Chelsfield Gv CCHDY M21 .... 127 D1 🡑
Chelston Av NEWH/MOS M40 .... 69 C3 🡑
Cheltenham Crs BRO M7 .... 82 A1
Cheltenham Rd CCHDY M21 .... 43 E2
Cheltenham St SLFD M6 .... 3 D2
Chelwood Dr DROY M43 .... 97 D3
Cheney Cl OP/CLY M11 .... 106 B2 🡑
Chepstow CCHDY M21 .... 43 E2 🡑
   SWIN M27 .... 59 C2
Chepstow St CMANE M1 .... 16 B5
Chepstow St South CMANE M1 .... 16 B5 🡑
Chequers Rd CCHDY M21 .... 126 A2 🡑
Cheriton Av SALE M33 .... 124 A4
Cherry Dr SWIN M27 .... 77 C1
Cherrytown Wk BRUN/LGST M13 ...... 28 A4 🡑
Cherry Tree Wk STRET M32 .... 113 C4 🡑
Chertsey Cl GTN M18 .... 107 C4 🡑
Cherwell Cl OLDS OL8 .... 72 A4
Chesham Rd ECC M30 .... 101 C1 🡑
Cheshire Cl STRET M32 .... 113 C4
Chesney Av CHAD OL9 .... 70 A3
Chesshyre Av ANC M4 .... 19 D2
Chessington Ri SWIN M27 .... 59 C2
Chester Av URM M41 .... 112 A2 🡑
Chestergate EDGY/DAV SK3 .... 138 A4 🡑
Chester Rd HULME M15 .... 24 C2
   OLDTF/WHR M16 .... 23 E5
   STRET M32 .... 32 A2
Chester St CHAD OL9 .... 54 A4
   HULME M15 .... 26 B2
   SWIN M27 .... 76 A2
Chesterton Gv DROY M43 .... 98 A3

Chestnut Av CCHDY M21 .... 126 B1 🡑
   DROY M43 .... 97 C2
Chestnut Gv FAIL M35 .... 88 B3 🡑
Chestnut Rd ECC M30 .... 90 A1
Chestnut St CHAD OL9 .... 70 B2
Chetham Cl SALO/ORD M5 .... 23 E3
Chetwynd Av URM M41 .... 111 C4 🡑
Chetwynd Cl SALE M33 .... 122 A3 🡑
Chevassut St HULME M15 .... 25 E3
Chevington Dr BKLY M9 .... 84 B3
Cheviot Av OLDS OL8 .... 73 C2
Cheviot Cl CHAD OL9 .... 53 C4 🡑
   SLFD M6 .... 95 C2 🡑
Cheviot St CSLFD M3 .... 6 B3
Chevril Cl HULME M15 .... 26 C3
Chevron Cl SALO/ORD M5 .... 13 E1
Chichester Rd HULME M15 .... 25 F5
Chiffon Wy CSLFD M3 .... 4 C4
Chilham Rd ECC M30 .... 92 B1
Chilham St SWIN M27 .... 76 A3 🡑
Chiltern Dr SWIN M27 .... 76 B3
Chilton Av CHAD OL9 .... 53 C3
Chilworth St RUSH/FAL M14 .... 47 E1
Chime Bank CHH M8 .... 84 A3
China La CMANE M1 .... 17 E3 🡑
Chinley Av NEWH/MOS M40 .... 86 A1 🡑
   STRET M32 .... 113 C2 🡑
Chinley St SLFD M6 .... 80 B4
Chinwell Vw BNG/LEV M19 .... 51 D3 🡑
Chippenham Rd ANC M4 .... 18 B1
Chipping Sq WGTN/LGST M12 .... 40 C3 🡑
Chipstead Av WGTN/LGST M12 .... 29 F5
Chiselhurst St CHH M8 .... 83 C2
Chisholm St OP/CLY M11 .... 106 B2
Chisledon Av CHH M8 .... 82 B3
Chislehurst Av URM M41 .... 111 C2
Choir St BRO M7 .... 5 E1
Cholmondeley Rd SLFD M6 .... 93 D1
Choral Gv BRO M7 .... 81 D4
Chorley Rd SWIN M27 .... 57 D4
Chorley St STRET M32 .... 32 A2
Chorley Wood Av BNG/LEV M19 ..... 131 D3 🡑
Chorlton Fold ECC M30 .... 75 D4
Chorlton Rd HULME M15 .... 25 D3
   OLDTF/WHR M16 .... 35 D1
Chorlton St CMANE M1 .... 17 D3 🡑
   OLDTF/WHR M16 .... 24 A5
Christchurch Av SALO/ORD M5 .... 13 F1
Christchurch Rd SALE M33 .... 121 C4
Christie St STRET M32 .... 115 C2
Christleton Av HTNM SK4 .... 133 D4
Christopher St NEWH/MOS M40 ...... 96 B1 🡑
   SALO/ORD M5 .... 13 E3 🡑
Chudleigh Rd CHH M8 .... 65 C3
Church Av NEWH/MOS M40 .... 87 C4 🡑
   SLFD M6 .... 94 B3
Church Dr PWCH M25 .... 61 D1
Churchfield Rd SLFD M6 .... 78 B4 🡑
Churchfields SALE M33 .... 121 D3
Churchgate STKP SK1 .... 138 B4
   URM M41 .... 111 C4
Churchgate Buildings CMANE M1 .... 18 A4 🡑
Churchill Av OLDTF/WHR M16 .... 44 C1 🡑
Churchill Crs RDSH SK5 .... 117 C4
Churchill St SLFD M6 .... 2 C5 🡑
   TRPK M17 .... 104 A2
Church La BKLY M9 .... 84 B1
   BNG/LEV M19 .... 131 D3 🡑
   BRO M7 .... 62 B4
   OLD OL1 .... 55 D2
   PWCH M25 .... 62 A1
   SALE M33 .... 122 A3
Church Rd ECC M30 .... 92 B3

HTNM SK4 .... **138** A3
URM M41 .... **110** A4
URM M41 .... **111** D4 ◫
URM M41 .... **120** A1
Churchside Cl *BKLY* M9 .... **66** B3 ◫
Church St *ANC* M4 .... **17** D1
CSLFD M3 .... **15** D1
DROY M43 .... **98** A4
ECC M30 .... **92** B3
FAIL M35 .... **88** B1
HTNM SK4 .... **138** A2 ◫
OLD OL1 .... **55** D2
STRET M32 .... **114** A4
SWIN M27 .... **76** A1 ◫
SWIN M27 .... **77** D1 ◫
Church Wk *SWIN* M27 .... **58** B1
Churnet St *NEWH/MOS* M40 .... **84** B4
Churston Av *BKLY* M9 .... **67** C1
Churton Av *RUSH/FAL* M14 .... **47** E2 ◫
Churton Rd *GTN* M18 .... **116** A2
Cicero St *BKLY* M9 .... **85** C1 ◫
Cinder St *ANC* M4 .... **8** A5 ◫
Cipher St *ANC* M4 .... **8** A4 ◫
Circle South *TRPK* M17 .... **105** C3
The Circuit *DID/WITH* M20 .... **129** C4
Circular Rd *DID/WITH* M20 .... **129** C4
PWCH M25 .... **62** B3
Circus St *CMANE* M1 .... **17** E3 ◫
Ciss La *URM* M41 .... **112** A3
Citrus Wy *SLFD* M6 .... **3** D5
City Rd *HULME* M15 .... **24** C4
City Rd East *HULME* M15 .... **26** A2
City Wk *SWIN* M27 .... **77** D1
Clague St *OP/CLY* M11 .... **10** C5
Claife Av *NEWH/MOS* M40 .... **68** B3 ◫
Clandon Av *ECC* M30 .... **90** B3
Clapham St *NEWH/MOS* M40 .... **87** C1
Clara St *CHAD* OL9 .... **72** A1
Claremont Av *DID/WITH* M20 .... **129** C4 ◫
HTNM SK4 .... **133** C4
Claremont Range *GTN* M18 .... **117** D1 ◫
Claremont Rd *OLDTF/WHR* M16 .... **35** F4
SALE M33 .... **123** C4
SLFD M6 .... **78** A4
Claremont St *FAIL* M35 .... **88** B1 ◫
OLDS OL8 .... **73** D3
Clarence Av *OLDS* OL8 .... **72** B1
TRPK M17 .... **102** B3
Clarence Rd *BRUN/LGST* M13 .... **39** F3
HTNM SK4 .... **132** B4
SWIN M27 .... **75** C2 ◫
Clarence St *BRO* M7 .... **4** B1
CMANW M2 .... **16** B5 ◫
Clarendon Crs *ECC* M30 .... **92** B2
SALE M33 .... **124** B4
Clarendon Rd *DTN/ASHW* M34 ...... **108** A2
ECC M30 .... **92** B3 ◫
OLDTF/WHR M16 .... **44** B2
SWIN M27 .... **76** B1
Clarendon Rd West *CCHDY* M21 .... **43** F2
Clarendon St *HULME* M15 .... **25** F3
RDSH SK5 .... **138** B2 ◫
Clare Rd *BNG/LEV* M19 .... **132** A1
RDSH SK5 .... **138** B1 ◫
Clare St *CMANE* M1 .... **27** F1
SALO/ORD M5 .... **14** B3 ◫
Claribel St *OP/CLY* M11 .... **19** E5
Claridge Rd *CCHDY* M21 .... **43** D3
Clarion St *ANC* M4 .... **8** A4
Clark Av *GTN* M18 .... **107** C4
Clarke Av *SALO/ORD* M5 .... **23** E2
Clark's Hl *PWCH* M25 .... **62** A1
Clarkson Cl *DTN/ASHW* M34 .... **119** D3

Clarkwell Cl *CHAD* OL9 .... **55** C1 ◫
Class St *OP/CLY* M11 .... **20** A2
Claude Av *SWIN* M27 .... **75** D1
Claude Rd *CCHDY* M21 .... **126** A3
Claude St *CHH* M8 .... **65** C4
ECC M30 .... **90** B1
SWIN M27 .... **75** D1 ◫
Claxton Av *BKLY* M9 .... **66** B2
Clay Bank *DROY* M43 .... **97** C4 ◫
Claybar Dr *ECC* M30 .... **92** A2
Clayburn Rd *HULME* M15 .... **25** F3
Claycourt Av *ECC* M30 .... **90** B1 ◫
Claymore St *GTN* M18 .... **107** C3
Clay St *OLDS* OL8............................ **73** C1
Claytonbrook Rd *OP/CLY* M11 ...... **96** A4
Clayton Cl *HULME* M15 .... **35** E1
Clayton Hall Rd *OP/CLY* M11 .... **96** A3 ◫
Clayton La *OP/CLY* M11 .... **21** E4
Clayton La South *OP/CLY* M11 ...... **31** D1
Clayton St *CHAD* OL9 .... **71** C2 ◫
FAIL M35 .... **88** B2 ◫
OP/CLY M11 .... **11** F4
Cleadon Av *GTN* M18 .... **116** A1
Cleavley St *ECC* M30 .... **90** B3
Clee Av *BRUN/LGST* M13 .... **50** A2
Cleethorpes Av *BKLY* M9 .... **65** D2 ◫
Clegg St *DROY* M43 .... **97** D4 ◫
MPL/ROM SK6 .... **141** D2 ◫
OLD OL1 .... **55** D3
OLDE OL4 .... **55** D3
Clementine Cl *SLFD* M6 .... **13** E1 ◫
Clement Scott Cl *BKLY* M9 .... **67** C4 ◫
Clement St *BRO* M7 .... **5** D1
HTNM SK4 .... **138** A2 ◫
Cleminson St *CSLFD* M3.................. **14** C1
Clevedon Av *URM* M41 .... **113** C3
Clevedon St *BKLY* M9 .... **85** C2
Cleveland Av *BNG/LEV* M19 .... **51** E2
SLFD M6 .... **93** D2
Cleveland Rd *CHH* M8 .... **65** D3
Cleveleys Av *CCHDY* M21 .... **127** C2 ◫
Cleveleys Gv *BRO* M7 .... **82** A2 ◫
Cleworth St *HULME* M15 .... **24** C2 ◫
Clibran St *CHH* M8 .... **83** D3
Cliff Av *BRO* M7 .... **81** C3
Cliff Crs *BRO* M7 .... **81** D2
Cliffdale Dr *CHH* M8 .... **65** C4 ◫
Clifford St *ECC* M30 .... **100** B1
SWIN M27 .... **77** D1 ◫
Clifton Av *ECC* M30 .... **91** D2 ◫
RUSH/FAL M14 .... **130** B1
Clifton Dr *SWIN* M27 .... **57** D1
Clifton Gv *SWIN* M27 .... **57** C3
Clifton House Rd *SWIN* M27 .... **58** A1 ◫
Clifton Rd *CCHDY* M21 .... **44** A5
ECC M30 .... **91** D2
PWCH M25 .... **61** C1
URM M41 .... **110** A3
Clifton St *FAIL* M35 .... **71** C4
NEWH/MOS M40 .... **10** A3
OLDTF/WHR M16 .... **24** C5 ◫
OLDTF/WHR M16 .... **34** C1
Clifton Vw *SWIN* M27 .... **58** A1
Cliftonville Dr *SLFD* M6 .... **77** D3
Clinton Av *RUSH/FAL* M14 .... **46** C3
Clinton Gdns *RUSH/FAL* M14 .... **46** C1
Clippers Quay *SALO/ORD* M5 .... **22** C4
Clitheroe Rd *BRUN/LGST* M13 ...... **40** A5
Clito St *BKLY* M9 .... **85** D1 ◫
Clively Av *SWIN* M27 .... **59** D4
Clive Rd *FAIL* M35 .... **88** A2
Clive St *ANC* M4.............................. **7** E4

OLDS OL8 .... 72 B3
Clivia Gv BRO M7 .... 81 D3 2
Cloak St CMANE M1 .... 27 D1
Clock House Av DROY M43 .... 97 C2
Clock St OLD OL9 .... 71 D3
Clough Dr PWCH M25 .... 61 D1
Cloughfield Av SALQ/ORD M5 .... 13 F5
Clough Ga OLDS OL8 .... 72 B3 2
Clough La PWCH M25 .... 61 D1
Clough Rd BKLY M9 .... 85 D1
  DROY M43 .... 98 B3
  FAIL M35 .... 89 C2
Clough St NEWH/MOS M40 .... 96 A1 2
The Clough RDSH SK5 .... 135 D3
Clough Top Rd BKLY M9 .... 68 A3
Clovelly Av OLDS OL8 .... 72 A3
Clovelly Rd CCHDY M21 .... 127 C1
  SWIN M27 .... 75 C2
Clovelly St NEWH/MOS M40 .... 87 D4 2
Clowes St CHAD OL9 .... 71 C3
  CSLFD M3 .... 15 F1
  WGTN/LGST M12 .... 30 C3
Club St OP/CLY M11 .... 107 D2
Clumber Rd GTN M18 .... 117 D1
Clydesdale Gdns OP/CLY M11 .... 20 C3
Clydesdale St OLDS OL8 .... 73 C1 2
Clyne St STRET M32 .... 32 A1
Coalshaw Green Rd CHAD OL9 .... 71 C2
Coatbridge St OP/CLY M11 .... 96 A4
Cobalt Av URM M41 .... 102 B3
Cobb Cl CHH M8 .... 64 A2
Cobble Bank BKLY M9 .... 66 B2 2
Cobden St BKLY M9 .... 67 C4
  CHAD OL9 .... 53 D2
  SLFD M6 .... 2 B1
Cob Hall Rd STRET M32 .... 114 A4 2
Cobham Av NEWH/MOS M40 .... 69 C3 2
Cobourg St CMANE M1 .... 17 E4
Coburg Av BRO M7 .... 4 C2
Cochrane Av WGTN/LGST M12 .... 29 F5
Cockcroft St BKLY M9 .... 66 B4
Coconut Gv SLFD M6 .... 2 C5
Coddington Av OP/CLY M11 .... 107 C1 2
Coghlan Cl OP/CLY M11 .... 21 F1 2
Colborne Av ECC M30 .... 90 B3
  RDSH SK5 .... 117 D2 2
Colbourne Av CHH M8 .... 64 B2 2
Colclough Cl NEWH/MOS M40 .... 86 B3 2
Coldhurst St OLD OL1 .... 55 C1
Coldstream Av BKLY M9 .... 66 B1 2
Colebrook Dr NEWH/MOS M40 .... 86 A3
Coleby Av OLDTF/WHR M16 .... 34 A3
Colenso St OLDS OL8 .... 72 B2
Coleridge Cl RDSH SK5 .... 117 C4
Coleridge Rd OLDTF/WHR M16 .... 34 A4
  RDSH SK5 .... 117 C4
Coleshill St NEWH/MOS M40 .... 9 E3
Cole St NEWH/MOS M40 .... 85 D1
Colgate Crs RUSH/FAL M14 .... 47 F5
Colgate La SALQ/ORD M5 .... 23 D4
Colgrove Av NEWH/MOS M40 .... 69 C3
Colina Dr CHH M8 .... 82 A4 2
Colindale Av BKLY M9 .... 67 C1
Colin Rd HTNM SK4 .... 138 A1 2
Coll Dr URM M41 .... 101 D4
College Av OLDS OL8 .... 72 B2
College Cft ECC M30 .... 92 B3 2
College Dr OLDTF/WHR M16 .... 44 B3 2
College Rd ECC M30 .... 93 C3 2
  OLDS OL8 .... 72 B1
  OLDTF/WHR M16 .... 44 B3
Colley St STRET M32 .... 32 A1
Collie Av SLFD M6 .... 81 C4

Collier Hl OLDS OL8 .... 72 B2
Collier Hill Av OLDS OL8 .... 72 A2
Collier St CSLFD M3 .... 5 F5
  CSLFD M3 .... 15 E5
  SLFD M6 .... 79 D3
  SWIN M27 .... 76 A2 2
Colliery St OP/CLY M11 .... 21 E4
  OP/CLY M11 .... 21 D3
Collin Av GTN M18 .... 116 A1
Collingburn Av SALQ/ORD M5 .... 23 E1
Collingham St CHH M8 .... 7 D2
Collington Cl WGTN/LGST M12 .... 40 C1
Collingwood Av DROY M43 .... 97 C2 2
Collingwood Dr SWIN M27 .... 77 C2
Collingwood Rd BNG/LEV M19 .... 50 A3
Collyhurst Rd NEWH/MOS M40 .... 7 F2
Collyhurst St NEWH/MOS M40 .... 8 B1
Colman Gdns SALQ/ORD M5 .... 23 F1
Colmore Dr BKLY M9 .... 68 A1
Columbia Av GTN M18 .... 117 D1
Columbia St OLDS OL8 .... 73 D1 3
Columbine St OP/CLY M11 .... 106 B2
Colwell Av STRET M32 .... 113 D4
Colwyn Av RUSH/FAL M14 .... 131 C1
Colwyn Crs RDSH SK5 .... 134 B4
Colwyn Rd SWIN M27 .... 75 C3 2
Colwyn St CHAD OL9 .... 54 B2
  SLFD M6 .... 2 B3
Combe Cl OP/CLY M11 .... 11 E4
Combermere Av DID/WITH M20 .... 129 C2 2
Comet St CMANE M1 .... 17 F3 2
Commercial Rd OLD OL1 .... 55 D3 2
Commercial St CHAD OL9 .... 54 A3 2
  HULME M15 .... 25 F1
Compass St OP/CLY M11 .... 106 A2 2
Compstall Av RUSH/FAL M14 .... 47 E2
Compstall Gv GTN M18 .... 107 C3
Comus St SALQ/ORD M5 .... 14 A4
Concert La CMANW M2 .... 16 C3
Concord Pl SLFD M6 .... 80 A4 2
Condor Cl DROY M43 .... 99 C2 2
Condor Pl SLFD M6 .... 80 A4 2
Congleton Av RUSH/FAL M14 .... 47 D2
Congou St CMANE M1 .... 18 A4 2
Congreave St OLD OL1 .... 55 C1
Coningsby Dr BKLY M9 .... 84 B1
Coniston Av BKLY M9 .... 84 B1 2
  OLDS OL8 .... 72 B2
Coniston Cl CHAD OL9 .... 53 C2
  DTN/ASHW M34 .... 118 B3
Coniston Rd RDSH SK5 .... 134 B3 2
  STRET M32 .... 114 A2
  SWIN M27 .... 76 B3
Coniston St NEWH/MOS M40 .... 87 C4 2
  SLFD M6 .... 3 F1
Connaught Av BNG/LEV M19 .... 131 C5
Connaught St CHAD OL9 .... 55 C3 2
Connie St OP/CLY M11 .... 106 A1
Connington Av BKLY M9 .... 66 B4
Conquest Cl WGTN/LGST M12 .... 30 B3
Conran St BKLY M9 .... 85 C2 2
Constable St GTN M18 .... 107 C3
Constance St HULME M15 .... 25 F1 2
Conway Av SWIN M27 .... 59 D2
Conway Cl OLDTF/WHR M16 .... 33 D5
Conway Gv CHAD OL9 .... 52 B1
Conway Rd URM M41 .... 111 D1
Conway St RDSH SK5 .... 138 A1
Conyngham Rd RUSH/FAL M14 .... 38 C3
Cooke St FAIL M35 .... 88 B1
Cook St CSLFD M3 .... 15 E1
  ECC M30 .... 91 C3 2
  EDGY/DAV SK3 .... 138 A4 2

Coomassie St *SLFD* M6 .... 2 A3
Co-operation St *FAIL* M35 .... 70 B4
Cooper St *CMANW* M2 .... 16 B3
   DROY M43 .... 97 C4 🔲
   STRET M32 .... 114 B4
Coop St *ANC* M4 .... 7 E5 🔲
Cope Cl *OP/CLY* M11 .... 107 C2 🔲
Copeland Av *SWIN* M27 .... 60 A4
Copeman Cl *BRUN/LGST* M13 ...... 28 A4
Copenhagen St *NEWH/MOS* M40 .. 86 A3 🔲
Copgrove Rd *CCHDY* M21 .... 126 B2 🔲
Copley Rd *CCHDY* M21 .... 43 D2
Copperas La *DROY* M43 .... 107 C1
Copperas St *ANC* M4 .... 17 D1
Coppice St *OLDS* OL8 .... 54 B4
The Coppice *PWCH* M25 .... 62 A1
   SWIN M27 .... 75 C4
Coppice Wk *DTN/ASHW* M34 ..... 119 D3
Copping St *WGTN/LGST* M12 ...... 30 A4
Coppleridge Dr *CHH* M8 .... 65 C3
Copplestone Dr *SALE* M33 .... 121 C4
Copson St *DID/WITH* M20 .... 129 D2
Copster Av *OLDS* OL8 .... 73 C2
Copster Hill Rd *OLDS* OL8 .... 73 C2
Copster Pl *OLDS* OL8 .... 73 C2
Copthall La *CHH* M8 .... 82 B1
Copthorne Crs *BRUN/LGST* M13 .. 49 F1
Coral St *BRUN/LGST* M13 .... 28 A2
Coram St *GTN* M18 .... 107 D3
   WGTN/LGST M12 .... 31 D4
Corbett St *OP/CLY* M11 .... 21 D1
Corby St *WGTN/LGST* M12 .... 31 D4
Cordingley Av *DROY* M43 .... 107 D1 🔲
Cordova Av *DTN/ASHW* M34 ...... 117 D2
Corelli St *NEWH/MOS* M40 .... 10 A2
Corinthian Av *BRO* M7 .... 81 C4
Corkland Rd *CCHDY* M21 .... 43 F5
Cork St *WGTN/LGST* M12 .... 19 D4
Cormallen Gv *FAIL* M35 .... 89 C2 🔲
Cornbrook Ct *HULME* M15 .... 24 C4
Cornbrook Gv *OLDTF/WHR* M16 .. 24 C5
Cornbrook Park Rd *HULME* M15 .. 24 B4 🔲
Cornbrook Rd *HULME* M15 .... 24 B2 🔲
Cornbrook Rd *OLDTF/WHR* M16 .. 24 C5
Corn Cl *BRUN/LGST* M13 .... 38 B1
Cornell St *ANC* M4 .... 7 F5
Cornet St *BRO* M7 .... 81 D3 🔲
Cornford Av *GTN* M18 .... 41 F4
Cornhill Av *URM* M41 .... 110 B2
Corn Hill La *DTN/ASHW* M34 ..... 108 A4
Cornhill Rd *URM* M41 .... 110 B2
Corn St *FAIL* M35 .... 87 D3 🔲
Cornwall Av *BNG/LEV* M19 .... 132 B1 🔲
Cornwall Crs *RDSH* SK5 .... 136 A3
Cornwall Rd *DROY* M43 .... 98 A2
Cornwall St *CHAD* OL9 .... 53 D4
   ECC M30 .... 91 C4 🔲
   OP/CLY M11 .... 106 B2
Corona Av *OLDS* OL8 .... 72 B2
Coronation Dr *DROY* M43 .... 97 D2
   FAIL M35 .... 88 A3 🔲
Coronation Sq *WGTN/LGST* M12 .. 18 B5 🔲
Coronation St *DTN/ASHW* M34 .. 119 C2
   OP/CLY M11 .... 106 A1 🔲
   RDSH SK5 .... 138 A1
   SALQ/ORD M5 .... 13 F4
   SWIN M27 .... 59 C4
Corporation Rd *DTN/ASHW* M34 ... 109 D4
Corporation St *ANC* M4 .... 6 C4
   CMANE M1 .... 16 B2
   CMANW M2 .... 16 B2
   STKP SK1 .... 138 B3 🔲
Corran Cl *ECC* M30 .... 90 B3 🔲
Corrie Crs *FWTH* BL4 .... 57 D1

Corrie Dr *FWTH* BL4 .... 57 D1
Corrie Rd *SWIN* M27 .... 59 C2 🔲
Corrie Wy *MPL/ROM* SK6 .... 137 C4
Corrigan St *GTN* M18 .... 107 C3 🔲
Corringham Rd *BNG/LEV* M19 .... 133 C2
Corwen Av *BKLY* M9 .... 85 C1
Corwen Cl *OLDS* OL8 .... 71 D3
Cosgrove Crs *FAIL* M35 .... 88 A4
Cosgrove Rd *FAIL* M35 .... 88 A4
Cotham St *CSLFD* M3 .... 6 A2
Cotswold Av *CHAD* OL9 .... 53 C4
Cotswold Dr *SLFD* M6 .... 2 A3
Cottage Gdns *MPL/ROM* SK6 .... 140 B2
Cottam Gv *SWIN* M27 .... 77 C2 🔲
Cottam St *OLD* OL1 .... 54 B1
Cottenham La *BRO* M7 .... 5 E2
Cottenham St *BRUN/LGST* M13 ... 27 F3
Cotterdale Cl *OLDTF/WHR* M16 ... 45 D2
Cotterill St *SLFD* M6 .... 13 D1
Cotter St *WGTN/LGST* M12 .... 28 A1
Cottesmore Dr *CHH* M8 .... 84 A1 🔲
Cottingham Rd *WGTN/LGST* M12 ... 29 E4
Cottonfield Rd *DID/WITH* M20 .... 130 A3
Cotton Hl *DID/WITH* M20 .... 130 A4
Cotton La *DID/WITH* M20 .... 130 A3
Cotton St *ANC* M4 .... 17 F1
Cotton Tree St *EDGY/DAV* SK3 .. 138 A4 🔲
Cottonwood Dr *SALE* M33 .... 121 C4 🔲
Coulsden Dr *BKLY* M9 .... 66 B2
Councillor St *OP/CLY* M11 .... 19 F2
Countess Gv *BRO* M7 .... 4 C1
   BRO M7 .... 81 D4 🔲
Countess Pl *PWCH* M25 .... 63 C1 🔲
Counthill Dr *CHH* M8 .... 64 A3 🔲
County St *CMANW* M2 .... 16 B3 🔲
   OLDS OL8 .... 72 A3
Coupland St *HULME* M15 .... 26 C5
Courier St *GTN* M18 .... 107 C3 🔲
Court Dr *NEWH/MOS* M40 .... 97 C1
Courtfield Av *BKLY* M9 .... 66 B1 🔲
Covent Gdn *STKP* SK1 .... 138 B4 🔲
Coverdale Crs *WGTN/LGST* M12 .. 29 D3
Cowan St *NEWH/MOS* M40 .... 19 D1
Cowburn St *CSLFD* M3 .... 6 B3
Cowesby St *RUSH/FAL* M14 .... 36 C5
Cow La *FAIL* M35 .... 88 A2
   SALE M33 .... 125 C3
   SALQ/ORD M5 .... 14 B3
Cowley St *NEWH/MOS* M40 .... 87 C3 🔲
Cowling St *BRO* M7 .... 79 D1
Crabbe St *ANC* M4 .... 7 D3 🔲
Crab La *BKLY* M9 .... 65 D1
Crabtree La *OP/CLY* M11 .... 96 B4
Cradley Av *OP/CLY* M11 .... 106 B1
Cragie St *CHH* M8 .... 82 B4
Craig Av *URM* M41 .... 110 A2
Craighall Av *BNG/LEV* M19 .... 50 B5
Craig Rd *GTN* M18 .... 116 A1
Craigslands Av *NEWH/MOS* M40 .. 86 A3
Craigwell Rd *PWCH* M25 .... 63 D3
Cramer St *NEWH/MOS* M40 .... 85 D4 🔲
Crammond Cl *NEWH/MOS* M40 ... 87 D3
Cranage Rd *BNG/LEV* M19 .... 51 F5
Cranbourne Rd *OLDTF/WHR* M16 .. 34 A2
Cranbourne St *SALQ/ORD* M5 .... 14 A3 🔲
Cranbrook Dr *PWCH* M25 .... 63 C3
Cranbrook Rd *ECC* M30 .... 90 A1
   GTN M18 .... 117 D2 🔲
Crane St *WGTN/LGST* M12 .... 18 B5
Cranfield Cl *NEWH/MOS* M40 .... 9 D5
Cranford Av *SALE* M33 .... 124 A3
   STRET M32 .... 32 A5
Cranford Cl *SLFD* M6 .... 77 D3 🔲

Cranleigh Dr SALE M33 ..... 123 C4
Cranlington Dr CHH M8 ..... 82 B3 ⁶
Cranmere Av BNG/LEV M19 ..... 116 A3 ⁹
Cranswick St RUSH/FAL M14 ..... 36 C5
Crantock St WGTN/LGST M12 ..... 41 E5
Craston Rd BRUN/LGST M13 ..... 49 F1
Craven Av SALQ/ORD M5 ..... 13 E4
Craven Dr SALQ/ORD M5 ..... 23 D3
Cravenhurst Av NEWH/MOS M40 ..... 11 E1
Craven Pl OP/CLY M11 ..... 96 A3 ⁶
Craven Rd RDSH SK5 ..... 134 B3 ⁸
Craven St OLD OL1 ..... 55 C1
  SALQ/ORD M5 ..... 14 B3
Cravenwood Rd CHH M8 ..... 83 C1
Crawford St ECC M30 ..... 91 D2
  NEWH/MOS M40 ..... 87 C4 ⁸
Crawley Av ECC M30 ..... 93 C2 ⁷
Craydon St OP/CLY M11 ..... 106 A3 ⁷
Crayfield Rd BNG/LEV M19 ..... 51 E5
Crayford Rd NEWH/MOS M40 ..... 11 E1
Crediton Cl HULME M15 ..... 26 B5
Cresbury St WGTN/LGST M12 ..... 28 C1
Crescent SALQ/ORD M5 ..... 14 C1
Crescent Av CHH M8 ..... 83 C1 ²
  PWCH M25 ..... 62 B3
  SWIN M27 ..... 77 D1 ⁶
Crescent Gv BNG/LEV M19 ..... 51 D3 ⁵
  PWCH M25 ..... 62 B3 ⁸
Crescent Range RUSH/FAL M14 ..... 38 B4
Crescent Rd CHAD OL9 ..... 70 A3
  CHH M8 ..... 83 C1
  STKP SK1 ..... 139 D2
Crescent St CHH M8 ..... 84 A1
The Crescent BNG/LEV M19 ..... 51 D3
  DROY M43 ..... 97 D4
  MPL/ROM SK6 ..... 140 B1
  PWCH M25 ..... 62 B1 ⁷
Cressfield Wy CCHDY M21 ..... 127 D2
Cressingham Rd STRET M32 ..... 113 D4
Cressington Cl SALQ/ORD M5 ..... 95 C3 ⁸
Cresswell Gv DID/WITH M20 ..... 129 C4
Crest St CSLFD M3 ..... 6 B4
The Crest DROY M43 ..... 108 A2
Crete St OLDS OL8 ..... 73 C4
Crimsworth Av OLDTF/WHR M16 ..... 43 E1
Cringleford Wk WGTN/LGST M12 ..... 40 A1
Cringle Hall Rd BNG/LEV M19 ..... 131 D3
Cringle Rd BNG/LEV M19 ..... 132 B2
Criterion St RDSH SK5 ..... 117 D3
Croft Bank GTN M18 ..... 107 C4 ⁴
Croft Brow OLDS OL8 ..... 73 C3
Croft Hill Rd NEWH/MOS M40 ..... 68 A4
Crofton Cl OLDS OL8 ..... 73 C2 ¹
  OLDTF/WHR M16 ..... 34 C4
  RUSH/FAL M14 ..... 37 E5
Crofts Bank Rd URM M41 ..... 111 C1
Croft St BRO M7 ..... 81 C4
  FAIL M35 ..... 71 C4
  OP/CLY M11 ..... 21 E2
The Croft OLDS OL8 ..... 73 C3
Cromarty Av CHAD OL9 ..... 70 B2 ¹
Cromer Av DID/WITH M20 ..... 129 C3
  DTN/ASHW M34 ..... 118 A2 ³
Cromer St OP/CLY M11 ..... 96 B4 ⁸
  STKP SK1 ..... 139 C3
Cromford Av STRET M32 ..... 113 D3
Cromhurst St CHH M8 ..... 83 C1 ⁹
Crompton Rd BNG/LEV M19 ..... 132 A2
Crompton St CHAD OL9 ..... 54 A2
  OLD OL1 ..... 55 C1
  SWIN M27 ..... 76 A1 ⁹
Cromwell Av OLDTF/WHR M16 ..... 44 A1
Cromwell Gv BNG/LEV M19 ..... 51 D3

BRO M7 ..... 81 C4 ⁷
Cromwell Rd ECC M30 ..... 91 C3 ²
  MPL/ROM SK6 ..... 136 B3
  PWCH M25 ..... 63 C1
  SLFD M6 ..... 3 D1
  STRET M32 ..... 115 C4
  SWIN M27 ..... 58 A4
Cromwell St OLD OL1 ..... 55 D3
Crondall St RUSH/FAL M14 ..... 36 C5
Cronshaw St BNG/LEV M19 ..... 132 B1 ²
Crookhill Dr CHH M8 ..... 82 B2 ⁸
Crookilley Wy MPL/ROM SK6 ..... 136 B4
  STKP SK1 ..... 139 D2
Crosby Rd NEWH/MOS M40 ..... 87 D4
  SLFD M6 ..... 78 B4 ²
Crosfield Gv GTN M18 ..... 116 B1 ²
Crossbank Cl BRUN/LGST M13 ..... 28 C5
Crossbank St CHAD OL9 ..... 55 C3 ⁶
  OLDS OL8 ..... 55 C3
Crosscliffe Cl OLDTF/WHR M16 ..... 36 A3
Crossdale Rd BKLY M9 ..... 67 C1
Crossfield Dr SWIN M27 ..... 58 A4
Crossford Br SALE M33 ..... 124 A2
Crossford St STRET M32 ..... 114 B4
Crosshill Cl OLDTF/WHR M16 ..... 36 A3
Cross Keys St ANC M4 ..... 7 E5
Crossland Rd CCHDY M21 ..... 126 A1
  DROY M43 ..... 98 A3
Crosslands PWCH M25 ..... 62 A2 ¹
Cross La DROY M43 ..... 99 D1
  GTN M18 ..... 106 B4
  SALQ/ORD M5 ..... 13 E1
Crossley Ct ANC M4 ..... 19 D2 ²
Crossley Rd BNG/LEV M19 ..... 132 A2
  SALE M33 ..... 123 C3
Crossley St GTN M18 ..... 31 F5
Cross Rd CCHDY M21 ..... 126 B2
Cross St CMANW M2 ..... 16 B2
  CSLFD M3 ..... 15 F1
  OLDTF/WHR M16 ..... 34 C1
  SALE M33 ..... 123 D3
  STRET M32 ..... 114 B3
  SWIN M27 ..... 60 B3
  URM M41 ..... 111 C4
  WALK M28 ..... 75 C2
Croughton Cl OP/CLY M11 ..... 106 B2 ²
Crowcroft Rd BRUN/LGST M13 ..... 40 C5
Crowden Rd NEWH/MOS M40 ..... 68 B3
Crowley Rd BKLY M9 ..... 85 D1
Crownhill Dr DROY M43 ..... 98 A3
Crown La ANC M4 ..... 7 D4
Crown Point Av NEWH/MOS M40 .. 87 C4 ⁸
Crown Sq CSLFD M3 ..... 15 F3
Crown St CSLFD M3 ..... 5 F5
  FAIL M35 ..... 88 B1
  HULME M15 ..... 25 E1
  MPL/ROM SK6 ..... 141 D1 ²
  NEWH/MOS M40 ..... 87 C4
Crowther Av SALQ/ORD M5 ..... 13 D4
Crowther St GTN M18 ..... 106 B4 ⁸
Crowthorn Rd HTNM SK4 ..... 133 D2
Croydon Dr NEWH/MOS M40 ..... 11 F2
Crumpsall La CHH M8 ..... 64 B4
Crumpsall V BKLY M9 ..... 66 A3
Crumpsall Wy CHH M8 ..... 65 D4 ¹
Cryer St DROY M43 ..... 99 C1
Cubley Rd BRO M7 ..... 82 A1
Cuddington Av DID/WITH M20 .. 129 C1 ²
Culand St WGTN/LGST M12 ..... 29 F4
Culcheth La NEWH/MOS M40 ..... 87 C4
Culford Cl WGTN/LGST M12 ..... 29 F5 ⁴
Cullen Gv BKLY M9 ..... 67 C2
Culmington Cl HULME M15 ..... 25 E5

Culross Av *NEWH/MOS* M40 .... 70 A4 🔢
Culverwell Dr *SALQ/ORD* M5 .... 13 E1
Cumberland Av *RDSH* SK5 .... 140 A1
SWIN M27 .... 58 B3
Cumberland Rd *BKLY* M9 .... 66 B4 🔢
URM M41 .... 111 C4
Cumberland St *BRO* M7 .... 4 C2
Cumbrae Gdns *SALQ/ORD* M5 .... 95 C4 🔢
Cumbrae Rd *BNG/LEV* M19 .... 116 A4 🔢
Cumbrian Cl *BRUN/LGST* M13 .... 28 A4 🔢
Cummings St *OLDS* OL8 .... 28 A3
Cunard Cl *BRUN/LGST* M13 .... 126 B3
Cundiff Rd *CCHDY* M21 .... 139 C4
Curate St *STKP* SK1 .... 75 C2
Curtels Cl *WALK* M28 .... 75 C2
Curtis Rd *BNG/LEV* M19 .... 116 A4
Curzon Av *RUSH/FAL* M14 .... 39 E3
Curzon Rd *BRO* M7 .... 81 D2
SALE M33 .... 123 D4 🔢
STRET M32 .... 113 C2
Curzon St *OLD* OL1 .... 55 D2
Cuthbert Av *BNG/LEV* M19 .... 51 E2
Cutland St *NEWH/MOS* M40 .... 86 A3
Cycle St *OP/CLY* M11 .... 21 E4
Cyclone St *OP/CLY* M11 .... 20 A4
Cygnus Av *BRO* M7 .... 4 B3
Cymbal St *RDSH* SK5 .... 53 D1
Cypress Av *CHAD* OL9 .... 98 A2
Cypress Rd *DROY* M43 .... 90 A1
ECC M30 .... 110 A2
Cyprus Cl *SALQ/ORD* M5 .... 12 B2
Cyprus St *STRET* M32 .... 114 B3
Cyril St *RUSH/FAL* M14 .... 37 E4
Cyrus St *NEWH/MOS* M40 .... 19 D1

D

Daccamill Dr *SWIN* M27 .... 76 B3
Dacre Av *CCHDY* M21 .... 43 F2
Dagenham Rd *RUSH/FAL* M14 .... 126 B3
Dagnall Av *CCHDY* M21 .... 83 C3
Daimler St *CHH* M8 .... 29 D1 🔢
Dainton St *WGTN/LGST* M12 .... 29 D1 🔢
Daintry Cl *HULME* M15 .... 26 A3 🔢
Daintry Rd *CHAD* OL9 .... 54 A2
Dairy St *CHAD* OL9 .... 53 D2
Daisy Av *BRUN/LGST* M13 .... 39 F2
Daisy Bank *NEWH/MOS* M40 .... 87 C4
Daisy Bank Av *SLFD* M6 .... 78 A3
Daisy Bank Rd *RUSH/FAL* M14 .... 38 C3
Daisy St *CHAD* OL9 .... 53 C1
CHAD OL9 .... 54 B2
Dakerwood Cl *NEWH/MOS* M40 .... 87 C4 🔢
Dakley St *OP/CLY* M11 .... 106 A2 🔢
Dakota Av *SALQ/ORD* M5 .... 105 C1
Dakota South *SALQ/ORD* M5 .... 12 A4
Dalbeattie St *BKLY* M9 .... 67 C2
Dalberg St *WGTN/LGST* M12 .... 28 C2
Dalbury Dr *NEWH/MOS* M40 .... 84 A4
Dalby Av *SWIN* M27 .... 76 A2 🔢
Dalby Gv *STKP* SK1 .... 139 C4
Dale Av *ECC* M30 .... 91 C2
Dales Av *CHH* M8 .... 64 B3
Dales Brow *SWIN* M27 .... 76 A3 🔢
Dales Park Dr *SWIN* M27 .... 75 D3 🔢
Dale St *CMANE* M1 .... 17 E2
SWIN M27 .... 76 A3 🔢
Dalham Av *BKLY* M9 .... 68 A3
Dalkeith Rd *RDSH* SK5 .... 134 B2 🔢
Dalkeith St *GTN* M18 .... 31 F4
Dallas Ct *SALQ/ORD* M5 .... 105 C1

Dalley Av *BRO* M7 .... 4 C2
Dalmahoy Cl *NEWH/MOS* M40 .... 87 C1
Dalmain Cl *CHH* M8 .... 82 B3 🔢
Dalmorton Rd *CCHDY* M21 .... 127 D1
Dalny St *BNG/LEV* M19 .... 51 E4
Dalston Av *FAIL* M35 .... 89 D1
Dalton Av *RUSH/FAL* M14 .... 47 D1
STRET M32 .... 112 B1
Dalton Dr *SWIN* M27 .... 78 B2
Dalton Gdns *URM* M41 .... 110 B2 🔢
Dalton St *ANC* M4 .... 7 F3
CHAD OL9 .... 53 D2
ECC M30 .... 91 D2
FAIL M35 .... 88 A1
SALE M33 .... 124 A3 🔢
Dalveen Av *URM* M41 .... 111 C1
Damask Av *CSLFD* M3 .... 4 C5
Dameral Cl *CHH* M8 .... 54 B1
Dame St *CHAD* OL9 .... 54 B1
Dam Head Dr *BKLY* M9 .... 67 C2
Damien St *BNG/LEV* M19 .... 51 E2
Danebank Ms *DTN/ASHW* M34 .... 118 B3
Danebank Wk *BRUN/LGST* M13 .... 27 F2 🔢
Danecroft Cl *BRUN/LGST* M13 .... 28 C5
Danefield Rd *SALE* M33 .... 124 A3
Daneholme Rd *BNG/LEV* M19 .... 131 C4
Dane Rd *DTN/ASHW* M34 .... 118 A3
SALE M33 .... 124 A3
Danesmoor Rd *DID/WITH* M20 .... 129 C4
Danes Rd *RUSH/FAL* M14 .... 48 C1
Dane St *OP/CLY* M11 .... 107 C2
Danesway *PWCH* M25 .... 63 D3
SWIN M27 .... 78 A3
Daneswood Av *BKLY* M9 .... 67 D3 🔢
Danett Cl *WGTN/LGST* M12 .... 55 C2 🔢
Dan Fold *OLD* OL1 .... 132 B1 🔢
Danforth Gv *BNG/LEV* M19 .... 132 B1 🔢
Daniel Adamson Rd *SALQ/ORD* M5 .. 104 B1
Daniel's La *STKP* SK1 .... 138 B3 🔢
Danson St *NEWH/MOS* M40 .... 9 E4
Dantall Av *BKLY* M9 .... 68 A2
Dante Cl *SLFD* M6 .... 93 C1
Dantzic St *ANC* M4 .... 7 D4
Dapple Gv *OP/CLY* M11 .... 20 C4
Darenth Cl *HULME* M15 .... 26 A4 🔢
Daresbury Rd *CCHDY* M21 .... 42 B4
Daresbury St *CHH* M8 .... 83 C2 🔢
Dargai St *OP/CLY* M11 .... 96 B4
Dargle Rd *SALE* M33 .... 123 D3
Dark La *WGTN/LGST* M12 .... 127 C3
Darley Av *CCHDY* M21 .... 101 C1 🔢
ECC M30 .... 33 F5
Darley Rd *OLDTF/WHR* M16 .... 19 F2
Darley St *OP/CLY* M11 .... 114 B1
STRET M32 .... 114 B1
Darlington Rd *DID/WITH* M20 .... 129 C3
Darnall Av *DID/WITH* M20 .... 129 C1
Darncombe Cl *OLDTF/WHR* M16 .... 36 A2
Darnley Av *SLFD* M6 .... 34 C2
Darnley St *OLDTF/WHR* M16 .... 34 C2
Darras Rd *GTN* M18 .... 116 A2
Dart Cl *CHAD* OL9 .... 52 B1
Dartford Av *ECC* M30 .... 90 B3
RDSH SK5 .... 135 C3
Dartford Cl *WGTN/LGST* M12 .... 29 D4
Dartford Rd *URM* M41 .... 111 C4
Dartmouth Cl *OLDS* OL8 .... 73 D1 🔢
Dartmouth Crs *RDSH* SK5 .... 136 A4 🔢
Dartmouth Rd *CCHDY* M21 .... 127 C1
Darton Av *NEWH/MOS* M40 .... 9 D4
Darwell Av *ECC* M30 .... 101 C1
Darwen St *OLDTF/WHR* M16 .... 1 D4
Dauntesy Av *SWIN* M27 .... 78 B2 🔢
Davenham Rd *RDSH* SK5 .... 117 D3

SALE M33 .... 122 A3
Davenhill Rd BNG/LEV M19 .... 132 A1
Davenport Av DID/WITH M20 ...... 129 D2
Davenport St DROY M43 .... 97 C4 🔢
Daventry Rd CCHDY M21 .... 45 D5
David's Rd DROY M43 .... 97 C3
David St RDSH SK5 .... 134 A1
Davies Rd MPL/ROM SK6 .... 140 B2 🔢
Davies St OLD OL1 .... 54 B1
Davis St ECC M30 .... 92 A4
Davy Av SWIN M27 .... 60 B3
Davyhulme Rd STRET M32 .... 114 A2
Davyhulme Rd East STRET M32 ... 114 B3
Davy St NEWH/MOS M40 .... 7 F2
Dawlish Av DROY M43 .... 97 C3
    RDSH SK5 .... 135 D4
Dawlish Rd CCHDY M21 .... 127 C1
    SALE M33 .... 122 A4
Dawnay St OP/CLY M11 .... 31 E1 🔢
Dawson St CSLFD M3 .... 6 A5 🔢
    CSLFD M3 .... 14 C5
    STKP SK1 .... 139 D2 🔢
    SWIN M27 .... 77 D1 🔢
Day Dr FAIL M35 .... 88 B3
Deacons Cl STKP SK1 .... 139 C4
Deacons Dr SLFD M6 .... 78 B3
Deal Av RDSH SK5 .... 135 D3
Deal Cl NEWH/MOS M40 .... 87 D4 🔢
Deal St CSLFD M3 .... 15 F1 🔢
    OLDTF/WHR M16 .... 33 F4
Deanbank Av BNG/LEV M19 .... 50 B5
Dean Brook Cl NEWH/MOS M40 ... 86 B2 🔢
Deanery Wy STKP SK1 .... 138 B3 🔢
Dean La NEWH/MOS M40 .... 86 B3
Dean Rd CSLFD M3 .... 5 F4
    GTN M18 .... 117 C1
Deanscourt Av SWIN M27 .... 76 A2
Deansgate CSLFD M3 .... 15 F4
    HULME M15 .... 25 F1
Deans Rd SWIN M27 .... 76 A2
Dean St CMANE M1 .... 17 F2
    FAIL M35 .... 88 A2
Deansway SWIN M27 .... 88 A2
Deanwater Cl BRUN/LGST M13 ..... 76 A2
Deanway NEWH/MOS M40 .... 86 A1
Dearmans Pl CSLFD M3 .... 15 F1
Dearne Dr STRET M32 .... 115 C3
Debdale La GTN M18 .... 117 D1
Debenham Av NEWH/MOS M40 .... 96 A1
Debenham Rd STRET M32 .... 113 C4
Deepcar St OP/CLY M11 .... 46 C5
Deepdale Av DID/WITH M20 .... 46 C5
Deepdale Cl RDSH SK5 .... 117 C4
Deepdale Dr SWIN M27 .... 78 B2
Deepdene St WGTN/LGST M12 .... 30 B4 🔢
Deeping Av OLDTF/WHR M16 .... 44 C1
Deerfold Cl GTN M18 .... 106 B4 🔢
Deerhurst Dr CHH M8 .... 82 B3
Deeroak Cl GTN M18 .... 31 F4
Deerpark Rd OLDTF/WHR M16 ..... 35 E4
Deer St CMANE M1 .... 18 A4
Deganwy Gv RDSH SK5 .... 134 B4 🔢
Deighton Av DID/WITH M20 .... 129 C1 🔢
Delacourt Rd RUSH/FAL M14 ..... 129 C1
Delafield Av WGTN/LGST M12 ...... 51 D1
Delahays Range GTN M18 .... 117 D1 🔢
Delaine Rd DID/WITH M20 .... 130 A3
Delamere Av SLFD M6 .... 78 A3
    STRET M32 .... 114 B3
    SWIN M27 .... 59 D2
Delamere Rd BNG/LEV M19 .... 51 E5
    DTN/ASHW M34 .... 118 B3

Delamere St OP/CLY M11 .... 107 D2 🔢
Delaunays Rd CHH M8 .... 65 D3
Dell Av SWIN M27 .... 78 B2
Dellcot Cl PWCH M25 .... 63 D3 🔢
    SLFD M6 .... 77 D4
Dell Side MPL/ROM SK6 .... 141 C2
Delside Av NEWH/MOS M40 .... 86 A1 🔢
Demesne Rd OLDTF/WHR M16 ..... 45 E2
Denbigh Pl SALQ/ORD M5 .... 13 D1
Denbigh Rd SWIN M27 .... 59 C3
Denbigh St OLDS OL8 .... 73 D2 🔢
Dencombe St BRUN/LGST M13 ..... 40 A3
Dene Hollow RDSH SK5 .... 118 A4
Denehurst St WGTN/LGST M12 .... 30 A3
Denewell Cl BRUN/LGST M13 .... 28 C5
Denham St BRUN/LGST M13 .... 39 D2
Denhill Rd HULME M15 .... 35 F1 🔢
Denis Av OLDTF/WHR M16 .... 45 E2
Denison Rd RUSH/FAL M14 .... 38 B4
Denison St RUSH/FAL M14 .... 38 A4 🔢
Deniston Rd HTNM SK4 .... 132 B4
Denmark Rd HULME M15 .... 36 C1
    SALE M33 .... 123 D3 🔢
Denmark St CHAD OL9 .... 54 A1
Denmark Wy CHAD OL9 .... 54 A1
Denmore Rd NEWH/MOS M40 ...... 69 C2
Dennington Dr URM M41 .... 111 C1
Dennison Av DID/WITH M20 .... 129 D2
Denshaw Av DTN/ASHW M34 ..... 109 D4
Densmore St FAIL M35 .... 88 A2 🔢
Denstone Av ECC M30 .... 92 A2
    URM M41 .... 111 C2
Denstone Rd RDSH SK5 .... 117 D4 🔢
    SLFD M6 .... 78 B4
    URM M41 .... 111 C2
Denton La CHAD OL9 .... 53 C4
Denver Av NEWH/MOS M40 .... 9 D3
Deramore St RUSH/FAL M14 .... 37 E4
Derby Av SLFD M6 .... 95 C3 🔢
Derby Ct CHAD OL9 .... 54 A4 🔢
Derby Gv BNG/LEV M19 .... 51 E3
Derby Rd RUSH/FAL M14 .... 130 A2 🔢
    SALE M33 .... 122 A3 🔢
    SLFD M6 .... 95 C3
    URM M41 .... 111 D2
Derbyshire Av STRET M32 .... 113 D2
Derbyshire Crs STRET M32 .... 113 D2
Derbyshire Gv STRET M32 .... 113 D2 🔢
Derbyshire La STRET M32 .... 114 A3
Derbyshire La West URM M41 ..... 113 C2
Derbyshire Rd NEWH/MOS M40 .... 96 B1
Derbyshire St OP/CLY M11 .... 106 A2 🔢
Derby St CHAD OL9 .... 54 A4
    CHAD OL9 .... 71 D2
    CHH M8 .... 6 A1
    DTN/ASHW M34 .... 119 D1
    FAIL M35 .... 70 B4 🔢
    PWCH M25 .... 62 A1
Derg St SLFD M6 .... 12 A1
Dermot Murphy Cl
    DID/WITH M20 .... 128 B3 🔢
Dernford Av BNG/LEV M19 .... 131 D4
Derwent Av CCHDY M21 .... 127 C4
    DROY M43 .... 97 C4
Derwent Cl CCHDY M21 .... 127 C4
    DTN/ASHW M34 .... 118 B3
Derwent Dr CHAD OL9 .... 53 C2 🔢
Derwent Rd STRET M32 .... 114 B2 🔢
Derwent St CHH M8 .... 84 A5 🔢
    OP/CLY M11 .... 96 B4 🔢
    SALQ/ORD M5 .... 14 B5
Desford Av OLDTF/WHR M16 ...... 44 B3
Dettingen St SLFD M6 .... 79 C3

Devas St *HULME* M15.............. 27 E5
Deverill Av *GTN* M18 .... 117 D1 ⑤
Devine Cl *CSLFD* M3 .... 4 C5
Devon Av *BNG/LEV* M19 .... 131 D1
Devon Cl *RDSH* SK5 .... 140 A1 ⑤
   SLFD M6 .... 93 C2
Devon Rd *DROY* M43 .... 98 A2
   FAIL M35 .... 88 A3
Devonshire Cl *URM* M41 ...... 112 A3 ⑤
Devonshire Rd *CCHDY* M21 ... 127 C1
   ECC M30 .... 92 A3 ⑤
   SLFD M6 .... 93 C2
Devonshire St *BRO* M7 .... 82 A3
   WGTN/LGST M12 .... 28 C4
Devonshire St East *FAIL* M35 ..... 87 D4 ⑤
Devonshire St North
   WGTN/LGST M12 .... 29 D2
Devonshire St South
   BRUN/LGST M13 .... 28 C5
Devon St *CHAD* OL9 .... 71 D1
   SWIN M27 .... 58 B3
Devon Wy *OLDS* OL8 .... 72 A3
Dewar Cl *OP/CLY* M11 .... 20 C3
Dewes Av *SWIN* M27 .... 59 D3 ⑤
Dewey St *OP/CLY* M11 .... 106 B2
Dewhurst St *CHH* M8............... 6 A2
Dew Wy *CHAD* OL9 .... 54 B2
Deyne Av *PWCH* M25 .... 62 B1
   RUSH/FAL M14 .... 38 A3
Deyne St *SALQ/ORD* M5......... 95 C3
Dickenson Rd *RUSH/FAL* M14....... 38 C5
Dickens Rd *ECC* M30 .... 91 D4 ⑤
Dickinson St *CMANE* M1 .... 16 C4
   CMANW M2 .... 16 B4 ⑤
Didley Sq *WGTN/LGST* M12 ... 31 D2 ⑤
Dillon Dr *WGTN/LGST* M12....... 29 F5
Dilston Cl *BRUN/LGST* M13 ..... 28 B3
Dilworth St *HULME* M15 .... 37 E1
Dingle Dr *DROY* M43 .... 98 B2
Dinnington Dr *CHH* M8 .... 83 C3 ⑤
Dinorwic Cl *CHH* M8................ 65 C3
Dinsdale Cl *NEWH/MOS* M40 ... 9 D5
Dinting Av *DID/WITH* M20 .... 129 C2 ⑤
Dinton St *HULME* M15 .... 24 B2
Disley Av *DID/WITH* M20 ...... 128 B3
Dixon Av *BRO* M7 .... 81 D3
Dixon Dr *SWIN* M27 .... 58 A1
Dixon St *NEWH/MOS* M40 .... 86 B3 ⑤
   SLFD M6 .... 79 D3
Dobcross Cl *BRUN/LGST* M13 .... 50 C1 ⑤
Dobroyd St *CHH* M8................ 83 C1
Dobson Cl *BRUN/LGST* M13....... 28 C4
Doddington Cl *OLDTF/WHR* M16 ..... 36 A3
Doddington La *SALQ/ORD* M5 .... 13 D4
Dodd St *SALQ/ORD* M5 .... 94 B3
Dodge HI *HTNM* SK4............. 138 A3
Dodworth Cl *HULME* M15 ...... 26 A4 ⑤
Doe Brow *SWIN* M27 .... 58 A1 ⑤
Dolbey St *SALQ/ORD* M5 ...... 95 C4 ⑤
Dolefield *CSLFD* M3 .... 15 F3
Dollond St *BKLY* M9 .... 67 C4
Dolphin PI *WGTN/LGST* M12 ... 28 B2
Dolphin St *WGTN/LGST* M12 ... 28 B2
Domett St *BKLY* M9 .... 66 A3
Donald St *CMANE* M1 .... 17 D5 ⑤
Don Av *SLFD* M6 .... 94 A3
Doncaster Av *DID/WITH* M20 ... 129 C2
Donleigh St *NEWH/MOS* M40 ... 87 D3
Donnington Rd *GTN* M18 ...... 107 C4 ⑤
Donnison St *WGTN/LGST* M12 ... 30 B4 ⑤
Donovan Av *NEWH/MOS* M40 ... 8 B1
Dorchester Av *PWCH* M25 ...... 63 C3
   URM M41 .... 112 B2 ⑤

Dorchester Rd *SWIN* M27 .... 76 B3
Dorclyn Av *URM* M41 .... 111 D3 ⑥
Dorfield Cl *MPL/ROM* SK6 .... 141 C2 ②
Doric Av *MPL/ROM* SK6 .... 140 B2
Doric Cl *OP/CLY* M11 .... 20 A3
Dorlan Av *GTN* M18 .... 117 D1
Dorman St *OP/CLY* M11 ...... 106 B2 ⑤
Dorney St *GTN* M18 .... 106 B4
Dorning Rd *SWIN* M27 .... 77 C2
Dorning St *ECC* M30 .... 91 D4 ⑤
Dorothy St *BRO* M7 .... 82 B2 ⑤
Dorris St *BNG/LEV* M19 .... 132 B1
Dorset Av *DTN/ASHW* M34 .... 109 C1
   RDSH SK5 .... 136 A4
   RUSH/FAL M14..................... 47 D2
Dorset Rd *BNG/LEV* M19 ...... 116 A4
   DROY M43 .... 97 D2 ②
   FAIL M35 .... 88 B4
Dorset St *CHAD* OL9 .... 54 A4
   STRET M32 .... 114 B4 ⑤
   SWIN M27 .... 58 B3
Dorsey St *ANC* M4 .... 17 E1 ⑥
Dorstone Cl *NEWH/MOS* M40....... 96 A1
Doughty Av *ECC* M30 .... 92 B2 ⑤
Douglas Av *STRET* M32 ...... 114 B2 ⑤
Douglas Gn *SLFD* M6 .... 80 A4
Douglas Rd *SWIN* M27 .... 75 C2
Douglas St *BRO* M7 .... 81 D3
   FAIL M35 .... 89 C2
   NEWH/MOS M40 .... 86 A2 ②
   SWIN M27 .... 77 C2
Doulton St *NEWH/MOS* M40 ... 87 C1 ⑤
Dounby Av *ECC* M30 .... 90 B2 ⑤
Douro St *NEWH/MOS* M40 ...... 85 D4
Dovecote *DROY* M43 .... 99 D2
Dovecote Ms *CCHDY* M21 .... 126 A1 ②
Dovedale Av *DID/WITH* M20 ... 129 C2
   DROY M43 .... 97 C3 ⑤
   ECC M30 .... 92 A2
   PWCH M25 .... 63 D2
   URM M41 .... 111 D3 ⑤
Dovedale Cl *FAIL* M35 .... 88 A2
Doveleys Rd *SLFD* M6 .... 79 C4 ⑤
Doveridge Gdns *SLFD* M6 ...... 2 B3 ⑤
Dover Pk *URM* M41 .... 111 D1
Dover Rd *SWIN* M27 .... 59 C3
Dover St *BRUN/LGST* M13 ...... 27 E4
   CHAD OL9 .... 54 A4 ⑤
   ECC M30 .... 90 B3
   RDSH SK5 .... 134 A2 ⑤
Dovestone Wk *NEWH/MOS* M40 ... 70 A4 ⑤
Doveston Rd *SALE* M33 .... 123 D3
Downfields *RDSH* SK5 .... 118 A4 ⑤
Downham Crs *PWCH* M25....... 63 D2
Downham Gdns *PWCH* M25 ..... 64 A2
Downham Rd *HTNM* SK4........ 133 D4
Downing St *CMANE* M1 .... 27 F1
Downley Dr *ANC* M4 .... 18 B1
The Downs *PWCH* M25 .... 62 A2
Dowry St *OLDS* OL8 .... 73 D2
Doyle Av *MPL/ROM* SK6 .... 140 B2
Drake Cl *OLD* OL1 .... 55 C1
Drake Ct *RDSH* SK5 .... 138 A1 ⑤
Drayfields *DROY* M43 .... 99 D3
Dresden St *NEWH/MOS* M40 ... 87 C1
Drewett St *NEWH/MOS* M40 ... 9 F2
Dreyfus Av *OP/CLY* M11 .... 96 A3
Driffield St *ECC* M30 .... 101 C1 ⑤
   RUSH/FAL M14..................... 36 C5
Drinkwater Rd *PWCH* M25 ..... 61 D4 ⑤
Driscoll St *BRUN/LGST* M13....... 40 B5
The Drive *BRO* M7 .... 63 C4
   MPL/ROM SK6 .... 140 B2

E

East Rd *CTN* M18 .... **41** F4
  STRET M32 .... **113** D1
  WGTN/LGST M12 .... **41** D5
Eastry Av *RDSH* SK5 .... **135** D3 🔢
East Union St *OLDTF/WHR* M16 ...... **24** B4
Eastville Gdns *BNG/LEV* M19 .... **131** C4 🔢
Eastwood Av *DROY* M43 .... **97** C4
  NEWH/MOS M40 .... **70** B4 🔢
  URM M41 .... **111** D3
Eastwood Rd *NEWH/MOS* M40 .... **70** B4
Eastwood St *DTN/ASHW* M34 ...... **109** D2 🔢
Eaton Rd *CHH* M8 .... **64** B4
Eaves La *CHAD* OL9 .... **53** C4
Ebberstone St *RUSH/FAL* M14 .... **47** D1
Ebden St *CMANE* M1 .... **17** E5 🔢
Ebenezer St *HULME* M15 .... **26** B2 🔢
Ebsworth St *NEWH/MOS* M40 .... **85** D1
Eccles Cl *OP/CLY* M11 .... **106** A1
Eccleshall St *OP/CLY* M11 .... **96** A4
Eccles New Rd *SALQ/ORD* M5 .... **93** D3
Eccles Old Rd *SLFD* M6 .... **2** A2
Eccles Rd *SWIN* M27 .... **76** B3
Eccleston Av *RUSH/FAL* M14 .... **47** E3
  SWIN M27 .... **75** D2 🔢
Eccleston St *FAIL* M35 .... **89** C1 🔢
Echo St *CMANE* M1 .... **17** E5
Eckford St *CHH* M8 .... **83** D3
Edale Av *DTN/ASHW* M34 .... **109** D2
  DTN/ASHW M34 .... **137** D1
  NEWH/MOS M40 .... **86** A1
  RDSH SK5 .... **118** A4
  URM M41 .... **110** B4
Edale Rd *STRET* M32 .... **113** D2
Edale St *SLFD* M6 .... **80** B4 🔢
Eddie Colman Cl *NEWH/MOS* M40 .. **86** B4 🔢
Eddisbury Av *DID/WITH* M20 .... **128** B1
Edenbridge Rd *NEWH/MOS* M40 .... **11** E1
Eden Cl *HULME* M15 .... **26** C4
Edenfield Rd *PWCH* M25 .... **64** A2
Edenhall Av *BNG/LEV* M19 .... **50** A3
Eden St *OLD* OL1 .... **55** C2
Edgbaston Dr *OLDTF/WHR* M16 ...... **32** C4
Edgedale Av *BNG/LEV* M19 .... **131** C4 🔢
Edgefield Av *BKLY* M9 .... **67** C3
Edgehill Cl *SALQ/ORD* M5 .... **2** B5
Edgehill Rd *SLFD* M6 .... **94** A2
Edgehill St *ANC* M4 .... **17** D1 🔢
Edge La *OP/CLY* M11 .... **96** B3
  STRET M32 .... **42** A4
Edge Lane Rd *OLD* OL1 .... **55** D1
Edgeley Rd *URM* M41 .... **120** A1
Edge St *ANC* M4 .... **17** D1
Edgeware Av *PWCH* M25 .... **64** B1
Edgeware Rd *CHAD* OL9 .... **70** A2 🔢
  ECC M30 .... **90** A1 🔢
Edgewater St *SALQ/ORD* M5 .... **94** B3 🔢
Edgeworth Dr *RUSH/FAL* M14 ...... **131** C3
Edgware Rd *NEWH/MOS* M40 .... **11** E2
Edilom Rd *CHH* M8 .... **64** A3
Edison Rd *ECC* M30 .... **101** C1
Edison St *OP/CLY* M11 .... **107** C2 🔢
Edith Av *RUSH/FAL* M14 .... **36** C3
Edith Cavell Cl *OP/CLY* M11 .... **96** A4
Edith St *OLDS* OL8 .... **73** D2
Edlin Cl *WGTN/LGST* M12 .... **29** F5
Edmonton Rd *NEWH/MOS* M40 .... **11** D1
Edmund Cl *HTNM* SK4 .... **138** A2 🔢
Edmund St *CSLFD* M3 .... **15** E1 🔢
  DROY M43 .... **108** A1
  FAIL M35 .... **88** B1 🔢
  SLFD M6 .... **95** C2
Edson Rd *CHH* M8 .... **64** B2 🔢
Edward Av *CCHDY* M21 .... **125** D2

MPL/ROM SK6 .... **141** C2
SLFD M6 .... **94** A2
Edward Charlton Rd
  OLDTF/WHR M16 .... **43** D1
Edward St *BKLY* M9 .... **85** C1
  BRO M7 .... **5** F2
  CHAD OL9 .... **53** C2
  CHAD OL9 .... **54** A3
  DROY M43 .... **108** A1 🔢
  DTN/ASHW M34 .... **109** D2
Edward Sutcliffe Cl *RUSH/FAL* M14... **47** D2
Edwin Rd *OP/CLY* M11 .... **19** F2
Eeasbrook *URM* M41 .... **111** D4
Egbert St *NEWH/MOS* M40 .... **86** B2
Egerton Crs *DID/WITH* M20 .... **129** D2 🔢
Egerton Dr *SALE* M33 .... **123** D4 🔢
Egerton Ms *RUSH/FAL* M14 .... **130** B3 🔢
Egerton Pk *WALK* M28 .... **74** B2
Egerton Rd *ECC* M30 .... **91** D1
  RUSH/FAL M14 .... **130** B1
Egerton Rd North *CCHDY* M21 .... **44** A2
  HTNM SK4 .... **133** C4
  OLDTF/WHR M16 .... **44** A1
Egerton Rd South *CCHDY* M21 .... **44** A5
  HTNM SK4 .... **133** C4
Egerton St *CSLFD* M3 .... **15** D2
  DROY M43 .... **98** B3
  DTN/ASHW M34 .... **109** D2
  ECC M30 .... **90** B3 🔢
  HULME M15 .... **25** D1 🔢
  PWCH M25 .... **63** C1 🔢
Egerton Ter *RUSH/FAL* M14 .... **130** B2 🔢
Eggington St *NEWH/MOS* M40 .... **84** A1
Egmont St *CHH* M8 .... **83** C1
  SLFD M6 .... **79** C3
Eida Wy *TRPK* M17 .... **104** A1
Eighth Av *OLDS* OL8 .... **72** B4
Eighth St *TRPK* M17 .... **104** B3 🔢
Eileen Gv *RUSH/FAL* M14 .... **48** A1
Eileen Gv West *RUSH/FAL* M14 ...... **47** F1
Elaine Av *BKLY* M9 .... **68** B3 🔢
Elbe St *WGTN/LGST* M12 .... **18** B5 🔢
Elbow St *BNG/LEV* M19 .... **51** D4
Elcot Cl *NEWH/MOS* M40 .... **84** A1 🔢
Elderfield Dr *MPL/ROM* SK6 .... **141** D1 🔢
Elder Gv *NEWH/MOS* M40 .... **70** B3 🔢
Eldermount Rd *BKLY* M9.................. **66** B3
Elderwood *CHAD* OL9 .... **52** A2 🔢
Eldon Pl *ECC* M30 .... **91** C4
Eldon St *OLDS* OL8 .... **55** D4
Eldridge Dr *NEWH/MOS* M40 .... **86** A4
Eleanor Rd *CCHDY* M21 .... **126** A1 🔢
Eleanor St *OLD* OL1 .... **54** B1
Electo St *OP/CLY* M11 .... **107** C2 🔢
Elevator Rd *TRPK* M17 .... **105** C3
Eleventh St *TRPK* M17 .... **104** B3
Elford Gv *GTN* M18 .... **118** A1
Elgar St *WGTN/LGST* M12 .... **41** D3
Eliot Rd *ECC* M30 .... **91** D4 🔢
Eli St *CHAD* OL9 .... **71** C2 🔢
Eliza Ann St *ECC* M30 .... **91** C4 🔢
  NEWH/MOS M40 .... **8** B1
Elizabeth Av *CHAD* OL9 .... **71** C2 🔢
Elizabeth Ct *RUSH/FAL* M14 .... **130** B3 🔢
Elizabeth St *CHH* M8 .... **82** B3
  DTN/ASHW M34 .... **119** D1
  SWIN M27 .... **58** B4
Eliza St *HULME* M15 .... **25** E3
Elkanagh Gdns *SLFD* M6 .... **2** A3
Ellanby Cl *RUSH/FAL* M14 .... **37** F5
Ellaston Dr *URM* M41 .... **111** D3 🔢
Ellastone Rd *SLFD* M6 .... **94** A1
Ellbourne Rd *BKLY* M9...................... **65** C2

Ellenbrook Cl *WGTN/LGST* M12 .... 31 E3
Ellen Gv *FWTH* BL4 .... 57 C1
Ellenhall Cl *BKLY* M9 .... 84 B1 **3**
Ellen St *CHAD* OL9 .... 54 B1
   DROY M43 .... 108 B1
Ellen Wilkinson Crs
   WGTN/LGST M12 .... 41 D1
Elleray Rd *SLFD* M6 .... 78 B4
Ellerby Av *SWIN* M27 .... 59 C2
Ellesmere Av *ECC* M30 .... 92 A3 **3**
Ellesmere Rd *CCHDY* M21 .... 44 A4
   ECC M30 .... 92 A1
Ellesmere Rd North *HTNM* SK4 ...... 133 C4
Ellesmere Rd South *CCHDY* M21 ..... 44 A4
Ellesmere St *ECC* M30 .... 91 D4 **6**
   FAIL M35 .... 88 B1 **3**
   HULME M15 .... 24 B2
   SWIN M27 .... 59 C4 **1**
   SWIN M27 .... 75 D2
Ellesmere Ter *RUSH/FAL* M14 .... 130 B2 **2**
Ellis St *BRO* M7 .... 5 E1
   HULME M15 .... 25 F4
Ellor St *SLFD* M6 .... 2 B4
Ellwood Rd *STKP* SK1 .... 139 C4 **3**
Elm Crs *WALK* M28 .... 74 A2
Elm Dr *DTN/ASHW* M34 .... 109 D4
   STRET M32 .... 113 D4
Elmfield Rd *DTN/ASHW* M34 .... 109 C1
Elmfield St *CHH* M8 .... 83 C3
Elmgate Gv *BNG/LEV* M19 .... 50 C4
Elm Gv *DROY* M43 .... 96 B3
   SALE M33 .... 123 C3
   URM M41 .... 112 A3
   WALK M28 .... 56 B4
Elmhurst Dr *BNG/LEV* M19 .... 131 D4
Elm Rd *OLDS* OL8 .... 72 B4
Elms Rd *HTNM* SK4 .... 132 B4
Elmstead Av *DID/WITH* M20 .... 129 C3
Elm St *ECC* M30 .... 91 D4 **7**
   FAIL M35 .... 88 B1
   MPL/ROM SK6 .... 141 D1
   SWIN M27 .... 58 A4 **4**
Elmswood Av *RUSH/FAL* M14 .... 46 B1
Elmsworth Av *BNG/LEV* M19 .... 51 F4
Elmton Rd *BKLY* M9 .... 67 C2 **1**
Elm Tree Cl *FAIL* M35 .... 89 D2
Elm Tree Rd *MPL/ROM* SK6 .... 140 D2
Elmwood Gv *BKLY* M9 .... 85 D2 **3**
Elsa Rd *BNG/LEV* M19 .... 116 A3 **3**
Elsdon Dr *GTN* M18 .... 106 B3
Elsdon Rd *BRUN/LGST* M13 .... 50 A1
Elsham Gdns *GTN* M18 .... 41 D2
Elsie St *BKLY* M9 .... 85 C1 **3**
Elsinore Cl *FAIL* M35 .... 89 D2 **2**
Elsinore Rd *OLDTF/WHR* M16 .... 33 D3
Elsma Rd *NEWH/MOS* M40 .... 97 C1 **1**
Elsmore Rd *RUSH/FAL* M14 .... 46 C4
Elstree Av *NEWH/MOS* M40 .... 11 F1
Elsworth Cl *CSLFD* M3 .... 6 C3
Eltham Dr *URM* M41 .... 111 C1
Eltham St *BNG/LEV* M19 .... 51 D2
Elton Av *BNG/LEV* M19 .... 132 A3
Elton St *BRO* M7 .... 5 D3
   STRET M32 .... 32 B1
Elton's Yd *BRO* M7 .... 5 D3 **3**
Elvate Crs *CHH* M8 .... 82 B4 **3**
Elverdon Cl *HULME* M15 .... 25 F5
Elvey St *NEWH/MOS* M40 .... 85 D4
Elwick Cl *OLDTF/WHR* M16 .... 36 A4
Ely Av *STRET* M32 .... 112 B2
Ely Crs *FAIL* M35 .... 88 B4
Elysian St *OP/CLY* M11 .... 106 A1
Ely St *CHAD* OL9 .... 53 D4 **2**

Emaline Gra *SLFD* M6 .... 95 C3 **6**
Ember St *OP/CLY* M11 .... 96 B3 **1**
Emerson Av *ECC* M30 .... 93 C2 **3**
Emerson St *SALQ/ORD* M5 .... 94 B3
Emery Av *CCHDY* M21 .... 127 C3
Emily Beavan Cl *OP/CLY* M11 .... 21 F3
Emily Pl *DROY* M43 .... 97 D4 **3**
Emley St *BNG/LEV* M19 .... 51 E3
Emlyn St *SWIN* M27 .... 75 D1 **3**
Emma St *OLDS* OL8 .... 73 D2 **3**
Emmett St East *NEWH/MOS* M40 ...... 85 C4
Emmott St *OLD* OL1 .... 55 D3 **3**
Emperor St *STKP* SK1 .... 139 C3 **4**
Empire St *CSLFD* M3 .... 6 B2
Empress St *CHH* M8 .... 82 B1 **3**
   OLDTF/WHR M16 .... 24 A4
Enbridge St *SALQ/ORD* M5 .... 12 C4
Encombe Pl *CSLFD* M3 .... 14 C1 **3**
Endcott Cl *GTN* M18 .... 31 E4
Enderby Rd *NEWH/MOS* M40 .... 69 C4
Endon Dr *CCHDY* M21 .... 46 A5
Endsleigh Rd *DID/WITH* M20 .... 130 A3
Endsor Cl *OLDTF/WHR* M16 .... 36 A4
Enfield Av *BNG/LEV* M19 .... 132 A3
   OLDS OL8 .... 73 C2
Enfield Cl *ECC* M30 .... 101 D1
Enfield Dr *OP/CLY* M11 .... 96 A3 **3**
Enfield Rd *ECC* M30 .... 91 D1
   SWIN M27 .... 76 A3
Engell Cl *GTN* M18 .... 106 A4
Engine St *CHAD* OL9 .... 71 D1 **3**
Enid Cl *BRO* M7 .... 81 D4 **3**
Ennerdale Av *SWIN* M27 .... 76 B3 **3**
Ennerdale Dr *SALE* M33 .... 122 A4 **2**
Ennerdale Rd *STRET* M32 .... 114 A2 **3**
Ennismore Av *ECC* M30 .... 93 C3
Enstone Dr *NEWH/MOS* M40 .... 69 D3 **3**
Entwisle Av *URM* M41 .... 110 B1
Entwisle St *SWIN* M27 .... 57 D4
Enver Rd *CHH* M8 .... 83 D1
Enville Rd *NEWH/MOS* M40 .... 68 B4
   SLFD M6 .... 79 C3
Enville St *BKLY* M9 .... 66 B2 **3**
Epping Cl *CHAD* OL9 .... 52 A1
Epping Dr *SALE* M33 .... 121 C4
Epping Rd *DTN/ASHW* M34 .... 118 B3 **1**
Epping St *HULME* M15 .... 26 C4
Eppleworth Ri *SWIN* M27 .... 59 C2 **3**
Epsley Cl *HULME* M15 .... 26 C4
Epworth St *CMANE* M1 .... 18 B3 **1**
Ercall Av *WGTN/LGST* M12 .... 29 F3
Erica Cl *RDSH* SK5 .... 134 B1
Eric Brook Cl *RUSH/FAL* M14 .... 37 D4
Erin St *OP/CLY* M11 .... 107 C2 **3**
Erith Cl *RDSH* SK5 .... 135 D3
Erlington Av *OLDTF/WHR* M16 .... 33 E5
Ermen Rd *ECC* M30 .... 101 C1
Ermington Dr *CHH* M8 .... 82 B3 **7**
Erneley Cl *WGTN/LGST* M12 .... 41 E4
Ernest St *PWCH* M25 .... 61 D1
Ernocroft Gv *GTN* M18 .... 107 C3 **3**
Errington Dr *BRO* M7 .... 4 C2
Errwood Crs *BNG/LEV* M19 .... 132 A1 **2**
Errwood Rd *BNG/LEV* M19 .... 132 A2
Erskine St *HULME* M15 .... 25 D4
Erwin St *NEWH/MOS* M40 .... 86 B3 **3**
Erwood Rd *HTNM* SK4 .... 131 D4
Eryngo St *STKP* SK1 .... 139 C4 **3**
Esk Cl *URM* M41 .... 110 A1
Eskdale Av *DID/WITH* M20 .... 129 C2 **3**
   OLDS OL8 .... 72 B1
Eskrigge Cl *BRO* M7 .... 82 B1 **3**
Esmond Rd *CHH* M8 .... 83 C2 **3**

Essex Av *DROY* M43 .... **98** A2
Essex Cl *FAIL* M35 .... **88** B4
Essex Rd *GTN* M18 .... **117** D1 🇧
  RDSH SK5 .... **136** A4 🇧
Essex St *CMANW* M2 .... **16** B2 🇧
Essex Wy *HULME* M15 .... **25** D5
Estate St *OLDS* OL8 .... **73** D1
Estate St South *OLDS* OL8 .... **73** D1 🇧
Eston St *BRUN/LGST* M13 .... **39** D2
Eswick St *OP/CLY* M11 .... **96** A4 🇧
Etchells St *STKP* SK1 .... **138** B4 🇧
Etchell St *NEWH/MOS* M40 .... **84** A4 🇧
Ethel Av *SWIN* M27 .... **77** D1 🇧
Ethel St *OLDS* OL8 .... **73** D2
Ethel Ter *BNG/LEV* M19 .... **51** D4
Etherow Av *NEWH/MOS* M40 ..... **70** B3 🇧
Etherstone St *CHH* M8 .... **84** A1
Eton Av *OLDS* OL8 .... **73** C1
Eton Cl *OLDTF/WHR* M16 .... **35** D1
Etruria Cl *BRUN/LGST* M13 .... **29** E5
Ettrick Cl *OP/CLY* M11 .... **106** B2
Euclid Cl *OP/CLY* M11 .... **19** F3
Europa Ga *TRPK* M17 .... **104** B3
Europa Wy *TRPK* M17 .... **104** B4
Euston Av *BKLY* M9 .... **68** A2
Evans Rd *ECC* M30 .... **90** A4 🇧
Evans St *CSLFD* M3 .... **5** F4
  OLD OL1 .... **55** D1 🇧
Evan St *NEWH/MOS* M40 .... **85** C4 🇧
Eva St *RUSH/FAL* M14 .... **38** A5
Evelyn St *RUSH/FAL* M14 .... **49** D5
Evening St *FAIL* M35 .... **88** B1
Evenley Cl *GTN* M18 .... **107** C3 🇧
Everard St *SALQ/ORD* M5 .... **24** B1
Everleigh Dr *BRO* M7 .... **82** B3 🇧
Everton Rd *OLDS* OL8 .... **72** B1
  RDSH SK5 .... **117** D3 🇧
Everton St *SWIN* M27 .... **76** A1 🇧
Every St *ANC* M4 .... **18** C3
Evesham Rd *BKLY* M9 .... **68** A3
Eve St *OLDS* OL8 .... **73** D3 🇧
Ewan St *GTN* M18 .... **106** B3
Ewart St *SALQ/ORD* M5 .... **12** C2
Ewhurst Av *SWIN* M27 .... **75** D3 🇧
Ewing Cl *CHH* M8 .... **65** C4
Exbury St *RUSH/FAL* M14 .... **130** B2
Exchange Quay *SALQ/ORD* M5 ... **23** D4
Exchange St *EDGY/DAV* SK3 .... **138** A4
Exeter Av *ECC* M30 .... **93** C1
Exeter Rd *RDSH* SK5 .... **136** A4
  URM M41 .... **111** D3
Exeter St *SLFD* M6 .... **95** C3
Exford Cl *NEWH/MOS* M40 .... **8** C4
  RDSH SK5 .... **134** B3 🇧
Exmouth Av *RDSH* SK5 .... **136** A4 🇧
Exmouth Rd *SALE* M33 .... **121** D4
Eynford Av *RDSH* SK5 .... **135** D3 🇧
Eyre St *HULME* M15 .... **26** C5

F

Faber St *ANC* M4 .... **7** D3
Factory La *BKLY* M9 .... **66** B4
  SALQ/ORD M5 .... **14** C2 🇧
Failsworth Rd *FAIL* M35 .... **89** D2
Fairbairn St *OP/CLY* M11 .... **20** A1
Fairbank Av *RUSH/FAL* M14 .... **37** E3
Fairbottom St *OLD* OL1 .... **55** D2 🇧
Fairbourne Rd *BNG/LEV* M19 .... **116** A4
Fairbrook Dr *SLFD* M6 .... **95** C3

Fairbrother St *SALQ/ORD* M5 .... **24** A2
Fairclough St *OP/CLY* M11 .... **11** D5
Fairfield Av *DROY* M43 .... **108** A1
Fairfield Rd *DROY* M43 .... **107** D1
  OP/CLY M11 .... **107** C2
Fairfields *OLDS* OL8 .... **73** C3
Fairfield Sq *DROY* M43 .... **108** A1
Fairfield St *CMANE* M1 .... **17** F5
  SLFD M6 .... **78** B4
Fairford Cl *RDSH* SK5 .... **134** B4
Fairford Wy *RDSH* SK5 .... **134** B4 🇧
Fairhaven Av *CCHDY* M21 .... **126** B1 🇧
Fairhaven St *WGTN/LGST* M12 .. **30** A4
Fairholme Av *URM* M41 .... **111** C4 🇧
Fairholme Rd *DID/WITH* M20 ... **130** A3
Fairhope Av *SLFD* M6 .... **93** D1
Fairisle Cl *OP/CLY* M11 .... **20** A1
Fairlawn *RUSH/FAL* M14 .... **36** C2
Fairlee Av *DROY* M43 .... **99** C4
Fairleigh Av *SLFD* M6 .... **94** A2
Fairless Rd *ECC* M30 .... **91** D4
Fairman Cl *OLDTF/WHR* M16 ..... **36** A4
Fairmount Rd *SWIN* M27 .... **74** B3
Fair Oak Rd *BNG/LEV* M19 ...... **131** D4
Fairstead Wk *OP/CLY* M11 .... **107** D2
Fair St *CMANE* M1 .... **18** A3
  SWIN M27 .... **59** C4
Fairview Av *BNG/LEV* M19 .... **50** B2
  DTN/ASHW M34 .... **118** A4
Fairview Cl *CHAD* OL9 .... **52** A1
Fairview Rd *DTN/ASHW* M34 ... **118** A3
Fairway *DROY* M43 .... **108** A1
  PWCH M25 .... **63** D3
  SWIN M27 .... **78** A2
The Fairway *NEWH/MOS* M40 ... **87** D1
Fairy La *CHH* M8 .... **82** A4
Falcon Av *URM* M41 .... **112** A3
Falcon Crs *SWIN* M27 .... **59** D3 🇧
Falcon Dr *CHAD* OL9 .... **54** A1
Falcon St *OLDS* OL8 .... **55** C4
Falfield Dr *CHH* M8 .... **83** D4
Falkland Av *NEWH/MOS* M40 ...... **9** D2
Fallowfield Av *SALQ/ORD* M5 .... **23** E1 🇧
Fallow Fields Dr *RDSH* SK5 ...... **118** A4
The Fallows *CHAD* OL9 .... **53** C4 🇧
Falmer St *GTN* M18 .... **107** D3
Falmouth Av *SALE* M33 .... **121** D4 🇧
Falmouth Crs *RDSH* SK5 .... **136** A4
Falmouth St *NEWH/MOS* M40 ... **10** A2
  OLDS OL8 .... **73** D1
Falsgrave Cl *NEWH/MOS* M40 ... **86** A4 🇧
Falston Av *NEWH/MOS* M40 ...... **69** D3
Faraday Av *CHH* M8 .... **83** C3
  SWIN M27 .... **60** B3
Faraday St *CMANE* M1 .... **17** E1 🇧
  CMANE M1 .... **17** E2 🇧
Far Cromwell Rd *MPL/ROM* SK6 .. **136** B3
Far La *GTN* M18 .... **116** B1
Far La *GTN* M18 .... **118** A1
Farley Wy *RDSH* SK5 .... **117** C4
Farm Av *STRET* M32 .... **113** C1
Farm Cl *HTNM* SK4 .... **133** C3
Farmfield *SALE* M33 .... **122** A3
Farm St *FAIL* M35 .... **87** D3
Farm Yd *BNG/LEV* M19 .... **51** D4
Farn Av *RDSH* SK5 .... **117** C3
Farnborough Rd *NEWH/MOS* M40 .. **8** C3
Farndon Rd *RDSH* SK5 .... **117** C3 🇧
Farnley St *WGTN/LGST* M12 ..... **30** C4
Farnworth Dr *RUSH/FAL* M14 ... **48** B1
Farrand Rd *OLDS* OL8 .... **71** D3
Farrant Rd *WGTN/LGST* M12 ... **40** C3
Farrar Rd *DROY* M43 .... **107** D1

Farrell St *CSLFD* M3 .... 5 E3
Farrer Rd *BRUN/LGST* M13 .... 40 A5
Farringdon St *SLFD* M6 .... 95 C2 ⬛
Farwood Cl *OLDTF/WHR* M16 .... 24 B5 ⬛
Fastnet St *OP/CLY* M11 .... 21 D5 ⬛
Faulkenhurst St *CHAD* OL9 .... 54 A1
Faulkner Rd *STRET* M32 .... 115 C3
Faulkner St *CMANE* M1 .... 16 C4
Faversham St *NEWH/MOS* M40 ... 86 B2
Fay Av *BKLY* M9 .... 68 B3
Featherstall Rd North *CHAD* OL9 ... 54 B1
　OLD OL1 .... 54 B1
Federation St *ANC* M4 .... 6 C5 ⬛
Fellbrigg Cl *WGTN* M18 .... 116 A2 ⬛
Felltop Dr *RDSH* SK5 .... 135 C4
Felthorpe Dr *CHH* M8 .... 82 B3
Fencegate Av *HTNM* SK4 .... 133 D4 ⬛
Fenchurch Av *NEWH/MOS* M40 ... 96 A1
Fencot Dr *WGTN/LGST* M12 .... 41 D3
Fenella St *BRUN/LGST* M13 .... 39 E2
Fenham Ct *NEWH/MOS* M40 .... 84 A4 ⬛
Fenmore Av *GTN* M18 .... 41 F4
Fennel St *ANC* M4 .... 6 B5
Fenney St *BRO* M7 .... 82 A3 ⬛
Fenney St East *BRO* M7 .... 82 A1 ⬛
Fenn St *HULME* M15 .... 25 E3
Fenwick St *HULME* M15 .... 26 C3
Ferdinand St *NEWH/MOS* M40 ... 8 C2 ⬛
Fernacre Av *SALE* M33 .... 124 A4
Fern Av *URM* M41 .... 110 A3
Fernbrook Cl *BRUN/LGST* M13 .... 29 D5
Fernclough Rd *BKLY* M9 .... 84 B3
Ferndale Gdns *BNG/LEV* M19 .... 131 C3 ⬛
Ferndene Rd *DID/WITH* M20 ...... 129 D4
Ferney Field Rd *CHAD* OL9 .... 52 B2
Ferngate Dr *DID/WITH* M20 .... 129 D3 ⬛
Fernhill Dr *GTN* M18 .... 41 F2
Fernholme Ct *OLDS* OL8 .... 72 A1 ⬛
Fernhurst Rd *DID/WITH* M20 ...... 130 A4
Fernie St *ANC* M4 .... 6 C3
Fernlea Crs *SWIN* M27 .... 76 A3
Fernleaf St *RUSH/FAL* M14 .... 37 D3 ⬛
Fernleigh Av *BNG/LEV* M19 .... 116 A1
Fernleigh Dr *OLDTF/WHR* M16 ... 24 B5
Fernside Av *DID/WITH* M20 .... 130 B4
Fern St *CHAD* OL9 .... 53 C1
　CHH M8 .... 6 C2
　OLDS OL8 .... 54 B4
Fernwood Av *GTN* M18 .... 116 B2 ⬛
Ferris St *OP/CLY* M11 .... 106 B1
Ferry St *OP/CLY* M11 .... 19 E4
Fettler Cl *SWIN* M27 .... 76 A2
Field Bank Gv *BNG/LEV* M19 ..... 51 F3
Fielden Av *CCHDY* M21 .... 43 D3
Fielden Rd *DID/WITH* M20 .... 128 B4
Fielders Wy *SWIN* M27 .... 58 A1 ⬛
Fieldfare Av *NEWH/MOS* M40 ... 11 F1
Fielding St *ECC* M30 .... 91 C4 ⬛
Field Rd *SALE* M33 .... 122 A3
Fields New Rd *CHAD* OL9 .... 53 C4
Field St *DROY* M43 .... 107 D1
　FAIL M35 .... 88 A2 ⬛
　GTN M18 .... 107 C3
　MPL/ROM SK6 .... 141 D2
　SLFD M6 .... 2 A5 ⬛
Fieldsway *OLDS* OL8 .... 73 C3
Field Vale Dr *RDSH* SK5 .... 118 A4
Fife Av *CHAD* OL9 .... 70 B1
Fifth Av *OLDS* OL8 .... 72 A3
　OP/CLY M11 .... 96 A3
　TRPK M17 .... 104 A4
Fifth St *TRPK* M17 .... 104 A4
Filby Wk *NEWH/MOS* M40 .... 9 E2

Filey Av *OLDTF/WHR* M16 .... 45 D1
　URM M41 .... 110 A1
Filey Dr *SLFD* M6 .... 78 B3
Filey Rd *RUSH/FAL* M14 .... 130 D1
Finborough Cl *OLDTF/WHR* M16 ... 35 F3
Finchley Av *NEWH/MOS* M40 ... 96 A1 ⬛
Finchley Gv *NEWH/MOS* M40 ... 68 A3
Finchley Rd *RUSH/FAL* M14 .... 47 F5
Finghall Rd *URM* M41 .... 110 B3
Finney Dr *CCHDY* M21 .... 126 A2
Finny Bank Rd *SALE* M33 .... 123 C3
Finsbury Av *NEWH/MOS* M40 ... 96 A1 ⬛
Finsbury Rd *RDSH* SK5 .... 134 A1
Finstock Cl *ECC* M30 .... 90 B4
Fintry Gv *ECC* M30 .... 91 D4
Firbeck Dr *ANC* M4 .... 8 C5
Firdale Av *NEWH/MOS* M40 ...... 70 A4
Firdale Wk *CHAD* OL9 .... 54 A2
Firefly Cl *CSLFD* M3 .... 14 C2
Fire Station Sq *SALQ/ORD* M5 ... 13 F1
Firethorn Av *BNG/LEV* M19 .... 131 D3 ⬛
　CHAD OL9 .... 53 D1
Fir Gv *BNG/LEV* M19 .... 50 C3
Fir Rd *SWIN* M27 .... 76 A3
Firs Av *FAIL* M35 .... 88 A2 ⬛
　OLDTF/WHR M16 .... 43 E1
Firsby Av *MPL/ROM* SK6 .... 141 D1
Firsby St *BNG/LEV* M19 .... 51 D3 ⬛
Firs Rd *SALE* M33 .... 122 A4 ⬛
First Av *OLDS* OL8 .... 72 B3
　OP/CLY M11 .... 96 B3
　SWIN M27 .... 75 D4
　TRPK M17 .... 104 B4
Fir St *ECC* M30 .... 91 D4
　FAIL M35 .... 88 A2 ⬛
　HTNM SK4 .... 138 A3
　NEWH/MOS M40 .... 8 C2
　OLDTF/WHR M16 .... 34 B2 ⬛
　SLFD M6 .... 2 A5
Firswood Dr *SWIN* M27 .... 76 A3
Firth St *OLD* OL1 .... 55 D3
Firwood Av *URM* M41 .... 113 C4
Firwood Pk *CHAD* OL9 .... 52 A2
Fisher St *OLD* OL1 .... 55 D1 ⬛
Fitton Av *CCHDY* M21 .... 126 B3
Fitton Crs *SWIN* M27 .... 58 B2
Fitzgeorge St *NEWH/MOS* M40 ... 8 A1
Fitzgerald Cl *PWCH* M25 .... 61 D3 ⬛
Fitzroy St *DROY* M43 .... 108 B3
Fitzwarren St *SALQ/ORD* M5 ...... 12 B1
　SLFD M6 .... 2 A4
Fitzwilliam St *BRO* M7 .... 5 D2
Flag Rw *ANC* M4 .... 7 E3 ⬛
Flagship Av *SALQ/ORD* M5 .... 13 E4 ⬛
Flamingo Cl *WGTN/LGST* M12 ... 31 D3 ⬛
Flashfields *PWCH* M25 .... 61 D4 ⬛
Flash St *NEWH/MOS* M40 .... 87 C3
Flatley Cl *HULME* M15 .... 26 C4
Flaxpool Cl *OLDTF/WHR* M16 .... 35 E3
Flax St *CSLFD* M3 .... 5 D4
Fleeson St *RUSH/FAL* M14 .... 38 A4
Fleet St *GTN* M18 .... 107 C3
Fletcher Av *SWIN* M27 .... 59 C2
Fletcher Cl *CHAD* OL9 .... 54 B3 ⬛
Fletcher Sq *CMANE* M1 .... 18 A3 ⬛
Fletcher St *NEWH/MOS* M40 ..... 85 D4 ⬛
　STKP SK1 .... 138 B4
Flint Cl *OP/CLY* M11 .... 21 F1
Flint St *DROY* M43 .... 98 B3
Flixton Rd *URM* M41 .... 110 A3
Flora Dr *BRO* M7 .... 5 D2
Flora St *BKLY* M9 .... 66 A2
　OLD OL1 .... 55 C2

Florence St *DROY* M43 .... 108 B1 🟦
  ECC M30 .... 90 B4
  FAIL M35 .... 88 B1 🟦
  HTNM SK4 .... 138 A3 🟦
  SALE M33 .... 123 D3
Florida St *OLDS* OL8 .... 55 C4
Floyd Av *CCHDY* M21 .... 127 C1
Floyer Rd *BKLY* M9 .... 67 C1
Fold Av *DROY* M43 .... 98 B3
Fold Gn *CHAD* OL9 .... 53 C3
Fold St *NEWH/MOS* M40 .... 86 A1
The Fold *BKLY* M9 .... 66 B2 🟦
  URM M41 .... 110 A2
Foleshill Av *BKLY* M9 .... 84 B2
Foliage Crs *RDSH* SK5 .... 135 D4
Foliage Gdns *RDSH* SK5 .... 136 A4 🟦
Foliage Rd *RDSH* SK5 .... 139 D1
Folkestone Rd *OP/CLY* M11 .... 96 B3
Folkestone Rd East *OP/CLY* M11 .. 96 B3
Folkestone Rd West *OP/CLY* M11 .. 96 A3
Follows St *GTN* M18 .... 106 B3 🟦
Folly La *SWIN* M27 .... 75 D4
Fontwell Cl *OLDTF/WHR* M16 .... 34 A5
Fooley Cl *DROY* M43 .... 107 C1
Forber Crs *GTN* M18 .... 116 A2
Forbes Rd *STKP* SK1 .... 139 D4
Forbes St *MPL/ROM* SK6 .... 141 D1 🟦
Ford La *SLFD* M6 .... 2 C2
Ford St *CSLFD* M3 .... 15 D1
  WGTN/LGST M12 .... 28 C3
Foreland Cl *NEWH/MOS* M40 ...... 84 B2
Forest Range *BNG/LEV* M19 .... 50 C4
Forest St *ECC* M30 .... 90 A1 🟦
  OLDS OL8 .... 73 D2
Forge La *OP/CLY* M11 .... 20 B1
Formby Av *CCHDY* M21 .... 127 C2
Formby Rd *SLFD* M6 .... 79 C4
Forrester St *WALK* M28 .... 74 A1
Forshaw Av *GTN* M18 .... 107 D3
Forshaw St *DTN/ASHW* M34 ...... 119 D1 🟦
Fortran Cl *SALO/ORD* M5 .... 13 C1
Fort Rd *PWCH* M25 .... 63 D3
Fortrose Av *BKLY* M9 .... 65 D2
Fortuna Gv *BNG/LEV* M19 .... 50 A5
Fortyacre Dr *MPL/ROM* SK6 .... 141 D2
Forum Gv *BRO* M7 .... 82 A4 🟦
Foster St *SALO/ORD* M5 .... 94 B4 🟦
Fotherby Dr *BKLY* M9 .... 66 B2
Foundry La *ANC* M4 .... 17 E1
Foundry St *CHAD* OL9 .... 55 C3
Fountains Rd *STRET* M32 .... 112 B2
Fountain St *CMANW* M2 .... 16 C3
  ECC M30 .... 101 D1 🟦
  OLD OL1 .... 55 C2 🟦
Fourth Av *CHAD* OL9 .... 53 C4
  OLDS OL8 .... 72 A4
  OP/CLY M11 .... 96 A2
  SWIN M27 .... 75 D4 🟦
Fourth St *TRPK* M17 .... 104 A4
Fourways *TRPK* M17 .... 103 C3
Four Yards *CMANW* M2 .... 16 B3 🟦
Fovant Crs *RDSH* SK5 .... 117 C4
Fowler Av *GTN* M18 .... 107 D2 🟦
Fowler St *OLDS* OL8 .... 72 A2
Foxbank St *BRUN/LGST* M13 ...... 39 E2
Foxbench Wk *CCHDY* M21 .... 127 D3
Foxdale St *OP/CLY* M11 .... 96 A4 🟦
Foxdenton Dr *URM* M41 .... 112 B2
Foxdenton La *MDTN* M24 .... 52 A3
Foxfield Dr *OLDS* OL8 .... 72 A4
Foxhall Rd *DTN/ASHW* M34 .... 119 D1
Fox Park Rd *OLDS* OL8 .... 72 A3 🟦
Fox St *ECC* M30 .... 92 B3 🟦

  OLDS OL8 .... 72 A3
Foxwood Gdns *BNG/LEV* M19 .... 131 C4 🟦
Foynes Cl *NEWH/MOS* M40 .... 84 B4 🟦
Framley Rd *CCHDY* M21 .... 128 B2
Fram St *BKLY* M9 .... 85 D1 🟦
  SLFD M6 .... 95 C3 🟦
Frances Av *ECC* M30 .... 92 A3 🟦
Francis Rd *DID/WITH* M20 .... 130 A4
Francis St *CSLFD* M3 .... 6 A3
  ECC M30 .... 91 D2
  FAIL M35 .... 88 B2 🟦
Frankby Cl *SWIN* M27 .... 78 A2 🟦
Frankland Cl *OP/CLY* M11 .... 21 E1
Franklin Cl *DTN/ASHW* M34 ...... 118 A3
Franklin Rd *DROY* M43 .... 98 A4 🟦
Franklin St *ECC* M30 .... 91 D3
  OLD OL1 .... 55 C1
Franklyn Rd *GTN* M18 .... 107 C3
Frank St *FAIL* M35 .... 88 A2
  SLFD M6 .... 2 B2 🟦
Franton Rd *OP/CLY* M11 .... 11 F5
Fraser Pl *TRPK* M17 .... 104 B4
Fraser Rd *CHH* M8 .... 64 B4
Fraser St *SWIN* M27 .... 59 C4
Frederick Rd *SLFD* M6 .... 3 F2
Frederick St *CHAD* OL9 .... 53 D1
  CSLFD M3 .... 15 E1
  OLDS OL8 .... 72 B1
Fred Tilson Cl *RUSH/FAL* M14 ..... 37 D5
Freeman Sq *HULME* M15 .... 26 C4
Freetown Cl *RUSH/FAL* M14 .... 36 C2
Fremantle Av *GTN* M18 .... 116 B2 🟦
French Barn La *BKLY* M9 .... 66 A2
Freshfield Cl *FAIL* M35 .... 89 C3
Freshville St *CMANE* M1 .... 17 F4 🟦
Freshwater St *GTN* M18 .... 107 C3 🟦
Freya Gv *SALO/ORD* M5 .... 14 A5
Friendship Av *GTN* M18 .... 117 C1 🟦
Frinton Av *NEWH/MOS* M40 .... 69 D2 🟦
Frith Rd *DID/WITH* M20 .... 130 A4
Frobisher Cl *BRUN/LGST* M13 .... 39 D1
Frobisher Pl *RDSH* SK5 .... 138 A1 🟦
Frodsham St *RUSH/FAL* M14 ...... 37 F5
Frome Av *URM* M41 .... 120 B1
Frome Dr *CHH* M8 .... 83 D2 🟦
Frostlands Rd *OLDTF/WHR* M16 .. 35 F3
Frost St *ANC* M4 .... 19 D2
  OLDS OL8 .... 73 C1
Froxmer St *GTN* M18 .... 106 A3
Fulham Av *NEWH/MOS* M40 .... 86 B4
Fulmer Dr *ANC* M4 .... 8 B5
Fulmere Ct *SWIN* M27 .... 75 D3 🟦
Fulneck Sq *DROY* M43 .... 108 A1
Fulwood Av *BKLY* M9 .... 67 D1 🟦
Furness Quay *SALO/ORD* M5 ...... 22 C1
Furness Rd *RUSH/FAL* M14 .... 48 B4
  URM M41 .... 111 D2
Furnival Cl *DTN/ASHW* M34 ..... 118 A3
Furnival Rd *GTN* M18 .... 106 A3
Furnival St *RDSH* SK5 .... 117 C3
Furrow Dr *ECC* M30 .... 90 B1 🟦
Fushia Gv *BRO* M7 .... 81 D3 🟦

G

Gable St *OP/CLY* M11 .... 20 A5 🟦
Gail Cl *FAIL* M35 .... 88 A4
Gainford Gdns *NEWH/MOS* M40 .. 68 B4 🟦
Gainford Rd *RDSH* SK5 .... 117 D4 🟦

Gainsborough Av
DID/WITH M20 .... 130 A4 🖫
  OLDS OL8 .... 73 C1
  STRET M32 .... 32 A5
Gainsborough Rd *DTN/ASHW* M34 .... 99 D4
Gainsborough Rd *BRO* M7 .... 82 A2
Gairloch Av *STRET* M32 .... 113 D3 🖫
Gair Rd *RDSH* SK5 .... 138 B1
Gaitskell Cl *WGTN/LGST* M12 .... 19 E3
Galbraith St *CMANE* M1 .... 17 D5 🖫
Gale Rd *PWCH* M25 .... 61 D2
Galgate Cl *HULME* M15 .... 25 D2
Galloway Dr *SWIN* M27 .... 58 B1
Galloway Rd *SWIN* M27 .... 75 D3 🖫
Galston St *OP/CLY* M11 .... 20 C5
Galsworthy Av *CHH* M8 .... 83 C4
Galvin Rd *BKLY* M9 .... 65 D2 🖫
Galway St *OLD* OL1 .... 55 D3 🖫
Garden Av *DROY* M43 .... 98 B3
  STRET M32 .... 114 B3
Garden La *CSLFD* M3 .... 5 F5
  CSLFD M3 .... 16 A2 🖫
Garden St *ANC* M4 .... 16 C1
  ECC M30 .... 92 A4
Garden Wall Cl *SALQ/ORD* M5 .... 14 A5
Gardner Rd *PWCH* M25 .... 61 D1
Gardner St *SLFD* M6 .... 3 D3
  WGTN/LGST M12 .... 31 E3
Garfield Av *BNG/LEV* M19 .... 51 F4
Garfield St *STKP* SK1 .... 139 C3 🖫
Garforth Av *ANC* M4 .... 8 B5
Garforth St *CHAD* OL9 .... 54 A2
Gargrave St *BRO* M7 .... 79 D1
Garlick St *CHAD* OL9 .... 55 C3 🖫
  GTN M18 .... 106 B4
Garnant Cl *BKLY* M9 .... 85 D1 🖫
Garner Dr *ECC* M30 .... 91 C2 🖫
  SLFD M6 .... 94 B2
Garnett St *STKP* SK1 .... 138 B4
Garratt Wy *GTN* M18 .... 106 A4
Garswood Rd *RUSH/FAL* M14 .... 46 B2
Garthorne Cl *OLDTF/WHR* M16 .... 35 D3
The Garth *SALQ/ORD* M5 .... 94 B3
Garthwaite Av *OLDS* OL8 .... 73 C2
Gartside St *CSLFD* M3 .... 15 F3
Garwood St *HULME* M15 .... 25 F2
Gascoyne St *RUSH/FAL* M14 .... 37 D4
Gaskell Rd *ECC* M30 .... 91 D4
Gaskell St *NEWH/MOS* M40 .... 87 D3 🖫
  SWIN M27 .... 58 B3 🖫
Gas St *HTNM* SK4 .... 138 A4 🖫
Gateshead Cl *RUSH/FAL* M14 .... 37 F3 🖫
Gate St *OP/CLY* M11 .... 106 A1
Gateway Crs *CHAD* OL9 .... 70 A1
Gateway Rd *GTN* M18 .... 106 A3 🖫
The Gateways *SWIN* M27 .... 58 B3 🖫
Gathurst St *GTN* M18 .... 107 C3 🖫
Gatley Av *RUSH/FAL* M14 .... 46 C3
Gatling Av *WGTN/LGST* M12 .... 51 D1
Gavin Av *SALQ/ORD* M5 .... 13 D2
Gaythorn St *SALQ/ORD* M5 .... 14 B2
Gee La *ECC* M30 .... 90 B2
Gemini Rd *SLFD* M6 .... 3 F1
Genista Gv *BRO* M7 .... 81 D3 🖫
George Leigh St *ANC* M4 .... 17 F1
George St *CHAD* OL9 .... 53 C2
  CMANE M1 .... 16 C3
  ECC M30 .... 91 C4
  FAIL M35 .... 88 B1
  OLD OL1 .... 55 C3 🖫
  PWCH M25 .... 62 B4
  STKP SK1 .... 139 C4 🖫
  URM M41 .... 112 A3

George St North *BRO* M7 .... 82 B1
George St South *BRO* M7 .... 82 A1
Georgette Dr *CSLFD* M3 .... 5 F4
Gerald Av *CHH* M8 .... 83 C1
Gerald Rd *SLFD* M6 .... 80 A4
Gerrard St *SLFD* M6 .... 3 D3
Gertrude Cl *SALQ/ORD* M5 .... 12 C4
Gervis St *NEWH/MOS* M40 .... 84 B4 🖫
Gibbon St *OP/CLY* M11 .... 20 C1
Gibb Rd *WALK* M28 .... 74 B2
Gibbs St *CSLFD* M3 .... 14 C2
Gibson Av *GTN* M18 .... 107 D2 🖫
Gibson Pl *ANC* M4 .... 6 C3
Gidlow St *GTN* M18 .... 107 C3 🖫
Gifford Av *BKLY* M9 .... 67 D1
  HULME M15 .... 25 F1 🖫
  SLFD M6 .... 12 A2 🖫
Gilda Brook Rd *ECC* M30 .... 93 C3
Gilda Crs *ECC* M30 .... 93 C3
Gildenhall *FAIL* M35 .... 89 C2
Gildridge Rd *OLDTF/WHR* M16 .... 45 F4
Giles St *WGTN/LGST* M12 .... 41 D3
Gillford Av *BKLY* M9 .... 85 D1 🖫
Gillingham Rd *ECC* M30 .... 90 B3
Gill St *BKLY* M9 .... 67 D4
  STKP SK1 .... 139 D2
Gillwood Dr *MPL/ROM* SK6 .... 141 D4
Gilman Cl *BKLY* M9 .... 66 A3 🖫
Gilman St *BKLY* M9 .... 66 A3 🖫
Gilmerton Dr *NEWH/MOS* M40 .... 87 C4 🖫
Gilmour Ter *BKLY* M9 .... 67 D4
Gilpin Rd *URM* M41 .... 112 B4
Giltbrook Av *NEWH/MOS* M40 .... 9 D1
Girton St *BRO* M7 .... 5 E2
Girvan Av *NEWH/MOS* M40.. .... 69 D3
Gisborn Dr *SLFD* M6 .... 79 D4 🖫
Gisburne Av *NEWH/MOS* M40 .... 69 D3 🖫
Givendale Dr *CHH* M8 .... 65 C3
Gladstone Cl *HULME* M15 .... 35 E2 🖫
Gladstone Rd *ECC* M30 .... 92 A3
  URM M41 .... 112 A3
Gladstone St *SWIN* M27 .... 77 C1
Gladys St *OLDTF/WHR* M16 .... 34 B2
Glamis Av *OP/CLY* M11 .... 11 F4
  STRET M32 .... 113 C3 🖫
Glanford Av *BKLY* M9 .... 65 C2 🖫
Glasshouse St *ANC* M4 .... 8 A4 🖫
Glastonbury Rd *STRET* M32 .... 112 B2
Glaswen Gv *RDSH* SK5 .... 138 B1 🖫
Gleaves Rd *ECC* M30 .... 92 A4
Gleave St *SALE* M33 .... 123 D3 🖫
Glebelands Rd *SALE* M33. .... 122 B3
Glebe Rd *URM* M41 .... 111 D3 🖫
Glebe St *CHAD* OL9 .... 71 C2
  STKP SK1 .... 139 C4 🖫
Gleden St *NEWH/MOS* M40 .... 23 D3
Gledhill Av *SALQ/ORD* M5 .... 23 D2
Gledhill St *DID/WITH* M20 .... 129 D2 🖫
Glemsford Cl *NEWH/MOS* M40 .... 86 B3 🖫
Glenacre Gdns *GTN* M18 .... 117 C2 🖫
Glenart *ECC* M30 .... 92 A3 🖫
Glen Av *BKLY* M9 .... 67 C4
  SALE M33 .... 123 C3
  SWIN M27 .... 75 D1
  WALK M28. .... 74 A1
Glenbarry Cl *BRUN/LGST* M13. .... 27 F4
Glenbarry St *WGTN/LGST* M12 .... 19 D5
Glencastle Rd *GTN* M18 .... 106 A4 🖫
  GTN M18 .... 116 B1 🖫
Glencoe St *OLDS* OL8 .... 72 A3 🖫
Glencross Av *CCHDY* M21 .... 43 D1
Glendale *SWIN* M27 .... 59 D3 🖫

Glendale Av *BNG/LEV* M19 .... **131** D3
Glendale Ct *OLDS* OL8 .... **73** D1
Glendale Rd *ECC* M30........... **93** C2
Glendene Av *DROY* M43 .... **99** C2
Glendinning St *SLFD* M6 .... **95** C3 🔟
Glendore *SALQ/ORD* M5 .... **94** A3 🖪
Glendower Dr *NEWH/MOS* M40........ **84** A4
Glenfyne Rd *SLFD* M6 .... **78** B4
Glenhaven Av *URM* M41 .... **111** C3
Glenhurst Rd *BNG/LEV* M19 .... **131** C4 🖪
Glenmore Dr *CHH* M8 .... **83** D2
   FAIL M35.................. **89** D1
Glenolden St *OP/CLY* M11 .... **96** B3
Glensdale Dr *NEWH/MOS* M40 ...... **70** A4 🖪
Glenside Av *GTN* M18................ **116** B2
Glenside Gdns *FAIL* M35 .... **89** C2
Glen St *SALQ/ORD* M5 .... **23** D1
Glenwood Dr *BKLY* M9 .... **85** C2 🖪
Glenwyn Av *BKLY* M9 .... **67** C1 🖪
Globe Cl *OLDTF/WHR* M16............ **35** D1
Gloucester Av *BNG/LEV* M19 .... **51** E5
Gloucester Pl *SLFD* M6 .... **3** D3 🖪
Gloucester Rd *DROY* M43 .... **98** A2
   DTN/ASHW M34........... **118** A3
   SLFD M6 .... **94** A1
   URM M41 .... **111** D4
Gloucester St *CMANE* M1 .... **26** B1 🖪
   SALQ/ORD M5 .... **14** A5
   SLFD M6 .... **3** D2
Gloucester St North *CHAD* OL9 ...... **54** A4 🖪
Glyneath Cl *OP/CLY* M11 .... **20** B4
Glynrene Dr *SWIN* M27 .... **57** C3
Godbert Av *CCHDY* M21 .... **127** C4
Goddard St *OLDS* OL8 .... **73** D1
Godfrey Av *DROY* M43............... **96** B2
Godfrey Range *GTN* M18 .... **117** D1 🖪
Godfrey Rd *SLFD* M6 .... **78** A4
Godlee Dr *SWIN* M27 .... **76** A2
Godley Cl *OP/CLY* M11 .... **106** A2
Godwin St *GTN* M18 .... **107** C3
Golborne Av *DID/WITH* M20 .... **128** B2
Goldenhill Av *OP/CLY* M11 .... **96** A2 🖪
Golden St *ECC* M30 .... **91** D4 🖪
Goldfinch Wy *DROY* M43............... **99** C2
Goldsmith Av *SALQ/ORD* M5 .... **94** B3 🖪
Goldsmith Rd *RDSH* SK5 .... **117** C4 🖪
Gold St *CMANE* M1 .... **17** D3 🖪
Golfview Dr *ECC* M30 .... **91** D1 🖪
Gooch Cl *OLDTF/WHR* M16 .... **35** E4
Goodiers Dr *SALQ/ORD* M5 .... **13** E4 🖪
Goodier St *NEWH/MOS* M40 .... **85** C4
Goodman St *BKLY* M9 .... **67** C4
Goodwill Cl *SWIN* M27 .... **76** B2
Goodwin Sq *BKLY* M9 .... **84** B2 🖪
Goodwood Dr *SWIN* M27 .... **77** D2
Goole St *OP/CLY* M11 .... **21** D4
Goostrey Av *DID/WITH* M20 .... **129** C1 🖪
Gordon Av *BNG/LEV* M19 .... **51** E4
   CHAD OL9 .... **71** C2
Gordon Pl *DID/WITH* M20 .... **129** D4
Gordon Rd *ECC* M30 .... **91** D2
   SALE M33 .... **123** D3
   SWIN M27 .... **75** C3
Gordon St *BRO* M7 .... **5** D2
   CHAD OL9 .... **70** B1
   GTN M18 .... **107** C3
   HTNM SK4 .... **138** A3
   OLDTF/WHR M16 .... **34** C2
Gore Av *FAIL* M35 .... **89** D2 🖪
   SALQ/ORD M5 .... **94** B3
Gorebrook Ct *WGTN/LGST* M12 ...... **41** D3 🖪
Gore Crs *SALQ/ORD* M5 .... **94** B2
Goredale Av *GTN* M18 .... **117** C2 🖪

Gore Dr *SLFD* M6........... **94** B2
Gorelan Rd *GTN* M18 .... **106** B4 🔟
Gore St *CMANE* M1 .... **17** E3 🖪
   CSLFD M3 .... **15** E2
   SLFD M6 .... **3** D3
Goring Av *GTN* M18 .... **106** B3
Gorse Av *DROY* M43 .... **99** C3
   STRET M32 .... **32** B4
Gorse Crs *STRET* M32 .... **32** B4 🖪
   STRET M32 .... **32** A4 🖪
Gorse Dr *STRET* M32........... **32** A4
Gorsefield Dr *SWIN* M27 .... **76** B2 🖪
Gorse La *STRET* M32................ **32** A4
Gorse Rd *SWIN* M27 .... **76** A3
Gorse St *CHAD* OL9 .... **70** B1
   STRET M32 .... **115** C2 🖪
Gorseway *RDSH* SK5 .... **139** D1
Gorsey Brow *STKP* SK1 .... **139** C4 🖪
Gorseyfields *DROY* M43 .... **108** A1
Gorsey Mount St *STKP* SK1 .... **139** C4
Gorton Crs *DTN/ASHW* M34 .... **119** C3
Gorton La *WGTN/LGST* M12............ **31** D3
Gorton Rd *OP/CLY* M11 .... **30** A1
   RDSH SK5 .... **134** B1
   WGTN/LGST M12 .... **30** C2
Gorton St *CHAD* OL9 .... **53** D3
   CSLFD M3 .... **6** A5 🖪
   ECC M30 .... **90** A4
   NEWH/MOS M40 .... **8** A1
Gosling Cl *OLDTF/WHR* M16 .... **36** A4
Gosport Sq *BRO* M7 .... **81** D4 🖪
Goulden Rd *DID/WITH* M20............ **129** C4
Goulden St *ANC* M4 .... **7** E5
   SLFD M6 .... **95** C3
Goulder Rd *GTN* M18 .... **117** C2
Gould St *ANC* M4............... **7** E3
Gowan Rd *OLDTF/WHR* M16............ **45** E4
Gowerdale Rd *RDSH* SK5 .... **136** A4 🖪
Gower St *SWIN* M27 .... **59** C4 🖪
Goyt Crs *MPL/ROM* SK6 .... **141** D2
   STKP SK1 .... **139** D2
Goyt Rd *STKP* SK1 .... **139** D2
Goyt Valley Rd *MPL/ROM* SK6 .... **141** D2
Grafton Av *ECC* M30 .... **93** C1
Grafton St *BRUN/LGST* M13 .... **27** F5
   FAIL M35 .... **88** B1
   HTNM SK4 .... **138** A2
Graham Rd *SLFD* M6 .... **94** A1
Graham St *OP/CLY* M11 .... **20** C5
Grainger Av *WGTN/LGST* M12 .... **40** C4
Grain Vw *SALQ/ORD* M5 .... **13** D4
Grammar School Rd *OLDS* OL8 .... **71** D2
Grampian Cl *CHAD* OL9 .... **53** C4
Granada Rd *DTN/ASHW* M34 .... **118** A2
Granby Rd *STRET* M32 .... **115** C4
   SWIN M27 .... **75** C2
Granby Rw *CMANE* M1 .... **17** E5
Granby St *CHAD* OL9 .... **71** C3
Grandale St *RUSH/FAL* M14 .... **38** A5
Grand Union Wy *ECC* M30 .... **101** D1
Grange Av *BNG/LEV* M19................ **50** B5
   ECC M30 .... **91** D1 🖪
   HTNM SK4 .... **133** C4
   OLDS OL8 .... **72** A1
   STRET M32 .... **114** B3
   SWIN M27 .... **57** D3 🖪
Grange Crs *URM* M41 .... **111** C4
Grange Dr *BKLY* M9 .... **67** D2
   ECC M30 .... **91** D1
Grangeforth Rd *CHH* M8............... **82** B1
Grangepark Rd *BKLY* M9 .... **67** D2
Grange Rd *CCHDY* M21 .... **43** D2
   URM M41 .... **111** C4

Grange St *CHAD* OL9 .... 55 C2
  FAIL M35 .... 87 D3
  SLFD M6 .... 95 C3
The Grange *RUSH/FAL* M14.. 38 A5
Grangethorpe Dr *BNG/LEV* M19 ..... 111 C2
Grangethorpe Rd *URM* M41........ 111 C2
Grangewood Dr *BKLY* M9 .... 84 B2
Granshaw St *NEWH/MOS* M40 ...... 9 E4
Gransmoor Av *OP/CLY* M11 .... 107 C2
Gransmoor Rd *OP/CLY* M11 .... 107 D2
Grant Cl *BKLY* M9 .... 66 B3
Grantham St *RUSH/FAL* M14 ...... 37 D5
Granville Av *BRO* M7 .... 82 A1 🗓
  OLDTF/WHR M16 .... 44 B2
Granville Cl *CHAD* OL9 .... 54 A2 🗓
Granville Rd *DTN/ASHW* M34 ..... 98 B4
  RUSH/FAL M14 .... 130 A1
  URM M41 .... 112 A1
Granville St *CHAD* OL9 .... 54 A1 🗓
  ECC M30 .... 91 C2
Grasmere Av *HTNM* SK4 .... 134 A3
  SWIN M27 .... 57 C3
Grasmere Crs *ECC* M30 .... 90 B1
Grasmere Rd *STRET* M32 .... 114 B2
  SWIN M27 .... 76 B3
Grasmere Cl *WGTN/LGST* M12 ..... 41 E5
Grasscroft *RDSH* SK5 .... 136 A3
Grasscroft Cl *RUSH/FAL* M14 ..... 46 B2
Grassfield Av *BRO* M7 .... 81 C3 🗓
Grassingham Gdns *SLFD* M6 ..... 2 A3 🗓
Grassington Av *NEWH/MOS* M40 ... 68 A2 🗓
Gratrix Av *SALQ/ORD* M5......... 23 F2
Gratrix St *GTN* M18 .... 117 C1 🗓
Gravel La *CSLFD* M3 .... 6 A5
Gravenmoor Dr *BRO* M7 .... 82 A3
Graver La *NEWH/MOS* M40 .... 87 D4 🗓
Greame St *RUSH/FAL* M14........ 36 B4
Great Ancoats St *ANC* M4........ 17 E1
Great Bridgewater St *CMANW* M2 .. 16 A5
Great Cheetham St East *BRO* M7.. 82 A2
Great Cheetham St West *BRO* M7... 81 C4
Great Clowes St *BRO* M7......... 81 D2
Great Ducie St *CSLFD* M3 .... 6 A3
Great Egerton St *STKP* SK1 ...... 138 A4 🗓
Great George St *CSLFD* M3 .... 14 C1
Great Jackson St *HULME* M15 .... 25 E1
Great John St *CSLFD* M3 .... 15 E4
Great Jones St *WGTN/LGST* M12 ... 30 A4
Great Marlborough St
  CMANE M1 .... 26 C1 🗓
Great Newton St *NEWH/MOS* M40 .. 87 C4
Great Portwood St *STKP* SK1..... 138 B3
Great Southern St *RUSH/FAL* M14... 37 E4
Great Stone Rd *STRET* M32....... 32 C5
Great St *CMANE* M1 .... 18 B4
Great Western St *RUSH/FAL* M14 .. 36 C3
Greaves Av *FAIL* M35 .... 88 A3 🗓
Greaves St *OLD* OL1 .... 55 D3
Grecian St *BRO* M7 .... 81 C4
Grecian St North *BRO* M7 .... 81 C3
Gredle Cl *URM* M41 .... 112 B3 🗓
Greek St *CMANE* M1 .... 27 E2
Green Av *SWIN* M27 .... 76 B3
Greenbank Av *SWIN* M27 .... 75 D3 🗓
Greenbank Rd *SALE* M33......... 122 A4
  SLFD M6 .... 95 C2
Greencroft Rd *ECC* M30 .... 90 B1
Greendale Dr *BKLY* M9.......... 67 C2
Green Dr *BNG/LEV* M19 .... 50 A4
Green End Rd *BNG/LEV* M19...... 131 C4
Greenfield Av *ECC* M30 .... 100 A1 🗓
  URM M41 .... 111 D3

Greenfield St *DTN/ASHW* M34 ...... 109 D2
Green Fold *GTN* M18 .... 107 D3
Greenford Ct *CHH* M8............ 83 C2
Greengate *CSLFD* M3 .... 6 A4
Greengate East *NEWH/MOS* M40 .... 69 C2
Greengate La *PWCH* M25 .... 62 A1
Greengate West *CSLFD* M3 .... 5 E4
Greenhalgh St *FAIL* M35 .... 87 C3 🗓
  HTNM SK4 .... 138 A3 🗓
Greenheys *DROY* M43 .... 98 A3
Greenheys La *HULME* M15 .... 36 B1
Greenheys La West *HULME* M15 .... 36 A1
Greenhill *PWCH* M25 .... 62 A1 🗓
Greenhill Av *SALE* M33......... 123 C3
Greenhill Rd *CHH* M8........... 83 C1 🗓
Greenholm Cl *NEWH/MOS* M40 ..... 69 D4 🗓
Greenhow St *DROY* M43 .... 107 D1
Greening Rd *BNG/LEV* M19 .... 51 F2
Greenland St *CHH* M8........... 82 B2
  SLFD M6 .... 95 C3 🗓
Green La *ECC* M30 .... 91 C3
  FAIL M35 .... 97 C1
  GTN M18 .... 106 B3
  OLDS OL8 .... 73 C3
  SALE M33 .... 122 A3
Greenlaw Ct *OLDTF/WHR* M16 ..... 34 B1 🗓
Greenlea Av *GTN* M18 .... 116 B2 🗓
Greenside *WALK* M28 .... 74 A4 🗓
Greenside Crs *DROY* M43 .... 97 D3 🗓
Greenside La *DROY* M43 .... 97 C2
Greenside St *OP/CLY* M11........ 106 A1
Greenstead Av *CHH* M8.......... 83 C1
Greenstone Dr *SLFD* M6 .... 79 D4 🗓
Green St *ECC* M30............. 100 B1
  OLDS OL8 .... 54 B3
  RUSH/FAL M14 .... 131 C2
  STRET M32 .... 124 A1 🗓
The Green *SWIN* M27 .... 59 D3
Greenthorne Av *HTNM* SK4 ...... 133 D2
Green Wk *OLDTF/WHR* M16 .... 44 B1 🗓
  STRET M32 .... 113 D3
Green Wks *PWCH* M25............ 63 C2
Greenwatch Cl *ECC* M30 .... 91 C4 🗓
Greenway Av *BNG/LEV* M19 .... 51 F5
Greenways *NEWH/MOS* M40 ...... 69 D4 🗓
Greenwich Cl *NEWH/MOS* M40 .... 96 B1
Greenwood Av *SWIN* M27 .... 59 D4 🗓
Greenwood St *OLDS* OL8 .... 73 D4 🗓
  SLFD M6 .... 2 B1
Greer St *OP/CLY* M11 .... 106 A1
Gregory St *OLDS* OL8 .... 72 A2
  WGTN/LGST M12 .... 30 A3
Gregory Wy *RDSH* SK5.......... 134 B3
Gregson Rd *RDSH* SK5.......... 134 A3 🗓
Greg St *RDSH* SK5 .... 134 A3
Grendale Av *STKP* SK1 .... 139 D4
Grendale Dr *OLDTF/WHR* M16 .... 24 B5
Grendon Av *OLDS* OL8 .... 73 C2
Grenham Av *HULME* M15 .... 24 C3
Gresford Cl *CCHDY* M21 .... 126 A1 🗓
Gresham Dr *CHAD* OL9 .... 54 A2 🗓
Greton Cl *BRUN/LGST* M13 ...... 39 F3
Greville St *BRUN/LGST* M13...... 39 F3
Greyhound Dr *SLFD* M6 .... 81 C4 🗓
Grey Mare La *OP/CLY* M11 ...... 20 C4 🗓
Greystoke Av *BNG/LEV* M19 ..... 116 A4
Greystoke La *FAIL* M35 .... 87 D3
Greystoke St *STKP* SK1 .... 139 C4
Greystone Av *OLDTF/WHR* M16 ... 46 B5
Grey St *DTN/ASHW* M34......... 119 D2
  PWCH M25 .... 63 C1 🗓
  WGTN/LGST M12 .... 29 F4
Greyswood Av *CHH* M8 .... 82 B3 🗓

Greytown Cl *SLFD* M6 .... 79 D4 ⒊
Griffin Ct *CSLFD* M3 .... 15 E1 ⒊
Griffin Gv *BNG/LEV* M19 .... 51 D5
Griffin Rd *FAIL* M35.............................. 87 D2
Griffin St *BRO* M7 .... 81 C3
Griffiths Cl *BRO* M7 .... 5 D2
Griffiths St *NEWH/MOS* M40 .... 87 C4 ⒑
Grimscott Cl *BKLY* M9 .... 67 D4 ⒉
Grimshaw Av *FAIL* M35 .... 89 C1
Grimshaw La *NEWH/MOS* M40....... 85 D4
Grimshaw St *FAIL* M35 .... 88 A1 ⒉
    STKP SK1 .... 139 D4 ⒉
Grindall Av *BKLY* M9 .... 68 B3
Grindley Av *CCHDY* M21 .... 127 D4
Grindlow St *BRUN/LGST* M13 .... 39 E1
Grindon Av *BRO* M7 .... 80 B3
Grinton Av *BRUN/LGST* M13 .... 49 F1
Grizebeck Cl *GTN* M18 .... 106 A3
Groby Rd *CCHDY* M21 .... 43 E5
Groby Rd North *DTN/ASHW* M34 .... 109 D1
Groby St *OLDS* OL8 .... 73 D2
Groom St *CMANE* M1 .... 27 E2 ⒈
Grosvenor Gdns *BRO* M7 .... 5 D2
Grosvenor Rd *ECC* M30 .... 90 A2 ⒈
    OLDTF/WHR M16 .... 45 D2
    SALE M33 .... 122 B4
    SWIN M27 .... 77 D2
    URM M41 .... 111 C3
Grosvenor Sq *BRO* M7 .... 5 D2
Grosvenor St *CMANE* M1 .... 27 E2
    DTN/ASHW M34 .... 119 D1
    PWCH M25 .... 63 C1
    STRET M32 .... 114 B3 ⒈
    SWIN M27 .... 58 B3 ⒏
Grove Av *FAIL* M35 .... 88 A4
Grove Cl *RUSH/FAL* M14 .... 38 A5
Grovehurst *SWIN* M27 .... 74 B3 ⒉
Grove St *BRO* M7 .... 82 A4
    DROY M43 .... 107 D1
The Grove *ECC* M30 .... 92 B4
Grundy Av *PWCH* M25 .... 61 C3
Guide Post Sq *BRUN/LGST* M13 ..... 28 C4 ⒈
Guide St *SALO/ORD* M5 .... 94 A4
Guido St *FAIL* M35 .... 88 A2
Guildford Rd *BNG/LEV* M19 .... 51 F2
    SLFD M6 .... 93 D1
    URM M41 .... 112 A1
Guildhall Cl *HULME* M15 .... 36 C1
Guilford Rd *ECC* M30 .... 90 B4
Guinness Rd *TRPK* M17 .... 103 C1
Gullane Cl *NEWH/MOS* M40 .... 87 C2
Gulvain Pl *CHAD* OL9 .... 52 B1 ⒈
Gunson St *NEWH/MOS* M40 .... 8 B4
Gun St *ANC* M4 .... 17 F1 ⒈
Gurner Av *SALO/ORD* M5...................... 23 F2
Gurney St *ANC* M4 .... 19 D2
Guy Fawkes St *SALO/ORD* M5 .... 23 E2
Guy St *BRO* M7 .... 82 B2 ⒎
Gwelo St *OP/CLY* M11 .... 11 D5
Gwenbury Av *STKP* SK1 .... 139 D4
Gwendor Av *CHH* M8 .... 64 B2
Gyte's La *BNG/LEV* M19 .... 116 A3

    NEWH/MOS M40 .... 96 A1 ⒉
Haddington Dr *BKLY* M9 .... 67 C2
Haddon Av *NEWH/MOS* M40 .... 70 A4
Haddon Rd *RDSH* SK5 .... 134 A2 ⒋
Haddon Hall Rd *DROY* M43 .... 97 C3 ⒉
Haddon Rd *CCHDY* M21 .... 127 D4 ⒈
    ECC M30 .... 101 C1
    SWIN M27 .... 75 C4
Haddon St *SLFD* M6 .... 80 B4
    STRET M32 .... 114 B1 ⒈
Hadfield Av *CHAD* OL9 .... 53 D4
Hadfield St *BRO* M7 .... 82 A3 ⒒
    OLDS OL8 .... 73 C2
    OLDTF/WHR M16 .... 24 B4
Hadley Av *BRUN/LGST* M13........... 49 F2
Hadley St *SLFD* M6 .... 80 B4 ⒈
Hadlow Gn *RDSH* SK5 .... 135 D3 ⒊
Hafton Rd *BRO* M7.......................... 80 B3
Hagley Rd *SALO/ORD* M5 .... 23 D4
Hague Rd *DID/WITH* M20 .... 129 C4
Hague St *NEWH/MOS* M40 .... 85 D4 ⒊
Haigh Av *HTNM* SK4 .... 138 A1
Haigh Pk *HTNM* SK4 .... 134 A4
Haig Rd *STRET* M32 .... 114 B2
Hailsham St *OP/CLY* M11 .... 20 A1 ⒈
Haldon Rd *DID/WITH* M20 .... 130 B4
Hale La *FAIL* M35 .... 88 A1
Hales Cl *DROY* M43 .... 97 D2
Halesden Rd *HTNM* SK4 .... 133 D4
Haley Cl *RDSH* SK5 .... 134 B1
Haley St *CHH* M8 .... 83 C2
Half Edge La *ECC* M30 .... 92 B2
Halford Dr *NEWH/MOS* M40 .... 86 B1
Halft St *CSLFD* M3 .... 5 F4 ⒈
Hallam Rd *NEWH/MOS* M40 .... 86 A3
Hall Av *RUSH/FAL* M14 .... 38 C5
    SALE M33 .... 122 A3
Hall Bank *ECC* M30 .... 91 C3
Hall Farm Av *URM* M41 .... 110 B2
Hall Gv *RUSH/FAL* M14 .... 38 C5
Halliday Rd *NEWH/MOS* M40 .... 11 E1
Halliford Rd *NEWH/MOS* M40........ 86 A3
Halliwell Av *OLDS* OL8 .... 73 C2
Halliwell La *CHH* M8 .... 82 B2
Halliwell Rd *PWCH* M25 .... 61 D4
Halliwell St *CHAD* OL9 .... 71 C3 ⒈
Halliwell St West *CHH* M8 .... 82 B2 ⒊
Hall Moss Rd *BKLY* M9 .... 68 A2
Hall Rd *RUSH/FAL* M14................... 38 C5
Hall St *CMANW* M2 .... 16 B4
    FAIL M35 .... 87 D3 ⒊
    STKP SK1 .... 139 C4
    SWIN M27 .... 58 B3 ⒎
Hallsville Rd *BNG/LEV* M19 .... 116 A4
Hallsworth Rd *ECC* M30 .... 90 B4 ⒈
Hallwood Av *SLFD* M6 .... 94 A1
Hallworth Av *DTN/ASHW* M34 ...... 98 B4
Hallworth Rd *CHH* M8 .... 83 D1 ⒈
Halmore Rd *NEWH/MOS* M40.......... 8 C5
Halsbury Cl *WGTN/LGST* M12 .... 29 E4
Halsey Cl *CHAD* OL9 .... 70 A2
Halsmere Dr *BKLY* M9 .... 67 C2 ⒉
Halstead Av *CCHDY* M21 .... 126 A2
    SLFD M6 .... 79 C4 ⒊
Halston Cl *RDSH* SK5 .... 138 B1 ⒏
Halston St *HULME* M15 .... 25 F4 ⒈
Halton Bank *SLFD* M6 .... 2 A2
Halton Rd *OP/CLY* M11 .... 96 A3
Halvis Gv *OLDTF/WHR* M16 .... 33 F5
Hambleton Dr *SALE* M33 .... 121 D4 ⒊
Hambridge Cl *CHH* M8 .... 83 C2 ⒊
Hamer Dr *OLDTF/WHR* M16 .... 34 C1
Hamer Hl *BKLY* M9 .... 66 A2 ⒈

H

Hacking St *BRO* M7 .... 82 A3
    PWCH M25 .... 62 A1 ⒋
Hackle St *OP/CLY* M11 .... 96 A3
Hackleton Cl *ANC* M4 .... 19 D2 ⒊
Hackness Rd *CCHDY* M21 .... 42 B5
Hackney Av *NEWH/MOS* M40 .... 11 F1

Hamerton Rd *NEWH/MOS* M40 .... **8** A2
Hamilcar Av *ECC* M30 .... **92** A3
Hamilton Cl *PWCH* M25 .... **62** A2 ☑
Hamilton Rd *BRUN/LGST* M13 .... **40** A4
  PWCH M25 .... **62** A2
Hamilton Sq *STKP* SK4 .... **138** A2 ☑
Hamilton St *BRO* M7 .... **81** D2 ☑
  CHAD OL9 .... **53** C2
  ECC M30 .... **90** B2 ☑
  OLDTF/WHR M16 .... **24** C5
  SWIN M27 .... **57** D3
Hamlet Dr *SALE* M33 .... **122** A3 ☑
Hammerside Rd *GTN* M18 .... **106** A3
Hammett Rd *CCHDY* M21 .... **126** A1 ☑
Hammond Av *HTNM* SK4 .... **134** A4
Hamnett St *OP/CLY* M11 .... **96** B4
Hampden Crs *GTN* M18 .... **106** A4
Hampden Gv *ECC* M30 .... **91** D3
Hampden Rd *PWCH* M25 .... **62** B1
Hampshire Rd *CHAD* OL9 .... **53** D4 ☑
  DROY M43 .... **98** A2
  RDSH SK5 .... **136** A4
Hampshire St *BRO* M7 .... **81** D3
Hampson Rd *STRET* M32 .... **114** A3
Hampson St *DROY* M43 .... **98** A3
  ECC M30 .... **90** B4
  NEWH/MOS M40 .... **8** C2 ☑
  SALQ/ORD M5 .... **14** B3
  SWIN M27 .... **59** C4 ☑
Hampton Rd *CCHDY* M21 .... **42** B4
  FAIL M35 .... **89** C1
  URM M41 .... **111** D4
Hampton St *OLDS* OL8 .... **72** B1
Hamsell Rd *BRUN/LGST* M13 ...... **28** A2
Hancock Cl *RUSH/FAL* M14 .... **37** F4
Hancock St *STRET* M32 .... **124** B1
Handel Av *URM* M41 .... **110** A3 ☑
Handforth Gv *BRUN/LGST* M13 .... **49** F2
Handforth Rd *RDSH* SK5 .... **134** B4
Handley Av *RUSH/FAL* M14 .... **47** E3
Handsworth St *WGTN/LGST* M12 .... **29** D1
Hanging Ditch *ANC* M4 .... **16** B1
Hankinson Wy *SLFD* M6 .... **2** C4
Hanlith Ms *BNG/LEV* M19 .... **131** D1
Hanlon St *CHH* M8 .... **82** B1
Hannah Baldwin Cl *OP/CLY* M11 .. **20** A4
Hannah St *WGTN/LGST* M12 ...... **51** D1
Hanover Ct *BRO* M7 .... **81** D2
Hanover Crs *RUSH/FAL* M14 .... **39** D3
Hanover Gdns *BRO* M7 .... **82** A1
Hanover St *ANC* M4 .... **6** C5
Hansdon Cl *CHH* M8 .... **83** C3 ☑
Hanson Ms *STKP* SK1 .... **139** D3
Hanson Rd *NEWH/MOS* M40 ...... **86** A2
Hanworth Cl *BRUN/LGST* M13 .... **27** F2
Hapton Av *STRET* M32 .... **114** B4
Hapton Pl *HTNM* SK4 .... **138** A2 ☑
Hapton St *BNG/LEV* M19 .... **51** D3 ☑
Harbern Cl *ECC* M30 .... **91** D1
Harcombe Rd *DID/WITH* M20 .... **130** A3
Harcourt Av *URM* M41 .... **112** B4
Harcourt Cl *URM* M41 .... **112** B4
Harcourt Rd *SALE* M33 .... **123** C3
Harcourt St *RDSH* SK5 .... **134** B1
  STRET M32 .... **115** C2 ☑
Hardcastle Av *CCHDY* M21 .... **127** C3
Hardicker St *BNG/LEV* M19 .... **132** B2
Harding St *ANC* M4 .... **18** C2
  CSLFD M3 .... **6** A5 ☑
  SLFD M6 .... **2** C1
  STKP SK1 .... **139** D4
Hardman Av *PWCH* M25 .... **63** D3
Hardman La *FAIL* M35 .... **88** A1

Hardman Rd *RDSH* SK5 .... **134** B1
Hardman St *CHAD* OL9 .... **71** D2
  CSLFD M3 .... **15** F3
  FAIL M35 .... **87** D2
Hardon Gv *BRUN/LGST* M13 ...... **50** A2
Hardrush Fold *FAIL* M35 .... **89** C3
Hardshaw Cl *BRUN/LGST* M13 .... **27** F3 ☑
Hardy Av *CCHDY* M21 .... **126** A1 ☑
Hardy Gv *SWIN* M27 .... **75** D4
Hardy La *CCHDY* M21 .... **126** B3
Hardy St *ECC* M30 .... **90** B4
Haredale Dr *CHH* M8 .... **83** D3 ☑
Harehill Cl *BRUN/LGST* M13 .... **27** F1
Hare St *ANC* M4 .... **17** D1 ☑
Harewood Gv *RDSH* SK5 .... **134** A1 ☑
Harewood Wy *SWIN* M27 .... **58** B3
Hargreave's St *ANC* M4 .... **7** D3
  CHAD OL9 .... **54** A3
  OLD OL1 .... **55** D2 ☑
Harkness St *WGTN/LGST* M12 .... **28** B2
Harland Dr *CHH* M8 .... **83** D2 ☑
Harley Av *RUSH/FAL* M14 .... **39** E4
Harley Rd *SALE* M33 .... **124** A4
Harley St *OP/CLY* M11 .... **106** B1
Harlow Dr *GTN* M18 .... **116** B2 ☑
Harmer Cl *NEWH/MOS* M40 ...... **86** A4
Harmsworth Dr *HTNM* SK4 ...... **132** B4
Harmsworth St *SLFD* M6 .... **95** C3
Harold Av *GTN* M18 .... **117** D1 ☑
Harold Priestnall Cl
  NEWH/MOS M40 .... **86** B3 ☑
Harold St *CHAD* OL9 .... **54** B2 ☑
  FAIL M35 .... **88** A2 ☑
  OLDTF/WHR M16 .... **24** B4
  PWCH M25 .... **61** D1
Harper St *OLDS* OL8 .... **73** C1
Harp Rd *TRPK* M17 .... **103** C1
Harp St *OP/CLY* M11 .... **106** B2
Harpurhey Rd *CHH* M8 .... **84** A1
Harriett St *ANC* M4 .... **8** B5
Harringay Rd *NEWH/MOS* M40 .... **86** B4
Harrington St *GTN* M18 .... **107** C4
Harris Av *DTN/ASHW* M34 .... **118** B2
  URM M41 .... **101** D4
Harris Cl *DTN/ASHW* M34............ **118** B2
Harrison Av *BNG/LEV* M19 .... **51** E2
Harrison St *ANC* M4 .... **18** C3
  BRO M7 .... **5** D2
  ECC M30 .... **100** A1
  OLD OL1 .... **55** D3 ☑
Harris St *CHH* M8 .... **5** F2
Harrogate Av *PWCH* M25 .... **63** D3
Harrogate Cl *OP/CLY* M11 .... **107** C2 ☑
Harrogate Dr *RDSH* SK5 .... **134** A1
Harrogate Rd *RDSH* SK5 .... **117** C4
Harrop St *GTN* M18 .... **107** D3
Harrow Av *BNG/LEV* M19 .... **132** A3 ☑
  OLDS OL8 .... **72** B2
Harrowby Dr *NEWH/MOS* M40.... **84** B4
Harrowby Rd *SWIN* M27 .... **76** A2
Harrow St *CHH* M8 .... **65** D4
Harry Hall Gdns *BRO* M7 .... **4** B3
Harry Rd *RDSH* SK5 .... **134** B1 ☑
Harry St *CHAD* OL9 .... **54** A3
Hart Av *DROY* M43 .... **98** B4
Harter St *CMANE* M1 .... **16** C4
Hartfield Cl *BRUN/LGST* M13 ...... **28** A3
Hartford Av *HTNM* SK4 .... **133** D3
Hartford Rd *URM* M41 .... **112** A1
Hart Hill Dr *SALQ/ORD* M5 .... **94** B2
Harthill St *CHH* M8 .... **82** B4
Hartington Cl *URM* M41 .... **112** A3 ☑
Hartington Dr *OP/CLY* M11.......... **11** F4

Hartington Rd *CCHDY* M21 .... **126** B1
  ECC M30 .... **90** A2 **2**
Hartington St *RUSH/FAL* M14........ **36** B4
Hartis Av *BRO* M7 .... **82** A3
Hartlepool Cl *RUSH/FAL* M14 .... **37** F4
Hartley Av *PWCH* M25 .... **63** C2
Hartley Rd *CCHDY* M21 .... **43** D3
Hartley St *NEWH/MOS* M40 .... **85** D1 **7**
Harton Av *GTN* M18 .... **116** A2 **2**
Hart Rd *RUSH/FAL* M14 .... **47** D2
Hartshead Cl *OP/CLY* M11 .... **108** A2 **1**
Hart St *CMANE* M1 .... **17** D4 **1**
  DROY M43 .... **98** A3
Hartswood Rd *DID/WITH* M20 ...... **130** B3
Hartwell Cl *OP/CLY* M11 .... **20** A5
Harvest Cl *SLFD* M6 .... **79** C4 **4**
Harvey Cl *OP/CLY* M11.................... **20** C5
Harvey St *STKP* SK1 .... **138** B4 **4**
Harwich Cl *BNG/LEV* M19 .... **51** E3 **1**
  RDSH SK5 .... **136** A3 **1**
Harwood Rd *BNG/LEV* M19 .... **131** C3 **2**
Harwood St *HTNM* SK4 .... **138** A2 **7**
Haslemere Rd *DID/WITH* M20 ...... **130** B3 **1**
  URM M41 .... **110** B4
Hasper Av *DID/WITH* M20 .... **129** C2
Hassall Av *DID/WITH* M20 .... **128** B1
Hassop Av *BRO* M7.......................... **80** A2
Hassop Cl *OP/CLY* M11.................... **19** F2
Hassop Rd *RDSH* SK5 .... **118** A4
Hastings Av *CCHDY* M21 .... **43** D5
Hastings Rd *ECC* M30 .... **90** A1
Hathaway Gdns *MPL/ROM* SK6 .... **141** D4
Hatherley Rd *DID/WITH* M20 .... **130** B3
Hatherop Cl *ECC* M30 .... **90** B4
Hathersage Rd *BRUN/LGST* M13 .. **38** C2
Hathersage St *CHAD* OL9 .... **54** A3
Hathershaw La *OLDS* OL8 .... **73** D2
Hatro Ct *URM* M41 .... **113** C4
Hatter St *ANC* M4 .... **7** E5
Hatton Av *BRO* M7 .... **4** C3
Hattons Ct *STRET* M32.................. **114** A2
Hattons Rd *TRPK* M17 .... **103** D3
Hatton St *STKP* SK1 .... **138** A3 **4**
  WGTN/LGST M12 .... **40** C4
Havana Cl *OP/CLY* M11 .... **20** A3
Havelock Dr *BRO* M7 .... **5** C1
Havelock St *OLDS* OL8 .... **55** D4 **2**
Haven Dr *DROY* M43 .... **97** C3
Havenscroft Av *ECC* M30 .... **101** D1
Haven St *SLFD* M6 .... **95** C4 **4**
Haverfield Rd *BKLY* M9 .... **67** C2
Haverford St *WGTN/LGST* M12...... **29** F3
Haversham Av *CHH* M8.................... **64** A3
Havers Rd *GTN* M18 .... **107** C4
Hawarden Av *OLDTF/WHR* M16 .... **44** A2
Hawes Av *RUSH/FAL* M14 .... **131** C2 **5**
  SWIN M27 .... **76** B3 **3**
Haweswater Cl *DTN/ASHW* M34 .. **118** A3 **1**
Hawkeshead Rd *CHH* M8 .... **83** D3 **3**
Hawkhurst Rd *BRUN/LGST* M13.... **40** A4
Hawkins St *RDSH* SK5 .... **138** A1
Hawkshaw Ct *SALQ/ORD* M5 .... **12** C3
Hawksley St *OLDS* OL8.................... **72** A2
Hawkstone Av *DROY* M43 .... **97** C2 **2**
Hawley St *BNG/LEV* M19 .... **132** B1 **3**
Haworth Dr *STRET* M32.................. **112** B2
Haworth Rd *GTN* M18 .... **116** A1
Hawsworth Cl *HULME* M15.............. **37** D1
Hawthorn Av *ECC* M30 .... **91** D2
  URM M41 .... **112** B4 **4**
Hawthorn Dr *SLFD* M6.................... **93** C1
  SWIN M27 .... **78** A2
Hawthorne Crs *OLDS* OL8 .... **73** D3 **3**

Hawthorne Dr *WALK* M28 .... **74** A2
Hawthorne Gv *CHAD* OL9 .... **53** D1 **2**
  MPL/ROM SK6 .... **141** C1
Hawthorn La *CCHDY* M21 .... **125** D1 **1**
  SALE M33 .... **121** D3
Hawthorn Rd *DROY* M43.................. **99** C3
  DTN/ASHW M34 .... **118** B1
  NEWH/MOS M40 .... **70** A4
  OLDS OL8 .... **71** D3
  STRET M32 .... **125** C1
Hawthorn Rd South *DROY* M43...... **99** C3
The Hawthorns *DTN/ASHW* M34 .. **109** D3
Hawthorn St *GTN* M18.................. **106** B3
Haxby Rd *GTN* M18 .... **116** B2
Haydn Av *RUSH/FAL* M14 .... **37** E3
Hayeswater Rd *URM* M41.............. **111** C2
Hayfield Cl *WGTN/LGST* M12........ **29** F2
Hayfield Rd *SLFD* M6 .... **93** D1
Hayley St *BRUN/LGST* M13 .... **39** F2 **1**
Hayling Rd *SALE* M33.................... **122** A4
Haymarket Cl *BRUN/LGST* M13 .... **28** B5
Haymond Cl *SLFD* M6...................... **80** A3
Hazel Av *OLDTF/WHR* M16 .... **44** C1
  SWIN M27 .... **77** C2
Hazelbank Av *DID/WITH* M20 ...... **129** D2
Hazelbottom Rd *CHH* M8 .... **83** D2
Hazel Cl *DROY* M43 .... **99** C3 **3**
Hazeldene Rd *NEWH/MOS* M40 .... **70** A4
Hazelfields *WALK* M28 .... **74** B2
Hazel Gv *CHAD* OL9........................ **53** D1
  URM M41 .... **112** A3
Hazelhurst Fold *WALK* M28 .... **75** C2
Hazelhurst Rd *WALK* M28 .... **74** B2
Hazel La *OLDS* OL8 .... **72** B3
Hazelmere Av *ECC* M30.................. **91** C1 **3**
Hazelmere Cl *ECC* M30 .... **102** A1 **3**
Hazelwood *CHAD* OL9 .... **52** A2 **2**
Headingley Dr *OLDTF/WHR* M16 .... **32** C4
Headingley Rd *RUSH/FAL* M14 .... **131** C2 **6**
Headlands St *PWCH* M25 .... **62** A4
Heald Av *RUSH/FAL* M14 .... **37** F4
Heald Gv *RUSH/FAL* M14 .... **37** F3
Heald Pl *RUSH/FAL* M14.................. **37** F4
Heald St *STKP* SK1........................ **139** C3
Healey Cl *BRO* M7 .... **81** C1
Heath Av *BRO* M7 .... **4** B2
Heathcote Rd *GTN* M18 .... **116** A1
Heather Av *DROY* M43 .... **99** C3
Heatherdale Dr *CHH* M8 .... **83** C3
Heather Gv *DROY* M43 .... **108** B1
Heatherside *RDSH* SK5 .... **118** A4 **8**
Heather St *OP/CLY* M11.................. **11** E5
Heatherway *SALE* M33 .... **121** D4
Heathfield Av *DTN/ASHW* M34 .... **119** D3 **2**
  HTNM SK4 .... **133** C4
Heathfield Dr *SWIN* M27................ **77** C2
Heathfield St *NEWH/MOS* M40 .... **87** C4 **11**
Heathland Rd *BRO* M7 .... **80** B1
Heathlands Dr *PWCH* M25 .... **62** A4
Heathside Rd *DID/WITH* M20 ...... **130** B4
Heath St *CHH* M8 .... **82** B2
Heatley Rd *DTN/ASHW* M34 .... **118** B3
Heaton Rd *DID/WITH* M20.............. **130** A2
Heaton St *BRO* M7 .... **82** A2
  DTN/ASHW M34 .... **119** D2
  PWCH M25 .... **63** C1
Hebden Av *SLFD* M6........................ **94** A2
Hector Rd *BRUN/LGST* M13.......... **40** B5
Hedges St *FAIL* M35 .... **89** C1
Helena St *SLFD* M6 .... **78** A4 **8**
Helen St *BRO* M7 .... **81** C4
  ECC M30 .... **100** B1
Helensville Av *SLFD* M6 .... **80** A4 **2**

Helga St *NEWH/MOS* M40 .... 8 C2
Helmet St *CMANE* M1 .... 18 B5
Helston St *NEWH/MOS* M40 .... 10 A2
Hembury Av *BNG/LEV* M19 .... 131 D3
Hemlock Av *OLDS* OL8 .... 73 C2 2
Hemming Dr *ECC* M30 .... 92 A4 1
Hemmington Dr *BKLY* M9 .... 84 B2
Hemmons Rd *WGTN/LGST* M12 .... 51 E1
Hemsley St *BKLY* M9 .... 67 C4
Hemsley St South *BKLY* M9 .... 85 C1
Hemswell Cl *SLFD* M6 .... 95 C1 4
Hemsworth Rd *GTN* M18 .... 116 B2
Henbury St *RUSH/FAL* M14 .... 36 C5
Henderson Av *SWIN* M27 .... 58 B4 3
Henderson St *BNG/LEV* M19 .... 132 B1
Hendham V *BKLY* M9 .... 84 A2
Hendon Rd *BKLY* M9 .... 66 A1 1
Hengist St *GTN* M18 .... 116 B1
Henley Av *OLDTF/WHR* M16 .... 33 E5
Henley Pl *BNG/LEV* M19 .... 132 A3
Henley St *CHAD* OL9 .... 71 C2
OLD OL1 .... 54 B1 2
Henniker St *SWIN* M27 .... 76 A3
Henrietta St *OLDTF/WHR* M16 ...... 34 B2
Henry St *ANC* M4 .... 17 E1
DROY M43 .... 98 A4 4
ECC M30 .... 91 C4 7
FAIL M35 .... 88 B2 4
OLDTF/WHR M16 .... 24 A5
Henshaw La *CHAD* OL9 .... 70 B3
Henshaw St *OLD* OL1 .... 55 C2
STRET M32 .... 114 B3 2
Henwood Rd *DID/WITH* M20 .... 130 A4
Heppleton Rd *NEWH/MOS* M40 .... 69 D3
Hepton St *OLD* OL1 .... 55 C1
Herbert St *CHAD* OL9 .... 53 D2 1
CHH M8 .... 82 B3 2
DROY M43 .... 97 D4
PWCH M25 .... 61 D1
STRET M32 .... 114 B3 2
Hereford Dr *PWCH* M25 .... 63 C3
SWIN M27 .... 76 B3
Hereford Gv *URM* M41 .... 111 C3
Hereford Rd *ECC* M30 .... 77 C4
RDSH SK5 .... 136 A4
Hereford St *CHAD* OL9 .... 53 D4
SALE M33 .... 123 D4 3
Hermitage Rd *CHH* M8 .... 65 C4
Hermon Av *OLDS* OL8 .... 73 C2
Herne St *OP/CLY* M11 .... 21 D5
Heron Ct *SLFD* M6 .... 93 D2
Herondale Cl *NEWH/MOS* M40 .... 86 B4 2
Heron Dr *DTN/ASHW* M34 .... 99 C4
Heron St *HULME* M15 .... 35 F1
OLDS OL8 .... 72 A2
SWIN M27 .... 59 C2
Herristone Rd *CHH* M8 .... 65 C3
Herrod Av *HTNM* SK4 .... 134 A4
Herschel St *NEWH/MOS* M40 .... 86 A1 3
Hersey St *SLFD* M6 .... 95 C3 4
Hertford Rd *BKLY* M9 .... 66 B4
Hesford Av *BKLY* M9 .... 85 D2
Hesketh St *HTNM* SK4 .... 138 A2 3
HTNM SK4 .... 138 A2 3
Hessel St *SALO/ORD* M5 .... 94 B4
Heston Av *BRUN/LGST* M13 .... 49 F2
Heston Dr *URM* M41 .... 111 C2
Heswall Av *DID/WITH* M20 .... 129 D2
Heswall Rd *RDSH* SK5 .... 117 D4
Hethorn St *NEWH/MOS* M40 .... 87 C4
Hetton Av *BRUN/LGST* M13 .... 49 F1
Hewart Cl *NEWH/MOS* M40 .... 8 B1
Hewitt Av *DTN/ASHW* M34 .... 117 D2

Hewitt St *CSLFD* M3 .... 25 F1
Hewlett Rd *CCHDY* M21 .... 42 C4
Hexham Cl *OLD* OL9 .... 54 A2 3
Heybury Cl *OP/CLY* M11 .... 20 A5
Heyford Av *NEWH/MOS* M40 .... 69 D3
Heyrod St *CMANE* M1 .... 18 A4
Heys Av *SWIN* M27 .... 57 C3
Heys Cl North *SWIN* M27 .... 57 C3 1
Heyscroft Rd *DID/WITH* M20 ...... 130 A3
Heysham Av *DID/WITH* M20 .... 128 B2
The Heys *RDSH* SK5 .... 118 A4
Heys Vw *PWCH* M25 .... 62 B1
Heywood Av *SWIN* M27 .... 59 D3 4
Heywood Gdns *PWCH* M25 .... 62 B1 5
Heywood Gv *SALE* M33 .... 123 C3
Heywood St *CHH* M8 .... 83 C3
FAIL M35 .... 87 D2
SWIN M27 .... 76 A1
Heywood Wy *SLFD* M6 .... 2 B4
Heyworth St *SALO/ORD* M5 .... 95 C4 3
Hibbert Av *DTN/ASHW* M34 .... 109 D4
Hibbert Crs *FAIL* M35 .... 89 C2
Hibbert St *HTNM* SK4 .... 134 A4
RUSH/FAL M14 .... 38 A5 1
Hibernia Wy *STRET* M32 .... 103 C4
Higginson Rd *RDSH* SK5 .... 134 A2
Higham Vw *SLFD* M6 .... 3 D3
High Ash Gv *DTN/ASHW* M34 ...... 109 D2 2
High Bank *GTN* M18 .... 107 C4
High Bank Crs *PWCH* M25 .... 63 C3
High Bank Gv *PWCH* M25 .... 63 C2
High Bank Rd *DROY* M43 .... 107 D1
SWIN M27 .... 77 D1
High Bank Side *STKP* SK1 .... 138 B4 8
Highbury Rd *HTNM* SK4 .... 133 C3
OLDTF/WHR M16 .... 45 F4
Highclere Av *CHH* M8 .... 82 B3 10
Highclere Rd *CHH* M8 .... 64 B3 2
Highcliffe Rd *BKLY* M9 .... 65 C2
Higher Ardwick *WGTN/LGST* M12 .... 28 B2
Higher Bents La *MPL/ROM* SK6 .. 141 D2 4
Higher Cambridge St *HULME* M15 .... 26 C3
Higher Chatham St *HULME* M15 .... 26 C3
Higher Cft *ECC* M30 .... 101 C1
Higher House Cl *CHAD* OL9 .... 71 C1
Higher Ormond St *HULME* M15 .... 27 D3 1
Higher Rd *URM* M41 .... 111 D3
Higher York St *BRUN/LGST* M13 .... 27 E3
Highfield Av *MPL/ROM* SK6 .... 141 D3
Highfield Cl *STRET* M32 .... 124 A1
Highfield Dr *ECC* M30 .... 91 D2
SWIN M27 .... 78 A2
URM M41 .... 111 C2 3
Highfield Park Rd *MPL/ROM* SK6 .... 141 C1
Highfield Pl *GTN* M18 .... 117 D1 10
Highfield Range *GTN* M18 .... 117 D1 11
Highfield Rd *BNG/LEV* M19 .... 51 F4 1
BNG/LEV M19 .... 116 A4
ECC M30 .... 91 D1
HTNM SK4 .... 133 D1
SLFD M6 .... 2 A4
STRET M32 .... 124 A1
Highfield St *BRO* M7 .... 82 B2
CHAD OL9 .... 54 B2
Highfield Ter *BKLY* M9 .... 84 B3 3
Highgate Av *URM* M41 .... 110 A1
Highgate Crs *GTN* M18 .... 116 B1
High La *CCHDY* M21 .... 43 E5
High Legh Rd *OP/CLY* M11 .... 106 B1
Highmead St *GTN* M18 .... 106 B4
Highmore Dr *BKLY* M9 .... 67 C2 3
High Peak St *NEWH/MOS* M40 ...... 86 B3
Highshore Dr *CHH* M8 .... 82 B2 9

Highstone Dr *CHH* M8 .... 84 A3 🔲
High St *ANC* M4 .... 16 C2
 DROY M43 .... 98 A4
 OLD OL1 .... 55 C2
 STKP SK1 .... 138 B4
Highworth Dr *NEWH/MOS* M40 ..... 69 D5 🔲
Higson Av *CCHDY* M21 .... 126 B2
 ECC M30 .... 101 C1
 MPL/ROM SK6 .... 141 D1
Hilary Av *OLDS* OL8 .... 73 D4
Hilbury Av *BKLY* M9 .... 66 B4
Hilda Gv *RDSH* SK5 .... 138 B1
Hilda St *CHAD* OL9 .... 54 B2
Hilden Ct *OLDTF/WHR* M16 ..... 34 C3
Hillam Cl *URM* M41 .... 112 B4
Hillbrook Av *NEWH/MOS* M40 .... 68 B3 🔲
Hillcourt St *CMANE* M1 .... 27 D2
Hill Crs *BKLY* M9 .... 65 C2
Hillcrest Dr *BNG/LEV* M19 .... 133 C2
Hillcrest Rd *PWCH* M25 .... 61 D3
Hillcroft Cl *CHH* M8 .... 83 C1 🔲
Hilldale Av *BKLY* M9 .... 66 B3
Hillfield Cl *BRUN/LGST* M13 .... 28 C5
Hillfield Cl *BRUN/LGST* M13 .... 28 C5
Hillgate Av *SALQ/ORD* M5 .... 23 C2
Hillier St *BKLY* M9 .... 85 C1
Hillier St North *BKLY* M9 .... 85 C1
Hillingdon Cl *OLDS* OL8 .... 71 D4
Hillingdon Dr *NEWH/MOS* M40 .... 68 B3
Hillingdon Rd *STRET* M32 .... 115 C4
Hillkirk St *OP/CLY* M11 .... 19 E2
Hill La *BKLY* M9 .... 66 B2
Hillman Cl *NEWH/MOS* M40 .... 84 B4 🔲
Hillside Av *BRO* M7 .... 80 A1 🔲
Hillside Cl *NEWH/MOS* M40 .... 68 A4
Hillside Dr *SWIN* M27 .... 78 B3
Hill St *BRO* M7 .... 81 D5 🔲
 DID/WITH M20 .... 129 D2
Hilltop Av *BKLY* M9 .... 66 B2
Hill Top Av *PWCH* M25 .... 62 B1
Hillview Rd *DTN/ASHW* M34 .... 118 A4
Hillwood Av *CHH* M8 .... 64 B2
Hilrose Av *URM* M41 .... 112 B3
Hilton Av *URM* M41 .... 111 D3
Hilton Dr *PWCH* M25 .... 62 B3 🔲
Hilton La *PWCH* M25 .... 62 A3
Hilton Sq *SWIN* M27 .... 59 C4
Hilton St *ANC* M4 .... 17 D1
 BRO M7 .... 81 D3
 CMANE M1 .... 17 E2
Hilton St North *BRO* M7 .... 81 D3
Himley Rd *OP/CLY* M11 .... 96 A2
Hinckley St *OP/CLY* M11 .... 20 A4 🔲
Hinde St *NEWH/MOS* M40 .... 86 A1
Hinton St *ANC* M4 .... 7 F4 🔲
 OLDS OL8 .... 55 D4 🔲
Hive St *OLDS* OL8 .... 71 D3
Hobart St *GTN* M18 .... 106 B2
Hobson St *FAIL* M35 .... 87 D3
 OLD OL1 .... 55 D5 🔲
 OP/CLY M11 .... 108 A2
 RDSH SK5 .... 117 D3
Hoddesdon St *CHH* M8 .... 83 D2
Hodge La *SLFD* M6 .... 12 B2
Hodge St *BKLY* M9 .... 67 D4
Hodgson St *CHH* M8 .... 82 B4
Hodson Rd *SWIN* M27 .... 58 A3 🔲
Hodson St *CSLFD* M3 .... 5 E5 🔲
Holbeck Gv *RUSH/FAL* M14 .... 39 E3
Holberton St *CHH* M8 .... 82 A4 🔲
Holborn Av *FAIL* M35 .... 89 D2 🔲
Holborn Dr *CHH* M8 .... 83 D4
Holborn St *STKP* SK1 .... 138 B4 🔲

Holbrook St *CMANE* M1 .... 17 D5 🔲
Holcombe Cl *SLFD* M6 .... 2 C5
Holcombe Rd *RUSH/FAL* M14 .... 131 C2 🔲
Holden Rd *BRO* M7 .... 63 D4
Holden St *OLDS* OL8 .... 73 D2 🔲
Holdgate Cl *HULME* M15 .... 25 F5
Holdsworth St *SWIN* M27 .... 75 D2
Holford Av *RUSH/FAL* M14 .... 47 E2
Holford St *SLFD* M6 .... 3 F1
Holker Cl *BRUN/LGST* M13 .... 39 D1
Holkham Cl *ANC* M4 .... 18 B1 🔲
Holland Rd *CHH* M8 .... 64 B3
Holland St *DTN/ASHW* M34 .... 119 D1
 NEWH/MOS M40 .... 9 D5
 SLFD M6 .... 80 A4
Holland St East *DTN/ASHW* M34 .... 119 D1
Holland St West *DTN/ASHW* M34 .... 119 D1
Hollin Bank *HTNM* SK4 .... 133 D2 🔲
Hollingworth Av
 NEWH/MOS M40 .... 70 B3 🔲
Hollingworth Rd *MPL/ROM* SK6 .... 141 C1
Hollingworth St *CHAD* OL9 .... 71 D2 🔲
Hollins Gv *WGTN/LGST* M12 .... 41 D4
Hollins Rd *OLDS* OL8 .... 72 A3
Hollinwood Av *NEWH/MOS* M40 .... 69 D3
Holloway Dr *WALK* M28 .... 57 C4
Hollow End *RDSH* SK5 .... 135 D2
Hollow Vale Dr *RDSH* SK5 .... 118 A4
Holly Av *URM* M41 .... 110 B3
Holly Bank Cl *HULME* M15 .... 24 B3 🔲
 HULME M15 .... 24 B4 🔲
Hollybush St *GTN* M18 .... 107 C3
Hollyedge Dr *PWCH* M25 .... 62 A3 🔲
Holly Gv *CHAD* OL9 .... 53 D1
Hollyhurst *WALK* M28 .... 74 B3
Holly La *OLDS* OL8 .... 72 A3 🔲
Holly Rd *HTNM* SK4 .... 133 C4
 SWIN M27 .... 75 D3
Holly St *DROY* M43 .... 96 B3
 OP/CLY M11 .... 19 E4
 STKP SK1 .... 139 C1
Holmbrook Wk *CHH* M8 .... 83 C3 🔲
Holmcroft Rd *GTN* M18 .... 116 B3
Holmdale Av *BNG/LEV* M19 .... 131 C4 🔲
Holme Park Wy *FAIL* M35 .... 89 D2
Holmfield Av *BKLY* M9 .... 85 D2
 PWCH M25 .... 63 C2
Holmfield Av West *NEWH/MOS* M40.. 85 D3
Holmfirth St *BRUN/LGST* M13 .... 40 A3
Holmlea Rd *DROY* M43 .... 97 C3
Holmleigh Av *BKLY* M9 .... 67 C4 🔲
Holmpark Rd *OP/CLY* M11 .... 107 D2 🔲
Holmwood Rd *DID/WITH* M20 .... 129 D4 🔲
Holroyd St *OP/CLY* M11 .... 21 D4 🔲
Holst Av *CHH* M8 .... 83 C3
Holtby St *BKLY* M9 .... 67 C4
Holt La *FAIL* M35 .... 89 C2
Holt Lane Ms *FAIL* M35 .... 89 C2
Holt St *ECC* M30 .... 101 C1
 NEWH/MOS M40 .... 85 D4
 SWIN M27 .... 58 B3 🔲
Holt Town *NEWH/MOS* M40 .... 19 E1
Holwood Dr *OLDTF/WHR* M16 .... 45 F5
Holyoake St *DROY* M43 .... 99 C3
Holyoak St *NEWH/MOS* M40.. .... 87 C3
Holyrood Dr *SWIN* M27 .... 75 C2
Holyrood St *NEWH/MOS* M40 .... 97 C1 🔲
Holywood St *RUSH/FAL* M14 .... 37 D4
Homebury Dr *OP/CLY* M11 .... 11 F5
Homerton Rd *NEWH/MOS* M40 .... 11 F5
Hometel *RUSH/FAL* M14 .... 48 B4
Honey St *CHH* M8 .... 7 D2
Honeywell La *OLDS* OL8 .... 73 D2

Honister Rd *BKLY* M9	85	D2
Honor St *BRUN/LGST* M13	40	A4
Hood St *ANC* M4	17	F1
Hooper St *STKP* SK1	138	A4 ☑
WGTN/LGST M12	19	D5
Hooton St *NEWH/MOS* M40	9	F3
Hope Av *STRET* M32	113	D2 ☑
Hopecourt Cl *SLFD* M6	94	A1 ☑
Hopedale Cl *OP/CLY* M11	20	B3
Hopedale Rd *RDSH* SK5	134	B3
Hopelea St *DID/WITH* M20	129	D2 ☑
Hope Park Cl *PWCH* M25	62	B2
Hope Park Rd *PWCH* M25	62	B2
Hope Rd *PWCH* M25	62	A3
RUSH/FAL M14	38	C3
Hopes Carr *STKP* SK1	138	B4
Hope St *BRO* M7	81	C2
CMANE M1	17	D3
ECC M30	92	B3 ☑
SALQ/ORD M5	14	A2
SWIN M27	77	C1
Hopkins St *WGTN/LGST* M12	40	C4
Hopkin St *OLD* OL1	55	D2 ☑
Hoppet La *DROY* M43	99	C3
Hopwood Av *ECC* M30	92	A2 ☑
Hopwood Rd *CSLFD* M3	5	F5 ☑
NEWH/MOS M40	86	A2
SWIN M27	77	D1 ☑
Horace Barnes Cl *RUSH/FAL* M14	36	C4
Horace Gv *HTNM* SK4	138	A1 ☑
Horatio St *GTN* M18	107	D3 ☑
Horbury Av *GTN* M18	116	B2
Hornbeam Cl *SALE* M33	121	C4
Hornbeam Rd *BNG/LEV* M19	51	F2
Hornby Rd *STRET* M32	32	B2
Hornby St *CHH* M8	6	A2
OLDS OL8	54	B4 ☑
Horncastle Rd *NEWH/MOS* M40	68	B4
Hornchurch St *HULME* M15	25	E4 ☑
Horne Dr *ANC* M4	18	A1
Horsedge St *OLD* OL1	55	D1
Horsefield Cl *CCHDY* M21	128	A2 ☑
Horseshoe La *CHAD* OL9	52	B3
Horsfield Wy *MPL/ROM* SK6	137	D3
Horsham St *SLFD* M6	95	C3 ☑
Horton Rd *RUSH/FAL* M14	47	D2
Hortree Rd *STRET* M32	115	C3
Horwood Crs *DID/WITH* M20	130	B4
Hoscar Dr *BNG/LEV* M19	131	C2
Hoskins Cl *WGTN/LGST* M12	41	D1
Hospital Rd *SWIN* M27	77	D2
Hothersall Rd *RDSH* SK5	134	B2 ☑
Hothersall St *BRO* M7	5	E3 ☑
Hotspur Cl *DID/WITH* M20	47	D5
Hough End Av *CCHDY* M21	127	C3 ☑
Houghend Crs *CCHDY* M21	128	A1 ☑
Hough Hall Rd *NEWH/MOS* M40	85	D1
Houghton Av *OLDS* OL8	72	B3 ☑
Houghton La *SWIN* M27	75	D4
Houghton Rd *CHH* M8	65	C4
Houghton St *SWIN* M27	78	B3 ☑
Houldsworth St *CMANE* M1	17	E1 ☑
RDSH SK5	134	A2
Houseley Av *OLD* OL9	71	C2
Houson St *OLDS* OL8	55	D4
Houston Pk *SALQ/ORD* M5	12	A3
Hoveden St *CHH* M8	6	A1
Hove Dr *RUSH/FAL* M14	131	C2
Hovey Cl *CHH* M8	82	B2 ☑
Hovis St *OP/CLY* M11	106	A1
Howard Av *ECC* M30	91	D2 ☑
HTNM SK4	133	C3
Howard St *CHH* M8	5	F1

SALQ/ORD M5	12	C4
STKP SK1	138	B3 ☑
STRET M32	114	B3
Howarth Av *SWIN* M27	75	C2 ☑
Howarth Cl *OP/CLY* M11	20	C3
Howarth St *OLDTF/WHR* M16	34	B2
Howden Cl *RDSH* SK5	117	C3
Howells Av *SALE* M33	123	C4
Howe St *BRO* M7	81	C2
Howgill St *OP/CLY* M11	96	B4
Hoy Dr *URM* M41	101	D4
Hoylake Cl *NEWH/MOS* M40	87	D1 ☑
Hoyland Cl *WGTN/LGST* M12	30	B4
Hoyle Av *OLDS* OL8	55	C4
Hoyle St *WGTN/LGST* M12	18	B5
Huddart Cl *SALQ/ORD* M5	13	F5
Hudson St *CHAD* OL9	71	C3
Hughes St *OP/CLY* M11	19	E5
Hugh Oldham Dr *BRO* M7	81	C3
Hugo St *NEWH/MOS* M40	86	A2
Hull Sq *CSLFD* M3	4	C5
Hulme Hall Rd *HULME* M15	24	C1
Hulme Pl *SALQ/ORD* M5	14	B2 ☑
Hulme Rd *DTN/ASHW* M34	118	B2
HTNM SK4	133	D4
Hulmes Rd *NEWH/MOS* M40	88	A4
Hulme St *HULME* M15	25	F2
OLDS OL8	73	C1
SALQ/ORD M5	14	B2
Hulme Wk *HULME* M15	26	A3
Hulton Dr *OLDTF/WHR* M16	35	E3
Hulton St *FAIL* M35	87	D2
SALQ/ORD M5	23	D1
Humberstone Av *HULME* M15	25	F2
Humber St *CHH* M8	83	D2 ☑
SALQ/ORD M5	94	B4
Hume St *BNG/LEV* M19	132	B1 ☑
Humphrey Crs *URM* M41	113	C3 ☑
Humphrey La *URM* M41	113	C3
Humphrey Pk *URM* M41	113	C4
Humphrey Rd *OLDTF/WHR* M16	33	F1
Humphrey St *CHH* M8	82	B1 ☑
Huncoat Av *HTNM* SK4	133	D3
Huncote Dr *BKLY* M9	67	C4 ☑
Hunmanby Av *HULME* M15	26	A2
Hunter's La *OLD* OL1	55	D3 ☑
Hunters Ms *SALE* M33	123	C4 ☑
Hunterston Av *ECC* M30	93	C4 ☑
Huntingdon Av *CHAD* OL9	53	D4 ☑
Huntingdon Crs *RDSH* SK5	136	A4 ☑
Hunt La *CHAD* OL9	52	B1
Huntley Rd *CHH* M8	64	A3
Hunts Rd *SLFD* M6	78	B4 ☑
Hunt St *BKLY* M9	66	B4
Hurdlow Av *BRO* M7	80	A2
Hurford Av *GTN* M18	106	B3 ☑
Hurstbourne Av *OP/CLY* M11	11	F4
Hurstbrook Dr *URM* M41	112	B2 ☑
Hurst St *CHAD* OL9	54	B2 ☑
RDSH SK5	134	A2
Hurstville Rd *CCHDY* M21	126	B3
Hurstway Dr *BKLY* M9	67	C2 ☑
Hus St *DROY* M43	107	D1
Huxley Av *CHH* M8	83	C3 ☑
Hyde Fold Cl *BNG/LEV* M19	131	D3
Hyde Gv *WGTN/LGST* M13	28	B5
Hyde Pl *BRUN/LGST* M13	28	B5
Hyde Rd *GTN* M18	31	E5
MDTN M24	52	A3
WGTN/LGST M12	30	B4
Hyde St *DROY* M43	99	C1
HULME M15	25	D5
Hydrangea Cl *SALE* M33	121	C4 ☑

Hythe Cl *RUSH/FAL* M14 .... **38** B5

NEWH/MOS M40 .... **86** A1

I

Iceland St *SLFD* M6 .... **12** A1 🔲
Ilex Gv *BRO* M7 .... **81** D3 🔢
Ilford St *OP/CLY* M11 .... **11** F5
Ilfracombe St *NEWH/MOS* M40 ...... **87** D3 🔢
Ilkley Cl *CHAD* OL9 .... **53** D3
Ilkley Crs *RDSH* SK5 .... **134** A1
Ilkley Dr *URM* M41 .... **110** A1
Ilkley St *NEWH/MOS* M40 .... **68** A4
Ilk St *OP/CLY* M11 .... **11** E5
Illona Dr *BRO* M7 .... **80** A1
Ince Cl *DID/WITH* M20 .... **129** D2 🔢
   HTNM SK4 .... **138** A2
Ince St *HTNM* SK4 .... **138** A2 🔢
Inchcape Dr *BKLY* M9 .... **65** D1 🔢
Inchfield Rd *NEWH/MOS* M40 .... **68** A4
Inchley Rd *BRUN/LGST* M13 .... **27** E2
Incline Cl *OLDS* OL8 .... **71** D3
Indigo St *SLFD* M6 .... **79** D4
Industry St *CHAD* OL9 .... **71** C1
Infant St *PWCH* M25 .... **63** C1 🔢
Ingham St *NEWH/MOS* M40 .... **97** C1 🔢
Inghamwood Cl *BRO* M7 .... **82** B3 🔢
Ingleby Av *BKLY* M9 .... **67** D1 🔢
Ingleby Ct *STRET* M32 .... **115** C4
Ingledene Av *BRO* M7 .... **64** A4 🔢
Ingleton Av *CHH* M8 .... **65** D3
Ingoldsby Av *RUSH/FAL* M14 .... **39** D2
Innes St *WGTN/LGST* M12 .... **41** E5
Innis Av *NEWH/MOS* M40 .... **87** C4
Instow Cl *BRUN/LGST* M13 .... **28** C4
Invar Rd *WALK* M28 .... **57** D4
Inverness Av *BKLY* M9 .... **68** A1 🔢
Iona Wy *URM* M41 .... **101** D4
Ionian Gdns *BRO* M7 .... **81** C4 🔢
Iqbal Cl *WGTN/LGST* M12 .... **41** D1
Iredine St *OP/CLY* M11 .... **96** A4 🔢
Iris St *OLDS* OL8 .... **73** D3
Irkdale St *CHH* M8 .... **84** A3
Irk St *ANC* M4 .... **7** D3
Irlam Av *ECC* M30 .... **91** D4
Irlam Rd *SALE* M33 .... **124** A4
Irlam Sq *SLFD* M6 .... **78** B4
Irlam St *NEWH/MOS* M40 .... **9** F1
Ironmonger La *OLD* OL1 .... **55** D3 🔢
Iron St *NEWH/MOS* M40 .... **9** E4
Irving St *OLDS* OL8 .... **71** D3 🔢
Irvin St *NEWH/MOS* M40 .... **87** C3
Irwell Av *ECC* M30 .... **92** B4
Irwell Gv *ECC* M30 .... **92** B4
Irwell Pl *ECC* M30 .... **92** B4 🔢
   SALQ/ORD M5 .... **14** A1
Irwell St *CHH* M8 .... **5** F2
   CSLFD M3 .... **15** D2
   SLFD M6 .... **80** A3
Isaac Cl *SALQ/ORD* M5 .... **12** C4
Isabella Cl *OLDTF/WHR* M16 .... **34** A2
Isaiah St *OLDS* OL8 .... **73** D1 🔢
Isca St *OP/CLY* M11 .... **20** A3
Isis Cl *BRO* M7 .... **80** A1
Islington St *CSLFD* M3 .... **15** D1 🔢
Islington Wy *CSLFD* M3 .... **14** C2
Isobel Cl *ECC* M30 .... **90** B4 🔢
Ivybridge Cl *BRUN/LGST* M13 .... **39** D1
Ivy Cl *DROY* M43 .... **97** D2
Ivygreen Rd *CCHDY* M21 .... **125** D1
Ivyleaf Sq *BRO* M7 .... **82** A3 🔢🔢
Ivy St *ECC* M30 .... **91** D4 🔢

J

Jack La *DROY* M43 .... **98** B3
   URM M41 .... **112** A3
Jackroom Dr *ANC* M4 .... **18** A2 🔢
Jackson Cl *OLDS* OL8 .... **55** C4 🔢
Jackson Ct *URM* M41 .... **110** A2
Jackson Crs *HULME* M15 .... **25** F2
Jackson Gdns *DTN/ASHW* M34 .... **119** D3
Jackson's Rw *CSLFD* M3 .... **16** A3
Jackson St *FAIL* M35 .... **87** D3
   SALE M33 .... **124** B4 🔢
   STRET M32 .... **114** A4
James Corbett Rd *SALQ/ORD* M5 ..... **94** A4 🔢
James Henry Av *SALQ/ORD* M5 .... **13** F4
James Leigh St *CMANE* M1 .... **16** C5 🔢
James St *DROY* M43 .... **98** B3
   FAIL M35 .... **89** C1
   NEWH/MOS M40 .... **9** D3
   SALQ/ORD M5 .... **14** C2
James St South *CHAD* OL9 .... **53** C2 🔢
Jammy La *CHAD* OL9 .... **54** A3
Jane St *CHAD* OL9 .... **53** D3
Japan St *BRO* M7 .... **82** B2
Jarmain St *WGTN/LGST* M12 .... **30** C2
Jasmine Av *DROY* M43 .... **99** C3 🔢
Jason St *ANC* M4 .... **7** E3
Jean Cl *BNG/LEV* M19 .... **51** D2
Jehlum Cl *CHH* M8 .... **83** D2
Jenkinson St *HULME* M15 .... **27** D2
Jenner Cl *HULME* M15 .... **25** F3
Jennings Av *SALQ/ORD* M5 .... **13** D5
Jennison Cl *GTN* M18 .... **31** E4
Jenny St *OLDS* OL8 .... **72** A3
Jersey Rd *RDSH* SK5 .... **138** B1
Jersey St *ANC* M4 .... **17** F1
Jerusalem Pl *CMANW* M2 .... **16** A4 🔢
Jesmond Av *PWCH* M25 .... **62** B3 🔢
Jespersen St *OLD* OL1 .... **55** D2
Jessamine Av *BRO* M7 .... **4** C2
Jessel Cl *BRUN/LGST* M13 .... **28** A3
Jessie St *NEWH/MOS* M40 .... **86** A3 🔢
Jessop St *GTN* M18 .... **106** B4
Jetson St *GTN* M18 .... **107** D3
Jinnah Cl *OP/CLY* M11 .... **106** A1
Joan St *NEWH/MOS* M40 .... **86** A2 🔢
Jobling St *OP/CLY* M11 .... **20** B4
Jocelyn St *NEWH/MOS* M40 .... **85** C3
Joddrell St *CSLFD* M3 .... **15** F3 🔢
John Atkinson Ct *SALQ/ORD* M5 ..... **94** B3 🔢
John Beeley Av *OP/CLY* M11 .... **106** B1 🔢
John Clynes Av *NEWH/MOS* M40 ..... **8** B3 🔢
John Dalton St *CSLFD* M3 .... **16** A2
John Foran Cl *NEWH/MOS* M40 .... **86** B3 🔢
John Gilbert Wy *TRPK* M17 .... **105** C4
John Heywood St *OP/CLY* M11 .... **21** E1
John Nash Crs *HULME* M15 .... **25** F4
Johnny King Cl *NEWH/MOS* M40 .. **84** B4 🔢🔢
Johns Cl *CCHDY* M21 .... **43** E5
Johnson's Sq *NEWH/MOS* M40 .... **8** C2 🔢
Johnson St *CSLFD* M3 .... **15** F1 🔢
   HULME M15 .... **24** C4
   SLFD M6 .... **78** B3 🔢
John St *ANC* M4 .... **17** D1
   BRO M7 .... **5** D1 🔢
   CHAD OL9 .... **55** C3
   CSLFD M3 .... **5** F5
   DROY M43 .... **107** D1
   ECC M30 .... **90** B4 🔢

FAIL M35	70 B4
SALE M33	123 D4
SWIN M27	77 C1
John William St *ECC* M30	92 B3
OP/CLY M11	96 A4 🔢
Joiner St *ANC* M4	17 D2
SALQ/ORD M5	14 B2 🔢
Jonas St *BKLY* M9	85 C1 🔢
BRO M7	5 E3
Jones St *SLFD* M6	2 A4
Jordan St *HULME* M15	25 F1
Josephine Dr *SWIN* M27	77 C2 🔢
Joseph St *ECC* M30	90 B4 🔢
FAIL M35	88 B1 🔢
Josslyn Rd *SALQ/ORD* M5	94 B2
Jo St *SALQ/ORD* M5	13 D2
Joules Ct *STKP* SK1	138 B4
Joule St *BKLY* M9	67 C4
Jowett St *RDSH* SK5	138 B1
Joyce St *NEWH/MOS* M40	86 B2
Joynson Av *BRO* M7	4 C2
Joynson St *SALE* M33	123 D4
Jubilee St *SLFD* M6	2 A4
Judson Av *CCHDY* M21	127 C4
Judy St *NEWH/MOS* M40	85 D1 🔢
Julia St *CSLFD* M3	6 A3
Julius St *BNG/LEV* M19	132 B1
Junction St *OLDS* OL8	73 C1 🔢
Juniper Bank *RDSH* SK5	135 C1
Juniper Cl *SALE* M33	122 B3
Jura Dr *URM* M41	102 A4
Jurby Av *BKLY* M9	66 A1
Jury St *CHH* M8	6 A2
Justin Cl *BRUN/LGST* M13	27 E2
Jutland St *CMANE* M1	17 F3

K

Kale St *BRUN/LGST* M13	27 F2
Kalima Gv *BRO* M7	81 D3 🔢
Kansas Av *SALQ/ORD* M5	105 C1
Kara St *SLFD* M6	95 C3
Kathkin Av *CHH* M8	65 D3
Kathleen Gv *RUSH/FAL* M14	48 B1 🔢
Kay Av *MPL/ROM* SK6	140 B2
Kay's Av *STKP* SK1	139 D4
Kays Gdns *CSLFD* M3	5 D5
Kay St *OP/CLY* M11	30 A1
SLFD M6	79 D3
Keadby Cl *ECC* M30	101 D1 🔢
Kearsley Av *CHH* M8	65 C3
Kearsley St *ECC* M30	90 B3 🔢
Kearton Dr *ECC* M30	93 C4
Keary Cl *GTN* M18	106 B3
Keaton Cl *SLFD* M6	95 C1 🔢
Keats Av *DROY* M43	98 A3
Keats Rd *ECC* M30	91 D4
Keble Av *OLDS* OL8	73 C2
Kedleston Av *RUSH/FAL* M14	39 E3
Keele Wk *NEWH/MOS* M40	8 B3
Keighley Av *DROY* M43	98 A2 🔢
Kelboro Av *DTN/ASHW* M34	109 D2
Kelbrook Rd *OP/CLY* M11	21 E4
Kellbrook Crs *BRO* M7	80 A1 🔢
Kelmarsh Cl *OP/CLY* M11	106 B3 🔢
Kelsall Dr *DROY* M43	97 D2
Kelsall St *CHAD* OL9	54 B3
WGTN/LGST M12	30 B3
Kelso Cl *OLDS* OL8	73 D4
Kelstern Av *BRUN/LGST* M13	39 E5 🔢
Kelstern Sq *BRUN/LGST* M13	39 E5

Kelvin Gv *CHH* M8	83 C3
Kelvington Dr *BKLY* M9	84 B3
Kelvin St *ANC* M4	17 D1
Kempley Cl *WGTN/LGST* M12	30 B3
Kempsey Ct *CHAD* OL9	53 C2
Kempsey St *CHAD* OL9	53 D2 🔢
Kempster St *BRO* M7	4 C1
Kempton Cl *DROY* M43	99 C3 🔢
Kempton Wy *CHAD* OL9	54 A2 🔢
Kenchester Av *OP/CLY* M11	106 B3 🔢
Kendall Rd *CHH* M8	64 B2
Kendal Rd *SLFD* M6	78 A4 🔢
STRET M32	114 B2
Kenilworth Av *DID/WITH* M20	128 B4 🔢
SWIN M27	59 D2
Kenilworth Dr *DTN/ASHW* M34	109 C1
Kenmere Gv *NEWH/MOS* M40	68 B4
Kennard Cl *BKLY* M9	67 D4 🔢
Kennedy Rd *SALQ/ORD* M5	94 A3
Kennedy St *CMANW* M2	16 B3
OLDS OL8	55 C4 🔢
Kennedy Wy *DTN/ASHW* M34	119 D3
Kenneth Sq *BRO* M7	82 A3 🔢
Kennington Av *NEWH/MOS* M40	11 F1 🔢
Kensington Av *CHAD* OL9	52 A1
RUSH/FAL M14	39 D3
Kensington Dr *SALQ/ORD* M5	94 B2 🔢
Kensington Gv *DTN/ASHW* M34	118 B1 🔢
Kensington Rd *CCHDY* M21	43 D2
FAIL M35	89 D1
OLDS OL8	72 B1
Kensington St *RUSH/FAL* M14	36 C4
Kenslow Av *CHH* M8	64 B3 🔢
Kent Av *CHAD* OL9	53 C3
DROY M43	97 C3
Kentford Dr *NEWH/MOS* M40	8 A1
Kenton Av *GTN* M18	116 A2
Kenton Cl *DTN/ASHW* M34	109 D2
Kent Rd *DTN/ASHW* M34	118 A3
FAIL M35	88 A3
Kent Rd East *RUSH/FAL* M14	39 D4
Kent Rd West *RUSH/FAL* M14	38 B5
Kent St *BRO* M7	5 D1
CMANW M2	16 B2 🔢
OLDS OL8	73 D1
SWIN M27	58 B3 🔢
Kenwick Dr *NEWH/MOS* M40	70 A3
Kenwood Av *BNG/LEV* M19	131 D3
Kenwood Cl *STRET* M32	115 C3 🔢
Kenwood Rd *RDSH* SK5	117 C3
STRET M32	115 C4
Kenwright St *ANC* M4	7 D5
Kenwyn St *NEWH/MOS* M40	9 F3
Kenyon Av *OLDS* OL8	73 D2 🔢
Kenyon La *NEWH/MOS* M40	86 A1
PWCH M25	63 C2
Kenyon St *GTN* M18	107 D3 🔢
Keppel Rd *CCHDY* M21	43 E4
Kerrera Dr *SALQ/ORD* M5	94 B3 🔢
Kerridge Dr *MPL/ROM* SK6	141 D1 🔢
Kerr St *BKLY* M9	66 B2
Kersal Av *SWIN* M27	78 A1
Kersal Bank *BRO* M7	81 C1
Kersal Cl *PWCH* M25	62 A4 🔢
Kersal Crag *BRO* M7	63 C4
Kersal Hall Av *BRO* M7	80 A1 🔢
Kersal Rd *PWCH* M25	62 A4
Kersal Vale Rd *SWIN* M27	61 D4
Kersal Wy *BRO* M7	80 B2
Kersh Av *BNG/LEV* M19	51 E5
Kershaw La *PWCH* M25	61 D3
Kershaw Dr *CHAD* OL9	69 D2
Kershaw Gv *DTN/ASHW* M34	108 B1

Kershaw La DTN/ASHW M34............... 99 C4
Kershaw Rd FAIL M35 .... 88 B1
Kershaw St DROY M43 .... 97 D4
Kershope Gv SALQ/ORD M5 .... 12 C4
Kesteven Rd BKLY M9 .... 84 B2
Keston Av BKLY M9 .... 68 A2 ▣
DROY M43 .... 97 D4
Keston Crs RDSH SK5 .... 135 D3
Kestrel Av DTN/ASHW M34 .... 99 C4
SWIN M27 .... 59 D3
Kestrel Rd TRPK M17 .... 102 B1
Keswick Av CHAD OL9 .... 53 C2
DTN/ASHW M34 .... 119 D1 ▣
Keswick Cl BRUN/LGST M13 .... 39 D1
Keswick Gv SLFD M6 .... 2 A4
Keswick Rd HTNM SK4 .... 133 D2
STRET M32 .... 114 A2
Kettering Rd BNG/LEV M19 .... 51 F2
Ketton Cl OP/CLY M11 .... 107 C2
Kevin St BNG/LEV M19 .... 51 E5
Kew Dr URM M41 .... 110 A1
Kew Gdns NEWH/MOS M40 .... 68 A4 ▣
Kew Rd FAIL M35 .... 89 C1
Keymer Av OP/CLY M11 .... 19 F1
Keynsham Rd OP/CLY M11 .... 11 E4
Keystone Cl SLFD M6 .... 95 C1
Key West Cl OP/CLY M11 .... 20 A3
Khartoum St OLDTF/WHR M16 .... 34 C3
OP/CLY M11 .... 96 B3 ▣
Kiel Cl ECC M30 .... 102 A1
Kildare Rd CCHDY M21 .... 45 D5
SWIN M27 .... 76 A2
Kilmington Dr CHH M8 .... 82 B3 ▣
Kiln Cft MPL/ROM SK6 .... 141 D4 ▣
Kilnside Dr BKLY M9 .... 84 B2
Kilnwick Cl OP/CLY M18 .... 41 F4 ▣
Kilrush Av ECC M30 .... 101 D1 ▣
Kilvert Dr SALE M33 .... 122 B4
Kilvert St TRPK M17 .... 22 B5
Kimberley St BRO M7 .... 82 A2 ▣
OLDS OL8 .... 72 A2
Kimbolton Cl WGTN/LGST M12 .... 31 D2
Kincardine Rd BRUN/LGST M13 .... 27 E2
Kincraig Cl OP/CLY M11 .... 96 A4
King Edward St BNG/LEV M19 .... 51 E3
ECC M30 .... 91 C3 ▣
SALQ/ORD M5 .... 13 F5
Kingfisher Av DTN/ASHW M34 .... 99 C4
Kingfisher Cl WGTN/LGST M12 .... 39 F1
Kingham Dr ANC M4 .... 8 B5
Kings Av CHH M8 .... 83 C1
Kingsbridge Rd BKLY M9 .... 84 A2
Kingsbrook Rd OLDTF/WHR M16 .... 45 E5
Kingsbury Rd OP/CLY M11 .... 96 A3 ▣
Kingscliffe St BKLY M9 .... 85 C2
King's Cl GTN M18 .... 107 D3 ▣
Kings Ct RDSH SK5 .... 138 B2
Kings Crs OLDTF/WHR M16 .... 33 E4
Kingsdale Rd DTN/ASHW M34 .... 118 A1
Kingsfold Av NEWH/MOS M40 .... 8 B2 ▣
Kingsford St SALQ/ORD M5 .... 94 B3
Kings Gv STRET M32 .... 32 B5
Kingshill Rd CCHDY M21 .... 126 A1
Kingsland Cl NEWH/MOS M40 .... 8 C3
Kings La STRET M32 .... 32 B5
Kingslea Rd DID/WITH M20 .... 130 A4
Kingsley Av BKLY M9 .... 85 D2
BRO M7 .... 80 A2
HTNM SK4 .... 138 A1 ▣
STRET M32 .... 32 A5
URM M41 .... 110 B3 ▣
Kingsley Cl DTN/ASHW M34 .... 119 D4
Kingsley Gv DTN/ASHW M34........... 109 C1

Kingsley Rd SWIN M27..................... 57 D4
Kingsmere Av BNG/LEV M19 .... 50 A4
Kingsmill Av BNG/LEV M19 .... 132 B1 ▣
Kings Rd CCHDY M21 .... 44 C5
CHAD OL9 .... 70 A2
DTN/ASHW M34 .... 108 A4
OLDS OL8 .... 55 D4
OLDTF/WHR M16 .... 34 A4
PWCH M25 .... 63 C3
STRET M32 .... 115 C3
Kings Ter STRET M32 .... 32 B5
Kingston Av CHAD OL9 .... 71 C1 ▣
BNG/LEV M19 .... 50 A4
Kingston Cl BRO M7 .... 81 D1 ▣
Kingston Dr SALE M33 .... 124 B4
URM M41 .... 120 B1
Kingston Gv BKLY M9 .... 67 D1 ▣
Kingston Rd FAIL M35 .... 89 D2
King St BRO M7 .... 82 A2
CHAD OL9 : .... 55 C2 ▣
CMANW M2 .... 16 A2
CSLFD M3 .... 5 F5
DROY M43 .... 108 A1
ECC M30 .... 92 B4 ▣
FAIL M35 .... 87 D3
SLFD M6 .... 78 B4
King St East STKP SK1 .... 138 B3 ▣
King St West CSLFD M3 .... 16 A2
Kingsway BNG/LEV M19 .... 50 A4
MPL/ROM SK6 .... 141 C2
STKP SK1.. 138 B3
STRET M32 .... 114 A4
SWIN M27 .... 78 A3
Kingsway Av BNG/LEV M19 .... 50 A4
Kingsway Cl OLDS OL8 .... 55 C4
Kingsway Crs BNG/LEV M19 .... 131 C4 ▣
Kingsway Pk URM M41 .... 111 D1
Kingswood Gv RDSH SK5 .... 117 D4 ▣
Kingswood Rd ECC M30 .... 90 B1
RUSH/FAL M14 .... 131 C2
King William St ECC M30 .... 90 A2 ▣
SALQ/ORD M5 .... 12 C5
Kinloch St OP/CLY M11 .... 10 C5
Kinmel Av RDSH SK5 .... 140 A1
Kinnaird Rd DID/WITH M20 .... 129 D4
Kinross Rd RUSH/FAL M14 .... 39 E4
Kintyre Av SALQ/ORD M5 .... 94 B4
Kintyre Cl OP/CLY M11 .... 96 A4 ▣
Kinver Rd NEWH/MOS M40 .... 69 C3
Kipling Av DROY M43 .... 98 A2
Kipling St BRO M7 .... 81 D3
Kippax St RUSH/FAL M14 .... 37 E5
Kirby Av CHAD OL9 .... 69 D2
SWIN M27 .... 75 D4 ▣
Kirkbank St CHAD OL9 .... 54 B1 ▣
Kirkby Av NEWH/MOS M40 .... 86 B2
Kirkdale Av NEWH/MOS M40 .... 69 D3 ▣
Kirkgate Cl NEWH/MOS M40 .... 8 B4 ▣
Kirkham Av GTN M18 .... 106 B3
Kirkham St OLDS OL8 .... 55 C2 ▣
SALQ/ORD M5 .... 95 C4
Kirkhaven Sq NEWH/MOS M40 .... 9 E2
Kirklinton Dr BKLY M9 .... 84 B3 ▣
Kirkman Av ECC M30 .... 101 C1
Kirkman Cl GTN M18 .... 116 B1
Kirkmanshulme La GTN M18 .... 41 F1 ▣
WGTN/LGST M12 .... 40 C2
Kirk Rd BNG/LEV M19 .... 132 B2
Kirkstall Rd URM M41 .... 112 A2
Kirkstall Sq BRUN/LGST M13.......... 28 A4
Kirkstead Cl OP/CLY M11 .... 20 C4
Kirkstile Pl SWIN M27 .... 58 A1
Kirkstone Rd NEWH/MOS M40 .... 69 C3
Kirk St GTN M18 .... 106 B4

Kirkway *BKLY* M9 .... 68 A1
Kirkwood Dr *NEWH/MOS* M40 .... 8 B2
Kirtley Av *ECC* M30 .... 91 D2
Kitepool St *ECC* M30 .... 90 A2 ②
Knaresborough Cl *RDSH* SK5 .... 117 C4 ②
Knightsbridge *STKP* SK1 .... 138 B3
Knightsbridge Cl *BRO* M7 .... 81 D1 ②
Kniveton Rd *WGTN/LGST* M12 .... 30 A3
Knoll St *BRO* M7 .... 81 D2
Knott St *SALQ/ORD* M5 .... 94 B4
Knowl Cl *DTN/ASHW* M34 .... 118 A3
Knowle Dr *PWCH* M25 .... 62 A3
Knowles Pl *HULME* M15 .... 26 B2
The Knowles *OLDS* OL8 .... 71 D4
Knowl St *OLDS* OL8 .... 72 A3
Knowsley Av *SALQ/ORD* M5 .... 13 E5
    URM M41 .... 111 C1
Knowsley Dr *SWIN* M27 .... 75 D3
Knowsley St *CHH* M8 .... 6 B3
Knutsford Av *HTNM* SK4 .... 133 D2
    OLDTF/WHR M16 .... 34 C3
Knutsford Rd *GTN* M18 .... 116 A1
Knutsford St *SLFD* M6 .... 95 C3
Kranj Wy *OLD* OL1 .... 55 D2

L

Labtec St *SWIN* M27 .... 59 D4
Laburnum Av *DTN/ASHW* M34 .... 99 C4
    ECC M30 .... 100 A1 ②
    FAIL M35 .... 88 B3
    SWIN M27 .... 76 A3 ②
Laburnum Rd *DTN/ASHW* M34 .... 117 D1
    GTN M18 .... 116 B1
    URM M41 .... 110 B1
Laburnum St *SLFD* M6 .... 2 A5
Lackford Dr *NEWH/MOS* M40 .... 8 B2
Lacrosse Av *OLDS* OL8 .... 72 A1
Lacy Gv *STRET* M32 .... 114 B4 ②
Lacy St *STRET* M32 .... 114 B4
Ladybarn Crs *RUSH/FAL* M14 .... 130 B2 ⑥
Ladybarn La *RUSH/FAL* M14 .... 130 B1
Ladybarn Rd *RUSH/FAL* M14 .... 48 C5
Ladysmith St *OLDS* OL8 .... 72 A2 ②
Ladythorn Ct *PWCH* M25 .... 62 A3 ②
Ladythorne Av *PWCH* M25 .... 62 A3 ②
Ladythorne Dr *PWCH* M25 .... 62 A3 ②
Lagos Cl *RUSH/FAL* M14 .... 36 C2
Laindon Rd *RUSH/FAL* M14 .... 39 E4
Lake Rd *TRPK* M17 .... 104 A1
Lakeside Cl *DTN* M18 .... 107 D3
Lake Vw *BKLY* M9 .... 68 A3
Lakin St *NEWH/MOS* M40 .... 86 A2
Lamb Cl *WGTN/LGST* M12 .... 40 A1
Lamb Ct *CSLFD* M3 .... 15 E1 ⑤
Lambert Dr *SALE* M33 .... 121 D3
Lambeth Av *FAIL* M35 .... 89 C1
Lambeth Rd *NEWH/MOS* M40 .... 96 A1 ⑥
    RDSH SK5 .... 134 B2 ②
Lamb La *CSLFD* M3 .... 15 E1
Lambs Fold *HTNM* SK4 .... 133 D4 ⑥
Lambton Rd *CCHDY* M21 .... 44 C5
    WALK M28 .... 75 C3 ②
Lambton St *ECC* M30 .... 90 B1
Lamburn Av *NEWH/MOS* M40 .... 69 D3 ⑦
Lamorna Cl *BRO* M7 .... 80 B1
Lamport Cl *CMANE* M1 .... 27 E1
Lampson St *CHH* M8 .... 5 F1 ⑤
Lamsholme Cl *BNG/LEV* M19 .... 51 D2 ⑤
Lanbury Dr *CHH* M8 .... 82 B2 ⑰②
Lancashire Hl *RDSH* SK5 .... 138 A2
Lancashire St *NEWH/MOS* M40 ...... 85 D4 ④
Lancaster Av *FAIL* M35 .... 88 A2
    URM M41 .... 112 A2 ④
Lancaster Dr *PWCH* M25 .... 63 C3
Lancaster Rd *DROY* M43 .... 97 D2
    SLFD M6 .... 77 D4
Lancaster St *CHAD* OL9 .... 71 C1
    STKP SK1 .... 139 C3
Lanchester St *NEWH/MOS* M40 .... 9 E4
Landcross Rd *RUSH/FAL* M14 .... 48 B4
Lander Gv *BKLY* M9 .... 67 D2
Landos Rd *NEWH/MOS* M40 .... 8 B4
Landsberg Rd *FAIL* M35 .... 89 D1
Lane End *ECC* M30 .... 92 B4
Lanfield Dr *CHH* M8 .... 82 B2 ⑬
Langcroft Dr *NEWH/MOS* M40 .... 87 C4 ⑫
Langdale Av *BNG/LEV* M19 .... 51 E5
    OLDS OL8 .... 72 B1
Langdale Rd *HTNM* SK4 .... 133 C3
    RUSH/FAL M14 .... 39 D3
    STRET M32 .... 114 A2 ⑨
Langfield Av *OLDTF/WHR* M16 .... 34 C4
Langfield Crs *DROY* M43 .... 99 C3 ③
Langford Rd *DID/WITH* M20 .... 129 C3 ⑤
Langham Ct *STRET* M32 .... 113 C1
Langham Rd *OLDS* OL8 .... 73 C1
    SLFD M6 .... 2 B5
Langholme Cl *HULME* M15 .... 25 D2 ②
Langholme Pl *ECC* M30 .... 90 B3 ⑤
Langland Cl *RDSH* SK5 .... 116 B3
Langland Dr *ECC* M30 .... 101 C2
Langley Cl *URM* M41 .... 112 A3
Langley Rd *RUSH/FAL* M14 .... 48 B3
    SWIN M27 .... 79 D1
Langley Rd South *SLFD* M6 .... 79 D3
Langness St *OP/CLY* M11 .... 96 A4 ②
Lango St *OLDTF/WHR* M16 .... 34 B4 ②
Langport Av *WGTN/LGST* M12 .... 29 E4
Langsett Av *SLFD* M6 .... 94 A4
Langshaw St *OLDTF/WHR* M16 .... 34 B2
    SLFD M6 .... 12 B2
Langside Av *BKLY* M9 .... 67 C3 ②
Langston St *CSLFD* M3 .... 6 A3
Langthorne St *BNG/LEV* M19 .... 132 B1 ①
Langton Cl *FAIL* M35 .... 89 D1
Langton St *SLFD* M6 .... 95 C3
Langworthy Rd *NEWH/MOS* M40 ...... 86 A2
    SLFD M6 .... 2 A3
Lanhill Dr *CHH* M8 .... 84 A3 ⑤
Lankro Wy *ECC* M30 .... 92 B4
Lansdale Gdns *BNG/LEV* M19 .... 131 C4 ⑦
Lansdale St *ECC* M30 .... 100 A1 ⑨
Lansdowne Av *DTN/ASHW* M34 .... 99 C4
Lansdowne Rd *CHAD* OL9 .... 54 A3
    CHH M8 .... 83 C1
    ECC M30 .... 91 D2
    SALE M33 .... 123 C3
Lanstead Dr *NEWH/MOS* M40 .... 9 E5
Lapwing La *DID/WITH* M20 .... 129 C4
    RDSH SK5 .... 136 A3
Larch Av *STRET* M32 .... 114 B4
    SWIN M27 .... 75 C3 ③
Larch Cl *FAIL* M35 .... 88 B3 ②
Larch Gv *CHAD* OL9 .... 53 D1 ③
    SWIN M27 .... 56 B3
Larch Rd *ECC* M30 .... 90 A1
Larch St *OLDS* OL8 .... 54 B3
Larchwood *CHAD* OL9 .... 52 A2
Larchwood Av *BKLY* M9 .... 85 D2 ④
Larks Ri *DROY* M43 .... 99 D2
Larmuth Av *CCHDY* M21 .... 127 C3
Larne Av *STRET* M32 .... 114 A3
Larne St *OP/CLY* M11 .... 21 D4

Lascar Av *SALQ/ORD* M5 .... **13** D4
Lashbrook Cl *NEWH/MOS* M40 .... **8** C1
Lassell St *OP/CLY* M11 .... **107** D2 🟦
Lastingham St *NEWH/MOS* M40 .... **87** C3 🟦
Latchmere Rd *RUSH/FAL* M14 .... **130** A1 🟦
Latham St *OP/CLY* M11 .... **107** D2
Lathbury Rd *BKLY* M9 .... **84** B3
Lathom Rd *DID/WITH* M20 .... **130** B2
Latrobe St *DROY* M43 .... **108** A1
Lauderdale Cres *BRUN/LGST* M13 ... **28** B4
Laundry St *SLFD* M6 .... **2** B1
Laurel Av *RUSH/FAL* M14 .... **46** C1
Laurel Bank Gdns *BKLY* M9 .... **66** B1
Laurel Gv *SALQ/ORD* M5 .... **94** A3 🟦
Laurel St *HTNM* SK4 .... **138** A3 🟦
Laurence Cl *WGTN/LGST* M12 .... **31** E3
Lausanne Rd *DID/WITH* M20 .... **129** D2
Lavender Cl *SALE* M33 .... **121** C4
Lavenders Brow *STKP* SK1 .... **138** B4 🟦
Lavenham Av *OP/CLY* M11 .... **96** B4 🟦
Lavington Gv *GTN* M18 .... **116** B1 🟦
Lavinia St *ECC* M30 .... **90** B3 🟦
Lawers Av *CHAD* OL9 .... **53** C1
Lawler Av *SALQ/ORD* M5 .... **23** E3
Lawn Dr *SALE* M33 .... **76** A2
Lawngreen Av *CCHDY* M21 .... **126** A2
Lawnside Ms *DID/WITH* M20 .... **129** C4
Lawnswood Dr *SWIN* M27 .... **77** D3 🟦
Lawnswood Park Rd *SWIN* M27 ..... **77** D3 🟦
Lawrence St *STKP* SK1 .... **138** A4 🟦
Lawson Cl *WALK* M28 .... **75** C2
Lawson Gv *SALE* M33 .... **123** C3
Lawson St *BKLY* M9 .... **66** A3
Lawton Cl *MPL/ROM* SK6 .... **141** D4 🟦
Lawton St *DROY* M43 .... **98** B3 🟦
   OP/CLY M11 .... **106** B2 🟦
Laxey St *NEWH/MOS* M40 .... **86** B2 🟦
Laycock Crs *FAIL* M35 .... **88** B3
Laycock Gv *FAIL* M35 .... **88** B2 🟦
Laystall St *CMANE* M1 .... **17** F2
Layton St *NEWH/MOS* M40 .... **9** D5
Leabank St *BNG/LEV* M19 .... **51** D2 🟦
Leabrook Dr *NEWH/MOS* M40 .... **88** A1
Leach St *GTN* M18 .... **31** F4
   PWCH M25 .... **61** D1
Lea Ct *FAIL* M35 .... **88** A2 🟦
Leacroft Rd *CCHDY* M21 .... **127** D4
Lea Dr *BKLY* M9 .... **67** D2
Leaford Av *DTN/ASHW* M34 .... **119** D1
Leaford Cl *DTN/ASHW* M34 .... **119** D1
Leaf St *HULME* M15 .... **26** A3
   RDSH SK5 .... **134** A2
Leagate *URM* M41 .... **112** A4
Leaholme Cl *NEWH/MOS* M40 .... **87** C4 🟦
Leak St *OLDTF/WHR* M16 .... **24** B3
Leamington Rd *ECC* M30 .... **90** B2
   RDSH SK5 .... **134** A2 🟦
   URM M41 .... **110** B2
Leamington St *OP/CLY* M11 .... **106** B2 🟦
Leander Cl *BKLY* M9 .... **67** C3
Leaside Dr *DID/WITH* M20 .... **130** B4
Lecester Rd *CHH* M8 .... **83** D3
Leconfield Dr *BKLY* M9 .... **67** C2
Ledbrooke Cl *SALQ/ORD* M5 .... **23** E1
Ledburn Cl *HULME* M15 .... **25** D3 🟦
Ledbury Av *URM* M41 .... **111** C2
Ledbury Rd *FAIL* M35 .... **97** C1 🟦
Lee Crs *STRET* M32 .... **115** C3
Lees St *DROY* M43 .... **98** B3
   GTN M18 .... **107** C3

   SWIN M27 .... **58** B4
Lee St *OLDS* OL8 .... **54** B3
   STKP SK1 .... **138** B4
Leeswood Av *CCHDY* M21 .... **127** C3 🟦
Leewood *SWIN* M27 .... **57** D1
Left Bank *CSLFD* M3 .... **15** F2 🟦
Legh Dr *DTN/ASHW* M34 .... **98** B4
Legh Rd *BRO* M7 .... **81** D1
Legh St *BRO* M7 .... **81** D1
   ECC M30 .... **91** C4
Legion Gv *BRO* M7 .... **82** A3 🟦
Legwood Ct *URM* M41 .... **111** C3 🟦
Leicester Av *BRO* M7 .... **64** B4 🟦
   DROY M43 .... **97** D2
Leicester Rd *BRO* M7 .... **82** A2
   FAIL M35 .... **89** C4
   SALE M33 .... **123** D4
Leicester St *RDSH* SK5 .... **117** C3
Leigh Av *SWIN* M27 .... **75** D4 🟦
Leighbrook Rd *RUSH/FAL* M14 ... **129** D1
Leigh St *BRO* M7 .... **81** D2
Leighton Rd *OLDTF/WHR* M16 .... **34** A3
Leighton St *NEWH/MOS* M40 .... **86** A1
Leinster Rd *SWIN* M27 .... **76** A2 🟦
Lena St *CMANE* M1 .... **17** E3
Leng Rd *NEWH/MOS* M40 .... **87** D4
Lenham Cl *RDSH* SK5 .... **135** D3
Lentmead Dr *NEWH/MOS* M40 .... **68** A4 🟦
Leopold Av *DID/WITH* M20 .... **129** C4 🟦
Leroy Dr *BKLY* M9 .... **66** B3
Lesley Rd *STRET* M32 .... **113** C4
Leslie Av *CHAD* OL9 .... **71** D2
Leslie Hough Wy *SLFD* M6 .... **3** F2
Leslie St *RUSH/FAL* M14 .... **37** E4
Lester St *STRET* M32 .... **114** B3
Letchworth St *RUSH/FAL* M14 .... **37** E5
Letham St *OLDS* OL8 .... **73** C3 🟦
Levedale Rd *BKLY* M9 .... **67** C1
Levenhurst Rd *CHH* M8 .... **82** B2
Levenshulme Rd *GTN* M18 .... **116** B1
Levenshulme Ter *BNG/LEV* M19 ... **51** D3 🟦
Levens St *NEWH/MOS* M40 .... **86** A2
   SLFD M6 .... **80** B4
Lever Av *SWIN* M27 .... **59** D3
Lever St *CMANE* M1 .... **17** D2 🟦
Lewis Av *BKLY* M9 .... **67** C4
   URM M41 .... **101** D3
Lewisham Av *NEWH/MOS* M40 ..... **11** F1
Lewis Dr *DROY* M43 .... **97** C3
   RDSH SK5 .... **117** D4
Lewis St *ECC* M30 .... **91** C4
   NEWH/MOS M40 .... **9** D3
Lewtas St *ECC* M30 .... **92** A4
Lexton Av *CHH* M8 .... **65** D3
Leybourne Av *BNG/LEV* M19 .... **51** F1
Leyburn Av *STRET* M32 .... **113** D3
   URM M41 .... **110** A4
Leyburn Rd *NEWH/MOS* M40 .... **69** C3
Leycroft St *CMANE* M1 .... **17** F4 🟦
   CMANE M1 .... **17** F3 🟦
Leyland St *STKP* SK1 .... **138** A4 🟦
   STKP SK1 .... **138** A4 🟦
Leyton Av *NEWH/MOS* M40 .... **86** B2 🟦
Library La *CHAD* OL9 .... **54** B1 🟦
Lichfield Av *RDSH* SK5 .... **134** A2
Lichfield Dr *CHH* M8 .... **83** D2 🟦
   PWCH M25 .... **63** C3
   SWIN M27 .... **76** B3 🟦
Lichfield Rd *ECC* M30 .... **92** B1 🟦
   URM M41 .... **111** D1
Lichfield St *SLFD* M6 .... **80** A4
Lidbrook Wk *WGTN/LGST* M12 .... **29** E4
Lidiard St *CHH* M8 .... **65** C4 🟦

Lifton Av *NEWH/MOS* M40 .... 9 E1
Lightbourne Av *SWIN* M27 .... 76 B2
Lightbowne Rd *NEWH/MOS* M40 ...... 86 B1
Light Oaks Rd *SLFD* M6 .... 93 D1
Lignum Av *CHAD* OL9 .... 53 D1
Lilac Av *SWIN* M27 .... 77 C1
Lilac Gv *CHAD* OL9 .... 53 D1
   NEWH/MOS M40 .... 68 A4 ▣
Lilac La *OLDS* OL8 .... 72 B3
Lila St *BKLY* M9 .... 85 D2 ▣
Lilford Cl *WGTN/LGST* M12 .... 30 C3
Lilian St *OLDTF/WHR* M16 .... 34 A2
Lillian Gv *RDSH* SK5 .... 134 B1 ▣
Lilmore Av *NEWH/MOS* M40 .... 87 C3
Lily La *BKLY* M9 .... 85 D2
Lily St *ECC* M30 .... 90 B4
Limbert Cir *CHH* M8 .... 66 A4 ▣
Lime Av *SWIN* M27 .... 75 C3 ▣
   URM M41 .... 110 B3
Lime Bank St *WGTN/LGST* M12 .... 19 D5
Limebrook Cl *OP/CLY* M11 .... 107 C2 ▣▣
Lime Cl *SLFD* M6 .... 2 C4
Lime Crs *OLDTF/WHR* M16 .... 33 E3
Limeditch Rd *FAIL* M35 .... 71 C4
Limefield Rd *BRO* M7 .... 63 D4
Limefield Ter *BNG/LEV* M19 .... 50 C3
Lime Ga *OLDS* OL8 .... 72 A3
Lime Gn *OLDS* OL8 .... 72 B4
Lime Gv *OLDTF/WHR* M16 .... 33 E2
Limehurst Av *DID/WITH* M20 .... 46 B5
Limekiln La *WGTN/LGST* M12 ...... 18 C5
Lime La *OLDS* OL8 .... 72 A4
Lime Rd *STRET* M32 .... 114 B4
Limerston Dr *NEWH/MOS* M40 ..... 85 D4
Limeside Rd *OLDS* OL8 .... 72 A3
Limestead Av *CHH* M8 .... 83 C1 ▣
Lime St *ECC* M30 .... 91 D4
   MPL/ROM SK6 .... 141 C1 ▣
   NEWH/MOS M40 .... 9 D3 ▣
Lime Tree Cl *URM* M41 .... 112 A4
Lime Tree Gv *FAIL* M35 .... 89 D2 ▣
Limley Gv *CCHDY* M21 .... 127 C2
Linby St *HULME* M15 .... 25 E2
Lincoln Av *BNG/LEV* M19 .... 51 F4
   DROY M43 .... 98 C4
   STRET M32 .... 112 B2
Lincoln Gv *BRUN/LGST* M13 .... 38 B1
Lincoln Rd *FAIL* M35 .... 89 C3 ▣
Lincoln St *BRUN/LGST* M13 .... 40 A3
   CHAD OL9 .... 53 D4
   ECC M30 .... 91 C4 ▣
Lindale Av *CHAD* OL9 .... 53 C3
   NEWH/MOS M40 .... 69 D3 ▣
Linden Av *DTN/ASHW* M34 .... 109 D2
   SLFD M6 .... 79 C3
   SWIN M27 .... 75 D2 ▣
Linden Dr *SALQ/ORD* M5 .... 13 D4
Linden Gv *RUSH/FAL* M14 .... 130 B1 ▣
Linden Pk *BNG/LEV* M19 .... 131 D1
Lindenwood *CHAD* OL9 .... 52 A1 ▣
Lindeth Av *GTN* M18 .... 116 B1
Lindfield Rd *RDSH* SK5 .... 117 D4 ▣
Lindinis Av *SALQ/ORD* M5 .... 13 C1
Lindleywood Rd *RUSH/FAL* M14 .. 131 C1
Lindon Wy *DROY* M43 .... 107 C1
Lindow Ct *MPL/ROM* SK6 .... 140 B2 ▣
Lindow Rd *OLDTF/WHR* M16 .... 43 F1
Lindrick Cl *NEWH/MOS* M40 .... 87 C2
Lindsay Av *BNG/LEV* M19 .... 50 A3
   SWIN M27 .... 76 A2 ▣
Lindsay Rd *BNG/LEV* M19 .... 131 D1
Lind St *NEWH/MOS* M40 .... 19 D1
Lindum Av *OLDTF/WHR* M16 .... 34 A3

Lindum St *RUSH/FAL* M14 .... 37 E5
Linen Ct *CSLFD* M3 .... 4 C4
Lines Rd *DROY* M43 .... 98 B4
Linfield St *OP/CLY* M11 .... 21 F2
Linford Av *NEWH/MOS* M40 .... 69 C3
Lingard La *MPL/ROM* SK6 .... 136 B4
Lingard St *RDSH* SK5 .... 134 B1
Lingcrest Rd *BNG/LEV* M19 .... 133 C2
Lingfield Rd *OP/CLY* M11 .... 96 A3
Link Av *URM* M41 .... 113 C4
Link La *OLDS* OL8 .... 73 C3
Links Av *FAIL* M35 .... 88 B4
Links Crs *PWCH* M25 .... 64 A3 ▣
Links Ri *URM* M41 .... 110 A1
The Links *NEWH/MOS* M40 .... 87 C2
Links Vw *PWCH* M25 .... 62 A4
Linksway *PWCH* M25 .... 63 D3
   SWIN M27 .... 77 C3 ▣
Linksway Cl *HTNM* SK4 .... 132 A4
The Link *RDSH* SK5 .... 136 A3
Linley Rd *SALE* M33 .... 123 C4
Linnet Cl *DTN/ASHW* M34 .... 99 C3
   WGTN/LGST M12 .... 40 A2
Linn St *CHH* M8 .... 65 C4
Linsley St *CSLFD* M3 .... 5 F5 ▣
Linstead Dr *CHH* M8 .... 82 B3 ▣▣
Linton Av *DTN/ASHW* M34 .... 118 A2
Linton Cl *WGTN/LGST* M12 .... 18 C4
Linton Rd *SALE* M33 .... 124 A3
Linwood Gv *WGTN/LGST* M12 ..... 50 C1
Linwood St *FAIL* M35 .... 87 C3 ▣
Lion Brow *BKLY* M9 .... 66 B3
Lion Fold La *BKLY* M9 .... 66 B2 ▣
Lions Dr *SWIN* M27 .... 77 C2
Lion St *BKLY* M9 .... 66 B3
Lisburn Av *CCHDY* M21 .... 44 B3
Lisburn Rd *NEWH/MOS* M40 .... 86 A1
Liscard Av *RUSH/FAL* M14 .... 47 E4
Lismore Wy *URM* M41 .... 101 D4
Lissadel St *SLFD* M6 .... 3 E2
Litcham Cl *CMANE* M1 .... 27 E1
Litchfield Gv *MANW* M28 .... 74 B2 ▣
Little Ancoats St *CMANE* M1 ...... 17 E1 ▣
Little David St *CMANE* M1 .... 17 D4
Little Ees La *SALE* M33 .... 122 B2
Little Egerton St *STKP* SK1 .... 138 B3 ▣
Littlegreen *SLFD* M6 .... 2 A3
Littlehaven Cl *WGTN/LGST* M12 ... 39 F1
Little Holme St *ANC* M4 .... 19 D3 ▣
Little John St *CSLFD* M3 .... 15 E4
Little Lever St *CMANE* M1 .... 17 E2 ▣
Little Moss La *SWIN* M27 .... 58 B3
Littlemoss Rd *DROY* M43 .... 99 C2
Little Nelson St *ANC* M4 .... 7 D4 ▣
Little Peter St *HULME* M15 .... 25 F1
Little Pitt St *CMANE* M1 .... 17 F2 ▣
Little Quay St *CSLFD* M3 .... 16 A3
Littleton Rd *BRO* M7 .... 80 A1
Little Underbank *STKP* SK1 .... 138 B4 ▣
Littlewood St *SLFD* M6 .... 95 C3 ▣▣
Liverpool Cl *RDSH* SK5 .... 134 A2 ▣
Liverpool Rd *CSLFD* M3 .... 15 D4
   ECC M30 .... 90 B4
Liverpool St *RDSH* SK5 .... 134 A2 ▣
   SLFD M6 .... 12 A1
Liverstudd Av *RDSH* SK5 .... 134 B1 ▣
Livesey St *ANC* M4 .... 8 A3
   BNG/LEV M19 .... 132 B1
Lizard St *CMANE* M1 .... 17 E2
Lizmar Ter *NEWH/MOS* M40 .... 85 D1
Lloyd Rd *BNG/LEV* M19 .... 132 B2
Lloyd St *CMANW* M2 .... 16 A3
Lloyd St North *RUSH/FAL* M14 .... 37 D2

Lloyd St South *RUSH/FAL* M14 .... 46 C3
Lockett Gdns *CSLFD* M3 .... 5 D5
Lockett St *CHH* M8 .... 5 F2
 SLFD M6 .... 80 A4 🔟
Lockhart Cl *WGTN/LGST* M12 .... 41 D1
Lockton Cl *CMANE* M1 .... 27 F1
 RDSH SK5 .... 134 A3
Lockwood St *WGTN/LGST* M12 .... 41 E5 🔟
Lodge Av *URM* M41 .... 112 A3
Lodge Fold *DROY* M43 .... 98 B3
Lodge Ri *DROY* M43 .... 98 B3
Lodgeside Cl *DROY* M43 .... 98 B3 🔟
Lodge St *NEWH/MOS* M40 .... 85 C4 🔟
Loganberry Av *SLFD* M6 .... 2 C4
Lois St *CHAD* OL9 .... 71 C3
Lomas St *FAIL* M35 .... 71 C4
Lomax St *CMANE* M1 .... 18 A2
Lombard Cl *MPL/ROM* SK6 .... 141 D1 🔟
Lombard Gv *RUSH/FAL* M14 .... 130 A1
Lombard St *OLD* OL1 .... 55 C2
Lomond Av *STRET* M32 .... 114 B2
London Pl *STKP* SK1 .... 138 B4 🔟
London Rd *CMANE* M1 .... 17 E4
London Sq *STKP* SK1 .... 138 B4 🔟
London St *SLFD* M6 .... 3 E1
Longacre St *CMANE* M1 .... 18 A4
Longbridge Rd *TRPK* M17 .... 103 C3
Longcroft Gv *DTN/ASHW* M34 ..... 108 B1
Longden Rd *WGTN/LGST* M12 .... 51 D1
Longfellow St *SLFD* M6 .... 4 A1
Longfield Av *URM* M41 .... 110 B3
Longfield Dr *URM* M41 .... 110 B3 🔟
Longford Av *STRET* M32 .... 115 C3
Longford Cl *STRET* M32 .... 115 C2 🔟
Longford Pl *RUSH/FAL* M14 .... 39 F3
Longford Rd *CCHDY* M21 .... 42 C3
 RDSH SK5 .... 117 D4
 STRET M32 .... 115 C2
Longford Rd West *RDSH* SK5 .... 116 B4
Longford St *GTN* M18 .... 106 B3 🔟
Longham Cl *OP/CLY* M11 .... 19 F3
Longhurst Rd *BKLY* M9 .... 65 D1
Long La *CHAD* OL9 .... 70 D1
Longley Dr *WALK* M28 .... 74 B3
Longley St *OLD* OL1 .... 55 D3 🔟
Longmead St *SLFD* M6 .... 78 B4
Long Millgate *ANC* M4 .... 6 C5
Longport Av *DID/WITH* M20 .... 129 C2
Longridge Pl *CSLFD* M3 .... 16 B1
Longshaw Av *SWIN* M27 .... 58 B4 🔟
Longsight Rd *GTN* M18 .... 41 F5
Long St *GTN* M18 .... 107 C3
 SWIN M27 .... 76 B2
Longton Av *DID/WITH* M20 .... 129 C4
Longton Rd *BKLY* M9 .... 66 A1
 SLFD M6 .... 78 A4
Longview Dr *SWIN* M27 .... 57 C4
Longwood Rd *TRPK* M17 .... 103 D3
Longworth St *CSLFD* M3 .... 15 F4
Lonsdale Av *RDSH* SK5 .... 117 D2
 SWIN M27 .... 75 D4 🔟
 URM M41 .... 110 B1
Lonsdale Rd *BNG/LEV* M19 .... 51 F2
 OLDS OL8 .... 71 D3
Lonsdale St *NEWH/MOS* M40 .... 87 C3
Loom St *ANC* M4 .... 17 F1
Lord Byron Sq *SALQ/ORD* M5 ..... 12 B3 🔟
Lord La *FAIL* M35 .... 88 B4
Lord Napier Dr *SALQ/ORD* M5 ...... 23 D2
Lord North St *NEWH/MOS* M40 ..... 9 F2
Lord's Av *SALQ/ORD* M5 .... 94 B3 🔟
Lordship Cl *BKLY* M9 .... 67 D4 🔟
Lordsmead St *HULME* M15 .... 24 C2 🔟

Lord St *ANC* M4 .... 6 C1
 BRO M7 .... 4 B1
 CSLFD M3 .... 6 B2
 DTN/ASHW M34 .... 118 A1
 OLD OL1 .... 55 D1
 STKP SK1 .... 138 B4 🔟
 STKP SK1 .... 138 A4 🔟
Loretto Rd *URM* M41 .... 112 B4
Loring St *NEWH/MOS* M40 .... 87 C4
Lorne Gv *URM* M41 .... 112 A3
Lorne Rd *RUSH/FAL* M14 .... 130 A1
Lorne St *ECC* M30 .... 100 B1 🔟
 OLDS OL8 .... 73 C1
Lostock Av *BNG/LEV* M19 .... 51 F4
 URM M41 .... 110 B2
Lostock Gv *STRET* M32 .... 113 D2
Lostock Rd *SALQ/ORD* M5 .... 95 C3
 URM M41 .... 111 D1
Lostock St *NEWH/MOS* M40 .... 8 C4
Lothian Av *ECC* M30 .... 90 B2 🔟
Lottie St *SWIN* M27 .... 77 C1
Loughfield *URM* M41 .... 110 A3 🔟
Louisa St *OP/CLY* M11 .... 106 B1
Louvain St *FAIL* M35 .... 88 A2
Love La *HTNM* SK4 .... 138 A3
Lowcock St *BRO* M7 .... 5 E2
Lowcroft Crs *CHAD* OL9 .... 52 B1
Lowcross Rd *NEWH/MOS* M40 ..... 86 A3 🔟
Lower Albion St *CMANE* M1 .... 17 E5
Lower Bents La *MPL/ROM* SK6 ... 141 D1
Lower Brook La *WALK* M28 .... 74 A4 🔟
Lower Brook St *CMANE* M1 .... 17 E4 🔟
Lower Broughton Rd *BRO* M7 .... 81 C4
Lower Byrom St *CSLFD* M3 .... 15 E4
Lower Carrs *STKP* SK1 .... 138 B4 🔟
Lower Chatham St *CMANE* M1 ..... 26 C1
 HULME M15 .... 26 C2
Lower Edge Av *OLD* OL1 .... 55 C1
Lower Hardman St *CSLFD* M3 ...... 15 E3
Lower Hillgate *STKP* SK1 .... 138 B4 🔟
Lower Moat Cl *HTNM* SK4 .... 138 A2
Lower Monton Rd *ECC* M30 .... 92 B3 🔟
Lower Mosley St *CMANW* M2 .... 16 A5
Lower Moss La *HULME* M15 .... 25 D2
Lower Ormond St *CMANE* M1 .... 26 C1
 HULME M15 .... 26 C2
Lower Park Rd *RUSH/FAL* M14 ..... 38 B3
Lower Seedley Rd *SLFD* M6 .... 95 C2
Lower Sutherland St *SWIN* M27 ... 76 A1
Lower Vickers St *NEWH/MOS* M40 ... 9 D4
Lower Victoria St *CHAD* OL9 ...... 53 D2 🔟
Lowestead Rd *OP/CLY* M11 .... 96 A3 🔟
Lowestoft St *RUSH/FAL* M14 .... 47 F1
Lowe St *STKP* SK1 .... 138 B4 🔟
Lowfield Av *DROY* M43 .... 97 D2
Lowick Gn *MPL/ROM* SK6 .... 137 D4 🔟
Lowlands Cl *MDTN* M24 .... 69 C1
Lowndes Wk *BRUN/LGST* M13 ... 28 A4 🔟
Lowry Dr *SWIN* M27 .... 58 B4
Lowther Av *GTN* M18 .... 41 F4
Lowther Cl *PWCH* M25 .... 62 A2 🔟
Lowther Rd *CHH* M8 .... 65 C4
 PWCH M25 .... 61 D2
Lowthorpe St *RUSH/FAL* M14 ...... 37 D5
Lowton Av *BKLY* M9 .... 85 D2
Low Wood Rd *DTN/ASHW* M34 .. 118 A1
Loxford St *HULME* M15 .... 26 B3
Lubeck St *BKLY* M9 .... 85 C1 🔟
Lucerne Cl *CHAD* OL9 .... 54 A3
Lucien Cl *WGTN/LGST* M12 .... 29 F5
Lucy St *BRO* M7 .... 81 C4
 HULME M15 .... 24 C4
Ludgate Hl *ANC* M4 .... 7 E4

Ludgate Rd *NEWH/MOS* M40 .... 96 A1
Ludgate St *ANC* M4 .... 7 D4
Ludlow Av *SWIN* M27 .... 59 C3
Luke Rd *DROY* M43 .... 98 B4
Lullington Rd *SLFD* M6 .... 94 B1
Lulworth Crs *FAIL* M35 .... 89 D1
Lulworth Rd *ECC* M30 .... 91 C3
Lumb La *DTN/ASHW* M34 .... 99 C4
Lumley Cl *RUSH/FAL* M14 .... 37 F3
Lumn's La *SWIN* M27 .... 60 A3
Luna St *ANC* M4 .... 17 E1
Lund St *OLDTF/WHR* M16 .... 24 A4
Lune St *OLDS* OL8 .... 73 C1
Lune Wy *RDSH* SK5 .... 134 B4
Lunn Av *GTN* M18 .... 107 D3
Lupton St *CSLFD* M3 .... 15 D1 🔢
Luton Rd *RDSH* SK5 .... 134 B1
Luxor Gv *DTN/ASHW* M34 .... 117 D2
Lyceum Pl *HULME* M15 .... 26 C2 🔢
Lydden Av *OP/CLY* M11 .... 96 B2 🔢
Lydgate Rd *DROY* M43 .... 97 C2
Lyme Gv *DROY* M43 .... 107 D1
Lyndale Av *RDSH* SK5 .... 117 D2
    SWIN M27 .... 75 D3 🔢
Lyndene Av *WALK* M28 .... 74 A1
Lyndhurst Av *CHAD* OL9 .... 52 B4
    MPL/ROM SK6 .... 141 D1
    PWCH M25 .... 64 A2 🔢
    URM M41 .... 111 C1
Lyndhurst Rd *OLDS* OL8 .... 72 B2
    RDSH SK5 .... 117 C3 🔢
    STRET M32 .... 113 D3
Lyndhurst St *SALQ/ORD* M5 .... 95 C3 🔢
Lynmouth Av *DID/WITH* M20 .... 129 C3 🔢
    OLDS OL8 .... 73 D2
    RDSH SK5 .... 134 A2 🔢
    URM M41 .... 120 B1 🔢
Lynmouth Gv *PWCH* M25 .... 61 D2
Lynn Av *SALE* M33 .... 124 B3
Lynn Dr *DROY* M43 .... 97 C3
Lynn St *CHAD* OL9 .... 72 A1
Lynthorpe Rd *NEWH/MOS* M40 .... 69 D3
Lynton Av *OLDS* OL8 .... 72 A3 🔢
    SWIN M27 .... 58 B4
Lynton Dr *BNG/LEV* M19 .... 131 D2
Lynton Rd *CCHDY* M21 .... 43 D3
    HTNM SK4 .... 132 B4
    SWIN M27 .... 58 B4 🔢
Lynton St *RUSH/FAL* M14 .... 47 F1 🔢
Lynway Dr *DID/WITH* M20 .... 129 D4
Lynwood Av *ECC* M30 .... 91 D3 🔢
    OLDTF/WHR M16 .... 44 B2
Lynwood Gv *DTN/ASHW* M34 .... 99 C4
    HTNM SK4 .... 133 C3 🔢
    SALE M33 .... 124 A4
Lyon Gv *WALK* M28 .... 74 A1
Lyons Fold *SALE* M33 .... 123 D3 🔢
Lyons Rd *TRPK* M17 .... 103 C2
Lyon St *SWIN* M27 .... 76 A2 🔢
Lysander Cl *RUSH/FAL* M14 .... 47 D5
Lytham Av *CCHDY* M21 .... 127 C2 🔢
Lytham Rd *RUSH/FAL* M14 .... 50 A3
Lyth St *RUSH/FAL* M14 .... 130 B2
Lytton Av *CHH* M8 .... 83 C3
Lytton Rd *DROY* M43 .... 98 A3 🔢

M

Mabel Av *WALK* M28 .... 74 A2
Mabel Rd *FAIL* M35 .... 71 C4
Mabel St *NEWH/MOS* M40 .... 87 D4 🔢

Mabfield Rd *RUSH/FAL* M14 .... 48 B3
Macauley Rd *OLDTF/WHR* M16 .... 43 F1
    RDSH SK5 .... 116 B4
Macdonald St *OLDS* OL8 .... 73 D1 🔢
Macfarren St *WGTN/LGST* M12 .... 40 C4
Mackenzie Rd *BRO* M7 .... 80 B3 🔢
Mackenzie St *WGTN/LGST* M12 .... 41 D4
Maclaren Dr *CHH* M8 .... 64 A3
Maclure Cl *OLDTF/WHR* M16 .... 35 E4 🔢
Maddison Rd *DROY* M43 .... 97 D4
Madeley Dr *CHAD* OL9 .... 53 D3 🔢
Madison Av *DTN/ASHW* M34 .... 109 C1
Madison St *GTN* M18 .... 107 C3
Mafeking St *OLDS* OL8 .... 72 A2 🔢
Magdala St *OLD* OL1 .... 55 C1
Magnolia Cl *SALE* M33 .... 121 C4
Magnolia Dr *CHH* M8 .... 83 C3 🔢
Magpie Cl *DROY* M43 .... 99 C2
Maher Gdns *HULME* M15 .... 35 E2
Maida St *BNG/LEV* M19 .... 51 E1
Maidford Cl *ANC* M4 .... 19 D2 🔢
    STRET M32 .... 115 C3 🔢
Maidstone Av *CCHDY* M21 .... 42 C4
Maidstone Ms *CCHDY* M21 .... 42 C4 🔢
Main Av *BNG/LEV* M19 .... 131 D2 🔢
    TRPK M17 .... 114 A1
Maine Rd *RUSH/FAL* M14 .... 37 D3
Mainprice Cl *SLFD* M6 .... 2 B3 🔢
Main Rd *CHAD* OL9 .... 54 A2
    SWIN M27 .... 60 B2
Main St *FAIL* M35 .... 88 B1
Major St *CMANE* M1 .... 17 D4
Makin St *CMANE* M1 .... 17 D5 🔢
Makkah Cl *NEWH/MOS* M40 .... 86 A4
Malby St *OLD* OL1 .... 55 D1
Malcolm Av *SWIN* M27 .... 59 C2 🔢
Malcolm Dr *SWIN* M27 .... 59 C3 🔢
Maldon Crs *SWIN* M27 .... 76 B3
Maldon Dr *ECC* M30 .... 92 A1 🔢
Maldwyn Av *CHH* M8 .... 65 C3
Maleham St *BRO* M7 .... 82 A3 🔢🔢
Mallard Cl *OLDS* OL8 .... 72 B3 🔢
Mallard St *CMANE* M1 .... 26 C1 🔢
Mallow St *HULME* M15 .... 25 E3
Malpas St *OLD* OL1 .... 55 D2
    WGTN/LGST M12 .... 30 C4
Malta St *ANC* M4 .... 18 C2
Malton Av *CCHDY* M21 .... 126 B1
Malton St *OLDS* OL8 .... 54 B4
Malt St *HULME* M15 .... 24 C2
Malvern Av *DROY* M43 .... 99 C3
    URM M41 .... 110 B3
Malvern Cl *SWIN* M27 .... 78 B3 🔢
Malvern Dr *SWIN* M27 .... 78 B3 🔢
Malvern Gv *DID/WITH* M20 .... 129 C3
    SLFD M6 .... 94 A2 🔢
Malvern St *HULME* M15 .... 24 C4
    OLDS OL8 .... 54 B4
Manby Rd *GTN* M18 .... 41 E3
Manby Sq *GTN* M18 .... 41 F3
Manchester Rd *CCHDY* M21 .... 43 E3
    CCHDY M21 .... 43 E4 🔢
    DROY M43 .... 97 C4
    DROY M43 .... 98 A4 🔢
    DTN/ASHW M34 .... 108 B2
    HTNM SK4 .... 133 D4
    OLDS OL8 .... 72 A1
    SWIN M27 .... 58 B2
Manchester Rd North
    DTN/ASHW M34 .... 119 C1
Manchester Rd South
    DTN/ASHW M34 .... 119 C2
Manchester St *OLDTF/WHR* M16 .... 24 B5

Mancunian Wy *WGTN/LGST* M12 .... **28** B1
Mandeville St *BNG/LEV* M19 .. **132** B1 🖭
Mandley Av *NEWH/MOS* M40 .... **69** D3 🖪
Mandley Park Av *BRO* M7................ **82** A2
Mangle St *CMANE* M1.................... **17** E2
Mango Pl *SLFD* M6 .... **3** D5
Manifold St *SLFD* M6 .... **3** E1
  SLFD M6 .... **80** B4 🖪
Manipur St *OP/CLY* M11 .... **20** A4
Manley Av *SWIN* M27 .... **58** B1
Manley Rd *CCHDY* M21 .... **43** F3
  OLDS OL8 .... **73** C1
Mannington Dr *BKLY* M9............... **84** A3
Mannock St *OLDS* OL8 .... **54** B3 🖪
Manor Av *OLDTF/WHR* M16 .... **44** C1
  SALE M33 .... **121** D4
  URM M41 .... **111** D4
Manor Cl *CHAD* OL9 .... **54** A1
Manor Ct *STRET* M32 .... **113** D4
Manor Rd *BNG/LEV* M19 .... **51** F2
  DROY M43 .... **97** C4
  DTN/ASHW M34 .... **108** D2
  RDSH SK5 .... **135** D4
  SALE M33 .... **123** D4
  SLFD M6 .... **94** B1
  STRET M32 .... **113** D4
  SWIN M27 .... **76** B3
Manor St *WGTN/LGST* M12 .... **28** A1
Mansfield Av *BKLY* M9 .... **66** B1
  DTN/ASHW M34 .... **109** D4
Mansfield Cl *DTN/ASHW* M34 ..... **109** D4 🖪
Mansfield Crs *DTN/ASHW* M34 .... **119** D1
Mansfield Dr *BKLY* M9 .... **67** C1 🖪
Mansfield Rd *BKLY* M9................... **66** B1
  URM M41 .... **110** A4
Mansford Dr *NEWH/MOS* M40 .... **85** D2 🖪
Manshaw Crs *OP/CLY* M11 .... **108** A2
Manshaw Rd *OP/CLY* M11 .... **108** A2
Manson Av *HULME* M15 .... **24** C2
Manswood Dr *CHH* M8 .... **83** C2
Manton Av *BKLY* M9 .... **68** B2
  DTN/ASHW M34 .... **118** A2
Manton Cl *CHH* M8......................... **82** B3
Manvers St *RDSH* SK5 .... **138** B2 🖪
Manwaring St *FAIL* M35 .... **88** A1 🖪
Maple Av *CCHDY* M21 .... **43** F5
  DTN/ASHW M34 .... **98** B4
  ECC M30 .... **90** A1
  STRET M32 .... **114** B4
Maple Cl *SLFD* M6 .... **2** B3
Maple Gv *FAIL* M35 .... **88** A4
  NEWH/MOS M40 .... **70** A3
Maple Rd *SWIN* M27 .... **76** A3
Maple St *OLDS* OL8 .... **72** A2
Maplin Cl *BRUN/LGST* M13 .... **28** A2
Marble St *CMANW* M2 .... **16** C2
Marbury Av *RUSH/FAL* M14 .... **47** E4
Marbury Rd *HTNM* SK4 .... **133** D2
Marcer Rd *NEWH/MOS* M40 .... **8** C5
Marchioness St *GTN* M18 .... **107** D3 🖪
Marchmont Cl *WGTN/LGST* M12.. **28** C4
Marchwood Av *CCHDY* M21 .... **45** D3
Marcliffe Dr *BNG/LEV* M19 .... **116** A4
Marcus Gv *RUSH/FAL* M14........... **48** B1
Mardale Av *DID/WITH* M20 .... **130** A4
  SWIN M27 .... **57** C3
Mardale Rd *SWIN* M27 .... **75** D3
Marfield *BKLY* M9 .... **67** C4 🖪
Marfield Av *CHAD* OL9 .... **53** C4 🖪
Margaret Ashton Cl *BKLY* M9 .. **85** D2 🖪
Margaret Rd *DROY* M43 .... **97** C3 🖪
Margaret St *OLDS* OL8 .... **71** D3

RDSH SK5 .... **134** A2
Margate Av *NEWH/MOS* M40 ..... **86** B4 🖪
Margate Rd *RDSH* SK5................. **134** B2 🖪
Margrove Rd *SLFD* M6 .... **94** A1
Marguerita Rd *NEWH/MOS* M40 .. **87** D4 🖪
Marham Cl *CCHDY* M21 .... **128** A3 🖪
Marie St *BRO* M7 .... **82** A2 🖪
Mariman Dr *CHH* M8 .... **65** C3
Marina Crs *OP/CLY* M11 .... **11** F4
Marina Rd *DROY* M43 .... **98** B3
  MPL/ROM SK6 .... **141** C1
Marion St *OLDS* OL8 .... **73** D2 🖪
Marjorie Cl *GTN* M18 .... **31** F4
Mark Av *SLFD* M6 .... **3** E1
Market Pl *STKP* SK1 .... **138** B2
Market St *CMANE* M1 .... **16** B2
  DROY M43 .... **98** B3
  SWIN M27 .... **59** C4 🖪
Market Wy *SLFD* M6 .... **2** B4
Markfield Av *BRUN/LGST* M13 .... **29** D5
Markham Cl *WGTN/LGST* M12 .... **19** D4
Markington St *RUSH/FAL* M14 .... **36** C5
Mark St *CHAD* OL9 .... **54** B2 🖪
Marland Crs *RDSH* SK5 .... **134** B1
Marland Fold La *OLDS* OL8 .... **73** D4 🖪
Marland St *CHAD* OL9 .... **71** C2 🖪
Marlborough Av *OLDTF/WHR* M16 ... **44** B2
Marlborough Dr *FAIL* M35 .... **88** A3
Marlborough Gv *DROY* M43 .... **99** C3 🖪
Marlborough Rd *BRO* M7 .... **82** B3 🖫
  ECC M30 .... **93** C1
  STRET M32 .... **114** A2
Marley Dr *SALE* M33 .... **123** C3 🖪
Marleyer Cl *NEWH/MOS* M40 ..... **87** C2 🖪
Marley Rd *BNG/LEV* M19 .... **132** B1
Marlinford Dr *NEWH/MOS* M40 ... **87** C4 🖫
Marlow Cl *URM* M41 .... **110** B1
Marlow Dr *SWIN* M27 .... **76** A3 🖪
Marlowe Wks *MPL/ROM* SK6 ...... **141** C3
Marlow Rd *BKLY* M9 .... **67** C4 🖪
Marmion Dr *CCHDY* M21 .... **126** A1 🖪
Marple Cl *OLDS* OL8 .... **72** B3 🖪
Marple Gv *STRET* M32 .... **114** A2
Marquis St *BNG/LEV* M19 .... **116** B4
Marriott St *DID/WITH* M20 .... **129** D3 🖪
Marron Pl *CMANW* M2 .... **16** A4 🖪
Marsden St *CMANW* M2 .... **16** B2
  ECC M30 .... **91** C2 🖪
Marshall Cl *BNG/LEV* M19 .... **50** C4
Marshall Stevens Wy *TRPK* M17 .. **103** D4
Marshall St *ANC* M4 .... **7** E5
  WGTN/LGST M12 .... **28** B3
Marsham Cl *BRUN/LGST* M13 .. **39** F2 🖪
Marshbrook Rd *URM* M41 .... **111** C2 🖪
Marsland Cl *DTN/ASHW* M34 ..... **118** B2
Marsland St *STKP* SK1 .... **138** B2 🖪
  STKP SK1 .... **139** C3 🖪
Marsland St North *BRO* M7 .... **82** A2
Marsland St South *BRO* M7 .... **82** B2
Mars St *CHAD* OL9 .... **54** A2
Marston Cl *FAIL* M35 .... **89** D3
Marston Rd *BRO* M7 .... **82** A1
  STRET M32 .... **115** C3
Marsworth Dr *ANC* M4 .... **18** B1 🖪
Martha St *CHAD* OL9 .... **54** B1
Martindale Crs *WGTN/LGST* M12 .. **29** F4
Martingale Wy *DROY* M43 .... **99** D3
Martin Rd *SWIN* M27 .... **59** D3
Martin St *SALQ/ORD* M5 .... **94** B3
Martlet Cl *RUSH/FAL* M14 .... **47** E4
Marton Gra *PWCH* M25 .... **63** D3
Marton Gv *HTNM* SK4 .... **134** A3
Mary France St *HULME* M15....... **25** E3

Mary St *CSLFD* M3 .... 6 A3
 DROY M43 .... 98 B4
 STKP SK1 .... 139 C3
Masboro St *CHH* M8 .... 82 B2 🗔
Masefield Av *PWCH* M25 .... 61 D2
Masefield Crs *DROY* M43 .... 98 A4 🗔
Masefield Gv *RDSH* SK5 .... 117 C4 🗔
Masefield Rd *DROY* M43 .... 98 A4
Mason St *ANC* M4 .... 7 E5
 CSLFD M3 .... 15 D2
Massey Av *FAIL* M35 .... 89 D1
Massey St *SALQ/ORD* M5 .... 14 B2
 STKP SK1 .... 138 B4 🗔
Mather Av *ECC* M30 .... 92 A3 🗔
 PWCH M25 .... 63 C4
Mather Rd *ECC* M30 .... 92 A3
Mather St *FAIL* M35 .... 87 D2
Matley Gn *RDSH* SK5 .... 136 A3
Matlock Av *BRO* M7 .... 80 A2
 DID/WITH M20 .... 128 B3 🗔
 URM M41 .... 120 B1
Matlock Rd *RDSH* SK5 .... 118 A4
 STRET M32 .... 113 C2
Matlock St *ECC* M30 .... 101 C1 🗔
Matt Busby Cl *SWIN* M27 .... 77 D2
Matthews La *BNG/LEV* M19 .... 51 D2
Matthew's St *WGTN/LGST* M12 .... 30 A2
Mattison St *OP/CLY* M11 .... 107 C2 🗔
Mauldeth Rd *BNG/LEV* M19 .... 131 C3
 DID/WITH M20 .... 130 A2
 RUSH/FAL M14 .... 130 A2
Mauldeth Rd West *CCHDY* M21 .... 128 A1
Maureen Av *CHH* M8 .... 83 C1 🗔
Maurice Dr *SLFD* M6 .... 2 A2
Maurice St *SLFD* M6 .... 2 B2
Mawdsley Dr *CHH* M8 .... 84 A1
Mayan Av *CSLFD* M3 .... 4 C5
Mayberth Av *CHH* M8 .... 65 C3
Maybury St *GTN* M18 .... 107 C3
Maycroft Av *DID/WITH* M20 .... 130 A4
Mayes St *ANC* M4 .... 6 C5
Mayfair Av *SLFD* M6 .... 93 D2
 URM M41 .... 110 B3
Mayfair Crs *FAIL* M35 .... 89 D1
Mayfield Av *RDSH* SK5 .... 134 B4
 STRET M32 .... 113 D4
 SWIN M27 .... 75 C3
Mayfield Gv *GTN* M18 .... 117 D2
 RDSH SK5 .... 134 B4
Mayfield Rd *BRO* M7 .... 62 B4
 OLDTF/WHR M16 .... 35 E5
Mayford St *BNG/LEV* M19 .... 51 D2
Maygate *OLD* OL1 .... 54 B1
May Gv *BNG/LEV* M19 .... 132 B1 🗔
Mayhill Dr *SLFD* M6 .... 93 C1 🗔
 WALK M28 .... 74 A1 🗔
Mayorlowe Av *RDSH* SK5 .... 140 A1
Mayor St *CHAD* OL9 .... 54 A2 🗔
Mayo St *WGTN/LGST* M12 .... 18 C5 🗔
Maypool Dr *RDSH* SK5 .... 134 B3 🗔
May Rd *OLDTF/WHR* M16 .... 35 D5
 SWIN M27 .... 77 D3
May St *ECC* M30 .... 91 C1
 NEWH/MOS M40 .... 87 C4
 OLDS OL8 .... 72 A1
Mayton St *OP/CLY* M11 .... 21 D5
Mayville Dr *DID/WITH* M20 .... 129 D4
Mcconnell St *NEWH/MOS* M40 .... 86 A2
Mccready Dr *SALQ/ORD* M5 .... 13 E4
Mclaren Ct *CCHDY* M21 .... 43 D1
Meachin Av *CCHDY* M21 .... 127 C3
Meade Cl *URM* M41 .... 111 C3 🗔

Meade Gv *BRUN/LGST* M13 .... 40 A4
Meade Hill Rd *PWCH* M25 .... 64 A2
Meadfoot Av *PWCH* M25 .... 63 C2
Meadfoot Rd *GTN* M18 .... 106 B3
Meadow Av *SWIN* M27 .... 59 D4
Meadow Bank *CCHDY* M21 .... 126 A2
 MPL/ROM SK6 .... 141 D2 🗔
Meadowbank Cl *FAIL* M35 .... 89 C3
Meadow Bank Ct *STRET* M32 .... 113 D4
Meadow Cl *STRET* M32 .... 115 C4
Meadow Ct *CCHDY* M21 .... 42 B5
Meadowgate *URM* M41 .... 111 D4
Meadowgate Rd *SLFD* M6 .... 93 D2
Meadow La *OLDS* OL8 .... 73 C3
Meadow Rd *BRO* M7 .... 4 B4
 URM M41 .... 111 D4
Meadows Rd *HTNM* SK4 .... 133 C3
 SALE M33 .... 124 A3
The Meadows *PWCH* M25 .... 62 B1
Meadow Wy *NEWH/MOS* M40 .... 68 A4
The Meads *CHAD* OL9 .... 53 C3
The Mead *CCHDY* M21 .... 126 B2 🗔
 SALQ/ORD M5 .... 95 C3
Meadway *CHAD* OL9 .... 70 A3
Mealhouse Brow *STKP* SK1 .... 138 B4 🗔
Meal St *HTNM* SK4 .... 138 A2
Measham Ms *CMANE* M1 .... 26 C1 🗔
Medlock Rd *FAIL* M35 .... 89 C4
Medlock St *DROY* M43 .... 98 A3
 HULME M15 .... 26 A1
Medway Cl *OLDS* OL8 .... 72 A2
 SALQ/ORD M5 .... 94 B2 🗔
Medway Rd *OLDS* OL8 .... 72 A2
Meech St *OP/CLY* M11 .... 106 A1
Mee's Sq *ECC* M30 .... 101 D1 🗔
Melanie Dr *RDSH* SK5 .... 134 B1
Melba St *OP/CLY* M11 .... 107 C1
Melbourne St *CHAD* OL9 .... 53 D2 🗔
 STRET M32 .... 114 B3 🗔
Melbourne St *BKLY* M9 .... 85 C1
 BRO M7 .... 82 A4 🗔
 CHAD OL9 .... 53 D2
 HULME M15 .... 25 E2
 RDSH SK5 .... 134 B1
 SWIN M27 .... 77 D1 🗔
Meldon Rd *BRUN/LGST* M13 .... 49 F1
Meldreth Dr *WGTN/LGST* M12 .... 40 B2
Meldrum St *OLDS* OL8 .... 73 D1
Melford Av *NEWH/MOS* M40 .... 70 A4
Melfort Av *STRET* M32 .... 115 C4
Melksham Cl *SALQ/ORD* M5 .... 13 E1 🗔
Melland Av *CCHDY* M21 .... 127 C4
Melland Rd *GTN* M18 .... 116 A2
Meller Rd *BRUN/LGST* M13 .... 50 B1
Melling Av *HTNM* SK4 .... 134 A3
Melling St *WGTN/LGST* M12 .... 41 D3
Mellors Rd *TRPK* M17 .... 103 D2
Mellor St *DROY* M43 .... 97 D4
 ECC M30 .... 91 D4
 FAIL M35 .... 87 D3
 NEWH/MOS M40 .... 8 C4
 PWCH M25 .... 61 D1
 STRET M32 .... 114 B1
Mellor Wy *CHAD* OL9 .... 71 D1
Mellowstone Dr *OLDTF/WHR* M16 .... 46 A3
Melloy Pl *CHH* M8 .... 7 D1
Melon Pl *SLFD* M6 .... 3 E5
Melrose Av *ECC* M30 .... 90 B1 🗔
Melrose St *NEWH/MOS* M40 .... 87 C4
Meltham Av *DID/WITH* M20 .... 129 C3
Melton Av *DTN/ASHW* M34 .... 118 A4
Melton Rd *CHH* M8 .... 64 A4
Melton St *BKLY* M9 .... 67 D4 🗔

Entry	Page
RDSH SK5	138 B1 7
Melville Cl *OP/CLY* M11	107 C2
Melville Rd *STRET* M32	113 D2
Melville St *CSLFD* M3	15 D1
Mendip Cl *CHAD* OL9	53 C4 8
HTNM SK4	138 A2
Mendip Rd *OLDS* OL8	72 B2 2
Menston Av *NEWH/MOS* M40	70 A4
Mentor St *BRUN/LGST* M13	50 B1
Mercer Rd *GTN* M18	106 B4
Mercer St *BNG/LEV* M19	51 E4
DROY M43	98 B5 8
Merchants Quay *SALQ/ORD* M5	22 C3
Mercury Wy *URM* M41	102 B4
Mere Av *DROY* M43	107 C1
SLFD M6	95 C3 13
Mere Cl *DTN/ASHW* M34	118 B3
Meredew Av *SWIN* M27	76 A3 8
Meredith St *RUSH/FAL* M14	130 B2 8
Mere Dr *SWIN* M27	59 C3
Merlewood Av *BNG/LEV* M19	133 C2
DTN/ASHW M34	98 B4 8
Merlewood Dr *SWIN* M27	75 C3 8
Merlyn Av *SALE* M33	124 A3
Merrill St *ANC* M4	19 D2
Merriman St *OLDTF/WHR* M16	35 E3
Merrybower Rd *BRO* M7	82 A1
Merrydale Av *ECC* M30	92 A1
Mersey Rd *SALE* M33	123 D3
Mersey Rd North *FAIL* M35	71 C4
Mersey Sq *STKP* SK1	138 A4 11
Mersey St *OP/CLY* M11	107 C1 8
OP/CLY M11	107 C2 12
STKP SK1	139 C3
Merton Av *OLDS* OL8	72 B2
Merton Dr *DROY* M43	97 C4
Merton Gv *CHAD* OL9	69 D2
Merton Rd *SALE* M33	123 C4
Merville Av *NEWH/MOS* M40	67 D4 8
Mervyn Rd *BRO* M7	80 A3
Merwood Gv *RUSH/FAL* M14	39 E3
Mesnefield Rd *BRO* M7	80 A1
Methuen St *WGTN/LGST* M12	41 E5
The Mews *NEWH/MOS* M40	9 F4
PWCH M25	62 B2 8
Meyrick Rd *SLFD* M6	2 C3
Michigan Av *SALQ/ORD* M5	12 A5
Middlebourne St *SLFD* M6	95 C3 14
Middlegate *NEWH/MOS* M40	69 C2 8
Middle Ga *OLDS* OL8	73 C3
Middleham St *RUSH/FAL* M14	47 D1 8
Middle Hillgate *STKP* SK1	138 B4 17
Middlesex Rd *BKLY* M9	66 B3
RDSH SK5	136 A3
Middlestone Dr *BKLY* M9	84 B2 8
Middleton Av *FAIL* M35	88 B2
Middleton Old Rd *BKLY* M9	66 B3 8
Middleton Rd *CHAD* OL9	52 B1
CHH M8	64 B3
RDSH SK5	117 D3
Middleton Rd West *CHAD* OL9	52 A1
Middlewood Gn *CHAD* OL9	53 C2
Middlewood St *SALQ/ORD* M5	14 B3
Midford Av *ECC* M30	90 B5 10
Midgley Av *GTN* M18	107 C3
Midgley St *SWIN* M27	75 D3 8
Midhurst Av *NEWH/MOS* M40	11 F2 8
Midland Rd *RDSH* SK5	117 D3
Midland St *WGTN/LGST* M12	29 D1
Midlothian St *OP/CLY* M11	11 E5
Midville Rd *OP/CLY* M11	96 A2
Midway St *BNG/LEV* M19	51 D2 8
Milan St *BRO* M7	82 A3
Mildred Av *PWCH* M25	63 C3
Mildred St *BRO* M7	81 C4
Miles St *WGTN/LGST* M12	30 C2
Milford Av *OLDS* OL8	72 A3 8
Milford Dr *BNG/LEV* M19	133 C2
Milford St *BKLY* M9	65 D1 8
SLFD M6	95 C4
Milk St *CMANW* M2	16 C2
Milkwood Gv *GTN* M18	116 B1 8
Millais St *NEWH/MOS* M40	68 A4
Millard St *CHAD* OL9	53 C2
Millbank St *CMANE* M1	18 A3
Millbeck St *HULME* M15	26 C3 8
Millbrook Av *DTN/ASHW* M34	119 D4
Mill Brow *BKLY* M9	66 A3
Miller Rd *OLDS* OL8	73 C2
Millers Ct *SALQ/ORD* M5	93 C3 8
Millers St *ECC* M30	91 C3
Miller St *ANC* M4	7 D5
Mill Ga *OLDS* OL8	72 B2
Millgate *STKP* SK1	138 B3 8
Mill Green St *WGTN/LGST* M12	18 C5 8
Millhall Cl *HULME* M15	25 E5
Millhead Av *NEWH/MOS* M40	9 E5
Mill La *CHAD* OL9	72 A1
FAIL M35	87 D3 8
RDSH SK5	118 A4
Millow St *ANC* M4	6 C4
Millstream La *DROY* M43	97 C2
Mill St *FAIL* M35	87 C2
OP/CLY M11	21 D5
SLFD M6	2 C2
Millwall Cl *GTN* M18	106 B4
Millwright St *NEWH/MOS* M40	86 B4
Milne Cl *WGTN/LGST* M12	31 D4
Milner St *OLDTF/WHR* M16	34 C3
SWIN M27	77 C1
Milne St *CHAD* OL9	53 D2
Milnrow Cl *CMANE* M1	27 F1
Milnthorpe St *SLFD* M6	80 A4
Milnthorpe Wy *WGTN/LGST* M12	29 F4
Milo St *BKLY* M9	66 B2 8
Milton Av *DROY* M43	98 A4 8
SALQ/ORD M5	94 B3 8
Milton Cl *STRET* M32	115 C2 8
Milton Dr *CHAD* OL9	53 C3
SALE M33	123 C3
Milton Gv *OLDTF/WHR* M16	44 A1
SALE M33	123 C3
Milton Pl *SLFD* M6	3 D4
Milton Rd *DTN/ASHW* M34	99 D4
STRET M32	115 C2 8
SWIN M27	57 D4
Milton St *BRO* M7	5 E2
ECC M30	91 D3
Milverton Rd *RUSH/FAL* M14	39 D3
Milwain Dr *HTNM* SK4	133 C3
Milwain Rd *BNG/LEV* M19	131 D1
STRET M32	114 A4
Mimosa Dr *SWIN* M27	58 B3 19
Mincing St *ANC* M4	7 D4 8
Minden Cl *SLFD* M6	79 C3
Minehead Av *DID/WITH* M20	128 B2
URM M41	120 B1
Minoan Gdns *BRO* M7	81 C4
Minor St *FAIL* M35	71 C4
OLDS OL8	55 C4
Minshull St *CMANE* M1	17 D3
Minshull St South *CMANE* M1	17 E4 8
Minton St *NEWH/MOS* M40	87 C1 8
Mirabel St *CSLFD* M3	6 A4
Mirfield Av *BKLY* M9	66 B1
OLDS OL8	73 C1 4

Mirfield Dr *ECC* M30 .... **91** D1
   URM M41 .... **111** C1 █
Mirfield Rd *BKLY* M9 .... **66** B1
Miriam St *FAIL* M35 .... **88** A4
   NEWH/MOS M40 .... **87** D3
Missouri Av *SALQ/ORD* M5 .... **95** C4
Mistletoe Gv *CSLFD* M3 .... **5** D4 █
Mitcham Av *BKLY* M9 .... **68** A2 █
Mitchells Quay *FAIL* M35 .... **88** A2 █
Mitchell St *ECC* M30 .... **91** C2
   NEWH/MOS M40 .... **86** B4
   OLD OL1 .... **54** B1
   OP/CLY M11 .... **20** B5
Mitcheson Gdns *SLFD* M6 .... **2** A3
Mitford Rd *RUSH/FAL* M14 .... **130** A2
Mitford St *STRET* M32 .... **114** A4
Mitre Rd *BRUN/LGST* M13 .... **40** A3
Mitre St *FAIL* M35 .... **88** B1
Moat Hall Av *ECC* M30 .... **100** A1
Mode Wheel Rd South
   SALQ/ORD M5 .... **94** B4
Modwen Rd *SALQ/ORD* M5 .... **23** E3
Mold St *OLD* OL1 .... **55** C1 █
Molyneux Rd *BNG/LEV* M19 ...... **116** A4
Mona Av *STRET* M32 .... **114** A2
Monart Rd *BKLY* M9 .... **67** C4
Mona St *SLFD* M6 .... **3** D2 █
Monica Av *CHH* M8 .... **64** B3
Monica Gv *BNG/LEV* M19 .... **50** A5
Monksdale Av *URM* M41 .... **110** B2 █
Monks Hall Gv *ECC* M30 .... **92** B3
Monkton Av *GTN* M18 .... **116** A3
Monkwood Dr *BKLY* M9 .... **85** C1 █
Monmouth Av *SALE* M33 .... **122** B4 █
Monmouth St *CHAD* OL9 .... **54** A4
   GTN M18 .... **107** C3 █
Monroe Cl *SLFD* M6 .... **95** C1 █
Monsal Av *BRO* M7 .... **80** A2 █
Monsall Rd *NEWH/MOS* M40 .... **85** C3
Monsall St *NEWH/MOS* M40 .... **84** B4
   OLDS OL8 .... **73** C2
Montague Rd *OLDTF/WHR* M16 ... **32** C1
Montana Sq *OP/CLY* M11 .... **107** C4
Montcliffe Crs *OLDTF/WHR* M16 ... **46** A3
Monteagle St *BKLY* M9 .... **65** D1 █
Montford St *SALQ/ORD* M5 .... **12** C4
Montgomery Rd *BRUN/LGST* M13 ... **50** A1
Montgomery St *OLDS* OL8 .... **71** D3
Monton Av *ECC* M30 .... **92** A2
Montondale *ECC* M30 .... **91** C2 █
Montonfields Rd *ECC* M30 .... **91** C2
Monton Gn *ECC* M30 .... **91** D1
Monton La *ECC* M30 .... **92** A3
Monton Mill Gdns *ECC* M30 .... **91** C2
Monton Rd *ECC* M30 .... **91** D2
   RDSH SK5 .... **140** A1 █
Monton St *RUSH/FAL* M14 .... **37** D3
Montreal St *BNG/LEV* M19 .... **51** E3
   OLDS OL8 .... **73** D1
Montrose Av *DID/WITH* M20 ..... **129** C4 █
   STRET M32 .... **113** D3
Montrose Crs *BNG/LEV* M19 .... **50** A5 █
Moon Gv *RUSH/FAL* M14 .... **38** C5
Moon St *CHAD* OL9 .... **54** A2 █
Moorcock Av *SWIN* M27 .... **77** D1 █
Moorcroft St *DROY* M43 .... **98** B4 █
   OLDS OL8 .... **72** A3
Moordale St *DID/WITH* M20 ...... **129** C4 █
Moordown Cl *CHH* M8 .... **83** D4 █
Moor End Av *BRO* M7 .... **81** C1 █
Moorfield Av *RUSH/FAL* M14 .... **130** A2 █
Moorfield Cl *SWIN* M27 .... **75** D3
Moorfield Rd *OLDS* OL8 .... **71** D3 █

SLFD M6 .... **78** B4
   SWIN M27 .... **75** C3 █
Moorfield St *DID/WITH* M20 ..... **129** D2 █
   DID/WITH M20 .... **129** D2 █
Moorgate Av *DID/WITH* M20 ..... **128** B3
Moorhead St *ANC* M4 .... **7** F4 █
Moorings Rd *TRPK* M17 .... **103** D1
The Moorings *WALK* M28 .... **74** A4
Moorland Av *CHH* M8 .... **64** B3
   DROY M43 .... **97** C4
Moorlands Av *URM* M41 .... **110** B2 █
Moor La *BRO* M7 .... **80** A1
   URM M41 .... **110** A2
Moorsholme Av *NEWH/MOS* M40 ... **86** A2 █
Moorside Av *DROY* M43 .... **99** C3 █
Moorside Crs *DROY* M43 .... **99** C3
Moorside Rd *BRO* M7 .... **63** C4
   CHH M8 .... **65** C4 █
   SWIN M27 .... **75** D1
   URM M41 .... **110** A2
Moorside St *DROY* M43 .... **98** B3
Moor St *ECC* M30 .... **90** B4
   SWIN M27 .... **76** B2
Moorton Av *BNG/LEV* M19 .... **131** D2
Moorton Pk *BNG/LEV* M19 .... **131** D2 █
Moorville Rd *SLFD* M6 .... **78** A4
Moorway Dr *BKLY* M9 .... **68** A1
Mora St *BKLY* M9 .... **85** D1
Moravian Fld *DROY* M43 .... **108** A1 █
Moray Rd *CHAD* OL9 .... **71** C1
Morbourne Cl *WGTN/LGST* M12 ... **29** E4
Morecambe Cl *NEWH/MOS* M40 ... **86** B3
Moreton Av *STRET* M32 .... **114** B3
Moreton St *CHAD* OL9 .... **52** B1
Morgan Pl *RDSH* SK5 .... **138** B1 █
Morland Rd *OLDTF/WHR* M16 .... **34** A3
Morley Av *RUSH/FAL* M14 .... **46** C3
   SWIN M27 .... **76** A3 █
Morningside Cl *DROY* M43 .... **107** D2
Mornington Crs *RUSH/FAL* M14 ... **47** D5
Mornington Rd *SALE* M33 .... **124** B4
Morpeth St *SWIN* M27 .... **76** A3
Morris St *DID/WITH* M20 .... **129** D2 █
Morrowfield Av *CHH* M8 .... **82** B2 █
Morse Rd *NEWH/MOS* M40 .... **86** B4
Mortimer Av *BKLY* M9 .... **67** C3
Mortlake Dr *NEWH/MOS* M40 ..... **86** B4
Morton St *FAIL* M35 .... **87** C2
   HTNM SK4 .... **138** A1
Morville Rd *CCHDY* M21 .... **44** C3
Morville St *CMANE* M1 .... **18** A4 █
Moseley Rd *BNG/LEV* M19 .... **50** A5
   RUSH/FAL M14 .... **49** D5
Mosley Rd *TRPK* M17 .... **104** A3
Mosley Rd North *TRPK* M17 ...... **104** A1
Mosley St *CMANW* M2 .... **16** B3 █
Moss Bank *CHH* M8 .... **83** C1
Moss Bank Av *DROY* M43 .... **99** C3
Moss Bank Ct *DROY* M43 .... **99** C3 █
Moss Bank Gv *SWIN* M27 .... **57** C3
Moss Bank Rd *SWIN* M27 .... **57** D3
Moss Brook Rd *BKLY* M9 .... **85** C2
Mossclough Ct *BKLY* M9 .... **85** C2 █
Moss Colliery Rd *SWIN* M27 .... **57** D2
Mosscot Wk *BRUN/LGST* M13 ..... **27** F1 █
Mossfield Dr *BKLY* M9 .... **68** A1
Mossfield Rd *SWIN* M27 .... **58** A3
Moss Grange Av *OLDTF/WHR* M16 ... **34** C3
Mosshall Cl *HULME* M15 .... **25** D4
Moss La *SWIN* M27 .... **57** D4
   URM M41 .... **101** D1
Moss La East *HULME* M15 .... **36** A2
Moss La West *HULME* M15 .... **35** E2

Mosslee Av *CHH* M8 .... 64 B2 ◨
Moss Lodge La *AULW* OL7 .... 99 D4
Moss Meadow Rd *SLFD* M6 .... 94 A1 ◨
Moss Park Rd *STRET* M32 .... 113 C3
Moss Rd *STRET* M32 .... 114 A2
Moss St *BRO* M7 .... N81 D4
   DTN/ASHW M34 .... 98 B4
Moss Vale Crs *STRET* M32 .... 112 B1 ◨
Moss Vale Rd *STRET* M32 .... 112 B2
   URM M41 .... 112 A3
Moston Bank Av *BKLY* M9 .... 85 C2
Moston La *BKLY* M9 .... 85 C1
   NEWH/MOS M40 .... 68 A4
Moston La East *NEWH/MOS* M40 . 69 D3
Moston St *BRO* M7 .... 82 B2 ◨
Mostyn Av *RUSH/FAL* M14 .... 131 C1 ◨
Motherwell Av *BNG/LEV* M19 ...... 50 C3 ◨
Mottram St *CCHDY* M21 .... 127 C4
Mough La *CHAD* OL9 .... 69 D2
Mouldsworth Av *DID/WITH* M20 .. 129 C2
   HTNM SK4 .... 133 D3
Moulton St *CHH* M8 .... 5 F2
Mouncey St *CMANE* M1 .... 26 C1 ◨
Mountain Ash Cl *SALE* M33 .... 121 C4 ◨
Mountain St *NEWH/MOS* M40 ..... 96 B1 ◨
   STKP SK1 .... 139 C3 ◨
Mountbatten St *GTN* M18 .... 106 A4 ◨
Mount Carmel Crs *SALQ/ORD* M5 . 24 A1 ◨
Mount Dr *URM* M41 .... 112 B3
Mountfield *PWCH* M25 .... 62 B1
Mountford Av *CHH* M8 .... 64 B3 ◨
Mount Rd *GTN* M18 .... 41 F1 ◨
   GTN M18 .... 106 A4 ◨
   GTN M18 .... 116 A1
Mountside Crs *PWCH* M25 .... 61 D1
Mount St *CMANW* M2 .... 16 B4
   CSLFD M3 .... 5 D4
   ECC M30 .... 101 C1 ◨
   SWIN M27 .... 76 B2
Mousell St *CHH* M8 .... 6 C2
Mowbray Av *PWCH* M25 .... 63 C3
Mowbray St *OLD* OL1 .... 55 D3 ◨
Moxley Rd *CHH* M8 .... 64 A4
Mozart Cl *ANC* M4 .... 8 B5
Muirfield Cl *NEWH/MOS* M40 ..... 87 C2
Mulberry Ms *HTNM* SK4 .... 138 A3 ◨
Mulberry Rd *SLFD* M6 .... 2 C5
Mulberry St *CMANW* M2 .... 16 A3
Mulberry Wk *DROY* M43 .... 107 C1
   SALE M33 .... 121 D3 ◨
Mulgrave Rd *WALK* M28 .... 74 A1
Mulgrave St *SWIN* M27 .... 57 D4 ◨
Mull Av *WGTN/LGST* M12 .... 40 A1
Mullion Cl *RDSH* SK5 .... 116 B3
Mulmount Cl *OLDS* OL8 .... 72 A2
Munday St *ANC* M4 .... 18 C2
Munster St *ANC* M4 .... 6 C4 ◨
Muriel St *BRO* M7 .... 81 D4
Murray St *ANC* M4 .... 18 A1
   BRO M7 .... 81 D3
Museum St *CMANW* M2 .... 16 A4 ◨
Muslin St *SALQ/ORD* M5 .... 14 B3
Myerscroft Cl *NEWH/MOS* M40 .. 87 D1
Myrtle Bank *PWCH* M25 .... 62 A4
Myrtle Cl *OLDS* OL8 .... 55 C4
Myrtle Gv *DROY* M43 .... 99 C3 ◨
   DTN/ASHW M34 .... 117 D2
   PWCH M25 .... 62 B3
Myrtleleaf Gv *SALQ/ORD* M5 ..... 94 B3 ◨
Myrtle Pl *BRO* M7 .... 4 A2
Myrtle St *OLDTF/WHR* M16 .... 34 B2 ◨
   OP/CLY M11 .... 19 F4
My St *SALQ/ORD* M5 .... 95 C4

N

Naburn Cl *RDSH* SK5 .... 136 A3 ◨
Naburn St *BRUN/LGST* M13 .... 38 C2
Nada Rd *CHH* M8 .... 64 B4 ◨
Nadine St *SLFD* M6 .... 95 C2
Nadin St *OLDS* OL8 .... 73 C2
Nall St *BNG/LEV* M19 .... 132 B2
Nameplate Cl *ECC* M30 .... 90 B3 ◨
Nancy St *HULME* M15 .... 24 C3
Nangreave St *SALQ/ORD* M5 ...... 14 C3 ◨
Nansen Av *ECC* M30 .... 91 C2 ◨
Nansen Cl *STRET* M32 .... 115 C1
Nansen St *OP/CLY* M11 .... 19 E5
   SLFD M6 .... 95 C3
   STRET M32 .... 114 B2
Nantwich Rd *RUSH/FAL* M14 ...... 47 D3
Napier Gn *SALQ/ORD* M5 .... 23 E1
Napier Rd *CCHDY* M21 .... 43 E5
   ECC M30 .... 91 C2
Napier St *SWIN* M27 .... 75 D2
Napier St East *OLDS* OL8 .... 54 B4
Napier St West *OLDS* OL8 .... 54 A4
Naples St *ANC* M4 .... 7 D4 ◨
Narbonne Av *ECC* M30 .... 93 C1
Narbuth Dr *CHH* M8 .... 82 B2 ◨
Naseby Av *BKLY* M9 .... 67 D1
Naseby Pl *PWCH* M25 .... 63 C1 ◨
Naseby Rd *RDSH* SK5 .... 134 A1
Nash Rd *TRPK* M17 .... 102 A1
Nash St *HULME* M15 .... 25 E4
Nasmyth Rd *ECC* M30 .... 101 C1
Nasmyth St *CHH* M8 .... 84 A4 ◨
Nately Rd *OLDTF/WHR* M16 .... 43 D1 ◨
Nathan Dr *CSLFD* M3 .... 5 E5
Naval St *ANC* M4 .... 18 A1
Nave Ct *SLFD* M6 .... 2 B1
Navenby Av *OLDTF/WHR* M16 ..... 34 A3
Naylor St *NEWH/MOS* M40 .... 8 C3
   OLD OL1 .... 55 C2
Neale Rd *CCHDY* M21 .... 126 A2
Neary Wy *URM* M41 .... 101 C4
Neath St *CHAD* OL9 .... 54 B2 ◨
Neden Cl *OP/CLY* M11 .... 21 E5 ◨
Needham Av *CCHDY* M21 .... 43 F5
Needwood Cl *NEWH/MOS* M40 ... 84 B4 ◨
Neenton Sq *WGTN/LGST* M12 .... 31 D2
Neild St *CMANE* M1 .... 17 F5
   OLDS OL8 .... 73 C1
Neill St *BRO* M7 .... 5 F2
Nell La *CCHDY* M21 .... 128 A3
Nelson Av *ECC* M30 .... 91 D2 ◨
Nelson Ct *HULME* M15 .... 35 E2
Nelson Dr *DROY* M43 .... 96 B3
Nelson Fold *SWIN* M27 .... 58 B4 ◨
Nelson St *BRO* M7 .... 81 D4 ◨
   ECC M30 .... 91 D3
   NEWH/MOS M40 .... 9 D2
   SALQ/ORD M5 .... 95 C4
   STRET M32 .... 114 B4
Nelson Wy *CHAD* OL9 .... 71 C1 ◨
Nelstrop Crs *HTNM* SK4 .... 133 D3 ◨
Nelstrop Rd *HTNM* SK4 .... 133 C3
Nelstrop Rd North *RDSH* SK5 ...... 133 D1
Nepaul Rd *BKLY* M9 .... 67 C4
Neptune Gdns *BRO* M7 .... 4 B1
   BRO M7 .... 81 D4 ◨
Neston St *OP/CLY* M11 .... 107 D2
Netherbury Cl *GTN* M18 .... 116 A2 ◨
Netherfield Cl *OLDS* OL8 .... 72 A1
Netherland St *SALQ/ORD* M5 ...... 12 C4

Nether St *WGTN/LGST* M12	18 A5 🔟
Netherton Rd *RUSH/FAL* M14	46 C4
Nethervale Dr *BKLY* M9	85 C2 3
Nettleford Rd *CCHDY* M21	128 A1
Nettleton Gv *BKLY* M9	67 D4 7
Nevile Rd *BRO* M7	80 B1
Neville St *CHAD* OL9	54 A2
Nevin Rd *NEWH/MOS* M40	69 D4
Newall St *CHAD* OL9	71 D3
Newark Av *RUSH/FAL* M14	37 E4 3
Newark Rd *RDSH* SK5	134 B4
SWIN M27	59 D3
New Bailey St *SLFD* M3	15 E2
Newbank Cha *CHAD* OL9	53 C1
New Bank St *WGTN/LGST* M12	29 F4
New Barton St *SLFD* M6	78 A4
Newbeck St *ANC* M4	7 D5 3
Newbold Cl *HULME* M15	26 B3 3
New Bridge La *STKP* SK1	138 B3
New Bridge St *CSLFD* M3	6 A4 🔟
Newburn Av *BKLY* M9	67 D1 3
Newbury Dr *ECC* M30	90 B2 7
URM M41	101 C4
Newcastle St *HULME* M15	26 B2 2
Newchurch St *OP/CLY* M11	20 A4 2
Newcliffe Rd *BKLY* M9	67 D1
Newcombe Cl *OP/CLY* M11	20 B2
Newcombe St *CSLFD* M3	6 B3 3
Newcroft *FAIL* M35	89 D3
Newcroft Crs *URM* M41	112 B4
Newcroft Dr *URM* M41	112 B4
Newcroft Rd *URM* M41	112 B4
New Cross St *SLFD* M6	94 A3
SWIN M27	77 C2
Newdale Rd *BNG/LEV* M19	51 E1
New Elizabeth St *CHH* M8	83 C1
New Elm Rd *CSLFD* M3	15 D5
Newgate St *ANC* M4	17 D1
New Hall Av *BRO* M7	81 D1
ECC M30	100 A2
New Hall Rd *BRO* M7	81 D1
Newhaven Av *OP/CLY* M11	107 D2
New Herbert St *SLFD* M6	78 A4 4
Newholme Rd *DID/WITH* M20	128 A4
Newington Av *CHH* M8	64 B2
New Islington *ANC* M4	18 B1
New Kings Head Yd *CSLFD* M3	6 A5 🔟
Newlands *FAIL* M35	97 C3
Newlands Dr *SWIN* M27	78 A3 🔟
Newland St *CHH* M8	65 D4
New La *ECC* M30	90 B3
New Lawns *RDSH* SK5	118 A4 3
Newlyn St *RUSH/FAL* M14	47 E1
New Market *CMANW* M2	16 B2
New Market La *CMANW* M2	16 B2
New Mount St *ANC* M4	7 D4 4
New Park Rd *SALQ/ORD* M5	23 E2
Newport Av *RDSH* SK5	134 A2
Newport Rd *CCHDY* M21	42 C3
Newport St *OLDS* OL8	54 B4
RUSH/FAL M14	37 E5
SLFD M6	95 C3
Newquay Av *RDSH* SK5	134 A2
New Quay St *CSLFD* M3	15 E2
New Rd *OLDS* OL8	73 C1
Newry Rd *ECC* M30	102 A1
Newsholme St *CHH* M8	82 B2
Newstead Av *DID/WITH* M20	130 B4
Newstead Gv *MPL/ROM* SK6	141 C3
Newstead Rd *URM* M41	112 A2
New St *DROY* M43	108 A1

ECC M30	91 C4
NEWH/MOS M40	9 F1
SWIN M27	59 C4
New Thomas St *SLFD* M6	2 C2 🔟
Newton Av *DID/WITH* M20	129 C3 3
WGTN/LGST M12	40 A2
Newton Rd *FAIL* M35	88 A4
URM M41	111 C3
Newton St *CMANE* M1	17 E2
DROY M43	99 C2
FAIL M35	87 C3 3
STRET M32	114 B4
Newtown Cl *OP/CLY* M11	21 E5
SWIN M27	58 B3 🔢
Newtown St *PWCH* M25	63 C1
New Union St *ANC* M4	18 A1
New Viaduct St *OP/CLY* M11	9 F5
Newville Dr *DID/WITH* M20	130 B4
New Wakefield St *CMANE* M1	26 C1 3
New Welcome St *HULME* M15	26 A3
New Zealand Rd *STKP* SK1	139 C4
Nicholas Cft *ANC* M4	16 C1
Nicholas Owen Cl *OP/CLY* M11	106 A1
Nicholas St *CMANW* M2	16 C3
Nicholson St *HTNM* SK4	138 A3 7
Nichols St *SLFD* M6	3 E3
Nicolas Rd *CCHDY* M21	42 C3
Nigel Rd *BKLY* M9	85 D2
Nightingale Dr *DTN/ASHW* M34	99 C3
Nile St *OLD* OL1	55 C1
Nile Ter *BRO* M7	81 D4 3
Nimble Nook *CHAD* OL9	53 C4
Nina Dr *NEWH/MOS* M40	69 C2
Nine Acre Dr *SALQ/ORD* M5	23 F2
Ninth Av *OLDS* OL8	72 B4
Niven St *WGTN/LGST* M12	28 A1
Nixon St *FAIL* M35	88 A2
No 11 Pas *DID/WITH* M20	128 B4 3
Noble St *OLDS* OL8	73 D1 3
Nolan St *BKLY* M9	85 C2
Nona St *SLFD* M6	95 C3 🔢
The Nook *ECC* M30	90 A2
Norbet Wk *BKLY* M9	85 C2 7
Norbreck Av *CCHDY* M21	126 B2 3
Norburn Rd *BRUN/LGST* M13	50 B1
Norbury Av *SLFD* M6	78 B4 4
Norbury Gv *SWIN* M27	58 B4
Norbury St *BRO* M7	82 A3
STKP SK1	138 B4 🔢
Norden Av *DID/WITH* M20	129 C3
Nordens Rd *CHAD* OL9	52 B1 3
Nordens St *CHAD* OL9	53 C1
Norfolk Av *DROY* M43	97 D2 3
DTN/ASHW M34	118 A3
GTN M18	116 A1 3
HTNM SK4	133 C3
Norfolk Crs *FAIL* M35	88 A3
Norfolk Rd *GTN* M18	116 A1
Norfolk St *CHAD* OL9	72 A1 🔟
CMANW M2	16 B2
SLFD M6	80 A4
Norley Av *STRET* M32	32 A5
Norley Dr *BNG/LEV* M19	116 A3 2
Normanby Gv *SWIN* M27	58 A4 3
Normanby St *RUSH/FAL* M14	37 D3
SWIN M27	58 A4
Norman Gv *RDSH* SK5	134 A2 3
WGTN/LGST M12	40 B2
Norman Rd *BRO* M7	82 A2 7
RUSH/FAL M14	48 C1
Norman Rd West *BKLY* M9	85 D2 7
Norman St *CHAD* OL9	54 B1 3
FAIL M35	71 C4

Normanton Av *SLFD* M6 .... 94 A2
Normanton Dr *BKLY* M9 .... 67 C2 🢔
Northallerton Rd *BRO* M7.................... 80 B3
Northampton Rd *NEWH/MOS* M40 .... 85 D3
North Av *BNG/LEV* M19 .... 131 D2
　URM M41 .... 102 A2
Northbank Gdns *BNG/LEV* M19 .... 131 C3
North Blackfield La *BRO* M7 .... 81 C1 🢔
Northbourne St *SLFD* M6 .... 95 C3 🢔
Northbrook Av *CHH* M8 .... 64 B1
North Broughton St *CSLFD* M3 ..... 15 E1 🢔
North Clifden La *BRO* M7 .... 82 A3
North Crs *NEWH/MOS* M40 .... 69 D2
　OP/CLY M11 .... 96 B2
North Dean St *SWIN* M27 .... 59 C4
Northdown Av *HULME* M15 .... 24 C3
North Dr *DTN/ASHW* M34 .... 99 C4
　SWIN M27 .... 77 D2
Northern Av *SWIN* M27 .... 60 A2
Northfield Av *NEWH/MOS* M40 .... 70 B3 🢔
Northfield Rd *NEWH/MOS* M40 .... 70 B3
North Ga *OLDS* OL8 .... 73 C2
North George St *CSLFD* M3 .... 4 C5
North Gv *BRUN/LGST* M13 .... 38 C1 🢔
　URM M41 .... 111 C4
North Harvey St *STKP* SK1 .... 138 B4 🢔
North Hill St *CSLFD* M3 .... 5 D4
Northland Rd *BKLY* M9 .... 68 C3
Northleigh Dr *PWCH* M25 .... 63 D2 🢔
Northleigh Rd *OLDTF/WHR* M16 .... 33 E5
North Lonsdale St *STRET* M32 ..... 115 C2 🢔
North Md *CCHDY* M21 .... 126 B2 🢔
Northmoor Rd *WGTN/LGST* M12 .... 40 C2
North Phoebe St *SALQ/ORD* M5 .... 13 F4
North Pl *STKP* SK1 .... 138 B4 🢔
North Rd *DTN/ASHW* M34 .... 99 C4
　OP/CLY M11 .... 96 A3
　STRET M32 .... 113 D1
　TRPK M17 .... 104 A4
North Star Dr *CSLFD* M3 .... 14 C2
North St *CHH* M8 .... 83 C4
Northumberland Cl
　OLDTF/WHR M16 .... 24 A5 🢔
Northumberland Crs
　OLDTF/WHR M16 .... 24 A5 🢔
Northumberland Rd
　OLDTF/WHR M16 .... 34 A2
　RDSH SK5 .... 135 D3
Northumberland St *BRO* M7 .... 81 D2
Northurst Dr *CHH* M8 .... 64 B2
Northway *DROY* M43 .... 108 A1
North Wy *RDSH* SK5 .... 136 A3
North Western Av *BNG/LEV* M19 .... 51 D5
　WGTN/LGST M12 .... 18 B5 🢔
Northwold Dr *BKLY* M9 .... 68 B2
Norton Av *DTN/ASHW* M34 .... 118 A2
　SALE M33 .... 121 D4
　URM M41 .... 111 D1
　WGTN/LGST M12 .... 41 E5
Norton Gra *PWCH* M25 .... 63 D2
Norton St *BRO* M7 .... 82 A2
　CMANE M1 .... 18 B3 🢔
　CSLFD M3 .... 6 A5
　NEWH/MOS M40 .... 9 F2
　OLDTF/WHR M16 .... 34 B3
Norville Av *NEWH/MOS* M40 .... 69 D2
Norway Gv *RDSH* SK5 .... 138 B1 🢔
Norway St *OP/CLY* M11 .... 19 E4
　SLFD M6 .... 95 C3
　STRET M32 .... 115 C2
Norwich Rd *STRET* M32 .... 112 B2
Norwood *PWCH* M25 .... 62 B3
Norwood Av *BRO* M7........................... 80 B1

Norwood Dr *SWIN* M27 .... 75 C2
Norwood Rd *STRET* M32 .... 115 C4
Nottingham Av *RDSH* SK5 .... 136 A3
Nottingham Cl *RDSH* SK5 .... 136 A4 🢔
Nottingham Dr *FAIL* M35 .... 89 C4
　RDSH SK5 .... 136 A3 🢔
Nuneaton Dr *NEWH/MOS* M40 .... 8 C3
Nuneham Av *DID/WITH* M20 .... 130 A2
Nunfield Cl *NEWH/MOS* M40 .... 68 B3
Nunthorpe Dr *CHH* M8 .... 84 A1 🢔
Nursery Rd *FAIL* M35 .... 89 C3
　URM M41 .... 110 B1
Nursery St *OLDTF/WHR* M16 .... 36 B5 🢔
　SLFD M6 .... 2 B2
Nuthurst Rd *NEWH/MOS* M40 .... 69 C3
Nutsford V *WGTN/LGST* M12 .... 41 D3
Nuttall St *OLDTF/WHR* M16 .... 24 A5
　OP/CLY M11 .... 31 D1

O

Oadby Cl *WGTN/LGST* M12 .... 40 C2
Oak Av *CCHDY* M21 .... 43 F5
　GTN M18 .... 117 C1 🢔
Oak Bank *BKLY* M9 .... 84 B1
　PWCH M25 .... 61 D4
Oak Bank Av *BKLY* M9 .... 67 D4
Oakbank Av *CHAD* OL9 .... 52 A1
Oakdene *SWIN* M27 .... 74 B5 🢔
Oakdene Av *HTNM* SK4 .... 133 D4 🢔
Oakdene St *BKLY* M9 .... 85 D1 🢔
Oak Dr *DTN/ASHW* M34 .... 118 A1
　RUSH/FAL M14 .... 49 D4
Oakfield *PWCH* M25 .... 63 D2
　SALE M33 .... 123 C4
Oakfield Av *DROY* M43 .... 97 D4
　OLDTF/WHR M16 .... 33 D5
　OLDTF/WHR M16 .... 34 C4
Oakfield Gv *GTN* M18 .... 116 B1
Oakfield St *CHH* M8 .... 83 C3
Oakford Av *NEWH/MOS* M40 .... 8 A3
Oak Gv *ECC* M30 .... 90 B4
　URM M41 .... 112 A3
Oakham Ms *BRO* M7 .... 63 C4 🢔
Oakhill Wy *CHH* M8 .... 82 B2
Oakhouse Dr *CCHDY* M21 .... 126 B2 🢔
Oakland Av *SLFD* M6 .... 93 C1
Oaklands Dr *SALE* M33 .... 123 C4 🢔
Oaklands Rd *BRO* M7 .... 80 A2
　SWIN M27 .... 75 C3
Oaklea Rd *SALE* M33 .... 122 A3
Oakleigh Av *BNG/LEV* M19 .... 131 D2 🢔
Oakley Cl *NEWH/MOS* M40 .... 87 C4
Oakley St *SALQ/ORD* M5 .... 94 B4
Oakmere St *ECC* M30 .... 91 C1 🢔
Oakmoor Dr *BRO* M7 .... 80 A1 🢔
Oak Rd *BRO* M7 .... 81 C3
　DID/WITH M20 .... 129 D4
　FAIL M35 .... 88 B3
　OLDS OL8 .... 72 A3
Oak St *ANC* M4 .... 17 E1 🢔
　ECC M30 .... 91 D4 🢔
　SWIN M27 .... 59 C4
Oakville Dr *SLFD* M6........................... 93 C1
Oakville Ter *NEWH/MOS* M40 .... 67 D4
Oakwell Dr *BRO* M7 .... 64 A4 🢔
Oakwell Man *BRO* M7 .... 64 A4
Oakwood *CHAD* OL9 .... 52 A2
Oakwood Av *DTN/ASHW* M34 .... 109 D4
　NEWH/MOS M40 .... 69 D4
　SWIN M27 .... 58 A1

Oakwood Dr *SLFD* M6 .... **77** D4
Oakworth St *BKLY* M9 .... **66** A2
Ockendon Dr *BKLY* M9 .... **85** C2 ▣
Octavia Dr *NEWH/MOS* M40 .... **96** A1
Odell St *OP/CLY* M11 .... **31** E1
Odessa Av *SLFD* M6 .... **77** D4
Odette St *GTN* M18 .... **116** A1 ▣
Offerton St *STKP* SK1 .... **139** D3 ▣
Ogden La *OP/CLY* M11 .... **106** B2
Ogden Rd *FAIL* M35 .... **88** B3
Ogden St *CHAD* OL9 .... **53** D1
    PWCH M25 .... **63** C1
    SWIN M27 .... **76** B2 ▣
Ohio Av *SALQ/ORD* M5 .... **12** B5
Okehampton Crs *SALE* M33 .... **121** D4
Okeover Rd *BRO* M7 .... **81** D1
Old Barton Rd *URM* M41 .... **101** C2
Old Birley St *HULME* M15 .... **26** A4
Old Broadway *DID/WITH* M20 ...... **130** A4
Oldbury Cl *NEWH/MOS* M40 .... **8** C4
Oldcastle Av *DID/WITH* M20 .... **129** C3
Old Church St *NEWH/MOS* M40 .... **86** B3
Old Crofts Bank *URM* M41 .... **111** C1
Old Elm St *BRUN/LGST* M13 ...... **28** B3 ▣
Oldershaw Dr *BKLY* M9 .... **84** B3 ▣
Old Farm Crs *DROY* M43 .... **107** D1
Oldfield Gv *SALE* M33 .... **124** A4 ▣
Oldfield Rd *SALE* M33 .... **124** A4
    SALQ/ORD M5 .... **14** B3
Oldfield St *OP/CLY* M11 .... **21** F2
Old Hall Dr *GTN* M18 .... **116** B1
Old Hall La *BRUN/LGST* M13 .... **50** A1
    RUSH/FAL M14 .... **48** C3
Old Hall Rd *BRO* M7 .... **81** D1
    NEWH/MOS M40 .... **86** B2
    STRET M32 .... **113** C1
Old Hall St *OP/CLY* M11 .... **107** C2 ▣
Old Hall Wy *OLD* OL1 .... **55** C3
Old La *CHAD* OL9 .... **71** D1
    OP/CLY M11 .... **106** A2
Old Malt La *DID/WITH* M20 .... **129** C2
Old Market St *BKLY* M9 .... **66** A3
Old Medlock St *CSLFD* M3 .... **15** D4 ▣
Old Mill Cl *SWIN* M27 .... **77** D1
Old Mill St *ANC* M4 .... **18** B2
Old Moat La *DID/WITH* M20 ...... **129** D2 ▣
Oldmoor Rd *MPL/ROM* SK6 .... **137** C4
Old Mount St *ANC* M4 .... **7** D4
Old Parrin La *ECC* M30 .... **90** B2 ▣
Old Rd *BKLY* M9 .... **66** B3
    FAIL M35 .... **88** A2
    HTNM SK4 .... **138** A2
Old School Dr *BKLY* M9 .... **66** A3 ▣
Old Shaw St *SALQ/ORD* M5 ...... **91** C4
Old Station St *ECC* M30 .... **91** C4 ▣
Old Wellington Rd *ECC* M30 .... **92** A3
Old York St *HULME* M15 .... **25** F4 ▣
Olebrook Cl *WGTN/LGST* M12 ...... **29** D4
Oliver St *OLD* OL1 .... **55** D3
    OP/CLY M11 .... **20** A4 ▣
Olive St *FAIL* M35 .... **88** A1 ▣
Olivia Gv *RUSH/FAL* M14 .... **38** C5
Ollerton Av *OLDTF/WHR* M16 .... **34** B3
    SALE M33 .... **121** D4

Ollier Av *WGTN/LGST* M12 .... **51** E1
Olney St *BRUN/LGST* M13 .... **38** C2
Olwen Av *WGTN/LGST* M12 ...... **40** C1 ▣
Olwen Crs *RDSH* SK5 .... **134** B3 ▣
Olympic Ct *SALQ/ORD* M5 .... **12** A4
Omer Av *BRUN/LGST* M13 .... **50** A1
Omer Dr *BNG/LEV* M19 .... **131** C2
Onslow Av *NEWH/MOS* M40 .... **70** A4
Onslow Cl *OLD* OL1 .... **55** C1 ▣
Opal St *BNG/LEV* M19 .... **132** B1 ▣
Orama Av *SLFD* M6 .... **93** C1
Orange St *SLFD* M6 .... **3** D3
Orchard Av *GTN* M18 .... **117** C1 ▣
Orchard Gv *DID/WITH* M20 .... **128** B4
Orchard Pl *SALE* M33 .... **123** D4 ▣
Orchard Rd *FAIL* M35 .... **88** B2
Orchard St *DID/WITH* M20 .... **128** B4 ▣
    SLFD M6 .... **3** D1
    STKP SK1 .... **138** B4 ▣
Orchid St *BKLY* M9 .... **84** B2
Ordsall Dr *SALQ/ORD* M5 .... **23** F2
Ordsall La *SALQ/ORD* M5 .... **14** C4
Oregon Cl *BRUN/LGST* M13 .... **28** A3
Orford Rd *NEWH/MOS* M40 .... **87** C4
Oriel Av *OLDS* OL8 .... **75** C2
Oriel Cl *CHAD* OL9 .... **71** C1
Orient Rd *SLFD* M6 .... **93** C1
Orient St *BRO* M7 .... **82** B2
Orion Pl *BRO* M7 .... **4** B2
Orkney Dr *URM* M41 .... **101** D4
Orlanda Av *SLFD* M6 .... **93** C1
Orlanda Dr *BRO* M7 .... **82** B3
Orme Av *SLFD* M6 .... **77** D4
Orme Cl *OP/CLY* M11 .... **19** F2
    URM M41 .... **112** B5 ▣
Ormerod Cl *MPL/ROM* SK6 .... **141** D4
Orme St *STKP* SK1 .... **139** D5 ▣
Ormonde Av *SLFD* M6 .... **93** D1
Ormsby Av *GTN* M18 .... **41** F3
Ormsgill St *HULME* M15 .... **26** A4
Ormskirk Av *DID/WITH* M20 .... **128** B3
Ormskirk Rd *RDSH* SK5 .... **134** B3 ▣
Oronsay Gv *SALQ/ORD* M5 .... **94** B4 ▣
Orphanage St *HTNM* SK4 .... **138** A2 ▣
Orpington Rd *BKLY* M9 .... **85** C2 ▣
Orrell St *OP/CLY* M11 .... **106** B1 ▣
Orrel St *SALQ/ORD* M5 .... **95** C3
Orsett Cl *NEWH/MOS* M40 .... **8** B3
Orthes Gv *HTNM* SK4 .... **133** D4
Orvietto Av *SLFD* M6 .... **93** C1
Orville Dr *BNG/LEV* M19 .... **131** D2
Orwell Av *DTN/ASHW* M34 .... **118** C2
Osborne St *SWIN* M27 .... **78** A2
Osborne Rd *BKLY* M9 .... **85** C2 ▣
    BNG/LEV M19 .... **50** B4
    OLDS OL8 .... **54** B4
    SLFD M6 .... **93** C2 ▣
Osborne St *CHAD* OL9 .... **54** A1
    MPL/ROM SK6 .... **140** A2
    NEWH/MOS M40 .... **8** A2
    SLFD M6 .... **2** A4
Oscar St *NEWH/MOS* M40 .... **86** A2
Oscroft Cl *CHH* M8 .... **82** B3 ▣
Osprey Cl *HULME* M15 .... **35** E1 ▣
Osprey Dr *DROY* M43 .... **99** C2
Ossory St *RUSH/FAL* M14 .... **37** F4
Ostlers Ga *DROY* M43 .... **99** D3
Ostrich La *PWCH* M25 .... **63** C2
Oswald Cl *SLFD* M6 .... **80** A4
Oswald La *CCHDY* M21 .... **43** E3
Oswald Rd *CCHDY* M21 .... **43** D4
Oswald St *ANC* M4 .... **6** C4

ANC M4 .... **18** C3 🔲
CHAD OL9 .... **54** B1
RDSH SK5 .... **117** D2
Othello Dr *ECC* M30 .... **91** D3 🔲
Otley Av *SLFD* M6 .... **94** A2
Otley Cl *CHAD* OL9 .... **53** D3 🔲
Otranto Av *SLFD* M6 .... **93** D1
Otterburn Cl *HULME* M15 .... **26** A4
Otter Dr *CHH* M8 .... **82** A4 🔟
Oulton Av *SALE* M33 .... **125** C4
Oundle Cl *RUSH/FAL* M14 .... **38** A4
Ouse St *SALQ/ORD* M5 .... **94** A4
Outram Sq *DROY* M43 .... **108** A1 🔒
Outrington Dr *OP/CLY* M11 .... **20** C5
Outwood Av *SWIN* M27 .... **57** D1
Overbridge Rd *BRO* M7 .... **5** F2
Overbrook Av *NEWH/MOS* M40 .... **84** B4 🔢
Overbrook Dr *PWCH* M25 .... **62** B2
Overdale *SWIN* M27 .... **77** C3
Overdale Rd *MPL/ROM* SK6 .... **141** D4
Overhill Rd *CHAD* OL9 .... **52** B1
Overlea Dr *BNG/LEV* M19 .... **131** C4
Overlinks Dr *SLFD* M6 .... **77** D4
Overstone Dr *CHH* M8 .... **82** B2 🔢
Owens Cl *CHAD* OL9 .... **52** A1 🔲
Owen St *ECC* M30 .... **90** B4
SLFD M6 .... **80** A4
Owler La *CHAD* OL9 .... **69** D2
Oxford Av *DROY* M43 .... **97** D2
Oxford Pl *RUSH/FAL* M14 .... **38** A3
Oxford Rd *BRUN/LGST* M13 .... **27** D3
CMANE M1 .... **26** C1
SLFD M6 .... **93** C1
Oxford St *CHAD* OL9 .... **53** D4
CMANE M1 .... **16** C5
CMANW M2 .... **16** B4
ECC M30 .... **92** A4
OLDTF/WHR M16 .... **35** D1 🔲
Oxley St *OP/CLY* M11 .... **20** C4
Oxney Rd *RUSH/FAL* M14 .... **38** A3
Oxton St *OP/CLY* M11 .... **107** D2 🔲

Pacific Wy *SALQ/ORD* M5 .... **104** A1
Packwood Cha *CHAD* OL9 .... **52** B1 🔲
Paddington Av *NEWH/MOS* M40 ... **86** B4 🔲
Paddington Cl *SLFD* M6 .... **2** C5
Paddison St *SWIN* M27 .... **76** A2 🔲
Paddock La *FAIL* M35 .... **88** B4
Paddock St *WGTN/LGST* M12 .... **28** A1
Padstow St *NEWH/MOS* M40 .... **9** F3
Paget St *NEWH/MOS* M40 .... **84** B4
Pagnall Ct *CHAD* OL9 .... **53** D5 🔲
Paignton Av *BNG/LEV* M19 .... **131** D3 🔲
Paignton Dr *SALE* M33 .... **121** D4
Paignton Gv *HTNM* SK4 .... **134** A2 🔲
Pailin Dr *DROY* M43 .... **99** C3
Palace Rd *SALE* M33 .... **123** C4 🔲
Palace St *CHAD* OL9 .... **54** A2 🔲
Palatine Av *DID/WITH* M20 .... **129** C3
Palatine Crs *DID/WITH* M20 .... **129** C4
Palatine Rd *DID/WITH* M20 .... **129** C2
Palfrey Pl *WGTN/LGST* M12 .... **28** B1
Pall Ml *CMANW* M2 .... **16** B3
Palm Cl *SALE* M33 .... **121** C4
Palmer Cl *OLDS* OL8 .... **73** D1
Palmerston Av *OLDTF/WHR* M16 ... **44** C2
Palmerston Cl *DTN/ASHW* M34 ..... **118** B2 🔲
Palmerston Rd *DTN/ASHW* M34 .... **118** B2
Palmerston St *WGTN/LGST* M12 ... **19** D3

Palmer St *BRO* M7 .... **81** C4 🔢
Palm Gv *CHAD* OL9 .... **53** D1
Palm St *BRUN/LGST* M13 .... **40** B5
DROY M43 .... **96** B3
Pandora St *DID/WITH* M20 .... **129** C4 🔲
Pangbourne Av *URM* M41 .... **112** A2 🔲
Panmure St *OLDS* OL8 .... **73** D1 🔲
Parbold Av *DID/WITH* M20 .... **129** C2
Parcel St *OP/CLY* M11 .... **20** A2
Paris Av *SALQ/ORD* M5 .... **23** E2
Parish Vw *SALQ/ORD* M5 .... **13** F4 🔲
Park Av *BNG/LEV* M19 .... **50** C3
BRO M7 .... **82** B1
FAIL M35 .... **87** D1
OLDTF/WHR M16 .... **34** A1
PWCH M25 .... **62** B1
SALE M33 .... **123** D3
URM M41 .... **111** C3 🔲
Park Brow Cl *CCHDY* M21 .... **127** C2 🔲
Park Crs *RUSH/FAL* M14 .... **38** B5
Parkdale Av *DTN/ASHW* M34 .... **109** D2
GTN M18 .... **116** A1 🔢
Park Dr *ECC* M30 .... **91** D1
OLDTF/WHR M16 .... **44** B1
Parker St *CMANE* M1 .... **17** D3
Parkfield *SALQ/ORD* M5 .... **94** B3 🔲
Parkfield Av *OLDS* OL8 .... **71** D3 🔲
PWCH M25 .... **63** D2 🔲
RUSH/FAL M14 .... **37** F4
URM M41 .... **110** B4 🔲
Parkfield Rd North
NEWH/MOS M40 .... **70** A3
Parkfield St *RUSH/FAL* M14 .... **37** F3
RUSH/FAL M14 .... **37** F5
Parkgate Dr *SWIN* M27 .... **77** D2 🔲
Park Gv *BNG/LEV* M19 .... **50** C3
Parkhill Av *CHH* M8 .... **65** D3
Park House Bridge Rd *SLFD* M6 .... **79** D3 🔲
Parkhouse St *OP/CLY* M11 .... **21** E5
Parkhurst Av *NEWH/MOS* M40 ..... **70** A4
Parkin St *WGTN/LGST* M12 .... **41** D4
Parklake Av *BRO* M7 .... **81** D1
The Parklands *HTNM* SK4 .... **138** D1
Park La *BRO* M7 .... **81** D1
OLDS OL8 .... **73** D3
SLFD M6 .... **78** A4
Park La West *SWIN* M27 .... **78** B2
Parkleigh Dr *NEWH/MOS* M40 ...... **70** A3
Park Ldg *BNG/LEV* M19 .... **50** C3
Park Ms *OLDTF/WHR* M16 .... **44** B1
Parkmount Rd *BKLY* M9 .... **67** C4
Park Pl *ANC* M4 .... **6** C3
SLFD M6 .... **93** C2
Park Range *RUSH/FAL* M14 .... **38** C5
Park Rd *DTN/ASHW* M34 .... **109** D1
ECC M30 .... **91** D1
HTNM SK4 .... **132** B4
OLDS OL8 .... **55** D4
PWCH M25 .... **63** D2
SALE M33 .... **123** C3
SLFD M6 .... **93** C1
STRET M32 .... **114** A2
Park Rd North *URM* M41 .... **111** C2
Park Rd South *URM* M41 .... **111** C3
Parkside Av *BRO* M7 .... **82** A1
ECC M30 .... **91** C4 🔢
FAIL M35 .... **88** A4
Parkside Rd *RUSH/FAL* M14 .... **46** B1
Parkside St *WGTN/LGST* M12 .... **28** B1 🔲
Park Sq *OLDTF/WHR* M16 .... **42** C1
Parkstead Dr *BKLY* M9 .... **84** B3 🔲
Parkstone Av *GTN* M18 .... **107** D3
Parkstone Dr *SLFD* M6 .... **77** D3 🔲

P

Park St *BRO* M7 .... 81 C1
  CSLFD M3 .... 6 B3
  CSLFD M3 .... 14 C2
  DROY M43 .... 99 C3 🔟
  DTN/ASHW M34 .... 119 D2
  MPL/ROM SK6 .... 141 D2
  OLDS OL8 .... 55 C4
  PWCH M25 .... 63 C1 🛑
  STKP SK1 .... 138 B3 🔟
  SWIN M27 .... 77 C2
Parksway *PWCH* M25 .... 63 C3
  SWIN M27 .... 78 A3 🛑
Park Vw *BKLY* M9 .... 84 A3
  DTN/ASHW M34 .... 109 D1 🛑
  RUSH/FAL M14 .... 131 C2 🔟
Park View Rd *PWCH* M25 .... 62 B2
Parkville Rd *DID/WITH* M20 .... 130 A4
Park Wy *STRET* M32 .... 112 B1
Parlane St *ANC* M4 .... 7 D3
Parneet Av *DID/WITH* M20 ..... 129 D3
Parrfield Rd *WALK* M28 .... 74 A2
Parrin La *ECC* M30 .... 91 C2
Parrot St *OP/CLY* M11 .... 96 A4 🛑
Parr St *ECC* M30 .... 91 D4
  OP/CLY M11 .... 107 C2 🔟
Parry Rd *WGTN/LGST* M12 ..... 40 C3
Parslow Av *CHH* M8 .... 83 C1 🛑
Parsonage CI *SALQ/ORD* M5 .... 14 A5 🛑
Parsonage La *CSLFD* M3 .... 16 A1 🛑
Parsonage St *DID/WITH* M20 . 130 A2
Parsonage St *CHH* M8 .... 64 B4 🛑
  HTNM SK4 .... 138 A3
  HULME M15 .... 35 F1
Parsons St *CHAD* OL9 .... 54 A3
Partington La *SWIN* M27 .... 76 A2
Partington PI *SALE* M33 .... 123 D4 🛑
Partington St *ECC* M30 .... 91 D2 🛑
  FAIL M35 .... 88 B2
  NEWH/MOS M40 .... 85 D4 🛑
  WALK M28 .... 75 C1
Partridge Ri *DROY* M43 .... 99 D2
Partridge St *STRET* M32 .... 32 B1
Parvet Av *DROY* M43 .... 97 D2
Pascal St *BNG/LEV* M19 .... 51 D5
Pass St *CHAD* OL9 .... 54 B3
Patchett St *WGTN/LGST* M12 . 30 A4 🛑
Patey St *WGTN/LGST* M12 ...... 41 D4
Paton Ct *BRO* M7 .... 4 A1
Paton St *CMANE* M1 .... 17 E3 🛑
Patten St *DID/WITH* M20 ...... 129 D2 🛑
Patterdale Av *URM* M41 .... 110 B1
Patterson Av *CCHDY* M21 ...... 42 C4
Pattishall CI *ANC* M4 .... 19 D3
Paulden Dr *FAIL* M35 .... 89 C2
Peace St *FAIL* M35 .... 71 C4 🛑
Peaceville Rd *BNG/LEV* M19 .... 50 A4
Peachey CI *OLDTF/WHR* M16 ... 36 A4
Peach Tree CI *BRO* M7 .... 82 B3 🛑
Peacock Av *SLFD* M6 .... 79 C4 🛑
Peacock CI *GTN* M18 .... 106 A3
Peacock Gv *GTN* M18 .... 116 B1
Peakdale Av *CHH* M8 .... 83 D1
Peakdale Rd *DROY* M43 .... 97 D2
Peaknaze CI *SWIN* M27 .... 77 D1 🔟
Peak St *CHAD* OL9 .... 54 A3
  CMANE M1 .... 17 F3
  STKP SK1 .... 139 C4
Pearl Av *BRO* M7 .... 64 A4
Pearn Rd *BNG/LEV* M19 .... 131 D4
Pearson St *RDSH* SK5 .... 138 B2 🛑
Pear Tree CI *SLFD* M6 .... 2 C5
Peary St *ANC* M4 .... 7 F3

Peatfield Av *SWIN* M27 .... 57 D3
Peckford Dr *NEWH/MOS* M40 . 86 A4 🛑
Peebles Dr *NEWH/MOS* M40 .... 96 B1
Peel Cross Rd *SALQ/ORD* M5 .. 12 C3
Peel Green Rd *ECC* M30 .... 100 B1
Peel Gv *WGTN/LGST* M12 .... 40 C2
Peel La *CHH* M8 .... 7 D1
Peel Moat Rd *HTNM* SK4 ..... 132 B4
Peel Mt *SLFD* M6 .... 3 F3
Peel St *CHAD* OL9 .... 53 D2
  DROY M43 .... 107 D1
  ECC M30 .... 92 B3
  FAIL M35 .... 87 D3 🛑
Pegasus Sq *BRO* M7 .... 4 B3
Pegwell Dr *BRO* M7 .... 82 A4
Pelham PI *CHH* M8 .... 65 D3
Pelham St *OLDS* OL8 .... 73 D3
Pellowe Rd *OLDS* OL8 .... 73 C1 🛑
Pelton Av *SWIN* M27 .... 57 D3 🛑
Pemberton St *OLDTF/WHR* M16 ... 34 B2
Pembridge Rd *BKLY* M9 .... 67 D1
Pembroke Av *ECC* M30 .... 91 D3 🛑
  SALE M33 .... 122 B4
Pembroke CI *BRUN/LGST* M13 .. 28 C4
Pembroke St *BRO* M7 .... 82 A3 🛑
  OLDS OL8 .... 54 B3 🛑
  SLFD M6 .... 95 C4 🛑
Pembry CI *RDSH* SK5 .... 135 D3
Pencombe CI *WGTN/LGST* M12 . 41 D2 🛑
Pencroft Wy *HULME* M15 .... 37 D1
Pendlebury CI *PWCH* M25 ...... 61 D3 🛑
Pendlebury Rd *SWIN* M27 ...... 77 C1
Pendlecroft Av *SWIN* M27 ...... 78 A2 🛑
Pendlegreen CI *OP/CLY* M11 ... 20 B5
Pendleton Wy *SLFD* M6 .... 2 C3
Pendleway *SWIN* M27 .... 59 C4
Pendragon PI *FAIL* M35 .... 89 C2
Penelope Rd *SLFD* M6 .... 78 B4 🛑
Penerly Dr *BKLY* M9 .... 84 B3 🛑
Penfair CI *OP/CLY* M11 .... 20 C3
Penfield CI *CMANE* M1 .... 27 E1
Penistone Av *BKLY* M9 .... 68 A2 🛑
  SLFD M6 .... 94 A2 🛑
Penketh Av *URM* M18 .... 41 E2
Pennell St *OP/CLY* M11 .... 96 B4 🛑
Pennine Av *CHAD* OL9 .... 53 C4
Pennine CI *BKLY* M9 .... 67 D1
Pennington St *CHAD* OL9 ...... 71 D2 🛑
  WGTN/LGST M12 .... 50 C2
Penn St *NEWH/MOS* M40 ...... 85 D1
  OLDS OL8 .... 54 B4
Penny Bridge La *URM* M41 .... 110 A3
Penny La *RDSH* SK5 .... 138 B3
Penrhyn Dr *PWCH* M25 .... 62 B1
Penrith Av *OLDS* OL8 .... 72 A2
  RDSH SK5 .... 117 D4
Penrod PI *SLFD* M6 .... 3 E1
Penroyson CI *WGTN/LGST* M12 . 30 B4 🛑
Pensarn Av *RUSH/FAL* M14 ... 131 C1
Pensarn Gv *RDSH* SK5 .... 138 B1 🔟
Pensby St *SWIN* M27 .... 78 A2
Penshurst Rd *RDSH* SK5 ...... 135 D3
Pentland Av *NEWH/MOS* M40 . 69 C3
Pentlands Av *BRO* M7 .... 81 D3
Penwortham St *NEWH/MOS* M40 . 10 A2
Penznance St *NEWH/MOS* M40 .. 9 F3
Pepperhill Rd *OLDTF/WHR* M16 . 36 A3
Percival CI *BRO* M7 .... 82 B3 🔟
Percival Rd *DROY* M43 .... 98 B4 🛑
Percy Dr *SALQ/ORD* M5 .... 23 F2
Percy St *HULME* M15 .... 25 D4
  STKP SK1 .... 138 B3 🔟
Peregrine Crs *DROY* M43 .... 99 C2

Perrygate Av *DID/WITH* M20 ...... **129** C3 🖪
Perth Av *CHAD* OL9 .... **71** C1
Perth St *SWIN* M27 .... **75** D2 🖪
Peru St *SLFD* M3 .... **4** C5
Peterborough St *GTN* M18 ...... **107** D3 🖪
Peter Moss Wy *BNG/LEV* M19 .... **116** A4
Peter St *CMANW* M2 .... **16** B4
    ECC M30 .... **91** D4
    OLD OL1 .... **55** D3
    STKP SK1 .... **139** C3 🖪
Petrel Cl *DROY* M43 .... **99** C2 🖪
Petrock Wk *NEWH/MOS* M40 .... **87** C4 🖪🖪
Petworth Rd *CHAD* OL9 .... **53** D3
Pevensey Rd *SLFD* M6 .... **79** C4
Peveril Crs *CCHDY* M21 .... **42** C2
Peveril Rd *SALQ/ORD* M5 ...... **94** B3
Pheasant Dr *CCHDY* M21 ...... **127** D2
Phelan Cl *NEWH/MOS* M40 .... **84** A4
Philip Av *DTN/ASHW* M34 ...... **109** D4
Philips Park Rd *OP/CLY* M11.... **19** F1
Philip St *ECC* M30 .... **91** D4
Phoebe St *SALQ/ORD* M5 ...... **23** E1
Phoenix St *CMANW* M2 ...... **16** C2 🖪
    OLD OL1 .... **55** C3
Phoenix Wy *URM* M41.......... **102** A3
Piccadilly *CMANE* M1 .... **17** D2 🖪
    STKP SK1 .... **138** B4
Pickering Cl *URM* M41 .... **110** B3 🖪
Pickford's Brow *STKP* SK1 ...... **138** B4 🖪🖪
Pickford St *ANC* M4 .... **17** F1
Pickmere Av *DID/WITH* M20 .... **129** D1 🖪
Pickmere Cl *DROY* M43 .... **98** B4 🖪
Picton Cl *CSLFD* M3 .... **5** E5
Picton St *BRO* M7 .... **5** D3
Piercy Av *BRO* M7 .... **4** C2
Piercy St *ANC* M4 .... **18** C2
    FAIL M35 .... **88** A2 🖪
Pigeon St *CMANE* M1 .... **17** F2
Pike Fold La *BKLY* M9 .... **66** A2
Pilgrim Dr *OP/CLY* M11 .... **20** B3
Pilkington Rd *BKLY* M9 .... **68** A3
Pilling St *NEWH/MOS* M40 .... **85** D4
Pimblett St *CSLFD* M3 .... **6** B3
Pimlico St *BRO* M7 .... **81** D3 🖪
Pimlott Gv *PWCH* M25 .... **61** D3
Pine Gv *ECC* M30 .... **92** A1
    RUSH/FAL M14.............. **39** F2
    SALE M33 .... **121** D3
    SWIN M27 .... **75** D2
Pinehurst Rd *NEWH/MOS* M40 .. **85** C4
Pine St *CHAD* OL9 .... **53** C1
    CMANE M1 .... **16** C3
Pinetop Cl *CCHDY* M21 .... **127** D2 🖪
Pine Tree Rd *OLDS* OL8 ...... **72** B4
Pinetree St *GTN* M18 .... **106** A4 🖪
Pinewood *CHAD* OL9 .... **52** A2
Pinewood Ct *SALE* M33 ...... **124** B4
Pinewood Rd *CCHDY* M21 .... **126** A2 🖪
Pinfold Av *BKLY* M9 .... **68** A3
Pink Bank La *WGTN/LGST* M12 .. **41** D2
Pin Mill Brow *WGTN/LGST* M12 .. **18** C4
Pinner Pl *BNG/LEV* M19 ...... **132** A3
Pinnington La *STRET* M32 ...... **114** B4 🖪
Pinnington Rd *GTN* M18 ...... **106** B3
Pioneer Rd *SWIN* M27 .... **60** B3 🖪
Pioneer St *OP/CLY* M11 .... **11** E5
Pipewell Av *GTN* M18.......... **106** A4
Pipit Cl *DTN/ASHW* M34 ...... **99** C3 🖪🖪
Pitman Cl *OP/CLY* M11.......... **21** D5
Pitsford Rd *NEWH/MOS* M40 .... **85** C4
Pit St *CHAD* OL9 .... **71** D1
Pittbrook St *WGTN/LGST* M12 .. **29** D1
Plainsfield Cl *OLDTF/WHR* M16 .. **36** A3

Plane Rd *FAIL* M35 .... **88** B4
Plantation St *GTN* M18 ...... **107** C4 🖪
Plant Cl *SALE* M33............ **123** C4
Plant St *CMANE* M1 .... **17** E3 🖪
Plate St *OLD* OL1 .... **55** D2 🖪
Plato St *CHAD* OL9 .... **54** B2
Plattbrook Cl *RUSH/FAL* M14 .. **47** F4
Platt La *RUSH/FAL* M14........ **46** B3
Playfair St *RUSH/FAL* M14.... **37** E3
Pleasant Rd *ECC* M30.......... **92** A4
Pleasant St *BKLY* M9 .... **84** B2
Pleasington Dr *NEWH/MOS* M40 .. **69** C3
Ploughbank Dr *CCHDY* M21 .. **127** D2
Plumbley Dr *OLDTF/WHR* M16 .. **34** B4
Plumbley St *OP/CLY* M11 .... **107** C2 🖪🖪
Plummer Av *CCHDY* M21........ **126** B3
Plumpton Wk *BRUN/LGST* M13 .. **40** A3 🖪
Plum St *OLDS* OL8 .... **54** B4
Pluto Cl *SLFD* M6 .... **4** A1 🖪
Plymouth Av *BRUN/LGST* M13 .. **39** E1
Plymouth Gv *BRUN/LGST* M13 .. **28** B5
Plymouth Gv West *BRUN/LGST* M13.. **39** D1
Plymouth Rd *SALE* M33........ **121** D4
Plymouth St *OLDS* OL8 .... **73** D1
Plymouth Vw *BRUN/LGST* M13 .. **28** B4
Plymtree Cl *CHH* M8 .... **64** A3
Pochin St *NEWH/MOS* M40 ...... **9** E3
Poland St *ANC* M4 .... **8** A5
Polefield Rd *BKLY* M9 .... **66** B3
Pole La *FAIL* M35................ **88** B1
Polesworth Cl *WGTN/LGST* M12 .. **30** C3
Police St *CMANW* M2 .... **16** A2
    ECC M30 .... **91** C3
Pollard St *ANC* M4 .... **18** B3
Pollard St East *NEWH/MOS* M40 .. **19** D1
Polletts Av *RDSH* SK5 .... **136** A3
Pollit Cft *MPL/ROM* SK6 ...... **141** D4
Pollitt Cl *WGTN/LGST* M12 .... **30** A4
Pollitts Cl *ECC* M30 .... **90** B3 🖪🖪
Polonia St *OLDS* OL8 .... **72** A2 🖪
Polruan Rd *CCHDY* M21........ **43** D2
Polworth Rd *BKLY* M9 .... **67** C4 🖪
Polygon Av *BRUN/LGST* M13 .. **28** B4
Polygon Rd *CHH* M8 .... **64** B4
Polygon St *BRUN/LGST* M13.. **28** B2
The Polygon *BRO* M7............ **81** C3
    ECC M30 .... **93** C3 🖪
Pomfret St *SLFD* M6 .... **78** A4 🖪
Pomona Crs *SALQ/ORD* M5 .... **23** E2
Pomona Strd *HULME* M15 .... **23** F4
Ponds Cl *CCHDY* M21............ **43** E3
Ponsford Av *BKLY* M9 .... **68** A2 🖪
Ponsonby Rd *STRET* M32 ...... **114** B2
Pontefract Cl *SWIN* M27 ...... **77** D2
Pool Fold *FAIL* M35 .... **89** C3 🖪
Pool St *OLDS* OL8 .... **73** D1
Poolton Rd *BKLY* M9 .... **65** D1
Poorfield St *OLDS* OL8 .... **55** C4 🖪
Poplar Av *BNG/LEV* M19 ...... **132** B2
    OLDS OL8 .... **72** B3
Poplar Dr *PWCH* M25 .... **62** A3 🖪
Poplar Gv *GTN* M18 .... **116** B1
    URM M41 .... **112** A3
Poplar Rd *ECC* M30 .... **92** A1
    STRET M32 .... **124** A1
    SWIN M27 .... **75** D2
Poplar St *FAIL* M35 .... **87** D3
    OP/CLY M11 .... **19** E5
Poplin Dr *CSLFD* M3 .... **5** F4
Porlock Av *DTN/ASHW* M34 .. **109** C1
Porlock Rd *URM* M41.......... **120** B3
Porter St *CHAD* OL9 .... **54** A4 🖪
Portland Crs *BRUN/LGST* M13 .. **39** D1

Portland Rd *BRUN/LGST* M13 .... 40 B4
  ECC M30 .... 92 B2
  STRET M32 .... 115 C1
  SWIN M27 .... 77 C2
Portland St *CMANE* M1 .... 16 C4
Portman Cl *OLDTF/WHR* M16 .... 35 E4
Portree Cl *ECC* M30 .... 90 B3 🖪
Portsmouth Cl *BRO* M7 .... 81 D4
Portsmouth St *BRUN/LGST* M13 ...... 27 F5 🖪
Port Soderick Av *SALO/ORD* M5 ...... 12 C2
Portstone Cl *OLDTF/WHR* M16 .... 35 F3
Port St *CMANE* M1 .... 17 E2
  OLDS OL8 .... 73 D1
  STKP SK1 .... 138 A4 🖪🖸
Portugal Rd *PWCH* M25 .... 62 B3 🖸
Portugal St *ANC* M4 .... 8 B4
Portugal St East *CMANE* M1 .... 18 A4
Portville Rd *BNG/LEV* M19 .... 51 D3
Portwood Pl *STKP* SK1 .... 138 B3 🖪🖸
Postal St *CMANE* M1 .... 17 E2 🖸
Postbridge Cl *BRUN/LGST* M13 .... 28 B4
Potato Whf *CSLFD* M3 .... 15 D5
Potters La *BKLY* M9 .... 85 C2
Pottery La *OP/CLY* M11 .... 30 C1
Pott St *SWIN* M27 .... 58 B3 🖸
Poulton St *OP/CLY* M11 .... 107 C2 🖽
Powell St *OLDTF/WHR* M16............... 34 B3
  OP/CLY M11 .... 96 B3
Powicke Dr *MPL/ROM* SK6 .... 141 D4
Powicke Wk *MPL/ROM* SK6 .... 141 D4
Poynter St *NEWH/MOS* M40 .... 69 C4 🖪
Poynton St *HULME* M15 .... 26 B4
Praed Rd *TRPK* M17 .... 104 A4
Premier Rd *CHH* M8 .... 6 A1
Premier St *OLDTF/WHR* M16 .... 34 C2
Prenton St *OP/CLY* M11 .... 107 C1
Prescot Rd *BKLY* M9 .... 84 B2 🖪
Press St *OP/CLY* M11 .... 106 B2
Prestage St *BNG/LEV* M19 .... 51 E1
  OLDTF/WHR M16 .... 34 C2 🖪
Prestbury Av *RUSH/FAL* M14 .... 46 B3
Prestbury Av *MPL/ROM* SK6 .... 141 C2
Preston Av *ECC* M30 .... 93 C2
Preston Cl *ECC* M30 .... 93 C2 🖪
Preston Rd *BNG/LEV* M19 .... 50 C5
Preston St *GTN* M18 .... 106 A3
Prestwich Hills *PWCH* M25 .... 62 A3
Prestwich Park Rd South
  PWCH M25 .... 62 A2
Prestwood Rd *SLFD* M6 .... 94 A1
Pretoria Rd *OLDS* OL8 .... 72 A2 🖪
Price St *ANC* M4 .... 19 D2 🖸
Prichard St *STRET* M32 .... 114 B3
Pridmouth Rd *DID/WITH* M20 .... 130 A3
Priestley Rd *WALK* M28 .... 75 C1
Primrose Av *URM* M41 .... 111 D3 🖸
Primrose Bank *OLDS* OL8 .... 55 C4
Primrose Dr *DROY* M43 .... 99 C3
Primrose St *ANC* M4 .... 7 F5 🖸
  OLDS OL8 .... 55 C4
Prince Albert Av *BNG/LEV* M19 ...... 51 D2 🖸
Princedom St *BKLY* M9 .... 85 C1
Prince's Br *SALO/ORD* M5 .... 15 D3
Princess Av *PWCH* M25 .... 63 C3
Princess Ct *CHAD* OL9 .... 70 A2
  HULME M15 .... 26 B4
  PWCH M25 .... 63 C3 🖸
  URM M41 .... 110 B3
Princess St *CMANE* M1 .... 16 C4
  ECC M30 .... 91 C3 🖪
  FAIL M35 .... 88 A2 🖽
  HULME M15 .... 24 C3
  NEWH/MOS M40 .... 9 E1 🖪

OP/CLY M11 .... 20 C1
  SLFD M6 .... 3 D2
  SWIN M27 .... 77 C2
Prince's St *STKP* SK1 .... 138 A4
Printer St *OLD* OL1 .... 55 D3 🖽🖪
  OP/CLY M11 .... 106 B1 🖸
Printon Av *BKLY* M9 .... 65 D2
Printworks La *BNG/LEV* M19 .... 116 A4
Priory Av *BRO* M7 .... 81 C3 🖸
  CCHDY M21 .... 43 F5 🖪
Priory Cl *OLDS* OL8 .... 72 B2
  SALE M33 .... 124 B3
Priory Ct *RDSH* SK5 .... 134 A1 🖸
Priory Gv *BRO* M7 .... 81 C3
  CHAD OL9 .... 71 C1 🖸
Priory La *RDSH* SK5 .... 134 A1
Priory Rd *SALE* M33 .... 124 B4
  SWIN M27 .... 58 A4
The Priory *BRO* M7 .... 81 C3
Pritchard St *CMANE* M1 .... 17 D5 🖸
Propps Hall Dr *FAIL* M35 .... 87 D3
Prospect Dr *FAIL* M35 .... 88 B4
Prospect Rd *CHAD* OL9 .... 54 A2
Prospect Vw *SWIN* M27 .... 77 C2 🖸
Prout St *WGTN/LGST* M12 .... 40 C4
Providence St *ANC* M4 .... 18 C3
Provident Av *BNG/LEV* M19 .... 116 A4 🖸
Provis Rd *CCHDY* M21 .... 126 B2
Pryme St *HULME* M15 .... 25 E1
Pullman Cl *BNG/LEV* M19 .... 51 F5
Pullman Dr *URM* M41 .... 112 B2 🖸
Purcell St *WGTN/LGST* M12 .... 40 C4
Purslow Cl *WGTN/LGST* M12 .... 19 E2
Pym St *ECC* M30 .... 91 D3 🖸
  NEWH/MOS M40 .... 85 D1 🖽
Pyramid Ct *BRO* M7 .... 81 D3 🖽
Pytha Fold Rd *DID/WITH* M20 .... 130 B4

Q

The Quadrant *BKLY* M9 .... 68 A2
  DROY M43 .... 97 D4
  STKP SK1 .... 139 D4
Quantock Cl *HTNM* SK4 .... 138 A3
  OLDTF/WHR M16 .... 35 E3 🖪
Quarmby Rd *GTN* M18 .... 117 D1 🖽🖸
The Quays *SALO/ORD* M5 .... 22 A2
Quay St *CSLFD* M3 .... 15 F1
  CSLFD M3 .... 15 E3
Quay Vw *SALO/ORD* M5...................... 12 C4
Quebec St *CHAD* OL9 .... 54 A1
Queens Av *GTN* M18 .... 31 F5 🖪
Queens Ct *NEWH/MOS* M40 .... 84 B4
Queen's Dr *PWCH* M25 .... 63 C3
Queensferry St *NEWH/MOS* M40....... 87 C3
Queen's Gv *WGTN/LGST* M12 .... 40 C3 🖸
Queensland Rd *GTN* M18 .... 31 F5
Queens Rd *CHAD* OL9 .... 53 C2
  CHH M8.. 83 D4
  NEWH/MOS M40 .... 9 E1
  URM M41 .... 111 D4
Queen St *CMANW* M2.......................... 16 A3
  CSLFD M3 .... 5 F5
  ECC M30 .... 92 B4 🖪
  FAIL M35 .... 88 A2
  OLD OL1 .... 55 D2
  SLFD M6 .... 78 B4
  STKP SK1 .... 139 C3 🖸
Queen St West *DID/WITH* M20 .... 129 D2 🖽🖸
Queensway *SWIN* M27 .... 59 C3
  URM M41 .... 112 A1

Queen Victoria St *ECC* M30 .... 91 C3 ☒
Quenby St *HULME* M15 .... 25 D3
Quendon Av *BRO* M7 .... 5 E2
Quilter Gv *BKLY* M9 .... 66 A3
Quinney Crs *OLDTF/WHR* M16 .... 36 B4
Quinn St *OP/CLY* M11 .... 20 C1
Quixall St *OP/CLY* M11 .... 20 C1

R

Raby St *OLDTF/WHR* M16 .... 35 F3
   RUSH/FAL M14 .... 36 B3
Rachel St *WGTN/LGST* M12 .... 28 B1
Radbourne Cl *WGTN/LGST* M12 ...... 30 C4
Radcliffe Park Crs *SLFD* M6 .... 78 A4 ☒
Radcliffe Park Rd *SLFD* M6 .... 77 D4
Radcliffe Rd *OLD* OL1 .... 55 D1
Radclyffe St *OLDG* OL9 .... 53 D1
Radford Dr *BKLY* M9 .... 85 C1 ☒
Radford St *BRO* M7 .... 81 C1
Radium St *ANC* M4 .... 7 F5
Radley St *DROY* M43 .... 107 C1
Radnor Av *DTN/ASHW* M34 .... 118 B2
Radnor St *CHAD* OL9 .... 54 A4
   GTN M18 .... 116 A1 ☒
   HULME M15 .... 36 B2 ☒
   STRET M32 .... 114 B3
Radstock Cl *RUSH/FAL* M14 .... 47 E4
Radstock Rd *STRET* M32 .... 114 A3
Raglan Av *SWIN* M27 .... 59 D3
Raglan Cl *OP/CLY* M11 .... 20 B3 ☒
Raglan St *STRET* M32 .... 113 D1
Rail Pl *HULME* M15 .... 26 C4 ☒
Railton Av *OLDTF/WHR* M16 .... 34 C4
Railton Ter *BKLY* M9 .... 85 D2 ☒
Railway Rd *CHAD* OL9 .... 54 B3
   CHAD OL9 .... 71 C3
   STRET M32 .... 32 A1
   URM M41 .... 111 D3
Railway St *GTN* M18 .... 106 A3
   HTNM SK4 .... 138 A3 ☒
Rainbow Cl *CCHDY* M21 .... 126 B2 ☒
Raincliff Av *BRUN/LGST* M13 .... 50 B2
Rainford Av *DID/WITH* M20 .... 129 C1
Rainforth St *BRUN/LGST* M13 .... 40 B4
Rainham Dr *CHH* M8 .... 83 C2
Rainham Wy *CHAD* OL9 .... 53 D3 ☒
   RDSH SK5 .... 135 D3
Rainow Av *DROY* M43 .... 107 C1 ☒
Rainsough Av *PWCH* M25 .... 61 D4
Rainsough Brow *PWCH* M25 .... 61 D4
Rainsough Cl *PWCH* M25 .... 62 A4
Rainwood *CHAD* OL9 .... 52 A1 ☒
Raja Cl *CHH* M8 .... 83 D2
Rake La *SWIN* M27 .... 58 B2
Raleigh Cl *DID/WITH* M20 .... 129 C4
   OLD OL1 .... 55 D1
Raleigh St *RDSH* SK5 .... 138 A1 ☒
   STRET M32 .... 114 B3
Ralli Cts *CSLFD* M3 .... 15 E2 ☒
Ralph Green St *CHAD* OL9 .... 71 D2
Ralph St *OP/CLY* M11 .... 96 B4 ☒
Ralston Cl *BRO* M7 .... 82 B1 ☒
Ralstone Av *OLDS* OL8 .... 73 D1
Ramsbury Dr *NEWH/MOS* M40 ...... 69 D3 ☒
Ramsdale Cl *OLD* OL1 .... 55 C2 ☒
Ramsden Cl *OLD* OL1 .... 55 C2 ☒
Ramsden Crs *OLD* OL1 .... 55 C2 ☒
Ramsden St *OLD* OL1 .... 55 C2
Ramsey Av *BNG/LEV* M19 .... 116 B4
Ramsey St *CHAD* OL9 .... 53 D4

Raby St *OLDTF/WHR* M16 .... ☒
   NEWH/MOS M40 .... 86 B2
Ramsgate Rd *NEWH/MOS* M40 ..... 96 A1
   RDSH SK5 .... 134 B2 ☒
Ramsgate St *BRO* M7 .... 82 A4
Ranbys Av *BKLY* M9 .... 67 D1
Randerson St *WGTN/LGST* M12 ... 28 A1 ☒
Randlesham St *PWCH* M25 .... 63 C1 ☒☒
Randolph St *BNG/LEV* M19 .... 51 D2
   OLDS OL8 .... 72 A3 ☒
Ranelagh Rd *SWIN* M27 .... 78 A2
Ranelagh St *OP/CLY* M11 .... 11 E5
Ranford Rd *BNG/LEV* M19 .... 132 A1
Range Rd *OLDTF/WHR* M16 .... 35 E5
Range St *OP/CLY* M11 .... 106 A1
Ransfield Rd *CCHDY* M21 .... 43 E3
Ranworth Cl *OP/CLY* M11 .... 20 B4
Ratcliffe St *BNG/LEV* M19 .... 51 E4
Rathan Rd *URM* M41 .... 111 C1
Rathbourne Av *BKLY* M9 .... 66 B2
Rathen Rd *DID/WITH* M20 .... 129 D4
Rathmore Av *NEWH/MOS* M40 ...... 85 C4 ☒
Rattenbury Ct *SLFD* M6 .... 78 A4 ☒
Raveley Av *RUSH/FAL* M14 .... 130 B1 ☒
Ravelston Dr *BKLY* M9 .... 84 B3
Raven Av *CHAD* OL9 .... 53 C4
Raven Cl *DROY* M43 .... 99 C2 ☒
Ravenhead Cl *RUSH/FAL* M14 .... 130 B1 ☒
Ravenoak Av *BNG/LEV* M19 .... 51 F5
Ravenoak Dr *FAIL* M35 .... 89 C1
Ravensbury St *OP/CLY* M11 .... 11 F5
Ravens Cl *PWCH* M25 .... 64 A3
Ravensdale Gdns *ECC* M30 .... 92 A2 ☒
Ravensdale St *RUSH/FAL* M14 ...... 38 A5
Ravenside Pk *CHAD* OL9 .... 53 C4
Ravenstone Dr *SALE* M33 .... 125 C4
Raven St *WGTN/LGST* M12 .... 18 B5
Ravensway *PWCH* M25 .... 63 D3
Ravenswood Dr *BKLY* M9 .... 67 C2 ☒
Ravenswood Rd *STRET* M32 .... 32 A1
Ravine Av *BKLY* M9 .... 85 C2
Rawcliffe Av *RUSH/FAL* M14 .... 37 E5
Rawdon Cl *BNG/LEV* M19 .... 51 F4 ☒
Rawkin Cl *HULME* M15 .... 25 F5
Rayburn Wy *CHH* M8 .... 83 C4
Raycroft Av *BKLY* M9 .... 68 A3
Raydon Av *NEWH/MOS* M40 .... 84 B4 ☒☒
Rayleigh Av *OP/CLY* M11 .... 107 D2 ☒
Raymond Av *CHAD* OL9 .... 71 D1
Raymond St *SWIN* M27 .... 58 B4 ☒
Rayner La *AULW* OL7 .... 99 D3 ☒
Rayson Hill Dr *BKLY* M9 .... 66 A3 ☒
Rayson St *BKLY* M9 .... 66 A3
Reabrook Av *WGTN/LGST* M12 ..... 30 A3
Reading Cl *OP/CLY* M11 .... 106 A1
Reading St *SLFD* M6 .... 80 B4
Reather Wk *NEWH/MOS* M40 .... 8 B3
Rebecca St *CHH* M8 .... 83 C1 ☒
Recreation Rd *FAIL* M35 .... 71 C4
Recreation St *PWCH* M25 .... 63 C1 ☒☒
Rectory Av *CHH* M8 .... 65 C4 ☒
   PWCH M25 .... 62 B1
Rectory Flds *STKP* SK1 .... 139 C4 ☒
Rectory Gdns *PWCH* M25 .... 62 B1
Rectory Gn *PWCH* M25 .... 62 A1
   STKP SK1 .... 139 C4 ☒
Rectory Gv *PWCH* M25 .... 62 B2
Rectory La *PWCH* M25 .... 62 A1
Rectory Rd *CHH* M8 .... 64 B4
Redacre Rd *GTN* M18 .... 107 C4
Red Bank *ANC* M4 .... 7 D3
Redbarn Cl *MPL/ROM* SK6 .... 141 D1
Redbrook Av *NEWH/MOS* M40 ...... 85 C4
Redby St *OP/CLY* M11 .... 31 F1

Redcar Av URM M41 ..... 110 A1
Redcar Rd SWIN M27 ..... 78 A2
Redclyffe Av RUSH/FAL M14 ..... 38 B4
Redclyffe Rd URM M41 ..... 101 D1
Redcote St NEWH/MOS M40 ..... 86 A1
Redcroft Rd SALE M33 ..... 122 A3
Reddaway Cl SLFD M6 ..... 80 A4
Reddish La GTN M18 ..... 117 C2
Reddish Rd RDSH SK5 ..... 134 B3
Reddish Vale Rd RDSH SK5 ..... 135 C2
Redesmere Cl DROY M43 ..... 98 B4
Redesmere Pk URM M41 ..... 120 B1
Redfern St ANC M4 ..... 6 C5
Redfield Cl OP/CLY M11 ..... 20 B3
Redford Rd CHH M8 ..... 64 B1
Redgate La WGTN/LGST M12 ..... 30 B5
Redhill Dr MPL/ROM SK6 ..... 140 B2
Redhill St ANC M4 ..... 17 F2
Redhouse La MPL/ROM SK6 ..... 141 D1
Redland Av RDSH SK5 ..... 134 B4
Redland Crs CCHDY M21 ..... 126 B3
Red Lion St ANC M4 ..... 17 D1
Redmere Gv RUSH/FAL M14 ..... 48 B5
Red Rose Ct SALE M33 ..... 123 D3
Red Rose Crs BNC/LEV M19 ..... 133 C2
Redruth St RUSH/FAL M14 ..... 47 F1
Redshaw Cl RUSH/FAL M14 ..... 49 D3
Redvers St OLD OL1 ..... 54 B1
  OP/CLY M11 ..... 19 F4
Redwood Dr CHH M8 ..... 83 D4
  MPL/ROM SK6 ..... 141 D2
Redwood St SLFD M6 ..... 2 B2
Reedshaw Rd BKLY M9 ..... 84 A3
Reed St GTN M18 ..... 106 B3
Reeves Rd CCHDY M21 ..... 126 B2
Regan Av CCHDY M21 ..... 127 D2
Regatta Cl CHAD OL9 ..... 71 C2
Regatta St SLFD M6 ..... 79 D3
Regency Cl NEWH/MOS M40 ..... 84 B4
  OLDS OL8 ..... 72 B1
Regent Av RUSH/FAL M14 ..... 46 B1
Regent Crs FAIL M35 ..... 88 A4
Regent Dr DTN/ASHW M34 ..... 119 D4
Regent Pl RUSH/FAL M14 ..... 38 A3
Regent Rd SALQ/ORD M5 ..... 13 E4
Regent Sq SALQ/ORD M5 ..... 13 F5
Regent St ECC M30 ..... 92 B4
  NEWH/MOS M40 ..... 87 D4
Reginald St ECC M30 ..... 100 A1
  OP/CLY M11 ..... 107 D2
  SWIN M27 ..... 57 D4
Reliance St NEWH/MOS M40 ..... 87 C3
Rendel Cl STRET M32 ..... 114 B3
Rennie Cl STRET M32 ..... 114 B3
Renshaw Av ECC M30 ..... 91 D4
Renshaw St ECC M30 ..... 91 D4
Renton Rd STRET M32 ..... 115 C3
Repton Av DROY M43 ..... 96 B2
  DTN/ASHW M34 ..... 118 A2
  NEWH/MOS M40 ..... 70 A4
  OLDS OL8 ..... 72 B2
Reservoir St CSLFD M3 ..... 5 F4
  SLFD M6 ..... 2 A5
Retiro St OLD OL1 ..... 55 D2
Reuben St HTNM SK4 ..... 138 A1
Reynard Rd CCHDY M21 ..... 126 B2
Reynell Rd BRUN/LGST M13 ..... 50 B1
Reyner St CMANE M1 ..... 16 C4
Reynolds Dr GTN M18 ..... 106 B3
Reynolds Rd OLDTF/WHR M16 ..... 34 A3
Rhine Dr CHH M8 ..... 82 A4
Rhodes Bank OLD OL1 ..... 55 D3
Rhodes St NEWH/MOS M40 ..... 9 E1

OLD OL1 ..... 55 D2
Rhos Av RUSH/FAL M14 ..... 131 C1
Ribble Rd OLDS OL8 ..... 72 A2
Ribblesdale Dr NEWH/MOS M40 ..... 84 A4
Ribchester Wk HULME M15 ..... 26 A4
Ribston St HULME M15 ..... 25 E4
Rice St CSLFD M3 ..... 15 E5
Richardson Rd ECC M30 ..... 92 A3
Richardson St OP/CLY M11 ..... 107 C2
Richard St FAIL M35 ..... 88 B2
  STKP SK1 ..... 138 B3
Richborough Cl BRO M7 ..... 82 A4
Richmond Av CHAD OL9 ..... 71 C1
  PWCH M25 ..... 63 C4
  URM M41 ..... 112 A3
Richmond Dr WALK M28 ..... 75 C1
Richmond Gv BRUN/LGST M13 ..... 39 D2
  ECC M30 ..... 92 A2
Richmond Gv East WGTN/LGST M12 ..... 39 F1
Richmond Rd DTN/ASHW M34 ..... 118 A2
  FAIL M35 ..... 89 C1
  RUSH/FAL M14 ..... 130 B1
  TRPK M17 ..... 103 C2
Richmond St CMANE M1 ..... 17 D4
  CSLFD M3 ..... 5 E4
  DROY M43 ..... 99 C3
Richmond Wk CHAD OL9 ..... 54 B3
Ridgefield CMANW M2 ..... 16 A2
  CMANW M2 ..... 16 A3
Ridgefield St FAIL M35 ..... 88 A3
Ridgeway SWIN M27 ..... 59 D4
Ridgeway St NEWH/MOS M40 ..... 9 D5
Ridgewood CHAD OL9 ..... 52 A1
Ridgewood Av NEWH/MOS M40 ..... 84 A4
Riding Fold La WALK M28 ..... 74 A4
Ridings St NEWH/MOS M40 ..... 85 D4
  OP/CLY M11 ..... 21 E4
Riding St CSLFD M3 ..... 15 E1
Ridings Wy CHAD OL9 ..... 53 D4
Ridsdale Av DID/WITH M20 ..... 129 C3
Rifle Rd SALE M33 ..... 125 D4
Rifle St OLD OL1 ..... 55 D1
Riga Rd RUSH/FAL M14 ..... 48 B4
Riga St ANC M4 ..... 7 D5
Rigby St BRO M7 ..... 81 D2
Rigel Pl BRO M7 ..... 4 B3
Rigel St ANC M4 ..... 8 B4
Rigton Cl WGTN/LGST M12 ..... 40 C1
Riley Wood Cl MPL/ROM SK6 ..... 141 D4
Rimmer Cl OP/CLY M11 ..... 19 F4
Rimmington Cl BKLY M9 ..... 68 A3
Rimworth Dr NEWH/MOS M40 ..... 8 B2
Ringcroft Gdns NEWH/MOS M40 ..... 68 B4
Ringfield Cl OLDTF/WHR M16 ..... 35 F3
Ringley St BKLY M9 ..... 84 B1
Ringlow Av SWIN M27 ..... 75 C2
Ringlow Park Rd SWIN M27 ..... 75 C3
Rings Cl FAIL M35 ..... 88 B3
Ringstead Dr NEWH/MOS M40 ..... 8 A2
Ringstone PWCH M25 ..... 62 A2
Ringwood Av DTN/ASHW M34 ..... 99 C4
  WGTN/LGST M12 ..... 51 E1
Rink St RUSH/FAL M14 ..... 131 C2
Ripley Cl ANC M4 ..... 18 C4
Ripon Cl CHAD OL9 ..... 53 D3
Ripon Crs STRET M32 ..... 112 B2
Ripon Gv SALE M33 ..... 122 B3
Ripon Rd STRET M32 ..... 112 B2
Ripon St HULME M15 ..... 36 C1
  OLD OL1 ..... 54 B1
Rippenden Av CCHDY M21 ..... 43 D2
Rippingham Rd DID/WITH M20 ..... 129 D2
Rishworth Dr NEWH/MOS M40 ..... 88 A1

Rising La *OLDS* OL8............... 73 C3
Risley Av *BKLY* M9 .... 84 B1
Risley St *OLD* OL1 .... 55 D1
Rita Av *RUSH/FAL* M14........... 37 E4
Ritson Cl *GTN* M18 .... 31 E3
Riverdale Rd *BKLY* M9 .... 65 C3
Riverpark Rd *NEWH/MOS* M40... 10 C3
River Pl *HULME* M15 .... 25 F1
Rivershill *SALE* M33 .... 123 C3
Riverside *BRO* M7.................. 4 B4
Riverside Dr *URM* M41 .... 120 B1
Rivers La *URM* M41 .... 101 C4
River St *HULME* M15 .... 26 A2
   STKP SK1............................ 139 D2
   WGTN/LGST M12 .... 18 B5
River Vw *RDSH* SK5 .... 135 C2
River View Cl *PWCH* M25 .... 61 D3 ▣
Rivington Av *SWIN* M27 .... 78 A1 ▣
Rivington Gv *DTN/ASHW* M34 ... 109 C1
Rivington Rd *SLFD* M6............ 94 A1
Rivington Wk *WGTN/LGST* M12 ... 40 A1 ▣
Roachwood Cl *CHAD* OL9 .... 52 A2
Robert Hall St *SALQ/ORD* M5 ... 13 E5
Robert Lawrence Ct *URM* M41 ... 110 A4 ▣
Robert Malcolm Cl *NEWH/MOS* M40... 8 C1
   NEWH/MOS M40 .... 84 B4 ▣▣
Roberts Av *RUSH/FAL* M14 .... 37 F3
Robertshaw Av *CCHDY* M21 ... 126 B5 ▣
Roberts St *ECC* M30 .... 91 D4
Robert St *CSLFD* M3.............. 6 B3
   FAIL M35 .... 71 C4 ▣
   NEWH/MOS M40 .... 85 D4
   OLDS OL8 .... 71 D3
   PWCH M25 .... 63 D1 ▣▣
Robin Cft *MPL/ROM* SK6 .... 140 B2 ▣
Robin Hood St *CHH* M8 .... 82 B1 ▣
Robins Cl *DROY* M43 .... 99 C2
Robinson St *CHAD* OL9 .... 53 D3
   OLDS OL8 .... 73 D2
Robin St *OLD* OL1 .... 55 C1 ▣
Robson Av *URM* M41 .... 102 A3
Robson St *OLD* OL1 .... 55 D3
Roby Rd *ECC* M30 .... 101 C1 ▣
Roby St *CMANE* M1 .... 17 E3
Rochdale Rd *ANC* M4 .... 7 E5
   BKLY M9 .... 66 B2
   NEWH/MOS M40 .... 8 A2
Rochester Av *PWCH* M25 .... 63 C3
Rochester Rd *URM* M41 .... 111 D1
Rockdove Av *HULME* M15 .... 26 A2
Rocket St *CSLFD* M3................ 15 D2
Rockfield Dr *BKLY* M9 .... 85 C1 ▣
Rockhampton St *GTN* M18 ...... 107 C4 ▣
Rockhouse Ct *ECC* M30 .... 101 D1 ▣
Rockingham Cl *WGTN/LGST* M12 ... 29 D4
Rocklyn Av *NEWH/MOS* M40 ..... 69 C3
Rockmead Dr *BKLY* M9 .... 67 C2
Rock Rd *URM* M41 .... 112 B3
Rock St *BRO* M7 .... 81 D3
   OLD OL1 .... 55 D2
   OP/CLY M11 .... 107 C2
Rocky La *ECC* M30 .... 91 D1
Roda St *BRO* M7 .... 85 D2 ▣
Rodenhurst Dr *NEWH/MOS* M40 ... 86 A3
Rodmell Av *NEWH/MOS* M40 ..... 84 B4 ▣▣
Rodmill Ct *RUSH/FAL* M14 .... 48 A4
Rodney St *ANC* M4 .... 8 B5
   CSLFD M3 .... 14 C2
Roe Gn *WALK* M28 .... 74 A1
Roe Green Av *WALK* M28 .... 74 A1
Roe St *ANC* M4 .... 8 A4
Roger Cl *MPL/ROM* SK6 .... 141 D4
Roger St *ANC* M4 .... 7 D3

Rokeby Av *STRET* M32........... 114 B4
Roker Av *BRUN/LGST* M13 ...... 50 A2
Roker Park Av *DTN/ASHW* M34 ... 109 D2
Roland Rd *RDSH* SK5 .... 134 B2 ▣
Rolla St *CSLFD* M3.................. 5 F5
Rolleston Av *NEWH/MOS* M40 ... 8 C5
Rolls Crs *HULME* M15............. 26 A4
Rollswood Dr *NEWH/MOS* M40 ... 86 A3 ▣
Roman Rd *FAIL* M35 .... 89 C1 ▣
   HTNM SK4 .... 138 A3 ▣
   OLDS OL8 .... 71 D4
   PWCH M25 .... 61 D4
Roman St *ANC* M4 .... 17 D1
Romer Av *NEWH/MOS* M40 ..... 70 A4 ▣
Rome Rd *NEWH/MOS* M40 .... 8 A4
Romford Cl *OLDS* OL8 .... 55 C4 ▣
Romford Rd *SALE* M33 .... 122 A3
Romiley St *SLFD* M6 .... 78 B4 ▣
   STKP SK1............................ 139 D3
Romley Rd *URM* M41 .... 111 D3
Romney St *NEWH/MOS* M40 ..... 86 A1
   SLFD M6 .... 80 A4
Romney Wy *RDSH* SK5 .... 135 D3
Romsley Cl *WGTN/LGST* M12..... 31 D3
Ronaldsay Gdns *SALQ/ORD* M5 ... 95 C4 ▣
Ronald St *OP/CLY* M11............ 96 B4
Rondin Cl *WGTN/LGST* M12 .... 19 E5
Rondin Rd *WGTN/LGST* M12 ..... 19 E5
Rookery Av *GTN* M18 .... 107 D3
Rooke St *ECC* M30 .... 100 A1
Rookfield Av *SALE* M33 .... 124 A4
Rope Wk *CSLFD* M3 .... 5 F4
Rosa Gv *BRO* M7 .... 81 D3
Rosamond Dr *CSLFD* M3 .... 15 D1
Rosamond St West *HULME* M15 ... 26 C3
Rosary Cl *OLDS* OL8 .... 73 D4
Roscoe St *OLD* OL1 .... 55 D3 ▣▣
Rosebank Rd *NEWH/MOS* M40 ... 11 E2
Roseberry St *OLDS* OL8 .... 54 B3 ▣
Rosebery St *RUSH/FAL* M14 ..... 36 B5
Rose Cottage Rd *DID/WITH* M20 ... 129 D2
Rosedale Rd *HTNM* SK4 .... 133 D4
   RUSH/FAL M14..................... 47 D2
Rosegate Cl *OLDTF/WHR* M16 ... 36 A4
Rose Hey La *FAIL* M35 .... 97 C1
Rose Hl *DTN/ASHW* M34 .... 119 D2
Rose Hill Av *NEWH/MOS* M40 ... 11 E2
Rosehill Cl *SLFD* M6 .... 2 B5
Rosehill Rd *SWIN* M27 .... 58 B3 ▣▣
Rosemary Gv *BRO* M7 .... 81 C4 ▣▣
Rosemary La *STKP* SK1 .... 139 C4 ▣
Roseneath Av *BNG/LEV* M19 ... 116 A4
Roseneath Rd *URM* M41 .... 111 C2
Rose St *CHAD* OL9 .... 71 C2
   RDSH SK5 .... 138 B2 ▣
Rosevale Av *BNG/LEV* M19 ..... 131 C4
Rosewell Cl *NEWH/MOS* M40 ..... 9 D2
Rose Wd *DTN/ASHW* M34 .... 119 D2
Rosewood Av *DROY* M43 .... 98 B3
Rosford Av *RUSH/FAL* M14 .... 47 E1
Rosina St *OP/CLY* M11........... 107 D2
Roslin St *OP/CLY* M11 .... 96 B3 ▣
Rossall Av *STRET* M32 .... 114 A2
Rossall Wy *SLFD* M6.............. 2 C3
Ross Av *BNG/LEV* M19 .... 50 B4
   CHAD OL9 .... 70 B2 ▣
Ross Dr *SWIN* M27 .... 58 A1
Rossendale Av *BKLY* M9 .... 67 D4 ▣
Ross Gv *URM* M41 .... 111 C3
Rossington St *NEWH/MOS* M40... 87 C4
Ross Lave La *DTN/ASHW* M34... 136 A1
Rosslyn Rd *CCHDY* M21 .... 43 D1
   NEWH/MOS M40 .... 68 A4

Ross St *OLDS* OL8 .... **54** B4
Rostherne Av *OLDTF/WHR* M16 .... **34** B4
  RUSH/FAL M14 .... **46** C4
Rostherne St *SLFD* M6 .... **95** C4 🔢
Roston Rd *BRO* M7 .... **82** A1 🔢
Rostron Av *WGTN/LGST* M12 ...... **29** E3
Rostron St *BNG/LEV* M19 .... **51** E4
Rothay Dr *RDSH* SK5 .... **134** B1
Rotherwood Av *STRET* M32 ...... **115** C2 🔢
Rothesay Av *CHH* M8 .... **64** A3
Rothman Cl *FAIL* M35 .... **87** C3
Rothwell St *FAIL* M35 .... **88** A3
  NEWH/MOS M40 .... **87** C3
Roughlee Av *SWIN* M27 .... **75** D2
Rousdon Cl *NEWH/MOS* M40 .... **84** B4 🔢
Rouse Ct *OP/CLY* M11 .... **20** B3
Rowan Av *OLDTF/WHR* M16 ...... **34** C5
  URM M41 .... **111** D2 🔢
Rowan Cl *FAIL* M35 .... **88** B4
  SLFD M6 .... **3** D5
Rowan Pl *PWCH* M25 .... **62** B2 🔢
Rowan Tree Rd *OLDS* OL8 .... **72** B4
Rowanwood *CHAD* OL9 .... **52** A2 🔢
Rowany Cl *PWCH* M25 .... **62** A3
Rowendale St *CMANE* M1 ...... **16** A5 🔢
Rowland Av *URM* M41 .... **112** A2 🔢
Rowland St *SALQ/ORD* M5 ...... **12** C4
Rowood Av *CHH* M8 .... **83** D3
  RDSH SK5 .... **117** D3 🔢
Rowsley Gv *RDSH* SK5 .... **134** B3
Rowsley Rd *ECC* M30 .... **101** C3
  STRET M32 .... **113** C2
Rowsley St *OP/CLY* M11 .... **19** F1
  SLFD M6 .... **80** B3 🔢
Roxburgh St *GTN* M18 .... **106** B4 🔢
Roxton Rd *HTNM* SK4 .... **133** C3
Royal Av *CCHDY* M21 .... **126** A2
  DROY M43 .... **98** B3
  URM M41 .... **111** D3
Royal Oak Yd *STKP* SK1 .... **138** B4 🔢
Royce Rd *HULME* M15 .... **25** E3
Roydale St *NEWH/MOS* M40 ...... **9** E4
Royds Cl *BRUN/LGST* M13 ...... **29** D5
Royd St *OLDS* OL8 .... **72** A1 🔢
Royle Cl *OLDS* OL8 .... **73** D2
Royle St *RUSH/FAL* M14 .... **130** B2
  SLFD M6 .... **12** C4 🔢
Royley Rd *OLDS* OL8 .... **73** C1
Royston Av *DTN/ASHW* M34 .... **117** D2
  OLDTF/WHR M16 .... **34** C4
Royston Rd *OLDTF/WHR* M16 .... **33** E4
  URM M41 .... **112** A2
Ruby St *HULME* M15 .... **26** C4
Rudcroft Cl *BRUN/LGST* M13 .... **27** F3
Rudd St *NEWH/MOS* M40 .... **86** A2
Rudford Av *OP/CLY* M11 .... **107** C1 🔢
Rudheath Av *DID/WITH* M20 .... **129** C2
Rudman Dr *SALQ/ORD* M5 .... **14** A5
Rudston Av *NEWH/MOS* M40 .... **68** B3 🔢
Rudyard Gv *HTNM* SK4 .... **133** D3
Rudyard Rd *SLFD* M6 .... **78** A4 🔢
Rudyard St *BRO* M7 .... **81** D3 🔢
Rufford Pl *GTN* M18 .... **117** C3 🔢
Rufford Rd *OLDTF/WHR* M16 .... **35** D4
Rufus St *RUSH/FAL* M14 .... **131** C2 🔢
Rugby Rd *SLFD* M6 .... **93** C2 🔢
Rugby St *CHH* M8 .... **5** F2
Rugeley St *SLFD* M6 .... **3** E1
  SLFD M6 .... **80** B3 🔢
Ruislip Av *NEWH/MOS* M40 ...... **85** C4
Runcorn St *HULME* M15 .... **24** B2
Runhall Cl *WGTN/LGST* M12 .... **31** D4
Runnymeade *SLFD* M6 .... **77** C3

Rupert St *NEWH/MOS* M40 .... **97** C1
  RDSH SK5 .... **134** A2
Rushbrooke Av *OP/CLY* M11 .... **96** A3 🔢
Rushden Rd *BNG/LEV* M19 ...... **51** F2 🔢
Rushen St *OP/CLY* M11 .... **96** A4 🔢
Rushfield Dr *BRUN/LGST* M13 .... **39** F5
Rushford Av *BNG/LEV* M19 ...... **50** C2
Rushford St *WGTN/LGST* M12 .... **40** C3
Rushley Av *BRO* M7 .... **80** B2
Rushmere Av *BNG/LEV* M19 ...... **51** E3
Rusholme Gv *RUSH/FAL* M14 .... **38** B5 🔢
Rusholme Pl *RUSH/FAL* M14 .... **38** A3
Rushton Gv *OP/CLY* M11 .... **107** C2
Rushwick Av *NEWH/MOS* M40 .... **85** C4
Ruskin Av *CHAD* OL9 .... **70** B2 🔢
  DTN/ASHW M34 .... **109** C2
  RUSH/FAL M14 .... **37** E3
Ruskin Crs *PWCH* M25 .... **61** D2
Ruskington Dr *BKLY* M9 .... **84** B2
Ruskin Rd *DROY* M43 .... **98** A3
  OLDTF/WHR M16 .... **34** A4
  PWCH M25 .... **61** C2
  RDSH SK5 .... **117** C4
Ruskin St *CHAD* OL9 .... **54** B1
Russell Av *OLDTF/WHR* M16 .... **45** D2
  SALE M33 .... **124** B4
Russell Rd *OLDTF/WHR* M16 .... **34** C5
  SLFD M6 .... **77** D2
Russell St *CHAD* OL9 .... **53** D2 🔢
  CHH M8 .... **5** F1
  ECC M30 .... **92** A3
  OLDTF/WHR M16 .... **36** B5
  PWCH M25 .... **63** C1
Russet Rd *BKLY* M9 .... **66** B4
Ruth Av *NEWH/MOS* M40 .... **70** A4
Ruthen La *OLDTF/WHR* M16 ...... **33** E5
Rutherford Av *RUSH/FAL* M14 .... **37** E4 🔢
Rutherglade Cl *NEWH/MOS* M40 .. **84** A3 🔢
Rutherglen Wk *NEWH/MOS* M40 .. **85** C4 🔢
Ruthin Cl *OLDS* OL8 .... **71** D3
Ruth St *GTN* M18 .... **116** B2
  OLD OL1 .... **55** D1
Rutland Av *DID/WITH* M20 ...... **129** C3
  OLDTF/WHR M16 .... **32** C5
  SWIN M27 .... **58** B3
  URM M41 .... **112** A3
Rutland Crs *RDSH* SK5 .... **136** B3
Rutland Dr *BRO* M7 .... **81** C1
Rutland La *SALE* M33 .... **125** D4
Rutland Rd *DROY* M43 .... **97** C3
  ECC M30 .... **92** B2
Rutland St *CHAD* OL9 .... **54** A4
  FAIL M35 .... **88** B1 🔢
  GTN M18 .... **107** C3 🔢
  SWIN M27 .... **58** A4
Ryall Av *SALQ/ORD* M5 .... **13** E5
Ryall Av South *SALQ/ORD* M5 .. **13** E5
Ryan St *OP/CLY* M11 .... **107** C2
Rydal Av *DROY* M43 .... **97** C4
  ECC M30 .... **90** B1
  SALE M33 .... **122** B4
  URM M41 .... **120** A1
Rydal Cl *DTN/ASHW* M34 .... **118** B3
Rydal Crs *SWIN* M27 .... **76** B3
Rydal St *STRET* M32 .... **114** B2 🔢
Ryder Av *GTN* M18 .... **116** B1
Ryder Brow *GTN* M18 .... **116** B1
Ryderbrow Rd *GTN* M18 .... **116** B1
Ryder St *NEWH/MOS* M40 .... **8** C1
Ryebank Rd *CCHDY* M21 .... **42** B4
Rye Bank Rd *OLDTF/WHR* M16 .. **33** E5
Rye Croft Av *SLFD* M6 .... **94** B2
Ryecroft Cl *CHAD* OL9 .... **70** B2
Ryecroft Rd *STRET* M32 .... **114** A4

Ryecroft Vw *DTN/ASHW* M34 ...... **109** C1 🔢
Ryedale Av *NEWH/MOS* M40 ...... **85** C4 🔢
Rylance St *OP/CLY* M11 .... **19** F4
Rylands St *GTN* M18 .... **107** C3 🔢
Rylane Wk *NEWH/MOS* M40 ...... **85** C4 🔢
Ryton Av *GTN* M18 .... **116** A2

S

Sabden Cl *NEWH/MOS* M40 .... **9** E4
Sabrina St *CHH* M8 .... **82** A4 🔢
Sackville St *CMANE* M1 .... **16** C4
  CSLFD M3 .... **15** E1
Saddle Gv *DROY* M43 .... **99** D2
Sadie Av *STRET* M32 .... **113** C1
Sagar St *CHH* M8 .... **6** A2
St Agnes Rd *BRUN/LGST* M13 ...... **50** B1
St Agnes St *RDSH* SK5 .... **117** D2 🔢
St Aidan's Gv *BRO* M7 .... **80** B3
St Alban's Av *HTNM* SK4 ...... **133** C4 🔢
  NEWH/MOS M40 .... **86** B4
St Albans Cl *OLDS* OL8 .... **73** D1
St Alban's Ter *CHH* M8 .... **82** B4 🔢
St Aldates *MPL/ROM* SK6 .... **141** D3
St Andrew's Av *DROY* M43 .... **97** C4
  ECC M30 .... **92** A4 🔢
St Andrew's Sq *CMANE* M1 .... **18** B4
St Andrew's St *CMANE* M1 .... **18** A4
St Anne's Av *SLFD* M6 .... **95** C2 🔢
St Annes Rd *CCHDY* M21 .... **126** B2
St Anne's St *NEWH/MOS* M40 .... **85** D3
St Anns Cl *PWCH* M25 .... **62** A2
St Ann's Rd *PWCH* M25 .... **61** D2
St Ann's Sq *CMANW* M2 .... **16** B2
St Ann's St *SWIN* M27 .... **76** A1 🔢
St Ann St *CMANW* M2 .... **16** A2
St Augustine St *NEWH/MOS* M40 .. **85** C4 🔢
St Austell Rd *OLDTF/WHR* M16 .. **45** E4
St Austell St *SWIN* M27 .... **78** A3
St Bartholomew's Dr *SALO/ORD* M5.. **14** A5
St Bees St *HULME* M15 .... **36** C2
  RUSH/FAL M14 .... **36** C2
St Benedict's Av *WGTN/LGST* M12 .. **30** A3
St Bernard's Av *SLFD* M6 ...... **81** C4 🔢
St Boniface Rd *BRO* M7 .... **4** A1
St Brannock's Rd *CCHDY* M21 .. **44** B3
St Brelades Dr *BRO* M7 .... **82** B1
St Brendan's Rd *DID/WITH* M20 .. **129** D2
St Brendan's Rd North
  DID/WITH M20 .... **129** D2
St Bride St *OLDTF/WHR* M16 ...... **34** C1
St Brides Wy *OLDTF/WHR* M16.... **34** C1
St Catherine's Dr *DID/WITH* M20.. **129** D2
St Chads Crs *OLDS* OL8 .... **72** B4
St Chad's Rd *DID/WITH* M20 .... **130** B2
St Chad's St *CHH* M8 .... **6** C2
St Christophers Cl *DID/WITH* M20 **128** B3 🔢
St Clement's Dr *SALQ/ORD* M5 .... **23** F1
St Clements Fold *URM* M41 ...... **112** A3 🔢
St Clement's Rd *CCHDY* M21 .... **126** A1
St Edmund's Rd *NEWH/MOS* M40 .. **85** C3
St Elisabeth's Wy *RDSH* SK5 .... **134** A2
St George's Crs *SLFD* M6 .... **93** C2 🔢
St George's Dr *NEWH/MOS* M40 .. **86** B2
St George's Rd *DROY* M43 .... **97** C2
  RUSH/FAL M14 .... **131** C2
  STRET M32 .... **113** C3
St George's Sq *CHAD* OL9 .... **70** A3
St George's Wy *SLFD* M6 .... **3** D1 🔢
St Helier's Dr *BRO* M7 .... **82** B1 🔢

St Hilda's Dr *OLD* OL1 .... **54** B1 🔢
St Hilda's Rd *OLDTF/WHR* M16.... **33** F1
St Ives Rd *RUSH/FAL* M14 .... **47** F1
St James' Ct *SLFD* M6 .... **93** D2 🔢
St James Rd *HTNM* SK4 .... **132** B4
St James's Rd *BRO* M7 .... **82** A3
St James's Sq *CMANW* M2 .... **16** B3 🔢
St James St *CMANE* M1 .... **16** C4 🔢
  CMANE M1 .... **16** C3 🔢
  ECC M30 .... **92** A3 🔢
St John's Av *DROY* M43 .... **98** B3
St John's Cl *BRO* M7 .... **81** D3 🔢
St John's Rd *BRUN/LGST* M13 .... **40** A3
  OLDTF/WHR M16 .... **34** B3
St John's St *BRO* M7 .... **81** D5 🔢
  CHAD OL9 .... **54** A4 🔢
St John St *CSLFD* M3 .... **15** F4
  ECC M30 .... **91** D4 🔢
  SWIN M27 .... **78** B3
St John's Wk *CHAD* OL9 .... **54** A3 🔢
St Joseph's Dr *SALO/ORD* M5 .. **13** E4
St Kilda's Av *DROY* M43 .... **97** D2
St Lawrence Quay *SALQ/ORD* M5 .. **22** B1
St Leonard's Rd *HTNM* SK4 .... **133** D4
St Lukes Ct *CHAD* OL9 .... **53** C2 🔢
St Luke's Rd *SLFD* M6 .... **94** B3
St Margaret's Av *BNG/LEV* M19 .. **131** D3 🔢
St Margaret's Rd *NEWH/MOS* M40 .. **69** D2
St Mark's La *CHH* M8 .... **82** B1 🔢
St Mark's Rd *BNG/LEV* M19 .... **116** A4
St Martin's Dr *DROY* M43 .... **97** D2 🔢
St Martin's Dr *BRO* M7 .... **82** B1 🔢
St Martins Rd *SALE* M33 .... **121** D3
St Marys Cl *PWCH* M25 .... **62** A1 🔢
  STKP SK1 .... **139** C4 🔢
St Mary's Ct *NEWH/MOS* M40 .. **86** B1 🔢
St Mary's Dr *RDSH* SK5 .... **134** B4
St Mary's Ga *CMANE* M1 .... **16** B1
St Mary's Hall Rd *CHH* M8........ **64** B4
St Mary's Parsonage *CSLFD* M3........ **16** A2
St Mary's Rd *ECC* M30 .... **92** B3
  NEWH/MOS M40 .... **86** B2
  PWCH M25 .... **62** A1
  SALE M33 .... **122** B4
St Mary's Cl *CSLFD* M3 .... **16** A2 🔢
  HULME M15 .... **35** F1
  OLD OL1 .... **55** D1
St Mary's Wy *OLD* OL1 .... **55** C2 🔢
  STKP SK1 .... **139** C3 🔢
St Michaels Ct *SALE* M33 .... **122** A3 🔢
St Michael's Sq *ANC* M4 .... **7** D4 🔢
St Modwen Rd *STRET* M32 ...... **102** B4
St Oswald's Rd *BNG/LEV* M19.... **51** E2
St Paul's Rd *BRO* M7 .... **63** C4
  DID/WITH M20 .... **130** A3
St Paul's St *STKP* SK1 .... **139** C2 🔢
St Petersgate *STKP* SK1 .... **138** A4 🔢
St Peter's Rd *SWIN* M27 .... **76** A2
St Peter's Sq *CMANW* M2 .... **16** B4 🔢
  STKP SK1 .... **138** A4 🔢
  STKP SK1 .... **138** B2 🔢
St Philip's Pl *CSLFD* M3 .... **14** C1 🔢
St Philip's Rd *GTN* M18 .... **116** B1 🔢
St Simon St *CSLFD* M3 .... **5** D3
St Stephen's Cl *BRUN/LGST* M13 .. **28** C5
St Stephen St *CSLFD* M3 .... **15** E1
St Stephens Vw *DROY* M43 ...... **98** A3
St Teresa's Rd *OLDTF/WHR* M16 .. **32** C1
St Thomas' Pl *CHH* M8.................. **7** D2
St Thomas's Cir *OLDS* OL8 ...... **54** B4 🔢
St Thomas St North *OLDS* OL8 .. **54** B4 🔢
St Thomas St South *OLDS* OL8 .. **54** B4 🔢
St Vincent St *ANC* M4 .... **18** B1

St Werburgh's Rd *CCHDY* M21 .... **44** B3
St Wilfrids St *HULME* M15 .... **25** E3
Salcombe Cl *SALE* M33 .... **122** A4 🎦
Salcombe Rd *OP/CLY* M11 .... **106** B1
Salford Ap *CSLFD* M3 .... **6** A5
Salisbury Dr *PWCH* M25 .... **63** C3 🎦
Salisbury Rd *CCHDY* M21 .... **43** F4
  ECC M30 .... **92** B1
  SWIN M27 .... **76** A2
  URM M41 .... **111** D1
Salisbury Rd *RDSH* SK5 .... **134** B1
  RUSH/FAL M14 .... **36** C3
Salmon St *ANC* M4 .... **17** D1
Salop St *SLFD* M6 .... **3** D2
Salteye Rd *ECC* M30 .... **90** A4
Saltford Av *ANC* M4 .... **18** B1
Saltire Gdns *BRO* M7 .... **82** A1 🎦
Saltney Av *DID/WITH* M16 .... **128** B2
Salutation St *HULME* M15 .... **26** B4
Sam Cowan Cl *RUSH/FAL* M14 .... **36** C4
Samian Gdns *BRO* M7 .... **81** C4 🎦
Sammy Cookson Cl *RUSH/FAL* M14... **37** D4
Samouth Cl *NEWH/MOS* M40 .... **8** C4 🎦
Sam Swire St *HULME* M15 .... **25** F5
Samuel Ogden St *CMANE* M1 .... **17** D5 🎦
Samuel St *BNG/LEV* M19 .... **51** E5
  FAIL M35 .... **88** B1
Sanby Av *GTN* M18 .... **116** A1
Sanby Rd *GTN* M18 .... **116** A1
Sanctuary Cl *HULME* M15 .... **37** E1 🎦
Sandal St *NEWH/MOS* M40 .... **9** F4
Sandbach Av *RUSH/FAL* M14 .... **46** B5
Sandbach Rd *RDSH* SK5 .... **117** C3 🎦
Sanderson Cl *WALK* M28 .... **74** B2 🎦
Sanderson St *NEWH/MOS* M40 .... **85** C4
Sanderstead Dr *BKLY* M9 .... **67** C2
Sandfold Av *GTN* M18 .... **106** B3 🎦
Sandford Station La *RDSH* SK5 .... **116** B3
Sandgate Av *OP/CLY* M11 .... **96** B3
Sandgate Dr *URM* M41 .... **111** C1
Sandgate Rd *CHAD* OL9 .... **53** D3 🎦
Sandheys Gv *GTN* M18 .... **117** C1
Sandhurst Av *DID/WITH* M20 .... **129** C3
Sandhutton Rd *BKLY* M9 .... **66** B4 🎦
Sandileigh Av *DID/WITH* M20 .... **129** D4
  RDSH SK5 .... **139** D1
Sandiway *MPL/ROM* SK6 .... **141** D2
Sandown Av *SLFD* M6 .... **95** C3 🎦
Sandown Crs *GTN* M18 .... **116** B3
Sandown Gdns *URM* M41 .... **110** A3
Sandown St *GTN* M18 .... **107** C3
Sandray Gv *SALQ/ORD* M5 .... **95** C4 🎦
Sandringham Av *DTN/ASHW* M34 ...... **109** D3
  DTN/ASHW M34 .... **118** A2 🎦
Sandringham Gra *PWCH* M25 .... **64** A2 🎦
Sandringham Rd *MPL/ROM* SK6 ...... **140** A2
Sandringham St *GTN* M18 .... **116** A1 🎦
Sandsend Cl *CHH* M8 .... **82** A4 🎦
Sandsend Rd *URM* M41 .... **111** C2
Sandstone Wy *CCHDY* M21 .... **127** D3 🎦
Sand St *NEWH/MOS* M40 .... **8** A2
Sandwell Dr *SALE* M33 .... **123** D3
Sandwich Rd *ECC* M30 .... **92** B2
Sandy Bank Rd *CHH* M8 .... **82** B1 🎦
Sandy Brow *BKLY* M9 .... **66** B3 🎦
Sandygate Cl *SWIN* M27 .... **76** A2 🎦
Sandy Gv *SLFD* M6 .... **95** C2
  SWIN M27 .... **76** B1
Sandyhill Rd *BKLY* M9 .... **65** C2
Sandylands Dr *PWCH* M25 .... **61** D4
Sandy La *CCHDY* M21 .... **126** B1
  DROY M43 .... **99** C2
  PWCH M25 .... **62** A3

  RDSH SK5 .... **138** B2
  SLFD M6 .... **95** C2
  STRET M32 .... **113** D4
Sandy Meade *PWCH* M25 .... **62** A2 🎦
Sandyway *PWCH* M25 .... **62** A2 🎦
Sandywell Cl *OP/CLY* M11 .... **106** B2
Sandywell St *OP/CLY* M11 .... **106** B1
Sanfold La *BNG/LEV* M19 .... **116** A3
Sangster Ct *SALQ/ORD* M5 .... **12** C4
Sankey Gv *BKLY* M9 .... **65** D2
Santiago St *RUSH/FAL* M14 .... **37** E5
Santley St *WGTN/LGST* M12 .... **41** D4
Santon Av *RUSH/FAL* M14 .... **131** C1
Sapling Rd *SWIN* M27 .... **75** D4
Sarah Ann St *OP/CLY* M11 .... **20** A2
Sarah St *ECC* M30 .... **90** B4 🎦
  OP/CLY M11 .... **20** B4 🎦
Sargent Dr *OLDTF/WHR* M16 .... **35** F2
Sargent Rd *MPL/ROM* SK6 .... **140** B3
Sark Rd *CCHDY* M21 .... **43** D2
Sarnesfield Cl *WGTN/LGST* M12 ...... **40** B2
Saturn Gv *SLFD* M6 .... **4** A1 🎦
Saunton Rd *OP/CLY* M11 .... **106** B1 🎦
Sawley Rd *NEWH/MOS* M40 .... **9** D2
Saxby St *SLFD* M6 .... **78** A4
Saxelby Dr *CHH* M8 .... **83** D3 🎦
Saxon Av *CHH* M8 .... **65** C3
Saxon Dr *CHAD* OL9 .... **52** A1
  DROY M43 .... **98** A3
Saxon St *DROY* M43 .... **98** B3
  NEWH/MOS M40 .... **9** F4
Saxwood Av *BKLY* M9 .... **66** B4
Scale St *SALQ/ORD* M5 .... **13** D3 🎦
Scarborough St *NEWH/MOS* M40 .. **86** A1 🎦
Scarcroft Rd *WGTN/LGST* M12 .... **31** D5
Scargill Rd *RUSH/FAL* M14 .... **48** B5
Scarisbrick Rd *BNG/LEV* M19 .... **50** A5
Scarsdale Rd *RUSH/FAL* M14 .... **39** E3
Scarsdale St *SLFD* M6 .... **3** F3
Schofield Rd *DROY* M43 .... **98** B4
  ECC M30 .... **90** A4
Schofield St *CSLFD* M3............ **88** B1 🎦
  FAIL M35 .... **88** B1 🎦
  OLDS OL8 .... **73** C2
  OP/CLY M11 .... **96** A3
Scholars Dr *DID/WITH* M20 .... **129** C2
Scholes Dr *NEWH/MOS* M40 .... **70** A3
Scholes La *PWCH* M25 .... **63** C2
Scholes St *CHAD* OL9 .... **71** C1
  FAIL M35 .... **71** C4
  SWIN M27 .... **77** C1 🎦
Scholes Wk *PWCH* M25 .... **62** B2
Scholfield Av *URM* M41 .... **112** B4 🎦
School Av *STRET* M32 .... **32** A5
School Ct *ANC* M4 .... **18** A1
School Gv *DID/WITH* M20 .... **130** B3
  PWCH M25 .... **62** A3
School Gv West *DID/WITH* M20 .. **130** A3 🎦
School La *BKLY* M9 .... **66** A3 🎦
  HTNM SK4 .... **133** C4
School Rd *ECC* M30 .... **101** C1 🎦
  FAIL M35 .... **88** B2
  OLDS OL8 .... **71** D3
  SALE M33 .... **123** C4
  STRET M32 .... **114** A3
Schools Rd *GTN* M18 .... **107** C4
School St *ANC* M4 .... **7** D4
  BRO M7 .... **5** E2
  ECC M30 .... **90** B4 🎦
  OLDS OL8 .... **54** B4
Score St *OP/CLY* M11 .... **20** C3
Scotforth Cl *HULME* M15 .... **25** E2 🎦
Scotland *ANC* M4 .... **6** C4

Scotland Hall Rd
  NEWH/MOS M40 .... **86** B4 🔟
Scotland St *NEWH/MOS* M40 ...... **87** C4
Scott Av *CCHDY* M21 .... **43** E2
  ECC M30 .... **91** C2 🔢
Scott Cl *RDSH* SK5 .... **138** B1 🔢
Scottfield *OLDS* OL8 .... **55** D4 🔢
Scottia Rd *ECC* M30 .... **100** B1
Scott Rd *DROY* M43 .... **98** A3
  PWCH M25 .... **61** D2
Scott St *OLDS* OL8........................ **55** D4
  SLFD M6 .... **4** A1
Scovell St *BRO* M7 .... **81** D3 🔢
Scropton St *NEWH/MOS* M40........ **84** B3
Seabrook Crs *URM* M41 .... **111** D1 🔢
Seabrook Rd *NEWH/MOS* M40 ...... **87** C4 🔢
Seacombe Av *RUSH/FAL* M14...... **47** D3
Seaford Rd *SLFD* M6 .... **80** B4
Sealand Dr *ECC* M30.................... **100** A1
Seale Av *DTN/ASHW* M34 .... **109** D2
Searby Rd *GTN* M18 .... **41** F3
Second Av *OLDS* OL8 .... **72** A3
  OP/CLY M11 .... **96** B3
  SWIN M27 .... **75** D4
  TRPK M17 .... **104** B4
Sedan Cl *SALO/ORD* M5 .... **13** D2
Seddon Av *GTN* M18 .... **106** B3
Seddon St *BNG/LEV* M19 .... **51** E2
Sedgeborough Rd *OLDTF/WHR* M16... **35** F4
Sedge Cl *RDSH* SK5 .... **135** C1 🔢
Sedgefield Cl *SALO/ORD* M5 .... **12** C1 🔢
Sedgeford Rd *NEWH/MOS* M40 ...... **84** B3
Sedgley Av *PWCH* M25 .... **63** C3
Sedgley Park Rd *PWCH* M25 .... **63** C3
Sedgley Rd *CHH* M8 .... **83** C1
Sedgley Park Rd *SLFD* M6............ **95** C3
Seedley Rd *SLFD* M6 .... **2** A3
Seedley St *RUSH/FAL* M14............ **37** E4
Seedley Ter *SLFD* M6 .... **95** C2
Seedley View Rd *SALO/ORD* M5 .. **95** C3 🔢
Sefton Cl *BRUN/LGST* M13 .... **27** F3
Sefton Crs *SALE* M33 .... **123** D3
Sefton Dr *SWIN* M27 .... **75** D3
  WALK M28.................................. **74** A3
Sefton Rd *CCHDY* M21 .... **43** F5
  SALE M33 .... **123** D4
  SWIN M27 .... **58** B4
Sefton St *CHAD* OL9 .... **71** C3
  CHH M8...................................... **83** C1
Selborne Rd *CCHDY* M21 .... **43** E4
Selby Cl *STRET* M32 .... **112** B3
Selby Dr *SLFD* M6 .... **93** D2
Selby Rd *STRET* M32.................... **113** C2
Selby St *OP/CLY* M11 .... **21** D3 🔢
Selden St *OLDS* OL8 .... **53** B4
Selhurst Av *OP/CLY* M11 .... **96** A3 🔢
Selkirk Av *OLDS* OL8...................... **72** B1
Selkirk Dr *BKLY* M9 .... **67** D2
Selkirk Rd *CHAD* OL9 .... **70** B1
Sellars Sq *DROY* M43 .... **108** A1
Sellers Wy *CHAD* OL9 .... **71** C3
Selsby Av *ECC* M30 .... **90** B3 🔢
Selston Rd *BKLY* M9 .... **65** D1
Selworthy Rd *OLDTF/WHR* M16.... **35** E3
Selwyn Av *BKLY* M9 .... **84** B1
Senior Av *RUSH/FAL* M14 .... **131** C2 🔢
Senior St *CSLFD* M3 .... **5** F4
Sepal Cl *RDSH* SK5...................... **118** A4
Sequoia St *BKLY* M9 .... **85** D1 🔢
  BKLY M9 .... **85** C1 🔢
Sevenoaks Av *HTNM* SK4 .... **132** A4
  URM M41 .... **111** D1
Sevenoaks Dr *SWIN* M27.............. **77** C3

Seventh Av *OLDS* OL8 .... **72** A4
Severn Rd *CHAD* OL9 .... **52** B1
  OLDS OL8.................................... **71** D4
Severn Wy *RDSH* SK5 .... **134** B3
Sewerby Cl *OLDTF/WHR* M16 ...... **36** A2
Sexa St *OP/CLY* M11 .... **106** B1
Seymour Av *OP/CLY* M11 .... **96** B3
Seymour Cl *OLDTF/WHR* M16 ...... **24** A5
Seymour Gv *OLDTF/WHR* M16 ...... **33** F3
Seymour Rd *CHH* M8 .... **64** B4
Seymour Rd South *OP/CLY* M11 .. **96** B3
Seymour St *DTN/ASHW* M34........ **119** D1
  GTN M18 .... **106** B3 🔢
Shackleton St *ECC* M30 .... **91** C2
Shackliffe Rd *NEWH/MOS* M40 .... **68** B3
Shaftesbury Av *ECC* M30 .... **101** C1
Shaftesbury Rd *CHH* M8 .... **83** C2
  SWIN M27 .... **76** B2
Shakespeare Av *DTN/ASHW* M34.... **137** D1
Shakespeare Crs *DROY* M43 .... **98** A3
  ECC M30 .... **91** D3
Shakespeare Rd *DROY* M43 .... **98** A3
  MPL/ROM SK6 .... **141** C2
  PWCH M25 .... **61** D2
  SWIN M27 .... **75** D1
Shakleton Av *BKLY* M9 .... **68** A2
Shaldon Dr *NEWH/MOS* M40 .... **97** C1
Shanklin Av *URM* M41 .... **111** C3 🔢
Shanklin Cl *CCHDY* M21 .... **43** D4
Shanley Ct *CHAD* OL9 .... **53** D1 🔢
Sharples St *HTNM* SK4 .... **138** A2
Sharp St *ANC* M4............................ **7** E4
  PWCH M25 .... **62** A1 🔢
Shawbrook Rd *BNG/LEV* M19...... **132** A4
Shawcross St *SLFD* M6 .... **12** A2
Shawe Hall Av *URM* M41 .... **120** A1
Shawe Hall Crs *URM* M41 .... **120** A1
Shawe Rd *URM* M41 .... **110** A3
Shawe Vw *URM* M41 .... **110** A3
Shawfield Cl *RUSH/FAL* M14........ **47** D5
Shawford Rd *NEWH/MOS* M40 ...... **69** C3
Shawgreen Cl *HULME* M15 .... **25** D3
Shaw Head Dr *FAIL* M35 .... **88** B3
Shawheath Cl *HULME* M15 .... **25** D4
Shawlea Av *BNG/LEV* M19 .... **131** C3 🔢
Shaw Rd *HTNM* SK4 .... **132** B4
Shaw St *CSLFD* M3 .... **6** B4
  OLD OL1 .... **55** D1
Shayfield Av *CHAD* OL9 .... **52** A1
Sheader Dr *SALO/ORD* M5............ **94** A3
Shearer Wy *SWIN* M27 .... **78** B2
Shearsby Cl *HULME* M15 .... **25** F5
Shearwater Gdns *ECC* M30.......... **100** A1
Sheepfoot La *PWCH* M25 .... **63** D2
Sheerness St *GTN* M18 .... **106** B4 🔢
Sheffield St *CMANE* M1 .... **17** F4
  HTNM SK4.................................. **138** A2
Shefford Cl *OP/CLY* M11 .... **20** B4
Shelderton Cl *NEWH/MOS* M40 .... **86** A2 🔢
Sheldon Dr *OP/CLY* M11................ **11** E5
Shelford Av *GTN* M18.................... **41** E3
Shelley Gv *DROY* M43 .... **98** A4
Shelley Rd *CHAD* OL9 .... **70** B2
  PWCH M25 .... **61** D2
  RDSH SK5 .... **116** B4
  SWIN M27 .... **75** D1
Shelley St *NEWH/MOS* M40.......... **87** C1
Shepherd St *BKLY* M9 .... **67** C4 🔢
Shepley St *CMANE* M1 .... **17** E4
  FAIL M35 .... **71** C4 🔢
Sheraton Rd *OLDS* OL8 .... **73** C1 🔢
Sherborne Rd *URM* M41 .... **112** A2
Sherborne St *CHH* M8 .... **82** B4

CSLFD M3 .... 6 A2
Sherborne St West CSLFD M3 .... 5 F3
Sherbourne St PWCH M25 .... 62 A1
Sherdley Ct CHH M8 .... 65 C4 🛭
Sherdley Rd CHH M8 .... 65 C4
Sheridan Wy URM CHAD OL9 .... 52 A1 🛭
Sheringham Dr SWIN M27 .... 76 B3
Sheringham Rd RUSH/FAL M14 ..... 130 B2 🛭
Sherlock St RUSH/FAL M14 .... 131 C2 🔟
Sherratt St ANC M4 .... 7 F5
Sherrington St WGTN/LGST M12 ...... 41 D4
Sherwell Rd BKLY M9 .... 65 D2
Sherwood Av BRO M7 .... 80 B2 🛭
DROY M43 .... 99 C3
RUSH/FAL M14 .... 48 B5 🛭
SALE M33 .... 124 B4 🛭
Sherwood Cl SALQ/ORD M5 .... 94 B2 🛭
Sherwood Dr SWIN M27 .... 77 D2
Sherwood Rd DTN/ASHW M34 ...... 118 B2
OLD OL1 .... 54 B1
RUSH/FAL M14 .... 48 B5
Shetland Rd NEWH/MOS M40 .... 8 C2
Shetland Wy URM M41 .... 101 D4
Shieldborn Dr BKLY M9 .... 84 B2
Shield Cl OLDS OL8 .... 55 C3
Shield Dr WALK M28 .... 75 C1
Shilford Dr ANC M4 .... 7 F4
Shipla Cl CHAD OL9 .... 55 C2
Shipley Av SLFD M6 .... 94 A2
Shippey St RUSH/FAL M14 .... 130 B3 🛭
Shiredale Dr BKLY M9 .... 84 B2
Shiregreen Av NEWH/MOS M40 ...... 84 A4 🛭
Shirehills PWCH M25 .... 62 A2
Shireoak Rd DID/WITH M20 .... 130 B2
The Shires DROY M43 .... 99 D2
Shirley Av BRO M7 .... 80 A2
CHAD OL9 .... 70 A3
DTN/ASHW M34 .... 109 C3
DTN/ASHW M34 .... 117 D2
ECC M30 .... 101 C1
STRET M32 .... 32 A4
SWIN M27 .... 78 A2
Shirley Rd CHH M8 .... 83 C2
Shoreditch Cl HTNM SK4 .... 132 B4
Shoreham Cl OLDTF/WHR M16 ...... 35 F2 🛭
Shorland St SWIN M27 .... 75 C2 🛭
Short Av DROY M43 .... 107 D1 🛭
Shortcroft St HULME M15 .... 26 A1
Short St ECC M30 .... 92 B3 🛭
BRO M7 .... 5 E3
HTNM SK4 .... 138 A2
Short St East HTNM SK4 .... 138 A2 🔟
Shrewsbury Rd DROY M43 .... 98 A3
PWCH M25 .... 62 A2
Shrewsbury St OLDTF/WHR M16 .... 24 B5
Shropshire Av RDSH SK5 .... 136 A3
Shropshire Rd FAIL M35 .... 89 C3 🛭
Shudehill ANC M4 .... 16 C1
Shuttle St ECC M30 .... 92 B3 🛭
Shuttleworth Cl OLDTF/WHR M16 ... 45 E5
Siam St OP/CLY M11 .... 20 A4
Sibley St GTN M18 .... 106 B4
Sibson Rd CCHDY M21 .... 43 D4
Sickle St CMANW M2 .... 16 C2 🛭
Sidbury Rd CCHDY M21 .... 127 C1
Siddall St OLD OL1 .... 55 D1 🛭
WGTN/LGST M12 .... 50 C1
Sidebotham St MPL/ROM SK6 ...... 141 D1 🛭
Sidebottom St DROY M43 .... 97 C4 🛭
Side St OLDS OL8 .... 72 A3
OP/CLY M11 .... 21 F2
The Sidings WALK M28 .... 74 A4 🛭
Sidley Av BKLY M9 .... 67 D1

Sidmouth Dr BKLY M9 .... 66 B3
Sidmouth Rd SALE M33 .... 121 D4
Sidmouth St CHAD OL9 .... 54 A4 🛭
DTN/ASHW M34 .... 109 D2 🛭
Sidney Rd BKLY M9 .... 66 B4
Sidney St CMANE M1 .... 27 D2
CSLFD M3 .... 15 D1 🛭
CSLFD M3 .... 16 A3 🛭
Signal Cl ECC M30 .... 90 B3 🔟
Signet Wk CHH M8 .... 83 D4
Silchester Dr NEWH/MOS M40 ...... 84 B3
Silfield Cl OP/CLY M11 .... 19 F3
Silkin Cl BRUN/LGST M13 .... 27 E2
Silkstone St OP/CLY M11 .... 106 A2 🛭
Silk St ANC M4 .... 7 F5
CSLFD M3 .... 4 C1
ECC M30 .... 92 B4
NEWH/MOS M40 .... 87 C3
Sillavan Wy CSLFD M3 .... 15 E1
Silton St BKLY M9 .... 85 D2
Silver Birch Gv SWIN M27 .... 77 D3
Silverbirch Wy FAIL M35 .... 88 B2 🛭
Silvercroft St HULME M15 .... 25 E1
Silverdale SWIN M27 .... 59 C3
Silverdale Av CHAD OL9 .... 53 C3
PWCH M25 .... 64 A3
Silverdale Rd CCHDY M21 .... 43 F4
Silverdale St OP/CLY M11 .... 107 D2
Silverlea Dr BKLY M9 .... 66 A3
Silverstone Dr NEWH/MOS M40 ...... 96 B1
Silver St CMANE M1 .... 16 C4 🛭
OLD OL1 .... 55 C3
Silverwell St NEWH/MOS M40 ...... 87 D4 🔟
Silverwood CHAD OL9 .... 52 A2 🛭
Silverwood Av CCHDY M21 .... 43 E5 🛭
Simeon St ANC M4 .... 7 E4 🛭
Simister Rd FAIL M35 .... 88 B2
Simister St BKLY M9 .... 85 C1 🔟
Simkin Wy OLDS OL8 .... 73 D4
Simms Cl CSLFD M3 .... 14 C1
Simon Freeman Cl
BNG/LEV M19 .... 133 C3 🛭
Simpson Av SWIN M27 .... 60 A3 🛭
Simpson St ANC M4 .... 7 E4
CHAD OL9 .... 71 D1 🛭
OP/CLY M11 .... 20 C3
Sindsley Rd SWIN M27 .... 57 D3
Singleton Cl BRO M7 .... 63 C4 🛭
Singleton Rd BRO M7 .... 63 C4
Sirdar St OP/CLY M11 .... 107 D1 🛭
Sirius Pl BRO M7 .... 4 C3
Sir Matt Busby Wy
OLDTF/WHR M16 .... 22 B5
Sir Richard Fairey Rd HTNM SK4 ... 132 B4
Sisson St FAIL M35 .... 88 B2 🛭
Sisters' St DROY M43 .... 108 A1
Sixth Av OLDS OL8 .... 72 A4
Sixth St TRPK M17 .... 104 B4 🛭
Skarratt Cl WGTN/LGST M12 .... 30 B3 🛭
Skelton Gv BRUN/LGST M13 .... 50 A2
Skelton Rd STRET M32 .... 114 B2
Skelwith Cl URM M41 .... 110 A1 🛭
Skerry Cl BRUN/LGST M13 .... 27 F2
Skerton Rd OLDTF/WHR M16 .... 33 E2
Skip Pl CSLFD M3 .... 6 C3
Skipton Av NEWH/MOS M40 .... 69 D3 🛭
Skye Rd URM M41 .... 101 D4
Slack La SWIN M27 .... 59 C4 🛭
Slack Rd BKLY M9 .... 66 B4
Slade Gv BRUN/LGST M13 .... 40 A5
Slade Hall Rd WGTN/LGST M12 ..... 50 C1
Slade La BNG/LEV M19 .... 50 B5
BRUN/LGST M13 .... 40 C5

Slaithwaite Dr *OP/CLY* M11 .... 96 A3 🔢
Slate La *DTN/ASHW* M34 .... 109 C1
Slater St *CHAD* OL9 .... 55 C3 🔢
   ECC M30 .... 90 B5 🔢
   FAIL M35 .... 70 B4
Slate Whf *HULME* M15 .... 15 D5 🔢
Sleaford Cl *NEWH/MOS* M40 .... 8 C3
Sledmere Cl *OP/CLY* M11 .... 20 C3
Sloane St *OP/CLY* M11 .... 20 C1
Smalldale Av *OLDTF/WHR* M16 .... 36 A5
Smallfield Dr *BKLY* M9 .... 84 B1 🔢
Smallridge Cl *NEWH/MOS* M40 .... 8 C4
Smallwood St *NEWH/MOS* M40 .... 87 C3 🔢
Smart St *WGTN/LGST* M12 .... 40 C4
Smeaton Cl *STRET* M32 .... 115 C3 🔢
Smeaton St *CHH* M8 .... 84 A3 🔢
Smedley La *CHH* M8 .... 83 D2
Smedley Rd *CHH* M8 .... 83 D3
   NEWH/MOS M40 .... 84 A4
Smedley St *CHH* M8 .... 83 C3
Smethurst St *BKLY* M9 .... 66 B4 🔢
Smith St *OLDTF/WHR* M16 .... 24 A3
Smithy La *CSLFD* M3 .... 16 A2 🔢
Smyrna St *SALO/ORD* M5 .... 95 C4
Snell St *ANC* M4 .... 18 C3
Snipe Wy *DTN/ASHW* M34 .... 99 D4
Snowden Av *URM* M4¹i 120 B1
Snowden St *OLDS* OL8 .... 73 D1 🔢
Snowdon Rd *ECC* M30 .... 93 C2
Soap St *ANC* M4 .... 17 D1
Solent Av *CHH* M8 .... 65 C3
Solway Cl *OLDS* OL8 .... 55 C4
   SWIN M27 .... 58 A1
Somerfield Rd *BKLY* M9 .... 66 B4
Somerford Av *DID/WITH* M20 .... 129 C1 🔢
Somerford Rd *RDSH* SK5 .... 118 A3
Somerset Cl *RDSH* SK5 .... 140 A1
Somerset Pl *SALE* M33 .... 123 D3 🔢
Somerset Rd *DROY* M43 .... 98 A2
   ECC M30 .... 93 C1
   FAIL M35 .... 88 A3 🔢
Somers Rd *RDSH* SK5 .... 117 D4
Sopwith Dr *RUSH/FAL* M14 .... 47 D3
Sorbus Cl *SLFD* M6 .... 13 E1
Sorrel Bank *SLFD* M6 .... 2 A2
Sorrell Bank *RDSH* SK5 .... 118 A4
Sorrel St *HULME* M15 .... 25 E3
Sorton St *CMANE* M1 .... 27 D1 🔢
Southall St *CSLFD* M3 .... 6 A3
Southampton Cl *BRO* M7 .... 81 D4 🔢
Southam St *BRO* M7 .... 82 B2 🔢
South Av *BNG/LEV* M19 .... 131 D2
   SWIN M27 .... 75 D4
Southbank Rd *BNG/LEV* M19 ..... 130 B4
Southbourne Av *URM* M41 .... 112 B3
Southbourne St *SLFD* M6 .... 95 C3 🔢
Southbrook Av *CHH* M8 .... 64 B2 🔢
Southcliffe Rd *RDSH* SK5 .... 134 B3 🔢
South Cliffe St *OP/CLY* M11 .... 107 D2 🔢
South Crs *NEWH/MOS* M40 .... 69 D2
   OP/CLY M11 .... 96 B3
Southcross Rd *GTN* M18 .... 116 B2 🔢
Southdown Crs *BKLY* M9 .... 68 A3
South Dr *CCHDY* M21 .... 126 B3
Southend Av *HULME* M15 .... 24 C4
Southern Av *HULME* M15 .... 24 C4
Southern Cl *DTN/ASHW* M34 ..... 137 C1
Southern Rd *SALE* M33 .... 123 C4
Southern St *CSLFD* M3 .... 15 F5 🔢
   SLFD M6 .... 95 C3
Southgarth Rd *SLFD* M6 .... 95 C2
Southgate *CCHDY* M21 .... 126 B2

   CSLFD M3 .... 16 A2 🔢
   HTNM SK4 .... 133 C4 🔢
   URM M41 .... 120 B1
Southgate College Land *CSLFD* M3... 16 A2
Southgate Rd *CHAD* OL9 .... 70 A2
Southgate St *OLD* OL1 .... 55 D3
South Gv *BRUN/LGST* M13 .... 38 C1
South Hall St *SALO/ORD* M5 .... 14 B5
South King St *CMANW* M2 .... 16 A2
   ECC M30 .... 90 B3
South Langworthy Rd
   SALO/ORD M5 .... 12 A2
Southlea Rd *DID/WITH* M20 ...... 130 B4
South Lonsdale St *RTRET* M32 ... 115 C2 🔢
South Meade *CCHDY* M21 .... 126 B3
   PWCH M25 .... 63 D3
   SWIN M27 .... 76 A3
Southmere Cl *BKLY* M9 .... 68 B3
South Mesnefield Rd *BRO* M7 .... 80 A2
Southmill St *CMANW* M2 .... 16 A4 🔢
South Pump St *CMANE* M1 .... 17 E4 🔢
South Radford St *BRO* M7 .... 80 A2
South Rd *RTRET* M32 .... 113 C1
   SWIN M27 .... 60 B3
South Rw *PWCH* M25 .... 61 D4 🔢
Southsea St *OP/CLY* M11 .... 106 B2 🔢
Southside *MPL/ROM* SK6 .... 137 C3
South St *OLDS* OL8 .... 71 D3
   OP/CLY M11 .... 21 E5
   WGTN/LGST M12 .... 29 F5
South Vw *RDSH* SK5 .... 117 D2 🔢
Southway *DROY* M43 .... 108 A1 🔢
   NEWH/MOS M40 .... 70 B3
South Wy *OLDS* OL8 .... 73 C3
Southwell St *BKLY* M9 .... 85 C2
South William St *CSLFD* M3 .... 14 C2 🔢
Southyard St *BNG/LEV* M19 .... 51 E5 🔢
Sovereign St *SLFD* M6 .... 2 C2
Spa Cl *RDSH* SK5 .... 134 A1
Sparkle St *CMANE* M1 .... 17 F3
Sparrow Cl *RDSH* SK5 .... 117 C5
Sparth Rd *NEWH/MOS* M40 .... 87 D4
Spaw St *CSLFD* M3 .... 15 E1
Spear St *CMANE* M1 .... 17 E2
Spectator St *ANC* M4 .... 18 C1
Spencer Av *OLDTF/WHR* M16 ..... 44 A2
Spencer St *CHAD* OL9 .... 71 D1
   ECC M30 .... 91 C4 🔢
   RDSH SK5 .... 134 B1
Spender Av *CHH* M8 .... 83 C3
Spennithorne Rd *URM* M41 .... 110 B3
The Spinney *URM* M41 .... 110 A3 🔢
Spreadbury St *NEWH/MOS* M40 ... 86 A2 🔢
Spring Bank Av *DTN/ASHW* M34 . 109 D2
Spring Bank St *OLDS* OL8 .... 72 A1 🔢
Spring Bridge Rd *OLDTF/WHR* M16... 46 A2
Spring Clough *SWIN* M27 .... 74 B4
Springfield Av *HTNM* SK4 .... 134 A2
Springfield Cl *FAIL* M35 .... 88 A1 🔢
Springfield La *CSLFD* M3 .... 5 F4
Springfield Rd *DROY* M43 .... 97 D2
Spring Gdns *CMANW* M2 .... 16 C2
   SLFD M6 .... 2 A4
   STKP SK1 .... 139 C4
Springhead Av *DID/WITH* M20 ... 129 C2 🔢
Springside *HTNM* SK4 .... 133 D2
Springs Rd *MDTN* M24 .... 52 A3
Spring St *WGTN/LGST* M12 .... 51 D1
Spring V *PWCH* M25 .... 62 A3
Springville Av *BKLY* M9 .... 85 D2 🔢
Springwell Cl *SLFD* M6 .... 95 C3 🔢
Springwood Av *SWIN* M27 .... 77 D3 🔢
Spruce St *HULME* M15 .... 25 E4

The Square SWIN M27 .... 76 A4
Squire Rd CHH M8 .... 82 B2
Stablefold WALK M28 .... 74 A4
Stableford Av ECC M30 .... 91 C1
The Stables DROY M43 .... 99 D2 🔟
Stable St CHAD OL9 .... 71 C3
Stafford Rd ECC M30 .... 92 A2
FAIL M35 .... 89 C4
SWIN M27 .... 76 B1
Stafford St CHAD OL9 .... 72 A1
Stag Pasture Rd OLDS OL8 .... 72 B4
Stainburn Rd OP/CLY M11 .... 21 E4
Stainer St WGTN/LGST M12 .... 40 C4
Stainforth St OP/CLY M11 .... 30 A1
Stainton Av GTN M18 .... 117 C1
Stakeford Dr CHH M8 .... 84 A1 🔟
Stalham Cl NEWH/MOS M40 .... 8 C3
Stamford Dr FAIL M35 .... 89 D4
Stamford Rd BRO M7 .... 80 B3
BRUN/LGST M13 .... 40 A5
DTN/ASHW M34 .... 109 D2
URM M41 .... 110 B5 🔟
Stamford St OLDTF/WHR M16 .... 34 C1 🔟
SALE M33 .... 123 C3
SWIN M27 .... 59 C4 🔟
Stanage Av BKLY M9 .... 67 D1 🔟
Stanbank St HTNM SK4 .... 138 A1
Stanbrook St BNG/LEV M19 .... 116 A4
Standish Rd RUSH/FAL M14 .... 48 C5
Stanhope Rd SLFD M6 .... 79 C3
Stanhope St BNG/LEV M19 .... 51 E4
RDSH SK5 .... 134 A2 🔟
Stanhope Wy FAIL M35 .... 88 A1 🔟
Stanhorne Av CHH M8 .... 65 C3
Stanier Av ECC M30 .... 91 D2
Stan Jolly Wk OP/CLY M11 .... 106 A1
Stanley Av RUSH/FAL M14 .... 38 B5
Stanley Cl OLDTF/WHR M16 .... 33 F1
Stanley Ct OLDTF/WHR M16 .... 34 A1 🔟
Stanley Gv URM M41 .... 111 D3
WGTN/LGST M12 .... 40 B3
Stanley Rd BRO M7 .... 82 A1
CHAD OL9 .... 71 D1
CHAD OL9 .... 72 A2 🔟
DTN/ASHW M34 .... 118 B2
ECC M30 .... 91 C4
OLDTF/WHR M16 .... 24 B5
SWIN M27 .... 77 C1
Stanley St BKLY M9 .... 85 C1 🔟
CHAD OL9 .... 53 D2 🔟
CHH M8 .... 7 D2
CSLFD M3 .... 15 E2
NEWH/MOS M40 .... 85 D4
OP/CLY M11 .... 107 C1
PWCH M25 .... 63 C1
SALQ/ORD M5 .... 15 D3
STKP SK1 .... 139 C3 🔟
Stanmore Av STRET M32 .... 113 D3 🔟
Stansby Gdns WGTN/LGST M12 .... 29 E4
Stansfield Rd FAIL M35 .... 71 C4
Stansfield St CHAD OL9 .... 53 D4 🔟
NEWH/MOS M40 .... 96 B1
OLD OL1 .... 55 C1
OP/CLY M11 .... 106 B1
Stanthorne Av DID/WITH M20 .... 129 C2 🔟
Stanton Av BRO M7 .... 80 B3
Stanton St CHAD OL9 .... 71 D2 🔟
OP/CLY M11 .... 96 A3
STRET M32 .... 114 B1
Stanway St BKLY M9 .... 85 C1 🔟
STRET M32 .... 114 B2
Stanwell Rd NEWH/MOS M40 .... 69 C4 🔟
SWIN M27 .... 76 A2

Stanwick Av BKLY M9 .... 65 C1
Stanworth Cl OLDTF/WHR M16 .... 35 E4
Stanyard Ct SALQ/ORD M5 .... 12 C4
Stapleford Cl SALE M33 .... 125 C4
Staplehurst Rd NEWH/MOS M40 .... 11 D1
Star Gv BRO M7 .... 82 A3 🔟
Starkie St WALK M28 .... 74 A1
Starling Cl DROY M43 .... 99 D2
Statford Av ECC M30 .... 101 C1 🔟
Statham St SLFD M6 .... 3 E4
Station Ap CMANE M1 .... 16 C5 🔟
Station Rd CHH M8 .... 65 C4
ECC M30 .... 91 C4
EDGY/DAV SK3 .... 138 A4
RDSH SK5 .... 117 C3
STRET M32 .... 114 B2
SWIN M27 .... 58 B4
URM M41 .... 111 D4
Station Vw BNG/LEV M19 .... 51 D4
Staton St OP/CLY M11 .... 106 A1
Staverton Cl BRUN/LGST M13 .... 28 A3
Staycott Cl OLDTF/WHR M16 .... 36 A3
Stedman Cl OP/CLY M11 .... 19 F3
Steeple Dr SALQ/ORD M5 .... 12 C3
Stelfox Av RUSH/FAL M14 .... 47 D3
Stelfox St ECC M30 .... 100 B1 🔟
Stella St BKLY M9 .... 65 D1
Stelling St GTN M18 .... 106 B4
Stenbury Cl RUSH/FAL M14 .... 38 A5
Stephenson Av DROY M43 .... 98 A4 🔟
Stephenson Rd STRET M32 .... 114 B4
Stephenson St FAIL M35 .... 71 C4
Stephens Rd DID/WITH M20 .... 130 A3
Stephen St CSLFD M3 .... 6 B2 🔟
URM M41 .... 112 A3
Stern Av SALQ/ORD M5 .... 13 D5
Stevenson Pl CMANE M1 .... 17 E2 🔟
Stevenson Rd SWIN M27 .... 76 A1
Stevenson Sq CMANE M1 .... 17 E2 🔟
Stevenson St CSLFD M3 .... 14 C3 🔟
Stilton Dr OP/CLY M11 .... 20 C4
Stirling Av DID/WITH M20 .... 128 B1
Stirling Rd CHAD OL9 .... 70 B1
Stirling St CHAD OL9 .... 54 A2
Stirrup Ga WALK M28 .... 74 A4 🔟
Stobart Av PWCH M25 .... 63 C3 🔟
Stockburn Dr FAIL M35 .... 89 D2
Stockdale Rd BKLY M9 .... 67 C1
Stockfield Rd CHAD OL9 .... 53 D2
Stockholm St OP/CLY M11 .... 11 E5
Stockland Cl BRUN/LGST M13 .... 27 E2
Stock La CHAD OL9 .... 53 D2
Stockport Rd BRUN/LGST M13 .... 40 B3
WGTN/LGST M12 .... 28 B3
Stockport Rd East MPL/ROM SK6 .... 141 D1
Stockport Rd West MPL/ROM SK6 .. 140 A2
Stocksfield Dr BKLY M9 .... 67 C2 🔟
Stocks St CHH M8 .... 7 D2
Stocks St East CHH M8 .... 7 D2
Stockton Rd CCHDY M21 .... 126 A1
Stockton St SWIN M27 .... 76 A2 🔟
Stokesay Cl SALE M33 .... 122 A4
Stokes St OP/CLY M11 .... 96 B4
Stonall Av HULME M15 .... 25 D3 🔟
Stoneacre Ct SWIN M27 .... 76 B2 🔟
Stonechat Cl DROY M43 .... 99 C2 🔟
Stonefield Dr CHH M8 .... 82 A4
Stonehead St BKLY M9 .... 85 D2 🔟
Stonehurst Cl WGTN/LGST M12 .... 30 C4
Stoneleigh Av SALE M33 .... 121 D4
Stonelow Cl HULME M15 .... 26 B3
Stone Pl RUSH/FAL M14 .... 38 B5 🔟

Stonesby Cl *OLDTF/WHR* M16 ...... **35** D3
Stone St *CSLFD* M3 ...... **15** F5
Stoneyfield Cl *OLDTF/WHR* M16 ...... **46** A2
Stoneygate Wk *OP/CLY* M11 ...... **106** B2
Stoneyhurst Cl *HULME* M15 ...... **26** A4
Stopford St *OP/CLY* M11 ...... **107** C2
Stores St *PWCH* M25 ...... **63** C1 🔟
Store St *CMANE* M1 ...... **18** A3
OP/CLY M11 ...... **31** F1
Stothard Rd *STRET* M32 ...... **113** D4
Stott La *SLFD* M6 ...... **93** D2
Stott Milne St *CHAD* OL9 ...... **53** D4
Stott Rd *CHAD* OL9 ...... **70** A2
SWIN M27 ...... **75** D3
Stott's La *NEWH/MOS* M40 ...... **87** D3
Stott St *NEWH/MOS* M40 ...... **87** D3
OP/CLY M11 ...... **20** A1
Stovell Av *WGTN/LGST* M12 ...... **51** D1
Stovell Rd *NEWH/MOS* M40 ...... **86** A1
Stowell St *SALQ/ORD* M5 ...... **95** C4 🔟
Stowfield Cl *BKLY* M9 ...... **65** D1
Stow Gdns *DID/WITH* M20 ...... **129** C3
Stracey St *NEWH/MOS* M40 ...... **9** E4
Strain Av *BKLY* M9 ...... **66** B3
Strand Ct *STRET* M32 ...... **124** A1 🔟
Stranton Dr *WALK* M28 ...... **75** C1
Stratford Av *DID/WITH* M20 ...... **128** B4 🔟
OLDS OL8 ...... **73** C2
Stratford Gdns *MPL/ROM* SK6 ...... **141** D2
Strathblane Cl *DID/WITH* M20 ...... **129** D2 🔟
Strathfield Dr *OP/CLY* M11 ...... **11** F5
Strathmere Av *STRET* M32 ...... **114** B3
Strathmore Av *CCHDY* M21 ...... **43** F2
Stratton Rd *OLDTF/WHR* M16 ...... **43** F2
SWIN M27 ...... **58** B3
Strawberry Bank *SLFD* M6 ...... **3** E3 🔟
Strawberry Hl *SLFD* M6 ...... **3** F3
Strawberry Rd *SLFD* M6 ...... **3** F3
Stray St *OP/CLY* M11 ...... **107** C1 🔟
Stream Ter *STKP* SK1 ...... **139** D4
Stretford Rd *HULME* M15 ...... **25** E4
OLDTF/WHR M16 ...... **24** A5
URM M41 ...... **111** C4
Stretton Av *STRET* M32 ...... **113** C2
Stretton Cl *NEWH/MOS* M40 ...... **84** B4 🔟
Stringer St *STKP* SK1 ...... **139** D4
Stroma Gdns *URM* M41 ...... **101** C4
Strong St *BRO* M7 ...... **5** E1
Stroud Av *ECC* M30 ...... **90** B4
Stuart Rd *STRET* M32 ...... **114** B2
Stuart St *OLDS* OL8 ...... **55** C4
OP/CLY M11 ...... **10** B5 🔟
Stuart St East *OP/CLY* M11 ...... **11** D5
STRET M32 ...... **113** C2
Style St *ANC* M4 ...... **7** D4
Sudbury Cl *OLDTF/WHR* M16 ...... **24** B5
Sudell St *ANC* M4 ...... **7** F4
Suffolk Av *DROY* M43 ...... **98** A2
Suffolk Dr *RDSH* SK5 ...... **136** A3
Suffolk St *CHAD* OL9 ...... **71** D1
SLFD M6 ...... **80** B4
Sulby Av *STRET* M32 ...... **115** C3
Sulby St *NEWH/MOS* M40 ...... **86** A1
Sullivan St *WGTN/LGST* M12 ...... **40** C5
Sulway Cl *SWIN* M27 ...... **77** C2 🔟
Sumac St *OP/CLY* M11 ...... **96** B3 🔟
Summer Av *URM* M41 ...... **112** A3
Summercroft *CHAD* OL9 ...... **71** D2 🔟
Summerfield Av *DROY* M43 ...... **97** C2 🔟
Summerfield Rd *WALK* M28 ...... **74** A2
Summer Pl *RUSH/FAL* M14 ...... **48** A1 🔟
Summerseat Cl *SALQ/ORD* M5 ...... **13** D5 🔟

Summers St *CHAD* OL9 ...... **54** A2
Summerville Av *BKLY* M9 ...... **85** D2 🔟
Summerville Rd *SLFD* M6 ...... **79** C4
Sumner Rd *SLFD* M6 ...... **78** B4
Sumner Wy *URM* M41 ...... **111** C3
Sunbury Dr *NEWH/MOS* M40 ...... **96** B1 🔟
Sunfield Rd *OLD* OL1 ...... **55** C1
Sunningdale Av *OP/CLY* M11 ...... **11** F5
Sunningdale Dr *SLFD* M6 ...... **77** C4
Sunningdale Rd *URM* M41 ...... **110** B4
Sunny Bank Av *DROY* M43 ...... **97** D4
Sunnybank Av *ECC* M30 ...... **92** B2
Sunny Bank Rd *BRUN/LGST* M13 ...... **39** F4
DROY M43 ...... **97** D4
Sunny Brow Rd *GTN* M18 ...... **106** A4
Sunny Dr *PWCH* M25 ...... **61** D1
Sunnylea Av *BNG/LEV* M19 ...... **131** C4 🔟
Sunnyside Av *DROY* M43 ...... **97** D1
Sunnyside Rd *DROY* M43 ...... **97** D2
Surbiton Rd *NEWH/MOS* M40 ...... **11** E1
NEWH/MOS M40 ...... **86** B4 🔟
Surrey Av *DROY* M43 ...... **97** D2
Surrey Rd *BKLY* M9 ...... **66** B3
Surrey St *BKLY* M9 ...... **66** A2 🔟
CHAD OL9 ...... **54** A4 🔟
Surrey Wy *RDSH* SK5 ...... **136** A4
Sussex Cl *CHAD* OL9 ...... **53** C3
SWIN M27 ...... **59** C3 🔟
Sussex Dr *DROY* M43 ...... **98** A2
Sussex St *BRO* M7 ...... **5** D2
CMANW M2 ...... **16** B2
Sutcliffe Av *WGTN/LGST* M12 ...... **51** D1
Sutcliffe St *OLDS* OL8 ...... **55** C4
Sutherland Cl *OLDS* OL8 ...... **73** D4 🔟
Sutherland Rd *OLDTF/WHR* M16 ...... **33** D5
Sutherland St *ECC* M30 ...... **90** B2
SWIN M27 ...... **58** A4
Suthers St *CHAD* OL9 ...... **54** A3
Sutton Dr *DROY* M43 ...... **97** C2
Sutton Rd *GTN* M18 ...... **116** A2
Swaine St *EDGY/DAV* SK3 ...... **138** A4 🔟
Swainsthorpe Dr *BKLY* M9 ...... **85** C1 🔟
Swallow St *OLDS* OL8 ...... **72** B3
OP/CLY M11 ...... **20** B2
WGTN/LGST M12 ...... **50** C1
Swanage Rd *ECC* M30 ...... **90** B2 🔟
Swanhill Cl *GTN* M18 ...... **107** D3 🔟
Swanley Av *NEWH/MOS* M40 ...... **85** C4
Swan St *ANC* M4 ...... **7** D5
Swarbrick Dr *PWCH* M25 ...... **61** D3
Swayfield Av *BRUN/LGST* M13 ...... **40** A4
Sweetnam Dr *OP/CLY* M11 ...... **21** F1
Swinbourne Gv *DID/WITH* M20 ...... **130** A2
Swinburne Av *DROY* M43 ...... **98** A2 🔟
Swinburne Gn *RDSH* SK5 ...... **116** B4
Swinburn St *BKLY* M9 ...... **67** D4 🔟
Swindells's St *OP/CLY* M11 ...... **107** C2 🔟
Swindon Gv *GTN* M18 ...... **106** B4
Swinfield Av *CCHDY* M21 ...... **125** D1 🔟
Swinstead Av *NEWH/MOS* M40 ...... **85** C4 🔟
Swinton Gv *BRUN/LGST* M13 ...... **38** B1
Swinton Hall Rd *SWIN* M27 ...... **77** C1
Swinton Park Rd *SLFD* M6 ...... **77** D4
Sycamore Av *CHAD* OL9 ...... **70** B1 🔟
Sycamore Dr *DROY* M43 ...... **99** C3
Sycamore Gv *FAIL* M35 ...... **89** D2
Sycamore Rd *ECC* M30 ...... **90** A1
Sydney Av *ECC* M30 ...... **90** A1
Sydney Jones Ct *NEWH/MOS* M40 ...... **69** C4
Sydney St *FAIL* M35 ...... **88** A2 🔟
SLFD M6 ...... **95** C3
STRET M32 ...... **114** B3
SWIN M27 ...... **75** D1

Sykes St *RDSH* SK5 .... **134** B1 🔲
Sylvan Av *FAIL* M35 .... **88** A4
  OLDTF/WHR M16 .... **34** C4
  URM M41 .... **111** D2
Sylvandale Av *BNG/LEV* M19 ...... **50** C3
Sylvan St *CHAD* OL9 .... **54** A2
Sylvia Gv *RDSH* SK5 .... **134** A2 🔲
Symms St *SLFD* M6 .... **3** E1 🔲
Symons Rd *SALE* M33 .... **123** D4
Symons St *BRO* M7 .... **82** A2
Syndall Av *WGTN/LGST* M12 .... **28** C3
Syndall St *WGTN/LGST* M12 .... **28** C3 🔲

T

Tabley Av *RUSH/FAL* M14 .... **47** F2
Tabley Gv *BRUN/LGST* M13 .... **50** A2
  RDSH SK5 .... **134** A2 🔲
Tabley St *SLFD* M6 .... **80** B4 🔲
Tackler Cl *SWIN* M27 .... **76** B2 🔲
Tagore Cl *BRUN/LGST* M13 .... **39** E3
Tahir Cl *CHH* M8 .... **83** D2 🔲
Talavera St *BRO* M7 .... **81** D4
Talbot Pl *OLDTF/WHR* M16 .... **33** F1
Talbot Rd *OLDTF/WHR* M16 .... **33** E1
  RUSH/FAL M14 .... **131** C2
  STRET M32 .... **32** A4
Talbot St *ECC* M30 .... **92** A4 🔲
Talford Gv *DID/WITH* M20 .... **129** C4 🔲
Talgarth Rd *NEWH/MOS* M40 ...... **8** A2
Tallarn Cl *DID/WITH* M20 .... **130** A2 🔲
Tallis St *WGTN/LGST* M12 .... **41** D4
Talmine Av *NEWH/MOS* M40 .... **85** C4 🔲
Tamarin Cl *SWIN* M27 .... **57** C3 🔲
Tamerton Dr *CHH* M8 .... **83** C3
Tame St *ANC* M4 .... **18** C3
Tamworth Av *SALQ/ORD* M5 .... **13** E5
Tamworth Ave West *SALQ/ORD* M5 .. **13** D5
Tamworth Cl *HULME* M15 .... **35** E1 🔲
Tamworth St *CHAD* OL9 .... **54** A4
  HULME M15 .... **35** E2 🔲
  STKP SK1 .... **139** D3
Tandlewood Ms
  NEWH/MOS M40 .... **87** C4 🔲
Tangmere Cl *NEWH/MOS* M40 ..... **69** C2 🔲
Tansey Gv *BRO* M7 .... **82** B2
Tansley Rd *CHH* M8 .... **65** C3
Tan Yard Brow *GTN* M18 .... **117** C1
Tanyard Gn *RDSH* SK5 .... **134** B4 🔲
Taplin Dr *GTN* M18 .... **106** A4 🔲
Tariff St *CMANE* M1 .... **17** F2
Tarporley Av *RUSH/FAL* M14 .... **46** C5
Tarrington Cl *WGTN/LGST* M12 .... **40** C1
Tartan St *OP/CLY* M11 .... **11** E5
Tarvin Cl *DID/WITH* M20 .... **129** C2
  HTNM SK4 .... **133** D2
Tarvin Dr *MPL/ROM* SK6 .... **141** C1
Tarvington Cl *NEWH/MOS* M40 ... **84** A3 🔲
Tasle Aly *CMANW* M2 .... **16** B3 🔲
Tatchbury Rd *FAIL* M35 .... **88** B4
Tatham Cl *BRUN/LGST* M13 .... **40** B5
Tattersall St *CHAD* OL9 .... **54** B3 🔲
Tatton Gv *DID/WITH* M20 .... **129** D3
Tatton Mere Dr *DROY* M43 .... **98** B4
Tatton Pl *SALE* M33 .... **123** D4
Tatton Rd North *HTNM* SK4 .... **133** C4
Tatton St *HULME* M15 .... **24** C3
  SALQ/ORD M5 .... **13** F5
  STKP SK1 .... **138** B4 🔲
Taunton Av *ECC* M30 .... **90** B2

RDSH SK5 .... **136** A4
  URM M41 .... **120** B1 🔲
Taunton St *ANC* M4 .... **19** D2
Tavern Court Av *FAIL* M35 .... **89** C2
Tavery Cl *ANC* M4 .... **18** B1 🔲
Tavistock Rd *SALE* M33 .... **121** D4
Tay Cl *OLDS* OL8 .... **55** C4
Taylor La *DTN/ASHW* M34 .... **119** D1
Taylor Rd *URM* M41 .... **102** A2
Taylorson St *SALQ/ORD* M5 .... **23** E3
Taylorson St South *SALQ/ORD* M5 .. **23** D4
Taylor's Rd *STRET* M32 .... **115** C1
Taylor St *CHAD* OL9 .... **53** C2
  DROY M43 .... **98** A4
  GTN M18 .... **106** A3
  PWCH M25 .... **63** C1
  RUSH/FAL M14 .... **48** A1
Teak Dr *FWTH* BL4 .... **57** D1
Tealby Av *OLDTF/WHR* M16 .... **34** A3
Tealby Rd *GTN* M18 .... **41** F3
Teasdale Cl *CHAD* OL9 .... **70** A2 🔲
Tebbutt St *ANC* M4 .... **7** F4 🔲
Teddington St *NEWH/MOS* M40 ... **69** C4
Teer St *NEWH/MOS* M40 .... **19** D1
Teesdale Av *URM* M41 .... **110** A1
Teignmouth St *NEWH/MOS* M40 .. **8** B1
Telfer Av *BRUN/LGST* M13 .... **49** E2
Telfer Rd *BRUN/LGST* M13 .... **49** E1
Telford St *CHH* M8 .... **84** A4
Tellson Cl *SLFD* M6 .... **78** B3 🔲
Tellson Crs *SLFD* M6 .... **78** B3
Temperance St *WGTN/LGST* M12 .. **18** A5
Temple Dr *SWIN* M27 .... **77** D2
Ten Acres La *NEWH/MOS* M40 ..... **86** A4
Tenax Rd *TRPK* M17 .... **103** D2
Tenbury Cl *SLFD* M6 .... **2** A4
Tenby Av *STRET* M32 .... **115** C1
Tenby Dr *SLFD* M6 .... **79** C4 🔲
Tenby Rd *OLDS* OL8 .... **71** D3
Teneriffe St *BRO* M7 .... **81** D4 🔲
Tennis St *OLDTF/WHR* M16 .... **33** E2
Tennyson Gdns *PWCH* M25 .... **61** D2 🔲
Tennyson St *DROY* M43 .... **98** A3
  RDSH SK5 .... **116** B4
  SWIN M27 .... **75** D2
Tennyson St *BRUN/LGST* M13 ..... **38** B1
  SLFD M6 .... **4** A1
Tenth St *TRPK* M17 .... **104** B3
Terence St *NEWH/MOS* M40 .... **87** D4
The Terrace *PWCH* M25 .... **62** B2 🔲
Terrington Cl *CCHDY* M21 .... **128** A2 🔲
Tetlow Gv *ECC* M30 .... **91** C4
Tetlow La *BRO* M7 .... **82** A1
Tetlow St *NEWH/MOS* M40 .... **87** D4 🔲
Teviot St *BRUN/LGST* M13 .... **39** F1
Teviot Wy *STKP* SK1 .... **138** B2 🔲
Tewkesbury Av *DROY* M43 .... **98** A2 🔲
  URM M41 .... **111** D2
Tewkesbury Dr *PWCH* M25 .... **63** C3
Tewkesbury Rd *NEWH/MOS* M40 .. **9** D4
Textile St *WGTN/LGST* M12 .... **31** D2
Textilose Rd *TRPK* M17 .... **103** D2
Thackeray Cl *CHH* M8 .... **83** C3 🔲
Thackeray Gv *DROY* M43 .... **98** A3
Thames Cl *OP/CLY* M11 .... **21** E5
Thanet Cl *BRO* M7 .... **82** A4 🔲
Thankerton Av *DTN/ASHW* M34.... **99** D4
Thatch Leach *CHAD* OL9 .... **53** D4
Thaxmead Dr *NEWH/MOS* M40 .... **96** B1 🔲
Theatre St *OLD* OL1 .... **55** D2 🔲
Thekla St *CHAD* OL9 .... **54** B1 🔲
Thelwall Av *RUSH/FAL* M14........ **46** B5
Thetford Dr *CHH* M8 .... **83** D2 🔲

Third Av OLDS OL8 .... 72 A3
  OP/CLY M11 .... 96 A3
  SWIN M27 .... 76 A4
  TRPK M17 .... 104 B4
Thirlmere Av STRET M32 .... 77 C2 ⑥
  SWIN M27 .... 77 C2 ⑥
Thirsfield Dr OP/CLY M11 .... 96 A3 ⑭
Thirsk St WGTN/LGST M12 .... 28 A1
Thistledown Cl ECC M30 .... 101 C1
Thomas Gibbon Cl STRET M32 .... 114 A4 ⑫
Thomas Johnson Cl ECC M30 .... 91 C4 ⑫
Thomas St ANC M4 .... 17 D1
  CHH M8 .... 82 B1
  STRET M32 .... 114 B2
Thompson Cl DTN/ASHW M34 .... 119 C2 ①
Thompson Ct DTN/ASHW M34 .... 118 B2 ⑥
Thompson La CHAD OL9 .... 71 C1
Thompson Rd DTN/ASHW M34 .... 118 B2
  TRPK M17 .... 102 A1
Thompson St ANC M4 .... 7 E5
  CHAD OL9 .... 54 B2 ⑥
  CSLFD M3 .... 6 A3
  NEWH/MOS M40 .... 85 D4 ⑦
Thomson Rd GTN M18 .... 116 A1
Thomson St BRUN/LGST M13 .... 28 B4 ①
Thoralby Cl WGTN/LGST M12 .... 40 C1
Thoresway Rd BRUN/LGST M13 .... 39 E5
Thor Gv SALQ/ORD M5 .... 14 B5
Thorley Cl CHAD OL9 .... 70 A3
Thorley Dr URM M41 .... 111 D3 ⑩
Thorley St FAIL M35 .... 88 B1
Thornage Dr NEWH/MOS M40 .... 8 B2 ②
Thorn Av FAIL M35 .... 88 B3
Thornbridge Av CCHDY M21 .... 126 B1 ⑪
Thornbury Rd STRET M32 .... 115 C1
Thornbury Wy GTN M18 .... 106 A4 ⑥
Thorncliff Av OLDS OL8 .... 73 C2
Thorncliffe Gv BNG/LEV M19 .... 116 A4
Thorncombe Rd OLDTF/WHR M16 ... 35 E4
Thorncross Cl HULME M15 .... 24 B2
Thornden Rd NEWH/MOS M40 .... 9 D2 ①
Thorne Av URM M41 .... 110 A2
Thorneycroft Av CCHDY M21 .... 126 B4
Thornfield Dr SWIN M27 .... 54 A4
Thornfield Rd BNG/LEV M19 .... 131 C4 ⑪
Thornfield St SALQ/ORD M5 .... 94 B4 ②
Thorngate Rd CHH M8 .... 83 C4 ①
Thorn Gv RUSH/FAL M14 .... 130 B1
Thornhill Cl DTN/ASHW M34 .... 118 A3 ②
Thornhill Rd DROY M43 .... 98 B3
Thornholme Cl GTN M18 .... 41 F4
Thorniley Brow ANC M4 .... 16 C1 ①
Thornlea Av OLDS OL8 .... 71 D4
  SWIN M27 .... 75 D3 ②
Thornleigh Rd RUSH/FAL M14 ...... 47 D4
Thornley La North RDSH SK5 .... 117 D2
Thornley La South RDSH SK5 .... 118 A3
Thornmere Cl SWIN M27 .... 57 C3 ②
Thorn Rd SWIN M27 .... 76 A3
Thornsett Cl BKLY M9 .... 85 C1 ⑮
The Thorns CCHDY M21 .... 126 B2 ⑦
Thornton Av DTN/ASHW M34 .... 109 C1
  URM M41 .... 110 A3
Thornton Rd RUSH/FAL M14 .... 47 D2
Thornton St NEWH/MOS M40 .... 8 B2
  OLDS OL8 .... 55 D4 ⑥
Thornton St North NEWH/MOS M40 ... 8 B1
  NEWH/MOS M40 .... 84 B1 ⑲
Thorntree Cl BKLY M9 .... 85 C2
Thornwood Av GTN M18 .... 117 C1 ⑧
Thorpe Av SWIN M27 .... 58 A4
Thorpebrook Rd NEWH/MOS M40 ... 86 A3
Thorpe Gv HTNM SK4 .... 133 D3

Thorpeness Sq GTN M18 .... 106 B3
Thorpe St OLDTF/WHR M16 .... 34 A2
Thorp Rd NEWH/MOS M40 .... 86 A3
Thorp St ECC M30 .... 100 B1
Thrapston Av DTN/ASHW M34 .... 99 D4
Throstles Cl DROY M43 .... 99 C2 ⑥
Thruxton Cl OLDTF/WHR M16 .... 35 F4 ①
Thurland St CHAD OL9 .... 52 A1 ②
Thurlby St BRUN/LGST M13 .... 39 D2 ①
Thurlestone Dr URM M41 .... 111 C2 ⑦
Thurloe St RUSH/FAL M14 .... 38 A4
Thurlow St SALQ/ORD M5 .... 12 B3
Thurlston Crs CHH M8 .... 83 D2 ⑧
Thurlwood Av DID/WITH M20 ...... 129 C2
Thursfield St SLFD M6 .... 80 B4
Tiber Av OLDS OL8 .... 72 A4
Tib La CMANW M2 .... 16 B3
Tib St ANC M4 .... 17 D2
Tideswell Av NEWH/MOS M40 .... 8 C3
Tideswell Rd DROY M43 .... 97 C2 ②
Tideway Cl SWIN M27 .... 79 D1
Tidworth Av ANC M4 .... 18 B1
Tilbury St OLD OL1 .... 55 C1
Tilney Av STRET M32 .... 115 C4
Timothy Cl SLFD M6 .... 93 D2 ③
Timperley St CHAD OL9 .... 54 B2 ⑦
  OP/CLY M11 .... 106 A1 ⑧
Timson St FAIL M35 .... 88 B2
Tindall St ECC M30 .... 100 B1
  RDSH SK5 .... 117 D2 ⑪
Tinningham Cl OP/CLY M11 .... 107 C2 ⑲
Tinshill Cl WGTN/LGST M12 .... 40 C1
Tinsley Cl NEWH/MOS M40 .... 9 E5
Tintern Av DID/WITH M20 .... 128 B4
  URM M41 .... 120 A1
Tintern Gv STKP SK1 .... 139 D4
Tintern St RUSH/FAL M14 .... 47 F1
Tirza Av BNG/LEV M19 .... 131 D2
Titherington Cl RDSH SK5 .... 116 B4 ①
Titterington Av CCHDY M21 .... 43 E1
Tiverton Rd URM M41 .... 112 A1
Tiviot Dr STKP SK1 .... 138 B3
Tiviot Wy RDSH SK5 .... 138 B2
Tivoli St CSLFD M3 .... 15 F3
Tobermory Cl OP/CLY M11 .... 96 B4 ⑦
Todd St ANC M4 .... 6 C5
  BRO M7 .... 81 D3
Toft Rd GTN M18 .... 116 A1
Togford Cl OLDTF/WHR M16 .... 35 F3 ①
Toledo St OP/CLY M11 .... 96 B4
Tollard Av NEWH/MOS M40 .... 84 B4 ⑳
Toll Bar St WGTN/LGST M12 .... 29 F4
Tollesbury Cl NEWH/MOS M40 .... 8 C1
Toll Gate Cl BRUN/LGST M13 .... 39 F2
Tolworth Dr CHH M8 .... 83 D2
Tomcroft La DTN/ASHW M34 ...... 119 D3
Tomlinson Cl OLDS OL8 .... 55 C4
Tomlinson St NEWH/MOS M40 ...... 69 C2 ③
Tommy Browell Cl RUSH/FAL M14 ... 37 D4
Tommy Taylor Cl
  NEWH/MOS M40 .... 87 C4 ⑰
Tonbridge Rd BNG/LEV M19 .... 132 B1
  RDSH SK5 .... 134 B3 ⑤
Tonge St WGTN/LGST M12 .... 29 D1
Tonman St CSLFD M3 .... 15 F4
Tootal Dr SLFD M6 .... 94 A2
Tootal Gv SLFD M6 .... 94 A3
Tootal Rd SALQ/ORD M5 .... 94 A3
Topaz St OP/CLY M11 .... 20 A2
Topley St BKLY M9 .... 84 A3
Top O' Th' Gn CHAD OL9 .... 72 A1
Torah St CHH M8 .... 6 C1
Torbay Rd CCHDY M21 .... 127 C1

URM M41 .... **112** A4
Torkington Av *SWIN* M27 .... **58** B4 **7**
Torquay Cl *BRUN/LGST* M13 .... **28** B5
Torrax Cl *SLFD* M6 .... **77** D3 **5**
Torrens St *SLFD* M6 .... **78** B4 **7**
Torrington Av *BKLY* M9 .... **68** A3 **1**
Torrington Rd *SWIN* M27 .... **77** D3
Totland Cl *WGTN/LGST* M12 .... **41** D4
Totnes Rd *CCHDY* M21 .... **127** C1
SALE M33 .... **121** D4
Tottington St *OP/CLY* M11 .... **96** A3 **15**
Totton Rd *FAIL* M35 .... **88** B2
Towcester Cl *ANC* M4 .... **19** D2 **7**
Towey Cl *GTN* M18 .... **106** B3
Townfield *URM* M41 .... **110** B4
Town Hall La *CMANW* M2 .... **16** B3 **7**
Town La *DTN/ASHW* M34 .... **119** D4
Townley St *CHH* M8 .... **82** B4 **4**
OP/CLY M11 .... **20** A4
Townsend Rd *SWIN* M27 .... **58** B4
Towton St *BKLY* M9 .... **85** C1
Towyn Av *SALQ/ORD* M5 .... **13** D1
Toxteth St *OP/CLY* M11 .... **107** C4
Tracey St *CHH* M8 .... **65** C4 **4**
Traders Av *URM* M41 .... **102** A3
Trafalgar Av *DTN/ASHW* M34 .... **109** C2
Trafalgar Gv *BRO* M7 .... **81** D4 **11**
Trafalgar Rd *SALE* M33 .... **124** A3 **6**
SLFD M6 .... **93** C2
Trafalgar St *BRO* M7 .... **82** A4
OLD L1 .... **55** C1
Trafford Av *URM* M41 .... **112** A2 **7**
Trafford Bank Rd
OLDTF/WHR M16 .... **24** A5 **3**
Trafford Gv *STRET* M32 .... **114** B4 **4**
Trafford Park Rd *TRPK* M17 .... **22** C5
Trafford Pl *HULME* M15 .... **24** C4
Trafford Rd *ECC* M30 .... **101** D1
SALQ/ORD M5 .... **23** D3
TRPK M17 .... **22** C5
Trafford St *CSLFD* M3 .... **15** F5
OLDS OL8 .... **55** C4 **8**
Trafford Wharf Rd *TRPK* M17 .... **104** A2
Trail St *SLFD* M6 .... **95** C3
Tram St *OP/CLY* M11 .... **106** A2
Tranmere Cl *GTN* M18 .... **31** F5
Transvaal St *OP/CLY* M11 .... **96** B4
Travis St *CMANE* M1 .... **18** A4
Tree Av *DROY* M43 .... **98** A2
Trenam Pl *SALQ/ORD* M5 .... **13** E1 **6**
Trenant Rd *SLFD* M6 .... **78** B4
Trent Av *CHAD* OL9 .... **52** A1
Trent Cl *RDSH* SK5 .... **136** A4
Trentham Gv *NEWH/MOS* M40 .... **68** A4
Trentham Rd *OLDTF/WHR* M16 ...... **33** D5 **1**
Trentham St *HULME* M15 .... **24** B2
SWIN M27 .... **58** A4 **8**
Tresco Av *STRET* M32 .... **115** C4
Trevelyan St *ECC* M30 .... **93** C3 **9**
Trevor Dr *NEWH/MOS* M40 .... **70** A3
Trevor Rd *ECC* M30 .... **90** B2
SWIN M27 .... **76** B3
Trevor St *OP/CLY* M11 .... **107** C2 **20**
Trimdon Cl *OP/CLY* M11 .... **21** F1
Trimley Av *NEWH/MOS* M40 .... **84** B4 **21**
Trinity St *OLD* OL1 .... **55** C1
Trinity Wy *CSLFD* M3 .... **15** E2
Triscombe Wy *OLDTF/WHR* M16 .... **35** E4
Tristam Cl *BRUN/LGST* M13 .... **28** A2 **2**
Trojan St *BRO* M7 .... **81** C4 **15**
Trough Ga *OLDS* OL8 .... **72** B3
Troutbeck Av *ANC* M4 .... **18** B1
Trowbridge Dr *NEWH/MOS* M40 ...... **69** C4

Trowtree Av *WGTN/LGST* M12 .... **29** F3
Troydale Dr *NEWH/MOS* M40 .... **86** A4
Trumpet St *CMANE* M1 .... **16** A5
Truro Av *RDSH* SK5 .... **136** A5
STRET M32 .... **115** C3
Trust Rd *GTN* M18 .... **116** A2
Tudbury Wy *CSLFD* M3 .... **5** D5
Tudor Av *BKLY* M9 .... **67** C4
CHAD OL9 .... **69** D2
Tudor Cl *RDSH* SK5 .... **134** A2
Tudor Ct *PWCH* M25 .... **63** C2
Tudor St *OLDS* OL8 .... **54** B4
Tuer St *BRUN/LGST* M13 .... **27** D4
Tuley St *OP/CLY* M11 .... **30** A1
Tulip Cl *CHAD* OL9 .... **52** A2
Tully Pl *CSLFD* M3 .... **5** F2 **1**
Tully St *BRO* M7 .... **82** A3 **18**
Tully St South *BRO* M7 .... **82** A3
Tulpen Sq *CHAD* OL9 .... **53** D2 **7**
Tunstall St *HTNM* SK4 .... **138** A3 **10**
OP/CLY M11 .... **107** C2 **21**
Tunstead Av *DID/WITH* M20 .... **128** B3
Turf La *CHAD* OL9 .... **70** B2
Turley St *CHH* M8 .... **83** D3 **8**
Turnbull Rd *BRUN/LGST* M13 .... **50** B2
GTN M18 .... **117** D2
Turnbury Cl *SALE* M33 .... **123** D3 **8**
Turncroft La *STKP* SK1 .... **139** C4
Turnell Wy *WALK* M28 .... **74** A4
Turner Av *FAIL* M35 .... **88** A3
Turner Dr *URM* M41 .... **112** B3
Turner La *MPL/ROM* SK6 .... **137** D3
Turner St *ANC* M4 .... **17** D1
BRO M7 .... **82** A2 **8**
GTN M18 .... **106** B4 **13**
HULME M15 .... **24** A3
OP/CLY M11 .... **96** A4
Turn Moss Rd *STRET* M32 .... **42** A5
Turton St *OP/CLY* M11 .... **106** B2 **9**
Tuscany Av *BRO* M7 .... **80** B1
Tutbury St *ANC* M4 .... **18** C3
Tuxford Wk *NEWH/MOS* M40 .... **84** B4 **22**
Tweedale Wy *CHAD* OL9 .... **71** C3
FAIL M35 .... **71** C4
Tweed Cl *OLDS* OL8 .... **55** C4
Tweedle Hill Rd *BKLY* M9 .... **65** D1
Twillbrook Dr *CSLFD* M3 .... **5** F4 **8**
Twining Rd *TRPK* M17 .... **102** A1
Tydden St *OLDS* OL8 .... **73** D2 **8**
Tyldesley St *RUSH/FAL* M14 .... **37** D4
Tymm St *NEWH/MOS* M40 .... **87** C1
Tyndall Av *NEWH/MOS* M40 .... **68** A4
Tynedale Cl *RDSH* SK5 .... **134** A4
Tyro St *OLDS* OL8 .... **73** D2 **7**
Tyrrel Rd *RDSH* SK5 .... **117** D2 **7**
Tysoe Gdns *CSLFD* M3 .... **5** D5
Tyson St *CHH* M8 .... **82** B1
Tytherington Dr *RDSH* SK5 .... **116** B4

U

Ukraine Rd *BRO* M7 .... **80** A3
Ulverston Av *CHAD* OL9 .... **53** C3
DID/WITH M20 .... **129** C2 **6**
Under La *CHAD* OL9 .... **71** D2
Underwood Cl *GTN* M18 .... **107** D3
Unicorn St *ECC* M30 .... **100** B1 **8**
Union St *ANC* M4 .... **17** D1 **5**
CHAD OL9 .... **71** D1
GTN M18 .... **107** C3 **15**
OLD OL1 .... **55** D3

RUSH/FAL M14 .... 37 F5
SLFD M6 .... 3 D1
SWIN M27 .... 76 A1 ⑥
WGTN/LGST M12 .... 28 B1
Union St West *CHAD* OL9 .... 55 C5
OLDS OL8 .... 55 C4
United Rd *OLDTF/WHR* M16 .... 32 A1
Unity Dr *BRO* M7 .... 82 A3
University Rd *SALQ/ORD* M5 .... 3 F5
SLFD M6 .... 3 F6
University Rd West *SALQ/ORD* M5 .. 3 F5
Unwin Av *GTN* M18 .... 116 B1
Upland Rd *OLDS* OL8 .... 73 C1
Upper Brook St *BRUN/LGST* M13 .. 27 E3
STKP SK1 .... 139 C4 ⑩
Upper Camp St *BRO* M7 .... 81 D4
Upper Chorlton Rd
OLDTF/WHR M16 .... 34 B5
Upper Cleminson St *CSLFD* M3 .... 14 C1
Upper Conran St *BKLY* M9 .... 85 C1
Upper Cyrus St *NEWH/MOS* M40 .. 19 E1
Upper Dover St *OP/CLY* M11 ...... 20 C2 ⑪
Upper Gloucester St *SLFD* M6 ...... 3 D3
Upper Helena St *NEWH/MOS* M40 .. 9 E5
Upper Kent Rd *RUSH/FAL* M14 ... 39 D4
Upper Kirby St *ANC* M4 .... 18 B2
Upper Lloyd St *RUSH/FAL* M14 ... 37 D4
Upper Medlock St *HULME* M15 .... 26 B3
Upper Monsall St *NEWH/MOS* M40 .. 85 C3
Upper Moss La *HULME* M15 .... 25 E4
Upper Park Rd *BRO* M7 .... 63 D4 ⑪
BRO M7 .... 64 B4 ⑥
RUSH/FAL M14 .... 38 C1
Upper West Gv *BRUN/LGST* M13 .. 38 C1
Upper Wharf St *SALQ/ORD* M5 .... 14 B2
Upper Wilton St *PWCH* M25 .... 63 C1 ⑭
Upton St *CMANE* M1 .... 17 E3 ⑥
Urmson St *OLDS* OL8 .... 73 D2
Urmston La *STRET* M32 .... 113 C4
Urmston Pk *URM* M41 .... 112 A3 ⑥

V

Vaal St *OLDS* OL8 .... 72 A2
Valance Cl *WGTN/LGST* M12 ...... 31 D3
Vale *SALE* M33 .... 125 C4
SWIN M27 .... 59 C4
Vale Dr *CHAD* OL9 .... 54 B3
PWCH M25 .... 62 A3
Vale La *FAIL* M35 .... 89 C4
Vale Rd *DROY* M43 .... 98 B2
Vale St *OP/CLY* M11 .... 96 A3
Vale Top Av *BKLY* M9 .... 85 D2 ⑬
Valetta Cl *RUSH/FAL* M14 .... 47 E5
Valley Rd *MPL/ROM* SK6 .... 140 B1
Vancouver Quay *SALQ/ORD* M5 .... 22 B1
Vandyke Av *SLFD* M6 .... 93 D2
Vane St *ECC* M30 .... 91 D3 ⑥
Varey St *GTN* M18 .... 106 B4 ⑭
Varley St *NEWH/MOS* M40 .... 9 D2
Varna St *OP/CLY* M11 .... 106 A1
Vauban Dr *SLFD* M6 .... 93 D2
Vaughan Av *NEWH/MOS* M40 ...... 86 A1 ⑥
Vaughan Rd *CCHDY* M21 .... 44 C5
Vaughan St *ECC* M30 .... 90 B2
WGTN/LGST M12 .... 30 B2
Vauxhall St *NEWH/MOS* M40 .... 7 F2
Vega St *CHH* M8 .... 5 F1

Velour Cl *CSLFD* M3 .... 4 C3
Vendale Av *SWIN* M27 .... 75 D3
Venetia St *NEWH/MOS* M40 ...... 87 C4 ⑱
Venice St *CMANE* M1 .... 17 D5 ⑥
SALE M33 .... 123 D3
Ventnor Av *BNG/LEV* M19 .... 133 C1 ⑥
SALE M33 .... 123 D3
Ventnor St *BKLY* M9 .... 84 B1
SLFD M6 .... 80 B4 ⑥
Ventura Cl *RUSH/FAL* M14 .... 47 D4
Venture Scout Wy *BRO* M7 ...... 82 B3 ⑰
Venwood Rd *PWCH* M25 .... 61 D3
Verdon St *ANC* M4 .... 6 C4
Verdun Av *SLFD* M6 .... 93 D2
Verdun Rd *ECC* M30 .... 90 B1
Verdure Cl *FAIL* M35 .... 89 D1
Vere St *SALQ/ORD* M5 .... 12 A3
Verity Cl *DID/WITH* M20 .... 129 D3
Verne Av *SWIN* M27 .... 76 A1
Vernon Av *ECC* M30 .... 92 B3 ⑩
STKP SK1 .... 139 D3
STRET M32 .... 114 B4
Vernon Dr *PWCH* M25 .... 62 A3
Vernon Rd *BRO* M7 .... 63 C4
DROY M43 .... 97 C3 ⑥
MPL/ROM SK6 .... 140 B3
Vernon St *BKLY* M9 .... 85 C2
BRO M7 .... 81 D4
OLDTF/WHR M16 .... 34 B1
Verona Dr *NEWH/MOS* M40 .... 96 A1
Vesper St *FAIL* M35 .... 89 C1
Vesta St *ANC* M4 .... 18 B2
Vestris Dr *SLFD* M6 .... 93 D2
Viaduct St *CSLFD* M3 .... 5 F5
EDGY/DAV SK3 .... 138 A4
WGTN/LGST M12 .... 19 D3
Vicarage Cl *SLFD* M6 .... 93 D2
Vicarage Gv *ECC* M30 .... 92 B3
Vicarage Rd *SWIN* M27 .... 76 A1
URM M41 .... 110 B1
Vicarage St *OLDS* OL8 .... 72 A3
Vicars Rd *CCHDY* M21 .... 126 A1
Vicars St *ECC* M30 .... 92 B3
Vicker Cl *SWIN* M27 .... 58 B3 ⑭
Vicker Gv *DID/WITH* M20 .... 128 B4
Vickers St *NEWH/MOS* M40 .... 9 E3
Victoria Av *BNG/LEV* M19 .... 50 C5
ECC M30 .... 92 B2 ②
MPL/ROM SK6 .... 141 D2
SWIN M27 .... 77 C1 ⑨
Victoria Av East *BKLY* M9 .... 67 D1
Victoria Bridge St *CSLFD* M3 .... 6 A5
Victoria Crs *ECC* M30 .... 92 B2
Victoria Gv *HTNM* SK4 .... 133 C4
RUSH/FAL M14 .... 130 A2
Victoria La *SWIN* M27 .... 75 D1
Victoria Ldg *BRO* M7 .... 81 C4 ⑯
Victoria Rd *BNG/LEV* M19 .... 50 B3
ECC M30 .... 92 A2
OLDTF/WHR M16 .... 45 D1
RUSH/FAL M14 .... 47 E5
SLFD M6 .... 93 C1
STKP SK1 .... 139 D2
STRET M32 .... 114 B3
URM M41 .... 110 B2
Victoria Station Ap *CSLFD* M3 ...... 6 B5
Victoria St *CHAD* OL9 .... 53 D2
CSLFD M3 .... 6 B5
FAIL M35 .... 87 D3
OP/CLY M11 .... 106 A1
Victoria Ter *WGTN/LGST* M12 ... 40 B2
Victor Mann St *OP/CLY* M11 ... 108 A2
Victor St *CSLFD* M3 .... 15 D1
NEWH/MOS M40 .... 8 A2

OLDS OL8 .... **71** D4
Victory Gv DTN/ASHW M34 ...... **109** C2 🔟
Victory St RUSH/FAL M14 .... **38** A5
Viking Cl OP/CLY M11 .... **20** A2
Village Ct TRPK M17 .... **104** A3
Village St BRO M7 .... **81** C4 🔢
Village Wy (Ashburton Rd East)
 TRPK M17 .... **103** D3
Villa Rd OLDS OL8 .... **73** D1
Villiers Dr OLDS OL8 .... **55** C4
Villiers St SLFD M6 .... **2** B1
Vinca Gv BRO M7 .... **81** D3 🔢
Vincent Av CCHDY M21 .... **43** D4
Vincent St BRO M7 .... **81** D2
 OP/CLY M11 .... **106** A1
Vine Av SWIN M27 .... **77** D1
Vine Cl SALE M33 .... **121** C4
Vine Ct STRET M32 .... **114** B4
Vine Fold NEWH/MOS M40 ...... **70** B4 🔢
Vine St BRO M7 .... **80** B1
 CHAD OL9 .... **71** D2
 ECC M30 .... **91** C4
 OP/CLY M11 .... **107** C2
Viola St OP/CLY M11 .... **96** B3
Violet St GTN M18 .... **107** D3
Virgil St HULME M15 .... **24** C3
Viscount St RUSH/FAL M14 ...... **38** A4
Vixen Cl CCHDY M21 .... **128** A2
Voltaire Av SLFD M6 .... **93** D2
Vorlich Dr CHAD OL9 .... **52** B1 🔢
Vyner Gv SALE M33 .... **122** B3

W

Waddington St CHAD OL9 ...... **54** A1
Wadeford Cl ANC M4 .... **8** A4 🔢
Wadeson Rd BRUN/LGST M13 ...... **27** F2
Wade Wk OP/CLY M11 .... **21** D5
Wadlow Cl CSLFD M3 .... **5** E4 ②
Wadsworth Ms DROY M43 ...... **97** D4 🔢
Waggoners Ct SWIN M27 ...... **76** B2 🔢
Wagstaffe Dr FAIL M35 .... **88** B2
Wain Cl ECC M30 .... **90** B3 🔢
Wainman St SLFD M6 .... **80** B4
Wainwright Av DTN/ASHW M34 ... **117** D2
Wainwright St OLDS OL8 ...... **55** C4 🔢
Wakefield Dr SWIN M27 .... **57** D1
Wakefield St CMANE M1 .... **26** C1 🔢
Wakeling Rd DTN/ASHW M34 ... **137** C1
Walcott Cl BRUN/LGST M13 ...... **39** D1
Wald Av RUSH/FAL M14 .... **131** C2
Walden Cl RUSH/FAL M14 .... **47** D5
Walderton Av NEWH/MOS M40 ... **86** A3
Walford St OLDTF/WHR M16 ...... **35** E3 ②
Walker Av FAIL M35 .... **89** D3 🔢
Walker Cl BKLY M9 .... **67** C1
 CHAD OL9 .... **70** B3
 ECC M30 .... **90** A1
Walker's Cft CSLFD M3 .... **6** B5
Walker's Rd OLDS OL8 .... **72** A3
Walker St OLDS OL8 .... **54** B3 🔢
 STKP SK1 .... **138** A4
Wallace Av RUSH/FAL M14 ...... **38** C5
Wallace St OLDS OL8 .... **73** D1 🔢
Wallasey Av RUSH/FAL M14 ...... **47** C4
Waller Av RUSH/FAL M14 .... **48** A5
Wallingford Rd URM M41 ...... **112** A3
Wallis St CHAD OL9 .... **71** C1
 NEWH/MOS M40 .... **87** C4 🔢
Wallness La SLFD M6 .... **4** A3
Wall St OLDS OL8 .... **55** D4

SLFD M6 .... **12** B1
Wall Wy GTN M18 .... **117** C1
Wallwork St OP/CLY M11 ...... **107** C1
 RDSH SK5 .... **117** D5 🔢
Wally Sq BRO M7 .... **82** A3 🔢
Walmersley Rd NEWH/MOS M40 ... **70** A3
Walmer St GTN M18 .... **107** C3
 RUSH/FAL M14 .... **37** F4
Walmer St East RUSH/FAL M14 ... **38** A4
Walmsley Gv URM M41 .... **111** D3 🔢
Walmsley St RDSH SK5 .... **138** B2 🔢
Walnut Cl SWIN M27 .... **57** D1
Walnut Rd ECC M30 .... **90** A1
Walnut St GTN M18 .... **106** B3
Walnut Wk STRET M32 .... **124** A1
Walsall St SLFD M6 .... **80** A4
Walsden St OP/CLY M11 .... **96** A3
Walsh Av BKLY M9 .... **66** B3 🔢
Walshaw Dr SWIN M27 .... **76** B2
Walsh St CHAD OL9 .... **53** D3
Walter St BKLY M9 .... **84** B1 🔢
 GTN M18 .... **107** C3
 OLDTF/WHR M16 .... **34** A2
 PWCH M25 .... **61** D1 🔢
Waltham Rd OLDTF/WHR M16 ...... **45** F3
Walton Hall Dr RDSH SK5 ...... **116** B4
Walwyn Cl STRET M32 .... **115** C4
Wandsworth Av OP/CLY M11 ...... **96** B1
Wansbeck Cl STRET M32 ...... **115** C4 🔢
Wansford St RUSH/FAL M14 ...... **37** D5
Wanstead Av BKLY M9 .... **68** A2
Warbeck Cl RDSH SK5 .... **118** A3
Warbeck Rd NEWH/MOS M40 ...... **69** D3
Warburton St ECC M30 .... **92** A4
 SALQ/ORD M5 .... **23** E3
Warden St NEWH/MOS M40 ...... **86** B3
Warde St HULME M15 .... **25** F4
Wardle Cl STRET M32 .... **115** C3
Wardle St NEWH/MOS M40 .... **9** D4
Wardley Av OLDTF/WHR M16 ...... **45** E5
Wardley Hall La WALK M28 ...... **74** A1
Wardley Hall Rd WALK M28 ...... **56** B4
Wardley St SWIN M27 .... **76** B3 ②
Ward Rd DROY M43 .... **98** B4
Ward St BKLY M9 .... **66** A3
 CHAD OL9 .... **54** A2
 FAIL M35 .... **88** A1
 MPL/ROM SK6 .... **141** D2
 NEWH/MOS M40 .... **85** D1
 OLD OL1 .... **54** B1
Wareham Gv ECC M30 .... **91** C2 🔢
Wareham St CHH M8 .... **65** D4 ②
Warford St ANC M4 .... **7** E3
Warley Rd OLDTF/WHR M16 ...... **32** C5
Warmington Dr WGTN/LGST M12 ... **29** E4
Warne Av DROY M43 .... **99** C3
Warnford Cl NEWH/MOS M40 ...... **96** B1
Warren Bank BKLY M9 .... **66** B2 🔢
Warren Bruce Rd TRPK M17 ...... **104** B3
Warren Cl DTN/ASHW M34 ...... **119** D3
Warren Dr SWIN M27 .... **75** D4
Warren Rd TRPK M17 .... **103** D3
Warren St BKLY M9 .... **66** A3 🔢
 BRO M7 .... **82** B1
 STKP SK1 .... **138** B3
Warrington Rd BKLY M9 .... **66** A1
Warwick Av BKLY M9 .... **57** D3
Warwick Ct OLDTF/WHR M16 ...... **33** C4
Warwick Dr URM M41 .... **110** B1
Warwick Gv DTN/ASHW M34 ...... **109** C1
Warwick Rd CCHDY M21 .... **43** E4
 FAIL M35 .... **88** B4

STRET M32 .... 32 C2
Warwick Rd South
  OLDTF/WHR M16 .... 32 C4
Warwick St ANC M4 .... 17 E1
  CHAD OL9 .... 54 A4
  CHAD OL9 .... 72 A1 🔢
  HULME M15 .... 25 F5
  PWCH M25 .... 61 D1 🔢
  SWIN M27 .... 58 B4
Wasdale Av URM M41 .... 110 B2
Wash Brook CHAD OL9 .... 71 D1
Washbrook Dr STRET M32 .... 113 D4
Washington St CHAD OL9 .... 54 A2 🔢
Waterbridge WALK M28 .... 74 A4
Waterfield Wy FAIL M35 .... 89 C3
Waterfront Quay SALQ/ORD M5 .. 22 C2
Watergate DTN/ASHW M34 .... 109 D1 🔢
Waterhouse Rd GTN M18 .... 117 C1
Water La DROY M43 .... 97 C4
Waterloo Rd BKLY M9 .... 66 A4
  CHH M8 .... 5 F1 🔢
  STKP SK1 .... 138 B4
Waterloo St CHH M8 .... 84 A1
  CMANE M1 .... 16 C4 🔢
  OLD OL1 .... 55 D2
Waterpark Rd BRO M7 .... 82 A1
Waterside TRPK M17 .... 22 A4
Waterslea ECC M30 .... 91 C3
Watersmeet STRET M32 .... 114 A1
Waterson Av NEWH/MOS M40 .... 86 A2
Water's Reach TRPK M17 .... 22 B4
Water St BKLY M9 .... 84 B1
  CSLFD M3 .... 14 C5
  STKP SK1 .... 139 C2
Watford St RUSH/FAL M14 .... 47 E2 🔢
Watkin Cl BRUN/LGST M13 .... 27 F4
Watkins Dr PWCH M25 .... 64 A2
Watkin St CSLFD M3 .... 5 D3
Watson Sq STKP SK1 .... 138 B4 🔢🔢
Watson St CMANW M2 .... 16 A5
  ECC M30 .... 91 C3
  SWIN M27 .... 58 B4
Watts St BNG/LEV M19 .... 132 B1
  CHAD OL9 .... 53 D2
  OLDS OL8 .... 72 B3
Waugh Av FAIL M35 .... 88 B3
Waverley Crs DROY M43 .... 98 A2
Waverley Rd BKLY M9 .... 85 D2
  SALE M33 .... 124 A3
  SWIN M27 .... 78 A2
Waverley Rd West NEWH/MOS M40 .. 85 D3
Waverton Av HTNM SK4 .... 133 D2
Waverton Rd RUSH/FAL M14 ...... 47 D3
Wavertree Rd BKLY M9 .... 66 A1
Wayfarers Wy SWIN M27 .... 76 A2
Wayland Rd GTN M18 .... 116 B2
Wayland Rd South RDSH SK5 ... 116 B2
Wayne Cl DROY M43 .... 99 C1 🔢
Wayne St OP/CLY M11 .... 107 C1 🔢
Weald Cl BRUN/LGST M13 .... 28 A3
Weaste Dr SLFD M6 .... 94 B2
Weaste La SALQ/ORD M5 .... 94 B4 🔢
  SLFD M6 .... 94 B2
Weaste Rd SALQ/ORD M5 .... 94 B4
Weatherall St North BRO M7 ..... 82 B2
Weatherley Cl OLDS OL8 .... 73 D4 🔢
Weaverham Cl BRUN/LGST M13 .. 40 B5 🔢
Webdale Dr NEWH/MOS M40 ..... 86 A2 🔢
Webster Gv PWCH M25 .... 61 D3
Webster St OLDS OL8 .... 55 D4
Wedgewood St NEWH/MOS M40 .. 10 A2
Wedgwood Rd SWIN M27 .... 59 D3
Weedall Av SALQ/ORD M5 .... 23 D3

Weir St FAIL M35 .... 88 A2
  HULME M15 .... 25 F5 🔢
Welbeck Av CHAD OL9 .... 69 D2
  URM M41 .... 112 A2
Welbeck Gv BRO M7 .... 82 A2
Welbeck Rd ECC M30 .... 92 A1
  RDSH SK5 .... 134 B1 🔢
  WALK M28 .... 74 B3
Welbeck St GTN M18 .... 106 B3
Welby St BRUN/LGST M13 .... 39 D2
Welcomb Cl MPL/ROM SK6 ...... 141 D1 🔢
Welcomb St OP/CLY M11 .... 31 F1
Weld Rd DID/WITH M20 .... 130 B2 🔢
Welford Gn RDSH SK5 .... 134 B4 🔢
Welford Rd CHH M8 .... 64 B1
Welford St SLFD M6 .... 3 F1
Welkin Rd MPL/ROM SK6 .... 140 B4
Welland Cl HULME M15 .... 24 C4 🔢
Welland St OP/CLY M11 .... 106 B1
  RDSH SK5 .... 117 D4
Weller Av CCHDY M21 .... 127 D2
Wellesley Av GTN M18 .... 106 B3 🔢
Wellfield Rd CHH M8 .... 83 C1 🔢
Wellgate Av BNG/LEV M19 .... 132 B1 🔢
Wellhead Cl HULME M15 .... 26 B5
Wellhouse Dr BKLY M9 .... 68 B2
Welling Rd NEWH/MOS M40 ...... 88 A1
Wellington Av OLDTF/WHR M16 ... 44 C2
Wellington Cl SALE M33 .... 124 A3
Wellington Crs OLDTF/WHR M16 ... 34 A5
Wellington Gv HULME M15 .... 25 D4 🔢
Wellington Rd CHH M8 .... 83 D1 🔢
  DID/WITH M20 .... 130 A2 🔢
  ECC M30 .... 92 B3
  OLDS OL8 .... 54 B4
  OLDTF/WHR M16 .... 45 E1
  RUSH/FAL M14 .... 130 A2
  SWIN M27 .... 76 B1
Wellington Rd North HTNM SK4 ... 132 B2
Wellington Rd South HTNM SK4 .. 138 A4
Wellington St CHAD OL9 .... 53 D1
  CSLFD M3 .... 5 D5
  FAIL M35 .... 71 C4 🔢
  GTN M18 .... 106 B4
  OLDE OL4 .... 55 D3
  STKP SK1 .... 138 B4
  STRET M32 .... 114 A4
Wellington St East BRO M7 .... 81 D2
Wellington St West BRO M7 ...... 81 D3
Wellington Ter SALQ/ORD M5 .... 94 B3 🔢
Well Md MPL/ROM SK6 .... 141 C2
Wellmead Cl CHH M8 .... 82 B4
Wellock St NEWH/MOS M40 ...... 85 D3
Wells Av PWCH M25 .... 63 C3
Wells Cl OP/CLY M11 .... 107 D1 🔢
Well St ANC M4 .... 16 C1
Wellwood Dr NEWH/MOS M40 ... 86 A2 🔢
Welney Rd OLDTF/WHR M16 ...... 33 F4
Welwyn Cl URM M41 .... 101 C4
Welwyn Dr SLFD M6 .... 77 C4
Wembley Gv RUSH/FAL M14 .... 48 A5
Wembley Rd GTN M18 .... 116 A1
Wembury St BKLY M9 .... 85 C1 🔢
Wembury St North BKLY M9 ...... 85 C1 🔢
Wem St CHAD OL9 .... 71 C1
Wemyss Av RDSH SK5 .... 117 D4 🔢
Wendover Rd URM M41 .... 111 C3
Wenfield Dr BKLY M9 .... 68 A2
Wenlock St SWIN M27 .... 75 D1
Wenlock Wy WGTN/LGST M12 .... 30 B3
Wensley Dr DID/WITH M20 .... 129 D4
Wensley Rd BRO M7 .... 62 A4
  RDSH SK5 .... 138 B1

Wentworth Av *GTN* M18 .... **107** C4 🖪
  SLFD M6 .... **94** A2
Wentworth Dr *SALE* M33 .... **122** B4
Wentworth Rd *ECC* M30 .... **92** B1
  RDSH SK5 .... **117** D4 🖪
  SWIN M27 .... **75** D3 🔟
Wenworth Av *URM* M41 .... **110** B4
Werneth Av *RUSH/FAL* M14 .... **47** E2
Werneth Crs *OLDS* OL8 .... **72** A1
Werneth Hall Rd *OLDS* OL8 .... **54** B4
Werneth St *STKP* SK1 .... **139** D3 🖪
Wesley Sq *URM* M41 .... **110** A3 🖪
Wesley St *ECC* M30 .... **91** C3 🖪
  FAIL M35 .... **71** C4 🖪
  OP/CLY M11 .... **20** C5
  STKP SK1 .... **138** B4 🔟
  STRET M32 .... **115** C1
  SWIN M27 .... **76** B1
West Ashton St *SALO/ORD* M5 ...... **12** B3
West Av *BNG/LEV* M19 .... **131** D2 🖪
  GTN M18 .... **107** C4 🖪
  NEWH/MOS M40 .... **69** D4
West Bank *OP/CLY* M11 .... **108** A2
Westbank Rd *DID/WITH* M20 .... **130** B4
West Bank St *SALO/ORD* M5 .... **14** A4
Westbourne Gv *BKLY* M9 .... **84** B1 🖪
  RDSH SK5 .... **134** B1 🗗
Westbourne Pk *URM* M41 .... **111** D2
Westbourne Range *GTN* M18 .... **117** D2
Westbourne Rd *ECC* M30 .... **90** B1
  RUSH/FAL M14 .... **130** B1
  URM M41 .... **111** D3
Westbourne St *CHAD* OL9 .... **54** B2
Westbrook Rd *SWIN* M27 .... **76** A2
  TRPK M17 .... **104** A2
Westbrook Sq *WCTN/LGST* M12 .... **31** D3 🖪
Westbury Rd *CHH* M8 .... **65** C4
West Canteen Rd *TRPK* M17 .... **114** A1
West Central Dr *SWIN* M27 .... **77** D2 🖪
West Charles St *SALO/ORD* M5 ...... **13** F2
Westcott Av *DID/WITH* M20 .... **129** C3
Westcourt Rd *SALE* M33 .... **122** B4 🖪
Westcraig Av *NEWH/MOS* M40 ...... **69** C2
West Craven St *SALO/ORD* M5 ...... **23** E1
West Crown Av *SALO/ORD* M5 ...... **13** F4
Westdale Gdns *BNG/LEV* M19 ...... **132** A4
Westdean Crs *BNG/LEV* M19 .... **131** D4
West Dean St *SALO/ORD* M5 .... **14** B3 🖪
West Dr *DROY* M43 .... **97** D4
  SLFD M6 .... **79** C3
  SWIN M27 .... **77** D2
West Duke St *SALO/ORD* M5 .... **14** C3
West Egerton St *SALO/ORD* M5 ..... **13** E5
West End St *CHAD* OL9 .... **54** B2
Westerham Av *SALO/ORD* M5 .... **13** D2
Western Av *SWIN* M27 .... **60** B3
Western Cir *BNG/LEV* M19 .... **131** D3
Western St *GTN* M18 .... **107** C3
  SLFD M6 .... **95** C2
Westfield *SLFD* M6 .... **95** C1
Westfield Rd *CCHDY* M21 .... **43** F4
  DROY M43 .... **97** C3 🖪
Westfield St *BRO* M7 .... **63** D4
  CHAD OL9 .... **54** A1
Westgate *URM* M41 .... **110** B4
Westgate Av *BKLY* M9 .... **66** A3 🖪
Westgate Dr *SWIN* M27 .... **76** B3
Westgate Rd *SLFD* M6 .... **93** D1
West Gv *BRUN/LGST* M13 .... **38** B1
West High St *SALO/ORD* M5 .... **13** D1
Westholm Av *HTNM* SK4 .... **132** B2
Westholme Rd *DID/WITH* M20 .... **129** D4
West Hope St *SALO/ORD* M5 .... **13** F2

Westinghouse Rd *TRPK* M17 .... **103** D3
West King St *CSLFD* M3 .... **5** E5
Westlake St *OP/CLY* M11 .... **106** A2 🖪
Westland Av *STKP* SK1 .... **139** D4 🖪
Westland Dr *BKLY* M9 .... **66** B1
The Westlands *SWIN* M27 .... **77** D3
Westlea Dr *GTN* M18 .... **116** B2
Westleigh Dr *PWCH* M25 .... **63** D2
Westleigh St *BKLY* M9 .... **67** C4
West Marwood St *BRO* M7 .... **82** A3 🔟
Westmead Dr *CHH* M8 .... **82** A4 🖪🖪
West Meade *CCHDY* M21 .... **126** A2
  PWCH M25 .... **63** D3 🖪
  SWIN M27 .... **76** A3
West Meadow *RDSH* SK5 .... **118** A4
Westmere Dr *BKLY* M9 .... **84** A3
Westminster Av *HTNM* SK4 .... **134** A3
  OLDTF/WHR M16 .... **44** B2
Westminster Rd *ECC* M30 .... **92** A2
  FAIL M35 .... **89** D1
  URM M41 .... **111** D1
Westminster St *BNG/LEV* M19 .... **51** E3 🖪
  HULME M15 .... **24** B2 🖪
  SWIN M27 .... **57** D4
Westmorland Cl *RDSH* SK5 .... **136** A3 🖪
Westmorland Dr *RDSH* SK5 .... **135** D3
Westmorland Rd *ECC* M30 .... **77** C4
  URM M41 .... **111** C4
West Mosley St *CMANW* M2 .... **16** C3
Westmount Cl *NEWH/MOS* M40 ... **84** A3 🖪
Weston Av *NEWH/MOS* M40 .... **70** A4
  SWIN M27 .... **58** B1 🖪
  URM M41 .... **110** B4 🖪
Weston Gv *HTNM* SK4 .... **133** C3
Weston St *NEWH/MOS* M40 .... **19** D1 🖪
  RDSH SK5 .... **138** A1 🖪
Westover Rd *URM* M41 .... **111** C2
Westover St *SWIN* M27 .... **58** A4
West Park Rd *STKP* SK1 .... **139** D3
West Park St *SALO/ORD* M5 .... **23** F1
West Pl *BNG/LEV* M19 .... **131** D2 🖪
Westray Crs *SALO/ORD* M5 .... **95** C4 🖪🔟
Westray Rd *BRUN/LGST* M13 .... **49** F2
West Rd *STRET* M32 .... **113** C1
West Rw *PWCH* M25 .... **61** D4 🖪
West St *CHAD* OL9 .... **54** B3
  FAIL M35 .... **88** A3
  OLD OL1 .... **55** C2 🖪
  OP/CLY M11 .... **21** E1
West Towers St *SLFD* M6 .... **12** A2
Westville Gdns *BNG/LEV* M19 .... **131** C4 🖪🖪
Westway *DROY* M43 .... **108** A2
Westwood Av *BRO* M7 .... **82** A1 🖪
  NEWH/MOS M40 .... **70** A4 🖪
  URM M41 .... **112** B4 🖪
Westwood Crs *ECC* M30 .... **90** B1
Westwood Dr *CHAD* OL9 .... **54** B2 🖪
  SWIN M27 .... **78** A3
Westwood Rd *STRET* M32 .... **113** D3
Westwood St *RUSH/FAL* M14 .... **36** B3
West Works Rd *TRPK* M17 .... **114** A1
Wetherall St *BNG/LEV* M19 .... **51** E4
Wetherby St *OP/CLY* M11 .... **107** C2
Weybourne Av *BKLY* M9 .... **68** A3
Weybourne Dr *MPL/ROM* SK6 .... **141** D1 🖪
Weybridge Rd *ANC* M4 .... **18** B1
Weybrook Rd *HTNM* SK4 .... **132** B2
Weylands Gv *SLFD* M6 .... **77** D4
Weymouth Rd *ECC* M30 .... **90** B2
Whalley Av *BNG/LEV* M19 .... **51** E2 🖪
  CCHDY M21 .... **127** C2
  OLDTF/WHR M16 .... **34** C4
  SALE M33 .... **124** A4

URM M41 .... 112 A2
Whalley Gv *OLDTF/WHR* M16 ...... 45 D1
Whalley Rd *OLDTF/WHR* M16 .... 34 C5
Whalley St *NEWH/MOS* M40 .... 8 C5
Wharfedale Av *NEWH/MOS* M40 ... 68 A4
Wharfedale Rd *RDSH* SK5 .... 134 A1
Wharf End *TRPK* M17 .... 22 C4
Wharf Rd *SALE* M33 .... 124 A4
Wharfside Av *ECC* M30 .... 101 D1 3
Wharfside Wy (Trafford Park Rd)
TRPK M17 .... 105 C3
Wharf St *CHAD* OL9 .... 71 D2
HTNM SK4 .... 138 A2
Wharton Av *CCHDY* M21 .... 127 D2 3
Wharton Ldg *ECC* M30 .... 92 A2
Wheat Cl *BRUN/LGST* M13 .... 38 B1
Wheater's Crs *BRO* M7 .... 4 B2
Wheater's St *BRO* M7 .... 4 B2
Wheater's Ter *BRO* M7 .... 4 C2
Wheatley Rd *SWIN* M27 .... 57 D3
Wheeldon St *RUSH/FAL* M14 .... 36 C5
Wheler St *OP/CLY* M11 .... 106 B1
Whernside Av *NEWH/MOS* M40 ...... 68 A4
Whernside Cl *HTNM* SK4 .... 138 A3
Whickham Cl *RUSH/FAL* M14 .... 37 F4
Whiley St *BRUN/LGST* M13 .... 40 A3
Whimberry Cl *SALQ/ORD* M5 .... 23 F1
Whirley Cl *HTNM* SK4 .... 133 D4
Whiston Dr *CHH* M8 .... 83 D1
Whitburn Av *BRUN/LGST* M13 .... 49 F1
Whitby Av *OLDTF/WHR* M16 .... 35 D5
RUSH/FAL M14 .... 131 C1
SLFD M6 .... 94 A2
URM M41 .... 112 A3
Whitby Rd *RUSH/FAL* M14 .... 130 B1
Whitchurch Dr *OLDTF/WHR* M16 .... 35 D1 3
Whitchurch Rd *DID/WITH* M20 .... 128 B2
Whitchurch St *CSLFD* M3 .... 5 F3 3
Whiteacres *SWIN* M27 .... 75 C2
White Bank Av *RDSH* SK5 .... 140 A1
White Bank Rd *OLDS* OL8 .... 72 B4
Whitebeam Cl *SLFD* M6 .... 4 B2
Whitebrook Rd *RUSH/FAL* M14 ..... 47 F4
Whitecar Av *NEWH/MOS* M40 .... 54 A4
White City Wy *OLDTF/WHR* M16 .... 23 D5
Whitecliff Cl *RUSH/FAL* M14 .... 38 A5
Whitefield Rd *MPL/ROM* SK6 .... 141 C1
SALE M33 .... 122 B4
Whitegate Av *CHAD* OL9 .... 70 B1
Whitegate Cl *NEWH/MOS* M40 .... 70 A4
Whitegate Dr *SALQ/ORD* M5 .... 94 B3 11
SWIN M27 .... 59 D3
Whitegate La *CHAD* OL9 .... 70 B1
Whitegate Rd *CHAD* OL9 .... 69 D2
Whitehall St *OLD* OL1 .... 55 D1
Whitehead Rd *CCHDY* M21 .... 125 D1 4
SWIN M27 .... 59 D3
Whitehill Dr *NEWH/MOS* M40 .... 86 A2
Whitehill St *HTNM* SK4 .... 138 A1
RDSH SK5 .... 134 B4 8
White House Av *CHH* M8 .... 64 A2
Whitekirk Cl *BRUN/LGST* M13 .... 27 F3
Whiteley St *CHAD* OL9 .... 71 D1
OP/CLY M11 .... 21 F1
Whitelow Rd *CCHDY* M21 .... 43 D5
White Moss Av *CCHDY* M21 .... 44 B5
Whitemoss Rd *BKLY* M9 .... 67 D1
White Moss Rd *BKLY* M9 .... 67 D1 3
Whiteoak Rd *RUSH/FAL* M14 ...... 130 A1
Whites Cft *SWIN* M27 .... 76 B1
Whiteside Cl *SALQ/ORD* M5 ...... 94 B3 12
White St *HULME* M15 .... 24 C4
SLFD M6 .... 95 C4

White Swallows Rd *SWIN* M27 ...... 77 D3 3
Whitethorn Av *OLDTF/WHR* M16 .... 34 C4
Whitewater Dr *BRO* M7 .... 79 D2
Whiteway St *BKLY* M9 .... 85 C2
Whitewillow Cl *FAIL* M35 .... 89 C3
Whitfield Cl *CSLFD* M3 .... 6 C2 3
Whitland Dr *OLDS* OL8 .... 71 D3 3
Whit La *SLFD* M6 .... 79 D3
Whitley Rd *NEWH/MOS* M40 .... 8 B1
Whitman St *BKLY* M9 .... 85 D1
Whitmore Rd *RUSH/FAL* M14 .... 47 E3
Whitnall Cl *OLDTF/WHR* M16 .... 35 F4
Whitsbury Av *GTN* M18 .... 116 B2
Whitstable Cl *CHAD* OL9 .... 53 D3
Whitstable Rd *NEWH/MOS* M40 .... 69 C4 3
Whitswood Cl *OLDTF/WHR* M16 .... 35 F4 2
Whittaker La *PWCH* M25 .... 63 C1
Whittaker St *CHAD* OL9 .... 53 D2
NEWH/MOS M40 .... 86 A1 7
WGTN/LGST M12 .... 19 D5
Whittingham Gv *OLD* OL1 .... 54 B1 3
Whittle's Cft *CMANE* M1 .... 17 F3 3
Whittle St *ANC* M4 .... 17 E1 5
SWIN M27 .... 76 A2
Whitwell Wy *GTN* M18 .... 106 A4 10
Whitworth La *RUSH/FAL* M14 .... 49 D3
Whitworth St *CMANE* M1 .... 17 D5
OP/CLY M11 .... 31 F1
Whitworth St East *OP/CLY* M11 ... 106 A2
Whitworth St West *CMANE* M1 ..... 26 A1
Whixhall Av *WGTN/LGST* M12 .... 29 F3
Wickentree La *FAIL* M35 .... 70 B4 3
FAIL M35 .... 71 C4 3
Wicket Gv *SWIN* M27 .... 58 A1 4
Widdop St *CHAD* OL9 .... 54 B2
Widecombe Cl *URM* M41 .... 110 B1 3
Widgeon Cl *RUSH/FAL* M14 .... 47 E5 3
Widnes St *OP/CLY* M11 .... 106 A2 3
Wigley St *WGTN/LGST* M12 .... 29 F2
Wigmore Rd *CHH* M8 .... 83 D2 3
Wigsby Av *NEWH/MOS* M40 .... 69 C4
Wilberforce Cl *HULME* M15 .... 25 F5
Wilbraham Rd *CCHDY* M21 .... 42 C4
RUSH/FAL M14 .... 46 C4
Wilburn St *SALQ/ORD* M5 .... 14 C4
Wilby St *CHH* M8 .... 83 D3
Wilcock Cl *OLDTF/WHR* M16 .... 35 F3
Wilcott Dr *SALE* M33 .... 122 A4
Wildcroft Av *NEWH/MOS* M40 .... 68 A4 3
Wilderswood Cl *DID/WITH* M20 ... 130 A4 2
Wild St *MPL/ROM* SK6 .... 141 D3
Wilfred Rd *ECC* M30 .... 100 A1
Wilfred St *NEWH/MOS* M40 .... 86 A1
Wilfrid St *SWIN* M27 .... 76 B1 3
Wilkinson Rd *HTNM* SK4 .... 138 A3
Willan Rd *BKLY* M9 .... 66 A1
ECC M30 .... 92 A3 3
Willaston Cl *CCHDY* M21 .... 126 A2
Willdale Cl *OP/CLY* M11 .... 10 C5
Willerby Rd *BRO* M7 .... 82 A4 15
Willesden Av *BRUN/LGST* M13 ...... 39 E4
William Chadwick Cl
NEWH/MOS M40 .... 8 B3
William Cl *URM* M41 .... 111 C4
William Kay Cl *HULME* M15 .... 35 F2
William Lister Cl *NEWH/MOS* M40 .. 96 B1 3
Williams Crs *CHAD* OL9 .... 70 B2
Williamson La *DROY* M43 .... 108 B1
Williamson St *ANC* M4 .... 7 E5
RDSH SK5 .... 134 B2 3
RDSH SK5 .... 134 A2 14
Williams Rd *GTN* M18 .... 106 A4
NEWH/MOS M40 .... 86 B2

Williams St *GTN* M18 .... **116** A1
William St *CSLFD* M3 .... **15** E1
   FAIL M35 .... **71** C4
   WGTN/LGST M12 .... **18** C5
Willock St *BRO* M7 .... **82** A3
Willoughby Cl *SALE* M33 .... **123** C4
Willow Av *RDSH* SK5 .... **138** B1
   URM M41 .... **112** A3
Willow Bank *RUSH/FAL* M14 .... **48** B5
Willowbrook Av *NEWH/MOS* M40 ... **86** A2 ⁊
Willow Ct *SALE* M33 .... **125** C4 ⁊
Willowdene Cl *NEWH/MOS* M40 ..... **84** A4 ⁊
Willow Fold *DROY* M43 .... **108** A3
Willow Gv *CHAD* OL9 .... **53** D1 ⁊
   GTN M18 .... **117** C1 ⁊
Willow Hill Rd *CHH* M8 .... **65** C3
Willow Rd *ECC* M30 .... **90** A1
Willows Dr *FAIL* M35 .... **97** D1
Willows Rd *SALQ/ORD* M5 .... **94** B3 ⁊⁊
The Willows *CCHDY* M21 .... **126** A2 ⁊
Willow St *CHH* M8 .... **5** F1
   OP/CLY M11 .... **20** C3
   SWIN M27 .... **75** D4 ⁊
   SWIN M27 .... **75** C3 ⁊
Wilma Av *BKLY* M9 .... **66** A1
Wilmcote Rd *NEWH/MOS* M40 .... **8** C1
Wilmington Rd *STRET* M32 .... **113** D3 ⁊
Wilmott St *HULME* M15 .... **26** B2 ⁊
Wilmslow Rd *DID/WITH* M20 .... **129** D4
   RUSH/FAL M14 .... **38** A3
Wilmur Av *BRO* M7 .... **82** A3
Wilpshire Av *WGTN/LGST* M12 ..... **41** E5
Wilson Av *SWIN* M27 .... **59** D3
Wilson Rd *BKLY* M9 .... **66** B4
Wilson St *BRUN/LGST* M13 .... **28** B4
   OLDS OL8 .... **73** C1
   OP/CLY M11 .... **21** D4
   SALE M33 .... **123** D4 ⁊
   STRET M32 .... **115** C1
Wilstborpe Cl *BNG/LEV* M19 .... **133** C3
Wilton Av *OLDTF/WHR* M16 .... **32** C4
   PWCH M25 .... **63** D3
   SWIN M27 .... **78** A2
Wilton Ct *DTN/ASHW* M34 .... **118** A1
Wilton Gv *DTN/ASHW* M34 .... **118** A1
Wilton Paddock *DTN/ASHW* M34 .. **118** A1
Wilton Pl *CSLFD* M3 .... **14** C1 ⁊
Wilton Rd *CCHDY* M21 .... **126** B1
   CHH M8 .... **65** C3
   SLFD M6 .... **93** D1
Wilton St *CHAD* OL9 .... **71** D2
   PWCH M25 .... **63** C1 ⁊⁊
   RDSH SK5 .... **117** D3
Wiltshire Av *RDSH* SK5 .... **140** A1
Wiltshire Rd *CHAD* OL9 .... **53** D4
   FAIL M35 .... **88** B3
Wiltshire St *BRO* M7 .... **82** A3
Wimbledon St *FAIL* M35 .... **89** D1
Wimborne Av *URM* M41 .... **111** D1
Wimpory St *OP/CLY* M11 .... **106** B2
Winchester Av *PWCH* M25 .... **63** C3 ⁊
Winchester Rd *ECC* M30 .... **93** C1
   SLFD M6 .... **94** A1
   URM M41 .... **111** D2
Wincombe St *RUSH/FAL* M14 .... **47** F1 ⁊
Windcroft Cl *OP/CLY* M11 .... **20** B4
Winder Dr *ANC* M4 .... **18** B2
Windermere Av *DTN/ASHW* M34 ... **118** A3
   SWIN M27 .... **77** C2 ⁊
Windermere Cl *OP/CLY* M11 .... **21** D5
   STRET M32 .... **114** A2 ⁊
Windermere Rd *URM* M41 .... **111** C4 ⁊
Winders Wy *SLFD* M6 .... **3** E2

Windle Av *CHH* M8 .... **64** B3
Windmill Av *SALQ/ORD* M5 .... **23** F1
Windmill Cl *DTN/ASHW* M34 .... **118** B3 ⁊
Windmill La *DTN/ASHW* M34 .... **118** A3
   RDSH SK5 .... **117** D4
Windmill St *CMANW* M2 .... **16** A4
Windrush Dr *BKLY* M9 .... **84** B2 ⁊
Windsor Av *CHAD* OL9 .... **71** C1
   FAIL M35 .... **89** D1 ⁊
   SALE M33 .... **123** D3 ⁊
   SWIN M27 .... **59** D3
Windsor Dr *DTN/ASHW* M34 .... **109** D1
Windsor Rd *BKLY* M9 .... **85** C2
   BNG/LEV M19 .... **50** C3
   DROY M43 .... **96** B3
   DTN/ASHW M34 .... **118** A2
   MPL/ROM SK6 .... **140** A2
   NEWH/MOS M40 .... **97** C1
   OLDS OL8 .... **54** B4
   PWCH M25 .... **64** A2
Windsor St *FAIL* M35 .... **89** C1 ⁊
   GTN M18 .... **116** A1
   NEWH/MOS M40 .... **97** C1 ⁊
   SALQ/ORD M5 .... **13** E3
Winfell Dr *NEWH/MOS* M40 .... **9** D4
Winfield Av *DID/WITH* M20 .... **130** B4
Winfield Dr *GTN* M18 .... **106** B3 ⁊⁊
Winford St *BKLY* M9 .... **85** C1 ⁊⁊
Wingfield Av *SWIN* M27 .... **77** C3
Wingfield St *STRET* M32 .... **114** B1
Winifred Rd *NEWH/MOS* M40.......... **86** B2
   URM M41 .... **111** C2
Winifred St *ECC* M30 .... **90** B4 ⁊
Winnie St *NEWH/MOS* M40 .... **86** A1
Winnipeg Quay *SALQ/ORD* M5 ..... **22** B1
The Winnows *DTN/ASHW* M34 ...... **119** D2
Winscombe Dr *NEWH/MOS* M40 ..... **8** B2
Winser St *CMANE* M1 .... **16** C5
Winsford Rd *RUSH/FAL* M14 .... **46** C3
Winslow St *OP/CLY* M11 .... **21** D5
Winstanley Rd *NEWH/MOS* M40 ..... **8** C4
   SALE M33 .... **124** A4
Winster Av *BRO* M7 .... **80** B3
   STRET M32 .... **113** C2
Winster Rd *ECC* M30 .... **100** B1
Winston Rd *BKLY* M9 .... **67** D4 ⁊⁊
   BKLY M9 .... **85** D1 ⁊⁊
   SALE M33 .... **122** B4
Winterbottom St *CHAD* OL9 .... **54** B2 ⁊
Winterdyne St *BKLY* M9 .... **85** C2 ⁊⁊
Winterford Av *BRUN/LGST* M13 ..... **39** D1
Winterford Rd *CHH* M8 .... **82** B2
Wintermans Rd *CCHDY* M21 .... **127** D3
Winterton Rd *RDSH* SK5 .... **118** A4 ⁊
Winthrop Av *NEWH/MOS* M40 .... **84** B2 ⁊⁊
Winton Av *DTN/ASHW* M34............ **109** D2
   NEWH/MOS M40 .... **69** D4 ⁊
Winton Rd *SLFD* M6 .... **78** B4
Wirral Cl *SWIN* M27 .... **59** C3 ⁊
Wiseley St *OP/CLY* M11 .... **19** F5 ⁊
Wiseman Ter *PWCH* M25 .... **63** C1 ⁊⁊
Wishaw Sq *CCHDY* M21 .... **128** A2 ⁊
Wisley Cl *RDSH* SK5 .... **134** B1
Wistaria Rd *GTN* M18 .... **106** B4
Withington Rd *CCHDY* M21 .... **127** D1 ⁊
   OLDTF/WHR M16 .... **35** D4
Withington St *SLFD* M6 .... **3** E4
Withins Rd *OLDS* OL8 .... **71** D3
Withycombe Pl *SLFD* M6 .... **80** A4 ⁊
Withy Gv *ANC* M4 .... **16** C1
Witley Dr *SALE* M33 .... **121** D3
Witterage Cl *WGTN/LGST* M12 ...... **30** B3 ⁊
Woburn Cl *OLDTF/WHR* M16........... **36** A4

Woburn Rd *STRET* M32 .... 42 C1
Woden's Av *SALQ/ORD* M5 .... 24 A1
Woden St *SALQ/ORD* M5 .... 24 B1
Wolfreton Crs *SWIN* M27 .... 59 C2
Wolseley Pl *DID/WITH* M20 .... 129 D4
Wolseley Rd *SALE* M33 .... 123 D3
Wolverton Av *OLDS* OL8 .... 72 B2
Wolveton St *OP/CLY* M11 .... 30 B1 ⑪
Woodbank Av *MPL/ROM* SK6 ...... 141 C2
Woodbourne Rd *HTNM* SK4 .... 133 C3 ③
Woodbray Av *BNG/LEV* M19 .... 131 C4 ⑬
Woodbridge Av *DTN/ASHW* M34 .. 109 D2
Woodcock Cl *DROY* M43 .... 99 C2 ⑧
Woodfield Cl *OLDS* OL8 .... 72 A1
Woodfield Crs *MPL/ROM* SK6 ...... 141 D3 ③
Woodfield Gv *ECC* M30 .... 91 C4
 SALE M33 .... 123 C3 ②
Woodfield Rd *CHH* M8 .... 65 C4 ⑪
 SLFD M6 .... 94 B1 ①
Woodfold Av *BNG/LEV* M19 .... 50 C2
Woodfold Rd *FAIL* M35 .... 89 C1
Woodford Av *ECC* M30 .... 90 B3
Woodford Dr *SWIN* M27 .... 58 A3
Woodgarth Av *NEWH/MOS* M40 .. 87 C4 ⑫
Woodgarth Dr *SWIN* M27 .... 76 A3
Woodgate Cl *MPL/ROM* SK6 .... 141 D2
Woodgate Rd *OLDTF/WHR* M16 ... 45 E3
Woodgrange Cl *SLFD* M6 .... 95 C3 ②
Woodhall Av *DID/WITH* M20 .... 129 C2 ⑦
Woodhall Crs *RDSH* SK5 .... 139 C1
Woodhall Rd *RDSH* SK5 .... 139 C1
Woodhall St *FAIL* M35 .... 88 B1
Woodhalt Rd *CHH* M8 .... 83 C1 ⑪
Woodhead Cl *OLDTF/WHR* M16 ... 35 E3
Woodhill Cl *WGTN/LGST* M12 ...... 41 E3
Woodhill Dr *PWCH* M25 .... 62 B3
Woodhill Gv *PWCH* M25 .... 62 B3
Woodhouse St *GTN* M18 .... 106 B4
 NEWH/MOS M40 .... 85 D4 ⑧
Woodland Av *GTN* M18 .... 117 C1
Woodland Crs *PWCH* M25 .... 62 B3
Woodland Rd *BNG/LEV* M19 ...... 132 A1
 GTN M18 .... 117 C1
Woodlands *FAIL* M35 .... 97 C1
 URM M41 .... 111 C2 ⑧
Woodlands Av *STRET* M32 .... 114 B3 ④
 SWIN M27 .... 75 C3 ⑦
Woodlands Rd *CHH* M8 .... 83 C1
 OLDTF/WHR M16 .... 45 E4
 SALE M33 .... 124 A4
Woodlands St *CHH* M8 .... 82 B1
Woodland St *GTN* M18 .... 31 E5
Woodlark Cl *SLFD* M3 .... 15 D2 ⑪
Woodlawn Ct *OLDTF/WHR* M16 ... 34 B5
Woodlea Av *BNG/LEV* M19 .... 131 C3
Woodleigh Dr *DROY* M43 .... 99 C1
Woodleigh St *BKLY* M9 .... 67 D4 ⑪
Woodliffe St *OLDTF/WHR* M16 .... 34 B1 ③
Woodman St *STKP* SK1 .... 158 A4 ⑯
Woodmere Dr *BKLY* M9 .... 67 C2 ⑧
Wood Rd *OLDTF/WHR* M16 .... 34 B5
Wood Rd North *OLDTF/WHR* M16 .. 34 A4
Woodside Av *BNG/LEV* M19 ...... 131 D4
Woodside Dr *SLFD* M6 .... 94 A2 ①
Woodside Rd *OLDTF/WHR* M16 ... 43 F1
Woodsmoor Rd *SWIN* M27 .... 75 D2 ③
Wood Sq *DROY* M43 .... 108 A1 ⑧
Woodstock Av *RDSH* SK5 .... 134 B4
Woodstock Dr *SWIN* M27 .... 77 C3 ⑧
 WALK M28 .... 74 A3
Woodstock Gn *RDSH* SK5 .... 135 C4
Woodstock Rd *NEWH/MOS* M40 .. 69 C4
 OLDTF/WHR M16 .... 33 E4

Woodstock St *OLDS* OL8 .... 55 D4
Wood St *CSLFD* M3 .... 15 F1
 ECC M30 .... 92 B4
 EDGY/DAV SK3 .... 138 A4
 OP/CLY M11 .... 21 F5
Woodthorpe Cl *PWCH* M25 .... 63 D3 ③
Woodthorpe Gra *PWCH* M25 ...... 63 D3 ④
Woodview Av *BNG/LEV* M19 ...... 131 D4 ③
Woodville Dr *SALE* M33 .... 123 C4
Woodville Gv *RDSH* SK5 .... 134 B3
Woodville Rd *SALE* M33 .... 123 C4 ⑧
Woodville Ter *NEWH/MOS* M40 ... 67 D4 ⑫
Woodward Pl *ANC* M4 .... 18 B1
Woodward Rd *PWCH* M25 .... 61 D3
Woodward St *ANC* M4 .... 18 B1
Woolden St *ECC* M30 .... 90 B2 ⑪
Woolfall Cl *WGTN/LGST* M12 ..... 30 B3 ③
Woollacot St *OLD* OL1 .... 55 D3 ⑬
Woollam Pl *CSLFD* M3 .... 15 D4 ②
Woolley St *CHH* M8 .... 6 B2
Worcester Av *RDSH* SK5 .... 136 A4
Worcester Rd *SLFD* M6 .... 94 A1
 SWIN M27 .... 57 D3
Worcester St *BRO* M7 .... 82 A3 ②①
 CHAD OL9 .... 53 D4
Wordsworth Av *CHH* M8 .... 83 C3 ⑩
 DROY M43 .... 97 D3
Wordsworth Gdns *PWCH* M25 ... 61 D2 ③
Wordsworth Rd *OLDTF/WHR* M16 .. 33 F4
 RDSH SK5 .... 116 B4
 SWIN M27 .... 57 D4
Wordsworth St *SLFD* M6 .... 4 A1
Workesleigh St *NEWH/MOS* M40 .. 87 C4 ②⑩
Worrall St *NEWH/MOS* M40 .... 86 A3 ⑧
 SALQ/ORD M5 .... 24 A1
Worsefold St *NEWH/MOS* M40 ... 86 A1 ⑪
Worsley Av *NEWH/MOS* M40 ..... 67 D4
Worsley Gv *BNG/LEV* M19 .... 51 D3
Worsley Rd *ECC* M30 .... 90 B3
 WALK M28 .... 74 A4
Worsley St *CSLFD* M3 .... 15 F5 ⑧
 HULME M15 .... 24 C1
 SWIN M27 .... 58 B3
 SWIN M27 .... 77 C2 ⑧
Worthing St *RUSH/FAL* M14 ...... 47 F1
Worthington Dr *BRO* M7 .... 63 D4 ②
Worthington St *NEWH/MOS* M40 .. 87 C1
 OLDTF/WHR M16 .... 34 A2
Wortley Av *SLFD* M6 .... 94 A2
Wortley Gv *NEWH/MOS* M40 ..... 68 B3
Wren Av *SWIN* M27 .... 59 D2
Wrenbury Av *DID/WITH* M20 .... 128 B2
Wren Cl *DTN/ASHW* M34 .... 99 C3
Wrexham Cl *OLDS* OL8 .... 71 D3 ⑧
Wright Robinson Cl *OP/CLY* M11 .... 19 F4
Wright St *CHAD* OL9 .... 53 D4
 FAIL M35 .... 88 B1 ⑧
 OLDTF/WHR M16 .... 24 A4
Wrigley Crs *FAIL* M35 .... 88 B2
Wrigley Head *FAIL* M35 .... 88 B1
Wrigley Head Crs *FAIL* M35 .... 88 B1 ⑪
Wroe St *CSLFD* M3 .... 14 C2 ⑪
 SWIN M27 .... 58 B2
Wrotham Cl *SALQ/ORD* M5 .... 13 D2 ⑪
Wroxham Av *DTN/ASHW* M34 ... 118 A2 ⑧
 URM M41 .... 110 B2
Wroxham Rd *BKLY* M9 .... 65 D2
Wyatt Av *SALQ/ORD* M5 .... 24 A1
Wyatt St *HTNM* SK4 .... 138 A3
Wychbury St *SALQ/ORD* M5 ...... 95 C3
Wycliffe Rd *URM* M41 .... 111 C3
Wycliffe St *ECC* M30 .... 91 C3 ⑦
Wycombe Av *GTN* M18 .... 107 C3

Wycombe Cl *URM* M41 .... 101 C4 ⑤
Wye Av *FAIL* M35 .... 88 B2 ②
Wye St *OLDS* OL8 .... 54 B4
Wykeham St *RUSH/FAL* M14 .... 37 D5
Wyndale Dr *FAIL* M35 .... 88 B4
Wyndale Rd *OLDS* OL8 .... 73 D2
Wyndham Av *SWIN* M27 .... 58 B3
Wynford Sq *SALO/ORD* M5 .... 12 A3
Wynne Av *SWIN* M27 .... 58 B2
Wynne Cl *OP/CLY* M11 .... 20 A5
Wynne St *SLFD* M6 .... 3 F2
Wynnstay Gv *RUSH/FAL* M14 ..... 48 B5
Wynnstay Rd *SALE* M33 .... 123 D4
Wyre St *CMANE* M1 .... 17 F5
Wythburn Av *CHH* M8 .... 84 A3 ⑩
  URM M41 .... 110 B2 ④
Wythburn St *SALO/ORD* M5 ..... 95 C3 ②②
Wythop Gdns *SALO/ORD* M5 ...... 12 C3
Wyvern Av *HTNM* SK4 .... 134 A4
Wyverne Rd *CCHDY* M21 .... 44 C5
Wyville Dr *SLFD* M6 .... 2 A3
  SWIN M27 .... 76 A3

Y

Yarburgh St *OLDTF/WHR* M16 ..... 35 E5
Yardley Av *STRET* M32 .... 113 C3
Yardley Cl *STRET* M32 .... 113 C3
Yasmin Gdns *OLD* OL1 .... 54 B1
Yates St *STKP* SK1 .... 139 D2
Yewdale *SWIN* M27 .... 59 D3 ⑧
Yew St *BRO* M7 .... 81 C3
  HULME M15 .... 25 D5
Yew Tree Av *BNG/LEV* M19 .... 51 D5
  RUSH/FAL M14 .... 46 C1
Yew Tree Dr *MPL/ROM* SK6 .... 140 B2
  PWCH M25 .... 62 B1
Yew Tree Rd *RUSH/FAL* M14 ..... 47 E1
York Av *OLDS* OL8 .... 72 B1
  OLDTF/WHR M16 .... 44 A1
  PWCH M25 .... 63 D3
  SALE M33 .... 123 D4
  SWIN M27 .... 57 D3
  URM M41 .... 112 A2 ⑧
York Rd *CCHDY* M21 .... 43 D5
  CHAD OL9 .... 52 B1
  DROY M43 .... 97 D2
  HTNM SK4 .... 132 B4
  SALE M33 .... 123 C4
Yorkshire St *CSLFD* M3 .... 15 F1 ①
York St *BKLY* M9 .... 85 C1
  BNG/LEV M19 .... 51 D5
  CHAD OL9 .... 55 C3
  CMANE M1 .... 16 C5
  CMANW M2 .... 16 C2
  HULME M15 .... 25 E2
Young St *CSLFD* M3 .... 15 F3

Z

Zebra St *BRO* M7 .... 82 B2 ②⓪
Zeta St *BKLY* M9 .... 85 D2
Zetland Rd *CCHDY* M21 .... 126 B1
Zion Crs *HULME* M15 .... 25 F4

Index - featured places

Abbey Hey Primary School
  GTN M18 .... 107 C4
Abbey Independent College
  CMANW M2 .... 16 B3
Abbey Tutorial College
  CMANW M2 .... 16 C2
Abbotsford Preparatory School
  URM M41 .... 110 A3
Abbott CP School
  NEWH/MOS M40 .... 8 A3
Abingdon Primary School
  RDSH SK5 .... 134 B2
Abraham Moss High School
  CHH M8 .... 83 C1
Ailsa Craig Medical Practice
  BRUN/LGST M13 .... 39 E4
Albany Trading Estate
  CCHDY M21 .... 43 F4
Albion Drive Clinic
  DROY M43 .... 98 A2
Albion Trading Estate
  SLFD M6 .... 2 C1
Alder Park CP School
  ECC M30 .... 90 B1
Aldwyn CP School
  DTN/ASHW M34 .... 99 C4
Alexandra Practice
  OLDTF/WHR M16 .... 45 E4
Al Kowsar Surgery
  OLDS OL8 .... 54 B4
Alliston House Medical Centre
  URM M41 .... 111 C3
All Saints Primary School
  GTN M18 .... 31 E4
All Saints Primary School
  NEWH/MOS M40 .... 87 C4
Alma Park Primary School
  BNG/LEV M19 .... 51 D5
Ancoats Hospital
  ANC M4 .... 18 B2
Anson Medical Centre
  RUSH/FAL M14 .... 39 D4
Apollo Theatre
  WGTN/LGST M12 .... 28 B3
Arcadia Sports Centre
  BNG/LEV M19 .... 50 C3
Ardath Israel Synagogue
  BRO M7 .... 64 A4
Arden Business Centre
  MPL/ROM SK6 .... 137 C3
Arden Primary School
  MPL/ROM SK6 .... 140 B2
Armitage C of E
  Primary School
  WGTN/LGST M12 .... 29 F3
Arndale Shopping Centre
  ANC M4 .... 16 C1
Arrow Trading Estate
  DTN/ASHW M34 .... 109 D4
Ashbury Primary School
  OP/CLY M11 .... 20 A4
Ashcroft Surgery
  BNG/LEV M19 .... 51 D3

Aspinall School
GTN M18 .... 117 C2

Astra Business Park
TRPK M17 .... 102 B1

Audenshaw CP School
DTN/ASHW M34 .... 109 C2

Audenshaw Hawthorns School
DTN/ASHW M34 .... 109 D4

Bank Meadow Primary School
WGTN/LGST M12 .... 19 D5

Baretrees CP School
CHAD OL9 .... 53 D1

Barlow Hall Primary School
CCHDY M21 .... 127 C4

Barn Gallery
CMANE M1 .... 16 C5

Barton Business Park
ECC M30 .... 91 C4

Barton Clough Primary School
STRET M32 .... 112 B1

BBC North
CMANE M1 .... 27 D1

Beech Road Gallery
CCHDY M21 .... 126 A1

Bents Lane Medical Practice
MPL/ROM SK6 .... 141 D1

Beth David School
PWCH M25 .... 62 B3

The Birches School
DID/WITH M20 .... 128 B4

Birchfields Primary School
RUSH/FAL M14 .... 50 A4

Bishop Bilsborrow RC Primary School
RUSH/FAL M14 .... 36 B5

Blue Coat C of E Secondary School
OLD OL1 .... 55 D2

Bnos Yisroel School
BRO M7 .... 82 A2

Bodmin Road Clinic
SALE M33 .... 121 D4

Bond Street Industrial Estate
WGTN/LGST M12 .... 18 A5

Booth Hall Childrens Hospital
BKLY M9 .... 67 D2

The Borchardt Medical Centre
DID/WITH M20 .... 128 B3

Bowker Vale Primary School
BKLY M9 .... 64 B1

Branwood Preparatory School
ECC M30 .... 92 A2

Bredbury Clinic
MPL/ROM SK6 .... 141 D1

Bredbury Green Primary School
MPL/ROM SK6 .... 141 D4

Brentnall Primary School
BRO M7 .... 81 D2

Bridgewater Concert Hall
CMANW M2 .... 16 B5

Bridgewater School
WALK M28 .... 74 A3

Brindale Primary School
RDSH SK5 .... 140 A1

Brinnington Health Centre
RDSH SK5 .... 136 A4

Briscoe Lane Junior & Infant School
NEWH/MOS M40 .... 86 B4

Broadfield County Primary School
OLDS OL8 .... 55 D4

Broadhurst CP School
NEWH/MOS M40 .... 87 C2

Broadoak Business Park
TRPK M17 .... 102 B2

Broadoak County Primary School
SWIN M27 .... 75 C3

Broadstone Hall Primary School
HTNM SK4 .... 133 D3

Broadway Industrial Estate
SALQ/ORD M5 .... 13 D5

Brookburn Primary School
CCHDY M21 .... 126 A2

Brooks Bar Medical Centre
OLDTF/WHR M16 .... 35 D2

Broughton Baths
BRO M7 .... 81 D3

Broughton Cricket Club
BRO M7 .... 81 D3

Broughton Recreation Centre
BRO M7 .... 81 D4

Brunswick Health Centre
BRUN/LGST M13 .... 28 A3

Buchanan Pet Surgery
ECC M30 .... 91 D2

Buile Hill High School
SLFD M6 .... 94 B1

Burgess Becker Primary School
BKLY M9 .... 85 C2

Burnage High School for Boys
BNG/LEV M19 .... 131 D4

Butterstile County Primary School
PWCH M25 .... 62 A3

CAB
ANC M4 .... 7 E5

Caius House School
URM M41 .... 111 C4

Cambridge Industrial Estate
BRO M7 .... 5 F2

Canterbury Road Junior & Infant School
URM M41 .... 111 D2

Canterbury Road Surgery
URM M41 .... 112 A2

Capital Road Surgery
OP/CLY M11 .... 107 C2

Cariocca Business Park
WGTN/LGST M12 .... 28 C3

Castlefield Gallery
CSLFD M3 .... 15 F5

Castle Hill School
RDSH SK5 .... 136 A3

Cavendish Road Primary School
DID/WITH M20 .... 129 C4

Cellar Vie the Ginnel Gallery
CMANW M2 .... 16 A3

Central Retail Park
ANC M4 .... 18 A2

Chadderton A F C
CHAD OL9 .... 53 D1

Chadderton Public Baths
CHAD OL9 .... 53 D2

Chadderton Town Health Centre
CHAD OL9 .... 53 D2

Chapel Street CP School
BNG/LEV M19 .... 51 F4

Charlestown CP School
SLFD M6 .... 3 E1

Charlestown Health Centre
BKLY M9 .... 68 A3

Charlestown Primary School
BKLY M9 .... 68 B2

Cheetham Community C of E School
BRO M7 .... 82 B2

Cheetham Hill Cricket Club
CHH M8 .... 64 A4

Cheethwood Community
& Sports Centre
CHH M8 .... 82 B3

Cheetwood Primary School
CHH M8 .... 5 F1

Chethams School of Music
CSLFD M3 .... 6 B5

Chevassut Primary School
HULME M15 .... 25 E2

Chinese Medical Centre
CSLFD M3 .... 15 F4

Chinese Traditional
Health Centre
URM M41 .... 110 B4

Choriton-cum-hardy C of E
Junior School
CCHDY M21 .... 43 D5

Choriton Cum Hardy
Cricket Club
CCHDY M21 .... 126 B3

Choriton Leisure Centre
CCHDY M21 .... 43 E2

Choriton Park Junior School
CCHDY M21 .... 127 C2

Christ Church C of E
Primary School
CHAD OL9 .... 53 C3

Christie Hospital & Holt Radium
Institute
DID/WITH M20 .... 129 D3

Christ the King RC School
NEWH/MOS M40 .... 87 C4

City College Manchester
CHH M8 .... 83 D1

City Course Trading Estate
OP/CLY M11 .... 31 D1

City Court Trading Estate
ANC M4 .... 8 A5

Civic Centre
OLD OL1 .... 55 C2

Civic Centre
SWIN M27 .... 76 A1

Claremont Road Junior
& Infant School
RUSH/FAL M14 .... 37 D5

Clarendon Clinic
SWIN M27 .... 76 B1

Clarendon Cottage School
ECC M30 .... 92 B2

Clarendon Primary School
ECC M30 .... 92 B2

Clarke Industrial Estate
STRET M32 .... 103 C4

Clayton Health Centre
OP/CLY M11 .... 21 F1

Clayton Industrial Estate
OP/CLY M11 .... 106 B2

Clifton Cricket Club
SWIN M27 .... 58 A1

Clifton Primary School
SWIN M27 .... 58 B2

Coldhurst Industrial Estate
OLD OL1 .... 55 C1

Coliseum Theatre
OLD OL1 .... 55 D2

Collegiate Medical Centre
CHH M8 .... 83 C2

Collyhurst Police Station
ANC M4 .... 7 F3

Coppice Industrial Estate
OLDS OL8 .... 54 B4

Coppice Junior School
OLDS OL8 .... 73 C1

Cornbrook Estate
HULME M15 .... 25 D1

Corpus Christi Junior
& Infant School
CHAD OL9 .... 71 D1

Crab Lane Primary School
BKLY M9 .... 65 D1

Craft Centre
ANC M4 .... 17 D1

Cravewood Primary School
CHH M8 .... 64 B4

Cromwell House Community
Mental Health Centre
ECC M30 .... 91 D3

Cromwell Special School
DTN/ASHW M34 .... 117 D3

Crosland Industrial Estate
MPL/ROM SK6 .... 141 C1

Crosslee County Primary School
BKLY M9 .... 67 D1

Crowcroft Park Primary School
WGTN/LGST M12 .... 41 D5

Crown Business Centre
FAIL M35 .... 88 B1

Crown Court
CMANE M1 .... 17 E3

Crown Industrial Estate
ANC M4 .... 8 A4

Crumpsall Lane Primary School
CHH M8 .... 65 C4

Dancehouse Theatre
& Northern Ballet Scool
CMANE M1 .... 26 C1

Dane Bank Primary School
DTN/ASHW M34 .... 118 A3

David Cuthbert
Business Centre
OP/CLY M11 .... 106 A2

David Medical Centre
CCHDY M21 .... 127 C3

The Deans CP School
SWIN M27 .... 76 A1

De La Salle College
SLFD M6 .... 94 A2

Denton West End
Junior & Infant School
DTN/ASHW M34 .... 118 A2

The Dogs Surgery
CMANE M1 .... 17 D4

Doocot Theatre
of Objects & Figures
OLDTF/WHR M16 .... 35 E5

Downing Street
Industrial Estate
CMANE M1 .... 27 F1

Droylsden Associated
Football Club
DROY M43 .... 98 A4

Droylsden High School for Girls
DROY M43 .... 97 C3

Droylsden Swimming Pool
DROY M43 .... 108 A1

Ducie High School
RUSH/FAL M14 .... 37 E2

Ducie Sports Centre
RUSH/FAL M14 .... 37 E2

Ebbefone Galleria
DID/WITH M20 .... 130 B4

Eccles College
ECC M30 .... 92 B1

Eccles Health Centre
ECC M30 .... 92 B4

Eccles Recreation Centre
ECC M30 .... 92 B4

Ellen Wilkinson High School
WGTN/LGST M12 .... 28 C3

Elsinore Business Centre
OLDTF/WHR M16 .... 33 D3

Empress Business Centre
  OLDTF/WHR M16 .... 24 B4
English Martyrs RC School
  URM M41 .... 111 C3
Enterprise Trading Estate
  TRPK M17 .... 103 C1
Eustace Street CP School
  CHAD OL9 .... 54 A1
The Eye Clinic
  CMANW M2 .... 16 B3
Failsworth County
  Upper School
  FAIL M35 .... 89 C2
Failsworth Health Centre
  FAIL M35 .... 88 A2
Failsworth Industrial Estate
  FAIL M35 .... 87 C3
Fairfield Girls High School
  DROY M43 .... 108 A1
Fairfield Road CP School
  DROY M43 .... 107 D1
Fairview Medical Centre
  URM M41 .... 111 C3
Fallowfield Medical Centre
  RUSH/FAL M14 .... 130 B1
Fallowfield Shopping Centre
  RUSH/FAL M14 .... 49 F4
Family Surgery
  RDSH SK5 .... 117 C4
Farjo Medical Centre
  CMANE M1 .... 17 D3
Ferneyfield School
  CHAD OL9 .... 52 B2
Fire Station
  ANC M4 .... 7 F5
Fir Tree Primary School
  RDSH SK5 .... 117 C3
Flixton Girls High School
  URM M41 .... 110 A3
Fourways Trading Estate
  TRPK M17 .... 103 C3
Freehold Community School
  CHAD OL9 .... 54 A4
The Friars Primary School
  CSLFD M3 .... 5 D4
The Gallery Bistro
  WGTN/LGST M12 .... 28 C3
The Gallery
  WGTN/LGST M12 .... 28 C1
Garrick Theatre
  EDGY/DAV SK3 .... 138 A4
Gateway Industrial Estate
  CMANE M1 .... 17 F3
George H Carnall
  Leisure Centre
  URM M41 .... 112 A1
Gloucester House
  Medical Centre
  URM M41 .... 111 D3
Gmex Centre
  CMANW M2 .... 16 A5
Gorse Bank School
  CHAD OL9 .... 52 B4
Gorse Hill Health Centre
  STRET M32 .... 115 C2
Gorse Hill Primary School
  STRET M32 .... 115 C1
Gorton Brook First School
  WGTN/LGST M12 .... 31 D4
Gorton Medical Centre
  GTN M18 .... 106 B4
Granada Studios Tour
  CSLFD M3 .... 15 E3
Granada Superbowl
  WALK M28 .... 75 C2

Grange Arts Centre
  (Oldham College)
  CHAD OL9 .... 54 B2
Grange School
  CHAD OL9 .... 55 C2
Grange School
  RUSH/FAL M14 .... 38 C5
Greater Manchester Museum
  of Science & Industry
  CSLFD M3 .... 15 E4
Green End Junior School
  BNG/LEV M19 .... 131 C4
Greenheys Business Centre
  HULME M15 .... 27 D5
Green Room Theatre
  CMANE M1 .... 16 B5
Greenside Primary School
  DROY M43 .... 97 D3
Greenside Trading Centre
  DROY M43 .... 98 A4
Greenwood Primary School
  ECC M30 .... 92 A1
Grosvenor Business Park
  MPL/ROM SK6 .... 137 D3
Grosvenor Road County
  Junior & Infant School
  SWIN M27 .... 77 D2
Grove Galleries
  HULME M15 .... 24 C2
Guinness Road Trading Estate
  TRPK M17 .... 102 B1
Hardman Fold School
  FAIL M35 .... 87 D2
Harper Mount Primary School
  BKLY M9 .... 84 A1
Harphurey Business Centre
  BKLY M9 .... 66 B4
Harp Trading Estate
  TRPK M17 .... 103 C1
Harpurhey Health Centre
  BKLY M9 .... 84 B1
Hartford Industrial Estate
  CHAD OL9 .... 54 A3
Hathershaw Secondary School
  OLDS OL8 .... 73 C3
Hazeidene Medical Centre
  NEWH/MOS M40 .... 70 A4
Heald Place Primary School
  RUSH/FAL M14 .... 37 F5
Heaton Moor Medical Centre
  HTNM SK4 .... 133 C4
Heaton Park Synagogue
  CHH M8 .... 64 B3
Heaton School
  HTNM SK4 .... 132 B4
Highbank Trading Estate
  OP/CLY M11 .... 106 B2
Higher Broughton Health Centre
  BRO M7 .... 82 A3
Higher Crumpsall & Higher
  Broughton Synagogue
  BRO M7 .... 82 A1
Higher Openshaw Community
  School
  OP/CLY M11 .... 106 B1
Highfield Primary School
  URM M41 .... 112 B3
Hm Prison Manchesterprison
  CSLFD M3 .... 6 B2
Hollywood Bowl
  NEWH/MOS M40 .... 69 D4
Holy Cross & All Saints
  R C Primary School
  ECC M30 .... 101 D1
Holy Name RC Primary School
  HULME M15 .... 37 D1

Holy Rosary RC Primary School
OLDS OL8.. **73** D3

Holy Trinity C of E
Primary School
BKLY M9 .... **85** C1

Houldsworth Golf Club
RDSH SK5 .... **134** A1

Houldsworth Medical Centre
RDSH SK5 .... **134** B2

Hubert House Jewish
Boys School
BRO M7 .... **81** D1

Hulme Grammar School
OLDS OL8 .... **72** B1

Hurstfield Industrial Estate
HTNM SK4 .... **134** A3

Huvys Gallery
BRO M7 .... **82** A2

Independent British Hospitals
RUSH/FAL M14 .... **38** C2

Inland Revenue Office
CSLFD M3 .... **15** F2

The Instructor College
STKP SK1 .... **138** B4

International Convention
Centre U/c
CMANW M2 .... **16** A4

International Swimming Pool
CMANE M1 .... **27** D3

Irwell Park High School
SLFD M6 .... **80** A4

Jewish High School for Girls
BRO M7 .... **81** D1

John Rylands University
CSLFD M3 .... **16** A3

Jubilee Surgery
OLDTF/WHR M16 .... **33** F2

Kaskenmoor School
OLDS OL8 .... **89** D1

Kersal High School
BRO M7 .... **80** A1

King David High School
CHH M8 .... **64** B4

King David Junior School
CHH M8 .... **64** B4

Kings Road Primary School
OLDTF/WHR M16 .... **33** D4

Kingsway CP School
URM M41 .... **112** A1

Ladybarn Primary School
DID/WITH M20 .... **130** B3

Ladywell Hospital
SALO/ORD M5 .... **93** C3

Ladywell Lodge
SALO/ORD M5 .... **93** C3

Lancashire County Cricket Club
STRET M32 .... **32** B3

Lancasterian School
DID/WITH M20 .... **128** A4

Lance Burn Health Centre
SLFD M6 .... **3** D5

Langworthy Clinic
SLFD M6 .... **12** A1

Langworthy Medical Practice
SLFD M6 .... **2** A3

Langworthy Road School
SLFD M6 .... **2** A4

Levenshulme Baths
BNG/LEV M19 .... **51** F3

Levenshulme Health Centre
BNG/LEV M19 .... **51** E3

Levenshulme High School
BNG/LEV M19 .... **132** A2

Library
OLD OL1 .... **55** D3

Light Oaks Infant School
SLFD M6 .... **93** D1

Lily Lane Junior & Infant School
NEWH/MOS M40 .... **86** A1

Little Moss High School
DROY M43 .... **99** C1

Longford Park School
STRET M32 .... **42** A2

Longford Trading Estate
STRET M32 .... **114** B2

Longsight Cricket Club
WGTN/LGST M12 .... **41** D4

Longsight Health Centre
BRUN/LGST M13 .... **40** A3

Longsight Industrial Estate
WGTN/LGST M12 .... **40** A2

Longsight Park School
WGTN/LGST M12 .... **29** F5

Loreto College
HULME M15 .... **35** F1

Lostock Clinic
STRET M32 .... **113** C2

Lower Broughton
Health Centre
BRO M7 .... **5** D2

Lower Kersal Primary School
BRO M7 .... **80** B3

Lowry Heritage Centre
(Art Gallery & Museum)
SALO/ORD M5 .... **14** A1

Lowry School
BRO M7 .... **81** D4

The Lyceum Musical Theatre
OLD OL1 .... **55** D3

Lyndhurst Primary School
OLDS OL8 .... **73** C2

Malbern Industrial Estate
DTN/ASHW M34 .... **119** C1

Manchester Air
& Space Museum
CSLFD M3 .... **15** F4

Manchester Cathedral
CSLFD M3 .... **6** B5

Manchester Central Hosp
& Community Care NHS Trust
BRUN/LGST M13 .... **38** A2

Manchester Centre for the Deaf
BRUN/LGST M13 .... **27** E3

Manchester Centre for Vision
BRUN/LGST M13 .... **37** F1

Manchester City Art Galleries
CMANW M2 .... **16** B3

Manchester City Council
CMANW M2 .... **16** B3

Manchester City Council
BKLY M9 .... **66** A2

Manchester City Council
BKLY M9 .... **68** A2

Manchester City Council
BKLY M9 .... **84** A2

Manchester City Council
BKLY M9 .... **85** C1

Manchester City Council
BNG/LEV M19 .... **131** C4

Manchester City Council
CHH M8 .... **83** C1

Manchester City Council
CMANE M1 .... **16** C5

Manchester City Council
CMANW M2 .... **17** D2

Manchester City Council
DID/WITH M20 .... **128** B3

Manchester City Council
DID/WITH M20 .... **129** D2

Manchester City Council
GTN M18 .... **106** A4

Manchester City Council
NEWH/MOS M40 .... **11** D3

Manchester City Council
  NEWH/MOS M40 .... 69 C3
Manchester City Council
  NEWH/MOS M40 .... 86 B4
Manchester City Council
  OLDTF/WHR M16 .... 36 B5
Manchester City Council
  OP/CLY M11 .... 30 B1
Manchester City Council
  OP/CLY M11 .... 107 C2
Manchester City Council
  WGTN/LGST M12 .... 29 F2
Manchester City Football Club
  RUSH/FAL M14 .... 47 F2
Manchester City Football Club
  RUSH/FAL M14 .... 47 D1
Manchester City
  Magistrates Court
  CSLFD M3 .... 15 F3
Manchester College of Arts
  & Technology
  BKLY M9 .... 85 D1
Manchester College of Arts
  & Technology
  CMANE M1 .... 17 E2
Manchester College of Arts
  & Technology
  OP/CLY M11 .... 31 E1
Manchester Computing School
  BRUN/LGST M13 .... 27 E3
Manchester Conference Centre
  CMANE M1 .... 17 E5
Manchester Grammar School
  BRUN/LGST M13 .... 49 E2
Manchester Health Authority
  HULME M15 .... 35 F1
Manchester High School
  for Girls
  RUSH/FAL M14 .... 48 B3
Manchester Industrial Centre
  CSLFD M3 .... 15 D4
Manchester Islamic High
  School for Girls
  CCHDY M21 .... 43 E5
Manchester Islamic High
  School for Girls
  CCHDY M21 .... 126 A1
Manchester Jewish
  Grammar School
  PWCH M25 .... 62 B2
Manchester Jewish Museum
  CHH M8 .... 7 D1
Manchester Junior Girls School
  BRO M7 .... 63 D4
Manchester Metropolitan
  University
  CMANE M1 .... 17 E4
Manchester Metropolitan
  University
  CMANE M1 .... 26 C2
Manchester Metropolitan
  University
  OLDTF/WHR M16 .... 46 A2
Manchester Metropolitan
  University
  PART M31 .... 120 A3
Manchester Metropolitan
  University
  RUSH/FAL M14 .... 38 A2
Manchester Metropolitan
  University
  RUSH/FAL M14 .... 48 C2
Manchester Reform Synagogue
  CSLFD M3 .... 16 A3
Manchester Road CP School
  DROY M43 .... 97 C4

Manchester Royal Infirmary
  BRUN/LGST M13 .... 38 A1
Manchester United
  Football Club
  OLDTF/WHR M16 .... 32 A1
Manchester United
  Football Club
  OLDTF/WHR M16 .... 105 C4
Manchester University
  BRUN/LGST M13 .... 28 B5
Manchester University
  HULME M15 .... 27 E5
Manchester Watersports Centre
  HULME M15 .... 25 D2
Manchester Youth Theatre
  HULME M15 .... 26 A4
Mancunian Community
  Health N H S Trust
  CCHDY M21 .... 43 E4
Mancunian Community
  Health N H S Trust
  NEWH/MOS M40 .... 86 B3
Mancunian Community
  Health N H S Trust
  OLDTF/WHR M16 .... 35 F4
Manley Park Infant School
  OLDTF/WHR M16 .... 44 B1
Manley Park Junior School
  OLDTF/WHR M16 .... 34 B5
Marjory Lees Health Centre
  OLD OL1 .... 55 D2
Market
  ANC M4 .... 16 C1
Market Hall
  OLD OL1 .... 55 C2
Marlborough Road School
  BRO M7 .... 82 B3
Mather Street Primary School
  FAIL M35 .... 87 D1
Mauldeth Medical Centre
  DID/WITH M20 .... 130 B2
Mauldeth Road Primary School
  DID/WITH M20 .... 130 B2
Maycroft Junior & Infant School
  RDSH SK5 .... 136 A3
Meadow Industrial Estate
  FAIL M35 .... 87 D3
The Meadows School
  MDTN M24 .... 67 D1
Medlock Infant School
  BRUN/LGST M13 .... 27 F2
Medlock Leisure Centre
  DROY M43 .... 98 B3
Megabowl
  OLDTF/WHR M16 .... 33 D1
Melland School
  RDSH SK5 .... 116 B3
Mersey Road Industrial Estate
  OLDS OL8 .... 71 D4
Mills Hill CP School
  CHAD OL9 .... 52 A1
Mills Hill Junior School
  CHAD OL9 .... 52 A1
Moat House School
  HTNM SK4 .... 138 A2
Monde Trading Estate
  TRPK M17 .... 103 C3
Montague Business Park
  OLDTF/WHR M16 .... 32 C2
Monton Bowling Club
  ECC M30 .... 92 A1
Monton Cricket Club
  ECC M30 .... 92 A1
Monton Medical Centre
  ECC M30 .... 91 C1
Moorlands Junior School
  SALE M33 .... 125 C4

Moorside High School
SWIN M27 .... **75** D2

Moorside Primary School
SWIN M27 .... **75** D2

Moravian College
DROY M43 .... **108** A1

Mosque
CHAD OL9 .... **54** A4

Mosque
CHH M8 .... **83** C2

Mosque
OLDTF/WHR M16 .... **34** C1

Mossfield Primary School
SWIN M27 .... **58** B4

**Moss Park Junior
& Infant School**
STRET M32 .... **113** D3

Moss Side Health Centre
RUSH/FAL M14 .... **36** C2

Moss Side Leisure Centre
HULME M15 .... **36** A1

Moston Brook High School
NEWH/MOS M40 .... **85** D3

Moston Fields Primary School
NEWH/MOS M40 .... **68** A4

Moston Indoor Market
NEWH/MOS M40 .... **85** D1

Moston Lane Primary School
NEWH/MOS M40 .... **85** D1

Mount Carmel RC Junior School
BKLY M9 .... **66** B3

Museum of Transport
CHH M8 .... **83** D3

**National Museum
of Labour History**
CMANE M1 .... **16** C4

Natural History Museum
OLDS OL8 .... **54** A4

Navigation Trading Estate
NEWH/MOS M40 .... **86** A4

Neville Street Industrial Estate
CHAD OL9 .... **54** A2

New Ardwick Sports Centre
BRUN/LGST M13 .... **29** E5

New Croft High School
SLFD M6 .... **2** B3

**New Hall Road Synagogue / Pinto
Talmudical Centre**
BRO M7 .... **81** C1

Newhaven Business Park
ECC M30 .... **92** A4

New Moston Primary School
NEWH/MOS M40 .... **70** A3

New Museum
OLD OL1 .... **55** C1

News (MEN) Arena
CSLFD M3 .... **6** B4

Newton Heath Cricket Club
NEWH/MOS M40 .... **87** D4

Newton Street Police Museum
CMANE M1 .... **17** E2

**Nicholas Varley
Community School**
NEWH/MOS M40 .... **9** E2

Norman House School
NEWH/MOS M40 .... **69** D2

North Area Sixth Form College
HTNM SK4 .... **132** B3

**North Chadderton
Comprehensive Lower School**
CHAD OL9 .... **53** C1

**North Grecian Street
Primary School**
BRO M7 .... **81** C4

North Heaton Primary School
HTNM SK4 .... **133** C3

**North Manchester
General Hospital**
CHH M8 .... **66** A4

**North Manchester High School
for Girls**
BKLY M9 .... **68** A3

North Manchester Synagogue
BRO M7 .... **82** A1

North Reddish Health Centre
RDSH SK5 .... **117** C4

North Reddish Infant School
RDSH SK5 .... **117** D4

North Trafford College
STRET M32 .... **32** B3

**North West Regional
Health Authority**
DID/WITH M20 .... **128** B4

Oakleigh Medical Centre
CHH M8 .... **65** D4

Oakwood High Lower School
CCHDY M21 .... **126** B4

Oakwood High School
SLFD M6 .... **78** A4

Odeon Theatre
CMANW M2 .... **16** B4

**Old Hall Drive Junior
& Infant School**
GTN M18 .... **116** A1

Oldham Central Clinic
CHAD OL9 .... **55** C3

Oldham College
CHAD OL9 .... **55** C2

Oldham County Court
OLD OL1 .... **55** C2

**Oldham Metropolitan
Borough Council**
CHAD OL9 .... **53** D2

**Oldham Metropolitan
Borough Council**
FAIL M35 .... **88** B2

**Oldham Metropolitan
Borough Council**
OLD OL1 .... **55** C1

**Oldham Owls Disabled
Sports Club**
CHAD OL9 .... **54** A1

Oldham Sixth Form College
CHAD OL9 .... **55** C3

Oldham Sports Centre
OLD OL1 .... **55** D2

Oldham West Business Centre
CHAD OL9 .... **53** D2

**Old Moat Junior
& Infant School**
DID/WITH M20 .... **129** C2

Old Trafford Infant School
OLDTF/WHR M16 .... **24** B4

Olympia Trading Estate
HULME M15 .... **25** F1

The Open University
CCHDY M21 .... **43** E3

Opera House
CSLFD M3 .... **15** F3

The Operating Theatre
STRET M32 .... **115** C2

Optimax Eye Care Clinic
CMANW M2 .... **16** B3

Orchard Trading Estate
SLFD M6 .... **79** D4

Ordsall Hall Museum
SALQ/ORD M5 .... **23** E3

Ordsall Health Centre
SALQ/ORD M5 .... **13** F5

Orion Trading Estate
TRPK M17 .... **103** C1

Orsall Sports Centre
SALQ/ORD M5 .... **23** D2

Osborne Trading Estate
CHAD OL9 .... 54 A1
Oswald Road Primary School
CCHDY M21 .... 43 D3
Our Lady of Mount RC
High School
SLFD M6 .... 94 B2
Our Ladys RC Primary School
OLDTF/WHR M16 .... 34 C4
Overdale Primary School
MPL/ROM SK6 .... 141 D4
O Y Y Lubavitch Girls School
BRO M7 .... 63 D4
Palace Theatre
CMANE M1 .... 16 C5
Palm Business Centre
CHAD OL9 .... 53 D2
Parish Church C of E
Junior School
OLD OL1 .... 55 D1
Park Road CP School
SALE M33 .... 123 C3
Park Surgery
OLDTF/WHR M16 .... 35 F5
Park View County
Primary School
PWCH M25 .... 62 B2
Park View Practice
RDSH SK5 .... 117 D4
Parkway Business Centre
OLDTF/WHR M16 .... 46 B3
Parkway Trading Estate
STRET M32 .... 103 C4
Patricroft C of E School
ECC M30 .... 91 C3
Peacock County
Primary School
GTN M18 .... 106 A3
Pear Mill Industrial Estate
MPL/ROM SK6 .... 140 A3
Peel Moat Recreation Centre
HTNM SK4 .... 132 B4
Pendlebury Health Centre
SWIN M27 .... 59 C3
Pendleton Medical Centre
SLFD M6 .... 2 C5
Peoples History Museum
CSLFD M3 .... 15 E2
Pike Fold Primary School
BKLY M9 .... 66 A2
Pinnacle Business Centre
HTNM SK4 .... 138 A2
Plant Hill High School
BKLY M9 .... 66 A1
Plasman Industrial Centre
BNG/LEV M19 .... 51 D4
Plymouth Court
Business Centre
BRUN/LGST M13 .... 38 C1
Plymouth Grove Primary School
BRUN/LGST M13 .... 39 E1
Poland Industrial Estate
ANC M4 .... 8 A5
PO Sorting Office
ANC M4 .... 7 F4
Prestwich Hebrew
Congregation Synagogue
PWCH M25 .... 62 B3
Primary School
BNG/LEV M19 .... 131 D2
Princess Christian College
RUSH/FAL M14 .... 48 A4
Propps Hall Primary School
FAIL M35 .... 88 A3
Queens Park Art Gallery
BKLY M9 .... 84 A3

Radclyffe County
Primary School
SALQ/ORD M5 .... 23 D1
The Radclyffe School
CHAD OL9 .... 52 B2
The Radclyffe School
CHAD OL9 .... 52 B3
Ravensbury CP School
OP/CLY M11 .... 11 E4
Reddish Vale School
RDSH SK5 .... 134 B2
Regal Industrial Estate
WGTN/LGST M12 .... 30 C2
Regent Trading Estate
CSLFD M3 .... 14 C2
Registry Office
CSLFD M3 .... 16 A3
Richmond Junior School
CHAD OL9 .... 54 B3
The Robert Darbishire Practice
RUSH/FAL M14 .... 38 A4
Roman Fort
CSLFD M3 .... 15 E5
Rosedale Shopping Centre
NEWH/MOS M40 .... 87 C4
Royal Exchange Clinic
CMANW M2 .... 16 B2
Royal Exchange Theatre
ANC M4 .... 7 D5
Royal Exchange Theatre County
ANC M4 .... 16 B1
Royal Manchester
Childrens Hospital
SWIN M27 .... 77 D2
Royal Northern College
of Music
HULME M15 .... 27 D3
Royce Primary School
HULME M15 .... 25 F5
Royce Trading Estate
TRPK M17 .... 102 B2
Russell Leite Theatre School
RUSH/FAL M14 .... 37 E3
St Agnes Primary School
BRUN/LGST M13 .... 40 B5
St Albans RC High School
GTN M18 .... 116 B3
St Alphonsus RC School
OLDTF/WHR M16 .... 24 C5
St Ambrose Barlow RC
High School
SWIN M27 .... 76 B2
St Andrews C of E
Primary School
BNG/LEV M19 .... 51 F5
St Andrews C of E School
ECC M30 .... 92 A4
St Andrews Medical Centre
ECC M30 .... 92 A3
St Annes Primary School
DTN/ASHW M34 .... 108 A2
St Annes RC School
ANC M4 .... 18 C2
St Anns RC Infant School
STRET M32 .... 114 B3
St Anns RC Junior School
STRET M32 .... 114 B3
St Antony High School
URM M41 .... 112 B3
St Augustine of Canterbury
RC School
OLDS OL8 .... 72 B2
St Augustines C of E
Primary School
NEWH/MOS M40 .... 85 C4
St Augustines C of E School
SWIN M27 .... 77 D1

St Barnabas C of E
  Primary School
  OP/CLY M11 .... **21** E5
St Bedes College
  OLDTF/WHR M16 .... **35** F5
St Bernadettes RC
  Primary School
  RDSH SK5 .... **139** D1
St Bernards Primary School
  BNG/LEV M19 .... **131** D3
St Boniface RC Junior
  & Infant School
  BRO M7 .... **81** C3
St Brigids RC Primary School
  OP/CLY M11 .... **20** C4
St Chads RC Primary School
  CHH M8 .... **83** C4
St Charles RC Primary School
  SWIN M27 .... **75** D1
St Chrysostoms C of E
  Primary School
  BRUN/LGST M13 .... **38** C1
St Clements C of E
  Primary School
  OP/CLY M11 .... **107** C2
St Clements C of E
  Primary School
  SALQ/ORD M5 .... **23** F1
St Cuthberts RC Infant School
  DID/WITH M20 .... **130** A4
St Cuthberts RC Junior School
  DID/WITH M20 .... **130** A4
St Dunstans RC Primary School
  NEWH/MOS M40 .... **86** A1
St Edmunds Junior
  & Infant School
  NEWH/MOS M40 .... **85** C3
St Edwards RC Primary School
  RUSH/FAL M14 .... **47** E1
St Elizabeths Primary School
  RDSH SK5 .... **133** D1
St Francis RC Primary School
  WGTN/LGST M12 .... **31** E2
St Gabriels Medical Centre
  PWCH M25 .... **63** D3
St Georges C of E
  Primary School
  SLFD M6 .... **80** A4
St Gilberts RC School
  ECC M30 .... **90** A3
St Gregorys RC High School
  DROY M43 .... **107** C1
St Herberts RC Primary School
  CHAD OL9 .... **53** C2
St Hildas C of E Primary School
  OLD OL1 .... **54** B1
St Hildas C of E Primary School
  PWCH M25 .... **63** C1
St Hugh of Lincoln Primary School
  STRET M32 .... **112** B2
St James C of E Primary School
  RUSH/FAL M14 .... **48** C2
St James RC Infant School
  SLFD M6 .... **2** B3
St James School
  NEWH/MOS M40 .... **8** B1
St James's Junior School
  SLFD M6 .... **2** B4
St John Bosco RC
  Primary School
  BKLY M9 .... **67** D2
St Johns Cathedral
  CSLFD M3 .... **15** D1
St Johns C of E Junior School
  FAIL M35 .... **89** C2
St Johns C of E Primary School
  FAIL M35 .... **88** B1

St Johns Primary School
  SLFD M6 .... **78** A3
St Johns RC Primary School
  CCHDY M21 .... **42** C3
St John Vianney Upper School
  OLDTF/WHR M16 .... **43** E1
St Josephs RC Junior
  & Infant School
  SALQ/ORD M5 .... **13** E5
St Josephs RC Junior
  & Infant School
  RDSH SK5 .... **134** A1
St Josephs RC Primary School
  BRUN/LGST M13 .... **39** E2
St Josephs RC Primary School
  STKP SK1 .... **138** B4
St Judes C of E Primary School
  ANC M4 .... **18** A1
St Kentigerns RC
  Primary School
  RUSH/FAL M14 .... **47** D4
St Lukes C of E Primary School
  SALQ/ORD M5 .... **94** B4
St Lukes C of E School
  CHAD OL9 .... **53** C2
St Lukes RC Primary School
  SLFD M6 .... **78** A4
St Lukes School
  WGTN/LGST M12 .... **29** E5
St Malachys School
  NEWH/MOS M40 .... **84** A4
St Margarets C of E
  Primary School
  OLDS OL8 .... **72** A3
St Margarets C of E
  Primary School
  OLDTF/WHR M16 .... **45** D1
St Mark's C of E Primary School
  NEWH/MOS M40 .... **9** D4
St Marks RC Primary School
  SWIN M27 .... **59** C3
St Martins School
  SALE M33 .... **122** A4
St Marys C of E Primary School
  NEWH/MOS M40 .... **69** C4
St Marys C of E Primary School
  RDSH SK5 .... **135** C3
St Mary's Hospital
  BRUN/LGST M13 .... **38** A2
St Marys Medical Centre
  OLD OL1 .... **55** D2
St Marys Primary School
  NEWH/MOS M40 .... **69** D2
St Mary's Primary School
  OLDTF/WHR M16 .... **35** F2
St Marys RC Infant School
  FAIL M35 .... **88** A3
St Marys RC Primary School
  BNG/LEV M19 .... **132** A1
St Mary's RC Primary School
  ECC M30 .... **92** A4
St Marys RC School
  HTNM SK4 .... **138** A3
St Marys School
  SWIN M27 .... **76** B1
St Marys School
  URM M41 .... **110** B1
St Matthews C of E
  Primary School
  STRET M32 .... **124** A1
St Matthews RC High School
  NEWH/MOS M40 .... **69** C3
St Monicas RC High School
  PWCH M25 .... **63** C2
St Patricks RC Infant School
  ANC M4 .... **8** A3

St Pauls C of E Primary School
  DID/WITH M20 .... 129 D3
St Pauls C of E Primary School
  SALQ/ORD M5 .... 13 E2
St Pauls Primary School
  RDSH SK5 .... 139 D1
St Peter & St John RC
  Primary School
  CSLFD M3 .... 5 D5
St Peters School C of E
  Primary School
  SWIN M27 .... 76 A1
St Philips C of E School
  CSLFD M3 .... 14 C2
St Phillips C of E Primary School
  HULME M15 .... 26 B3
St Phillips RC Primary School
  BRO M7 .... 63 C4
St Roberts RC School
  BRUN/LGST M13 .... 40 B5
St Sebastians RC School
  SLFD M6 .... 80 A4
St Stephens RC School
  DROY M43 .... 98 A3
St Teresas RC Primary School
  OLDTF/WHR M16 .... 33 D5
St Thomas Aquinas RC
  High School
  OLDTF/WHR M16 .... 45 E3
St Thomas Aquinas RC
  High & Upper School
  CCHDY M21 .... 127 D2
St Thomas Primary School
  CHH M8 .... 84 A1
St Vincent De Paul High School
  RUSH/FAL M14 .... 38 C4
St Wilfrids RC Primary School
  HULME M15 .... 25 E3
St Willibrords RC School
  OP/CLY M11 .... 96 A2
Sale Cricket Club
  SALE M33 .... 124 B4
Sale Leisure Centre
  SALE M33 .... 124 A4
Salford City Council
  BRO M7 .... 81 D2
Salford City Council
  CSLFD M3 .... 5 E3
Salford City Council
  ECC M30 .... 92 B3
Salford City Council
  SALQ/ORD M5 .... 14 A5
Salford City Council
  SALQ/ORD M5 .... 22 C2
Salford City Council
  SALQ/ORD M5 .... 94 A3
Salford City Council
  SLFD M6 .... 80 B4
Salford City Council
  SLFD M6 .... 93 D2
Salford City Council
  SLFD M6 .... 95 C1
Salford City Council
  SWIN M27 .... 76 B1
Salford City Council
  SWIN M27 .... 77 C1
Salford City Council
  SWIN M27 .... 77 C2
Salford College
  ECC M30 .... 90 A3
Salford College
  SALQ/ORD M5 .... 23 D2
Salford College
  SLFD M6 .... 3 E4
Salford College
  SLFD M6 .... 3 F2

Salford College
  SWIN M27 .... 57 C3
Salford County Court
  SALQ/ORD M5 .... 12 C3
Salford Medical Centre
  SLFD M6 .... 95 C2
Salford Royal Hospitals
  NHS Trust
  SLFD M6 .... 93 D2
Salford Rugby Club
  SALQ/ORD M5 .... 94 B3
Salford Town Hall
  CSLFD M3 .... 15 D1
Salford & Trafford
  Health Authority
  ECC M30 .... 92 B3
Salford University
  Business Park
  SLFD M6 .... 3 F2
Salvation Army
  BRUN/LGST M13 .... 27 E2
Saviour C of E Primary School
  NEWH/MOS M40 .... 84 A4
Seaford Industrial Estate
  SLFD M6 .... 3 E2
Sedgley Park CP School
  PWCH M25 .... 63 D3
Seedley Primary School
  SLFD M6 .... 95 C3
Severnside Trading Estate
  TRPK M17 .... 103 D4
Seymour Park Primary School
  OLDTF/WHR M16 .... 33 F2
Seymour Road Primary School
  OP/CLY M11 .... 96 B4
Shandon Clinic
  HULME M15 .... 37 D1
Shawgrove School
  DID/WITH M20 .... 128 B3
Shena Simon College
  CMANE M1 .... 17 D4
Shiv Lodge Medical Centre
  BRUN/LGST M13 .... 40 A3
Showcase Cinemas Belle Vue
  WGTN/LGST M12 .... 31 E5
Shree Swaminarayan Temple
  OLDS OL8 .... 55 C4
Sikh Temple
  OLDTF/WHR M16 .... 35 D3
Sikh Temple
  RUSH/FAL M14 .... 37 D2
Silverdale Primary School
  SWIN M27 .... 59 D3
Slough Industrial Estate
  SALQ/ORD M5 .... 14 B5
Sorrel Group Practice
  SLFD M6 .... 93 C2
South Chadderton
  Secondary School
  CHAD OL9 .... 70 B2
Southern Cross School
  CCHDY M21 .... 127 C4
South Failsworth County School
  FAIL M35 .... 88 A4
Southfield Industrial Estate
  TRPK M17 .... 104 A4
South Manchester Synagogue
  RUSH/FAL M14 .... 48 B4
South Reddish Medical Centre
  RDSH SK5 .... 138 B1
South Trafford College
  SALE M33 .... 121 C4
South West Manchester
  Cricket Club
  CCHDY M21 .... 44 A4
The Spindles Shopping Centre
  OLD OL1 .... 55 C3

Sports Hall
OLDS OL8 .... 55 C3
Springfield Business Centre
CSLFD M3 .... 6 A4
Spurley Hey High School
GTN M18 .... 116 A3
Stanley Grove Primary School
WGTN/LGST M12 .... 40 B3
Stanley Road Primary School
CHAD OL9 .... 71 D1
Stansfield Road Junior School
FAIL M35 .... 89 C1
Star Industrial Estate
OLDS OL8 .... 55 C4
Stockport County Court
STKP SK1 .... 138 B4
**Stockport Metropolitan
Borough Council**
RDSH SK5 .... 134 B2
**Stonecourt Great
& New Synagogue**
BRO M7 .... 63 D4
Stretford Grammar School
STRET M32 .... 115 C4
Stretford High School
STRET M32 .... 32 A3
Stretford Memorial Hospital
OLDTF/WHR M16 .... 33 F5
Sugden Sports Centre
CMANE M1 .... 27 D2
Summerville Primary School
SLFD M6 .... 78 B4
Surrey Lodge Group Practice
RUSH/FAL M14 .... 38 C3
Swinton Cricket Club
SWIN M27 .... 77 C2
Swinton High School
SWIN M27 .... 58 A4
Swinton Industrial Estate
SWIN M27 .... 77 C1
Swinton Leisure Centre
SWIN M27 .... 76 B1
Synagogue
BRO M7 .... 80 B1
Talbot Court Medical Practice
STRET M32 .... 115 C2
Talmah Torah Jewish School
BRO M7 .... 81 D2
**Tameside & Glossop
Health Authority**
DROY M43 .... 108 A1
**Tameside Metropolitan
Borough Council**
DTN/ASHW M34 .... 109 C1
Tame Valley Primary School
MPL/ROM SK6 .... 136 A2
Tavistock Industrial Estate
OP/CLY M11 .... 106 B3
Taylors Sports Club
ECC M30 .... 92 A4
Telford School
BKLY M9 .... 66 A1
Temple Junior School
CHH M8 .... 83 C3
Temple Street Infant School
CHH M8 .... 83 C3
Thames Industrial Estate
WGTN/LGST M12 .... 28 C1
Tian Guan Temple
NEWH/MOS M40 .... 9 E2
Tib Lane Gallery
CMANW M2 .... 16 B3
**Tootal Drive County
Primary School**
SALO/ORD M5 .... 94 A3
Town Square Shopping Centre
OLD OL1 .... 55 D3

Trading Centre
CHH M8 .... 83 C4
Trading Estate
ANC M4 .... 7 F4
Trading Estate
SALO/ORD M5 .... 24 B1
Trafalgar Business Park
BRO M7 .... 5 E1
Trafford Area Health Authority
SALE M33 .... 123 D4
Trafford Football Club
URM M41 .... 110 A4
Trafford Healthcare NHS Trust
URM M41 .... 110 A2
**Trafford Metropolitan
Borough Council**
OLDTF/WHR M16 .... 33 F2
**Trafford Metropolitan
Borough Council**
SALE M33 .... 123 D4
**Trafford Metropolitan
Borough Council**
STRET M32 .... 114 A3
**Trafford Metropolitan
Borough Council**
STRET M32 .... 114 A2
**Trafford Metropolitan
Borough Council**
URM M41 .... 110 A3
**Trafford Metropolitan
Borough Council**
URM M41 .... 111 D3
Trafford M V R F C C
SALE M33 .... 123 C2
Trinity C of E High School
HULME M15 .... 26 C4
UMIST
CMANE M1 .... 17 E5
United Synagogue
CHH M8 .... 64 A2
University College Salford
CSLFD M3 .... 4 C5
**University Dental Hospital
of Manchester**
HULME M15 .... 27 D4
University of Manchester
BRUN/LGST M13 .... 27 F5
University of Manchester
HULME M15 .... 27 E4
University of Manchester
HULME M15 .... 37 F1
University of Manchester
RUSH/FAL M14 .... 39 D4
University of Manchester
RUSH/FAL M14 .... 48 C3
University of Manchester
RUSH/FAL M14 .... 48 C2
University of Manchester
RUSH/FAL M14 .... 49 D4
**University of Manchester
Institute of Science
& Technology**
BRUN/LGST M13 .... 27 E2
University of Salford
SALO/ORD M5 .... 3 F4
University of Salford
SLFD M6 .... 4 B4
Urmston Grammar School
URM M41 .... 111 C2
Urmston Group Practice
URM M41 .... 111 C4
Urmston Infant School
URM M41 .... 111 C3
Urmston Junior School
URM M41 .... 111 C3
Urmston Leisure Centre
URM M41 .... 110 B3

Vaishali Medical Centre
CCHDY M21 .... **43** F5
Varley Street Clinic
NEWH/MOS M40 .... **9** D2
Vauxhall Industrial Estate
RDSH SK5 .... **134** A3
Vauxhall Industrial Estate
RDSH SK5 .... **138** B1
Vernon Industrial Estate
STKP SK1 .... **138** B3
Vernon Industrial Estate
STKP SK1 .... **139** C3
Vernon Park Primary School
STKP SK1 .... **139** C4
Victoria Industrial Estate
ANC M4 .... **18** C2
Victoria Medical Centre
URM M41 .... **111** D3
Victoria Park Infant School
STRET M32 .... **114** A3
Victoria Park Junior School
STRET M32 .... **114** B3
Victoria Trading Estate
CHAD OL9 .... **71** D2
Virgin Cinemas
EDGY/DAV SK3 .... **138** A4
Virgin Cinemas
SALQ/ORD M5 .... **22** C4
Wadeson Junior School
BRUN/LGST M13 .... **28** A2
Wardley C of E School
SWIN M27 .... **57** D3
Wardley Industrial Estate
WALK M28 .... **57** C4
Waterloo Industrial Park
STKP SK1 .... **138** B4
Waters Edge Business Park
SALQ/ORD M5 .... **23** E3
Watersports Centre
SALQ/ORD M5 .... **22** C2
Waybridge Industrial Estate
SALQ/ORD M5 .... **104** B1
Weaste Trading Estate
SALQ/ORD M5 .... **94** B3
Webster Junior School
RUSH/FAL M14 .... **37** D2
Wellfield Junior School
SALE M33 .... **122** B3
Wellfield Medical Centre
CHH M8 .... **82** B1
Wentworth High School
ECC M30 .... **92** B1
Werneth Cricket Bowling
& Tennis Club
OLDS OL8 .... **72** B1
Werneth Infant School
OLDS OL8 .... **72** B1
Werneth Jamia Mosque
OLDS OL8 .... **54** A4
Werneth Private
Preparatory School
OLDS OL8 .... **54** B4
Werneth School
MPL/ROM SK6 .... **141** D3
Westbrook Trading Estate
TRPK M17 .... **104** B2
West End Trading Estate
SWIN M27 .... **58** B4
West Gorton Medical Centre
WGTN/LGST M12 .... **30** A3

West Liverpool Street School
SLFD M6 .... **12** B1
Westpoint Medical Centre
BNG/LEV M19 .... **50** B3
Westwood Business Centre
CHAD OL9 .... **54** B3
Westwood Industrial Estate
CHAD OL9 .... **54** A2
Westwood Park Primary School
ECC M30 .... **90** B2
Westwood Primary School
CHAD OL9 .... **54** B2
Whalley Range Football Club
CCHDY M21 .... **45** D5
Whalley Range High School
for Girls
OLDTF/WHR M16 .... **46** A5
Wharfside Business Centre
TRPK M17 .... **22** B4
White City Retail Park
OLDTF/WHR M16 .... **32** C1
Whitegate End Primary School
CHAD OL9 .... **70** A2
Whitehill Primary School
HTNM SK4 .... **138** A1
Whitley Road Medical Centre
NEWH/MOS M40 .... **8** B1
Whitworth Art Gallery
HULME M15 .... **37** F2
Whitworth Park School
RUSH/FAL M14 .... **37** D2
Wilbraham Infant School
RUSH/FAL M14 .... **47** D3
Willan Industrial Estate
SALQ/ORD M5 .... **12** A3
William Hulmes Grammar
School
OLDTF/WHR M16 .... **46** A3
Wilmslow Road Medical Centre
RUSH/FAL M14 .... **38** B5
Windmill Medical Practice
DTN/ASHW M34 .... **117** D2
Windsor High School
SLFD M6 .... **13** D1
Withington Bowling Club
RUSH/FAL M14 .... **130** A2
Withington Girls School
RUSH/FAL M14 .... **129** D1
Withington Hospital
DID/WITH M20 .... **128** B3
Withington Swimming Baths
DID/WITH M20 .... **129** D3
Woodhouse Primary School
URM M41 .... **110** A1
Wright Robinson High School
GTN M18 .... **107** D3
Xaverian College
RUSH/FAL M14 .... **38** B4
Yew Tree Junior
& Infant School
CHAD OL9 .... **70** D2
YHA
CSLFD M3 .... **15** E5
Y Sport & Leisure Centre
CSLFD M3 .... **15** E4
Zakaria Mosque
OLDTF/WHR M16 .... **45** D2

Page 51

D3
1 Chinwell Vw
2 Crescent Ov
3 Firsby St
4 Hapton St
5 Levenshulme Ter

F4
1 Highfield Rd
2 Rawdon Cl

Page 54

B3
1 Allen St
2 Bisley St
3 Fletcher Cl
4 Mannock St
5 Pembroke St
6 Richmond Wk
7 Rosebery St
8 Tattersall St
9 Walker St

B4
1 Bright St
2 Burnaby St
3 Hornby St
4 St Thomas's Cir
5 St Thomas North
6 St Thomas South

Page 55

D4
1 Back Scott St
2 Havelock St
3 Hinton St
4 Scottfield
5 Thornton St

Page 81

D3
1 Buddleia Gv
2 Clivia Gv
3 Cornet St
4 Fushia Gv
5 Genista Gv
6 Hill St
7 Ilex Gv
8 Kalima Gv
9 Pimlico Cl
10 Pyramid Ct
11 Rudyard St
12 St John's Cl
13 St John's St
14 Scovell St
15 Vinca Gv

D4
1 Back Camp St
2 Burland Cl
3 Carter St
4 Countess Gv
5 Enid Cl
6 Gosport Sq
7 Nelson St
8 Nile Ter
9 Southampton Cl
10 Teneriffe St
11 Trafalgar Ct

Page 82

A4
1 Ashworth St
2 Benson Cl
3 Canonsleigh Cl
4 Cascade Dr
5 Colina Dr
6 Forum Gv
7 Hilton St
8 Holberton St
9 Melbourne St
10 Otter Dr
11 Richborough Cl
12 Sabrina St
13 Sandsend Cl
14 Thanet Cl
15 Westmead Dr
16 Willerby Rd

Page 51

B1
1 Back St Mark's La
2 Bank St
3 Bourget St
4 Empress St
5 Eskrigge Cl
6 Humphrey St
7 Ralston Cl
8 Robin Hood St
9 St Helier's Dr
10 St Mark's La
11 St Martin's Dr
12 Sandy Bank Rd

B3
1 Back Halliwell La
2 Barry Lawson Cl
3 Broomfield Dr
4 Carstairs Cl
5 Crookhill Dr
6 Dorothy St
7 Guy St
8 Halliwell St West
9 Highshore Dr
10 Hovey Cl
11 Inghamwood Cl
12 Lanbury Dr
13 Lanfield Dr
14 Masboro St
15 Morrowfield Av
16 Moston St
17 Narbuth Dr
18 Overstone Dr
19 Southam St
20 Zebra St

C1
1 Avebury St
2 Axford Cl
3 Brakenhurst Dr
4 Chiseldon Av
5 Cranlington Dr
6 Dalmain Cl
7 Errmington Dr
8 Everleigh Dr
9 Greyswood Av
10 Highclere Av
11 Kilmington Dr
12 Linstead Dr
13 Marlborough Rd
14 Oscroft Cl
15 Peach Tree Cl
16 Percival Cl
17 Venture Scout Wy

Page 83

D2
1 Blanwood Dr
2 Frome St
3 Harland Dr
4 Humber St
5 Lichfield Dr
6 Tahir Cl
7 Thetford Dr
8 Thurlston Crs
9 Wigmore Rd

Page 84

B3
1 Kirklinton Dr
2 Oldershaw Dr
3 Parkstead Dr
4 Penerly Dr

B4
1 Ailsa Cl
2 Aldbourne Cl
3 Anslow Cl
4 Bishop Marshall Cl
5 Burnett Cl
6 Foreland Cl
7 Foynes Cl
8 Gervis Cl
9 Hillman Cl
10 Johnny King Cl
11 Needwood Cl
12 Overbrook Av
13 Raydon Av
14 Regency Cl
15 Robert Malcolm Cl
16 Rodmell Av
17 Rousdon Cl
18 Stretton Cl
19 Thornton St North
20 Tollard Av
21 Trimley Av
22 Tuxford St
23 Winthrop Av

Page 85

D2
1 Benton St
2 Brantwood Ter
3 Elmwood Av
4 Larchwood Av
5 Lila St
6 Margaret Ashton Cl
7 Norman Rd West
8 Railton Ter
9 Roda St
10 Springville Av
11 Stonehead St
12 Summerville Av
13 Vale Top Av

Page 86

B5
1 Boringdon Cl
2 Colclough Cl
3 Dixon St
4 Dulverton St
5 Erwin St
6 Glemsford Cl
7 Harold Priestnall Cl
8 John Foran Cl

Page 87

D3
1 Albert St West
2 Brook St
3 Corn St
4 Gaskell St
5 Hall St
6 Ilfracombe St
7 Mill La
8 Peel St

D4
1 Bardsley St
2 Charlield St
3 Clovelly St
4 Deal Cl
5 Devonshire St East
6 Graver La
7 Leaholme St
8 Mabel St
9 Marguerita Rd
10 Silverwell St
11 Tetlow St
12 Woodgarth Av

Page 88

B2
1 Casson St
2 Clayton St
3 Francis St
4 Henry St
5 Laycock Gv
6 Richard St
7 Silverbirch Wy
8 Sisson St
9 Wye Av

Page 90

B2
1 Albany Rd
2 Beaufort St
3 Brindley St
4 Dounby Av
5 Hamilton St
6 Lothian Av
7 Newbury Dr
8 Old Parrin La
9 School St
10 Swanage Rd
11 Woolden St

B5
1 Annisdale Cl
2 Brodie Cl
3 Bromsgrove Av
4 Cleavley St
5 Corran St
6 Egerton St
7 Kearsley St
8 Langholme Pl
9 Lavinia St
10 Midford Av
11 Nameplate Cl
12 Pollitts Cl
13 Portree St
14 Selsby Av
15 Signal Cl
16 Slater St
17 Wain Cl

Page 91

D1
1 Brentwood Dr
2 Golfview Dr
3 Grange Av

D4
1 Alba Cl
2 Bradburn Cl
3 Dickens Rd
4 Dorning St
5 Eliot Rd
6 Ellesmere St
7 Elm St
8 Golden St
9 Ivy St
10 Oak St
11 St John St

Page 92

B5
1 Birkdale Gv
2 Cambridge Av
3 Castle St
4 Clarendon Rd
5 College Cft
6 Fox St
7 Hope St
8 Lower Monton Rd
9 Shuttle St
10 Vernon Av

Page 94

B3
1 Buckingham Av
2 Calvert St
3 Edgewater
4 Goldsmith Av
5 John Atkinson Ct
6 Lord's Av
7 Milton Av
8 Myrtleleaf Gv
9 Parkfield
10 Wellington Ter
11 Whitegate Dr
12 Whiteside Cl
13 Willows Rd

Page 95

C5
1 Alexander St
2 Baltic St
3 Cressington Cl
4 Derby Av
5 Emaline Gv
6 Fram St
7 Glendinning St
8 Greenland St
9 Hersey St
10 Horsham St
11 Littlewood St
12 Lyndhurst St
13 Mere Av
14 Middlebourne St
15 Nona St
16 Northbourne St
17 Sandown St
18 Seedley View Rd
19 Southbourne St
20 Springwell Cl
21 Woodgrange Cl
22 Wythburn St

D1
1 Maurice St

D5
1 Iceland St
2 Langham Rd
3 Wall St

Page 96

A3
1 Alminstone Cl
2 Assheton Crs
3 Christopher St
4 Mountain St
5 Sunbury Dr
6 Thaxmead Dr
7 William Lister Cl

B3
1 Ember St
2 Khartoum St
3 Roslin St
4 Sumac St
5 Wandsworth Av

Page 106

B1
1 Aldermoor Cl
2 John Beeley Av
3 Kenchester Av
4 Orrell St
5 Printer St
6 Saunton Rd
7 Stansfield St

B3
1 Ansell Cl
2 Azalea Av
3 Barrass St
4 Follows St
5 Hurford Av
6 Longford St
7 Reynolds Dr
8 Sandiford Av
9 Seymour St
10 Wellesley Av
11 Winfield Dr

B4
1 Acheson St
2 Argyle St
3 Ashkirk St
4 Brogan St
5 Broxwood Cl
6 Chapman Ms
7 Cheddar St
8 Crowther St
9 Deerfold Cl
10 Corelan St
11 Roxburgh St
12 Sheerness St
13 Turner St
14 Varey St
15 Wallworth Av

Page 107

C3
1 Annable Rd
2 Compstall Gv
3 Corrigan St
4 Courier St
5 Emocroft Gv
6 Evenley Cl
7 Freshwater St
8 Gathurst St
9 Gidlow St
10 Monmouth St
11 Rutland St
12 Rylands St
13 Union St

D2
1 Delamere St
2 Fowler Av
3 Gibson Av
4 Holmpark Rd
5 Lassell St
6 Oxton St
7 Rayleigh Av
8 Reginald St
9 South Cliffe St

Page 110

B3
1 Chassen Av
2 Kingsley Av
3 Longfield Dr
4 Pickering Cl
5 Stamford Rd

Page 111

D2
1 Rowan Av

D3
1 Atkinson Rd
2 Braddon Av
3 Brentwood Av
4 Dorclyn Av
5 Dovedale Av
6 Ellaston Dr
7 Glebe Rd
8 Hilton Av
9 Primrose Av
10 Thorley Dr
11 Walmsley Gv

Page 117

D2
1 Arras Gv
2 Ashfield Gv
3 Birtles Av
4 Bispham Av
5 Brook Green La
6 Burnfield Rd
7 Colborne Av
8 Cranbrook Rd
9 St Agnes St
10 South Vw
11 Tindall St

D4
1 Burnham Av
2 Campbell St
3 Denstone Rd
4 Gainford Rd
5 Kingswood Cv
6 Lindfield Rd
7 Tyrrel Rd
8 Wemyss Av
9 Wentworth Rd

Page 129

D3
1 Bridgelea Ms
2 Brownacre St
3 Candleford Rd
4 Ferngate Dr
5 Marriott St

Page 130

B2
1 Birchacre Gv
2 Egerton Ter
3 Elizabeth Ct
4 Ellesmere Ter
5 Ladybarn Crs
6 Meredith St
7 Sheringham Rd
8 Shippey St
9 Weld Rd

Page 131

D1
1 Auckland Rd
2 Craighall Av
3 Deanbank Av
4 Edenhall Av
5 Paignton Av

D3
1 Ascot Pde
2 Avon Rd
3 Baldwin Rd
4 Bibby La
5 Chorley Wood Av
6 Church La
7 Firethorn Av
8 St Margaret's Av

Page 134

B3
1 Brendon Av
2 Broom Av
3 Broomfield Cl
4 Brunton Rd
5 Coniston Rd
6 Craven Rd
7 Dumbarton Cl
8 Exford Cl
9 Maypool Dr
10 Ormskirk Rd
11 Southcliffe Rd

Page 138

B1
1 Acacia Gv
2 Bangor St
3 Broughton Rd
4 Clare Rd
5 Glaswen Gv
6 Halston Cl
7 Melton St
8 Morgan Pl
9 Norway Gv
10 Pensarn Gv
11 Scott Cl

B3
1 Avenue St
2 Back Water St
3 Brewery St
4 Corporation St
5 Daniel's La
6 Deanery Wy
7 King St East
8 Little Egerton St
9 Millgate
10 Park St
11 Percy St
12 Portwood Pl

B4
1 Banbury St
2 Covent Gdn
3 Etchells St
4 Harvey St
5 High Bank Side
6 Holborn St
7 Lavenders Brow
8 Little Underbank
9 London Pl
10 London Sq
11 Lord St
12 Lower Carrs
13 Lower Hillgate
14 Lowe St
15 Massey St
16 Mealhouse Brow
17 Middle Hillgate
18 Norbury St
19 North Harvey St
20 North Pl
21 Orchard St
22 Pickford's Brow
23 Royal Oak Yd
24 St Peter's Sq
25 Tatton St
26 Watson Sq
27 Wesley St

Page 139

D2
1 Dawson St

Notes

Notes